# THE ASCENSION OF THE MESSIAH IN LUKAN CHRISTOLOGY

BY

A.W. ZWIEP

BRILL
LEIDEN · NEW YORK · KÖLN

This book is printed on acid-free paper.

BT
500
.Z94
1997

ISSN   0167-9732
ISBN   90 04 10897 1

# THE ASCENSION OF
# THE MESSIAH
# IN LUKAN CHRISTOLOGY

# SUPPLEMENTS TO
# NOVUM TESTAMENTUM

VOLUME LXXXVII

*parentibus uxori liberis*

# TABLE OF CONTENTS

Preface ........................................................ XI
Abbreviations ................................................. XII

CHAPTER ONE

## *FORSCHUNGSBERICHT*

a. Introduction ............................................. 1
b. The Origins of Modern Ascension-*Forschung* .................... 1
c. From V. Larrañaga to J.G. Davies ........................... 7
d. Ascension-*Forschung* in the Period of *Redaktionsgeschichte* ........ 12
e. The Contribution of G. Lohfink and the Subsequent Debate ........ 20
f. Recent Developments ...................................... 28
g. Conclusions ............................................. 33

CHAPTER TWO

## RAPTURE-PRESERVATION IN EARLY JEWISH SOURCES

a. Introduction ............................................. 36
b. The Enoch Tradition ...................................... 41
c. Enoch, Metatron, and the Heavenly Son of Man ............... 51
d. The Elijah Tradition ...................................... 58
e. The Moses Tradition ...................................... 64
f. Ezra, Baruch, Phinehas (and Melchizedek) ................... 71
g. Summary and Conclusions ................................. 76

CHAPTER THREE

## THE RAPTURE CHRISTOLOGY OF LUKE-ACTS (I)

a. Introduction ............................................. 80
b. Lk 9:51 ................................................. 80
c. Lk 24:50-53 ............................................. 86
d. Acts 1:1-14,21-22 ....................................... 94

e. Acts 3:19-21 .......................................... 109
f. Conclusions ........................................... 115
    Table 1. The Macro-Structure of Lk 24-Acts 1 ................. 118

CHAPTER FOUR

## RESURRECTION, EXALTATION AND ASCENSION IN EARLY CHRISTIANITY

a. Introduction .......................................... 119
b. The Resurrection-Exaltation Paradigm ........................ 121
c. The Ascension-Exaltation Paradigm (Mk 16:19) ................. 131
d. The Descent-Ascent Paradigm (Fourth Gospel) ................. 133
e. Other Ascension Texts ................................... 138
f. Summary and Conclusions ................................ 143

CHAPTER FIVE

## RESURRECTION, EXALTATION AND ASCENSION IN LUKE-ACTS

a. Introduction .......................................... 145
b. The Gospel of Luke (Lk 22:69; 23:42-43; 24:26) ............... 147
c. The Book of Acts (Acts 2:32-36; 5:31; 13:30-37) ............... 153
d. The Nature of the Lukan Post-Resurrection Appearances .......... 159
e. Summary and Conclusions ................................ 163

CHAPTER SIX

## THE RAPTURE CHRISTOLOGY OF LUKE-ACTS (II)

a. Introduction .......................................... 167
b. The Ascension and the Closure of the Time of Jesus ............. 169
c. The Apologetic Function of the Forty Days ..................... 171
d. The Ascension and the Expectation of the Parousia .............. 175
e. The Ascension and the Outpouring of the Spirit ................. 182
f. The Question of Sources ................................. 185
g. Conclusions .......................................... 192

Summary, Final Remarks and Conclusions ........................ 194

Bibliographies  . . . . . . . . . . . . . . . . . . . . . . . . . . . . . . . . . . . . . . . . . . . . . . .  200

a. The Ascension in Luke-Acts. A Bibliography 1900-1996  . . . . . . . . .  200
b. Texts, Translations, and Critical Editions. Lexical Aids, etc  . . . . . . . .  216
c. General Bibliography  . . . . . . . . . . . . . . . . . . . . . . . . . . . . . . . . . . . .  226

Index of Passages  . . . . . . . . . . . . . . . . . . . . . . . . . . . . . . . . . . . . . . . . .  260

a. OT and Apocrypha  . . . . . . . . . . . . . . . . . . . . . . . . . . . . . . . . . . . . .  260
b. Jewish Pseudepigrapha  . . . . . . . . . . . . . . . . . . . . . . . . . . . . . . . . . .  264
c. Dead Sea Scrolls, Philo, Josephus, Rabbinic Writings etc.  . . . . . . . . .  268
d. New Testament  . . . . . . . . . . . . . . . . . . . . . . . . . . . . . . . . . . . . . . . .  270
e. Early Christian and Gnostic Writings  . . . . . . . . . . . . . . . . . . . . . . . .  280
f. Classical and Other Ancient Writings  . . . . . . . . . . . . . . . . . . . . . . . .  282

Index of  Modern Authors  . . . . . . . . . . . . . . . . . . . . . . . . . . . . . . . . . . .  285

PREFACE

The present work is a revision of my doctoral dissertation accepted by the University of Durham (UK) in July 1996. I am especially grateful to my promotor, Prof. Dr. J.D.G. Dunn, who supervised my dissertation with great care and interest. At times his patience was severely put to the test, when I provided him with a 'foretaste of the things to come' in the form of preliminary drafts, rather than completed chapters. Hopefully, his longing for the final consummation has now been satisfied. I am also grateful to Dr. L.T. Stuckenbruck (Durham) and Dr. L.C.E. Alexander (Sheffield), who acted as examiners and were so kind to give some helpful advices for the further production of my thesis.

Of those who have read (parts of) the manuscript, I am particularly indebted to Drs. G. van den Brink (Doorn) and Mr. M. Rotman (Soest) for many helpful criticisms and corrections. Appreciation is due to Drs. P. Rosseneu (Leefdaal, Belgium), who helped me out many times when library services failed; to Drs. M.J. de Haan (Spijkenisse) for his patient assistance in PC matters, and to B. and S. McNeal (Strijen) for correcting the manuscript.

Thanks are due to Prof. Dr. D.P. Moessner, Prof. Dr. A.J. Malherbe and the editorial board of the Supplement Series of *Novum Testamentum* for accepting this book in the series, and to Dr. D.E. Orton of Brill's publishing house.

Finally, I would like to extend my thanks to my parents, my wife Cisca, and our two children, without whose support and encouragement this time-consuming project would not have been possible. To them I dedicate this book.

*March 1997*                                                                 A.W.Z.

Where possible, abbreviations have been those in S.M. Schwertner, *Internationales Abkürzungsverzeichnis für Theologie und Grenzgebiete* (Berlin, New York: W. de Gruyter, ²1992) xli + 488pp., with the exception of the Pseudepigrapha, which are abbreviated according to J.H. Charlesworth (ed.), *The Old Testament Pseudepigrapha* 1 (Garden City, NY: Doubleday, 1983) xlv-xlvii. For Philo and Josephus the conventions of the *Theologische Real-Enzyklopädie* are followed; unless otherwise indicated, patristic authors are quoted from Migne's edition, classical authors from the Loeb series. Abbreviated titles of patristic and classical authors should be sufficiently clear to recognise. In addition the following abbreviations have been used (* indicates an abbreviation replacing an existing *IATG*-abbreviation):

| | |
|---|---|
| *Apg* | Apostelgeschichte |
| BAFCS | The Book of Acts in Its First-Century Setting (ed. B.W. Winter). |
| Bauer | W. Bauer, *Griechisch-deutsches Wörterbuch zu den Schriften des Neuen Testaments und der übrigen urchristlichen Literatur* (Berlin: W. de Gruyter, ⁶1988). |
| BDR | F. Blass, A. Debrunner, *Grammatik des neutestamentlichen Griechisch* (bearbeitet v. F. Rehkopf; GTL; Göttingen: Vandenhoeck & Ruprecht, ¹⁷1990). |
| Beg | *The Beginnings of Christianity 1. The Acts of the Apostles* (eds. F.J. Foakes-Jackson, K. Lake; London: Macmillan, 1920-1933) 5 vols. |
| BENT | Beiträge zur Einleitung in das Neue Testament (A. Harnack). |
| *CUP | Cambridge University Press (Cambridge). |
| *DJG* | *Dictionary of Jesus and the Gospels* (eds. J.B. Green, S. McKnight, I.H. Marshall) (1992). |
| EvAp | *Evangelia Apocrypha* (ed. C. Tischendorf). |
| Field | *Origenis Hexaplorum quae supersunt* (ed. F. Field) 2 vols. |
| *FilNT* | *Filología Neotestamentaria* (Córdoba). |
| FPsG | *Fragmenta pseudepigraphorum quae supersunt graeca una cum historicorum et auctorum Judaeorum hellenistarum fragmentis* (ed. A.M. Denis). |
| *HJP* | E. Schürer, *The History of the Jewish People in the Age of Jesus Christ (175 B.C.-A.D. 135)* (A New English Version Revised and Edited by G. Vermes, F. Millar, P. Vermes and M. Black; Edinburgh: T.& T. Clark, 1973-1987) 4 vols. |
| *IBP | Institut Biblique Pontifical (Roma). |
| *IKT* | *Internationaal katholiek tijdschrift/Communio* |
| IVP | Inter-Varsity Press (Leicester). |
| KBW | Katholisches Bibelwerk (Stuttgart). |
| LSJM | H.G. Liddell, R. Scott, *et alii*, *A Greek-English Lexicon* (rev. ed. 1996). |
| MBib | Miscellanea Biblica (Roma). |

MGM W.F. Moulton, A.S. Geden, H.K. Moulton, *Concordance to the Greek Testament* (⁵1978).

MM J.H. Moulton, G. Milligan, *The Vocabulary of the Greek Testament* (1930).

*NBG *Bijbel. Vertaling in opdracht van het Nederlandsch Bijbelgenootschap, bewerkt door de daartoe benoemde commissies* (Leeuwarden: Jongbloed-Zetka, [1951]).

NRSV *The Holy Bible Containing the Old and New Testaments. New Revised Standard Version. Catholic Edition* (Thomas Nelson: 1989; London: G. Chapman, 1993).

OUP Oxford University Press (Oxford, New York).

PNT.N De Prediking van het Nieuwe Testament (Nijkerk).

RLU *Die Bibel oder die ganze Heilige Schrift des Alten und Neuen Testaments nach der Übersetzung Martin Luthers. Mit Apokryphen* (Stuttgart: Deutsche Bibelstiftung, 1975).

Spg Sacra Pagina (Collegeville, MN).

*SV *Bijbel, dat is de ganse Heilige Schrift bevattende al de kanonieke boeken van het Oude en Nieuwe Testament. Door last van de Hoog-mogende Heren Staten-Generaal enz.* (1618-1619) (Leeuwarden: A. Jongbloed, z.j.).

Thayer J.H. Thayer, *A Greek-English Lexicon of the New Testament* (²1889; repr. n.d.).

TPI Trinity Press International (Valley Forge, Philadelphia).

UMI University Microfilms International (Ann Arbor, MI, London).

WBC Word Biblical Commentary (Dallas, TX).

WBG Wissenschaftlichte Buchgesellschaft (Darmstadt).

WH *The New Testament in Greek* (ed. Westcott-Hort).

*WV *De Bijbel uit de grondtekst vertaald. Willibrord-vertaling* ('s Hertogenbosch: KBS, herziene uitgave 1995).

# CHAPTER ONE

# FORSCHUNGSBERICHT

a. *Introduction*

Except for some concise survey articles, an up-to-date overview study of the Lukan ascension narratives in NT scholarship is lacking[1]. The purpose of the present chapter is to fill this gap and to clear the ground for further investigation so as to gain a clear picture of the critical issues involved[2]. Since D.F. Strauß as 'der eigentliche Vater einer kritischen und zugleich traditionsgeschichtlichen Auslegung der Himmelfahrtsgeschichte' (G. Lohfink)[3] has exercised an immense influence upon all subsequent scholarship, he forms a natural starting-point for our survey[4].

b. *The Origins of Modern Ascension-Forschung*

D.F. Strauß (1808-1874) has given ample treatment of the ascension in volume two of his *Leben Jesu kritisch bearbeitet*[5]. Averse to the orthodox supernatural

---

[1] The most extensive is V. Larrañaga, *L'Ascension de Notre-Seigneur dans le Nouveau Testament* (SPIB 50; Roma: IBP, 1938) 8-129, covering the period from H.S. Reimarus to 1938, with an introductory section on the first centuries. See further F. Bovon, *Luc le théologien. Vingt-cinq ans de recherches (1950-1975)* (MoBi; Neuchatel, Paris: Delachaux & Niestlé, 1978) 181-191, and the updated but rather inaccurate tr. by K. McKinney; *Luke the Theologian. Thirty-Three Years of Research (1950-1983)* (PThM 12; Allison Park, PA: Pickwick, 1987) 170-177.441-446. A more comprehensive survey of ascension scholarship is found in my original Ph.D.-thesis (University of Durham 1996) 8-54.

[2] If, in what follows, a particular interpretation of Lk 24:50-53 stands or falls with a text-critical decision, this is briefly indicated by the designation 'shorter/longer text', dependent upon its treatment of the words καὶ ἀνεφέρετο εἰς τὸν οὐρανὸν v.51 (and προσκυνήσαντες αὐτὸν v.52). For a separate discussion of the text of the ascension narratives, see A.W. Zwiep, 'The Text of the Ascension Narratives (Lk 24:50-53; Acts 1:1-2,9-11)', *NTS* 42 (1996) 219-244.

[3] G. Lohfink, *Die Himmelfahrt Jesu. Untersuchungen zu den Himmelfahrts- und Erhöhungstexten bei Lukas* (StANT 26; München: Kösel, 1971) 21.

[4] For a full bibliography, see *infra* Bibliography (a). To reduce the number of footnotes page numbers of works under discussion usually are given in the body of the text (in parentheses).

[5] D.F. Strauß, *Das Leben Jesu kritisch bearbeitet* 2 (Tübingen: J.C.B. Mohr/Paul Siebeck, 1835-36; [4]1840) 642-662.

explanation of the ascension as a physical elevation into the air—an idea he rejected with much the same zeal as the idea of the resurrection as 'eine natürliche Wiederbelebung'—and equally dissatisfied with the rationalist attempts to eliminate the miraculous elements from the story so as to arrive at a 'natural' explanation, Strauß set out to interpret the ascension in terms of 'myth' (i.e. as an expression of a theological idea)[1]. While the first impression of the ascension narrative is admittedly that it reports a literal elevation of Jesus into the sky (where God lives), Strauß claimed that the underlying conception of heaven as a superior region in the atmosphere belonged to the childish imagery of the ancient world, which was incompatible with the modern view of reality: 'Wer zu Gott und in den Bezirk der Seligen kommen will, der, das wissen wir, macht einen überflüssigen Umweg, wenn er zu diesem Behuf in die höheren Luftschichten sich emporschwingen zu müssen meint, und diesen wird Jesus, je vertrauter er mit Gott und göttlichen Dingen war, gewiß nicht gemacht haben, noch Gott ihn denselben haben machen lassen' (2, 652).

With equal vigour, however, Strauß repudiated the superficial constructs of the rationalists because their solutions were forced and in gross conflict with the meaning of the words.

A typical example of the rationalist approach is H.E.G. Paulus (1761-1851). He believed that Jesus had not died on the cross but had only slipped into a coma. After the crucifixion, not being mortally wounded by the spear thrust, he was removed from the cross and placed in the tomb where aromatic spices soon made him regain conscience. He could leave the grave because an earthquake removed the stone. He then stayed forty days in the company of his disciples. At the end of this period he departed from them and with his last strength walked off into a mist cloud on the mountain, where he finally succumbed to the injuries of his body. The disciples then mistook two casual passers-by (who were in fact two accomplices from Jesus' secret followers in Jerusalem) for angelic messengers[2].

In an effort to move beyond the impasse in which the orthodox-rationalist

---

[1] In this respect, Strauß was particularly indebted to K.A. Hase, *Das Leben Jesu. Lehrbuch zunächst für akademische Vorlesungen* (Leipzig: Breitkopf & Härtel, 1829, [5]1865) 11-13.267-284, who, unwilling to assign the origins of the resurrection and ascension story to fraud on the part of the disciples, as did H.S. Reimarus [see A. Schweitzer, *Geschichte der Leben-Jesu-Forschung* (UTB.W 1302; Tübingen: J.C.B. Mohr/Paul Siebeck, 1906, [9]1984) 62-63; Larrañaga, *Ascension* 18-20], assigned it rather to the creative activity of the early Christian community (282).

[2] H.E.G. Paulus, *Das Leben Jesu als Grundlage einer reinen Geschichte des Urchristentums* 1/2 (Heidelberg: C.F. Winter, 1828) 280ff., 318ff. For other rationalist explanations, see Strauß, *Leben Jesu KB* 2, 653-655 (e.g. ἐπήρθη Acts 1:9 as 'ein bloßes Sichaufrichten'!); Schweitzer, *Leben-Jesu-Forschung* 83-84 (K.F. Bahrdt), 86-87 (K.H. Venturini); Larrañaga, *Ascension* 28-33 (H.E.G. Paulus, F.D.E. Schleiermacher).

controversy of his time had ended up, Strauß claimed that the ascension narratives were never meant to be taken as *ad litteram* reports as his opponents did. Paul and the traditionally alleged eyewitnesses, Matthew and John, were obviously unacquainted with a visible ascension (2, 655-658) and the accounts that describe the ascension as a physical, visible act performed by Jesus and observed by the disciples are mutually contradictory. In Mk 16:19 Jesus seems to depart from a room in Jerusalem immediately after a meal; in Lk 24:50 somewhere in the open ἔξω ἕως εἰς Βηθανίαν (= *Textus Receptus*). Both texts date the ascension on Easter Sunday; Acts 1:3 forty days later.

Strauß, alternatively, suggested that the ascension was the result of a more or less unconscious mythologising process. In line with the early community's tendency to make Jesus agree with OT predictions, the ascension was to be regarded as a mythical expression of its belief in Jesus' heavenly exaltation based on the OT Scripture. But while the dominant tradition in the primitive Church expressed no more than the logical implication of Ps 110:1, viz. 'daß Jesus sich zur rechten Gottes erhoben habe, ohne über das Wie etwas zu bestimmen, oder sich die Auffahrt dahin als eine sichtbare vorzustellen' (2, 661), the ascension tradition had been developed out of the Son of Man tradition and the expectation of his parousia on the clouds. To reconstruct its tradition-historical genesis the angelic words must be read in reverse: 'wie Jesus dereinst vom Himmel wiederkommen wird, so wird er wohl auch dahin gegangen sein' (2, 661).

Later Strauß refined his theory and sketched how in his view the Gospel post-Easter appearance stories had come into development[1]. He argued that in the earliest kerygma the visions of the risen Jesus, which were in fact psychologically induced 'subjective visions' (i.e. hallucinations), were regarded as evidence of Jesus' resurrection-exaltation, his entrance into the new messianic life. As Jesus was now in possession of immortal life, made occasional appearances from heaven and was expected to return soon, the idea of an ascension (in the sense of a final departure) found no soil. But in the course of history the Christian community began to realise that Jesus had ceased to manifest himself any longer as he had done in the early days of the Church. The appearance to Paul seemed to be the last of its kind (2, 154). Thus the idea of an intermediate post-resurrection state (i.e. Jesus risen but not yet exalted) grew naturally out of the experience of the early Church. As on the one hand it was not desirable to allow for too much time between the resurrection

---

[1] Strauß, *Das Leben Jesu für das deutsche Volk bearbeitet* 2 (Volksausgabe in unverkürzter Form; Stuttgart: Emil Strauß, A. Kröner, 1864, [16]o.J.) 148-162.

and exaltation, and on the other hand a sufficiently elongated period of time was required to encompass the various appearance stories of the risen Lord and to have the apostles fully instructed ('Weder der Unglaube, noch der Unverstand werden mit Einem Schlage gewichen sein ...', 2, 155), the number forty, being a sacred number in Jewish and early Christian circles (cf. Ex 16:35; 24:18; 1 Kings 19:8; Lk 4:2; 4 Ezra 14:42), was a natural choice for the early Church to fix the date of Jesus' final departure (2, 155).

The idea that the ascension myth had come into development in the early Church was further developed by A. Harnack (1851-1930)[1]. He applied himself to investigate and reconstruct the historical circumstances in which the ascension myth (or legend) could have developed. He argued that the ascension legend was the culmination of a three-stage process of materialisation of the traditional belief in Jesus' resurrection-exaltation (126-129). While the ascension in the oldest preaching (1 Cor 15; Mt 28; Mk 16:1-8) had no separate place from the resurrection-exaltation, Luke, while composing his Gospel, replaced this primitive tradition (against his better knowledge) with an inferior one, that is, the ascension tradition preserved in Lk 9:51 and 24:50-53 (shorter text!) (cf. *supra* 1 n.2), which according to Harnack referred to an invisible ascension on Easter Sunday (128). When Luke wrote Acts he substituted this secondary tradition (once more against his better knowledge!) with the detailed narrative of Acts 1:3,9-11, which describes a visible ascension on the Mount of Olives after forty days, reminiscent of the Elijah narrative. Ancient though this tradition was, it could not possibly have originated in the circle of the Eleven (the alleged eyewitnesses). The period when the apostles, under the pressure of persecutions, were forced to leave Jerusalem and the Church came under the direction of James, must have provided the best conditions for the wild and uncontrolled growth of the ascension legend (127)[2].

As much a historian as Harnack, E. Meyer equally tried to reconstruct the tradition-historical framework of the ascension narrative but he arrived at a very opposite conclusion[3]. While Harnack (and Strauß for that matter) had opted for a pre-Lukan origin, Meyer regarded Acts 1:2-14 practically *in toto* as a second-century interpolation. Had Luke consistently followed the conventions of contemporary Greek historiography he would have continued the resumé of his former treatise (introduced by μέν, Acts 1:1) with a statement

---

[1] A. Harnack, *Die Apostelgeschichte* (BENT 3; Leipzig: J.C. Hinrichs, 1908).

[2] For a more detailed analysis of Harnack's views regarding the ascension (including further literature), see Larrañaga, *Ascension* 48-50.64-74, and my Ph.D.-thesis, 12-14.

[3] E. Meyer, *Ursprung und Anfänge des Christentums* 1 (Stuttgart: J.G. Cotta, 1921, [4,5]1924; repr. Darmstadt: WBG, 1962) 34-46.

about the content of his second book (introduced by δέ). Its absence together with a number of other textual incongruities[1] convinced Meyer that the passage had been heavily reworked: 'An der Tatsache, daß hier eine große Interpolation vorliegt, daß in die Worte des Lukas ein ihm ganz fremder Bericht hineingeflickt ist und die ursprüngliche Fortsetzung der Eingangsworte dem zum Opfer gefallen ist, ist nicht zu rütteln: so wie der Text jetzt lautet, hat nie ein Mensch seine Gedanken formuliert, sei es mündlich, sei es schriftlich' (1, 36)[2]. Given the various attempts to define the period of post-resurrection appearances in Gnostic circles—the Ophites and Valentinians, e.g., prolonged the risen Lord's instructions to a period of 18 months[3]—Meyer suspected a Gnostic provenance of Acts 1:2-5 (1, 40). Like Acts 1:2-5, the ascension narrative proper (Acts 1:6-14) is secondary, as is shown by its independent position in the text (οἱ μὲν συνελθόντες, v.6 contradicts συναλιζόμενος, v.4) and inconsistencies and doublets in the narrative (e.g. the totally unnecessary question about the Kingdom after the disciples had been fully instructed about it for forty days, and the double mention of the Spirit). In comparison with vv.3-5 the ascension pericope is the older (yet post-Lukan!) piece of tradition. Luke's own perspective was found in Lk 24 and Acts 10:34-43, where he shows no awareness of a longer period of appearances and restricts the appearances exclusively to Easter Sunday[4].

Interpolation hypotheses in one form or another have been defended by a number of authors. The wide variety of hypotheses forbids an easy classification. Especially influential has been an article by Ph.H. Menoud[5]. Menoud regarded the entire section from

---

[1] Such as what διὰ πνεύματος ἁγίου (v.2) refers to (a verse which in the present text is practically untranslatable), the clumsy transition from the main clause into several incongruous relative clauses ('ein wahres Satzungeheuer', 1, 38), the chronological discrepancy with Lk 24, the erroneous attribution of a Baptist logion to Jesus (v.5; cf. Mk 1:3), etc.

[2] The variant solution of B.W. Bacon, 'The Ascension in Luke and Acts', *Exp.* (Series 7) 7 (1909) 254-261, to regard Acts 1:3 as an interjected parenthesis (so that the forty days are subsequent to the ascension), has won but little support. See M.S. Enslin, 'The Ascension Story', *JBL* 47 (1928) 63-64, and J.M. Creed, 'The Text and Interpretation of Acts i,1-2', *JThS* 35 (1934) 180, for a critique.

[3] See *inter alios* W. Bauer, *Das Leben Jesu im Zeitalter der neutestamentlichen Apokryphen* (Tübingen: J.C.B. Mohr/Paul Siebeck, 1909; repr. Darmstadt: WBG, 1965) 275-279, and *infra* 97-98.

[4] Later Meyer, *Ursprung* 3, 12 Anm.1 admitted that he had overlooked Acts 13:31, which explicitly mentions post-Easter appearances over an extended period of time (ἐπὶ ἡμέρας πλείους). But he simply consigned this piece of conflicting evidence to Luke's careless taking over of a source without integrating it into his thought.

[5] Ph.H. Menoud, 'Remarques sur les textes de l'ascension dans Luc-Acts', in: W. Eltester

Lk 24:50 to Acts 1:5 as an interpolation by a second-century redactor in Rome. Luke-Acts must have been a one-volume work, with the original text running straight from Lk 24:49 to Acts 1:6, thus forming a coherent narrative. When at the formation of the canon (second century AD) Luke-Acts for the sake of convenience was separated into two parts, the books were provided with a fitting conclusion (Lk 24:50-53) and an appropriate beginning (Acts 1:1-5). Later, Menoud would revoke his interpolation thesis (*infra* 14).

In response to Meyer, W. Michaelis[1] pointed out that the words δι' ἡμερῶν τεσσεράκοντα (Acts 1:3) did not as in the later Gnostic line of interpretation signify an uninterrupted period of Jesus living together with his disciples but a period 'über den Zeitraum von 40 Tagen verteilt in einzelnen τεκμήρια' (τεκμήρια standing for the individual appearances) (102)[2]. Says Michaelis: 'Also keine Daueroffenbarung des Auferstandenen, keine Konkurrenz und Steigerung seines Erdenlebens, keine esoterische Vertiefung seiner Logia, sondern die Reihe der in der Urgemeinde bekannten Offenbarungen des Auferstandenen ist gemeint' (102-103).

Since Lk 24:50-53 (shorter text!) describes an 'apostolic christophany' in the vicinity of Bethany (106-107) and Acts 1 is a departure scene (distinguished from other appearance stories only in that it rounds off the *final* appearance), there is no real conflict because they simply relate to two separate occasions[3]. Nor is there a discrepancy between the primitive kerygma (which, with Luke, does not restrict the appearances to one single day, cf. 1 Cor 15) and Luke (who, with the old kerygma, does not know of a continuous post-Easter presence of Jesus but only of various isolated traditional units describing post-Easter appearances). As the appearance to Paul on the Damascus road indicates, the primitive Church apparently did not experience the ascension as a final break.

Michaelis in his turn was criticised by A. Fridrichsen for ignoring the strong literary unity of Lk 24:35-53 and Acts 1:4-11, firmly established by their common subject-matter and motifs[4]. From a literary point of view it is quite clear that the function of Lk 24:50-53 is to describe a final farewell scene (the

---

(Hrsg.), *Neutestamentliche Studien für R. Bultmann* (BZNW 21; Berlin: A. Töpelmann, 1954, [2]1957) 148-156. More authors are listed in my Ph.D.-thesis, 14 n.23 and 15f. n.28.

[1] W. Michaelis, 'Zur Überlieferung der Himmelfahrtsgeschichte', *ThBl* 4 (1925) 101-109.

[2] Likewise Acts 13:31 ἐπὶ ἡμέρας πλείους (103). Michaelis, 'Überlieferung' 103 regarded Acts 10:41 D E it sa mae (ἡμέρας τεσσεράκοντα '40 Tage lang') as a later interpolation, contra Th. Zahn, *Die Apostelgeschichte des Lucas* 1 (KNT 5; Leipzig: A. Deichert, Werner Scholl, [3,4]1920) 359.

[3] Likewise (unless indicated otherwise with shorter text): A.R.C. Leaney, E. Lohse, E.E. Ellis, O. Betz (longer text!), M.D. Goulder (longer text!).

[4] A. Fridrichsen, 'Die Himmelfahrt bei Lukas', *ThBl* 6 (1927) 337-341.

appropriate conclusion of the travel section 9:51ff.) and not, as Michaelis suggested, a temporary departure of Jesus only to return on later occasions. Although the timing differs the two accounts agree in that the intermediate state of the risen Lord is portrayed in rather massive terms. Fridrichsen detected here a 'Vergröberung der Vorstellung vom Auferstandenen' (339) and a 'Konkretisierung ... des Erhöhungsvorganges' (340) and suspected that 'hier eine volkstümliche, materialisierende und legendenfrohe Entwicklung früh eingesetzt hat und hinter Lukas liegt' (339). But whether or not there was ever a pre-Lukan tradition of a visible ascension of Jesus he left undecided (340)[1].

> Here we must also make reference of an important article by G. Bertram in a *Festschrift* to A. Deissmann[2]. Bertram argued that among the various models (*Darstellungsformen*) which the early Church used to express belief in Jesus' entrance into the heavenly glory—resurrection, ascension from the grave (empty tomb), ascension after a shorter or longer period, appearances, parousia—the conception of an immediate 'ascension from the cross' (EvPe 5:19) must have been prominent in the oldest strata, but was supplanted soon by more developed ideas. Yet some traces of this primitive conception are found in the NT (e.g. in Lk 23:43; 24:26, and texts that juxtapose death and life, cross and glory, without mentioning the resurrection: Phil 2:5ff., Rom 5:10; 2 Cor 4:4; Gal 3:1; 1 Cor 1:23; 2:2; Heb 1:3)[3].

c. *From V. Larrañaga to J.G. Davies*

The publication in 1938 of the massive doctoral dissertation of the Spanish Jesuit V. Larrañaga launched a new phase in the study of the ascension narratives[4]. Larrañaga developed his arguments in response to the triple-tradition theory of A. Harnack and the interpolation hypothesis of E. Meyer (v).

As Harnack's theory was, to a large extent, dependent upon his text-critical stance (the shorter text of Lk 24:51), Larrañaga made a detailed study of the MSS tradition and early patristic evidence in order to establish the original text

---

[1] See also L. Brun, *Die Auferstehung Christi in der urchristlichen Überlieferung* (Oslo: H. Aschehoug & Co (W. Nygaard); Giessen: A. Töpelmann, 1925) 97, and Enslin, 'Ascension' 60-73. According to Enslin, the story of the forty days (and consequently the tradition of an ascension distinct from the resurrection) could become the standard of Christian theology, since Scripture was believed not to contradict Scripture: 'Harmony has usually been purchased at the expense of historical accuracy' (73)..

[2] G. Bertram, 'Die Himmelfahrt Jesu vom Kreuz aus und der glaube an seine Auferstehung', in: K.L. Schmidt (Hrsg.), *Festgabe für Adolf Deissmann zum 60. Geburtstag* (Tübingen: J.C.B. Mohr/Paul Siebeck, 1927) 187-217.

[3] U. Holzmeister, 'Der Tag der Himmelfahrt des Herrn', *ZKTh* 55 (1931) 46-54 provides a convenient list of patristic texts brought forward in support of the 'ascension from the cross' (includes critique).

[4] Larrañaga, *Ascension*.

of the ascension narratives (131-213). Contrary to the popular opinion of the time (established by *inter alios* WH and Tischendorf), he arrived at the conclusion that the original text of Lk 24:50-53 and Acts 1:2,9 was best represented in the Alexandrian text-type ('la recension orientale'), that is, including the words καὶ ἀνεφέρετο εἰς τὸν οὐρανόν (Lk 24:51) and ἀνελήμφθη (Acts 1:2), their absence in the Western tradition reflecting an unfortunate attempt to alleviate the assumed chronological tension between Lk 24:50-53 and Acts 1:3.

In opposition to Meyer, Larrañaga demonstrated on the basis of a meticulous statistical analysis of Luke's vocabulary and idiom that Acts 1:1-14 formed an integral part of Luke-Acts (219-269, esp. 230-231).

In an attempt to refute Meyer's assertion that the absence of δέ in the prologue of Acts pointed to textual corruption, Larrañaga made a detailed analysis of transitionary prologues ('prologue-transitions') in contemporary Greek literature to prove that the use of μέν-*solitarium* was not an irregular device in Greek preface writing (270-329). In the Hellenistic period, he distinguished three types: (1) The most common type marks the perimeters separating the two volumes by means of a double summary, viz. of the preceding book(s) and of the following book, usually with a μὲν ... δέ construction[1]; (2) A second type marks the transition by means of a single summary, viz. of the preceding book, without anticipating the content of what will follow, usually with a μὲν ... δέ construction[2]; (3) A third type marks the transition by merely indicating the content of the following, the μὲν ... δέ construction generally being replaced by an initial δέ[3]. Acts 1:1-3 is a prologue of the second type: it only refers back to the content of the former book without specifying the content of the present book. Luke preferred the second to the first since he wished to relate in more detail what had happened before the ascension (325). That the corresponding δὲ is lacking is not inconsistent with Luke's style. Larrañaga quite boldly concluded: 'Le prologue-transition de *Act* 1,1-3, point de mire des attaques des critiques qui y voient une interpolation, n'offre aucune irrégularité par rapport aux méthodes littéraires de

---

[1] Polybius, *Hist* II 1,1-4; III 1,1-3; IV 1,1-3; DiodS, *Hist* I 42,1-2; II 1,1; III 1,1-2; IV 1,1.5; XIX 1,10; XX 2,3; DionHal, *AntRom* I 90,2; cf. VII 73-VIII 1; Philo, *VitMos* 2,1; 3,1; *SpecLeg* 2; *Plant* 2; *QPL* 2; Josephus, *Ap* II 1 (1-2); Artemidorus, *Oneirocriticum* 2,1; Eusebius, *HistEccl* 2 (1-2).

[2] Josephus, *Ant* VIII i,1 (1-2); XIII i,1 (1); Herodian, *Hist* 3,1; 4,1; 5,1; 6,1; 7,1; 8,1; Xenophon, *Anabasis* II 1,1-2; III 1,1-2; IV 1,1-2; V 1,1-2; VII 1,1-2. On the disputed authenticity of the prologues to Xenophon's *Anabasis*, see Larrañaga, *Ascension* 301-306.

[3] Appian, *RomHist* 7,1; 2,1; DiodS, *Hist* V 2,1; Eusebius, *HistEccl* 8 (1).

l'historiographie grecque' (631). Since Lk 24:44-53 and Acts 1:1-14 correspond in structure and Acts 1 does not attempt to rectify the former account (364-367), both passages describe the same events (contra Michaelis). The notion of the forty days (which Larrañaga on the basis of a very extensive analysis of OT, NT and patristic data took as a historically exact date) does not run counter to Lk 24, because there is a time gap assumed in Lk 24:44, which separates the ascension chronologically from the preceding events (448-461).

Larrañaga, finally, claimed that Harnack's theory that the two passages were the result of legendary evolution was irreconcilable with Harnack's own early dating of the Book of Acts (between 58 and 62 AD). A legend would require considerable time to emerge. If the ascension story were a legend, its development would have taken much longer than only three decades (remember the eyewitnesses!)[1].

In many respects concurring with Larrañaga, P. Benoit claimed in a very influential article[2] that, taken by itself, the ascension narrative (Acts 1:9-11) provides no serious difficulties to the interpreter: the story as such is clear and '... il n'y a rien en elle qui ne puisse être admis par quiconque ne rejette pas a

---

[1] Taking δι᾽ ἡμερῶν τεσσεράκοντα to denote individual appearances spread over forty days, W. Tom, 'Waar was Jezus gedurende de veertig dagen tusschen Zijn opstanding en hemelvaart?', *GThT* 39 (1938) 404-411, raised the question where Jesus was during the forty days at times he did not appear to the disciples. As Scripture articulated no other goal for this period than the instruction of the disciples and to convince them of the reality of his resurrection, it had no independent significance for Christ himself (e.g. a continuous, progressive glorification and spiritualisation of his body; Jesus received a σῶμα πνευματικόν at the resurrection). Accordingly, whenever Christ appeared to the disciples, he appeared from heaven and afterwards ascended thither. Acts 1:9 describes Christ's final appearance and ascension. C.J. Goslinga, 'Een herhaalde Hemelvaart?', *GThT* 39 (1938) 557-560, objected that Tom undermined the unique character of the ascension as a salvation-historical event (558), and was at risk to interfere with the once-for-all character of Pentecost. Tom in return responded that the idea of provisional ascensions did not necessarily jeopardise the once-for-all character of the (definitive) ascension, as Scripture is silent on Christ's whereabouts during the forty day period [Tom, 'Nog eens: waar was Jezus ...', *GThT* 40 (1939) 303-306]. Unlike the incarnation and the resurrection, he maintained, the ascension is (only) a local transfer (304-306). Goslinga objected that it is not justified to speak of *the* ascension if Jesus in fact had ascended at least ten times [Goslinga, 'Tot op den dag, in welken Hij opgenomen is', *GThT* 40 (1939) 519-522]. After the resurrection, Christ could only increase in glory, not decrease (not even temporarily) (522). Tom finally suggested to distinguish Jesus' assumption ('opneming') on Easter-day from his glorification ('verheerlijking') forty days later, when he received his full glory [Tom, 'Het vraagteeken gehandhaafd', *GThT* 41 (1940) 129-131].

[2] P. Benoit, 'L'Ascension' (1949); repr. in: idem, *Exégèse et Théologie* 1 (Paris: Cerf, 1961) 363-411. See also idem, 'Ascension', *VThB* (²1971) 87-91.

priori la possibilité du surnaturel et du miracle' (363-364). The physical resurrection was the only way the risen Lord could convince his disciples of the inauguration of the messianic reign. An immediate assumption into heaven on the analogy of Enoch and Elijah or the Roman emperors would not have convinced the disciples of Jesus' triumph over death. Most primitive traditions regard the resurrection and the exaltation at the right hand of the Father as two practically simultaneous events, two complementary stages of the glorification of the Lord.

Benoit rejected the idea that the primitive Church conceived of Jesus' victory over death in merely spiritual (non-corporeal) terms because this would be unacceptable for a faith rooted in Judaism and contradicted by the NT evidence (377-391). Luke may have received the information about the forty days after the closing of his first volume (399)[1]. It should perhaps not be pushed in all its literalness, although the historical reality of the ascension is firmly established by the very precise location of the event: on the Mount of Olives, at some point on the road to Bethany (400). Theologically speaking, we should distinguish two different aspects of Christ's entrance into his glorious life, viz. the invisible exaltation at the right hand of the Father on the day of his resurrection (followed by appearances of the risen Lord from heaven) and the visible ascension forty days later as the conclusion of the period of appearances (401)[2]. Compared to the exaltation, Jesus' visible departure is only of secondary importance, 'une concession indulgente faite à notre faiblesse d'êtres sensibles' (402)[3]. This explains why the other NT writers mention the exaltation without alluding to the ascension. For Luke, the ascension is not the occasion of Jesus' exaltation or glorification, but his final departure, which concludes the period of appearances from heaven (405)[4].

Despite the relative frequency with which Larrañaga and Benoit are quoted in literature, one cannot say that their conclusions have met with general acceptance. Scholarship in general felt more attracted to the relatively negative

---

[1] Likewise D.F. Strauß, K.A. Hase, F. Blass, H.H. Wendt, A. Plummer, B.H. Streeter, M.S. Enslin, C.F.D. Moule, C.S.C. Williams, B. Reicke.

[2] A distinction adopted by J. Heuschen, *De bijbel over Hemelvaart* (4) (Roermond, Maaseik: J.J. Romen, 1960) 43-79.80-100, a study otherwise strongly dependent upon Benoit.

[3] Cf. B.M. Metzger, 'The Ascension of Jesus Christ', in: idem, *Historical and Literary Studies. Pagan, Jewish and Christian* (NTTS 8; Leiden: E.J. Brill; Grand Rapids: Eerdmans, 1968) 86: 'At Jesus' final appearance to his followers he rose from their midst ... *for didactic reasons*, in order to make his last act symbolically intelligible' (italics mine). Further P. Brunner, 'The Ascension of Christ. Myth or Reality?', *Dialog* 1 (1962) 39.

[4] Followed by J.A.T. Robinson, *Jesus and His Coming. The Emergence of a Doctrine* (London: SCM, 1957) 134-136.

judgement of the ascension story by R. Bultmann, who in the 40s and the 50s of this century was working on his demythologising program. The ascension was represented in his work as a stock-example of a mythological worldview, which did not lend itself easily to an existential interpretation and therefore was to be eliminated[1].

Generally speaking, the scene up to now had largely been dominated by German scholarship, Larrañaga and Benoit notwithstanding. The English-speaking world did not play a role of significance in the debate. In the beginning of this century H.B. Swete wrote two books on a more popular level, one on the appearances, the other on the ascension (or, more precisely, on the present ascended status of Christ)[2], but all in all the contribution of British scholarship in particular had been small.

A first breakthrough was effected by a brief article by A.M. Ramsey, in which he questioned the theory that the resurrection and the ascension in the apostolic preaching were two separate events in time[3]. He argued that the allusions in Acts (Acts 2:32,33; 5:30,31) and the epistles (Rom 8:34; Col 3:1; Phil 2:8,9; Eph 1:19-20; 1 Tim 3:16; 1 Pet 3:21,22 and Hebrews) do not give a clear testimony to a belief that there had been an ascension, distinct in time from the resurrection; in the Fourth Gospel, death, resurrection, and ascension (visible in Jn 6:62; 20:17) are drawn together as in one single act (140-142). Like Mt 28 and Mk (14:62; 16:7), Acts 1 describes a theophany (that is, a manifestation of the already ascended Lord) (143).

The first major critical study on the ascension by a British scholar was the book that resulted from the 1958 Bampton Lectures by J.G. Davies[4]. Starting from the premise that allusions to the ascension may take a great variety of forms, he boldly asserted that '... there is scarcely a New Testament writer who does not testify to the Ascension ...' (56). Taking ὑψόω (and ὑπερυψόω) in its primary meaning ('a movement from a lower to a higher level'), he suggested that we have here an equivalent of ἀναβαίνω, which, if the context warrants it,

---

[1] See R. Bultmann, *Neues Testament und Mythologie. Das Problem der Entmythologisierung der neutestamentlichen Verkündigung* (hrsg. v. E. Jüngel; BEvTh 96; München: Chr. Kaiser, 1941; repr. ³1988).

[2] H.B. Swete, *The Appearances of our Lord after the Passion. A Study in the Earliest Christian Tradition* (London: Macmillan, 1907); idem, *The Ascended Christ. A Study in the Earliest Christian Teaching* (London: Macmillan, 1910).

[3] A.M. Ramsey, 'What was the Ascension?' (1951); repr. in: D.E. Nineham, *et alii*, *Historicity and Chronology in the New Testament* (TCSPCK 6; London: SPCK, 1965) 135-144.

[4] J.G. Davies, *He Ascended into Heaven. A Study in the History of Doctrine* (BaL 1958; London: Lutterworth, 1958). For what follows see esp. 15-68.

may be taken as a reference to the ascension (e.g. Rom 10:6,7; Phil 2:8-11; Acts 2:33) (28-29). As the NT never uses ὑψόω of the resurrection alone, exaltation texts confirm belief in the ascension as an act distinct from the resurrection. Similarly, session (Col 3:1) and parousia texts (1 Thess 1:10; 2 Thess 1:7) presuppose belief in the ascension as an accomplished fact.

Davies further argued that ἐγείρω and its synonym ἀνίστημι, when used of the resurrection, do not imply an immediate entry into heaven but only a restoration to earthly life (30-34), inferring on the basis of LXX-constructs as ἀναστὰς ἀνάβηθι (Gen 35:1; Josh 8:1; Jer 31:6; 1 Macc 9:8) that ἀνίστημι is used differently from ἀναβαίνω: '*anastasis* precedes *anabasis*' (33, his italics). Having thus taken (and mixed up!) exaltation, session, and parousia texts as evidence of belief in the ascension, Davies took recourse to the evangelists' alleged use of prefigurement to substantiate his thesis (the ascension precedes the coming outpouring of the Spirit on the disciples, as much as Elijah's ascension preceded the empowerment of Elisha; the transfiguration story bears strong resemblances to the ascension story)[1]. The christological titles (Son of Man, Messiah) presuppose the ascension (36-39.43). Luke, the only NT writer to describe the occasion and circumstances of the ascension, may have shaped his stories around a Raphael typology in Lk 24 (Tob 12) and an Elijah typology in Acts 1. The notion of forty days is not a chronological but a typological statement, pointing to the connection with the Elijah story (1 Kings 19:8 LXX). 'There is no reason to suppose that in doing so he expected his readers to press the details literally or that he thought that this involved any serious contradiction of what he had previously written' (53).

d. *Ascension-Forschung in the Period of Redaktionsgeschichte*
The introduction, in the mid-1950s, of the method of *Redaktionsgeschichte*, developed as far as Lukan studies are concerned by H. Conzelmann (Luke) and E. Haenchen (Acts), signalled an important turning-point in the study of the ascension narratives. Whereas earlier scholarship had been predominantly concerned with the history of tradition and the place of the ascension in the NT preaching, Conzelmann and Haenchen focused their attention on the contribution Luke—as a theologian in his own rights—had made in the process of selecting, organising and editing his materials.

According to Conzelmann[2] the author of Luke-Acts, writing in a period in

---

[1] Cf. Davies, *Ascended* 15-26; idem, 'The Prefigurement of the Ascension in the Third Gospel', *JThS* 6 (1955) 229-233.
[2] H. Conzelmann, *Die Mitte der Zeit. Studien zur Theologie des Lukas* (BHTh 17; Tübingen: J.C.B. Mohr/Paul Siebeck, 1954, [6]1977).

which the delay of the parousia of Christ had caused a serious crisis in the Christian community, sought to come to terms with the ongoing history by offering a philosophy of history that accounted for the past (the life of Jesus) and the actual experience of the Church. Luke categorised biblical history into three sharply differentiated periods: the period of Israel (from creation, concluded by the ministry of John the Baptist, Lk 16:16), the period of Jesus (a period considered free from the influence of Satan, *grosso modo* from Satan's departure in Lk 4:13 to his reappearance in 22:3; cf. also Lk 4:16-20; Acts 10:38) (158) and the period of the Church (between ascension and parousia) (1-11). Luke transferred the parousia to the indefinite future. Instead of maintaining fervent *Naherwartung*, Luke showed that the delay was divinely planned, that the End would be 'sudden' (*plötzlich*) rather than 'soon' (*bald*), and that the cardinal virtue for the Christian community in the present was that of ὑπομονή (87-127). The ascension, in this construction, signals the end of the second epoch of salvation history (the period of Jesus) and the opening of the third (the period of the Church). More precisely, Conzelmann marked the period of post-Easter appearances up to the ascension as 'eine heilige Zeit zwischen den Zeiten' (189) and the period between ascension and Pentecost as 'ein geistloser Zwischenraum' (171, with H. von Baer)[1].

In a similar attempt to uncover the peculiarities of Luke's story, Haenchen[2] observed that in comparison with later apocryphal ascension stories (e.g. in the Gospel of Peter), Luke's version was very discrete and devoid of legendary details and personal impressions: 'unsere Geschichte ist unsentimental und von fast befremdender Nüchternheit' (157). Haenchen believed Luke was not the first to tell the story of the ascension, although he failed to provide firm evidence to sustain his thesis. The tradition of the forty days enabled Luke to commence his second book with the Risen One giving directions for the future (instead of the disciples being left alone)[3]. The narrative focus is on the event

---

[1] Conzelmann was *inter alios* followed by Grässer, *Das Problem der Parusieverzögerung in den synoptischen Evangelien und in der Apostelgeschichte* (BZNW 22; Berlin, New York: W. de Gruyter, 1957, ³1977) 178-215; idem, 'Die Parusieerwartung in der Apostelgeschichte', in: J. Kremer (éd.), *Les Actes des Apôtres. Traditions, rédaction, théologie* (BEThL 48; Gembloux: Duculot, 1979) 99-127.

[2] E. Haenchen, *Die Apostelgeschichte* (KEK III¹⁷; Göttingen: Vandenhoeck & Ruprecht, 1956, ⁷1977) 142-158.

[3] Later, Haenchen, 'Judentum und Christentum in der Apostelgeschichte', *ZNW* 54 (1963) 157-161; cf. idem, 'The Book of Acts as Source Material for the History of Early Christianity', in: L.E. Keck, J.L. Martyn (eds.), *Studies in Luke-Acts. Essays Presented in Honor of Paul Schubert* (Nashville, New York: Abingdon, 1966) 260-261, corroborated his thesis: Luke took up the tradition of the forty days to give a believable portrayal of the

itself and the angelic message. The story does not clarify the ascension but tries to correct the disciples' attitude (the problem of *Naherwartung*) (157). It was not Luke's goal to give a spectacular account of the ascension: 'Nicht der Historiker und nicht der fromme Erzähler Lukas, sondern der verantwortungsbewußte Christ, der seinen Brüdern zu dem gottgewollten Verständnis ihrer Existenz verhelfen wollte, hat die Gestalt dieses Abschnitts geformt, wenn man es einmal so überspißt ausdrücken darf' (158). This explains the absence in Acts 1 of the disciples' reaction (cf. Lk 24:4!) and of the blessing gesture (Lk 24:51): their personal relation to Jesus was subordinate to their role as representatives of the Christian community who need to grasp the proper relation between ascension and parousia. Luke replaced the expectation of the imminent parousia with an attitude, 'welche auf jede Datierung der Parusie verzichtet und insofern nicht mehr im Sehen lebt, sondern sich hier mit dem Unanschaulichen bescheidet' (158).

Whereas Haenchen believed that Luke had drawn the forty days from a source, Ph.H. Menoud[1], who earlier had defended a second-century provenance of the forty days (*supra* 5-6), in 1962 rejected his former thesis and was by now convinced that the number forty was a Lukan creation, a theological, not a chronological statement. He admitted by now that the few stylistic arguments and the total lack of MSS support for his 'single volume theory' formed too narrow a basis for his case. Had the forty days been inserted, it is not clear why, seeing that it did not play a significant role at that time.

In defence of his revised thesis he adduced three arguments: (1) Jesus addresses himself to the Twelve (not to the wider circle of disciples): the function of the forty days of instruction is to authenticate their role as custodians of the faith (149-150); (2) The number forty has strongly symbolic associations (150-152); (3) The fortieth day after the resurrection is not a Christian date, neither for Luke (who does not immediately link the forty days to the ascension) nor for the Christian Church of the first three centuries, which did not celebrate the ascension as a distinct day (152-154)[2].

---

message of the resurrection, which for Luke was the dividing issue between Judaism and Christianity (Acts 4:2).

[1] Menoud, 'Pendant Quarante Jours', in: W.C. van Unnik (ed.), *Neotestamentica et Patristica* (FS O. Cullmann; NT.S 6; Leiden: E.J. Brill, 1962) 148-156.

[2] According to G. Kretschmar, 'Himmelfahrt und Pfingsten', *ZKG* 66 (1954/55) 209-254, the custom of the Eastern Syriac and Palestinian Church (up to the fourth century AD) to celebrate the ascension on the fiftieth day after Easter (that is, on the day of Pentecost), represents an ancient liturgical tradition, independent from Luke-Acts, which may reach back into first-century Palestine, and even antedate Luke-Acts (211.246f.). The festival of Pentecost is derived from the ascension festival on the fiftieth day. As from the fourth century

Redaction criticism positively contributed to the understanding of the ascension narrative in that it made clear that Lk 24 and Acts 1 were in themselves carefully structured. P. Schubert, e.g., showed that the structure of Lk 24 as a whole was determined by literary and theological concerns, in particular a proof-from-prophecy pattern, and noted a progressive change of attitude of the disciples in chapter 24, beginning with their state of perplexity (v.4) and ending with their continuous praise of God in the temple (v.53) (176-177)[1].

P.A. van Stempvoort[2] made it clear that Lk 24 and Acts 1 were two different yet complementary interpretations of the ascension[3]. Lk 24:50-53 (longer text) is a 'doxology with the refined style of worship' (36-37.39), portraying Jesus as a blessing priest (following the example of Sir 50), who fulfils the unfinished *leitourgia* of Zechariah at the beginning of the Gospel. The description of Acts 1:9-11, on the other hand, is 'hard and realistic, leading into the future, but at the same time into the history of the Church, beginning from Jerusalem' (39). The typically Lukan realism of the narrative surfaces in the concrete description of the event by ἐπήρθη, the emphasis on the visibility of the event,

---

AD this tradition had to make room for the canonical chronology of Acts 1. The celebration of Pentecost in the primitive Church is very similar to that of the community of the covenant at Qumran and similar sectarian groupings (as e.g. in the Book of Jubilees). References are found in Holzmeister, 'Tag' 61-67; Kretschmar, 'Himmelfahrt' 209-211. Kretschmar's thesis was criticised by Lohfink, *Himmelfahrt* 137-144.

[1] P. Schubert, 'The Structure and Significance of Luke 24', in: Eltester (Hrsg.), *Neutestamentliche Studien* 165-186.

[2] Van Stempvoort, 'The Interpretation of the Ascension in Luke and Acts', *NTS* 5 (1958/59) 30-42.

[3] Van Stempvoort argued that ἀνελήμφθη (Acts 1:2) ought to be taken in its normal meaning 'to die, to be taken up in the sense of to pass away, removal out of this world' (32), and concluded 'that Acts i,2 do not speak about the 'ascension' in the developed technical sense, but about the 'passing away and being taken up' in the sense of Luke ix,51' (33). J. Dupont, '᾽ΑΝΕΛΗΜΦΘΗ (Act.i.2)' (1961); repr. in: idem, *Études sur les Actes des Apôtres* (LeDiv 45; Paris: Cerf, 1967) 477-480, criticised Van Stempvoort's thesis on several grounds: (1) the technical meaning of ἀναλαμβάνω is attested in NT (Acts 1:11,22; 1 Tim 3:16; Mk 16:19) and LXX (2 Kings 2:9-11; 1 Macc 2:58; Sir 48:9) and is required by the immediate context (Acts 1:9-11,22); (2) ῎Αχρι ἧς ἡμέρας ... ἀνελήμφθη should not be interpreted in the light of Lk 9:51, where ἀνάλημψις has admittedly a broader meaning (including passion, death, resurrection and ascension). The closer parallel is rather Acts 1:22. Since Luke says that his former treatise ends with the 'day on which he was taken up', ἀνελήμφθη must refer to the ascension; (3) The ascension took place 'after having instructed' his disciples. The parallel is between Acts 1:4 and Lk 24:49 (the command to stay in Jerusalem, which in both sections *precedes* the ascension). See further *infra* 30 n.3.

and particularly in the verb ὑπολαμβάνω ('to take up by getting under', 37-38, according to Liddell and Scott). Van Stempvoort writes: 'If we follow the normal meaning of ὑπολαμβ[άνω] in this way, the cloud is not a fog cloud hiding a mystery but a royal chariot showing the reality of the disappearance of Christ' (38). The Acts version ('the ecclesiastical and historical interpretation [of the ascension]', 39) attempts to explain why the christophanies had ceased, why the end had not yet come and why the disciples had to stay in Jerusalem 'where the prophets were killed' (39).

In opposition to the view that Luke's theological program was dominated by the delay of the imminent parousia (H. Conzelmann and E. Grässer), E. Franklin espoused the view that Luke's eschatological outlook was determined by the central significance of the ascension as the climax of redemptive history[1]. Through a number of editorial changes (Lk 22:69; 21:27; 21:7; 19:28-29,37; 19:38 (13:35); 9:31; 9:26; Acts 7:56) (192-194), Luke wished to make clear that the ascension rather than the parousia was God's decisive eschatological act in the history of the Jewish people[2]: 'The Ascension ... becomes for Luke the entry of Jesus into his full authority. He now enters into his glory (24.26): now, God has made him 'both Lord and Christ' (Acts 2.33-36): he is 'Lord of all' (Acts 10.36): the prophecy of Psalm 110.1 now finds fulfilment (Acts 2.34)' (194-195). The parousia will only reveal what is already a reality in heaven.

In a subsequent study Franklin argued in a similar vein that the ascension is an expression of belief in the *present* Lordship of Jesus[3]. For Luke, it is not the resurrection, but the ascension which marks the moment of Christ's glorification. In defence of his thesis he argued: (1) Luke's resurrection appearances are devoid of any hint of glorification; (2) The cloud, as the sign and means of Jesus' entry into heaven, witnesses to the glorification; (3) The ascension and the outpouring of the Spirit are not simply a series of events, but the ascension actually enables the gift of the Spirit, which testifies to the exaltation (Acts 2:33); (4) The lack of theophany marks is due to Luke's belief that the glorification took place in heaven, not on earth (31-32). Without the ascension Jesus would have been no other than one of the prophets.

In his study of the architecture of Luke-Acts and the principle of balance,

---

[1] E. Franklin, 'The Ascension and the Eschatology of Luke-Acts', *SJTh* 23 (1970) 191-200.

[2] Similarly, E.A. Laverdiere, 'The Ascension of the Risen Lord', *BiTod* 95 (1978) 1553-1559.

[3] Franklin, *Christ the Lord. A Study in the Purpose and Theology of Luke-Acts* (London: SPCK, 1975) 9-47.

C.H. Talbert attributed the ascension narratives for the most part to the artistic hand of Luke and circumscribed the ascension as a guarantee device to ascertain the corporeality of the ascension and the continuity of the dying and rising one with the ascending one, against a docetic tendency which advocated a spiritual ascension[1].

Meanwhile, with all the emphasis on the creative role of Luke, the search for a pre-Lukan ascension tradition continued[2]. G. Haufe raised the possibility that the earthly Jesus had already expected his *Entrückung*. On the basis of the rapture-preservation pattern in the Jewish rapture stories of Enoch, Elijah, Moses, Baruch and Ezra, he concluded that only those historical figures which were physically taken up to God could exercise an eschatological role[3]. He then concluded: 'Wußte sich Jesus zum Menschensohn designiert, dessen baldiges Kommen auf den Wolken des Himmels feststand, so muß er zuvor seine persönliche Entrückung erwartet haben' (112)[4]. F. Hahn[5] argued that the ascension in Acts 1:9-11 was patterned after the OT rapture narratives and regarded Jesus' present status in heaven as transient, 'bis zur Übernahme seiner eigentlichen Funktion in der Endzeit' (126), a primitive (pre-Lukan) conception that originally competed with the view that Jesus was exalted from his resurrection onwards[6]. R.H. Fuller also argued that 'the central statement [of Lk

---

[1] C.H. Talbert, *Literary Patterns, Theological Themes, and the Genre of Luke-Acts* (SBL.MS 20; Missoula, MO: Scholars, 1974) 58-65.112-116. See also idem, *Luke and the Gnostics. An Examination of the Lukan Purpose* (Nashville, New York: Abingdon, 1966) 17-19.27-32. In another essay he presents the ascension as a reflection on a mistaken identification of Jesus' ἀνάλημψις and his parousia, see Talbert, 'The Redaction Critical Quest for Luke the Theologian', in: *Jesus and Man's Hope* 1 (Perspective; Pittsburgh, PN: Pittsburgh Theological Seminary, 1970) 176-178.

[2] In a brief article G. Bouwman, 'Die Erhöhung Jesu in der lukanischen Theologie', *BZ NS* 14 (1970) 257-263, made some important methodological remarks with particular reference to the exaltation christology of Luke-Acts. See also the criteria developed by F. Hahn, 'Das Problem alter christologischer Überlieferungen in der Apostelgeschichte unter besonderer Berücksichtigung von Act 3,19-21', in: Kremer (éd.), *Actes* 131-135.

[3] G. Haufe, 'Entrückung und eschatologische Funktion im Spätjudentum', *ZRGG* 13 (1961) 105-113.

[4] A critique of Haufe's central statement is found in A. Strobel, *Kerygma und Apokalyptik. Ein religionsgeschichtlicher und theologischer Beitrag zur Christusfrage* (Göttingen: Vandenhoeck & Ruprecht, 1967) 64-71.

[5] Hahn, *Christologische Hoheitstitel. Ihre Geschichte im frühen Christentum* (FRLANT 83; Göttingen: Vandenhoeck & Ruprecht, 1963, ²1964) 126-132.

[6] Hahn's view was criticised by Ph. Vielhauer, 'Ein Weg zur neutestamentlichen Christologie? Prüfung der Thesen Ferdinand Hahns', in: idem, *Aufsätze zum Neuen Testament* (TB 31; München: Chr. Kaiser, 1965) 141-198, esp. 167-175.

24:50-53] ('and was carried up into heaven') may well be based on a primitive kerygmatic formula, belonging to the Palestinian-Aramaic christological stratum'[1].

The most daring attempts in this period to defend a pre-Lukan origin were undertaken by G. Schille and R. Pesch. Schille[2] attempted to determine the *Sitz im Leben* of Acts 1:3-12 as a cult-etiology of the Jerusalem Church on the fortieth day after the Passover, on which occasion the local Christian community used to reflect on the ascension of Christ (184-190). He argued that the function of Acts 1:9-11 was to recall to mind the most elementary facts of an otherwise known fact and that it may have been taken out of larger narrative unit. According to Schille various elements betrayed a liturgical concern: (1) The fact that the *Quadragesima* (usually understood as a period of preparation) follows rather than precedes Easter suggests that a specific day is in view. Since the date of Pentecost had been established according to the Jewish calender, not for historical but for liturgical reasons, the same may be the case with the date of the ascension; (2) The unexpected συνέρχεσθαι (v.6) may be taken as *terminus technicus* for the coming together of the Christian community in worship (1 Cor 11:18,20; 14:23,26; cf. Acts 10:27; 16:13; 28:17) (186); (3) The sudden transition to v.9 is rather awkward. The setting has changed (mealtime setting, v.4; Mount of Olives) and the dialogue scene (vv.4-8) makes room for a descriptive part (vv.9-11). Schille comments: 'Hatte Lukas die Darstellung durch das Essen und den Dialog menschlich aufgelockert, so halten die streng objektivierenden Verse 9-11 alle derartigen Züge nieder, ein Stilbruch, den ich mir nur mit überlieferungsgeschichtlichen Erwägungen erklären kann' (187); (4) Vv.6-8 are an appendix to the proemium (which contains a variety of traditional material), which comes in the place of a conventional preview of the book. Where the excursus ends traditional material may be expected; (5) The actual description of Jesus' rapture, brief and concise, reflects an almost hymnal structure (*parallelismus membrorum*, chiasms). In the present context the reference to the parousia is unexpected (a command to await the outpouring of the Spirit in Jerusalem, v.4, Lk 24:49, would be more in place); (6) V.12 does not add new material. This may indicate the presence of a source in the previous verses. That the distance is measured 'a sabbath day's journey' from Jerusalem may also reflect a liturgical concern: 'Schon der

---

[1] R.H. Fuller, *The Formation of the Resurrection Narratives* (Philadelphia: Fortress, 1971, [2]1980) 120-130 (quotation from 122-123). Fuller held Luke responsible for having changed the traditional sequence resurrection-assumption-appearances into resurrection-appearances-assumption (= ascension).

[2] G. Schille, 'Die Himmelfahrt', *ZNW* 57 (1966) 183-199.

Gedanke, eine Entfernung an der Sabbatgesetzlichkeit zu messen, obgleich das Berichtete nicht dem Anspruch erhebt, an einem Sabbat geschehen zu sein, ist seltsam. Wer den Rekurs auf das lukanische Unwissen für verfehlt hält—schon die Bezeichnung 'Sabbatweg' offenbart ein bestimmtes, allerdings merkwürdiges Wissen -, wird hier noch einmal ein irgendwie gottesdienstliches Moment angezeigt finden' (190). The specific location on the Mount of Olives (different from Lk 24:50 Bethany) is not due to the author's supposed lack of knowledge of local geography but stems from tradition. Schille concludes: 'Die Erzählung war eine Jerusalemer Ortsüberlieferung. Für die Erinnerung an eine Entrückung vom Ölberg aus war zuerst Jerusalems Gemeinde zuständig' (191)[1].

A critique of Schille's thesis was offered by S.G. Wilson[2]. He criticised him in the first place for ignoring the fact that the language and style of Acts 1:9-11 were predominantly Lukan, which makes it highly probable that the narrative is a Lukan construction rather than a piece of tradition (269). The fortieth day is simply Luke's attempt to fill up the hiatus between Easter and Pentecost. There is no linguistic evidence that συνέρχεσθαι (Acts 1:6) has the technical meaning of 'coming together to worship' (272-273). The narrative is brief not because of its supposed mnemonic function but because the emphasis is on the proper response of the disciples to the ascension rather than on the event itself (273). Wilson concluded 'that there is no good reason to suppose that Acts 1:9-11 is a unit of pre-Lukan tradition whose original *Sitz im Leben* was the worship of the early Jerusalem Christians. Much of the evidence points to a Lukan origin, and certainly none of it is irreconcilable with this view' (274). Luke was not concerned with the problem of the delay of the parousia (a remark addressed against Haenchen) since οὕτως ἐλεύσεται ὃν τρόπον is hardly an adequate answer to men expecting an imminent parousia. 'Rather, they are an answer to those who were inclined to deny that there would be any Parousia at all. Luke is not dealing with the problem of 'Naherwartung' as such. He is dealing with a problem that arose as a result of a disappointed

---

[1] In view of Kretschmar's thesis that the early Church did not attach any significance to the feast of ascension (*supra* 14-15 n.2), Schille argued that ancient Jerusalem traditions may have survived the catastrophes of the Jewish Revolt (Bar Kochba) in two ways, viz. by their adoption in non-Jewish churches (as e.g. the Markan Passion narrative, and the feast of Pentecost), or (which he believed was the case with the ascension) through their survival in the recollection of the Jerusalem Church (195).

[2] S.G. Wilson, 'The Ascension. A Critique and an Interpretation', *ZNW* 59 (1968) 269-281; repr. in: idem, *The Gentiles and the Gentile Mission in Luke-Acts* (MSSNTS 23; Cambridge: CUP, 1973) 88-107.

'Naherwartung,' namely a denial that the End would come at all. In the face of this denial Luke firmly reasserts that the End will come (v.11)' (277). Luke responded to two issues, namely the fervent renewal of false apocalyptic hopes (the imminent parousia, *praesumptio*) and loss of faith (denial of the parousia, *desperatio*).

The second effort to uncover a pre-Lukan stratum of the ascension story is that of R. Pesch[1]. He argued that despite its Lukan form and style Luke had made abundant use of source material in the ascension story. In addition to the material drawn from the Synoptic tradition (so e.g. the mealtime setting), traditional material is found in the notion of the forty days (following Haenchen) (13-14), the ascension (15-18), the promise of the Spirit and the missionary command (18-19). Vv.9-11 come from Luke's hand, except v.9b (καὶ νεφέλη ὑπέλαβεν αὐτὸν ἀπὸ τῶν ὀφθαλμῶν αὐτῶν) which is traditional (12-13). Because Acts 1:1-11 reflects a more Lukan style than Lk 24:50-53, source material is easier to recover in the latter passage. Lk 24 is inspired by the Elijah narrative and Sir 50:20-22, whereas Acts 1 only reflects an Elijah tradition. On the basis of a stylistic analysis Pesch made the following (hypothetical) reconstruction of the pre-Lukan source:

καὶ (ὁ Ἰησοῦς) παρέστησεν ἑαυτὸν ζῶντα ... ἐν πολλοῖς τεκμηριοῖς,
δι᾽ ἡμερῶν τεσσαράκοντα ὀπτανόμενος αὐτοῖς.
καὶ συναλιζόμενος παρήγγειλεν αὐτοῖς ἀπὸ Ἱεροσολύμων μὴ χωρίζεσθαι
ἀλλὰ περιμένειν· καθίσατε ἐν τῇ πόλει,
ἕως οὗ ἐνδύσησθε ἐξ ὕψους δύναμιν.
ἐξήγαγεν δὲ αὐτοὺς (ἔξω) ἕως πρὸς Βηθανίαν,
καὶ διέστη ἀπ᾽ αὐτῶν καὶ ἀνεφέρετο εἰς τὸν οὐρανόν
καὶ νεφέλη ὑπέλαβεν αὐτὸν ἀπὸ τῶν ὀφθαλμῶν αὐτῶν (17)[2].

In addition, Pesch observed that as early as the pre-Lukan tradition the ascension was connected with the conferring of the Spirit (18-19).

### e. *The Contribution of G. Lohfink and the Subsequent Debate*
The most comprehensive analysis of the Lukan ascension and exaltation texts so far is the doctoral dissertation of G. Lohfink[3], which is the first serious systematic attempt to take the *religionsgeschichtliche* parallels into account as

---

[1] R. Pesch, 'Der Anfang der Apostelgeschichte (Apg 1,1-11)', *EKK. V* 3 (Zürich: Benziger; Neukirchen: Neukirchener, 1971) 7-35.

[2] German translation in Pesch, *Die Apostelgeschichte* 1 (EKK 5; Neukirchen-Vluyn: Neukirchener; Zürich: Benzinger, 1986) 76 (where he partly resumes his thesis, 72-77).

[3] G. Lohfink, *Die Himmelfahrt Jesu. Untersuchungen zu den Himmelfahrts- und Erhöhungstexten bei Lukas* (StANT 26; München: Kösel, 1971).

a basis for understanding the Lukan ascension narratives[1] and to provide clear definitions and descriptions of the various ascension forms in antiquity[2].

Surveying Graeco-Roman literature (32-50), Lohfink identified two different types of ascension, viz. the heavenly journey of the soul (*Himmelsreise der Seele*) and the rapture (*Entrückung*). The first reports the transportation of a soul (ψυχή, πνεῦμα) into the heavenly realm either in ecstasy or at the end of one's life. The narrative focus of the heavenly journey story is on the events during the upward journey itself or the arrival in the heavenly world rather than on the destiny and is (necessarily so) always reported (sometimes quite dramatically) from the perspective of the traveller himself.

Unlike the heavenly journeys the accent of rapture stories is on the spatial *terminus a quo* and *terminus ad quem*: a person is taken away *from the human world* and transported *to the world of the gods*. They are always told from an earth-bound perspective, which implies that nothing more is reported than human beings could reasonably tell from their earthly perspective (sometimes bystanders simply infer from one's sudden vanishing that a rapture has taken place). Rapture narratives may describe the *locus dramatis* in quite some detail and usually heavily emphasise the role of witnesses. Furthermore, a rapture is experienced by the whole person: body and soul are taken up into heaven. Graeco-Roman rapture stories employ a variety of technical terms, of which ἀφανίζομαι and its cognates have become the most favourite (42-43)[3]. Literary motifs of a rapture include: mountain, pyre, flash of lightning, storm, chariot, eagle, cloud(s), accompanying phenomena (*Begleitmotive*, such as solar eclipse, earthquake etc.), heavenly confirmation, subsequent veneration and institution of a cult (42-49).

OT and early Judaism (51-74) also distinguish between heavenly journey (TAb B 7:19-8:3) and rapture (Gen 5:24; 2 Kings 2; 2 En 67; 4 Ezra 14; 2 Bar 76), but in addition know of two other types of ascensions, viz. the final

---

[1] Shortly after Lohfink, A. Schmitt, *Entrückung-Aufnahme-Himmelfahrt. Untersuchungen zu einem Vorstellungsbereich im AT* (FzB 10; Stuttgart: KBW, 1973, [2]1976) analysed the OT rapture and assumption texts and concluded: 'Entrückung, Aufnahme und Himmelfahrt im AT demonstrieren deutlich, daß mit diesem Vorstellungsbereich die Grundlagen für die neutestamentlichen Himmelfahrts- und Erhöhungstexte gegeben sind' (346). See also idem, 'Zum Thema 'Entrückung' im Alten Testament', *BZ NF* 26 (1982) 34-49.

[2] Significant preliminary work in the *religionsgeschichtliche* field has been done by E. Rohde, W. Bousset, C. Höhn, H. Diels, E. Bickermann, R. Holland, H. Schrade, St. Lösch, A.S. Pease, and G. Strecker. For bibliographic details, see Bibliography (a) and (c).

[3] Cf. G. Friedrich, 'Lk 9,51 und die Entrückungschristologie des Lukas', in: P. Hoffmann, N. Brox, W. Pesch (Hrsg.), *Orientierung an Jesus. Zur Theologie der Synoptiker* (FS J. Schmid; Freiburg: Herder, 1973) 53-54.

assumption of the soul at death (TAb B 14:6-7) and the ascent at the conclusion of an (angelic) appearance (Tob 12:20-22). As Jewish heavenly journeys purport to be revelatory, they never conclude (as in the Graeco-Roman tradition) the earthly life of the person involved: the traveller is supposed to deliver the divine oracles to his fellow people and his descendants. Like the pagan heavenly journeys this type of story is told from the perspective of the traveller himself. The Jewish sources lay much emphasis on the physical nature of an ascension. Not only the soul but the whole body is—in line with Jewish anthropology—taken up into heaven[1]. Jewish heavenly journey stories very often employ rapture terminology (e.g. GkApEzra 5:7), even though a clear distinction exists between the concepts themselves. The assumption of the soul (*Aufnahme der Seele*) is a final departure of the soul from the body, from earthly life (TAb B 14:6-7; LAE 32-37; TJud 9:3; 10:2; TJob 52), that is, only the soul is taken up into heaven, the body remains in the grave (54).

Unlike the heavenly journeys and assumptions of the soul, a rapture is concerned with a physical taking up of a human being into Paradise or heaven as the final conclusion of his earthly life (Enoch, Elijah, Ezra and Baruch). The ascent after an appearance of a heavenly being (an angel, the angel of YHWH or YHWH himself) is in fact a *return* to heaven (Gen 17:22; 35:13; Jub 32:20; *PJ* 3:17; Jud 6:21; Tob 12:20-22 S; TAb B 4:4). In Jewish tradition the same form-critical motifs occur as in the pagan narratives.

On the basis of this evidence Lohfink concludes that, form-critically, Luke's ascension narrative belongs to the rapture type (*Entrückung*). This is clear from the mountain motif (Acts 1:12), the farewell setting (Acts 1:6-8), the cloud (Acts 1:9), the *proskynesis* (Lk 24:52), the heavenly confirmation (Acts 1:11), the adoration (Lk 24:53), the narrative perspective (seen from the by-standing witnesses), and the final departure setting ('a cloud took him from their eyes'). Ἀναλαμβάνομαι (Acts 1:2,11,22; cf. Lk 9:51) is the most important rapture term of the LXX.

Lohfink then turns to NT writings other than Luke-Acts to analyse the theological significance of ascension and exaltation (80-146). In the earliest traditions resurrection and exaltation were placed in one event. Texts like Eph 4:8-10; 1 Tim 3:16 and 1 Pet 3:19,22, despite describing a heavenly ascent, do not conceptualise it in visible terms and are therefore, *stricto sensu*, not

---

[1] E.g. TAb B 7:18 ἐν σώματι. Lohfink, *Himmelfahrt* 53 comments: 'Mann muß wohl von dem Prinzip ausgehen, daß überall, wo nicht ausdrücklich das Gegenteil gesagt wird, die Reise ἐν σώματι geschieht. Selbst wenn vom 'Geist' oder der 'Seele' die Rede ist, muß damit gerechnet werden, daß die alttestamentliche Vorstellung von der רוח beziehungsweise der נפש bestimmend geblieben ist'.

*Entrückungstexte.* Lohfink concludes that there was no tradition independent from Luke-Acts that knows of a visible ascension of Jesus in front of witnesses, distinct in time from the resurrection. Texts like 1 Cor 15:3-8 and Mt 28:18-20 even seem to contradict the Lukan conception (95). The same verdict goes for the early patristic writings. It is only as late as Justin (*Apol* 1,50) and Irenaeus (*AdvHaer* I 10,1; II 32,3; III 10,6; 12,1.5; 16,8; 17,2; V 31,2; *Dem* 41; 83; 84) that the Lukan conception is carried through, albeit parallel to the exaltation kerygma, which persisted into the fifth century AD (145).

In a chapter discussing the form-critical aspects of the Lukan ascension texts Lohfink observes that the final part of Luke (24:36-53) consists of three components (147-148): (a) narrative (vv.36-43) = recognition scene; (b) speech of Jesus (vv.44-49) = teaching scene; (c) narrative (vv.50-53) = farewell scene. Lohfink suggests that (c) does not belong to the original tradition for the following reasons: first of all, there is no compelling relationship between (a) and (c). The recognition scene suggests a first appearance rather than a last departure (c). The farewell scene does not need to be introduced by the recognition scene. Secondly, (b) does need a conclusion (c), but since the teaching scene (according to Lohfink) is a Lukan composition one cannot hold that (a) and (c) belong together. Thirdly, the form recognition scene + teaching scene is traditional (Jn 20:19-23; 21:1-23; Acts 10:34-43). Fourthly, when (a) + (b) is traditional, there is much to say for understanding (c) as a Lukan composition. Adding a conclusion to an appearance scene is a distinctly Lukan technique[1]. Finally, καὶ ἦσαν διὰ παντὸς ἐν τῷ ἱερῷ εὐλογοῦντες τὸν θεόν (v.53) is a typical Lukan summary (151).

Lohfink concludes that the original textual components of the ascension narrative of Lk 24:50-53 are a very small part of the whole. Acts 1:3 is a Lukan summary of Lk 24:50-53 (the forty days are Lukan redaction, see our discussion *infra* 186-188); the search for tradition should therefore concentrate on vv.9-11. There are only two elements that the two Lukan ascension narratives have in common, viz. the actual description of the ascension (ἀνεφέρετο εἰς τὸν οὐρανόν Lk 24:51 and ἐπήρθη Acts 1:9) and its location on the Mount of Olives (if ἕως πρὸς Βηθανίαν be so understood). From a tradition-critical view, however, the two Lukan accounts differ. Lk 24 is determined by the motifs of benediction and *proskynesis*, Acts 1 by the cloud motif. The function of the cloud is to conceal, to convey, and to symbolise

---

[1] Lk 1:38; 2:15; 9:33; 24:31; Acts 10:7; 12:10. But see the correction by M.C. Parsons, *The Departure of Jesus in Luke-Acts. The Ascension Narratives in Context* (JSNT.S 21; Sheffield: JSOT, 1987) 59-61.

God's presence (187-193)[1]. Since the motifs, as they stand, fit their contexts so perfectly it is highly unlikely that Luke had two different ascension traditions at his disposal, which he reworked separately[2]. Other doublets (such as the conversion narrative of Paul) are equally Lukan constructs[3]. It is also unlikely that Luke disposed of only one ascension tradition containing the motifs of benediction, *proskynesis* and the cloud together, which he subsequently separated into two different accounts. It is impossible that the *proskynesis* (the definite response, recognition) stems from the same tradition as the angels' scene (which suggest an indefinite, open future). The only solution (according to Lohfink) is that the two accounts are both the result of Luke's composition technique.

In a thorough *motivkritische* analysis Lohfink further reduces the materials eligible for the redaction-critical quest to the mere concept of the ascension, i.e. the words ἀνεφέρετο and ἐπήρθη (210). This raises the question where Luke got his theme from. Having investigated the other Lukan ascension and exaltation texts (Lk 9:51; Acts 1:1f.; 1:21; 3:19-21; 2:32-35; 5:30-32; 13:32f.; Lk 24:26), Lohfink comes to the conclusion that the only Lukan texts that have an exaltation background are Acts 2:32-35; 5:30-32 and 13:32f. Without denying that Luke may have had access to the original exaltation tradition he asserts that Luke 'historicised' the exaltation in terms of an ascension: '(...) aus einem unsichtbaren Vorgang wird ein Ereignis, das bezeugt werden kann' (240). In other words, Luke is responsible for having converted the *Erhöhungskerygma* into a rapture story. The two ascension accounts, then, go back to Luke himself, not to earlier tradition.

Lohfink closes his study with some remarks on the question of historicity, which he feels assumes an unfortunate distinction between historical-unhistorical, and which wrongly assumes that Luke's concern is the reporting of an event (*Ereignis*) and that this event is a *historical* one. Luke's realistic picturing cannot be pressed as to describe a historical event in time and space (276-283)[4].

---

[1] Likewise: J. Luzarraga, *Las Tradiciones de la Nube en la Biblia y en el judaismo primitivo* (AnBib 54; Roma: IBP, 1973) 220-225. Luzarraga's study has been reviewed and introduced to English readers by L. Sabourin, 'The Biblical Cloud. Terminology and Traditions', *BTB* 4 (1974) 290-311.

[2] So e.g. Davies, *Ascended* 49.

[3] Lohfink, *Paulus vor Damaskus. Arbeitsweisen der neueren Bibelwissenschaft dargestellt an den Texten Apg 9,1-19; 22,3-21; 26,9-18* (SBS 4; Stuttgart: KBW, 1965).

[4] The question of historicity has been a matter of sharp debate between D.W. Gooding and J.D.G. Dunn. Gooding, 'Demythologizing Old and New, and Luke's Description of the Ascension. A Layman's Appraisal', *IBSt* 2 (1980) 95-119, sharply criticised the what he

Lohfink has put his mark upon a number of exegetes, such as E. Kränkl[1], J.M. Guillaume[2], M. Dömer[3], J. Hug[4], and J. Zmijewski[5].

While the vast majority of NT scholars has accepted Lohfink's form-critical assessment of the ascension as an *Entrückungserzählung*, K. Berger[6] put forward the view that Lk 24 represents the pattern 'resurrection-manifestation-ascent to heaven' ('Auferweckung, Sichtbarwerden und Hinaufgehen in den Himmel', 474) (as in Rev 11:3-13; EvPe 10), while the narrative of Acts 1 forms the conclusion of an appearance (171)[7]. Similarly, J.F. Maile criticised Lohfink for placing the ascension narratives too firmly in the category of rapture stories and suggested the influence of the form of an 'ascension at the end of an appearance' and of the OT parting scenes[8]. All in all, however, alternative form-critical assessments remain exceptions.

Lohfink's attempt to assign the entire narrative to Luke's creative activity, however, met with much stronger opposition. F. Hahn[9] objected to the straightforward identification of resurrection and exaltation and repeated his

---

called 'new generation of demythologizers' for 'not believing what Luke has written', and criticised Dunn in particular, who in a passing comment had suggested that the ascension was a (literal) description depending on a first century cosmology no longer possible to us; see Dunn, 'Demythologizing—The Problem of Myth in the New Testament', in: I.H. Marshall (ed.), *New Testament Interpretation. Essays on Principles and Methods* (Exeter: Paternoster, 1977, [2]1979) 285-307 (the critical passage on p.300). See further his responding article, Dunn, 'Demythologizing the Ascension. A Reply to Professor Gooding', *IBSt* 3 (1981) 15-27.

[1] E. Kränkl, *Jesus der Knecht Gottes. Die heilsgeschichtliche Stellung Jesu in den Reden der Apostelgeschichte* (BU 8; Regensburg: F. Pustet, 1972) 149-166.

[2] J.M. Guillaume, *Luc interprète des anciennes traditions sur la résurrection de Jésus* (EtB; Paris: Librairie Lecoffre, J. Gabalda, 1979) 203-262, with a more positive appraisal of the influence of the Jewish rapture and vindication-exaltation texts.

[3] M. Dömer, *Das Heil Gottes. Studien zur Theologie des lukanischen Doppelwerkes* (BBB 51; Köln, Bonn: P. Hanstein, 1978) 95-128, but preferring the term *Aufnahme* to *Entrückung* or *Himmelfahrt* (108 Anm.43).

[4] J. Hug, *La Finale de l'Évangile de Marc (Mc 16,9-20)* (EtB; Paris: J. Gabalda, 1978) 128-153.

[5] J. Zmijewski, *Die Apostelgeschichte übersetzt und erklärt* (RNT 5; Regensburg: F. Pustet, 1994) esp. 68-72.

[6] K. Berger, *Die Auferstehung des Propheten und die Erhöhung des Menschensohnes* (StUNT 13; Göttingen: Vandenhoeck & Ruprecht, 1976) 170-174.471-475.

[7] For a brief critique of Berger's thesis, see A. Weiser, 'Himmelfahrt Christi I. Neues Testament', *TRE* 15 (1986) 332.

[8] J.F. Maile, 'The Ascension in Luke-Acts', *TynB* 37 (1986) 40-44.

[9] Hahn, 'Die Himmelfahrt Jesu. Ein Gespräch mit Gerhard Lohfink', *Bib.* 55 (1974) 418-426.

earlier thesis that exaltation and ascension traditions may have coexisted (422-423) (*supra* 17). One should reckon with pliable borders between visual (as in the ascension narratives) and invisible representations of the ascension (as in the cosmic ascension texts of Colossians, Ephesians, 1 Timothy and 1 Peter) (423). Perhaps the fact that the period of appearances had come to a close (1 Cor 15:5-10) has played a constitutive role. With a view to Mk 2:20; Acts 3:20f.; 1 Thess 1:10; Rev 12:5; Jn 20:17 and Barn 15:9, Hahn suggested that one should allow for much more diversity in the earliest (pre-Lukan) strata than Lohfink was willing to admit (424). The Gnostic attempts to assign a specific term to the period of appearances are unlikely to be totally dependent upon Luke (425).

F. Bovon[1] similarly felt that Lohfink had overstated his case and challenged the legitimacy of distinguishing the (visible) ascension from the (invisible) exaltation. In this respect the conception of the Fourth Gospel and Hebrews may be closer to Luke-Acts than Lohfink was willing to concede. Was Luke really the only writer to 'historicise' the exaltation?[2] Jewish Christian texts as EvPe 9:35-42 and Barn 15:9 may reflect the same intention to squeeze the exaltation into salvation history (188)[3].

Generally speaking, Lohfink's case for redaction was felt to be more convincing for Lk 24:50-53 than for Acts 1. M.C. Parsons, for one, remarked: '... whatever pristine tradition may have existed prior to Luke is irrecoverable from the heavily redacted passage in Luke 24.50-53'[4], but he continued his quest for sources in Acts 1. On the basis of the peculiar vocabulary of Acts 1:9 (βλεπόντων αὐτῶν, ἐπαίρω, ὑπολαμβάνω, νεφέλη, ὀφθαλμός) and extra-biblical texts like Mk 16:19, Codex Bobiensis on Mk 16:3 and Barn 15:9, which in Parsons' view might well provide independent evidence of an ascension tradition (140-149), Parsons concluded that the present text '... may best be explained as the result of an ascension scene which was transmitted through the tradition and compressed in the Gospel to construct a leave-taking scene along the lines of a biblical farewell account, and expanded in Acts by formal elements of heavenly assumption stories' (62).

In addition to disapproval of Lohfink's redaction-critical thesis, criticism

---

[1] Bovon, *Luc le théologien* 181-190.

[2] Cf. Bovon, 'Himmelfahrt Christi', *EKL* 2 (³1989) 522-523, where he is more cautious.

[3] G. Schneider, *Die Apostelgeschichte 1. Einleitung. Kommentar zu Kap.1,1-8,40* (HThK 5; Freiburg: Herder, 1980) 209-211. Cf. Schille, *Apg* 75-76, who accepts Lohfink's form-critical assessment but thinks he decided too rash for redaction.

[4] Parsons, *Departure* 63. Likewise R.J. Dillon, *From Eye-Witnesses to Ministers of the Word. Tradition and Composition in Luke 24* (AnBib 82; Roma: IBP, 1978) 220.

was levelled against his *Verhältnisbestimmung* of the resurrection-exaltation-ascension complex, so e.g. R.F. O'Toole[1], L. Goppelt[2], M.C. Parsons[3], and K. Giles[4]. In this respect the studies of J.G. Lygre, J.A. Fitzmyer and J.F. Maile deserve particular mention.

Lygre argued in his doctoral dissertation that both the resurrection and the ascension are essential aspects of Jesus' exaltation-enthronement[5]. Defining resurrection as 'God's raising Jesus from the dead' (6.60), ascension as 'Jesus' being lifted up from earth to heaven' (137; cf. 6), and exaltation as 'God's granting Jesus sovereign status' (6.61), Lygre concluded:

> 'Although resurrection and ascension are distinguished in Luke's presentation and given individual identities, they are to be considered as aspects not of one another, but of exaltation-enthronement. Luke uses exaltation-enthronement to express dynamically God's act in granting sovereign authority to the crucified, raised and ascended Jesus' (196)[6].

In line with Benoit, Fitzmyer stressed the importance of making the proper distinctions between the various assertions about the ascension[7]. In the earliest traditions references to Christ's existence following his burial were cast in terms of his exaltation (that is, his being taken up to the glorious presence of the Father), sometimes without an express mention of the resurrection (Phil 2:8-11; 1 Tim 3:16; the Johannine exaltation texts), sometimes with it (Acts 2:33; 5:30-31; cf. Rom 6:4). Belief in Christ's glorious exaltation is implied in NT texts that simply refer to his presence in heaven without specifying how he arrived there (1 Thess 1:10; 4:16; Rev 1:12-18 etc.), and in references to the resurrection without a mention of the exaltation (1 Cor 15:3-5) (410-413).

In dealing with the ascension two sorts of references are to be distinguished: texts that allude to Jesus' exaltation as an ascension (Heb 4:14; 9:24; 1 Pet

---

[1] R.F. O'Toole, 'Luke's Understanding of Jesus' Resurrection-Ascension-Exaltation', *BTB* 9 (1979) 106-114.

[2] L. Goppelt, *Theologie des Neuen Testaments* (hrsg. v. J. Roloff; UTB 850; Göttingen: Vandenhoeck & Ruprecht, 1976, ³1978) 293-294.

[3] Parsons, *Departure* 149.

[4] K. Giles, 'Ascension', *DJG* (1992) 46-50.

[5] J.G. Lygre, *Exaltation. Considered with Reference to the Resurrection and Ascension in Luke-Acts* (Diss. Princeton Theological Seminary, 1975).

[6] Cf. also Lygre, *Exaltation* 205. Along similar lines M. Korn, *Die Geschichte Jesu in veränderter Zeit. Studien zur bleibenden Bedeutung Jesu im lukanischen Doppelwerk* (WUNT 2/51; Tübingen: J.C.B. Mohr/Paul Siebeck, 1993) 169.269.

[7] J.A. Fitzmyer, 'The Ascension of Christ and Pentecost', *TS* 45 (1984) 409-440; idem, *The Gospel According to Luke X-XXIV. Introduction, Translation, and Notes* (AncB 28A; Garden City, NY: Doubleday, 1985) 1586-1593.

3:22; Rom 10:6-8; Eph 4:7-11; Jn 20:17) (413-416) and texts that describe or depict the ascension (Lk 24:50-51; Acts 1:9-11; Mk 16:19) (416-421). Lk 24:50-51 (longer text) utilises the apparently more primitive expressions of the ascension, couched in the passive, and describes an Easter Sunday evening ascension. In Acts 1:9-11 Luke situates the ascension in space and time with the aid of apocalyptic stage-props (clouds, angel-interpreters). 'The exaltation is already pre-Lucan, even if the graphic details of its mode are not' (420-421). Since the resurrection of Jesus is never presented in the NT as a return to his physical, terrestrial life as e.g. in the case of Lazarus, the question arises, from where Jesus appeared to his disciples. Lk 24:26 (οὐχὶ ταῦτα ἔδει παθεῖν τὸν χριστὸν καὶ εἰσελθεῖν εἰς τὴν δόξαν αὐτοῦ;) suggests Jesus had already entered the glorious presence of the Father before his conversation with the Emmaus disciples, so that the 'spatial' *terminus a quo* of his appearances was his Father's glory (cf. Rom 6:4), the difference with Paul's Damascus road experience being only temporal (postpentecostal *vs.* prepentecostal) (422). This may find confirmation in the fact that Jesus was not immediately recognised when he appeared: 'one must recall what Paul says of the difference between a 'physical body' sown in death and a 'spiritual body' raised therefrom ([1 Cor] 15,42-44)' (423). The ascension is 'nothing more than *the* appearance from glory in which Christ took his final leave from the community of his followers' (424, his emphasis)[1]. The forty days (a round number) are preparatory to the more important fiftieth day. The interval is not meant for some development of Jesus' role in salvation history, but for the instruction of the disciples (438).

J.F. Maile[2] likewise argued that both Lk 24 and Acts 1 describe the conclusion of the resurrection appearances of the already exalted Lord (39-44) and that Luke in this respect is in agreement with the rest of the NT in that he marks the resurrection as the occasion of Jesus' exaltation (44-48). Maile defined the ascension as a *confirmation* of the exaltation of Christ and his present Lordship. The ascension, according to Maile, explains the continuity between the ministry of Jesus and that of the Church and forms the culmination of the resurrection appearances. Following Menoud and Lohfink with respect to the redactional character of the number 40, Maile calls the forty days 'a vital vehicle for conveying Luke's theology of continuity' (48-54).

f. *Recent Developments*
We have already referred to the study of M.C. Parsons on several occasions.

---

[1] Fitzmyer, *Luke* 2, 1588.
[2] Maile, 'Ascension' 29-59.

His major contribution is in the area of literary criticism[1]. With the help of the tools of traditional historical criticism (textual, form, source, and redaction criticism = diachronic analysis) and narrative analysis (narrative and canonical criticism = synchronic analysis) he has tried to determine how Lk 24:50-53 and Acts 1:1-11 function (both independently from each other and taken together) in their historical, literary and canonical context (18-25). Text-critically, Parsons defended the shorter reading of Lk 24:50-53 on the basis of a supposed tendency on the part of the scribe of $\mathfrak{P}^{75}$, the oldest extant copy of Luke (29-52). As neither the OT theophany stories nor the primitive apostolic commissioning scenes—the most likely candidates for the *Gattung* of Lk 24:50-53—had a fixed pattern of conclusion, Parsons suggested that 'Luke was forced to look elsewhere to bring his final story to a proper dénouement. Having already used the form of the biblical farewell address in Luke 22, it is most natural that he return there at the end of his Gospel. By delaying the concluding elements to this point in the narrative, Luke is able to tie the entire passion, resurrection, and departure of Jesus into an *inclusio* introduced by the farewell address of Luke 22 and concluded by the departure of Jesus in the pattern of a departing hero in Luke 24' (58).

With the help of M. Torgovnick's literary theory on narrative closure techniques[2], Parsons studied closure and plot development in Luke. Through the device of *circularity* (= 'the recalling at the end of a story of characters, settings, or situations which have not recurred since the beginning', 73), Luke connects the infancy narrative (Lk 1-2) with the resurrection narrative (Lk 24)[3]. Parsons comments: 'Certainly the painting evangelist of the Third Gospel has effectively related the end of his story to the beginning, and in so doing has drawn his own circle on the Gospel canvas. The narrator ends the narrative where it started and the readers, already familiar with the Gospel, are able to know the place and the story perhaps for the first time' (77). The pattern of *parallelism* (= the relationship between the ending and the middle of a narrative work, 77), which helps to develop the plot of the narrative and leads to its

---

[1] See F.S. Spencer, 'Acts and Modern Literary Approaches', in: B.W. Winter, A.D. Clarke (eds.), *The Book of Acts in Its Ancient Literary Setting* (BAFCS 1; Grand Rapids: Eerdmans; Carlisle: Paternoster, 1993) 381-414, for a general assessment of literary approaches to the Book of Acts.

[2] M. Torgovnick, *Closure in the Novel* (Princeton: Princeton University Press, 1981).

[3] So the priestly blessing (Lk 1:23; 24:51), the return to Jerusalem (Lk 2:45; 24:33,52), the role of heavenly beings (as characters in the story, Lk 1:11,26; 2:13 and the resurrection narrative), the emphasis on the pious people of God and the dominant role of the temple and Jerusalem in the opening and closing chapters of the Gospel.

denouement, is developed in the Gospel through conflict scenes (mealtime conflicts, misunderstandings by the disciples and temple and synagogue confrontation scenes), the motif of prophecy and fulfilment, and the journey motif (78-93).

In the ascension narrative itself the following literary devices seem to have been employed by the author: the device of *linkage* or interlacing[1] is particularly prominent in Lk 24 and Acts 1, and serves to connect the story of Jesus with the story of his followers. The literary device of *incompletion* presents themes which do not find fulfilment in the Gospel. Thus the expectation of salvation of Israel and the promises of the infancy narratives are left unresolved in the Gospel. And the promise of Jesus' ἀνάλημψις (Lk 9:51) does not (!) find its fulfilment in the Gospel (95)[2]. Of the two types of closure developed by Torgovnick—the *overview ending*, in which either the narrator's and reader's understanding is superior to the characters, or the conclusion is related 'from a point much later in or more cosmic in knowledge than that available to the novel's character' and the *close-up ending*, in which there is no temporal gap between the body of the narrative and its conclusion (96)—Lk 24:50-53 falls under the latter category. It is a 'silent' scene which creates distance between the reader and the story (as in Lk 1:1-4).

In the Book of Acts[3] the narrative plot is developed through *circularity* (the prominent position of the Kingdom of God in the beginning and ending of Acts, Acts 1:3,6; 28:23,31; the connection between the command of worldwide mission, Acts 1:8, and the activity of Paul in Rome, Acts 28:23-31; the term διδάσκω, Acts 1:1; 28:31) and *parallelism* (Luke's treatment of the Jews, an acceptance or rejection pattern, conflict scenes, the Christian community in Acts). In Acts Luke employs an empty centre narrative patterning (about a character who is 'absent but curiously present ... around which both the major

---

[1] Cf. Dupont, 'La question du plan des Actes des Apôtres à la lumière d'un texte de Lucien de Samosate' (1979); repr. in: idem, *Nouvelles Études sur les Actes des Apôtres* (LeDiv 118; Paris: Cerf, 1984) 24-36, providing extensive examples of interlacing in Luke-Acts.

[2] Here, it should be noted, Parsons is particularly dependent on his text-critical stance. If the longer text is original, as I have argued elsewhere (see Zwiep, 'Text', 219-244), we do not have incompletion but parallelism.

[3] As for Acts 1:2, Parsons (defending the authenticity of ἀνελήμφθη) believes the word was intentionally, but erroneously, removed from the text to harmonise the text with (the shorter reading of) Lk 24:51. Taking up and partially modifying Van Stempvoort's arguments and responding to Dupont's criticisms (*supra* 15 n.3), Parsons argued that Luke would have the word refer to Jesus' entire journey back to God (burial, resurrection, exaltation), but that later (Western) revisers erroneously interpreted it as a reference to the ascension. Augustine may be blamed for the excision of the ascension in the Western tradition.

action and the various characters' thoughts revolve'[1]): Jesus himself is gone but his impact is still there.

The device of *reverse linkage* (in which a sequel refers to its predecessor) is employed in various ways: Acts 1-Lk 24; Acts 1-Lk 9; and Acts 1 and the resurrection narratives. '(...) The narrative beginning of Acts has sufficient reverse linkage with the Gospel that the readers are constantly called upon to remember the story of Jesus, while learning about the story of the early church' (173). The *viewpoint* at the beginning of the narrative (which provides access from the world of the reader to the world of the text) moves from an external point of view to an internal point of view: 'When Jesus is lifted up and a cloud removes him out of the sight of the disciples, he is also removed out of the sight of the narrator and reader as well' (175). Whereas in Luke it is the narrator who orients the presentation of the event (= external focalisation), the Acts narrative is viewed from the perspective of the disciples (= internal focalisation).

The device of *defamiliarisation* (challenging norms held by—in our case—favourable characters) is found in Jesus' response to the disciples' question (vv.6-8) and the angels' rhetorical question (v.10). The narrator employed this device in order to correct two insufficient values held by the disciples and the implied readers regarding the place of Israel in the kingdom of God and the significance of the ascension. The *primacy effect* (the effect of the reader's first impression of a character, either favourable or negative) is employed here in a positive sense: '... the apostles are presented in a very favorable light; their values are corrected, but they are *still* Jesus' chosen witnesses and spokespersons' (183, his emphasis).

In the concluding section Parsons analyses the departure of Jesus in canonical context. The similarities and differences between the two narratives are best explained, not in terms of interpolation or source theories, but in terms of their literary function.

The literary device of *redundancy* enabled Luke to tie his two volumes together and to move his story ahead (191-198). The temporal discrepancy is to be explained on literary grounds. The mention of the forty days would be inappropriate at the end of the Gospel because this would destroy the effect of the close-up ending (which has no temporal gap between the ending and the body of the novel); it is, however, appropriate in an overview scene such as Acts 1 (194-195)[2].

---

[1] M. Kreiswirth, quoted by Parsons, *Departure* 161.

[2] Parsons is followed by *inter alios* R.C. Tannehill, *The Narrative Unity of Luke-Acts. A Literary Interpretation* (Foundations and Facets; Philadelphia: Fortress, 1986) 1, 298-301

At the risk of oversimplifying and thereby misrepresenting the intention of the authors, we confine our discussion of M.É. Boismard and A. Lamouille to their contribution to the ascension narratives. For the sake of fairness it must be borne in mind that their conclusions form part of a larger theory on the composition of Luke-Acts as a whole[1]. Some preliminary clarifications, however, are indispensable.

According to the authors, the Book of Acts in its present form has come into existence in three successive editorial stages (Act I, Act II and Act III), whereby each editor has to a greater or lesser extent used and modified written sources. The composition of Act I (1, 3-30), written around 60-62 AD by an unknown Jewish Christian, goes back to a period in which Luke-Acts was still a one-volume book. Act I had a Document P (of predominantly Petrine traditions) at his disposal for the first part of Acts (the exploits of Peter, Acts 1:6-12:25 except 9:1-30) and a travel account for the second (the exploits of Paul, Acts 9:1-30; 13:1-28:31). For both sections he also had access to a Document J, comprising Baptist traditions. Act I, in turn, provided the main source for Act II (1, 31-43), a rewritten and polished version of Act I composed by Luke the Physician, the traditional companion of Paul, in the eighth decade of the first century AD (1, 41-43). He rewrote his source with the help of Document P and the original Document J. The result corresponds to the Western text. Act III (1, 43-51) marks the final stage of composition, in the last decade of the first century, probably in Rome (1, 50-51). The editor used Act II, Document P, Act I, and the travel account. His text concurs with the Alexandrian text.

The oldest version of the ascension (Document P) corresponds to Lk 24:50-53 minus the words ἐγένετο ἐν τῷ εὐλογεῖν αὐτὸν αὐτούς (v.51) (2, 27-31). This description is reminiscent of the Elijah narrative, although the author did not purposely portray Jesus as the New Elijah (2, 28.29). He sees Jesus as the New High Priest of the New Covenant (cf. the blessing gesture based on Lev 9:22; Sir 45:15; 50:20; fulfilling Ps 110:4; cf. Heb 5:1) and as King (the motif of *proskynesis*), both elements inspired by Ps 110 (King: Ps 110:1; Priest: Ps 110:4). The royal element finds confirmation in the location of the event in Bethany (as a fulfilment of Lk 19:38). Since in Document P the ascension is the only and final post-Easter appearance, the joy of the disciples (v.52) is inspired by the recognition that their Master lives forever (this would otherwise be a bit

---

(following Parsons' original Ph.D.-thesis); (1990) 2, 9-25.

[1] For what follows, see M.-É. Boismard, A. Lamouille, *Les Actes des deux apôtres* (EtB; Paris: Librairie Lecoffre, J. Gabalda, 1990) 2, 27-31.93-97.142-143.201; 3, 35-40. For a convenient summary of their theory, see idem, *Actes* 1, 3-51; 3, 7-26.

awkward after Jesus' final departure): 'La joie qui les envahit n'est pas autre que la joie paschale, la joie de la résurrection' (2, 30). The disciples are continuously present in the temple (v.53) at the hours of prayer (Acts 3:1), 'c'est à dire à l'heure où l'on immolait l'agneau du sacrifice (Ex 29:38-42) et où un prêtre allait déposer l'encens sur l'autel des parfums (Lc 1,8-20; cf. Ex 30,1-9)' (2, 30). In sum, the intention of the author is to make it clear that Jesus fulfils the double oracle of Ps 110:1,4 'Sit at My right hand ... You are priest forever' (2, 31).

The next editorial stage is found in Acts 1:6-14a, which is the result of the rewriting of Document P (Lk 24:50-53) by Act I (2, 93-97). The worship in the temple (Lk 24:53) has now made room for private worship (Acts 1:14), reflecting the state of affairs of the editor. In Act I Jesus is identified as the New Elijah (confirmed by the parallels between Acts 1:6-14a and 2 Kings 2). The cloud motif (absent in Lk 24:50-53) betrays the influence of the Danielic Son of Man, and the location of the event at the Mount of Olives alludes to Zech 14:4. The phrase 'was removed away from their eyes' (Acts 1:9) marks Jesus' definitive separation from his disciples. Its wording reminds us of the 'removal of the bride' (Lk 5:35), an occasion of sadness. That Jesus' ascension likewise evokes sadness is confirmed by the fact that Act I does not recall the motif of joy.

The author of Act II (= Luke) is responsible for fusing Document P and Act I together. To avoid a discrepancy between Luke and Acts he adopted Act I unalteredly and transformed Document P into a final departure scene by excising καὶ ἀνεφέρετο εἰς τὸν οὐρανόν and προσκυνήσαντες αὐτὸν. This (Lukan!) text survived in the primitive Western text (2, 142-143). In the final stage of composition (Act III) (2, 201) the omitted words were reinserted by the final editor (2, 142).

### g. *Conclusions*

Drawing together the lines of this survey we are now in a position to define the direction and progress of modern Ascension-*Forschung* and to situate the present study. There appears to be a general agreement that the author of Luke-Acts is, to a significant degree, responsible for the style and formulation of the ascension pericopae (Lk 24:50-53; Acts 1:1-12). This has been demonstrated conclusively by the investigations of V. Larrañaga and G. Lohfink and has been reaffirmed by the literary-critical analysis of M.C. Parsons. One of the continuing controversies revolves around the question whether and to what extent Luke is also responsible for their *content*. Is the ascension story a free creation of the author or can it be traced back to a pre-Lukan stage of tradition-history? And if so, in what form did it exist?

A further area of agreement is the general recognition of the key role of the ascension in the narrative structure and in the theological outlook of Luke. But authors who have recently treated the issue are far from unanimous in their assessment of what the ascension means theologically or christologically: does it constitute the moment of Christ's exaltation (and if so, does that mean a denigration of the resurrection?) or is it an 'afterthought' with no real christological implications? And, granted that the ascension is important to Luke, why is it an apparently marginal belief in the rest of the NT and early Christian thinking?

A third point of agreement which is virtually undisputed since the work of Lohfink is that the Lukan ascension story is presented as a rapture story (*Entrückungserzählung*).

There are three further areas in the study of the ascension narratives that require closer examination.

First of all, the textual criticism of the ascension narratives. The modern consensus to regard the 'longer (non-Western) text' to be authentic has been challenged by M.C. Parsons and M.-É. Boismard and A. Lamouille. I have treated the issue elsewhere (cf. *supra* 1 n.2). In what follows I will build on that study.

Secondly, whereas the bearing of Graeco-Roman rapture stories (Lohfink) and the OT rapture stories (Schmitt) on the Lukan narrative have received ample treatment in contemporary scholarship, the impact of early Jewish ('intertestamental') literature has received relatively little attention[1]. As I shall argue below, pre-Christian (or at least pre-Lukan) Judaism may provide at least as plausible a horizon of understanding (if not a better one) for the interpretation of the ascension as the Graeco-Roman rapture tradition.

Thirdly, closely related to this, the predominant tendency of scholarship since Strauß has been to establish the meaning of the ascension in the light of the resurrection-exaltation kerygma, that is, *in concreto*, as a narrative expression of Jesus' *exaltatio ad dexteram Dei* (Ps 110:1). This tends to inhibit an understanding of the ascension from a different perspective and not rarely leads to a minimising of the importance of the ascension in its own right and/or in a different constellation. We must bear in mind that from the perspective of *Religionsgeschichte*, strictly speaking, resurrection and ascension (in the sense of a bodily *Entrückung*) are competitive (not to say mutually exclusive)

---

[1] This is true of Lukan scholarship in general. A promising first step in a new direction is the study of E. Reinmuth, *Pseudo-Philo und Lukas. Studien zum Liber Antiquitatum Biblicarum und seiner Bedeutung für die Interpretation des lukanischen Doppelwerks* (WUNT 74; Tübingen: J.C.B. Mohr/Paul Siebeck, 1994).

conceptualisations: a person who is taken up alive into heaven does not die and consequently need not be resuscitated. If his earthly existence is to be continued at all (!), in Jewish belief a return from heaven rather than a resurrection from the dead would be the proper way to resume life on earth! This implies that it may be premature to define the *Verhältnisbestimmung* of resurrection and ascension in the light of each other. This is only a second step, the first step being to establish their meaning both in their own right.

The present investigation will be pursued along the following lines. First of all it will be necessary to explore the wider first-century context of understanding to have a general appreciation of how and to what extent first-century Jews and Christians employed ascension language (or, more accurately, rapture language) (chapter two). Then we will turn to the writings of Luke for an initial appreciation of his 'rapture christology' (chapter three). Since the ascension pericopae are framed in the narrative context of the resurrection, the outpouring of the Spirit and the parousia, we will have to define the meaning of the ascension in relation to the resurrection-exaltation complex (chapters four and five). Finally, we must assess the role of the ascension in Luke's larger theological program and try to define what Luke's 'rapture christology' adds to our understanding of NT christology (chapter six). We will then round off our inquiry by making some final remarks and stating the conclusions that emerge from our investigation.

CHAPTER TWO

RAPTURE-PRESERVATION IN EARLY JEWISH SOURCES

a. *Introduction*

Within the large range of ascension stories in antiquity, the Lukan ascension narratives (Lk 24:50-53; Acts 1:9-11) belong form-critically to the type of rapture stories (*Entrückungserzählungen*)[1], that is, they purport to report Jesus' bodily translation into the 'beyond' as the conclusion of his earthly life without the intervention of death[2].

Rapture stories in this strict sense of the term appear to have been a well-established motif in the literary traditions of the ancient Orient from very early

---

[1] Despite common language and motifs, the lines of demarcation between rapture (*Entrückung*) and other types of ascensions are quite neatly drawn on the conceptual level. This makes it relatively easy to trace rapture traditions: a rapture is definitive (unlike a heavenly journey) and bodily (unlike an ecstatic experience or an assumption of the soul after death); it involves a transportation to heaven, or at least to a far-away region that under normal circumstances is unattainable for mortal human beings, such as Elysium (Homer, *Odyssey* 4,563), the Isles of the Blessed Ones (Hesiod, *Erga* 171), Dilmun, Paradise, etc. (unlike a miraculous terrestrial transportation from one place to another), and, most importantly, there is no death experience (unlike an assumption of the soul). For a useful description of the various forms and types of ascensions, see G. Lohfink, *Die Himmelfahrt Jesu. Untersuchungen zu den Himmelfahrts- und Erhöhungstexten bei Lukas* (StANT 26; München: Kösel, 1971) 32-79, and also the *RAC*-articles by C. Colpe (see *infra* bibliography).

[2] It seems to me that the reservation of Ph. Vielhauer, 'Ein Weg zur neutestamentlichen Christologie? Prüfung der Thesen Ferdinand Hahns', in: idem, *Aufsätze zum Neuen Testament* (TB 31; München: Chr. Kaiser, 1965) 169, to classify the ascension of Jesus as an *Entrückung*, 'da es sich ja nicht um Aufnahme in den Himmel ohne vorherigen Tod handle', is unwarranted. This is not to say that other sets of terminology did not slide into rapture contexts. Not infrequently death terminology is used for persons taken up alive into heaven (e.g. Jub 7:39; 4 Ezra 7:15; 8:5; 10:34; 2 Bar 44:2; 46:1; 78:5; 84:1; *LAB* 48:1, etc.). Cf. also K. Berger, *Die Auferstehung des Propheten und die Erhöhung des Menschensohnes* (StUNT 13; Göttingen: Vandenhoeck & Ruprecht, 1976) 113[e] and 388-389 Anm.516. This is not *per se* indicative of different sources or of *Sachkritik*. With Lohfink it must be stressed that between the various genres exists a careful distinction, contra A.F. Segal, 'Heavenly Ascent in Hellenistic Judaism, Early Christianity and Their Environment', *ANRW* II 23,2 (1980) 1345 n.33, who believes Lohfink distinguishes too closely between the genres of heavenly journeys.

times[1]. In a Sumerian creation and deluge text (ed. Civil 144; tr. 145; ANET 44, 254-261 tr. Kramer) the pious king Ziusudra is taken up by the gods Anu and Enlil after the great flood because he had pleased them with his past conduct. They bestow immortal life upon him ('life like that of a god ... breath eternal like that of a god'), after which they translate him [mu-un-tìl-eš 'they (i.e. Anu and Enlil) caused to dwell' or 'they settle'; from the root tìl] to the land of Dilmun, 'the place where the sun rises'[2], so that he does not experience death.

Likewise, in the Akkadian Gilgamesh Epic 11 (ed. Campbell Morgan 64 translit., plate 50 text; tr. Speiser 189-196), which provides a Babylonian-Assyrian version of the Sumerian flood and rapture myth, the god Enlil blesses the priest Utnapishtim and his wife (note the expansion!) after the great flood, bestows divine life on them and then takes [leqû(m)] the couple to make them reside [(w)ašābu(m), cf. AHw III 1483 3] at their future residence far away 'at the mouth of the rivers' [ina pi-i nārāti].

In the Hellenistic period the ancient Sumerian myth of king Ziusudra found its way into the now lost writings of the Babylonian priest Berossus (340-270 BC), fragments of which have been preserved by Eusebius. After the great flood, Xisuthros (the Greek equivalent of Ziusudra), his wife, his daughter and the ship's captain (note again the expansion!) disembark and disappear[3]. When those who had stayed behind in the ship set out to look for them, they are informed by a heavenly voice that Xisuthros and his company, because of his piety, now dwell with the gods (i.e. in heaven)[4]. They are then commanded to install a religious cult[5].

---

[1] See e.g. A. Schmitt, *Entrückung-Aufnahme-Himmelfahrt. Untersuchungen zu einem Vorstellungsbereich im AT* (FzB 10; Stuttgart: KBW, 1973, [2]1976) 4-45; cf. G. Strecker, 'Entrückung', *RAC* 5 (1962) 470-471.

[2] On the mythological function and historical location of Dilmun, see E. Burrows, *Tilmun, Bahrein, Paradise* (Zusatzbemerkungen von A. Deimel; BibOr 30; Roma: IBP, 1928); S.N. Kramer, 'Dilmun, the Land of the Living', *BASOR* 96 (1944) 18-28; P.B. Cornwall, 'On the Location of Dilmun', *BASOR* 103 (1946) 3-11; Schmitt, *Entrückung* 9-11.

[3] Eusebius, *Chronicon* I 3,2 (PG 19, 115); I 7,1 (PG 19, 122). The element of disappearance is a typical Hellenistic rapture motif, see Lohfink, *Himmelfahrt* 41; Schmitt, *Entrückung* 18-20.

[4] P. Grelot, 'La Légende d'Hénoch dans les Apocryphes et dans la Bible. Son origine et signification', *RSR* 46 (1958) 12.

[5] Further rapture stories in antiquity are found in Indian and Persian literature. Cf. J. Scheftelowitz, 'Der Seelen- und Unsterblichkeitsglaube im Alten Testament', *ARW* 16 (1916/19) 216ff.; V. Larrañaga, *L'Ascension de Notre-Seigneur dans le Nouveau Testament* (SPIB 50; Roma: IBP, 1938) 85-87. Strictly speaking, the heavenly ascension stories of the Egyptian Pharaohs cannot be classified as rapture stories because they are *post-mortem* ascensions. See Schmitt, *Entrückung* 36-43; Colpe, 'Jenseitsfahrt', *RAC* 17 (1995) 411-413.

Rapture stories were particularly favourite among the Greeks and the Romans[1]. In the Homeric tradition Ganymede, because of his beauty, was taken up to the realm of the gods to become the cupbearer of Zeus [Homer, *Ilias* 20,233-235; Ovid, *Metamorphoses* 10,159-161; cf. Dosiades (FGH 458 fgm 5)]. Menelaos was promised to escape death and to be transferred to Elysium because he was Helen's husband and the son-in-law of Zeus (Homer, *Odyssey* 4,561-565; cf. Euripides, *Helena* 1676-1677). Hesiod relates the rapture of the heroes of the fourth generation (*Erga* 167-173), and Philostratus has a most vivid rapture story about Apollonius of Tyana (*VitAp* 8,29-30). Among the most popular and well-remembered rapture stories of the Greeks and the Romans were those about Heracles, the son of Zeus and Alkmene (Apollodorus, *Bibliotheca* II 7,7; DiodS, *Hist* IV 38,5; Euripides, *Heraclidae* 910; *Lysias* 2,11; Lucian, *Cynicus* 13; *Hermotimus* 7; Cicero, *Tusculanae* I 14,32), and about Romulus, the founder of Rome (Apollodorus, *Bibliotheca* II 7,7; DiodS, *Hist* IV 38,5; Euripides, *Heraclidae* 910; *Lysias* 2,11; Lucian, *Cynicus* 13; *Hermotimus* 7; Cicero, *Tusculanae* I 14,32).

The few examples just referred to very well illustrate the relatively wide diffusion of rapture thinking in the ancient world. Especially in the Greek and Roman tradition, rapture seems to have crystallised into a literary convention, with differences only in the *dramatis personae* and in the descriptive details[2]. When Cicero declares, *Suscepit autem vita hominum consuetudoque communis ut beneficiis excellentis viros in caelum fama ac voluntate tollerent* (*DeoNat* II 14,62; cf. III 16,39), he does not seem to make a gross overstatement (cf. also Petronius, *Satyricon* 17; Seneca, *Apocolocyntosis* 9).

---

References to the king's physical ascension and his union with the solar disc are to be understood as euphemistic affirmations about his death. The enthronement of Tutmosis III (ANET 446) is depicted with the imagery and style of a heavenly ascent. For more (postbiblical) *religionsgeschichtliche* parallels, see H. Wißmann, 'Entrückung I. Religionsgeschichtlich', *TRE* 9 (1982) 680-683, and the *RAC*-articles of Colpe (bibliography).

[1] In addition to the authors cited *supra* 21 n.2, Graeco-Roman rapture texts are found in: D. Roloff, *Gottähnlichkeit, Vergöttlichung und Erhöhung zu seligem Leben. Untersuchungen zur Herkunft der platonischen Angleichung an Gott* (UaLG 4; Berlin: W. de Gruyter, 1970) *passim*; Lohfink, *Himmelfahrt* 32-50; G. Friedrich, 'Lk 9,51 und die Entrückungschristologie des Lukas', in: P. Hoffmann, N. Brox, W. Pesch (Hrsg.), *Orientierung an Jesus. Zur Theologie der Synoptiker* (FS J. Schmid; Freiburg: Herder, 1973) 51-54; P.W. van der Horst, 'Hellenistic Parallels to the Acts of the Apostles (1,1-26)', *ZNW* 74 (1983) 19-23.

[2] As Lohfink, *Himmelfahrt* 49-50 has demonstrated, even professed sceptics of rapture speculations employed the rapture scheme. Lohfink distinguishes rationalisations, spiritualisations and rapture satires.

A recurrent, if not standard feature, in the Hellenistic rapture stories is that the heavenly assumption is regarded as the gateway to immortality and the means of deification[1]. D. Roloff explains this as follows: 'Da bei einer anthropomorphen Gottesvorstellung die Unsterblichkeit das wesentliche Merkmal des Göttlichen ist, bedeutet die Aufhebung des Todes als die Aufhebung dessen, was den Heros vom Göttlichen trennt, seinen Übergang ins Göttliche, seine Erhebung zur Göttlichkeit'[2]. G. Lohfink claims in a similar vein: 'Entrückung und Vergöttlichung sind im hellenistischen Denken so fest miteinander verbunden, daß die Entrückung oft das eigentliche Kriterium dafür bildet, ob ein Mensch vergöttlicht wurde oder nicht'[3].

This being the case, we might wonder whether in a tradition where the lines between mortals and the gods were more sharply drawn (as in the Jewish-Christian monotheistic tradition) rapture stories were read with the same set of assumptions and connotations in mind as in a polytheistic context. Similarities of language and form do not necessarily imply ideological correspondence. Although in Hellenistic Judaism, e.g., historical figures of Israel's past were occasionally elevated, even up to the status of θεός[4], there is little evidence (at least in the period relevant to the present investigation) that this has affected or compromised its basic belief in monotheism, because it perceived this type of divinity in an attenuated, non-literal, sense[5]. A literalistic conception would be

---

[1] A brief inventory of the terminology used in connection with rapture suffices to illustrate what is really a tendency in Graeco-Roman rapture stories: ἐκθειάζω: Herodian of Syria, *Hist* IV 2,1; θεοποιέω: DionHal, *AntRom* II 56,6; cf. Pindar, *NemOd* 10,7; cf. Euripides, *Andromache* 1256; θεός γίγνομαι: Plutarch, *Romulus* 27,8; Arrian, *Anabasis* VII 27,3; Lucian, *Hermotimus* 7; DioCass, *RomHist* LII 35,5; LXVI 17,3; DiogLaert, *Lives* VIII 2,68.69; *deum facio*: Ovid, *Metamorphoses* 14,607; Seneca, *Apocolocyntosis* 11; cf. Augustine, *CivDei* 18,21; *deum fio*: Cicero, *RePub* 2,10 (17f.); Seneca, *Apocolocyntosis* 8-9; Suetonius, *Vespasian* 23,4. Further: Ovid, *Metamorphoses* 8,218-220. Cf. further: ἰσόθεος: DiodS, *Hist* IV 58,6; ἀντίθεος: Homer, *Ilias* 20,232.

[2] Roloff, *Gottähnlichkeit* 84.

[3] Lohfink, *Himmelfahrt* 46. See further A.S. Pease, 'Some Aspects of Invisibility', *HSCP* 53 (1942) 12-21 (on the connection disappearance-deification); C.H. Talbert, 'The Concept of Immortals in Mediterranean Antiquity', *JBL* 94 (1975) 419-436.

[4] See e.g. Philo, *Sacr* 9; *QPL* 43; cf. *Som* 2,189; *VitMos* 1,158; *Quaest in Ex* 2,29. Cf. also the much later Metatron tradition, where the translated Enoch is called 'the lesser Yahweh' (3 En 12:5; 48:7 C; 48:1 D [90]). On Ps-Phoc 104, see Van der Horst, 'Pseudo-Phocylides. A New Translation and Introduction', *OTP* 2, 570.

[5] On the issue, see Segal, *Two Powers in Heaven. Early Rabbinic Reports about Christianity and Gnosticism* (SJLA 25; Leiden: E.J. Brill, 1977); J.D.G. Dunn, *Christology in the Making. An Inquiry into the Origins of the Doctrine of the Incarnation* (London: SCM, 1980, ²1989) xxviii-xxxi, 16-22; idem, 'Was Christianity a Monotheistic Faith from the

near to blasphemy to the Jewish mind. Granted that rapture thinking has found an accepted place in OT-Jewish belief and provides the conceptual horizon of understanding for the ascension of Jesus in Luke-Acts, the critical question is how rapture thinking *functioned* within a first-century Jewish (and Christian) context. Did first-century Jews and Christians consider rapture also as a means of deification and as the commencement of an immortal existence in glory? How (and how successfully) was rapture thinking integrated into the Jewish and Christian world of beliefs? Before we can define the significance of the fact that rapture claims were made about Jesus, it will be necessary to explore the larger framework in which first-century Judaism before and during the emergence of Christianity conceptualised its canonical and postbiblical rapture traditions.

> For the sake of methodological clarity I will, in what follows, adhere as strictly as possible to the narrow definition of 'rapture' offered in the opening paragraph of this chapter. Although first-century Judaism has an impressive list of historical figures 'exalted to heaven' or with a heavenly status, this must be carefully distinguished from the concept of rapture in the proper sense. Heavenly exaltation imagery very often is no more than a metaphorical expression of praise and is not necessarily connected with the end of one's life (if it has a 'historical' *Sitz im Leben* at all), whereas 'rapture' language was usually taken quite literally. As a consequence heavenly exaltation imagery will be discussed only in so far as it is used in the context of a rapture. The same restriction goes for the apotheioses of the Roman emperors[1], the 'disappearance' of Wisdom (1 En 42; 4 Ezra 5:9ff.; 2 Bar 48:33,36), and the throne speculations in the Hekaloth literature. Even if a great deal of the traditions contained therein may reach back into the first century AD, we must be aware that we have here a different conceptualisation or formal category[2].

---

Beginning?, *SJTh* 35 (1982) 303-336; idem, *The Parting of the Ways between Christianity and Judaism and their Significance for the Character of Christianity* (London: SCM; Philadelphia: TPI, 1991) 163-229; L.W. Hurtado, *One God, One Lord. Early Christian Devotion and Ancient Jewish Monotheism* (London: SCM, 1988) (n.1 on pp.129-130 on pagan monotheism is important!); idem, 'What Do We Mean by 'First-Century Jewish Monotheism'?', *SBL.SP* 32 (1993) 348-368; P.A. Rainbow, 'Jewish Monotheism as the Matrix for New Testament Christology. A Review Article', *NT* 33 (1993) 78-91; P.M. Casey, *From Jewish Prophet to Gentile God. The Origins and Development of New Testament Christology* (ECL 1985-86; Cambridge: J. Clarke; Louisville, KN: Westminster, J. Knox: 1991) 92-93; L.T. Stuckenbruck, *Angel Veneration and Christology. A Study in Early Judaism and in the Christology of the Apocalypse of John* (WUNT 2/70; Tübingen: J.C.B. Mohr/Paul Siebeck, 1995).

[1] See E. Bickermann, 'Die römische Kaiserapotheose', *ARW* 27 (1929) 1-27; S. Weinstock, *Divus Julius* (Oxford: Clarendon, 1971); L. Kreitzer, 'Apotheiosis of the Roman Emperor', *BA* 53 (1990) 210-217.

[2] See D.J. Halperin, *The Faces of the Chariot. Early Jewish Responses to Ezekiel's Vision* (TSAJ 16; Tübingen: J.C.B. Mohr/Paul Siebeck, 1988).

b. *The Enoch Tradition*

In what is probably the oldest known text related to the name Enoch (Gen 5:21-24), a brief biographical note has been preserved about Enoch's sudden disappearance: 'Enoch walked with God; and he was no more, because God took him (away)' (v.24 חנוך את־האלהים ואיננו כי־לקח אתו אלהים ויתהלך)[1]. Although it does not explicitly say that Enoch did not die there is great unanimity among the interpreters up to the period pertinent to our investigation (first century AD) that Enoch did escape death and was bodily transferred from human society into the divine realm.

In later rabbinic literature it is sometimes explicitly denied that Enoch did not die[2], but these statements are apologetically motivated[3]. That MT thinks of Enoch's departure from life in terms of an *Entrückung* may be inferred from the following: (1) If the absence of the stereotyped 'and he died' (וימת Gen 5:5,8,11,14,17,20,27,31) is given its full force, the implication is: 'he did not die'; (2) If the Enoch tradition is structured in conscious opposition to the Utnapishtim myth, one would hardly expect Enoch to suffer a different fate. Note that לקח, which in due course became the favourite Hebrew rapture term (cf. 2 Kings 2:(3,5,)9,10; Hebr Sir 44:16; 49:14), is analogous to the Akk. *leqû(m)*, the verb used to describe Utnapishtim's rapture, Gilgamesh Epic 11,196[4]; (3) Form-critically, the motif of 'absence' often prepares for, or is used in conjunction with a rapture[5]; (4) The earliest doubts as to the nature of Enoch's departure from earthly life are from a later period (it is

---

[1] The allusive brevity of the text may indicate that already some speculations about Enoch in one form or another were circulating [J.C. VanderKam, *Enoch and the Growth of an Apocalyptic Tradition* (CBQ.MS 16; Washington: Catholic Biblical Association of America, 1984) 23-51], but it would be difficult to define their exact form and content.

[2] TO Gen 5:24 (ed. Aberbach-Grossfeld 48-49); BerR 25:1 (ed. Theodor-Albeck 1, 238-239; tr. Freedman-Simon 1, 205). More examples are found in Bill. 3, 744-745. Among modern commentators: U. Cassuto, *A Commentary on the Book of Genesis 1. From Adam to Noah Genesis I-VI,8* (Translated from the Hebrew by I. Abrahams; Jerusalem: Magnes, 1944, ET 1961) 285-286; N.M. Sarna, בראשית *Genesis* (JPSTC; Philadelphia, New York, Jerusalem: JPS, 5749/1989) 43, who take the phrase as a euphemism for (premature) death. Also Berger, *Auferstehung* 570 Anm.416.

[3] Namely, to counter the growing popularity of Enoch in Jewish (and Jewish-Christian) sectarian groupings. On the (ambivalent) role of Enoch in rabbinic literature, see L. Ginzberg, *The Legends of the Jews* 1 (ET H. Szold; Philadelphia: JPS, 1909) 122-140; 6 (1928) 150-166; Bill. 3, 744-745; M. Himmelfarb, 'A Report on Enoch in Rabbinic Literature', *SBL.SP* (1978) 259-269.

[4] So H.H. Schmid, לקח *lqh* nehmen, *THAT* 1 (1984) 878-879; but see the reservations of Schmitt, *Entrückung* 312-313.

[5] 2 Kings 2:17; Chariton 3,3; Pausanias, *Periegesis* VI 9,7-8 (cf. Plutarch, *Romulus* 28,6); AntLib 33,4; DiodS, *Hist* IV 38,5; DionHal, *AntRom* I 64,4; DiogLaert, *Lives* VIII 2,68. See further Bickermann, 'Das leere Grab' (1924); repr. in: idem, *Studies in Jewish and Christian History* 3 (AGJU 9; Leiden: E.J. Brill, 1986) 70-81.

doubtful whether Wis 4:10 can be used as evidence, see *infra* 44-45).

The underlying conviction seems to be that Enoch because of his outstanding piety, vividly expressed in the double 'Enoch walked with האלהים' (vv.22,24; cf. Gen 6:9; Mal 2:6)[1], did not descend into Sheol—the otherwise inescapable fate of mortal men[2]—but continued to live in God's company even after his earthly existence had come to an end.

Despite this quite laudable picture of Enoch drawn by the author of Gen 5:24, there is no further mention of Enoch in the Hebrew Bible, except for his (unavoidable) naming in a genealogy (1 Chron 1:3). This reticence may be explained by the supposed Babylonian background of the Enoch myth[3], his pre-Israelite (pre-Abrahamic) status, and the fact that the Enoch speculations developed in predominantly sectarian circles.

In LXX, on the other hand—composed in a period in which Enoch became a figure of increasing prominence in apocalyptic circles—the brief Enoch tradition of Gen 5 is slightly expanded and reinterpreted with the help of Greek rapture terminology[4]. The crude anthropomorphic 'walked with God' (Gen 5:22,24) is replaced by a less offensive reference to his God-pleasing life (εὐηρέστησεν τῷ θεῷ, cf. Gen 6:9 LXX), thereby focusing more strongly on

---

[1] There is room for some doubt as to the original meaning of האלהים. The use of the article in האלהים (vv.22,24a) seems to contrast to the anarthrous אלהים in v.24b. J. Skinner, *Genesis* (ICC; Edinburgh: T.&T. Clark, 1910, ²1930) 131 suggests we have here a trace of polytheism ('walked with *the gods*'). A parallel is provided in Enmeduranki's association with the gods Shamash and Adad, see the discussion in VanderKam, *Enoch* 38-45. On the other hand, in view of Enoch's close contacts with angels in later apocalyptic literature, Enochic circles seem to have taken the phrase to mean that Enoch 'walked with *the angels*' (cf. Jub 4:21; Gesenius 40). But whatever the precise reference is, Enoch is marked by his contact with the heavenly world.

[2] Cf. J. Jeremias, ᾅδης, *ThWNT* 1 (1933) 146-150; D.S. Russell, *The Method and Message of Jewish Apocalyptic* (London: SCM, 1964) 353-390; G. Fohrer, 'Das Geschick des Menschen nach dem Tode im Alten Testament' (1968); repr. in: idem, *Studien zu alttestamentlichen Texten und Themen (1966-1972)* (BZAW 155; Berlin, New York: W. de Gruyter, 1981) 188-202 (literature 190 Anm.1).

[3] See W. Bousset, *Die Religion des Judentums im späthellenistischen Zeitalter* (hrsg. v. H. Gressmann; HNT 21; Tübingen: J.C.B. Mohr/Paul Siebeck, ⁴1966) 490-491; Grelot, 'La géographie mythique d'Hénoch et ses sources orientales', *RB* 65 (1958) 33-69; idem, 'Légende' 5-26.181-210; VanderKam, 'Enoch Traditions in Jubilees and Other Second-Century Sources', *SBL.SP* (1978) 229-230; idem, *Enoch*. This would for instance account for Enoch's traditional association with astrology.

[4] Schmitt, 'Die Angaben über Henoch Gen 5,21-24 in der LXX', in: J. Schreiner (Hrsg.), *Wort, Lied und Gottesanspruch. Beiträge zur Septuaginta* (FS J. Ziegler; FzB 1; Würzburg: Echter, 1972) 161-169.

Enoch's piety which led to his assumption[1]. His mysterious 'taking away' is now explicitly described in terms of rapture or translation (μετατίθημι)[2], whereby the motive of absence is replaced by the (more powerful!) motif of unsuccessful search (οὐχ ηὑρίσκετο), a typical *topos* of Hellenistic rapture stories[3].

The Enoch story is twice referred to in the book of Sirach, viz. at the beginning (Sir 44:16)[4] and the end (Sir 49:14) of the *laus patrum* (Sir 44:1-49:16)[5]. Though Sir 44:16b (ולקח אות דעת לדור ודור[ין]) is overrun with syntactical obscurity[6], its intention may not be difficult to uncover if we bear in mind that the Enoch speculations preserved in the various books of Enoch and the Book of Jubilees reach back beyond the date of composition of (Hebrew) Sirach and thus may well shed light on the brief (catchword-like) notice of Sir 44:16b[7]: Enoch is spoken of as a 'sign' (Eth. *te'emert*, Heb. אות) in Jub 4:24 (cf. 10:17); his 'knowledge' is spoken of in Jub 4:17-24 and is a major theme in

---

[1] As in the targumic tradition. See TO Gen 5:24 (ed. Aberbach-Grossfeld 48-49); Targum Neofiti 1 Gen 5:24 (ed. McNamara 70; Diez-Macho 30-31); TPsJ Gen 5:24 (ed. Clarke 6-7; tr. Maher 36).

[2] Μετατίθημι is otherwise unattested as a rapture term, but cf. μεθίστασθαι and μετακομίζω; see Schmitt, 'Angaben' 166-168. Μετατίθημι has become the standard Greek term to describe Enoch's rapture, Sir 44:16; 49:14 *v.l.*; cf. Wis 4:10; Heb 11:5 (2x); 1 Clem 9:3; Justin, *Dial* 19 (PG 6, 516); ActPil 9:25 (EvAp 331).

[3] Friedrich, 'Entrückungschristologie' 54.

[4] This verse is missing in Syr and some Hebrew MSS. Schmitt, *Entrückung* 176-178 and D. Lührmann, 'Henoch und die Metanoia', *ZNW* 66 (1975) 107-109 advocate the authenticity of the verse. V.16a (חנוך [נמצא] תמים והתהלך עם ייי) (Hebr) corresponds to Gen 5:24a MT with the exception of נמצא תמים, which is obviously a scribal interpolation from v.17, G. Sauer, *Jesus Sirach (Ben Sira)* (JSHRZ 3/5; Gütersloh: G. Mohn, 1976) 615 Anm.16a;

[5] The suggestion of Schmitt, *Entrückung* 177 and P.W. Shekan, A.A. Di Lella, *The Wisdom of Ben Sira. A New Translation with Notes by P.W. Shekan, Introduction and Commentary by A.A. Di Lella* (AncB 39; Garden City, NY: Doubleday, 1987) 499, that we have here an *inclusio* would carry more conviction had Enoch actually rounded off the *laus patrum*, but his name is followed by that of Joseph, Shem, Seth and Adam (Sir 49:14-16) and Adam explicitly marks the climax (Sir 49:16). Cf. G.H. Box, W.O.E. Oesterley, 'The Book of Sirach', *APOT* 1, 506, who follow Syr, contrasting Adam not only to Shem and Seth, but also to Enoch. But see the criticisms of S.D. Fraade, *Enosh and His Generation. Pre-Israelite Hero and History in Postbiblical Interpretation* (SBL.MS 30; Chico, CA: Scholars, 1984) 12 n.23.

[6] E.g., is אות דעת לדור ודור apposite to the entire preceding phrase (implying that the proposition to be made concerns Enoch's translation) or just to its subject, חנוך (so that Enoch himself, i.e. his entire pious life, is its logical subject)? And, further, whose 'knowledge' is in view, Enoch's or that of future generations?

[7] Cf. H. Odeberg, Ἐνώχ, *ThWNT* 2 (1935) 554-555.

the various books attributed to Enoch. According to Sirach, then, Enoch was an initiate into the divine mysteries of the universe and the course of human history, whose encyclopaedic knowledge marked him as a very pious person who was rewarded appropriately with a heavenly assumption[1] (the LXX rendering ὑπόδειγμα μετανοίας ταῖς γενεαῖς 'an example of repentance to all generations' reflects the influence of Alexandrian (allegorising) exegesis, cf. Philo, *Abr* 17; ClemAlex, *Stromata* 2,15 (70,1); GCS 52/2, 150). In Sir 49:14 Enoch's fortune is for the first time implicitly compared to Elijah's (וגם הוא 'he too', cf. 48:9-12).

It is a matter of debate whether Wis 4:10-14 has to be taken as a direct reference to Enoch[2] or as a general description of the δίκαιος of v.7[3]. Its language is reminiscent of Gen 5:24 and Sir 44:16 LXX. That the author does not explicitly mention Enoch's name may well be in line with his tendency elsewhere to avoid the mention of proper names of historical persons (10:1,3-6,10,13,16; 11:1; 12:3; 14:6; 15:14; 18:5,21; 19:14,17). The immediate context, on the other hand, does not necessarily require that the reference is to the 'historical Enoch'. The issue at hand is the problem of theodicy, posed by the untimely death (!) of a righteous person (cf. Eccles 7:15; 8:14). There is, as far as I know, no tradition prior to Wis 4:10-14 which justifies Enoch's early departure from life in terms of divine preventive action, as later e.g. in BerR 25:1 (ed. Theodor-Albeck 1, 238-239; tr. Freedman-Simon 1, 205); Cyprian, *Mort* 23 (PL 4, 598-599). In Is 57:1-2, however, the righteous one (הצדיק ὁ δίκαιος) is said to be taken away by God 'to be spared from evil' (NIV) (כי־מפני הרעה נאסף הצדיק ἀπὸ γὰρ προσώπου ἀδικίας ἦρται ὁ δίκαιος). If Is 57:1-2 was in the mind of the author of Wisdom at vv.11,14, it is all the more reasonable that v.10 likewise refers to 'the righteous one', rather than to Enoch. On balance, then, it would seem that Wis 4:10-14 is concerned with the righteous one in general[4]. In either case, however, the *tertium comparationis* is not the mode of departure

---

[1] From the LXX rendering לקח/μετατίθημι (Sir 44:16) and לקח/ἀναλαμβάνω (Sir 49:14) it may be surmised that Greek rapture terminology was still flexible and/or that in 49:14 the translator was influenced (consciously or not) by the rapture terminology of Elijah. The *v.l.* μετετέθη (49:14 A S) is a harmonisation under the influence of Sir 44:16 and Gen 5:24. The underlying comparison with Elijah (καὶ, i.e. like Elijah) speaks for the authenticity of ἀνελήμφθη. The addition of the *terminus a quo* ἀπὸ τῆς γῆς (not in Hebr Sir) betrays again the influence of Greek rapture terminology.

[2] So S. Holmes, 'Wisdom of Solomon', *APOT* 1, 541 n.10; Lührmann, 'Henoch' 110-111; D.M. Winston, *The Wisdom of Solomon. A New Translation with Introduction and Commentary* (AncB 43; Garden City, NY: Doubleday, 1979) 139.

[3] So Schmitt, *Entrückung* 181-184; idem, 'Der frühe Tod des Gerechten nach Weish 4,7-19. Ein Psalmthema in weisheitlicher Fassung', in: E. Haag, F.-L. Hossfeld (Hrsg.), *Freude an der Weisung des Herrn. Beiträge zur Theologie der Psalmen* (FS H. Groß; SBB 13; Stuttgart: KBW, 1986, ²1987) 334-338.347; C. Larcher, *Le Livre de la Sagesse ou La Sagesse de Salomon* 2 (EtB Ns 3; Paris: Librairie Lecoffre, J. Gabalda, 1984) 330-331.

[4] To this, compare Ps 49:16 and 73:24, where the Psalmist likewise seems to choose his

from life (contrary to the righteous one, Enoch did not experience death at all), but its motive: both Enoch and the righteous one that died an untimely death departed from life because of God's pleasure[1].

Outside the 'canonical' confines of MT and LXX, Enoch's intensive association with האלהים has given rise to more speculative reflections on the mystic experiences he was supposed to have had in the period leading up to his final assumption and afterwards. In the pseudepigraphic Enoch literature, where Enoch has become *the* central figure of apocalyptic speculations, these revelatory experiences usually take the form of short term visits to heaven or of ecstatic visions in which Enoch travels through the heavenly world 'in the spirit', after which he returns to the earth to deliver his divine knowledge to his descendants, sanctioned as it is by heaven itself. In the Book of Watchers it says:

'Before these things (happened) Enoch was hidden [Eth. *takabta* Gr. ἐλήμφθη], and no one of the children of the people knew by what he was hidden and where he was. And his dwelling place as well as his activities were with the Watchers and the holy ones; and (so) were his days' (1 En 12:1-2; ed. Knibb 1, 40-41; tr. Isaac 19).

It is disputed whether this is a reference to Enoch's final departure at the end of his life[2] or to a pre-rapture heavenly journey during his lifetime[3]. In its present literary setting the latter seems to be the most feasible option (cf. Jub 4:21), so that the subsequent journeyings through the heavenly world also took place during Enoch's lifetime, but since BW is a composite document[4], it is difficult to reach definite conclusions. In any case, Enoch associates with good and bad angels and assumes the role of an intermediate figure who announces judgement on the fallen angels (cf. Gen 6:1-4) and prays for mercy on their

words with allusion to Enoch's translation. See on these Psalms Schmitt, *Entrückung* 193-252 (Ps 49); 253-309 (Ps 73); H.J. Kraus, *Psalmen* 1 (BK 15; Neukirchen-Vluyn: Neukirchener, 1961, ⁵1978) 522-523 (Ps 49:16); 2, 671-673 (Ps 73:24); P. Casetti, *Gibt es ein Leben vor dem Tod? Eine Auslegung von Psalm 49* (OBO 44; Freiburg, Schweiz: Universitätsverlag; Göttingen: Vandenhoeck & Ruprecht, 1982); H. Irsigler, *Psalm 73. Monolog eines Weisen. Text, Programm, Struktur* (MUS.ATSAT 20; St. Ottilien: EOS, 1984).

[1] See further Schmitt, 'Frühe Tod' 325-347, who suggests the influence of the Greek-hellenistic consolation literature (*Konsolationsliteratur*) on the author of Wisdom.

[2] M. Black, *The Book of Enoch or 1 Enoch. A New English Edition with Commentary and Textual Notes* (SVTP 7; Leiden: E.J. Brill, 1985) 141-142.

[3] Grelot, 'Légende' 21 n.55; VanderKam, *Enoch* 130-131.

[4] G.W.E. Nickelsburg, 'The Bible Rewritten and Expanded', in: M.E. Stone (ed.), *Jewish Writings of the Second Temple Period. Apocrypha, Pseudepigrapha, Qumran Sectarian Writings, Philo, Josephus* (CRI 2/2; Assen: Van Gorcum; Philadelphia: Fortress, 1984) 90-93; VanderKam, *Enoch* 110.

behalf (but unsuccessfully; cf. 2 En 7:4-5) (1 En 1-13). In a series of (visionary) heavenly journeys (1 En 17-36) he is granted insight into the secrets of the universe, the destiny of the fallen angels, and the final judgement of the righteous and the wicked. In 12:4 he is called 'the scribe of righteousness'[1].

In the Astronomical Writings (1 En 72-82) Enoch passes astronomical insights, granted to him by the angel Uriel, to his son Methuselah (76:14; 79:1; 82:1; cf. 81:5). In what is probably an addition to the original composition (chapters 80-81)[2], Enoch's final departure from life and its timing are announced in advance by angelic mediation. Before the event takes place, Enoch is to deliver his final instructions to his descendants:

> 'We shall let you stay with your son [= Methuselah] for one year, so that you may teach your children another law and write it down for them and give all of them a warning; and in the second year, you shall be taken away from (among) all of them' (1 En 81:6; ed. Knibb 1, 268-269; tr. Isaac 59)[3].

In the Dream Visions (1 En 83-90) Enoch observes the visionary appearance of '(a being) in the form of a snow-white person' from heaven, accompanied by three other celestial beings, who seize him in order to rescue him from the coming destruction (the flood):

> 'Those ones which had come out last seized me by my hand and took me ['anše 'ûnî] from the generations of the earth, lifted me up into a high place, and showed me a high tower above the earth, and all the hills were firm. (One of them) said to me, 'Stay here until you see everything that will happen to these elephants, camels, and donkeys, as well as to the bovids—all of them' (1 En 87:3-4; ed. Knibb 1, 293-394; tr. Isaac 63-64).

What follows is a typical apocalyptic presentation of the course of sacred history (88:1-90:42)[4].

In Jub 4:16-26 we have a picture of Enoch very similar to that in the various books attributed to Enoch. Enoch is portrayed here as the first man who learned

---

[1] Cf. (with varying words in the original) 1 En 15:1; 93:1 [= 4QEn$^g$ ar II, 22]; 4QEnGiants$^a$ frag 8,3; 4QEnGiants$^b$ ar II, 14; Jub 4:23; TAb B 11:3; 2 En 23:1-4; 40:13; 53:2; 64:5; 68:2; ApPaul 20). On Enoch's role as writer, see VanderKam, *Enoch* 104-106. See further H. Bietenhard, *Die himmlische Welt in Urchristentum und Spätjudentum* (WUNT 2; Tübingen: J.C.B. Mohr/Paul Siebeck, 1951) 231-254, on the heavenly books and tablets.

[2] VanderKam, *Enoch* 78-79.106-109 (following R.H. Charles).

[3] That this verse refers to Enoch's ascent is disputed by Black, *1 Enoch* 19.142.253, who thinks Enoch is here miraculously transported back to the earth from Paradise, afterwards to return thither for a second time.

[4] See Russell, *Method* 217-234; C. Rowland, *The Open Heaven. A Study of Apocalyptic in Judaism and Early Christianity* (London: SPCK, 1982) 136-155.

'writing and knowledge and wisdom' (v.17)[1]. He is the recipient of divine visionary revelations concerning the correct reckoning of time (vv.17,18) and the past and future destiny of the generations 'until the day of judgment' (v.19). To preserve his visions as a testimony for later generations, he wrote them down in books (vv.19,21; cf. 21:10). After his marriage with Edni and the birth of Methuselah (v.20), he resided for a period of six jubilees (i.e. the 300 years of Gen 5:22) with the heavenly angels, who showed him 'everything which is on earth and in the heavens, the dominion of the sun' (v.21), after which he wrote down his visions to bear witness against the Watchers (the fallen angels) (v.22). At the end of his life he was taken up by the angels and transported to 'the garden of Eden'[2], where he carried on his function as scribe:

> 'And he [= Enoch] was taken [*taneš'a*] from among the children of men, and we [= the accompanying angels] led him to the garden of Eden for greatness and honor. And behold, he is there writing condemnation and judgment of the world, and all of the evils of the children of men' (Jub 4:23; ed. Milik 12; tr. Wintermute 62-63).

Because of Enoch's presence the flood did not cover the Garden of Eden (v.24)[3]. Enoch is claimed to perform the function of a priest in a mountain sanctuary (v.25)[4].

Another post-rapture tradition about Enoch is found in 1QGenApocr 2-5 (parallelled in 1 En 106-107), where Enoch is consulted by his son Methuselah about the disputed legitimacy of Lamech's son Noah[5]. As Lamech suspects his

---

[1] Cf. Jub 8:2; 11:16; 47:9. On the heavenly origin of Enoch's learning to write, cf. 1 En 81:1-2; 92:1. There is no claim in the Enoch literature that he was the *first* to learn writing. VanderKam, 'Enoch Traditions' 233 suggests Jubilees is here partially dependent upon 1 En 92:1 (or 82:1-3) but had also access to other data. But why could this not be a deduction by the author of Jubilees himself? On Enoch's 'firsts', see further VanderKam, *Enoch* 180-184.

[2] Though Enoch's post-rapture destiny (the garden of Eden) is explicitly identified as a place on earth (Jub 4:24,26), it is beyond the normal reach of other human beings and thus confirms to the formal pattern. For the use of death terminology in Jub 7:39, see *supra* 36 n.2.

[3] So the oldest extant MS, EMML 3. R.H. Charles' text (*APOT* 2, 19) is based on a corrupt text. See VanderKam, 'Enoch Traditions' 236; idem, *Enoch* 10 n.27; Wintermute, 'Jubilees' 63 n.*k*. Cf. 4QPsJub^c (4Q227) line 6 (ed. Milik 12; tr. García Martínez 245). However, the alternate reading would fit into the Enoch tradition as well: judgement (the Flood) arrives, because Enoch reported the evil deeds of his generation (Jub 4:24; 10:17) (cf. Grelot, 'Légende' 14).

[4] On the location of the sanctuary, see Grelot, 'Géographie' 45-47; Berger, *Das Buch der Jubiläen* (JSHRZ 2/3; Gütersloh: G. Mohn, 1981) 346 Anm.26a.

[5] The chronology of Gen 5:21-31 would admittedly allow for an overlap of the life of Enoch and Noah's birth (cf. VanderKam, *Enoch* 176-177) and the presence of Enoch in 'Parvaim' could be taken in a strictly historical-geographical sense (2 Chron 3:6). But the present mutilated MS runs from Gen 5:28-15:4 and is likely to have contained a report on

wife Bithenosh has conceived by one of the fallen angels, he urges his father Methuselah to visit his father Enoch to discover the truth (2:19-21b). Methuselah then travels 'through the length of the land of Parvaim' (מת לפרוין לארך) (ed./tr. Fitzmyer 44-46), that is, to Paradise[1], where he finds Enoch and presents his case (2:21b-23). Though the MS here is badly transmitted, Enoch apparently has given a reassuring answer (5:4,10; 1 En 106:18). Methuselah then returns to Lamech and tells him that Noah is indeed his legitimate son (5:24-25). In this story, incidentally, a double motive may be present, viz. the Jewish monotheistic refusal to attribute to Noah a divine origin, and the tendency to accredit Enoch with superhuman knowledge.

The conviction that Enoch was still alive somewhere evolved quite naturally in speculations about his post-rapture activities. In 1 En 89:52 the prophet Elijah is rescued from the anger of the people by God, who transports him to heaven alive, where Enoch is: '(The Lord of the sheep) caused him [= Elijah] to ascend to me [= Enoch]'. Enoch then foresees the reentry of the two of them at the Day of judgement, presumably in the role of witnesses:

'Thereafter, those three who were wearing snow-white (clothes), the former ones who had caused me to go up, grabbed me by my hand—also holding the hand of that ram [= Elijah] holding me—and I ascended [other MSS: they elevated me]; they set me down in the midst of those sheep prior to the occurrence of this judgment' (1 En 90:31; ed. Knibb 1, 336-337; tr. Isaac 71).

In addition to this very old piece of evidence (second century BC), the author of 4 Ezra (writing in the last decade of the first century AD) expects an eschatological appearance of Enoch and Elijah at the time of the manifestation of the Messiah (cf. 14:9):

*Et videbunt qui recepti sunt homines, qui mortem non gustaverunt a nativitate sua* [= Enoch and Elijah[2]], *et mutabitur cor inhabitantium et convertetur in sensum alium* (4 Ezra 6:26; ed. Klijn 40; tr. Metzger 535).

Their task is not defined but it seems to be preparatory to the coming day of judgement. Further evidence of belief in Enoch's future return is found in the patristic literature. Although Rev 11:3-12 seems to envision a return of Moses and Elijah, patristic authors sometimes identify the two witnesses as *Enoch* and

---

Enoch's final assumption (cf. '... and with the Holy Ones is his lot apportioned', 2:20-21).

[1] According to the par. passage, Enoch's 'dwelling-place is among the angels ... at the ends of the earth' (1 En 106:7-8); according to 1 En 60:23, in the 'garden of the righteous'. For the identification of Parvaim with Paradise, see Grelot, 'Parwaim des Chroniques à l'Apocryphe de Genèse', *VT* 11 (1961) 30-38; idem, 'Retour au Parwaim', *VT* 14 (1964) 155-163; cf. idem, 'Géographie' 33-69; Fitzmyer, *Genesis Apocryphon* 83-84 (brief survey).

[2] Enoch and Elijah are the only feasible candidates. Perhaps Moses (see *infra* 64-71).

Elijah[1]. Since the identification with Enoch is not immediately obvious from the text it is possible, and indeed likely, that early Christian writers took over this idea from Judaism.

But despite this evidence, belief in Enoch's return was not very widespread, as is clear from the complete silence in the Similitudes (1 En 37-71) and the Slavonic and Hebrew Books of Enoch.

Before we turn to a discussion of the Similitudes, we will first consider the further development of the Enoch myth in 2 (Slavonic) Enoch, since, as we will discuss, this represents a stream of tradition which is closer to the traditions discussed thus far than the Similitudes. Despite the uncertain date and provenance, 2 Enoch is likely to contain much pre-AD 70 material, as C. Böttrich has recently argued[2]. As in 1 Enoch, it elaborates on Enoch's heavenly journeys preceding his departure from life[3]. In 2 En 67:1-3 (in both the longer and the shorter recension) we have a rapture story which draws very close to Luke's version of the ascension (and transfiguration!):

'While Enoch was talking to his people, [...] the Lord sent darkness onto the earth, and it became dark and covered the men who were standing with Enoch. And the angels hurried and the angels grasped Enoch and carried him up to the highest heaven, and the LORD received him and made him stand in front of his face for eternity. And the darkness departed from the earth, and it became light. And the people looked, and they understood how Enoch had been taken away. And they glorified God. And they went away into their homes' [2 En 67:1-3 A; ed. Vaillant 64 tr. 65 (XVIII); tr. Andersen 195][4].

Cf. also 68:1-7; 36:2-3; 55:1-3. In both 2 En 67 and Lk 24:50-53 the ascension episode closes the book[5]. Typical rapture motives include the motif of the

---

[1] Tertullian, *Anima* 50 (PL 2, 735); Ps-Cyprian, *MontSinSion* 5 (PL 4, 913); ApEl 4:7-19; 5:32; ApocPet 2; Irenaeus, *AdvHaer* V 5,1 (PG 7, 1134; SC 153, 62); Hippolytus, *CommDan* 22 (PG 10, 655); *De Antichristo* 43 (PG 10, 762). Further references are found in W. Bousset, *Der Antichrist in der Überlieferung des Judenthums des neuen Testaments und der alten Kirche. Ein Beitrag zur Auslegung der Apocalypse* (Göttingen: Vandenhoeck & Ruprecht, 1895) *passim*; Berger, *Auferstehung* 296-297 Anm.182 *et passim* (Teil 1); R.J. Bauckham, 'The Martyrdom of Enoch and Elijah. Jewish or Christian?', *JBL* 95 (1976) 447-458; Black, 'The 'Two Witnesses' of Rev.11.3f. in Jewish and Christian Apocalyptic Tradition', in: E. Bammel, C.K. Barrett, W.D. Davies (eds.), *Donum Gentilicum. New Testament Studies in Honour of D. Daube* (Oxford: OUP, 1978) 227-237.

[2] C. Böttrich, 'Recent Studies in the *Slavonic Book of Enoch*', *JSPE* 9 (1991) 35-42.

[3] Note that in (the seventh) heaven, Enoch's body is transformed (2 En 22:8-10). According to 2 En 24:1 Enoch receives a position even closer to God than Gabriel. But notice also that this is temporary (for the duration of his instructions) and that it is emphasised that Enoch is still a human being, 2 En 39:3-5.

[4] Andersen's A-text (= MS BAN 45.13.4) should not be confused with Charles' A.

[5] Even if 2 En 68:1-73:9 is an authentic part of the original book, it serves as an appendix

cloud, the presence of angels, the spectator narrative perspective, and the role of witnesses (v.1 'his people ... the men who were standing with Enoch'; in Luke-Acts the disciples). More striking resemblances include:

- conversation setting
  2 En 67:1 'While Enoch was talking to his people'
  Acts 1:9 καὶ ταῦτα εἰπὼν
- the act of rapture described
  2 En 67:2 'carried him up to the highest heaven'
  Lk 24:51 καὶ ἀνεφέρετο εἰς τὸν οὐρανόν
  Acts 1:9 ἐπήρθη
- in front of eyewitnesses
  2 En 67:3 'And the people looked'
  Acts 1:10 καὶ ὡς ἀτενίζοντες ἦσαν
- explanatory comment
  2 En 67:3 'how Enoch had been taken away'
  Acts 1:11 οὗτος ὁ Ἰησοῦς ὁ ἀναλημφθεὶς ἀφ' ὑμῶν εἰς τὸν οὐρανὸν
- joyous response in praise of God
  2 En 67:3 'And they glorified God'
  Lk 24:53 εὐλογοῦντες τὸν θεόν
- the return of the eyewitnesses
  2 En 67:3 'And they went away into their homes'
  Lk 24:52 ὑπέστρεψαν εἰς Ἰερουσαλὴμ (into the temple)
  Acts 1:12 ὑπέστρεψαν εἰς Ἰερουσαλὴμ (into the upper room)

That Enoch 'stands in front of his face for eternity' (v.2; 21:3; 22:5,7; cf. 39:8; 42:6; as the angels do: 21:1; cf. 18:8 ) suggests his continuous priestly activity in heaven (cf. Num 16:9; Deut 10:8; 17:12; 18:5; 1 Kings 8:11; 2 Chron 5:14; 29:11; Ezek 44:15), a feature already hinted at in Jub 4:25[1].

Despite the close agreements between 2 Enoch 67 and the ascension in Luke-Acts, they probably represent two independent rapture traditions. The differences should not be overlooked: Enoch's ascension takes place in darkness; the cloud is not the medium of translation, but covers the bystanders. Enoch is carried off by angels. Unlike Acts 1:10-11, the angels are not *angeli interpretes* (the people understand from themselves what had happened, v.3) but his accompanying agents. Jesus receives (divine!) adoration (*proskynesis*),

---

to 2 En 1-67. The Old Slavonic MSS VL 125 and NLB 151/443 end after 67:3 with 'To our God be glory forever. Amen'. Cf. the liturgical addition of ἀμήν in the MSS tradition of Lk 24:53.

[1] Cf. 2 En 64:5 'For the LORD has chosen you, to appoint you to be the one who reveals, who carries away our sins', that is, in his function as a priest. Is the recurrent act of blessing (2 En 56:1; 57:2; 64:4 J) perhaps another parallel to Lk 24:50-53, where Jesus figures as a blessing priest?

Enoch does not. Yet the common structure suggests we have here an already well established narration scheme on which these rapture stories are patterned[1].

c. *Enoch, Metatron, and the Heavenly Son of Man*
If we pursue our inquiry into the development of the Enoch myth beyond the chronological limits set to the present investigation (late first-century AD) we soon find evidence of a growing tendency in some sectarian circles to exalt the figure of Enoch beyond recognition and to attribute to him an angelic and even divine status. According to Targum Pseudo-Jonathan on Gen 5:24 (fifth-sixth century AD) Enoch, after his ascension, was identified (appointed) as the archangel Metatron[2]:

'Enoch worshiped in truth before the Lord, and behold he was not with the inhabitants of the earth because he was taken away and he ascended to the firmament at the command of the Lord, and he was called Metatron, the Great Scribe' (TPsJ Gen 5:24; ed. Clarke 6-7; tr. Maher 36-37).

The most extravagant development of the Enoch myth is found in the Hebrew Book of Enoch, where Enoch upon entering the seventh heaven is transformed into an angelic being of immense proportions (3 En 9:2-5; cf. 15:1-2 A) and is instituted on a heavenly throne as God's vice-gerent:

'I have appointed Metatron my servant as a prince and a ruler over all the denizens of the heights, apart from the eight great, honored, and terrible princes who are called YHWH by the name of their king' (3 En 10:3; ed. Odeberg יו; tr. Alexander 264).

The usual designation of the celestial Enoch in 3 Enoch is 'Metatron, Prince of the Divine Presence' (1:9; 3:1; 5:1 etc.); in 12:5 he is even called 'the lesser YHWH'. See further 48:1-12 C[3]. However, the identification of Enoch with

---

[1] In the following texts little is made of Enoch beyond recital of the biblical account or inclusion of his name in a list of other righteous persons: *LAB* 1:16 (ed. Harrington 62); TIsaac 3:16 (where Enoch is called 'the perfect'); HelSynPr 12:55 (ConstAp VIII 12,21); 16:8 (ConstAp VIII 41,4); cf. 7:3; 8:3; 1 Clem 9:3; Gregory-Nazianzus, *Epitaph* 92,1 (PG 38, 57); ActPil 16:6-7 (EvAp 281-282).

[2] J.T. Milik (with the collaboration of M. Black), *The Books of Enoch. Aramaic Fragments of Qumran Cave 4* (Oxford: Clarendon, 1976) 125-135. On the various attempts to decipher the meaning of the name Metatron, see S. Liebermann, 'Metatron, The Meaning of His Name and His Functions', in: I. Gruenwald, *Apocalyptic and Merkabah Mysticism* (AGJU 14; Leiden: E.J. Brill, 1980) 235-241.

[3] 3 En 16 (the dethronement of Metatron) hardly squares with the tendency of chapters 3-15 and is probably a later addition, as suggests P. Alexander, '3 (Hebrew Apocalypse of) Enoch', *OTP* 1, 268 n.*a*.

Metatron cannot be dated earlier than 450 AD[1].

However, a situation not dissimilar from the Enoch-Metatron tradition is found in the (Ethiopic) Book of Similitudes (1 En 37-71), where Enoch's ascension culminates in his institution as the heavenly Son of Man. After Enoch's third apocalyptic discourse (1 En 58:1-69:29) the extant Ethiopic MSS continue with a description of Enoch's final translation into heaven (1 En 70-71)[2]. The first two verses have a third person summary description of Enoch's ascension, in terms reminiscent of Elijah (and Ezekiel?):

> 'And it came to pass after this (that), while he [= Enoch] was living, his name [= his person, he] was lifted from those who dwell upon the dry ground to the presence of that Son of Man [*walda 'eguāla 'emaheyāw*] *and* to the presence of the Lord of Spirits. And he was lifted on the chariots of the spirit, and (his) name vanished among them' (1 En 70:1-2; ed. Knibb 1, 208; tr. Knibb 2, 165)[3].

This brief description is immediately followed by a more specific description in the first person:

> 'And from that day I was not counted among them, and he placed me between two winds, between the north and the west, where the angels took the cords to measure for me the place for the chosen and the righteous. And I there saw the first fathers and the righteous who from (the beginning of) the world dwelt in that place' (1 En 70:3-4; ed. Knibb 1, 208-209; tr. Knibb 2, 165).

---

[1] Maher, *Pseudo-Jonathan* 37 n.10.

[2] 1 En 39:3 contains (at least in its present literary context) a brief description of a heavenly journey.

[3] Italics are Knibb's, comments in square brackets mine. The *terminus ad quem* of Enoch's ascension is, according to the best reading, 'the presence of that Son of Man and ... of the Lord of Spirits', that is, the heavenly realm, the abode of God and the Son of Man [so Charles, 'Book of Enoch', *APOT* 2, 235; E. Sjöberg, *Der Menschensohn im äthiopischen Henochbuch* (SHVL 41; Lund: C.W.K. Gleerup, 1946, ²1956) 147; Knibb, *Enoch* 1, 208; 2, 165; J.J. Collins, "The Heavenly Representative'. The 'Son of Man' in the Similitudes of Enoch', in: G.W.E. Nickelsburg, J.J. Collins (eds.), *Ideal Figures in Ancient Judaism. Profiles and Paradigms* (SCS 12; Missoula, MO: Scholars, 1980) 123-124; Isaac, *OTP* 1, 49; S. Uhlig, *Das äthiopische Henochbuch* (JSHRZ 5/6; Gütersloh: G. Mohn, 1984) 631]. A. Caquot, 'Remarques sur les chapitres 70 et 71 du livre éthiopien d'Hénoch', in: L. Monloubou (éd.), *Apocalypses et Theologie de l'Esperance* (Congres de Toulouse 1975; LeDiv 95; Paris: Cerf, 1977) 113 (following MS Abbadianus 55) translates: 'Il arriva ensuite que le nom de ce fils d'homme fut élevé de son vivant auprès du Seigneur des esprit', and understands the expression 'son of man' as a non-titular reference to Enoch. Black, *1 Enoch* 250 suspects (on the basis of Eth^v) an inner Eth. corruption of an original *semu lawalda 'eguāla ['emma] 'eyāw* ... ('the name of a son of man (= Enoch) was raised up to the Lord of spirits') redrafted by (perhaps) a Christian scribe to *semu 'eyāw* ... ('his name alive was raised up to the Son of Man and to the Lord of spirits').

We have here an obvious exception to Lohfink's thesis that a rapture '... niemals aus der Perspektive dessen erzählt [wird], der entrückt wird'[1]. Enoch is carried away by angels (cf. 1 En 87:3; 90.31; Jub 4:23; 2 En 3:1; 67:2) to a region 'between two winds, between the north and the west', i.e. in the northwest ('the place for the chosen and the righteous ... where the first fathers and the righteous dwell')[2], that is, to Paradise (cf. 60:8; 61:12)[3]. 1 En 71:1-4 describes (still in the first person) Enoch's further translation 'into heaven'[4], where he, impressed by what he sees, bows down in adoration for the Lord of Spirits. He is then initiated by the archangel Michael into the mysteries of the universe. From v.5 onwards Enoch is again carried off to a higher level, to 'the heaven of heavens' (Charles, Isaac), where he sees the palace of God ('the Head of Days') covered in fire and continuously surrounded by angelic beings. Enoch then describes the appearance of Michael, Raphael, Gabriel and Phanuel, accompanied by thousands of holy angels coming out of the house, and the appearance of the Head of Days: 'and with them the Head of Days, his head white and pure like wool, and his garments indescribable' (v.10). Impressed by the appearance Enoch falls upon his face: 'My whole body melted, and my spirit was transformed' (v.11). He then blesses and glorifies God. Then the angel (or the Head of Days, MSS differ)[5] says (in the extant MSS) to Enoch: 'You are the Son of Man [walda be'esī] who was born to righteousness', and then he continues to describe the function of the Son of Man (v.15)[6]. As the text

---

[1] Lohfink, *Himmelfahrt* 38.

[2] So Jeremias, παράδεισος, *ThWNT* 5 (1954) 765.

[3] So Jeremias, *ThWNT* 5, 764-766.769; Sjöberg, *Menschensohn* 148. Probably the different *termini ad quem* ('the presence of the Son of Man and the Lord of Spirits' v.1, and 'the place for the chosen and the righteous' v.3) should not be pressed. Both indicate a region somewhere in the heavenly world.

[4] I take the whole portrayal as a three-stage translation from Paradise (70:4) via 'the heavens' (71:1) into 'the heaven of heavens' (71:5). For a defence of the unity of chapters 70-71, see R. Otto, *Reich Gottes und Menschensohn. Ein religionsgeschichtlicher Versuch* (München: C.H. Beck, 1934, ²1940) 155-163; Sjöberg, *Menschensohn* 159-166.

[5] V.14: 'the angel' (Eth^M) or 'he' (the Head of Days, v.13) (Eth^m q, 8mss).

[6] The Eth. text has different words for what in most English versions is usually indiscriminately rendered 'Son of Man', viz. *walda sab'e* ('descendant of man', 46:2,3,4; 48:2); *walda 'eguāla 'emaheyāw* ('descendant of the race of those born of woman', 62:7,9,14; 63:11; 69:26,27; 70:1; 71:17); *walda be'esī* ('descendant of man', 62:5; 71:14; 69:29 twice); *walda be'esīt* ('descendant of woman' 62:5; 69:29 in two MSS). These variant Eth. expressions are most likely translation variants of the Gr. ὁ υἱὸς τοῦ ἀνθρώπου or the Hebr. אדם בן. See Colpe, ὁ υἱὸς τοῦ ἀνθρώπου, *ThWNT* 8 (1969) 425-428; Casey, 'The Use of the Term 'Son of Man' in the Similitudes of Enoch', *JSJ* 7 (1976) 17-18; C.C. Caragounis, *The Son of Man. Vision and Interpretation* (WUNT 2/38; Tübingen: J.C.B.

stands Enoch is addressed in v.16 with language elsewhere used in respect of the Son of Man (46:3):

'And all ... will walk according to your way, inasmuch as righteousness will never leave you; with you will be their dwelling, and with you their lot, and they will not be separated from you, for ever and ever and ever' (1 En 71:16; ed. Knibb 1, 214; tr. Knibb 2, 167).

The chapter closes with the promise of eternal bliss for the righteous in the presence of the Son of Man:

'And so there will be length of days with that Son of Man [*walda 'eguāla 'emaheyāw*], and the righteous will have peace, and the righteous will have an upright way, in the name of the Lord of Spirits for ever and ever' (1 En 71:17; ed. Knibb 1, 214-215; tr. Knibb 2, 167). Cf. 62:14-16.

As the text stands Enoch's translation into heaven culminates in his exaltation or enthronement as Son of Man. Enoch is now identified as the Son of Man, as E. Sjöberg has argued circumstantially[1], and his ascension accordingly provides the occasion for his glorification/exaltation. It is however very doubtful whether the present (post-Christian!) Ethiopic text is a faithful reproduction of its (Semitic) *Vorlage*.

The difficulties are conveniently summed up by C.C. Caragounis[2]. a) The awkward transition from v.13 to v.14 makes it very likely that the present text is mutilated and originally contained a fragment describing the appearance of the Son of Man with the Head of Days, and Enoch asking about the Son of Man (46:2), in response to which the angel utters vv.14-17[3]. b) Whereas the Head of Days is the grammatical subject of 'came' in v.13, in v.14 it is the interpreting angel, rather than the Head of Days (who is being referred to in the third personal pronoun). c) This is indeed the case in the MS translated by Knibb. d) The second personal pronoun destroys the natural flow of thought. e) That the author would have God come up to Enoch (rather than the reverse) is an idea offensive in itself. That he has God inform Enoch that he (Enoch) was the central figure of the former Parables, is very incongruous. f) V.15 is quite incongruous after v.14, if the Son of Man is Enoch and the speaker the Head of Days. On the other hand, it makes good sense

---

Mohr/Paul Siebeck, 1986) 106 n.115. Contra Isaac, *OTP* 1, 50 n.*s*, who distinguishes between 'Son of Man' and 'son of man'. The use of these words in the rest of the Similitudes does not confirm this distinction.

[1] Sjöberg, *Menschensohn* 147-189. Likewise Casey, *Son of Man. The Interpretation and Influence of Daniel 7* (London: SPCK, 1979) 99-107; N. Perrin, *Rediscovering the Teaching of Jesus* (New York, Evanston: Harper & Row, 1967) 168; G. Haufe, 'Entrückung und eschatologische Funktion im Spätjudentum', *ZRGG* 13 (1961) 107.

[2] For what follows see Caragounis, *Son of Man* 110-112 n.121.

[3] Charles, *APOT* 2, 237 comments after v.13: '[Lost passage wherein the Son of Man was described as accompanying the Head of Days, and Enoch asked one of the angels (as in xlvi.3) concerning the Son of Man as to who he was.]'

when the speaker is the angel, and the subject of 'proclaims' is the Son of Man. g) Vv.14-17 are best understood as a proclamation to Enoch about the Son of Man, rather than an address of the angel to Enoch telling him who he was h) The reversion to the third personal pronoun in v.17 (that Son of Man) is in line with the entire work. It may indicate a tampering has taken place in regard to vv.14,16, facilitated by the address to Enoch in v.15. i) The whole portrayal of the Son of Man in the Parables is inapplicable to Enoch's person.

Although there is no MSS evidence to sustain the theory of a lost fragment between v.13 and 14, the internal (stylistic) grounds mentioned make it very likely that the present text is mutilated[1]. If so, the textual corruption may have been carried out by a Jewish scribe with a special interest in the figure of Enoch, answering the Christian identification of Jesus as Son of Man[2].

If, however, the text should be taken as it stands—the absence of MSS evidence is a serious objection against emendation!—there is the problem how the portrayal of Enoch as Son of Man in chapters 70-71 matches with the picture of Enoch as *distinct* from the Son of Man in the rest of the Similitudes (esp. 1 En 46). In theory it is of course possible that a redactor has uncritically integrated quite competing traditions without much alteration and without smoothing away internal discrepancies. But that only sharpens the problem. Whoever was responsible for the passage on Enoch's exaltation (either the original author or a later interpolator, in either case someone with the highest respect for Enoch) could not have overlooked the fact that the equation of Enoch and the Son of Man is quite untypical, if not contrary, to the *Tendenz* of the rest of the Similitudes. It gives the impression of being a *Fremdkörper* and is at least unexpected in the present book[3]. The text makes an anachronistic impression. The awkward connection to the rest of the Similitudes suggests that chapters 70-71 have not been always part of the Similitudes but are a later[4]

---

[1] So Charles, *APOT* 2, 237; H. Appel, *Die Komposition des äthiopischen Henochbuches* (BFChTh 10/3; Gütersloh: C. Bertelsmann, 1906) 43-45; A.L. Moore, *The Parousia in the New Testament* (NT.S 13; Leiden: E.J. Brill, 1966) 23; Caragounis, *Son of Man* 110 n.121*a*.

[2] Cf. Bietenhard, *Himmlische Welt* 147-148.

[3] Sjöberg, *Menschensohn* 147-189 argues that the equation of Enoch and the Son of Man is not in conflict with their distinctiveness elsewhere in the Similitudes, if they are understood in terms of exaltation (i.e. Enoch is now exalted to something he was not before), so that there is no conflict between a pre-existent Son of Man in heaven and Enoch (a mere human being) on earth. If Enoch were his incarnation (and thus on earth being a Son of Man) this would be difficult. Now he is only called Son of Man in heaven (which, Sjöberg admits, remains a bit of a difficulty to modern readers). The acclamation 'you are the Son of Man' may be understood in the old Israelite enthronement sayings in which 'you are king' means 'you are installed as king'.

[4] Contra Black, 'The Eschatology of the Similitudes of Enoch', *JThS* 3 (1952) 1-10,

interpolation[1]. Its *Sitz im Leben* may again be (sectarian) Jewish apologetic against the Christian identification of Jesus as the Son of Man.

If the former arguments are invalid, there is another difficulty. Even if Enoch was identified as the Son of Man and chapters 70-71 were an integral part of the Similitudes, there remains the difficulty of dating the Similitudes as a whole. The absence of fragments of the Similitudes at the caves of Qumran—significant in the light of the interest taken in the person of Enoch in the Qumran community: fragments of all other constituent parts of 1 Enoch have been found—suggests at least a date in the second half of the first century AD[2], that is, in roughly the same period as the composition of Luke-Acts. Since there is no unambiguous pre-Christian (pre-Lukan) evidence that Enoch's ascension was understood as the occasion of his exaltation/enthronement as Son of Man[3] and positive evidence that Luke knew the Similitudes fails[4], the

---

followed by Perrin, *Rediscovering* 167, who hold chapters 70-71 to be older.

[1] So Black, 'Aramaic Barnasha and the 'Son of Man'', *ET* 95 (1984) 201; Caragounis, *Son of Man* 93-94 (following Black); J. Theisohn, *Der auserwählte Richter. Untersuchungen zum traditionsgeschichtlichen Ort der Menschensohngestalt der Bilderreden des Äthiopischen Henoch* (StUNT 12; Göttingen: Vandenhoeck & Ruprecht, 1975) 216 Anm.4 (!).

[2] *HJP* 2, 505; 3/1, 256-259; Dunn, *Christology* xxxix, n.81; 76-78.297-298 n.79.

[3] Even if it were the case in 1 En 70-71, it remains difficult to establish how influential this text was in its environment. The attention given to it in modern scholarship does not secure its popularity in its original setting!

[4] Some line of contact of the Similitudes with Matthew (19:28; 25:31) has been positively confirmed by Theisohn, *Richter* 149-201, but in the case of Luke-Acts it seems not possible to convey positive evidence which proves Lukan dependency. Charles' list of references of supposed influence of 1 Enoch on the NT (Charles, *APOT* 2, 180-181)—except for Acts 10:4 // 1 En 99:3 all from the Similitudes—on a closer look cannot prove Lukan dependency on the Similitudes, as all references can be explained in terms of a common source, or a more likely OT candidate. Lk 1:52 // 1 En 46:4 (Sir 10:14; Job 12:19; 5:11; Ezek 21:31); Lk 9:35 // 1 En 40:5 (cf. 45:3,4; 49:2,4) (Ps 2:7; Is 42:1; cf. 1QpHab 9:12); Lk 18:7 // 1 En 47:1-2 (Judg 11:36; Ps 21:3 LXX; Sir 35:22; cf. 2 Pet 3:9); Lk 21:28 // 1 En 51:2 (cf. 2 Bar 23:7; cf. Is 63:4; Ps 111:9; Dan 4:34; see further Bill. 2, 256); Lk 23:35 // 1 En 40:5 (cf. Lk 9:35; Is 42:1; Jn 1:34; 1 Pet 2:4 [see I.H. Marshall, *Commentary on Luke* (NIGTC; Grand Rapids: Eerdmans, 1978) 869]; Acts 3:14 // 1 En 53:6 (2 Sam 23:3; Is 32:1; 53:11; Zech 9:9; cf. PssSol 17:35); Acts 4:12 // 1 En 48:7 [cf. 1 Cor 6:11; Herm(v) IV 2,4; cf. E. Haenchen, *Die Apostelgeschichte* (KEK III[17]; Göttingen: Vandenhoeck & Ruprecht, 1956, [7]1977) 215-216]; Acts 17:31 // 1 En 41:9 (variant readings!) (Dan 7:13ff.; cf. Ps 9:9; 96:13; 98:9). Nestle-Aland's index of *loci citati vel allegati* (NA[27], 804-805) lists three supposed Lukan allusions to the Similitudes (1 En 39:4 // Lk 16:9; 1 En 51:2 // Lk 21:28; 1 En 63:10 // Lk 16:9), but again none of them provides sufficient proof for the claim that Luke knew or used the Similitudes. We must therefore assume the independence of Luke-Acts and the Similitudes (cf. Dunn, *Christology* 77-78.298f. nn.82-86).

corollary is that 1 En 70-71 does not contribute to the understanding of the ascension of Jesus in Luke-Acts.

Putting things in perspective, it must be stressed that in marked contrast to the central significance of Enoch in some apocalyptic circles Enoch's role in other first-century Jewish and Christian sources is limited. Admittedly, in the age of Hellenism Enoch, like so many other biblical figures, became an instrument of Jewish propaganda[1], but many texts simply repeat no more than the biblical affirmation of his piety and his subsequent being taken away, or refer to the Enoch literature. For Philo, the interest in the figure of Enoch is mainly for the virtues and spiritual lessons he stands for[2]. Josephus refers to Enoch only with much restraint and reshapes the biblical Enoch story in terms of a Greek rapture [*Ant* I iii,2 (79); iii,4 (85-86); IX ii,2 (28)][3]. And as for the NT, it should be noted that it does not engage in the wild speculations of Enochic circles either. Except for his (unavoidable) mentioning in the Lukan genealogy (Lk 3:37) he is only referred to in Heb 11:5 and Jud 14. In Heb 11:5

---

[1] E.g. Ps-Eup 8-9 (as quoted by Eusebius, *PraepEv* IX 17,2-9; ed. Holladay 175), where Enoch, in conscious opposition to Egyptian and Greek claims, is claimed to have discovered astrology and is identified with Atlas, who in Greek opinion had discovered astrology.

[2] For Philo, Enoch symbolises virtue and understanding. The triad Enosh-Enoch-Noah stands for ἐλπίς-μετάνοια (καὶ βελτίωσις)-δικαιόσυνη (*Abr* 17-26; cf. *Praem* 15-21), but this triad stands on a lower level than Abraham-Isaac-Jacob, who represent διδασκαλικὴ ἀρετή-φυσικὴ ἀρετή-ἀσκητικὴ ἀρετή (*Abr* 11), see E.R. Goodenough, *By Light, Light. The Mystic Gospel of Hellenistic Judaism* (New Haven: 1935, repr. Amsterdam: Philo, 1969) 121-152. In line with his allegorising tendency, Philo 'spiritualises' Enoch's rapture. In *Quaest in Gn* 1,86 Philo associates Enoch's translation to heaven with that of Moses (*protopropheta*) and Elijah, but clearly as an ascent of the soul distinct from the body. Enoch's rapture marks a transition 'from dead life to immortality' (*Mut* 38; cf. *Praem* 17) or *ex sensibili visibilique loco ad incorpoream et intelligibilem ideam* (*Quaest in Gn* 1,86), his conversion (*Abr* 18). That Enoch was found no more resembles the fact that wise men are always difficult to find because they are rare and withdraw from the crowds (*Abr* 20-23). See further R.A. Kraft, 'Philo (Josephus, Sirach and Wisdom of Solomon) on Enoch', *SBL.SP* (1978) 253-257; Luciani, 'Le vicende di Enoc nell'interpretazione di Filone Alessandrino', *RivBib* 31 (1983) 43-68; P. Borgen, 'Heavenly Ascent in Philo. An Examination of Selected Passages', in: J.H. Charlesworth, C.A. Evans (eds.), *The Pseudepigrapha and Early Biblical Interpretation* (JSNT.S 83; Studies in Scripture in Early Judaism and Christianity 2; Sheffield: JSOT, 1993) 246-268.

[3] In the genealogy he comments: (...) οὗτος [= Enoch] ζήσας πέντε καὶ ἑξήκοντα πρὸς τοῖς τριακοσίοις ἀνεχώρησε πρὸς τὸ θεῖον, ὅθεν οὐδὲ τελευτὴν αὐτοῦ ἀναγεγράφασι, *Ant* I iii,4 (85); cf. IV viii,48 (326). In discussing Elijah's departure from life he has Enoch (and Elijah) simply disappear from the world, *Ant* IX ii,2 (28). The idea of 'disappearance' is the most common *terminus technicus* in Hellenistic rapture stories (Lohfink, *Himmelfahrt* 41).

Enoch is given a place among the faithful and praised on account of his faith during his earthly life[1]. As in Gen 5:24, the author is silent on Enoch's post-rapture status. The author of Jude is well aware of the existence of the Enoch traditions—Jud 14 is understood best as a reference to 1 En 1:9—but makes no mention of his rapture or his alleged heavenly journeys. This restraint may well have been for christological reasons[2]. Significantly, his name is absent in the lists of Mk 6:15; 8:28.

### d. *The Elijah Tradition*

The elaborate and detailed report of Elijah's ascent to heaven (2 Kings 2:1-18) stands in marked contrast to the brevity of the account of Enoch's rapture (Gen 5:24). The author—with an almost embarrassing lack of restraint—dramatically pictures the details of Elijah's separation from Elisha by 'a chariot of fire and horses of fire' and his assumption 'in a whirlwind into heaven'.

> After the introductory statement (v.1) Elijah and Elisha are portrayed in a rapid change of scenes as wandering from Gilgal (v.1b) via Bethel (v.2) and Jericho (v.4) towards the Jordan (v.6), where Elisha, in contrast with the 50 prophets who stayed behind (v.7), accompanies his master to the very end. At the Jordan, Elijah (who, incidentally, seems to be quite informed about the event to take place!) takes his mantle, rolls it up, and divides the water so that they can cross over on dry ground (cf. Moses) (v.8). In response to Elijah's offer to grant his pupil a wish, Elisha asks for 'a double share of Elijah's spirit' (v.9; cf. Deut 21:17). Elijah attaches a condition[3] to the wish: 'if you see me ...' (v.10). The actual rapture report is brief but dramatic: 'As they continued walking and talking, a chariot of fire and horses of fire separated the two of them, and Elijah ascended in a whirlwind into heaven' (v.11). Witnessing the event, Elisha cries in response: 'Father, father! The chariots of Israel and its horsemen!' (13:14; cf. 6:17; 7:6)[4], and, seeing Elijah no more, takes his garments and rends them in two, thus demonstrating symbolically the final separation (v.12)[5]. At his return at the bank of the river Elisha repeats the miracle his master performed, thereby showing that his wish has been fulfilled (vv.13-14). The prophets acknowledge Elisha as rightful successor of Elijah (v.15). The narrative concludes with the unsuccessful search for the body of Elijah (vv.16-18).

---

[1] See Lührmann, 'Henoch' 103-116.

[2] W. Adler, 'Enoch in Early Christian Literature', *SBL.SP* (1978) 271-275; *HJP* 3/1, 260-264.

[3] So Schmitt, *Entrückung* 72-74; contra K. Galling, 'Der Ehrenname Elisas und die Entrückung Elias', *ZThK* 53 (1956) 140-141.

[4] See Galling, 'Ehrenname' 129-148; M.A. Beek, 'The Meaning of the Expression 'The Chariots and Horsemen of Israel' (2 Kings 2:12)', *OTS* 17 (1972) 1-10; Schmitt, *Entrückung* 114-119.

[5] Schmitt, *Entrückung* 118-119.

Form-critically, the narrative is to be classified as a 'prophetic calling story'[1], marking the transition from the ministry of Elijah to that of Elisha[2]. In the present literary context the focus is emphatically on the successor, Elisha[3]. The scope of the entire section—well expressed by the prophets of Jericho: נחה רוח אליהו על־אלישע (v.15)—is to establish the succession of the prophetic ministry from Elijah to Elisha.

The entire narrative is chiastically structured around v.11, which thus forms the pivot of the story[4]. Elijah's ascension marks the conclusion of his earthly career and is *conditio sine qua non* for the transfer of his spirit to Elisha, the fulfilment of which is closely related to Elisha's seeing Elijah go to heaven.

New in comparison with the biblical Enoch story, where the medium of translation remained unmentioned, is that Elijah is taken up (this is implied) in a fiery chariot drawn by fiery horses (cf. Sir 48:9; LivPro 21:15; GkApEzra 7:6; cf. SibOr 2,187)[5], which is of course a most fitting end for the prophet whose career is characterised by fire (1 Kings 18:38; 2 Kings 1:10,12; Sir 48:1,3)![6]. According to 1 Macc 2:58 Elijah's ascension was a reward for his

---

[1] Schmitt, *Entrückung* 130-133. E. Haag, 'Die Himmelfahrt des Elias nach 2 Kön 2,1-15', *TThZ* 78 (1969) 31 rejects the classification 'Prophetenlegende' and calls the story a 'lehrhafte Erzählung' (following O.H. Steck). Schmitt, *Entrückung* 133-134 regards vv.16-18 as originally independent from vv.2-15 and classifies them as a 'prophetic anecdote'. See further T.R. Hobbs, *2 Kings* (WBC 13; Dallas, TX: Word, 1984) 15-19 for other attempts to classify the story (with reservations).

[2] The story is usually assigned to the so-called Elisha-cycle rather than to the Elijah-cycle. This form-critical assessment is criticised by C. Houtman, 'Elia's hemelvaart. Notities over en naar aanleiding van 2 Koningen 2:1-18', *NThT* 32 (1978) 295-298, who concludes 'dat 2 Kon. 2:1-18 *zowel* het verhaal over het einde van Elia *als* het verhaal over het begin van Elia is. Het vormt de schakel tussen de verhalen rondom Elia en de verhalen rondom Elisa' (298, my emphasis).

[3] Note the threefold mention of Elisha's loyalty to his master (vv.2,4,6), the double reference to Elisha's foreknowledge of his master's imminent rapture (vv.3,4), the quest for a double share of Elijah's spirit which marks him as a firstborn and legal successor (v.9), his ability to repeat the miracle of the splitting of the waters, which serves as a proof that he received Elijah's spirit (vv.13-14), the acknowledgement of his authority (v.15), and the emphasis on the superiority of spiritual insight (vv.16-18).

[4] For a more detailed analysis, see Hobbs, *2 Kings* 17-19.

[5] See Houtman, 'Elia's hemelvaart' 284-286.

[6] Schmitt, *Entrückung* 93-96 has convincingly demonstrated that the motif of the 'fiery chariots and the fiery horses' belongs to the OT theophany tradition. That Elijah is carried off 'in a whirlwind' (בסערה vv.1,11) is puzzling, since it seems to compete with the fiery chariot. Do we have here two different sources? Is the mention of a whirlwind perhaps a rationalisation? It should be noted, at any rate, that we have here a motif which occurs with some frequency in Greek rapture stories [Homer, *Odyssey* 20,63-66; *HomHym* 5,208;

zeal for the Law (cf. 2 Kings 19:10,14)[1].

A not insignificant question is raised by the LXX rendering ὡς εἰς τὸν οὐρανόν in 2 Kings 2:1,11. Does ὡς express criticism on Elijah's ascension, as if the LXX-translator were embarrassed and rationalised the text? This is possible[2]. But it should be noted that ὡς qualifies εἰς τὸν οὐρανόν rather than ἀνελήμφθη, that is, *stricto sensu* the issue under attack is the *terminus ad quem*, not the rapture event itself. After all, why would a translator apologise for a story which Greeks of all people would appreciate the most? Another possibility deserves attention. In obvious competition with the view that Elijah was now in heaven (that is, in God's presence) some rabbinic sources express the opinion that he lived somewhere hidden on earth (e.g. on Mount Carmel) or in Paradise, awaiting his future return (references in Bill. 4/2, 765-766). R. Yose ben Chalafta (± 130-160 AD) denied that Elijah went to heaven on dogmatic grounds, since this contradicted Ps 115:16, where it is said that heaven is God's dwelling-place, not man's (Suk 5a; tr. I.W. Slotki, in: *Soncino Talmud* 15). Syr has in vv.1,11 שמיא לצית 'towards heaven, heavenwards' (TFormProph 2 Kings 2:1,11; ed. Sperber 2, 273-274; tr. Harrington-Saldarini 266-267). This debate may go back to the days of LXX on the following grounds: (1) the same *v.l.* is found in some MSS of 1 Macc 2:58 (undoubtedly under the influence of the present passage)[3]; (2) in Sir 48:9 LXX (+ Vg) both *termini ad quem* מעלה and [מן]רום are omitted[4] (Syr again has 'heavenwards'); (3) Sir 48:12 replaces a *terminus ad quem* 'in the (heavenly) chambers' (v.12) by the medium/agency 'in a whirlwind'. This all lends weight to the suggestion that the LXX translator did not so much criticise Elijah's rapture as such, but that he wanted to express his unwillingness to believe Elijah was in heaven.

As in the case of Enoch, Elijah's non-conventional departure from the world and the conviction that he was alive somewhere formed a natural springboard for belief in the possibility of his return and renewed activity among the people. The earliest expression of belief in a return of Elijah is found in Mal 3:23-24

---

Sophocles, *OedCol* 1659f.; DiodS, *Hist* III 60,3; DionHal, *AntRom* II 56,2; Livy, *AUC* I 16,2; Horace, *Carm* I 2,42-48; Plutarch, *Romulus* 27,7; Dosiades (FGH 458 fgm 5)], but which in the OT is used in the context of a theophany (cf. Nahum 1:3; Zech 9:14; Ps 18:11; 50:3; Ezek 1:4; Ps 104:3).

[1] Perhaps 1 Macc 4:46 and 14:41 also have Elijah in mind. So e.g. A. Wiener, *The Prophet Elijah in the Development of Judaism. A Depth-Psychological Study* (Littman Library of Jewish Civilization; London, Henley, Boston: Routledge & Kegan Paul, 1978) 38.

[2] Schmitt, *Entrückung* (53.142.)145-151; Ginzberg, *Legends* 6, 322-323 n.32; J.A. Goldstein, *1 Maccabees. A New Translation with Introduction and Commentary* (AncB 41; Garden City, NY: Doubleday, 1976) 241 n.58. One should compare DiodS, *Hist* II 20,1: ἠφάνισεν ... ὡς εἰς θεοὺς; Plutarch, *Romulus* 27,5: ὡς ἀνηρπασμένον εἰς θεοὺς.

[3] For the attestation of ὡς, see ed. Kappler 61. Codex V has ἕως, which is certainly secondary, see Schmitt, *Entrückung* 146 Anm.205. Critical judgement is divergent. Rahlfs 1046 rejects ὡς; H.B. Swete 3, 601 and Kappler 61 accept it.

[4] Although מעלה could be left untranslated, because the idea was probably included in the prep. 'Ἀνα- and [מן]רום may not have been in LXX's copy. The fact that in 2 Kings 2:1,11 and 2 Macc 2:58 the *terminus ad quem* is likewise a matter of dispute is suggestive.

MT[1], where God promises to send the prophet Elijah 'before the great and terrible day of the LORD comes' (לפני בוא יום יהוה הגדול והנורא), to prepare the covenant people for God's visitation at the day of judgement[2]. His specific task is here described as והשיב לב־אבות על־בנים ולב בנים על־אבותם, i.e. 'to turn the heart of fathers to the children, and the heart of the children to their fathers', envisaging a reconciliation between the generations (so LXX), or 'to turn the heart of the fathers (to God) with the children, and the heart of the children (to God) with their fathers', thus restoring the covenant community[3].

In Sir 48:9-12 the ascension of Elijah and the Malachi prophecy have merged into a coherent picture[4]. Beyond Mal 3:23-24 Elijah is now expected 'to restore the tribes of Israel' (להכין שבטי ישראל καὶ καταστῆσαι φυλὰς Ιακωβ), a task elsewhere ascribed to the Servant of YHWH (Is 49:6 ונצירי ישראל להשיב להקים את־שבטי יעקב στῆσαι τὰς φυλὰς Ιακωβ καὶ τὴν διασπορὰν τοῦ Ισραηλ ἐπιστρέψαι) (cf. Ezek 47:13-48:29; PssSol 17:28). Unfortunately, the Hebrew text of v.11 has been badly damaged. Line 'a' probably read ... ומ[ת] אשר ראך 'blessed he who sees you and dies', but what follows (perhaps an explanatory comment) is so mutilated that it is impossible to restore the original text beyond the level of conjecture. This is complicated by the fact that LXX suffered from several editorial operations. Given the use of the second person in vv.4-10, Elijah rather than YHWH is addressed. The reference is more likely to the return of Elijah than to his earthly life[5]. The sense of the

---

[1] A later addition according to a scholarly majority. For a defence of the authenticity of Mal 3:22-24, see G.Ch. Aalders, *Oud-Testamentische Kanoniek* (Kampen: J.H. Kok, 1952) 284; P.A. Verhoef, *Maleachi* (COT; Kampen: J.H. Kok, 1972) 266-267.

[2] The suggestion that Malachi here foresees a *personal* return of the historical Elijah has however not gone unchallenged. Especially in the light of the association of Elijah with John the Baptist (Mk 9:13 // Mt 17:12; Lk 1:17; 7:27) and the analogy with 'the prophet like Moses', his words are sometimes taken as to announce the manifestation of an Elijah-like figure, rather than a reappearance of Elijah himself, so e.g. C.F. Keil, *Die Zwölf kleinen Propheten* (BC; Leipzig: Dörffling & Franke, [3]1888) 715; Verhoef, *Maleachi* 271-272. The mere designation of this eschatological figure as אליה הנביא (MT) would not be an obstacle for later exegetes to interpret this person as 'someone like Elijah'. It is, however, interesting to see that LXX renders אליה הנביא as Ηλιαν τὸν Θεσβίτην (cf. 1 Kings 17:1), thereby suggestively strengthening the reference to the historical Elijah.

[3] Verhoef, *Maleachi* 273-274.

[4] Except for the suppression of the *termini ad quem* (*supra* 60), the variations between LXX and its original are of minor significance. Λαῖλαψ (vv.9,12 LXX) and συσσεισμός (2 Kings 2:1,11) are translation variants for סערה (Job 38:1). LXX (+ Vg) adds πυρὸς (but not in v.12; cf. vv.1,3). Some LXX MSS (+ Vg) omit καὶ, possibly to strengthen the identity of the 'whirlwind' and the 'chariots of fiery horses'.

[5] With Shekan, Di Lella, *Ben Sira* 534, contra Box, Oesterley, *APOT* 1, 501 n.11.

words may be best captured in the translation: 'blessed he who has seen you before he dies'[1]. For an author alien to the idea of an afterlife such as Ben Sira[2], it makes good sense to call a blessing upon those who will see Elijah before they die, i.e. experience the blessing of his preparatory actions before the Day of the Lord and thus witness the dawn of the age of salvation.

The intertestamental pseudepigrapha contain but a few references to Elijah's ascent into heaven. 1 En 89:53 (Dream Visions) most likely has Elijah in view, who is taken up into heaven by 'the Lord of the sheep' to protect him from his adversaries. In 90:31 Elijah is probably to be identified with 'that ram'[3], but he is largely overshadowed by the figure of Enoch (which is, of course, hardly surprising in a corpus in which Enoch figures as the prominent hero of Israel's past). 1 En 93:8 (Apocalypse of Weeks) possibly refers to the ascension of Elijah, but as in the Dream Visions, he is not mentioned by name. 4 Ezra 6:26 (cf. 14:9) also refers to the ascension and eschatological reappearance of Elijah (and Enoch).

In comparison with the dramatic description of 2 Kings 2, Josephus gives an extremely sober report on Elijah's end (τελευτή) in *Ant* IX ii,2 (28). No mention of chariots of fire and fiery horses, no whirlwind, no dramatic action whatsoever. Instead, Josephus interprets the biblical account with the help of Greek rapture terminology and speaks twice rather vaguely about Elijah's becoming 'invisible' and about the fact that nobody knows of his (and Enoch's) death. The *terminus ad quem* remains vague:

> Κατ᾿ ἐκεῖνον δὲ τὸν καιρὸν (= during the reign of the wicked king Joram) Ἠλίας ἐξ ἀνθρώπων ἠφανίσθη καὶ οὐδεὶς ἔγνω μέχρι τῆς σήμερον αὐτοῦ τὴν τελευτήν· μαθητὴν δὲ Ἐλισσαῖον κατέλιπεν, ὡς καὶ πρότερον ἐδηλώσαμεν. Περὶ μέντοι γε Ἠλία καὶ Ἐνώχου τοῦ γενομένου πρὸ τῆς ἐπομβρίας ἐν ταῖς ἱεραῖς ἀναγέγραπται βίβλοις, ὅτι γεγόνασιν ἀφανεῖς, θάνατον δ᾿ αὐτῶν οὐδεὶς οἶδεν [*Ant* IX ii,2 (28)].

His modesty may be due to his rationalising tendency[4], although he does not go

---

[1] To limit the blessing to a particular individual in Israel's past makes little or no sense (why, if e.g. Elisha were in view, refer to his death?). Rather the blessing should be understood in general terms (LXX has the plural) as a reference to those who are alive when Elijah returns.

[2] Shekan, Di Lella, *Ben Sira* 530.534 and especially 83-87; further Box, Oesterley, *APOT* 1, 501. V.11c LXX (καὶ γὰρ ἡμεῖς ζωῇ ζησόμεθα) is certainly a later insertion by Ben Sira's grandson.

[3] Black, *1 Enoch* 279 (in opposition to J.T. Milik).

[4] So R. Marcus, in: LCL 326, 17 n.c. For a general treatment, see H.R. Moehring, 'Rationalization of Miracles in the Writings of Flavius Josephus', in: E.A. Livingstone (ed.), *StEv* 6 (TU 112; Berlin: Akademie, 1973) 376-383.

so far as to deny Elijah's rapture. According to some traditions, Elijah made occasional post-rapture appearances from heaven (2 Chron 21:12 seemed to suggest that at that time he was still alive). Josephus seems to be familiar with such a tradition [*Ant* IX v,2 (99)][1], but this does not seem to be eschatologically qualified.

In the writings of Philo, Elijah and his ascension do not play a significant role (see *Imm* 136-139).

The NT, on the other hand, gives ample evidence of popular belief in the return of Elijah: as a rumour reaching king Herod (Mk 6:15 // Lk 9:8); as a popular speculation noticed by the disciples (Mk 8:28 // Mt 16:14 // Lk 9:19); as a question addressed to John the Baptist (Jn 1:21). Beyond the popular level, the scribes appear to believe in Elijah's return before the establishment of the messianic kingdom (Mk 9:11-13 // Mt 17:10-13)[2]. Possibly Elijah's appearance on the Mount of Transfiguration (Mk 9:2-10parr.) also reflects this tradition[3].

Summarising, first-century Judaism and emergent Christianity were quite familiar with the idea that Elijah since his spectacular ascent to heaven was reserved there by God for a future reentry. At the end of time he would return from heaven to perform his role in the eschatological drama, be it as forerunner of the Messiah or as a Messianic figure himself[4]. How this bears on the ascension theme in Luke-Acts will be discussed in chapters three and six.

---

[1] According to the interpretation of Ginzberg, *Legends* 4, 202. But this is disputable!

[2] Despite J.A.T. Robinson, 'Elijah, John and Jesus. An Essay in Detection' (1958); repr. in: idem, *Twelve New Testament Studies* (SBT 34; London: SCM, 1962) 28-52; M. Faierstein, 'Why Do the Scribes Say That Elijah Must Come First?', *JBL* 100 (1981) 75-86 [response by D. Allison, 'Elijah Must Come First', *JBL* 103 (1984) 256-258] and Fitzmyer, 'More about Elijah Coming First', *JBL* 104 (1985) 295-296, this seems to be the correct understanding of the words. It is difficult to see why the scribes were made mouthpiece if this did not originate with them.

[3] The tradition of Elijah's ascent and return is further taken up in GkApEzra 7:6; LivPro 21:15; ActPil 15:1 (EvAp 264-265.319); Pes 5b; TPsJ Deut 30:4 (ed. Clarke 246; tr. Etheridge 2, 653); Justin, *Dial* 49 (PG 6, 581-584; *Elias redivivus*); Tertullian, *Res* 22 (PL 2, 825); cf. Lactantius, *Inst* VII 17,1-3; Commodian, *CarmDuoPop* 833-864.

[4] In post-70 AD rabbinic Judaism Elijah has become one of the most popular religious figures, who as a heavenly scribe writes down the origin and deeds of men in a book, renders service to the deceased patriarchs of Israel, occasionally conducts the souls of the righteous into the Garden of Eden, and, above all, acts as an intercessor and helper in times of need, especially for the weak and oppressed (perhaps already in Mk 15:34-35). Different from Enoch-Metatron, according to later mysticism Elijah did not experience a transformation of his body so that he could easily return to the earth to help people in need [J. Gutmann, M. Aberbach, *et alii*, 'Elijah', *EJ* 6 (1971) 638].

## e. *The Moses Tradition*

Given the straightforward description of Moses' death and burial in Deut 34:5-8 it may come somewhat as a surprise to find in some circles an expressed belief that Moses in fact had *not* died but had been bodily transferred to heaven. Yet among the various legends about Moses' final days there is a rather persistent tradition—embroidering on the biblical affirmation that 'no one knows his burial place to this day' (Deut 34:6)—that Moses had been bodily taken up into the heavenly sanctuary[1]. SifDev 357, e.g., preserves an anonymous tradition of Moses' escape from death and his present priestly activity in heaven:

ויש אומרים לא מת משה אלא עומד ומשרת למעלה
נאמר כאן שם ונאמר להלן ויהי שם עם הי ‎[2].

According to MHG Gen 5:24 (drawing upon a supposedly Tannaitic source) Moses was one of the three choice persons who entered heaven alive:

תאנא שלשה עלו ושימשו במרום. ואלו הן חנוך ומשה ואליהו ‎[3].

In Yalkut Shim'oni God grants Moses the quite exceptional privilege of ascending to heaven (i.e. alive) instead of descending into Sheol as all other creatures:

---

[1] References to Moses' mysterious death and/or (bodily) assumption are collected in: Bill. 1, 754-756; Ginzberg, *Legends* 3, 463-481; 5, 148-168 (see index in vol. 7 *s.v.* Moses); P. Volz, *Die Eschatologie der jüdischen Gemeinde in neutestamentlichen Zeitalter nach den Quellen der rabbinischen, apokalyptischen und apokryphen Literatur dargestellt* (Tübingen: J.C.B. Mohr/Paul Siebeck, [2]1934) 194-195.197; Jeremias, Μωυσῆς, *ThWNT* 4 (1942) 858-860; W.A. Meeks, *The Prophet-King. Moses Traditions and the Johannine Christology* (NT.S 14; Leiden: E.J. Brill, 1967) 122-125.156-159.209-214.244-254; *FPsG* 63-67; Lohfink, *Himmelfahrt* 61-69; S.E. Loewenstamm, 'The Death of Moses' (1958), rev. in: Nickelsburg (ed.), *Studies on the Testament of Abraham* (SCS 6; Missoula, MO: SBL, 1972) 185-217; J.D. Purvis, 'Samaritan Traditions on the Death of Moses', in: Nickelsburg (ed.), *Studies on the Testament of Moses* (SCS 4; Cambridge, MA: SBL, 1973) 93-117; K. Haacker, P. Schäfer, 'Nachbiblische Traditionen vom Tod des Mose', in: O. Betz, K. Haacker, M. Hengel (Hrsg.), *Josephus Studien. Untersuchungen zu Josephus, dem antiken Judentum und dem Neuen Testament* (FS O. Michel; Göttingen: Vandenhoeck & Ruprecht, 1974) 147-174; *HJP* 3/1, 284-286; J.E. Fossum, *The Name of God and the Angel of the Lord. Samaritan and Jewish Concepts of Intermediation and the Origin of Gnosticism* (WUNT 36; Tübingen: J.C.B. Mohr/Paul Siebeck, 1985) 129-144 (the ascension of the Prophet like Moses according to the Dositheans).

[2] SifDev 357 (ed. Finkelstein 428; tr. Hammer 381). Par. MTann 224; Sot 13b.

[3] MHG Gen 5:24 (ed. Margulies 132 (קלב); tr. Jeremias, *ThWNT* 4, 860. On the disputed authenticity, see Himmelfarb, 'Report' 259.

אמר לו הקב//ה למשה
כל הבריות יורדות לשאול שנאמר כל יורדי דומה
ואתה עולה שנאמר עלה אל הר העברים וגו/[1]

In Christian circles Augustine makes a passing reference to the doctrine that Moses did not die, though he cautiously hands it down as a (minority) opinion of others:

> *Non desunt, qui etiam Moysen asserant vivere; quia scriptum est eius sepulcrum non inveniri, et apparuit cum Domino in monte, ubi et Elias fuit, quem mortuum legimus non esse, sed raptum* (Augustine, *CommJoh* 74,2; CChr.SL 36, 681)[2].

The critical question for the present investigation—how far does this tradition reach back?—is complicated by a number of methodological problems. In so far as this tradition has been taken up in the Christian tradition, it stands under the suspicion of drawing out the conclusion of what Moses' appearance at the Transfiguration and his eschatological return in Rev 11:3-12 seemed to imply. Furthermore, the Moses tradition is a complex one and it is here that a proper distinction of the various 'ascension forms' becomes most imperative. While Moses' ascent on Sinai to receive the Law (Ex 24) was widely interpreted as an ascent to heaven, in the course of which Moses was enthroned as king and was even deified[3], this tradition should be carefully distinguished from the speculations about his rapture, because it represents a heavenly journey type of ascension, that is, a temporary visit to heaven during his lifetime to receive divine revelations, rather than an *Entrückung* that concludes his earthly life[4].

Similar reservations should be urged against Moses' heavenly exaltation in the so-called 'Throne Vision' in Ezekiel the Tragedian (second century BC)[5],

---

[1] y Num 27:12 (ed. Landau 2, 958; tr. Meeks, *Prophet-King* 209-210).

[2] The appeal to Moses' appearance on the Mount of Transfiguration is of course an argument of specifically *Christian* provenance. Cf. Ambrose, *De Cain et Abel* I 2,8 (PL 14, 337). Contra Lohfink, *Himmelfahrt* 68, Jerome (*CommAmos* III 9,6; CChr.SL 76, 340) cannot be taken as to support the tradition of Moses' bodily rapture: though he associates Moses with Enoch and Elijah, it should be noted that he immediately passes over to include Paul's experience as well. The common denominator of all four is the fact that each of them has been in heaven some way or another (Enoch and Elijah by means of their bodily assumption, Moses after his mysterious burial and Paul during a mystical experience).

[3] Philo, *Quaest in Ex* 2,29 (see Meeks, *Prophet-King* 122-125). Cf. Jub 1:1-4,26; prologue; *LAB* 32:9 (ed. Harrington 248); 2 Bar 59:5-11.

[4] See on Moses' Sinai ascents, Meeks, *Prophet-King*. It is disputed whether Ps-Orph 32-36 describes an apotheosis of Moses. Possibly the reference is to God rather than Moses.

[5] EzekTrag [as quoted by Eusebius, *PraepEv* IX 29 and ClemAlex, *Stromata* 1,23 (155,1-7) (GCS 52/2, 96-98), both citing Alexander Polyhistor (*FPsG* 210f.)] describes a heavenly exaltation vision of Moses, describing his investiture as king and his installation to the

which is no more than a metaphorical description of Moses' exaltation with a different historical reference, viz. his role as leader of the Exodus. Furthermore, given the plain affirmation of Scripture it is unlikely that the belief that Moses had not died was a very widespread tradition. Besides, if Moses is said to ascend to heaven at the end of his life, this does not necessarily conflict with the tradition of his death as long as it remains within the conceptual borders of an assumption of the soul. Such traditions are e.g. preserved in the so-called Assumption of Moses[1], the writings of Philo[2], and in the so-called 'duplex Moses tradition'[3]; texts which, despite their abundant use of rapture terminology, are little more than solemn affirmations of Moses' death and the subsequent passing of his soul into heaven. Unlike the Enoch and Elijah

---

prophetic office). Interestingly, this 'exaltation' is neither connected with the Sinai ascent nor with his final assumption. On this passage see further Van der Horst, 'Moses' Throne Vision in Ezekiel the Dramaturg', *JJS* 34 (1983) 21-29; H. Jacobson, *The* Exagoge *of Ezekiel* (Cambridge: CUP, 1983) 89-97.

[1] AsMos 10:12 (ed. Tromp 20). Charles, 'The Assumption of Moses', *APOT* 2, 422 takes *receptionem* as an addition by the editor, who combined the 'Testament of Moses' (which told of Moses' death) and 'the Assumption of Moses' (which told of Moses' assumption). With Tromp, however, the *m* is more likely to be an abbreviated *mea* [so also Haacker, Schäfer, 'Nachbiblische Traditionen' 160 Anm.31 (contra A. Ceriani); cf. E. Brandenburger, *Himmelfahrt Moses* (JSHRZ 5/2; Gütersloh: G. Mohn, 1976) 77-78 Anm.12a], rather than an incongruous case ending. In the extant text it is thus apposite to *a morte*: *a morte receptione mea*, i.e. 'from (my) death, (that is) my assumption', 'from (my) death, (that is) the assumption of my soul' (to heaven, I would suggest, not, as Tromp, *Assumption* 239 suggests, to the realm of death). J. Priest, 'Testament of Moses. A New Translation and Introduction', *OTP* 1, 933 n.*h*, translates 'my death and burial', but this has not much to commend it. Tromp has an excellent discussion on pp.270-285 on the lost ending of the Assumption of Moses. A more audacious attempt to reconstruct the content of the lost ending is undertaken by Bauckham, *Jude and the Relatives of Jesus in the Early Church* (Edinburgh: T. &T. Clark, 1990) 235-280.

[2] Though Philo explicitly compares Moses' end with the fate of Enoch and Elijah (*Quaest in Gn* 1,86), this may mean no more than that all three departed life in a non-conventional way. In the actual description of Moses' departure, Philo is clearly thinking of an assumption *of his soul* (*VitMos* 2,288). Moses' final ascent is a transition from mortal to immortal life, whereby his imprisoned soul leaves the body (*Virt* 76). This however does not prevent Philo in the dramatic description in *VitMos* 2,291 from using rapture terminology (including the heavenly chariot as a means of transportation).

It should be noted, incidentally, that Moses' final 'ascent' to deity is patterned after his earlier ascents on Sinai, rather than the reverse. This means that not the rapture/assumption scheme, but Moses' heavenly ascents bring in the notion of exaltation-deification.

[3] ClemAlex, *Stromata* 6,15 (132,2-3) (GCS 52/2, 498); Origen, *HomJos* 2,1; Euodius, *EpAug* 158,6 (*FPsG* 65-66) (cf. Lohfink, *Himmelfahrt* 66-67).

traditions, which could expand quite uncontrolledly due to Scripture's silence, anyone who deviated from the biblical Moses tradition would have to account for it.

Josephus is our oldest source for the belief that Moses escaped death and was translated. At the end of his section on the life of Moses[1], Josephus relates how Moses bids the people farewell and accompanied by the elders of Israel, Eleazar and Joshua, ascends Mount Abaris [*Ant* IV viii,48 (325)]. Having left the elders behind, Moses, Eleazar and Joshua move to a higher location. Josephus then continues:

(Moses) ἀσπαζομένου δὲ καὶ τὸν Ἐλεάζαρον αὐτοῦ καὶ τὸν Ἰησοῦν καὶ προσομιλοῦντος ἔτι, νέφους αἰφνίδιον (suddenly) ὑπὲρ αὐτὸν στάντος ἀφανίζεται (he disappeared) κατά τινος φάραγγος (in a ravine)· γέγραφε δ' αὐτὸν ἐν ταῖς ἱεραῖς βίβλοις τεθνεῶτα, δείσας μὴ δι' ὑπερβολὴν τῆς περὶ αὐτὸν ἀρετῆς πρὸς τὸ θεῖον αὐτὸν ἀναχωρῆσαι (that he went back to the deity) τολμήσωσιν εἰπεῖν [Josephus, *Ant* IV viii,48 (326)].

A number of formal criteria suggests that this is a typical rapture report: ἀφανίζομαι, which Josephus uses also for Elijah and Enoch [*Ant* IX ii,2 (28)], is the most common *terminus technicus* for a Greek rapture[2]. The otherwise unparalleled phrase πρὸς τὸ θεῖον ... ἀναχωρῆσαι is exactly the same as the one used in the case of Enoch [*Ant* I iii,4 (85); cf. III v,7 (96) (hypothetically of Moses)]. The notion of 'suddenness' (αἰφνίδιον)[3] and the cloud motif are standard features in Hellenistic rapture stories (cf. esp. Apollodorus, *Bibliotheca* II 7,7; DionHal, *AntRom* I 77,2). The incident, furthermore, is viewed from a spectator perspective. And although the location of the event, on a mountain, was dictated by the biblical tradition it is nevertheless a happy coincidence that the same motif abundantly appears in Graeco-Roman rapture stories[4]. Most striking, finally, is that Josephus bypasses the biblical description of Moses' burial.

That this is a rapture report about Moses in the strict sense has, however, not gone unchallenged[5]. It has been suggested that Josephus clearly speaks about

---

[1] On Josephus' general treatment of Moses, see L.H. Feldman, 'Josephus' Portrait of Moses', *JQR* 82 (1992) 285-328; 83 (1992) 7-50; 83 (1993) 301-330.

[2] References in Friedrich, 'Entrückungschristologie' 54 Anm.60.

[3] Livy, *AUC* I 16,1 (*subito*); DiodS, *Hist* II 20,1 (ταχέως); III 60,3 (ἐξαίφνης); Plutarch, *Romulus* 27,5; *Camillus* 33,7 (ἄφνω); cf. 1 Cor 15:52 (ἐν ἀτόμῳ, ἐν ῥιπῇ ὀφθαλμοῦ); 2 Bar 46:2 ('quickly').

[4] References in Lohfink, *Himmelfahrt* 43.

[5] It has been questioned e.g. by Haacker, Schäfer, 'Nachbiblische Traditionen' 147-151; J.D. Tabor, "Returning to Divinity'. Josephus's Portrayal of the Disappearances of Enoch, Elijah, and Moses', *JBL* 108 (1989) 225-238.

Moses' end in terms of death elsewhere [*Ant* IV viii,49 (330)], and that the unusual *terminus ad quem* (a φάραγξ) rules out the possibility of Moses' assumption into heaven or Paradise[1]. If Josephus employs rapture language, it is argued, it is to communicate Moses' death. A closer look, however, reveals that these arguments cannot be decisive. The use of death terminology as such is not *per se* incompatible with a belief in a bodily rapture, as we pointed out earlier (*supra* 36 n.2). The *terminus ad quem* has obviously been derived from the biblical account, which makes explicit mention of Moses' death and burial 'in a valley [(א)יג] in the land of Moab' (Deut 34:6). This has been misunderstood by LXX, who took יג as a *nomen proprium* (Γαι). It should be noted that elsewhere LXX renders the Hebrew יג by φάραγξ[2], which, in turn, not only means 'valley' but also 'ravine'[3]. For Hellenistic readers there would be nothing surprising about a rapture into a valley or ravine, given the ancient tradition of 'cave raptures'[4]. Moreover, the Palestinian Targumic tradition on Deut 33:21 speaks explicitly of the preparation of the *cave* for Moses' burial (TPsJ Deut 33:21; ed. Clarke 253; tr. Etheridge 2, 679; SifDev 355; ed. Finkelstein 418; tr. Hammer 372; MTann 219). This is, of course, a different tradition, but it proves that there is nothing spectacular about linking Moses' end with a valley, a ravine or the like. Josephus' rapture story, then, would appeal to the Greeks and Romans, without leaving the terminological confines of the biblical narrative[5].

Others[6], admitting that we have here a reference to Moses' rapture, suggest that Josephus dissociates himself from this tradition, taking the second part of

---

[1] Haacker, Schäfer, 'Nachbiblische Traditionen' 150 Anm.13-15, esp. Anm.14.

[2] Deut 4:46; Josh 15:78 (2x); 2 Chron 14:9; 26:9; 2 Ezra 12:15 LXX // Neh 2:15 MT; 13:13 LXX // Neh 3:13 MT; 21:30 *v.l.* // Neh 11:30 MT; Ps 59:2 // 60:2 MT; Zech 14:5 (2x); Is 22:1,5; 40:4 (= Lk 3:5); Jer 7:31,32 (2x); 39:35 // 32:35 MT; Ezek 6:3; 31:12; 35:8; 36:4.

[3] 1 En 24:2; 26:3,4 (2x),5,6; 27:1; 30:1,3; LetAris 118:3; Josephus, *BJ* I vii,4 (147); VI ii,8 (161); TIss 1:5; SibOr 3,457.682.

[4] See E. Rohde, *Psyche. Seelencult und Unsterblichkeitsglaube der Griechen* 1 (Tübingen: J.C.B. Mohr/Paul Siebeck, 1893, [9.10]1925) 128-145; Strecker, 'Entrückung' 467-468, with reference to Homer, *Ilias* 2,546-550; Philostratus, *VitAp* 8,30; Pausanias, *Periegesis* IX 37,7; cf. 39,2; Apollodorus, *Bibliotheca* III 2,2; DiodS, *Hist* V 59,4; Sophocles, *OedCol* 1661f., 1681; Herodotus, *Hist* 4,94-96; DiodS, *Hist* IV 82,6.

[5] Cf. ClemAlex, *Stromata* 6,15 (132,2) (GCS 52/2, 498) (φάραγξ!).

[6] Bill. 1, 753; Jeremias, *ThWNT* 4, 859; Lohfink, *Himmelfahrt* 61-69; Talbert, 'Immortality' 424-425; Feldman, in: M.R. James, *The Biblical Antiquities of Philo. Translated from the Old Latin Version* (Library of Biblical Studies, 1917; repr. New York: Ktav, 1971) cvi; Tromp, *Assumption* 284. Admittedly Josephus distances himself from the idea in *Ant* III v,7 (95-97), but there the situation is different (the ascent on Mount Sinai to receive the Law).

the text to be Josephus' dismissal of the tradition, interpreting the phrase to mean something like: 'Moses was caught up (it is said), but this cannot be true, because he wrote in the scriptures that he died'. However, Josephus does not assign the rapture speculation to popular belief—as he did *expressis verbis* in *Ant* III v,7 (95-98)!—but he simply records what he believed to be the facts. Since the facts, however, so obviously run counter with the biblical record of Moses' death, he is forced to give an explanation of this apparent discrepancy. This is what he does in what follows. The following rendering of the rather ambiguous Greek brings to the surface that which seems to be at the heart of the issue (with italics to indicate where the emphasis is): 'but he wrote[1] himself in the holy scriptures that he died, for fear people would venture to say that it was *on account of his outstanding virtue* that he went (back) to the deity [= was taken up into heaven]'. In other words, Moses, knowing in advance of his coming rapture (like Elijah!), apparently wanted to avoid any notion of merit on his own part[2].

The crucial remaining question is why Josephus, familiar with the biblical tradition of Moses' death and burial, deliberately deviates from 'the plain words of Scripture'. The answer must either be that Josephus either reinterpreted the biblical Moses tradition himself in view of his Hellenistic readership, as he did with Enoch and Elijah, or that he was acquainted with a particular tradition of Moses' bodily assumption[3]. In both cases, the existence of a tradition of Moses' bodily rapture is brought back at least to the end of the first century AD[4].

---

[1] Γέγραφε has a personal subject here (he, i.e. Moses). For a formal 'it is written' Josephus usually has γέγραπται [see K.H. Rengstorf, *A Complete Concordance to Flavius Josephus* 1 (Leiden: E.J. Brill, 1973) *s.v.* γράφω]. MS L has in fact γέγραπται, Lat. *scriptum est* (ed. Niese 1, 290 Anm.1).

[2] A speculation already prepared for in *Ant* III v,7 (97) (cf. *LAB* 12:2 ed. Harrington 126). Josephus' otherwise laudable portrait of Moses (*supra* 67 n.1) would of course prepare his Hellenistic readers for such a dramatic denouement.

[3] Haufe, 'Entrückung' 109. Meeks, *Prophet-King* 140-141, believes that Josephus rationalises an account of Moses' ascension, and concludes: 'Josephus here makes himself mouthpiece, not of the tradition that Moses was translated, ... but of a tradition that already fears that that notion leads to idolatry' (141).

[4] If our line of interpretation is correct and Josephus claims a rapture for Enoch, Elijah *and* Moses, the thesis of Tabor, 'Returning' 225-238, followed by Feldman, 'Josephus' Portrait of Elijah', *SJOT* 8 (1994) 80-81, that Josephus shows an ambivalence with regard to the raptures of Enoch and Elijah because he wished to prevent them from being regarded superior to Moses (who had died), cannot stand. Perhaps *LAB* 19:16 (ed. Harrington 164) (cf. 20:2 ed. Harrington 166) consciously opposes the view that Moses had not died [cf. C. Perrot, P.-M. Bogaert, avec la collaboration de D.J. Harrington (eds.), *Pseudo-Philon. Les antiquités*

If we have rightly interpreted Josephus' account, the perplexing question of whether Moses' appearance at the Mount of Transfiguration (Mk 9:4 // Mt 17:3 // Lk 9:30) implies his previous rapture into heaven may be answered more confidently in the positive. If, furthermore, we may take the Transfiguration scene to be a 'scene of eschatological anticipation'[1], we then have a clear analogy of the *Henoch et Elias redituri* tradition, following the rapture-preservation-(eschatological) return pattern[2]. Later Christian sources affirm a future return of Moses (Rev 11:3-12; SibOr 5,256-257?).

The crucial issue is whether the doctrine of Moses' eschatological return is a Christian innovation on the basis of the Enoch and Elijah speculations or a deduction from current Jewish expectations. Unfortunately, we are on rather unsteady ground here because the expectation of the 'prophet *like* Moses'[3] would be a natural alternative to a return of Moses *in personam*. In addition, sources that affirm a personal return of Moses are late and, in the case of the few rabbinic sources that speak of Moses' eschatological reentry[4], are connected with his future resurrection from the dead, not with his rapture. In Samaritanism, an eschatological return of Moses is expected in the medieval Book of Joshua:

'And he (Moses) informed the children of Israel concerning the deluge of fire, and the day of vengeance and reward, and defined the time of his return unto them. Then he announced what should happen unto every tribe, and that he would marshal them complete in the days of final perfection and completion' (tr. O.T. Crane, quoted from Meeks, *Prophet-King* 246-247).

If the fivefold prayer for the coming of Moses in Memar Marqah 2:8 (משה ייתי בשלם נביה רבה ed. MacDonald 1, 40; tr. 2, 63) also envisages an eschatological role for Moses, this tradition goes back at least to as far as the

---

*bibliques* 2 (SC 230; Paris: Cerf, 1976) 136; Harrington, 'Pseudo-Philo', *OTP* 2, 328 n.*u.*]. That Ps-Philo has Moses die *super excelsam terram* [= on Mount Abarim] *et in lumine totius orbis* (contrary to the biblical account) may be for apologetic reasons, viz. to have Moses' death publicly confirmed; cf. TMos 1:15. If so, the suggestion of Haacker, Schäfer, 'Nachbiblische Traditionen' 155-156, that *LAB* 19 marks a transition *to* an *Entrückungsvorstellung*, can be taken in reverse (i.e. a relics of a rapture tradition).

[1] Marshall, *Commentary* 384.

[2] Note that Josephus does not reflect upon Moses' post-rapture status and activities.

[3] See H.M. Teeple, *The Mosaic Eschatological Prophet* (SBL.MS 10; Philadelphia: SBL, 1957); F. Hahn, *Christologische Hoheitstitel. Ihre Geschichte im frühen Christentum* (FRLANT 83; Göttingen: Vandenhoeck & Ruprecht, 1963, [2]1964) 356-371.

[4] DebR 3:17 (ed. Mirkin 69; tr. Freedman-Simon 7, 88); SifDev 355 (ed. Finkelstein 418; tr. Hammer 372-373); TPsJ Deut 33:21 (ed. Clarke 253; tr. Etheridge 2, 679); AgBer 67 (ed. Jellinek 4, 91-93); MTann 219 (according to R. Yohanan ben Zakkai, first century AD!).

fourth century AD[1]. This would find confirmation if, as Meeks argues, for Marqah the Taheb figure was identical with Moses rather than with the prophet like him[2], a suggestion which has much to commend it, since in Samaritan theology Moses is the central figure after whom there would not again arise a prophet like him (Deut 34:10)[3]. References to eschatological figures would thus naturally be interpreted in terms of a return of Moses himself. On the other hand, the privilege to escape death is explicitly denied to Moses in Memar Marqah 5:2 (does the polemic presuppose assertion?) and much is made of his mysterious death (which is described as an ascent of his spirit/soul)[4].

In sum, the tradition of Moses' rapture can be traced back to the first century AD—to an author who is otherwise very close to Luke!—but it nevertheless remains an isolated and probably most controversial belief[5]. Finally, anticipating our discussion further on, it should be noted that in the biblical Moses tradition the number 'forty' figures frequently in connection with the ascents on Mount Sinai (not his final ascent!) to denote a period of preparation (fasting, Ex 24:18; 34:28; Deut 9:9,18,25; 10:10)[6].

### f. Ezra, Baruch, Phinehas (and Melchizedek)
While the rapture speculations about Enoch, Elijah and Moses were to a greater or lesser extent grounded in affirmations of OT Scripture, there is no direct OT point of departure which sanctioned speculations about the idea of Ezra's bodily assumption into heaven[7]. In that respect we have here a

---

[1] MacDonald, *Memar Marqah* 1, xx.

[2] Meeks, *Prophet-King* 246-254, who notes for instance the exact parallelism of Memar Marqah 2:8 (the prayer for the coming of Moses) and 1:9 (the prayer for the coming of the Taheb).

[3] For an introduction to the role of Moses in Samaritan theology, see MacDonald, *The Theology of the Samaritans* (NTLi; London: SCM, 1964) 147-222. On Samaritan eschatology in particular, see F. Dexinger, 'Samaritan Eschatology', in: A.D. Crown (ed.), *The Samaritans* (Tübingen: J.C.B. Mohr/Paul Siebeck, 1989) 266-292.

[4] See MacDonald, *Theology* 215-222; Meeks, *Prophet-King* 244-246; Purvis, 'Samaritan Traditions' 93-117; Haacker, Schäfer, 'Nachbiblische Traditionen' 160-164.

[5] Cf. also M. Hengel, 'Setze dich zu meiner Rechten! Die Inthronisation Christi zur Rechten Gottes und Psalm 110,1', in: M. Philonenko (éd.), *Le Trône de Dieu* (WUNT 69; Tübingen: J.C.B. Mohr/Paul Siebeck, 1993) 171-174, who arrives at a similar conclusion with regard to the heavenly enthronement of Moses.

[6] Surveying the Moses tradition as a whole, it appears that his ascent on Mt. Sinai to receive the Law is the key event, on which his final ascension is patterned, not *vice versa*.

[7] The OT does not mention Ezra's death. According to Josephus, *Ant* XI v,5 (158), Ezra died as an old man and was buried with great magnificence in Jerusalem. Rabbinic sources say Ezra died in Persia (Ginzberg, *Legends* 4, 446). That Ezra had died was obviously general

*traditionsgeschichtliches* novum. However, what is true of apocalyptic writings in general—the tendency to make great men of the past spokesmen of their own theology—applies to the idea of bodily assumptions as well. Given the prominence of apocalyptic traditions about Enoch, it must have been only a matter of time before other (more prominent and less controversial) historical figures were claimed to have received heavenly revelations and were believed to have been granted the privilege of being bodily taken up into heaven. It is likely that Ezra's activity as priest (Ezra 7:1-5,11,12,21; 10:10,16; Neh 8:2,9; 12:26) and scribe (Ezra 7:6; Neh 8:2,5,14; 12:36; cf. 4 Ezra 12:37-38; 14:19-26,48 longer text) made him an eligible candidate for apocalyptic speculations (cf. Enoch's scribal activities!).

The very first (and only) tradition about Ezra's bodily assumption is mentioned as late as the last decade of the first century AD, viz. in the Fourth Book of Ezra. Yet, for three reasons, we must take notice of 4 Ezra. Firstly, with the exception of chapters 1-2 and 15-16, which are Christian additions, 4 Ezra 3-14 is a genuinely Jewish document, representing a stream of Jewish tradition which is more or less independent from Christianity[1]. Secondly, the description of Ezra's rapture shares some striking elements with 2 Baruch and 2 Enoch, which gives us reason to believe that the three writings have made use of a conventional scheme, probably in existence somewhere in the second half of the first century AD. Thirdly, as we will argue below, the same traditional scheme may have been used by Luke in his portrayal of the ascension of Jesus.

In chapter 8, which hints at Ezra's assumption (8:20 *adsumeretur*), Ezra is informed about his future destiny, which will involve access to Paradise (v.52 *vobis enim apertus est paradisus*) and immortality (v.53 *et [mors] absconsa est*, sc. *a vobis*). In the seventh vision (4 Ezra 14:1-48), in which Ezra represents a New Moses, Ezra is commanded by the Lord to make final preparations for his departure from the world because the ageing world is rapidly approaching its end (14:1-18):

> 'And now I say to you: Lay up in your heart the signs that I have shown you, the dreams that you have seen, and the interpretations that you have heard; for you shall be taken up (*recipieris*) from among men, and henceforth you shall live with my Son and with those who are like you (*cum similibus tuis*), until the times are ended (*usquequo finiantur tempora*)' (4 Ezra 14:7-9; ed. Klijn 87; tr. Metzger 553).

Fearing that divine knowledge will disappear after his departure, Ezra asks

---

opinion. The site of his tomb was a matter of debate [see A. Ben-Yaacob, 'Ezra', *EJ* 6 (1971) 1107].

[1] This, of course, does not rule out the possibility of Christian interpolations. But the idea of Ezra's rapture is certainly not Christian.

permission to put in writing that which is necessary for future generations, a request which is granted to him (vv.19-26). At the end of his farewell-address to the people (vv.27-36), he urges them, in accordance with God's command, not to seek him for forty days (vv.23,36,42,44,45)[1]. Accompanied by five other men who were trained to write rapidly (vv.24,37), Ezra goes to the field, where the next day a voice from heaven commands him to open his mouth and to drink a cup of wisdom. Then knowledge flows from his lips and under divine inspiration he dictates 94 books (i.e. 24 OT books and 70 esoteric apocalyptic works). The Latin text ends with a remark about Ezra's obedience to publish 24 books and to keep the rest secret: *et feci sic* (v.48). The Syriac version (preserved in the Milan Peshitta MS dating to the sixth or seventh century AD), however, continues:

> '... in the seventh year of the sixth week, five thousand years and three months and twelve days after creation. At that time Ezra was caught up, and taken to the place of those who are like him, after he had written all these things. And he was called the Scribe of the knowledge of the Most High for ever and ever' (cf. Eth., Arab 1, Arm.) (4 Ezra 14:48 *v.l.*; tr. Metzger 555 n.*p.*).

No doubt this reading represents the lost ending which was cut out when chapters 15-16 were added[2]. Earlier, we made a brief reference of the allusion to Enoch and Elijah in 4 Ezra 6:26 (*et videbunt qui recepti sunt homines, qui mortem non gustaverunt a nativitate sua*). Possibly Enoch and Elijah were in the author's mind in 4 Ezra 8:51 as well, where Ezra is commanded to focus on his own destiny, rather than on that of the unrighteous and to inquire concerning the glory of 'those like him' (*de similibus tuis inquire gloriam*). The typical qualification 'those like you' also occurs in 4 Ezra 14:9 and 14:48. That Ezra is associated with the Messiah (*filius meus*) and with Enoch and Elijah marks his importance in the eyes of the author of 4 Ezra. Ezra's assumption (*receptio*) is understood as a translation to the heavenly realm where the Messiah and Enoch and Elijah dwell[3]. Although there is no explicit mention of

---

[1] Forty days on the analogy of the forty days of Moses' stay on Sinai, H.R. Balz, τεσσεράκοντα κτλ., *ThWNT* 8 (1969) 137.

[2] J.M. Myers, *I and II Esdras. Introduction, Translation and Commentary* (AncB 42; Garden City, NY: Doubleday, 1974) 329; Stone, *Fourth Ezra* (Hermeneia; Minneapolis, MN: Fortress, 1990) 442.

[3] Whereas Enoch and Elijah are in heaven by virtue of their rapture, the presence of the Messiah in heaven should be understood in terms of his pre-existence (cf. 4 Ezra 12:32; 13:26). Likewise: Myers, *2 Esdras* 127; A. Barbi, *Il Cristo celeste presente nella Chiesa. Tradizione e Redazione in Atti 3,19-21* (AnBib 64; Roma: IBP, 1979) 70-71; Caragounis, *Son of Man* 129; Stone, 'The Question of the Messiah in 4 Ezra' (1968/1988); repr. in: idem, *Selected Studies in Pseudepigrapha and Apocrypha. With Special Reference to the Armenian*

Ezra's body being taken up to heaven this is implied by his close association with Enoch and Elijah, even though occasionally his departure is described in terms of death (7:15; 8:5; 10:34) (*supra* 36 n.2). That a chronological limit is set on Ezra's presence in heaven (*usquequo finiantur tempora*) suggests an expected return of Ezra in the end ('the decisive point in the eschatological sequence' (Stone), i.e. the inauguration of the Messianic Kingdom[1]).

The Second (Syriac) Apocalypse of Baruch, a Jewish apocalyptic work dating from around 100 AD, preserves a tradition about the *Entrückung* of Baruch, which draws very close to that of Ezra (2 Bar 48:30; 76:1-5; cf. 43:2; 46:7). Whatever the literary relationship between the two books is, whether one was using the other or both were drawing upon a common source, the fact that both works claim an assumption for its main character is significant in itself, as it demonstrates the tendency to 'conventionalise' the rapture-preservation scheme.

Baruch is known in the biblical tradition as a scribe (ספר Jer 36:26,32 MT), the secretary of Jeremiah. As with Ezra[2], this may have facilitated the choice of him as recipient of divine revelations, as preserved in the various works under his name. The crucial passage on Baruch's rapture is found in 2 Bar 76:1-5:

> 'And he [= the *angelus interpres*] answered and said to me [= Baruch]: Since the revelation of this vision has been explained to you as you prayed for, hear the word of the Most High that you know that which will happen to you after these things. For you will surely depart from this world, nevertheless not to death but to be kept unto (the end) of times [*ad reservationem temporum*]. Therefore, go up to the top of this mountain, and all countries of this earth will pass before you, as well as the likeness of the inhabited world, and the top of the mountains, and the depths of the valleys, and the depths of the seas, and the number of rivers, so that you may see that which you leave and whither you go. This will happen after forty days [*hoc autem continget post quadraginta dies*]. Go, therefore, now during these days and instruct the people as much as you can so that they may learn lest they die in the last times, but may learn so that they live in the last times' (2 Bar 76:1-5; ed. Kmosko 1199-1201; tr. Klijn 646).

The passage is styled after a Moses typology (cf. Deut 34:1-3). It is announced that Baruch will escape death[3] to be 'kept unto (the end) of times' (v.2), that is,

---

*Tradition* (SVTP 9; Leiden, New York, København, Köln: E.J. Brill, 1991) 318.322.

[1] Cf. Stone, 'Coherence and Inconsistency in the Apocalypses. The Case of 'The End' in 4 Ezra' (1983); repr. in: idem, *Selected Studies* 333-347.

[2] According to Jewish tradition, Ezra was a student of the Law in Babylonia under Baruch, cf. G.F. Moore, *Judaism in the First Centuries of the Christian Era. The Age of the Tannaim* 1 (Schocken 294; New York: Schocken, 1927; repr. 1971) 6-7.

[3] Even though in 2 Bar 44:2; 78:5; 84:1 death terminology is used for Baruch. H.H. Mallau, 'Baruch/Baruchschriften', *TRE* 5 (1980) 273, suggests this is indicative of different

he will be physically taken up into heaven, where he will be preserved unto the end of times (i.e. the day of judgement). At the final judgement he will stand up as a witness (13:3; cf. 25:1)[1]. As in 4 Ezra 14, a forty day period of final instructions precedes the assumption (v.4)[2].

A few decades before 4 Ezra and 2 Baruch, Ps-Philo's *Liber Antiquitatum Biblicarum*, a rewriting of biblical history, preserved a tradition about the rapture of Phinehas, the son of Eleazar the priest, the wording of which is reminiscent of Elijah:

> 'And now rise up and go from here and dwell in Danaben on the mountain and dwell there many years. And I will command my eagle, and he will nourish you [= Phinehas] there, and you will not come down to mankind until [*quousque*] the time arrives and you be tested in that time; and you will shut up the heaven then, and by your mouth it will be opened up. And afterward you will be lifted up [*elevaberis*] into the place where those who were before you [*priores tui*] lifted up, and you will be there until [*quousque*] I remember the world. Then I will make you all come, and you will taste what is death [*gustabitis quod est mortis*]. And Phinehas went up and did all that the LORD commanded him' (*LAB* 48:1-2; ed. Harrington 320 tr. OTP 2, 362).

If *priores tui* is taken in a strict chronological sense, at least Enoch and perhaps Moses are included[3]. Their common 'zeal for the law' has led later interpreters to equate Phinehas and Elijah (Phinehas: Num 25:11; Sir 45:23; 1 Macc 2:54; 4 Macc 18:12; Elijah: Sir 48:2; 1 Macc 2:58)[4], but it remains a matter of dispute whether *LAB* 48:1 already identifies the two[5]. The interesting thing of the brief

---

sources or traditions, but see our comments *supra* 36 n.2.

[1] Except for the ambiguous 55:6, there is no explicit mention of Baruch's *return* to earth, but unless we are to assume that the judgement takes place in heaven, this is implied. A comparison with 4 Ezra would confirm this.

[2] On the further treatment of Baruch in Jewish sources, see Ginzberg, *Legends* 4, 322-325 (including a discussion on Baruch's tomb); 6, 411-412 (n.66. rabbinic references to Baruch's never having tasted death).

[3] So Black, 'Two Witnesses' 232.

[4] They are identified in PRE 29; 47 (ed. Braude נׁא, קׁנׁף; tr. Friedlander 213-214.317); TPsJ Ex 6:18 (ed. Clarke 72; tr. Etheridge 1, 459); TPsJ Deut 30:4 (ed. Clarke 246; tr. Etheridge 2, 653); BemR 21:3 (ed. Mirkin 2, 279; tr. Freedman-Simon 6, 828-830); Origen, *CommJoh* 6,7. (PG 14, 225); y Num 25:11 (ed. Landau 2, 771).

[5] According to R. Hayward, 'Phinehas—the same is Elijah. The Origin of a Rabbinic Tradition', *JJS* 29 (1978) 22-38, the Palestinian Targum is the first Jewish tradition to equate Phinehas with Elijah; according to Jeremias, *ThWNT* 2, 935 Anm.38, the equation is post-Christian. See on this issue further Ginzberg, *Legends* 4, 195; 6, 316-317 n.3; Bill. 4/2, 790-791; Hengel, *Die Zeloten. Untersuchungen zur jüdischen Freiheitsbewegung in der Zeit von Herodes I. bis 70 n.Chr.* (AGSU 1; Leiden, Köln: E.J. Brill, 1961) 167-172; Willems, 'Textes rabbiniques' 99-101.

note is that it is patterned on the rapture-preservation paradigm. As with the Messiah in 4 Ezra (and 2 Baruch) the hour of his death is postponed.

A further development of the conventional rapture-preservation scheme is found in the Melchizedek story in 2 En 71-72[1] (in both the longer and shorter recension), the date of which unfortunately cannot be established with any certainty[2]. Melchizedek, the foreseen successor of the priest Nir, the son of Methuselah, experienced a miraculous birth under bizarre circumstances (2 En 71). After forty days in Nir's tent, the angel Michael comes down to translate the wonder-child into Edem, to preserve him from the coming flood, after which he will be established as (arch)priest of the future (71:29). A striking difference between the J and A recension is that the former expects 'another Melchizedek' (71:34,37; 72:6 J), whereas the latter seems to envisage an eschatological role for Melchizedek himself: 'Melkisedek will be the head of the priests in another generation' (71:33,37; 72:2 A). 2 En 71:11 A regards the rapture of the child to be born as some sort of punishment: 'I shall receive [the child Melchizedek] in paradise, so that you will not be the father of a gift of God'. The themes are reminiscent of Ezra's and Baruch's translation: a period of forty days preceding the rapture, a translation into heaven, a period of divine preservation which culminates in an eschatological role[3].

g. *Summary and Conclusions*

The Talmudic treatise *Derekh Erez Zutta* preserves a catalogue in which the number of rapture candidates is fixed:

'There were nine who entered the Garden of Eden alive, viz.: Enoch the son of Yered, Elijah, the Messiah, Eliezer the servant of Abraham, Hiram, king of Tyre, Ebed-melech the Cushite, Jabez the son of R. Juda the Prince, Bithiah the daughter of Pharaoh, and Serach, the daughter of Asher. Some say: Also R. Joshua b. Levi' (DEZ 1:18; ed. Higger 68-70; tr. Cohen 2, 570)[4].

Whatever the value of this otherwise obscure list, it is significant that the number of raptures is limited to *only* nine or ten persons. A noticeable expansion in comparison with the OT, yes, but in the light of the sheer innumerable rapture stories in the Jewish *Umwelt*, esp. in the Graeco-Roman world, quite a modest figure. This concurs with what our late first-century sources show. With the names of Enoch, Elijah, Moses, Ezra, Baruch and

---

[1] 2 En 71-72 [ed./tr. Vaillant 69-84 (XXII-XXIII)]. Cf. also Epiphanius, *AdvHaer* 1,3, *Haer* 40,7 (PG 41, 687-688) (on Seth).

[2] Böttrich, 'Slavonic Enoch' 40-41, argues that the Melchizedek material goes back to a pre-AD 70 setting.

[3] On other Melchizedek speculations, see O. Michel, Μελχισεδέκ, *ThWNT* 4 (1942) 573-575; F.L. Horton, *The Melchizedek Tradition. A Critical Examination of the Sources to the Fifth Century A.D. and in the Epistle to the Hebrews* (MSSNTS 30; Cambridge, London, New York, Melbourne: CUP, 1976).

[4] For similar lists (of later date) see Himmelfarb, 'Report' 261-262.

Phinehas (and perhaps Melchizedek) the Jewish rapture list seems to be exhausted[1]. Despite the inclusion of the Messiah in the list of DEZ 1, there is no indisputable first-century evidence that the Messiah was expected to be caught up at the end of his life[2]. 'Rapture belief' always seems to have remained something of a *Fremdkörper* in Jewish biblical faith. This reticence may be due to a large extent to a desire to avoid the religious associations attached to the pagan rapture stories (deification and immortalisation). Moreover, the prevailing conviction of first-century Judaism (if we may generalise here) was that, at death, the soul separated from the body and that the body would rest in the grave (Gen 3:19!) awaiting the resurrection. Further, the crude cosmology which seems to underlie rapture belief would not invite general acceptance. After all, any serious rapture claim would need an empty tomb or at least the absence of a corpse. In this respect the more refined 'assumption of the soul' type of ascension lent itself much more to integration into the OT-Jewish context of belief. Yet the fact is that the translation stories of Enoch and Elijah did obtain a place in the scriptures and tradition of Israel, so that the community of faith had to accept them *nolens volens*. This, in turn, must have cleared the way for a more positive appraisal of the rapture phenomenon as a miraculous act of divine intervention which befell only a few elect of outstanding piety: Enoch because of his praiseworthy walk with God; Elijah because of his zeal for the Law, and so on.

In the foregoing analysis we have seen that in the course of time the assumption stories of Enoch and Elijah have merged quite spontaneously with

---

[1] Other rapture claims cannot be traced back with any confidence to the first century AD, see Haufe, 'Entrückung' 110-112. In later times the prophet Jeremiah was believed to have escaped death by means of a bodily rapture and to fulfil an eschatological task (e.g. Victorinus of Pettau, *CommApc* 11,3, CSEL 49, 98, and see the references in Berger, *Auferstehung* 256-257 Anm.72). But, despite Berger, it seems that this belief cannot be traced back to the first century AD (2 Macc 2:4-8; 15:14-16; and Mt 16:14 are insufficient proof).

[2] In some sources we have the idea of the Messiah being caught up as a child (Rev 12:5; Ber 2:4 (5a); Bill. 1, 83; 2, 339-340). In view of the parallel passage in 4 Ezra 7:28-29, where the Messiah is said to die at the end of the messianic kingdom, the Messiah's expected return to/in glory in 2 Bar 30:1 should not be understood as an *Entrückung*, but as an assumption of the soul. The Messiah's movement in this spurious text seems to be from earth to heaven, so Bogaert, *Apocalypse de Baruch. Introduction, traduction du Syriac et commentaire* 2 (SC 145; Paris: Cerf, 1969) 65; Klijn, *Die syrische Baruch-Apokalypse* (JSHRZ 5/2; Gütersloh: G. Mohn, 1976) 142; M. de Goeij, *Jozef en Aseneth. Apokalyps van Baruch* (De Pseudepigrafen 2; Kampen: J.H. Kok, 1981) 86, rather than from heaven to earth, so V. Ryssel, 'Die Apokalypsen des Baruch', *APAT* 2, 246; cf. Charles, *APOT* 2, 498. If we may take the text to denote the Messiah's departure 'into glory' rather than 'with glory' (Klijn, *OTP* 1, 631) we have here an interesting parallel to Lk 24:26. See *infra* 151-153.

current end-time expectations into a comprehensive conception of the course of eschatological events. It should not go unnoticed that this has effected a slight reassessment of the *function* of rapture. Whereas in the original Enoch and Elijah stories their rapture was in itself a crown to their career, later their rapture was seen as a precursory event which set them temporarily aside as it were for a future task in the eschaton.

As is particularly clear in the case of Enoch, but the point may be illustrated by the other rapture stories as well, the rapture form, in due course, attracted other ascension forms, which simply added to the original tradition, so that rapture, heavenly journey, ecstatic experiences and even assumption of the soul terminology were applied to one and the same historical figure, yet without blurring the distinction between the various conceptions.

At the end of a very complex tradition-history, the contours of which we have sketched only in the broadest outlines without exploring the mutual influences which shaped the material, we are confronted with a comparatively clear narrative model. Although there is a great variety in the particulars (the length of the period preceding the ascension, the accompanying circumstances of the event, the *terminus ad quem*, etc.), the basic structure which underlies the various rapture stories we have investigated is constant. The rapture, the occurrence of which is often mediated in advance by a divine revelation, is usually preceded by a limited period of final instructions, be it one year (1 En 81:5ff.), 40 days (4 Ezra 14:23,36,42,44,45; 2 Bar 76:4; cf. 2 En 72:1), or 30 days (cf. 2 En 36:1f. heavenly journey). When the rapture itself is reported, free use is made of standard rapture motives (mountain, chariot, clouds, etc.) and terminology. The post-rapture condition is an intermediate state in which the person is preserved in heaven until the day of judgement, when he is expected to reappear to perform some role in the eschatological drama (usually as a witness or, in the case of Elijah, as a precursor of the Messiah/the Lord).

On the reasons for the quite remarkable upsurge of rapture speculations in the late first century AD we can only speculate. Presumably the various crises which befell the Jewish nation at large (the Jewish war, the destruction of the temple) would create an atmosphere in which an imminent expectation of the day of the Lord would be quite intense and speculations about the unfolding of the eschatological drama would easily evolve in speculations about the role of favourite saints of the past in the future events[1]. How widespread such rapture-

---

[1] With regard to the rationale for Ezra' eschatological return, if after the destruction of the temple the hope for the rebuilding of the temple increased or (as in apocalyptic speculations) God was expected to build an eschatological temple—then there is a sufficiently clear rationale for the rapture of Ezra the temple-builder: as rebuilder of the first, he should be

preservation speculations were is difficult to determine, but the fact that their basic message was informed by OT Scripture (Gen 5:24; 2 Kings 2; Mal 3; Moses' Sinai ascents) gives us reason to believe that first-century readers were quite familiar with the general idea of a person rapt up to heaven in preservation for the end. It is perhaps not unfair to say that in Jewish thinking rapture (ascension) and parousia (i.e. a return from heaven) were seen together as two sides of one coin. Seen in this light, the similarity with the events described in the opening verses of the Book of Acts is most striking: Jesus, after a period of forty days of final instructions (Acts 1:3) is taken up into heaven, where he is kept until the end of times (Acts 3:21) to make his appearance again at the parousia (Acts 1:11; 3:20-21). It seems then that the Jewish rapture-preservation scheme provides a very plausible context of comparison and horizon of understanding for a *sachgemässe* understanding of the ascension of Jesus.

---

involved in the rebuilding of the last. If so, he would need to be preserved until the end, i.e. until the restoration of the eschatological temple. This would accord with the (exaggerated!) claim by G. Haufe that eschatological figures can obtain eschatological functions only by virtue of a bodily rapture-preservation. As for Baruch, 2 Baruch does seem to expect the rebuilding of the temple (e.g. 32:2-4), but Baruch is not remembered as a temple-builder. Probably Baruch's capacity as a scribe invited eschatological expectations.

# CHAPTER THREE

# THE RAPTURE CHRISTOLOGY OF LUKE-ACTS (I)

a. *Introduction*

Having submitted that the OT-Jewish rapture-preservation paradigm provides the primary context of understanding for the Lukan ascension narratives we now arrive at the point where we must study Luke's work in more detail to test the validity of this hypothesis. Following the narrative sequence of Luke-Acts to get as much as possible an 'inside' view of how the author develops his argument, we will analyse the major clusters of ascension texts in Luke's two-volume work (Lk 9:51; 24:50-53; Acts 1:1-14,21-22; 3:19-21) in an attempt to sketch the contours of what we, for the sake of convenience, will call Luke's 'rapture christology'. This initial exploration of the ascension texts, in which we are primarily interested in the significance of the ascension in itself, prepares for a discussion of the role of the ascension in the larger perspective of Luke's theology *in toto*, and notably in comparison with the primitive exaltation kerygma (chapters four and five) and the role of the present and the future in Luke's concept of salvation history (chapter six).

b. *Lk 9:51*

The first[1] overt allusion in Luke's narrative sequence to the ascension of Jesus is found strategically at the beginning of the travel-section, introducing a pericope which is otherwise strongly reminiscent of the figure of Elijah (Lk 9:51-56)[2]. The actual introductory words (v.51) recall the opening words of Elijah's rapture story:

Lk 9:51   Ἐγένετο δὲ ἐν τῷ συμπληροῦσθαι τὰς ἡμέρας τῆς ἀναλήμψεως αὐτοῦ καὶ αὐτὸς τὸ πρόσωπον ἐστήρισεν τοῦ πορεύεσθαι εἰς Ἰερουσαλήμ.

2 Kgs 2:1   Καὶ ἐγένετο ἐν τῷ ἀνάγειν κύριον τὸν Ηλιου ἐν συσσεισμῷ ὡς εἰς τὸν οὐρανὸν καὶ ἐπορεύθη ...

---

[1] Lk 5:35 does not refer to the ascension, since for Luke the ascension is not an occasion for grief, but for joy and worship (Lk 24:52,53). On Mk 2:20 see *infra* 138-140. Texts like Lk 19:12 and 20:19 refer to the ascension by implication at the most.

[2] See T.L. Brodie, 'The Departure for Jerusalem (Luke 9,51-56) as a Rhetorical Imitation of Elijah's Departure for the Jordan (2 Kgs 1,1-2,6)', *Bib.* 70 (1989) 96-109.

Since this is obviously a Lukan composition (cf. Acts 2:1)[1], the verse plays an important role in uncovering Luke's own perspective on the matter. Unfortunately, however, opinions about the meaning of the opening clause differ widely. Does Luke refer to the event described at the end of his Gospel (the ascension) or does he have a wider range in view? Why does he speak of the *days* (plural) of Jesus' ἀνάλημψις? And what does it mean that they are 'being (completely) filled up'? Three issues, then, require a further examination: the meaning of ἀνάλημψις, the use of the plural, and the meaning of the phrase as a whole.

When used in the context of an assumption into heaven, the noun ἀνάλημψις (a NT hapax) is the technical term to describe a *receptio animae*, which is no more than a solemn way of describing one's *death*: PssSal 4:18; TLev 18:3 (Christian interpolation?); Ps-Clement, *Homiliae* 3,47 (PG 2, 141); a Christian inscription from Aphrodisias[2]; and the references to the assumption of Moses in *FPsG* 63-64 (cf. TMos 10:12). There is no unambiguous pre-NT attestation of ἀνάλημψις in the technical sense of 'rapture'[3].

The cognate verb ἀναλαμβάνω, on the other hand, is used in a much wider semantic field. Like the noun, it is used in the context of an assumption of the soul (TAb A 7; cf. 17; TAb B 7; 4 Bar 9:3; Philo, *VitMos* 2,291)[4]. In addition the term is used to describe the end of an appearance of a heavenly being (TAb A 4), and it is a common term to describe a (temporary) heavenly journey (TAb B 7; 8; GkApEzra 1:7). It is also used for a terrestrial translocation (Ezek 3:12-15; 8:3; 11:1,24). Finally and most significantly, the verb ἀναλαμβάνομαι is the standard LXX term for the ascension of Elijah: 2 Kings 2:10,11; 1 Macc 2:58; Sir 48:9; 49:14 (Enoch with Elijah terminology). Ἀναλαμβάνομαι is used with reference to Jesus in Acts 1:2,11,22; Mk 16:19; 1 Tim 3:16.

---

[1] H. Flender, *Heil und Geschichte in der Theologie des Lukas* (BEvTh 41; München: Chr. Kaiser, 1965, ²1968) 35; G. Lohfink, *Die Himmelfahrt Jesu. Untersuchungen zu den Himmelfahrts- und Erhöhungstexten bei Lukas* (StANT 26; München: Kösel, 1971) 212-217; M. Dömer, *Das Heil Gottes. Studien zur Theologie des lukanischen Doppelwerkes* (BBB 51; Köln, Bonn: P. Hanstein, 1978) 83 Anm.36; J. Jeremias, *Die Sprache des Lukasevangeliums. Redaktion und Tradition im Nicht-Markusstof des dritten Evangeliums* (KEK Sonderband; Göttingen: Vandenhoeck & Ruprecht, 1980) 179; J. Nolland, *Luke 9:21-18:34* (WBC 35B; Dallas, TX: Word, 1993) 534.

[2] See H. Grégoire, 'Du nouveau sur la hiérarchie de la secte Montaniste d'après une inscription grecque trouvée près de Philadelphie en Lydie', *Byzantion* 2 (1925) 331.

[3] G. Friedrich, 'Lk 9,51 und die Entrückungschristologie des Lukas', in: P. Hoffmann, N. Brox, W. Pesch (Hrsg.), *Orientierung an Jesus. Zur Theologie der Synoptiker* (FS J. Schmid; Freiburg: Herder, 1973) 71. In post-NT literature ἀνάλημψις is often used as 'ascension' (PGL 110), but under canonical influence.

[4] See further ClemAlex, *Stromata* 6,15 (132,2) (GCS 52/2, 498; *FPsG* 65); Justin, *Dial* 80 (PG 6, 665); EvPe 5:19 (ed. Vaganay 254-256); a Christian inscription in Grégoire, 'Inscription' 330; cf. Origen, *CommMatt* 140 (PG 13, 1793); ActJ 102 (16) (ed. Bonnet 202; Junod-Kaestli 1, 215); Eusebius, *HistEccl* V xvi,14 (LCL 153, 478-479).

This brief inventory shows the wide range of connotation of the verb ἀναλαμβάνομαι. Interestingly enough, the instances brought forward are all from a (Hellenistic) Jewish or Jewish Christian milieu. In the period relevant to the present investigation I have not been able to find a rapture text with ἀνάλημψις or ἀναλαμβάνομαι outside the Jewish or Christian realm[1]. If Luke's wording rings a bell, it is a Jewish or biblical one; if a historical figure comes to mind, it is Elijah!

However, many authors who have treated the verse under consideration are reluctant to claim an immediate or exclusive influence of the Elijah tradition upon v.51, mainly because of the use of the plural 'days', which seems to imply that the ἀνάλημψις of Jesus (unlike Elijah's) stretches out over several days or weeks. The next question, then, is: what does Luke refer to? Without any claim for completeness—the following list is illustrative rather than exhaustive—the following options have been advanced:

(1) Jesus' death[2];
(2) Jesus' passion, death and resurrection[3];
(3) his entire transit from earth to heaven through death-resurrection-ascension[4];

---

[1] MM 35 s.v. ἀναλαμβάνω. Cf. Lohfink, *Himmelfahrt* 42. I cannot confirm the (inadvertent?) remark of M.C. Parsons, *The Departure of Jesus in Luke-Acts. The Ascension Narratives in Context* (JSNT.S 21; Sheffield: JSOT, 1987) 110 'that the word ἀναλαμβάνω is commonly used in ancient Jewish *and pagan* assumption stories' (emphasis mine).

[2] Bede, *ExpLuc* 3,9 (PG 92, 459); Calvin, *CommHarmEv*, 525; D. Plooij, 'The Ascension in the 'Western' Textual Tradition', *MNAW.L* 67 A/2 (Amsterdam: Noord-Hollandsche, 1929) 49-50 (cf. 56-57); G. Delling, πλήρης, πληρόω κτλ., *ThWNT* 6 (1959) 307; J. Schmid, *Das Evangelium nach Lukas übersetzt und erklärt* (RNT 3; Regensburg: F. Pustet, 1940, ⁴1960) 176; Friedrich, 'Entrückungschristologie' 70-74.

[3] W. Michaelis, *Die Erscheinungen des Auferstandenen* (Basel: H. Majer, 1944) 82.143 Anm.93 (perhaps including the resurrection, but not the ascension).

[4] So most commentators. See the authors cited in Friedrich, 'Entrückungschristologie' 70-71 Anm.146, and J.L. Resseguie, 'Interpretation of Luke's Central Section (Luke 9.51-19.44) since 1856', *SBTh* 5 (1975) 30-31 n.156. In addition to their lists (post-1980): J. Kremer, ἀναλαμβάνω, ἀνάλημψις, *EWNT* 1 (1980) 201; J.A. Fitzmyer, *The Gospel According to Luke I-IX. Introduction, Translation, and Notes* (AncB 28; Garden City, NY: Doubleday, 1981) 827-828; R. Maddox, *The Purpose of Luke-Acts* (Studies of the New Testament and Its World; Edinburgh: T.&T. Clark, 1982) 156 n.145; E. Schweizer, *Das Evangelium nach Lukas* (NTD 3; Göttingen: Vandenhoeck & Ruprecht, 1982, ²1986) 110; D.L. Tiede, *Luke* (ACNT; Minneapolis, MN: Augsburg, 1988) 197; W. Wiefel, *Das Evangelium nach Lukas* (ThHK 3; Berlin: Evangelische, 1988) 190; C.F. Evans, *Saint Luke* (TPI NT Commentaries; London: SCM; Philadelphia: TPI, 1990) 435-436; G. Petzke, *Das Sondergut des Evangeliums nach Lukas* (ZWKB; Zürich: Theologischer, 1990) 105; L.T. Johnson, *The Gospel of Luke* (SPg 3; Collegeville, MN: Liturgical, 1991) 162; Nolland, *Luke* 2, 534-535.

(4) as under (3), including the journey to Jerusalem[1];
(5) the ascension[2];
(6) his acceptance among the people[3];
(7) his pilgrimage[4].

Of these, options (6) and (7) must be rejected since they ignore the wider Lukan context. The other five options can be divided into those views that regard the ἀνάλημψις as a complex event stretching out over a longer period of time (2-4) and those that take it as a more or less punctiliar action (1 and 5), so that the next critical question to be answered is whether or not we have here a complex event. If so, the conclusion that Luke distinguishes the event described in Lk 24:51 // Acts 1:9 from the ἀνάλημψις of Jesus in the present verse is hard to avoid. The apparent discrepancy is usually resolved in tradition-historical terms, i.e. Lk 9:51 is held to reflect an older tradition which Luke failed to assimilate with his own conception.

The view that ἀνάλημψις refers to a longer period of time is based first and foremost on the use of the plural ἡμέραι and the present tense ἐν τῷ συμπληροῦσθαι, which suggests that the 'days of the ἀνάλημψις' are

---

[1] J.H. Davies, 'The Purpose of the Central Section of St. Luke's Gospel', in: F.L. Cross (ed.), *StEv* 2 (TU 87; Berlin: Akademie, 1964) 164-165.

[2] In addition to the authors cited in Friedrich, 'Entrückungschristologie' 48 Anm.1-2: (post-1980) F. Schnider, 'Himmelfahrt Jesu—Ende oder Anfang? Zum Verständnis des lukanischen Doppelwerkes', in: P.-G. Müller, W. Stenger (Hrsg.), *Kontinuität und Einheit* (FS F. Mußner; Freiburg: Herder, 1981) 167-168 Anm.15; Parsons, *Departure* 107-110 (only at first reading! an ingenious and forced interpretation!); A.D. Baum, *Lukas als Historiker der letzten Jesusreise* (TVGMS 379; Wuppertal, Zürich: Brockhaus, 1993) 350-359; J. van Bruggen, *Lucas. Het evangelie als voorgeschiedenis* (CNT derde serie; Kampen: J.H. Kok, 1993) 206-207; H. Schürmann, *Das Lukasevangelium 2/1. Kommentar zu Kap.9,51-11,54* (HThK 3; Freiburg, Basel, Wien: Herder, 1993) 24-26. E. Mayer, *Die Reiseerzählung des Lukas (Lk 9,51-19,10). Entscheidung in der Wüste* (EHS.T 554; Frankfurt etc.: P. Lang, 1996) 69-73 (translating 'Tage *zur* Himmelfahrt', taking τῆς ἀναλήμψεως as an objective genitive).

[3] K. Wieseler, *Chronologische Synopse der vier Evangelien* (Hamburg: 1843) 325; idem, *Beiträge zur richtigen Würdigung der Evangelien und der evangelischen Geschichte* (Gotha: 1869) 130 (i.e. acceptance among the Galileans or Israel in general).

[4] Tracing the phrase back to a Semitic original. So e.g. Plooij, 'Ascension' 50 and A.J. Wensinck in Plooij, 'Ascension' 56-57, who translate 'when the time of His pilgrimage had come', a view also defended by B. Reicke, 'Instruction and Discussion in the Travel Narrative', in: K. Aland (ed.), *StEv* 1 (TU 73; Berlin: Akademie, 1959) 211 (ἀνάλημψις = מעלה) and D. Flusser, 'Lukas 9:51-56. Ein hebräisches Fragment', in: W.C. Weinrich (ed.), *The New Testament Age. Essays in Honor of Bo Reicke* 1 (Macon, MA: Mercer University Press, 1984) 167-169 (who takes ἀνάλημψις as a pre-Lukan mistranslation of עליה 'pilgrimage') (but recognising that in the present context the reference is to the ascension).

*already* being filled up, or at least very soon will be. Yet this view is not without serious difficulties. Luke uses the cognate verb ἀναλαμβάνομαι (the standard LXX rapture term for Elijah's ascension) unambiguously to denote Jesus' ascension in Acts 1:(2,)11,22, and he never elsewhere speaks of Jesus' ascension in terms of a longer period. On the contrary, he speaks *expressis verbis* of it as a single day event (Acts 1:2,22). Unless we are to disregard this irregularity as a Lukan 'slip of the pen' we need to clarify *why* Luke expresses himself in this particular way.

First of all it must be stressed that the plural 'days' does not *necessarily* imply that the ἀνάλημψις took place over a longer period of time. A.D. Baum has recently drawn attention to a comparable OT idiom which utilises the plural 'days' where the event in view (death) clearly refers to a single day, and concluded:

> 'In allen genannten Stellen [= Gen 47:29; Deut 31:14; 1 Kings 2:1] weist der Plural *Tage* keineswegs auf einen sich über eine längere Zeitperiode ausdehnenden Sterbeprozeß hin, sondern bringt zum Ausdruck, daß der Tod in Kürze eintreten wird, daß die verbleibenden Tage ganz im Zeichen des nahen Todes stehen, dessen exaktes Eintrittsdatum noch nicht bekannt ist'[1].

He then suggests that Luke has taken over this idiom and that he replaced death by ascension. Yet this still does not satisfactorily explain why Luke expressed himself in this way: it shows the elliptic nature of the construction, but fails to clarify why Luke did not use a less ambiguous and more correct expression.

There is, however, another way of solving the problem. Rather than 'the days of ... are/were approaching', the closer parallel to Lk 9:51 is found in the common OT expression 'the days ... are/were fulfilled ...'. One way to further qualify this construction is by appending an adjective or qualitative genitive. So e.g. Esther 1:5 ὅτε δὲ ἀνεπληρώθησαν αἱ ἡμέραι τοῦ γάμου 'when the days of the feast (v.3) were fulfilled', i.e. when the period of feasting was over (aor.), and Is 60:20 καὶ ἀναπληρωθήσονται αἱ ἡμέραι τοῦ πέντους σου 'and the days of your mourning will be fulfilled', i.e. the period of mourning will be over. Luke employs this type e.g. in Lk 1:23: καὶ ἐγένετο ὡς ἐπλήσθησαν αἱ ἡμέραι τῆς λειτουργίας αὐτοῦ 'and it happened when the days of his service were fulfilled', i.e. the period of Zechariah's priestly ministry—from Sabbath to Sabbath (Bill. 2, 55-68; *HJP* 2, 292)—had come to an end (aor.)[2].

Another way to qualify the construction is by adding a ל *cum infinitivo*-

---

[1] Baum, *Lukas* 357. Also Van Bruggen, *Lucas* 207-208, who regards this as solemn language, and Schürmann, *Lukasevangelium* 2/1, 24 Anm.9.

[2] See also Lev 12:4,6 (Lk 2:22); Tob 8:20 BA; 10:1 BA. Further Lev 25:29,30; Num 6:13; 2 Sam 7:12; Tob 14:5 BA; 1 Chron 17:11; Lam 4:18. Cf. Lk 21:24; Jn 7:8.

construction (in Greek a τοῦ + substantival infinitive), which expresses the purpose of the period under discussion. E.g. Gen 25:24 ἐπληρώθησαν αἱ ἡμέραι τοῦ τεκεῖν αὐτήν 'the days were fulfilled to give birth', i.e. the period leading up to the day of childbirth was over, the day of childbirth had arrived (aor.). Luke uses this formula in 2:6 ἐγένετο δὲ ... ἐπλήσθησαν αἱ ἡμέραι τοῦ τεκεῖν αὐτήν 'and it happened ... that the days were fulfilled to give birth', i.e. the period leading up to the day of the birth was fulfilled, the birthday of John had arrived (aor.); 2:21 καὶ ὅτε ἐπλήσθησαν αἱ ἡμέραι ὀκτὼ τοῦ περιτεμεῖν αὐτὸν 'and when the days were fulfilled, eight, to circumcise him', i.e. the period preceding the circumcision had come to an end, the day of circumcision, the eighth day, had arrived (aor.)[1].

The first impression of Lk 9:51 is that it represents the first type, τῆς ἀναλήμψεως representing a qualitative genitive ('the days which constitute his ἀνάλημψις'), but, as we already noted, this does not correspond with the meaning with which Luke uses the corresponding verb. Once it is recognised that a construction of the *second* type underlies the expression, however, the difficulties easily disappear and a clear picture emerges. This can be made clear by the following (hypothetical) reconstruction[2]. The Hebrew archetype underlying the Greek would run:

ויהי במלאות הימים להלקחו

The normal way to render this in Greek would be:

᾽Εγένετο δὲ ἐν τῷ (συμ)πληροῦσθαι τὰς ἡμέρας τοῦ ἀναληφθῆναι αὐτόν.

If we compare this with Luke's construction it appears that the only irregularity is that Luke uses a noun (τῆς ἀναλήμψεως αὐτοῦ), where an infinitival clause (τοῦ ἀναληφθῆναι αὐτόν) would be expected. Tentatively, it may be suggested that Luke chose the noun-form in order to strengthen the parallelising of v.51 to v.31, to create a noun-allusion to both the biblical Moses (ἔξοδος) and the Elijah tradition (ἀνάλημψις). What he did not realise, or took for granted, was that in so doing the syntax of the phrase became hopelessly ambiguous. What he *says* is that 'the days of the ἀνάλημψις' are being filled up (that is, strictly speaking from 9:51 onwards); what he *intends* to say (if our hypothesis is correct) is that the period leading up to the ascension is

---

[1] Cf. Lk 1:57; cf. also Jer 25:34 MT (Jer 32:34 LXX).

[2] I do not suggest that Luke is translating from a Hebrew or Aramaic source, contra the authors cited *supra* 83 n.4. On the contrary, Luke apparently was not sensitive enough to the underlying Hebrew construction, so that he could easily confuse the translation differences.

being (completely)[1] filled up and that this period finds its completion in the ascension[2]. The emphasis thus placed on the ascension accords with Luke's composition technique in Lk 24 and Acts 1, where the ascension (at least from a literary perspective) forms the climax of the book and of Jesus' earthly career (Acts 1:2,22): Luke views the events related in the second half of his Gospel *sub specie ascensionis*[3].

Since v.51 is patterned after v.31, the question arises how the ἀνάλημψις of Jesus relates to his ἔξοδος referred to in v.31. The choice of these *termini* is not coincidental, of course: ἀνάλημψις recalls the biblical Elijah tradition, ἔξοδος is derived from the biblical Moses tradition, perfectly fitting in the context of the Transfiguration scene. Ἔξοδος is not attested as a rapture term[4]. It may be used occasionally as a euphemism for death. However, in the sense of 'end of life, death' it is rare in classical Greek[5]. In fact, in all the relevant texts ἔξοδος may mean no more than 'departure from life' or 'end of life'[6] without specifying its mode: Wis 3:2; 7:6; Philo, *Virt* 77; Josephus, *Ant* IV viii,2 (189); 2 Pet 1:15; Justin, *Dial* 105 (PG 6, 721). In addition the possibility must be emphasised that we have here a progressive parallelism, the statement in v.51 (ascension) expanding the imagery of v.31 (departure from life).

c. *Lk 24:50-53*

Chapter 24 is made up of three clearly distinguished parts, viz. the story of the Empty Tomb (vv.1-11,12), the Emmaus story (vv.13-35), and the final section on the last appearance of Jesus to his disciples (vv.36-53). Form-critically, the final section can be divided into a recognition scene (vv.36-43), a teaching scene (vv.44-49) and a departure scene (vv.50-53). Vv.50-53 round off the appearance that began in v.36, but also chapter 24 as a whole and, in fact, the

---

[1] The prefix συν- is most likely due to Luke, see *infra* 101 + n.2.

[2] Perhaps a similar mistranslation underlies Acts 2:1. The construction τὴν ἡμέραν τῆς πεντηκοστῆς is Lukan (Acts 20:16). The present tense of συμπληροῦσθαι is perhaps best understood as denoting the process of completion, meaning something like 'when the day of Pentecost came' (NIV) or 'while ... was running its course' (NEB).

[3] The concept accordingly does *not* concur with the Johannine δοξασθῆναι, contra Th. Zahn, *Das Evangelium des Lucas* (KNT 3; Leipzig: A. Deichert, Werner Scholl, 1913, [3.4]1920) 397; E.E. Ellis, *The Gospel of Luke* (NCeB; Grand Rapids: Eerdmans; London: Marshall, Morgan & Scott, 1966, [2]1974) 152; W. Grundmann, *Das Evangelium nach Lukas* (ThHK 3; Berlin: Evangelische, 1961, [10]1984) 201; Wiefel, *Lukas* 190 Anm.10; Evans, *Luke* 436. See our treatment of the Johannine ascension and exaltation complex, *infra* 133-138.

[4] And should accordingly not be taken as an immediate reference to the ascension, contra C.H. Talbert, *Literary Patterns, Theological Themes, and the Genre of Luke-Acts* (SBL.MS 20; Missoula, MO: Scholars, 1974) 62.

[5] Michaelis, ὁδος, ὁδηγός κτλ., *ThWNT* 5 (1954) 108 (+ Anm. 3) quotes only Epictetus IV 4,38, and (6th century AD) Bishop Abraham of Hermonthis (Christian!).

[6] Cf. Michaelis, *ThWNT* 5, 111.

entire Gospel[1].

*V 50*   The final departure scene is tied to the preceding verses by the copulative δέ. After the farewell speech (vv.44-49), Jesus leads his disciples outside the walls of Jerusalem along the road to Bethany, a route they had taken on many occasions (21:37; 22:39). From the larger context, it seems that a larger group than the Eleven is in view (cf. v.33 τοὺς ἕνδεκα καὶ τοὺς σὺν αὐτοῖς, and the requirements for apostleship in Acts 1:22), although (as is especially clear in Acts 1) Luke's primary interest is in the Eleven[2]. That Jesus 'led them out' (ἐξήγαγεν ... αὐτοὺς) is understood by many authors to reflect an Exodus typology, which presents Jesus as a New Moses, leading his people out to the promised land (see the commentaries *ad loc.*). But the comparison is weak: those who are led out will soon afterwards return to the city. In a more general line of reasoning Lohfink argues that Luke purposely used this word for its biblical and theological connotations and traces it to the influence of the Emmaus story (vv.15,28-29)[3]. But again the analogy is superficial: in v.15 we have a συμπορεύεσθαι, in v.28 a πορρώτερον πορεύεσθαι. A more immediate Lukan concern may be to stress the active role of Jesus as the one who, until the end, is in control of what happens and firmly guides the disciples to the events to come. Is there perhaps a connection with the journey motif in 2 Kings 2?

When they arrive at the site, Jesus raises his hands in a benediction gesture and imparts God's blessing upon those present. The motif of blessing plays no significant role in the Graeco-Roman world and is not found in its rapture stories[4]. A Jewish parallel is found in 2 En 56:1; 57:2; 64:4, but as a rapture *topos* it is exceptional[5]. A more likely background is provided by the priestly blessing of Simeon at the close of the *laus patrum* (Sir 50:19-23). Note the following points of contact:

---

[1]   A brief survey and critique of the various form-critical assessments of the finale of Luke's Gospel is found in Parsons, *Departure* 52-58.215-217.

[2]   Contra V. Larrañaga, *L'Ascension de Notre-Seigneur dans le Nouveau Testament* (SPIB 50; Roma: IBP, 1938) 375-380 and A. Wikenhauser, *Die Apostelgeschichte übersetzt und erklärt* (RNT 5; Regensburg: F. Pustet, 1938, ⁴1961) 29, who suggest that the apostles were the only eyewitnesses.

[3]   Lohfink, *Himmelfahrt* 164.

[4]   H.W. Beyer, εὐλογέω, εὐλογητός κτλ., *ThWNT* 2 (1935) 751-752.

[5]   Tob 12:16-22 (an εὐλογία at the end of an angelic appearance) parallels v.52 rather than v.50. Cf. Josephus, *Ant* IV viii,44 (302) and 48 (320), where Moses at the end of his life blesses the tribes of Israel (but not in the immediate context of his assumption).

| Sir 50:20-23 | | Lk 24:50-53 | |
|---|---|---|---|
| v.20 | ἐπῆρεν | v.50 | καὶ ἐπάρας |
| | χεῖρας αὐτοῦ ... | | τὰς χεῖρας αὐτοῦ |
| | δοῦναι εὐλογίαν | | εὐλόγησεν αὐτούς |
| v.21 | ἐν προσκυνήσει | v.52 | προσκυνήσαντες αὐτὸν |
| v.22 | εὐλογήσατε | v.53 | εὐλογοῦντες |
| | τὸν θεὸν | | τὸν θεόν |
| v.23 | εὐφροσύνην | v.52 | μετὰ χαρᾶς μεγάλης |

Especially the elsewhere unattested triad εὐλογία (= blessing)-προσκύνησις-εὐλογία (= thanksgiving) should remove all doubt that the finale of Ben Sira sets its imprint upon Luke's Gospel finale[1]. As the eulogy of Simeon (Sir 50) surpasses all previous descriptions of Israel's saints in length and praise (Sir 44:1-49:16), so Luke suggests that Jesus is the climax and fulfilment of Israel's sacred history. In view of the influence of Sir 50 upon the present passage, the blessing is that of a priest (cf. Lev 9:22), rather than that of a patriarch (Gen 48; Deut 33, etc.) or a king (1 Kings 8:54-61)[2]. That this depicts a priestly symbolism is strengthened by the apparently conscious parallelising of Lk 24 with the opening chapters of the Gospel, in particular with the unsuccessful blessing of the priest Zechariah: what Zechariah was unable to do, Jesus now performs in a most dramatic way[3].

The *locus dramatis* of the ascension is situated somewhere ἕως πρὸς Βηθανίαν, that is, not in Bethany itself[4], but 'up to the point where the road goes to Bethany'[5]. Bethany was a small village on the eastern slope of the

---

[1] R. Pesch, 'Der Anfang der Apostelgeschichte (Apg 1,1-11)', *EKK.V* 3 (Neukirchen: Neukirchener; Zürich: Benziger, 1971) 16; Lohfink, *Himmelfahrt* 167-169; R.J. Dillon, *From Eye-Witnesses to Ministers of the Word. Tradition and Composition in Luke 24* (AnBib 82; Roma: IBP, 1978) 220-224; Dömer, *Heil Gottes* 108; I.H. Marshall, *Commentary on Luke* (NIGTC; Grand Rapids: Eerdmans, 1978) 908-909.

[2] P.A. van Stempvoort, 'The Interpretation of the Ascension in Luke and Acts', *NTS* 5 (1958/59) 35; H. Schlier, 'Jesu Himmelfahrt nach den lukanischen Schriften' (1961); repr. in: idem, *Besinnung auf das Neue Testament. Exegetische Aufsätze und Vorträge* 2 (Freiburg, Basel, Wien: Herder, 1964) 229-230; cf. also J. Ernst, *Das Evangelium des Lukas übersetzt und erklärt* (RNT 3; Regensburg: F. Pustet, 1977, ²1993) 514. The priestly symbolism is questioned by Lohfink, *Himmelfahrt* 169 Anm.14. But the literary parallel to Sir 50 should remove all doubt.

[3] For further parallelisms between Lk 24 and Lk 1-2, see Parsons, *Departure* 73-77.

[4] So e.g. R.D. Kaylor, *The Ascension Motif in Luke-Acts, the Epistle to the Hebrews and the Fourth Gospel* (Diss. Duke University, 1964) 27-28.

[5] B. Weiss, *Die Evangelien des Markus und Lukas* (KEK II⁹; Göttingen: Vandenhoeck & Ruprecht, 1876, ⁴1901) 692; Zahn, *Lucas* 732 (+ Anm.87); followed by L. Brun, *Die Auferstehung Christi in der urchristlichen Überlieferung* (Oslo: H. Aschehoug & Co (W.

Mount of Olives. According to Jn 11:18, it was 15 stadia = 2.775 km from Jerusalem. Overlooking, for the moment, the question to what extent Luke was aware of the local geography[1], we can infer from Lk 19:29 and Acts 1:12 that he situated Bethany on the Mount of Olives. This concurs with Luke's geographical perspective elsewhere[2]. For Luke, Bethany is still in the vicinity of Jerusalem: 'he led them out as far as to Bethany, that is, *only* as far as to Bethany'. Cf. Acts 1:12, where the Mount of Olives is qualified as ὅ ἐστιν ἐγγὺς (!) Ἰερουσαλὴμ σαββάτου ἔχον ὁδόν. In Luke-Acts, all the post-Easter appearances (including the one that leads to the ascension) take place in or around Jerusalem[3].

The *chronology* of the departure scene is most puzzling. The continuous narrative sequence leaves the unbiased reader with the impression that the ascension took place on Easter Sunday itself (v.1 τῇ δὲ μιᾷ τῶν σαββάτων ὄρθρου βαθέως; v.13 ἐν αὐτῇ τῇ ἡμέρᾳ; v.33 αὐτῇ τῇ ὥρᾳ; v.36 ταῦτα δὲ αὐτῶν λαλούντων). This, however, does not square with Acts 1, where the ascension follows forty days after the resurrection (cf. Acts 13:31 'many days'). And if we press the chronology of Lk 24 a little bit further, the ascension took place at night (cf. v.29 κέκλικεν ἤδη ἡ ἡμέρα!)[4]. But unlike

---

Nygaard); Giessen: A. Töpelmann, 1925) 90; Larrañaga, *Ascension* 409-416; BDR 239₃; Van Bruggen, *Lucas* 416 (reading ἕως εἰς Βηθανίαν!). On the alleged difference between εἰς and πρός, see Hesychius, *Quaest* 60 (PG 93, 1448); Zahn, *Lucas* 732 Anm.87. Lohfink, *Himmelfahrt* 166 qualified this negatively as 'historisierende Exegese', but this should not obscure the fact that the description concurs well with local geography. On the other hand, I fail to see any exegetical proof for the suggestion of J.G. Lygre, *Exaltation. Considered with Reference to the Resurrection and Ascension in Luke-Acts* (Diss. Princeton Theological Seminary, 1975) 21, that 'the expression ἕως πρὸς Βηθανίαν suggests a raised locale (cf. Lk. 9:28; Acts 1:12) and sets the tone for the author's use of ἐπαίρω, διίστημι, and ἀναφέρω'.

[1] A hyper-critical assessment is found in C.C. McCown, 'Gospel Geography. Fiction, Fact, and Truth', *JBL* 60 (1941) 1-25; German tr. 'Geographie der Evangelien. Fiktion, Tatsache und Wahrheit', in: G. Braumann (Hrsg.), *Das Lukasevangelium. Die redaktions- und kompositionsgeschichtliche Forschung* (WdF 280; Darmstadt: WBG, 1974) 13-42. For a more positive appraisal of Luke's geographical knowledge of Palestine, see M. Hengel, 'Der Historiker Lukas und die Geographie Palästinas in der Apg.', *ZDPV* 99 (1983) 147-183.

[2] E. Lohmeyer, 'Galiläa und Jerusalem bei Lukas' (1936); partially repr. in: Braumann (Hrsg.), *Lukasevangelium* 7-12; H. Conzelmann, *Die Mitte der Zeit. Studien zur Theologie des Lukas* (BHTh 17; Tübingen: J.C.B. Mohr/Paul Siebeck, 1954, ⁶1977) 12-86; Fitzmyer, *Luke* 1, 164-172.

[3] Similarly, Emmaus (Lk 24:13) may be distanced *only* 60 stadia from Jerusalem.

[4] E. Meyer, *Ursprung und Anfänge des Christentums* 1 (Stuttgart: J.G. Cotta, 1921, ⁵1924; repr. Darmstadt: WBG, 1962) 32; H.J. Cadbury, *The Making of Luke-Acts* (New York:

the Transfiguration (cf. Lk 9:28,37) and Enoch's rapture in 2 En 67:1 nothing else in the narrative suggests that it took place in darkness. It is therefore not surprising that various solutions have been offered which attempt to alleviate the chronological tension between Lk 24 and Acts 1.

First of all, the most radical solution simply disclaims that Luke is responsible for both versions and asserts that foreign material (either here or in Acts 1, or in both passages) has been *interpolated* into the text (cf. *supra* 5f. n.5 for authors). But studies in the language and idiom of the text (V. Larrañaga), redaction criticism (G. Lohfink) and literary criticism (M.C. Parsons) have contributed, each in their own way, to the now almost general recognition that Lk 24:50-53 and Acts 1 belong to the original work;

Secondly, in Lk 24:51 and Acts 1:9 we simply have accounts of *two separate events* (*supra* 6 + n.3). This theory usually goes hand in hand with a rejection of the words καὶ ἀνεφέρετο εἰς τὸν οὐρανόν (v.51)[1]. But, as has often been noted, the close parallelism between Lk 24:36-53 and Acts 1:1-14 is decidedly against it, and the case for the authenticity of the shorter text fails to convince, as I have shown elsewhere[2];

Thirdly, after completing the Gospel, Luke received *new information* (notably about the forty days) (*supra* 10 + n.1). This option gains in plausibility as time separating the publication of the Book of Acts from that of Luke's Gospel increases. If, as e.g. W.G. Kümmel suggests[3], a considerable length of time (a decade or so) divides the two books, the suggestion that Luke received additional information or had come to revise his own chronology himself, is not implausible. But the detailed parallelisms between the two volumes suggest that Luke composed Acts with a view to the Gospel *and vice versa*[4]. This

---

Macmillan, 1927; repr. London: SPCK, 1958) 249-250; M.S. Enslin, 'The Ascension Story', *JBL* 47 (1928) 61; J.G. Davies, *He Ascended into Heaven. A Study in the History of Doctrine* (BaL 1958; London: Lutterworth, 1958) 48; Evans, *Luke* 928.

[1] O. Betz, 'Entrückung II. Biblische und frühjüdische Zeit', *TRE* 9 (1982) 688 and M.D. Goulder, *Luke. A New Paradigm* 2 (JSNT.S 20; Sheffield: JSOT, 1989) 790.798 are notable exceptions. The suggestion of Goulder that the use of a different verb suggests a different occasion is not convincing, given Luke's clear preference for variation [cf. Cadbury, 'Four Features of Lucan Style', in: L.E. Keck, J.L. Martyn (eds.), *Studies in Luke-Acts. Essays Presented in Honor of Paul Schubert* (Nashville, New York: Abingdon, 1966) 88-97]. Did Luke perhaps cross out ἀναφέρω from Mk 9:1 // Lk 9:28 to insert the verb here?

[2] See A.W. Zwiep, 'The Text of the Ascension Narratives (Lk 24:50-53; Acts 1:1-2,9-11)', *NTS* 42 (1996) 219-244.

[3] W.G. Kümmel, *Einleitung in das Neue Testament* (Heidelberg: Quelle & Meyer, 1963, [21]1983) 153-154.

[4] Talbert, *Patterns*; Pesch, *Die Apostelgeschichte* 1 (EKK 5; Neukirchen-Vluyn:

suggests a carefully planned overall-composition (cf. *infra* 118 table 1). Since Luke does not give us a hint that in Acts 1 he corrects his earlier chronology, we may assume that the chronology of Acts is not due to Luke's better knowledge;

Fourthly, there is a *chronological break* in the story-line of Lk 24. This option has attracted various scholars. Some would locate the break between vv.43 and 44[1], others after v.49[2], others again would assume several breaks[3]. The difficulty with placing a break in vv.36-53 is that the events related in Acts 1 (the missionary command and the command to remain in Jerusalem) all take place on the day of the ascension (*infra* 102);

Fifthly, perhaps Luke was familiar with *two distinct traditions* which he reworked separately, without passing his judgement upon them. That he did not harmonise the chronology could reflect Luke's commitment to his sources[4]. But we are sufficiently informed about Luke's treatment of his sources (Mark and Q) to know that this is precisely what he does *not* do[5].

The problem of the conflicting dates is not easily solved. The least unsatisfactory solution seems to be the fourth view, which I would adopt with

---

Neukirchener; Zürich: Benzinger, 1986) 24-25; R.C. Tannehill, *The Narrative Unity of Luke-Acts. A Literary Interpretation* (Philadelphia, Minneapolis, MN: Fortress, 1986-1990) 2 vols.; Marshall, 'Acts and the 'Former Treatise'', in: B.W. Winter, A.D. Clarke (eds.), *The Book of Acts in Its Ancient Literary Setting* (BAFCS 1; Grand Rapids: Eerdmans; Carlisle: Paternoster, 1993) 163-182.

[1] Bengel, *Gnomon* 311; Zahn, *Lucas* 727-728 Anm.77; J.H. Bernard, 'Assumption and Ascension', *ERE* 2 (1930) 155; E. Klostermann, *Das Lukasevangelium* (HNT 5; Tübingen: J.C.B. Mohr/Paul Siebeck, 1919, ³1975) 239; Larrañaga, *Ascension* 448-461.632-633; H. Graß, *Ostergeschehen und Osterberichte* (Göttingen: Vandenhoeck & Ruprecht, 1956, ³1964) 44; Schmid, *Lukas* 361; D.P. Fuller, *Easter Faith and History* (Grand Rapids: Eerdmans, 1965) 231-232; P. Seidensticker, *Die Auferstehung Jesu in der Botschaft der Evangelisten. Ein traditionsgeschichtlicher Versuch zum Problem der Sicherung der Osterbotschaft in der apostolischen Zeit* (SBS 26; Stuttgart: KBW, 1967, ²1968) 99 Anm.69; B.K. Donne, 'The Significance of the Ascension of Jesus Christ in the New Testament', *SJTh* 30 (1977) 558; Dömer, *Heil Gottes* 99.

[2] A. Loisy, *L'Évangile selon Luc* (Paris: E. Nourry, 1924) 591; Marshall, 'The Resurrection of Jesus in Luke', *TynB* 24 (1973) 93; idem, *Commentary* 904.

[3] A. Plummer, *The Gospel According to S. Luke* (ICC; Edinburgh: T.&T. Clark, 1896, ⁵1922) 564 (after v.43 and v.49).

[4] Davies, *Ascended* 49.

[5] An alternative solution is offered by Talbert, *Patterns* 78-79, who explains the chronological tension due to the Greek aversion of *absolute* symmetry. But could these Greeks appreciate a contradictory structure? Giving one event two dates seems to involve more than only a lack of symmetry.

due reservation. The chronological framework of Lk 24 is to be regarded as the result of Luke's compact story-telling technique, by which he draws together various elements to form a single uninterrupted story-line[1]. The *effect* is that the ascension is firmly tied to the resurrection and appearance story. If Luke is indeed responsible for compressing the narrative sequence, attempts to locate breaking-points in the narrative are likely to fail, since he would have removed them on purpose. One is reminded of the freedom with which Luke sets the events of Lk 4:1ff. or Acts 9-11 in sequence[2]. That a temporal discrepancy resulted was evidently of no concern for him[3].

*V.51* It is during the act of blessing (ἐν τῷ εὐλογεῖν αὐτὸν αὐτούς), that Jesus departs from his disciples. The actual description of the ascension is brief: 'Jesus departed from them and was carried up into heaven' (NRSV). Διέστη ἀπ᾽ αὐτῶν is to be understood on the analogy of the earlier withdrawal and appearance (v.31 καὶ αὐτὸς ἄφαντος ἐγένετο ἀπ᾽ αὐτῶν; cf. v.36 αὐτὸς ἔστη ἐν μέσῳ αὐτῶν): Jesus departed from them by suddenly vanishing from the scene (cf. Acts 12:10). It is only in the interpretive words καὶ ἀνεφέρετο εἰς τὸν οὐρανόν—an explanatory comment from behind the scenes as it were—that the act of withdrawal is interpreted as an ascension, or better, given the passive, as a rapture (*Entrückung*)[4]. Ἀναφέρομαι (εἰς τὸν οὐρανόν) is occasionally used as a rapture term in Hellenistic rapture stories [Plutarch, *Numa* 2,3; AntLib 25,4; Hesiod, fgm 148; Apollonius Rhodius, *Argonautica* (rec. H. Keil) IV 57.58 p.264,17 (Bauer 124-125); cf. DioCass, *RomHist* LVI 42,3]. The imperfect tense ἀνεφέρετο seems to suggest a gradual departure[5] and is materially parallelled in Acts 1:10 ὡς ἀτενίζοντες ἦσαν εἰς τὸν οὐρανὸν πορευομένου αὐτοῦ. Anticipating our discussion of Acts 1:9, it

---

[1] Van Bruggen, *Lucas* 417-418.

[2] Cf. G. Stählin, *Die Apostelgeschichte* (NTD 5; Göttingen: Vandenhoeck & Ruprecht, 1962, ⁷1980) 13, and other commentaries *ad loc.*

[3] Cf. J.F. Maile, 'The Ascension in Luke-Acts', *TynB* 37 (1986) 34-35. This I find more plausible than the suggestion of S.G. Wilson, 'The Ascension. A Critique and an Interpretation', *ZNW* 59 (1968) 271 n.13, that by the time Luke came to write Acts he had simply forgotten what he had written in the Gospel.

[4] The passive expresses divine action. This is a standard feature of Hellenistic and Jewish rapture stories and makes the suggestion of J. Luzarraga, *Las Tradiciones de la Nube en la Biblia y en el judaismo primitivo* (AnBib 54; Roma: IBP, 1973) 221-222, to take both verbs as a middle voice—ἀναφέρομαι (*se mueve*) and ἐπαίρομαι (*se elevó*)—most unlikely.

[5] Zahn, *Lucas* 732; Brun, *Auferstehung* 90; Stempvoort, 'Ascension' 36; Marshall, *Commentary* 909; J.T. Nielsen, *Het Evangelie naar Lucas* 2 (PNT.N; Nijkerk: Callenbach, 1983) 267.

may be considered whether we have here a καὶ-*epexegeticum*: 'he withdrew from them by being carried off into heaven'.

*V.52*    The disciples did not experience Jesus' departure as a sorrowful event but as an occasion for adoration, joy and worship. The return to Jerusalem—a strong editorial feature of Luke[1]—is a logical step in obedience to the command of the risen Lord to remain in the city (v.49). But perhaps the return of Elisha after Elijah's ascension is being hinted at as well (2 Kings 2:12-14).

For the first time in Luke's Gospel προσκύνησις is offered to Jesus (notably in his absence!)[2]. In Greek sources προσκυνέω is a commonly used term for the veneration of the gods (LSJM 1518). Occasionally it occurs in Hellenistic rapture stories as an act of recognition of the divinity of the person involved (Sophocles, *OedCol* 1654; Plutarch, *Romulus* 27,8; Lucian, *MortPer* 39). Adoration of the person taken up to heaven is an element which is absent in the Jewish rapture traditions, for obvious reasons (*supra* 39-40)[3]. Lohfink has therefore suggested the influence of a Hellenistic scheme upon Luke. If, however, Luke's portrayal of the closing pericope is determined by Sir 50:19-23, as we have suggested above, the apparent strength of the argument loses its force. Rather than a conventional rapture *topos*, the act of *proskynesis* is inspired by Sir 50:21. That the notion of *proskynesis* is not inspired by a Hellenistic rapture scheme is further corroborated by the suggestion that the element of *proskynesis* comes from a post-Easter appearance tradition also attested to by Mt 28:17 (probably traditional!), which is the closest parallel to Lk 24:52[4]. We have here the connection appearance-*proskynesis*, not the

---

[1]  Ὑποστρέφω is used 33x in Luke-Acts, and only 4x in the rest of the NT (MGM 981).

[2] Lohfink, *Himmelfahrt* 171-174, has convincingly demonstrated how Luke, different from the other evangelists, consistently avoids *proskynesis* for the earthly Jesus and reserves the motif of *proskynesis* for the end of his Gospel. On this, see also Lohfink, 'Gab es im Gottesdienst der neutestamentlichen Gemeinde eine Anbetung Christi?', *BZ* 18 (1974) 161-179.

[3] But cf. Jud 13:20. Is the *proskynesis* in 2 Kings 2:15 an incidental parallel?

[4] Lk 24:52 is the only instance in which Luke uses προσκυνέω with the accusative (there is no difference in meaning with the dative). Different from Luke, Matthew develops the προσκύνησις motif as act of recognition proper to any stage in Jesus' ministry. He normally uses the dative construction (Mt 2:2,8,11; 4:9; 8:2; 9:18; 14:33; 15:25; 18:26; 28:9) and twice the absolute (Mt 20:20; 28:17, with variations in the MSS tradition). In the only indisputable instance in which Matthew uses the accusative (Mt 4:10) he follows his source (Q Lk 4:8 = Deut 6:13). It is therefore reasonable to assume that the formulation in the absolute, especially Mt 28:17, has been drawn from a pre-Matthean source. This would suggest a common appearance tradition including the notion of *proskynesis*.

connection rapture-*proskynesis*. This means that with the notion of *proskynesis* Luke remains wholly within the confines of biblical Judaism.

*V.53* In closing the Gospel with the description of the disciples' constant presence in the temple[1], where they are fully taken up with worshipping God (recall the description of Anna in 2:37!), Luke underlines the *heilsgeschichtliche* continuity of the early Christian community with Israel[2] and prepares his Gentile readership for his presentation in Acts 1-5 of the Jerusalem Church as not yet emancipated from Judaism (cf. Acts 2:46-47; 3:1; 5:42). Although διὰ παντὸς (*sc.* χρόνου) should not be taken in strictly literal terms, more seems to be involved than simple attendance at the regular hours of prayer[3]. At any rate, this historical reminiscence serves Luke as a means to show that the Jesus event did not cause a break with Judaism[4].

### d. *Acts 1:1-14,21-22*

The parallel structure of Lk 24:36-53 and Acts 1:1-14—a school example of Lucian's principle of interlacing (*ArtConscr* 55)[5]—suggests that these are reports about the same events. Structurally, the general description of v.3 (events between resurrection and ascension) marks a smooth transition from the larger time-span of vv.1-2 (events from the beginning of Jesus' ministry to the end) to the narrower time-span of vv.4-14 (events on the day of the ascension).

*Vv.1-2* In accordance with the literary conventions of his time, Luke

---

[1] On the analogy of Acts 2:46-47 (cf. 5:42; Lk 2:37), ἦσαν should be taken with διὰ παντὸς ἐν τῷ ἱερῷ rather than with εὐλογοῦντες (*constructio periphrastica*). The emphasis is on the disciples' *presence* in the temple. The temple, of course, is seen here as a house of prayer, a place of worship (τὸ ἱερόν rather than ναός).

[2] L. Goppelt, *Theologie des Neuen Testaments* (hrsg. v. J. Roloff; UTB 850; Göttingen: Vandenhoeck & Ruprecht, 1976, [3]1978) 620-621.

[3] Calvin, *CommHarmEv*, 828; Zahn, *Lucas* 733 Anm.91. The summarising character of the statement does of course not permit a more exact topographical description (but cf. Acts 3:11; 5:12).

[4] On the whole Luke has a positive view of the temple, see F.D. Weinert, 'The Meaning of the Temple in Luke-Acts', *BTB* 11 (1981) 85-89. But the Jesus event has transformed the relation to the temple [cf. G. Schrenk, ἱερός, τὸ ἱερόν κτλ., *ThWNT* 3 (1938) 241-247]. It should be noted that the temple is *not* the place where the Spirit will be poured out!

[5] See J. Dupont, 'La question du plan des Actes des Apôtres à la lumière d'un texte de Lucien de Samosate' (1979); repr. in: idem, *Nouvelles Études sur les Actes des Apôtres* (LeDiv 118; Paris: Cerf, 1984) 24-36; W.C. van Unnik, 'Luke's Second Book and the Rules of Hellenistic Historiography', in: J. Kremer (éd.), *Les Actes des Apôtres. Traditions, rédaction, théologie* (BEThL 48; Gembloux: Duculot, 1979) 54-55.

commences his 'second book' with a brief summary of the preceding book before he plunges into the sequel of events related in the Gospel (vv.1-2)[1]. He describes his Gospel as a treatise περὶ πάντων ... ὧν ἤρξατο ὁ Ἰησοῦς ποιεῖν τε καὶ διδάσκειν κτλ., that is, a full account of the Jesus tradition (cf. Lk 1:1-4). The claim of completeness (πάντων; cf. Lk 1:3 πᾶσιν; and esp. Acts 10:39 ἡμεῖς μάρτυρες πάντων ὧν ἐποίησεν) is typically Lukan. It is quite suggestive that in comparison with his sources Luke's presentation is more comprehensive than that of his predecessors. Beyond Mark and Q, e.g., Luke recounts the birth, the resurrection and the ascension of Jesus. Although, strictly speaking, none of these events can be said to be 'acts and teachings' of Jesus, they lend some weight to the suggestion that πάντων is more than only a rhetorical device.

If there is a special point in ἤρξατο[2], it may be suggested that we have here a variation on the typical Lukan tendency to tag Jesus' ministry with a *terminus a quo* and a *terminus ad quem* (e.g. Acts 1:22)[3], and that consequently the end-term ἄχρι ἧς ἡμέρας ... ἀνελήμφθη, rather than some implied sort of continuation ('what Jesus *continued* to do'), is its complement. To bring out this meaning, ἤρξατο is best rendered as an adverbial construct, 'from the beginning': 'I have written on all that Jesus did from the beginning (cf. Lk 1:2 ἀπ' ἀρχῆς) until the day he was taken up' (my translation), which is of course a fair summary of what he did in his Gospel[4].

---

[1] Our focus is on the preface only in so far as it has relevance for understanding Luke's rapture christology. The wider issues of interpretation of the prefaces to Luke-Acts have been dealt with sufficiently by Cadbury, 'Commentary on the Preface of Luke', *Beg* 2 (1922) 489-510; G. Klein, 'Lukas 1,1-4 als theologisches Programm' (1964); repr. in: Braumann (Hrsg.), *Lukasevangelium* 170-203; Dillon, 'Previewing Luke's Project from His Prologue (Luke 1:1-4)', *CBQ* 43 (1981) 205-227; and L.C.E. Alexander, *The Preface to Luke's Gospel. Literary Convention and Social Context in Luke 1.1-4 and Acts 1.1* (MSSNTS 78; Cambridge, New York: CUP, 1993), and need no further elaboration here (see the bibliography and discussion in Nolland, *Luke* 1, 3-12). For the preface to Acts in relation to Hellenistic preface-writing, see in addition to the still useful investigation of Larrañaga, *Ascension* 270-333, and the literature cited in G. Schneider, *Die Apostelgeschichte 1. Einleitung. Kommentar zu Kap.1,1-8,40* (HThK 5; Freiburg: Herder, 1980) 188-189; D.W. Palmer, 'The Literary Background of Ac 1.1-14', *NTS* 33 (1987) 427-428; Alexander, *Preface* 142-146.

[2] This is denied by authors who treat it as a redundant auxiliary, so that ἤρξατο ... ποιεῖν corresponds more or less with ἐποίησεν (Bauer 227; BDR 419.3; 392.2₉).

[3] E. Samain, 'La notion de APXH dans l'oeuvre lucanienne', in: F. Neirynck (éd.), *L'Évangile de Luc—The Gospel of Luke. Revised and Enlarged Edition of L'Évangile de Luc. Problèmes littéraires et théologiques* (BEThL 32; Leuven: Leuven University Press, Peeters, 1973, ²1989) 209-238.327.

[4] For the various positions, see the commentaries *ad loc.*

In the light of the foregoing discussion on the meaning of ἀνάλημψις / ἀναλαμβάνομαι in Lk 9:51, there can be little doubt that ἄχρι ἧς ἡμέρας ... ἀνελήμφθη (= ἄχρι τῆς ἡμέρας ἐν ᾗ ... ἀνελήμφθη BDR 294)[1] is a deliberate reference to the day of the ascension described at the end of the Gospel. The preposition ἄχρι is used accordingly in an inclusive sense (i.e. the day of the ascension is included in the Gospel narrative)[2]. The instruction of the apostles (ἐντειλάμενος τοῖς ἀποστόλοις) reads as a natural flash-back to Lk 24:44-49, that is, to the (implied) commandment for universal mission and the commandment to remain in Jerusalem until Pentecost[3]. The election of the apostles through the Holy Spirit (διὰ πνεύματος ἁγίου οὓς ἐξελέξατο = οὓς ἐξελέξατο διὰ πνεύματος ἁγίου)[4] has no counterpart in Lk 24 and should probably be translated as a pluperfect 'which he *had* chosen' (on an earlier occasion, that is, on the occasion of Lk 6:12-16). In addition to the obvious

---

[1] Whether ἄχρι ἧς ἡμέρας ... ἀνελήμφθη marks the end of the book (ἐποιησάμην ... ἄχρι ἧς ἡμέρας) or marks the conclusion of the earthly ministry of Jesus (ἤρξατο ... ποιεῖν τε καὶ διδάσκειν ... ἄχρι ἧς ἡμέρας) is difficult to decide, since for Luke these *termini ad quem* overlap. But in the light of Luke's idiom elsewhere (Acts 1:22; cf. 10:37-38; Lk 1:2; 3:23; 23:5; cf. also Lk 24:47; Acts 1:8; 11:15), one is inclined to regard the latter as the most probable option. Moreover, v.3 is a description of Jesus' ministry, not a recapitulation of the Gospel narrative.

[2] Contra Michaelis, 'Zur Überlieferung der Himmelfahrtsgeschichte', *ThBl* 4 (1925) 106-107, and B.D. Ehrman, *The Orthodox Corruption of Scripture. The Effect of Early Christological Controversies on the Text of the New Testament* (New York, Oxford: OUP, 1993) 229, both in the interest of a defence of the shorter text in Lk 24:51. See v.22 (!), and Lk 1:20; 17:27. An inclusive temporal *terminus ad quem* is normal in Hellenistic prologues: Polybius, *Hist* II 1,1-3; IV 1,1-2; Xenophon, *Anabasis* III 1,1; IV 1,1; cf. VII 1,1 (?); DiodS, *Hist* XX 2,3; Appian, *RomHist* 7,1.

[3] This is a more natural understanding of the verse than to understand ἐντειλάμενος as a reference to Lk 6:13 [G. Bouwman, 'Der Anfang der Apostelgeschichte und der 'westliche' Text', in: T. Baarda, A. Hilhorst, G.P. Luttikhuizen, A.S. van der Woude (eds.), *Text and Testimony. Essays in Honour of A.F.J. Klijn* (Kampen: J.H. Kok, 1988) 49] or to the Last Supper Scene [Parsons, *Departure* 132 (+ 247 n.119)].

[4] Since this construction is not uncommon in Luke-Acts, this view is to be preferred to constructs that link διὰ πνεύματος ἁγίου with the post-Easter commandments [ἐντειλάμενος ... διὰ πνεύματος ἁγίου, e.g. F.F. Bruce, *The Acts of the Apostles. Greek Text with Introduction and Commentary* (Grand Rapids: Eerdmans; Leicester: Apollos, 1951, ³1990) 99, and C.K. Barrett, *The Acts of the Apostles 1. Preliminary Introduction and Commentary on Acts I-XIV* (ICC; Edinburgh: T.&T. Clark, 1994) 69] or that regard the position of διὰ πνεύματος ἁγίου as intentionally ambivalent [e.g. W. Schmithals, *Die Apostelgeschichte des Lukas* (ZBK.NT 3/2; Zürich: Theologischer, 1982) 20; L.T. Johnson, *The Acts of the Apostles* (SPg 5; Collegeville, MN: Liturgical, 1992) 24; J. Zmijewski, *Die Apostelgeschichte übersetzt und erklärt* (RNT 5; Regensburg: F. Pustet, 1994) 46-47].

christological point (Jesus is one who acts through the Spirit), Luke's motive for inserting the election of the apostles διὰ πνεύματος ἁγίου may be to stress that they are the legitimate custodians of the faith (see further on v.3).

*V.3* Though from a formal perspective Luke has by now sufficiently recapitulated the events leading up to the ascension (vv.1-2), he does not proceed with stating the content of his δεύτερος λόγος as would be expected after the current literary conventions, but he continues reporting what had happened in the period between the resurrection and the ascension. In line with the presentation in the Gospel narrative, the post-Easter period is characterised by the manifestations of the risen Lord to the apostles. Note how the focus is emphatically on the apostles: it is to them (οἷς καὶ, with καὶ for the sake of emphasis, BDR 442.8) that he showed himself alive and to them that the instructions concerning the Kingdom of God were given. In this way Luke reassures his readership that the apostles were fully instructed by the risen Lord and thus are the authentic witnesses of the Gospel[1]. Jesus showed himself alive to them ἐν πολλοῖς τεκμηρίοις 'by many (convincing) proofs'[2]. The τεκμήρια are probably demonstrative acts done during the appearances, such as the showing of his hands and feet and the eating of fish, rather than the appearances as such[3]. Παρέστησεν ἑαυτὸν ζῶντα is Luke's reformulation of the traditional ὤφθη (1 Cor 15:5-8).

Different from Luke's earlier account, an interval of forty days now separates the ascension from the resurrection. There is no strict parallel to the forty days in Hellenistic rapture stories[4], but, as we noted in the previous chapter, the Jewish-biblical rapture tradition provides ample parallels. This again suggests that we are in a Jewish environment.

---

[1] See Talbert, *Luke and the Gnostics. An Examination of the Lukan Purpose* (Nashville, New York: Abingdon, 1966) 17-32, who shows that Luke has consciously organised Acts 1 and Luke-Acts in its entirety around the theme of apostolic witness.

[2] Cf. Wis 5:11 (with σημεῖον); 19:13; 3 Macc 3:24; Josephus, *Ant* V i,13 (39); XVII v,6 (128); see further D.L. Mealand, 'The Phrase 'Many Proofs' in Acts 1,3 and in Hellenistic Writers', *ZNW* 80 (1989) 134-135, who has shown that the combination πολλα τεκμηρια is normal Hellenistic Greek. Bruce, *Acts* 100 refers to Aristotle's definition of τεκμήριον as ἀναγκαῖον σημεῖον 'a compelling sign', *Rhetorica* I 2,16).

[3] With Lohfink, *Himmelfahrt* 152-153; Dömer, *Heil Gottes* 112; J. Roloff, *Die Apostelgeschichte* (NTD 5; Göttingen: Vandenhoeck & Ruprecht, 1981) 20. Contra E. Haenchen, *Die Apostelgeschichte* (KEK III[17]; Göttingen: Vandenhoeck & Ruprecht, 1956, [7]1977) 147.

[4] P.W. van der Horst, 'Hellenistic Parallels to the Acts of the Apostles (1,1-26)', *ZNW* 74 (1983) 19.

*Stricto sensu*, the notion of the forty days does not fix the date of the ascension. The traditional date of the ascension 'on the fortieth day' can only be deduced by implication from the narrative sequence (δι᾽ ἡμερῶν τεσσεράκοντα v.3 ... καὶ ... παρήγγειλεν v.4 ... οἱ μὲν ... ἠρώτων v.6 ... εἶπεν δὲ v.7 ... καὶ ταῦτα εἰπὼν κτλ. v.9). As a date of the ascension it would be expected at vv.9-12 but there it is absent. The absence of the forty days in Luke's Gospel and in the rest of Acts (although it would have been appropriate in Acts 10:41 and 13:31) suggests that Luke did not intend to date the ascension exactly on the fortieth day. Furthermore, the typological force of the number forty prevents taking it as an exact date[1]. The forty days rather delimit the *period* of appearances and final instructions before the ascension[2]. The idea is not that of an uninterrupted period in which Jesus was permanently present (this would require the temporal accusative ἡμέρας τεσσεράκοντα, cf. Chrysostom, *ActHom* 1,4; PG 60, 18). Δι᾽ ἡμερῶν τεσσεράκοντα rather suggests that a series of appearances took place 'over a period of forty days' (BDR 223₃), cf. Acts 13:31.

The notion of the forty days is perhaps the most puzzling part of the Lukan ascension story. As we noted earlier, it does not fit the chronology of the Gospel very well (*supra* 89-92). With the exception of a harmonising textual variant in Acts 10:41[3], the forty days of appearances is unique in Luke-Acts and the NT. Acts 13:31 defines the duration of the appearances of the risen Lord more generally as ἐπὶ ἡμέρας πλείους[4]. The next attestation of the forty days after Luke is found in Tertullian (*Apol* 21; PL 1, 402). In addition, there were alternative ascension dates in circulation from very early times. The

---

[1] Contra Larrañaga, *Ascension* 448-461, who made a strenuous effort to show that the forty days should be taken as an exact date. The church fathers who accept the canonical chronology are divided on whether the ascension took place 'on the fortieth day' or not. A number of them take up the notion of the forty days as an approximate number, i.e. without necessarily dating the ascension 'on the fortieth day', others take the forty days as exact chronology (i.e. 'on the fortieth day'); see the references in U. Holzmeister, 'Der Tag der Himmelfahrt des Herrn', *ZKTh* 55 (1931) 69-74.

[2] Δι᾽ ἡμερῶν τεσσεράκοντα is to be construed with the following ὀπτανόμενος αὐτοῖς κτλ. rather than with the preceding παρέστησεν (so SV), as is suggested by 13:31.

[3] Ἡμέρας μ´ D (E) it syʰ** sa mae; cf. B.M. Metzger, *A Textual Commentary on the Greek New Testament* (Stuttgart: Deutsche Bibelgesellschaft, UBS, 1971, ²1994) 335. The Western reading seems to misunderstand Acts 1:3 as denoting a period of uninterrupted conversation of Jesus with the disciples: συνεστράφημεν ... ἡμέρας μ´.

[4] Ἐπὶ ἡμέρας πλείους is a stylistic variation of Luke (cf. Acts 21:10; 24:17; 25:14; 27:20; cf. Acts 18:20; 20:9; 24:4,11; 25:6; ἐπὶ πολλὰς ἡμέρας Acts 16:18, cf. Heb 11:30). Outside Luke-Acts the combination διὰ + ἡμέρα (Lk 9:37 WH mg D; Acts 1:3; 27:5) occurs only in Mk 2:1; 13:2 D W it; 14:58 (= Mt 26:61).

Ethiopic *Epistula Apostolorum* (mid-second century AD) dates the ascension on the resurrection day itself [EpAp(Eth) 18 (29) tr. Schmidt 60; 51 (62) tr. Schmidt 154; also Mk 16:3 *k* (NA²⁷ *apparatus*)]. According to the testimony of Irenaeus, Gnostic groupings such as the Valentinians, the Ophites and the Sethians believed that after his resurrection Jesus had conversed with his disciples for 18 months [*AdvHaer* I 3,2 (PG 7, 469; SC 264, 52); I 30,14 (PG 7, 703; SC 264, 382-384)]. In the Ethiopic version of the Ascension of Isaiah the ascension of Christ occurs 545 days after his resurrection on the third day (AscenIs 9:16 tr. Knibb 170)¹, in the Apocryphon of James after 550 days (ApocJas 2:19-24 tr. NHL 30; 14:30 tr. NHL 35). According to Pistis Sophia, Jesus remained in the company of his disciples eleven years after the resurrection, before (in the twelfth year) he ascended to heaven (Pistis Sophia 1; NTApo 1, 177-178).

In the light of our previous discussion of the Jewish rapture-preservation traditions, it seems that we can be a little more specific as to the background of the forty days. The forty days that precede the ascension of Jesus have their parallel in the Jewish rapture traditions: the forty days are forty days of preparation, in which the disciples are fully instructed in view of the period to come, in which their Master will be absent². In rabbinic sources, learning and teaching 40 times suggests reliable instruction³. On the question whether Luke has drawn the forty days from a source, see our discussion *infra* 186ff.

The instructions concerning τὰ περὶ τῆς βασιλείας τοῦ θεοῦ—a Lukan summary of the content of the Christian Gospel—provide the link between the story of Jesus (Lk 4:13; 16:16 etc.) and the story of the church (but the latter in an expanded meaning, including τὰ περὶ τοῦ Ἰησοῦ) (Acts 8:12; 14:22; 19:8; 20:25; 28:23,31).

*Vv.4-5*  Καὶ συναλιζόμενος παρήγγειλεν κτλ. marks the transition from the general description of the period of the post-Easter appearances (v.3) to the description of what happened on one particular occasion⁴, namely, the final

---

¹ The words 'and will remain in that world for five hundred and forty-five days' are absent in a Latin MS (Lat2) and in the Slavonic version. M.A. Knibb (*OTP* 2, 170 n.*v*) suspects the words have been added under the influence of the Valentinian and Ophite tradition (18 months, i.e. approximately 545 days). Or were the disputed words erased because of the contradiction with the canonical chronology?

² Luke's employment of the number 40 elsewhere in his work (MGM 939) does not seem to shed much light on it.

³ References are found in H.R. Balz, τεσσεράκοντα κτλ., *ThWNT* 8 (1969) 137.

⁴ So e.g. H.J. Holtzmann, *Die Apostelgeschichte* (HC I/2; Freiburg: 1889; Tübingen, Leipzig: J.C.B. Mohr/Paul Siebeck, ³1901) 24. Contra D.J. Williams, *Acts* (NIBC 5; Peabody,

appearance of the risen Lord to his disciples on the day of the ascension (vv.4-14). Acts 1:4-5 is materially parallelled by Lk 24:36-49. The present participle συναλιζόμενος denotes action prior to the aorist indicative παρήγγειλεν: συναλιζόμενος παρήγγειλεν = συνηλίσθη καὶ παρήγγειλεν (cf. BDR 339.2b with reference to Acts 4:34).

The meaning of συναλιζόμενος[1] is disputed. Under the influence of H.J. Cadbury, it has been argued that συναλιζόμενος is only an orthographic variant of συναυλιζόμενος 'spending the night with', hence: 'being with, staying with' (d: *convivens*)[2]. If this is correct, the present tense may be taken to denote an uninterrupted period of Jesus' presence among his disciples[3]. The problem with this interpretation is that it is difficult to imagine how this meaning would apply to only one person (Jesus being the subject of the sentence) and hardly tallies with the interpretation offered above on the meaning of δι᾽ ἡμερῶν τεσσεράκοντα[4]. A more plausible meaning of the verb is 'eating salt together with' (from συν- and ἁλίζω), hence: 'eating together' (*convescens*)[5]. As in the parallel passages Lk 24:43 and Acts 10:41, we have here a mealtime setting (cf. Chrysostom, *ActHom* 1,4; PG 60, 19;

---

MA: Hendrickson, 1985, ²1990) 21.

[1] The MSS evidence is in strong support of the reading συναλιζόμενος. The reading συναλισκόμενος μετ᾽ αὐτῶν 'being taken captive together with them' (D*) makes no sense and is probably a transcriptional error for συναναλισκόμενος μετ᾽ αὐτῶν (presumably) 'consuming together' or συναλιζόμενος (μετ᾽ αὐτῶν). In the MS it is corrected into the likewise incomprehensible συναλισγόμενος μετ᾽ αὐτῶν 'being sullied with them'. The variant reading συναυλιζόμενος [for its attestation see M.-É Boismard, A. Lamouille, *Le Texte Occidental des Actes des apôtres* 2 (Paris: Éditions Recherche sur les Civilisations 17, 1984) 3] is 'an alleviation by conjecture, perhaps regarded as a mere improvement in spelling', J.H. Ropes, *The Text of Acts* (Beg 3; London: Macmillan, 1926) 2 n.4.

[2] Cadbury, 'Lexical Notes on Luke-Acts 3. Luke's Interest in Lodging', *JBL* 45 (1926) 310-317, followed by Lake, Cadbury, *The Acts of the Apostles. English Translation and Commentary* (Beg 4; London: Macmillan, 1933) 4-6; C.F.D. Moule, 'The Post-Resurrection Appearances in the Light of Festival Pilgrimages', *NTS* 4 (1957/58) 60; Metzger, *Commentary* 241-242; Schneider, *Apg* 1, 196 Anm.*a* + 199.

[3] An inference Enslin, 'Ascension' 63-64 draws from Cadbury's argument.

[4] Likewise to be rejected is the view which derives the word from συναλίζω 'bring together, collect, assemble', pass. 'come together, assemble' (cf. LSJM 1694) (Bengel, *Gnomon* 435 *conventum agens*). This meaning is not attested in the middle voice.

[5] This meaning is attested in Ps-Clement, *Homiliae* 13,4 (cf. 11); *Recogn* 7,29; Origen, Hexapla Ps 140:4 (ed. Field 2, 297). See further LSJM 1694 συνἁλίζω (B) pass. 'eat salt with, eat at the same table with', with reference to Acts 1:4. The form without μετ᾽ αὐτῶν is *lectio difficilior*; D it sy have specified an object to συναλιζόμενος: μετ᾽ αὐτῶν.

Theophylact, *ExpAct* 1,4; PG 125, 508; Ps-Oecumenius, *CommAct* 1,4; PG 118, 48)[1]. The usual objection that the sense 'to eat with' is unknown in the first century AD may well be overruled by the suggestion that Luke is responsible for having added the prefix σύν (a favourite of Luke)[2] to the more familiar ἁλίζω/-ομαι (Mk 9:49 // Mt 5:13; Lev 2:13; Tob 6:5 S; Is 47:2 A; Ezek 16:4)[3]. As in Lk 24:43, the mealtime scenario may serve to underline the reality of the (physical) resurrection of Jesus (cf. also IgnSm 3:3), although a more dominant concern seems be to stress the apostles' intimate fellowship with the risen Lord in view of their future mission (Acts 10:40-42).

The present infinitive μὴ χωρίζεσθαι corresponds, if reverted into direct speech, to the aorist imperative μὴ χωρίσατε 'do not depart (from Jerusalem)' and expresses negatively what Lk 24:49 καθίσατε ἐν τῇ πόλει said positively. The non-signalled transition to direct discourse is attested elsewhere in Luke-Acts (Lk 5:14; Acts 14:22; 17:3; 23:22) and Hellenistic literature[4].

Ἡ ἐπαγγελία τοῦ πατρὸς is used here in a double sense: the disciples are to await 'the promise of the Father', that which the Father has promised (*promissum*), i.e. the Spirit. The qualification 'which you heard from me' takes ἐπαγγελία as the act of promising (*promissio*). By inserting 'which you heard from me', Luke connects the command to wait, drawn from Lk 24 and put in indirect speech, with the Jesus logion about the coming Spirit baptism (v.5). In the Gospel tradition this saying is unanimously preserved as a Baptist logion (Q Lk 3:16 // Mt 3:11; Mk 1:8; cf. Jn 1:26), but here the saying is attributed to Jesus (cf. 11:16 where Luke calls it a ῥῆμα τοῦ κυρίου). Except for the parallel text Lk 24:49[5], it is difficult to find the reference in Luke's Gospel or

---

[1] Among modern interpreters *inter alios* O. Bauernfeind, *Kommentar und Studien zur Apostelgeschichte* (hrsg. v. V. Metelmann; WUNT 22; Tübingen: J.C.B. Mohr/Paul Siebeck, 1980) 334 (cf. 20 undecided); Marshall, *The Acts of the Apostles. An Introduction and Commentary* (TNTC 5; Leicester: IVP; Grand Rapids: Eerdmans, 1980) 59; Roloff, *Apg* 21; Schmithals, *Apg* 21; G. Schille, *Die Apostelgeschichte des Lukas* (ThHK 5; Berlin: Evangelische, 1983, [2]1984) 69; Bruce, *Acts* 101; Johnson, *Acts* 25; Zmijewski, *Apg* 53-54.

[2] Mt 4x; Mk 6x; Lk 23x; Jn 3x; Acts 52x; rest 42x (MGM 1109-1110). Luke *adds* συν- to the simple verb in Lk 5:15 (Mk 1:45); 6:49 (Mt 7:27); 12:2 (Mt 10:26); 23:49 (Mt 27:55); cf. 4:38 [Mk 1:30 // Mt 8:14]; 22:4 (Mk 14:10; Mt 26:15). He *substitutes* συν- for another preposition in 9:1 (Mk 6:7; Mt 10:1); 20:5 (Mk 11:31 // Mt 21:25); 22:10 (Mk 14:13).

[3] The form can thus be satisfactorily explained by an inner-Greek mechanism, despite C.C. Torrey, *The Composition and Date of Acts* (HThS 1; Cambridge, MA: Harvard University Press, 1916) 23, who treats it as an Aramaism, and M. Wilcox, *The Semitisms of Acts* (Oxford: Clarendon, 1965) 106-109, who in partial support of Torrey suggests the possibility of Syriacism.

[4] See the references in Van der Horst, 'Parallels' 19-20.

[5] So H.H. Wendt, *Die Apostelgeschichte* (KEK II[8]; Göttingen: Vandenhoeck & Ruprecht,

elsewhere in the synoptic tradition Luke alludes to (perhaps Lk 11:13). Since Luke is familiar with the Baptist ascription of the logion and yet attributes it to Jesus in the present context, it is likely that he had received it from the tradition as a word of Jesus[1].

The ὅτι-clause explains why the apostles are to remain in Jerusalem: they must remain there because (ὅτι)[2] they will soon be baptised in the Holy Spirit (the Jesus logion is quoted in full, the emphasis is on the Spirit baptism). The time indication οὐ μετὰ πολλὰς ταύτας ἡμέρας[3] (a litotes for μετὰ ὀλίγας ταύτας ἡμέρας) may be regarded as the logical inference Luke made from the command to stay in Jerusalem until the disciples were empowered with power from above (Lk 24:49). He thereby links the present occasion (the ascension!) more closely to the day of Pentecost[4].

*Vv.6-8*     The introductory words οἱ μὲν οὖν συνελθόντες probably do not introduce a new occasion ('when they had come together, they asked him' NRSV), but explicate the subject of the sentence: 'they who had come together (οἱ συνελθόντες) asked him' (cf. 2:41; 8:4; 11:19) (Vg). Note that in the parallel passage Lk 24:47-49 the command to wait in Jerusalem for the coming

---

1880, [4]1899) 65; Holtzmann, *Apg* 24.

[1] According to Pesch, *Apg* 1, 65, Luke is responsible for the attribution to Jesus. Haenchen, *Apg* 149, and cf. Bauernfeind, *Apg* 335 ('möglich, aber nicht nachweisbar'), think that already in pre-Lukan tradition the saying was restyled as a Jesus logion.

[2] WV(first edition) treats ὅτι as a *recitativum* (no longer in the revised edition).

[3] Cf. Josephus, *Ant* I xix,5 (294); *Ant* V ix,3 (328), and Ex 2:23; 4:19. Van der Horst, 'Parallels' 20, refers to Pap Oxy VIII 1121,12 (without litotes). F. Blass, *Acta apostolorum sive Lucae ad Theophilum liber alter. Editio philologica apparatu critico, commentario perpetuo, indice verborum illustrata* (Göttingen: Vandenhoeck & Ruprecht, 1895) 43 and Menoud, 'Remarques sur les textes de l'ascension dans Luc-Acts', in: W. Eltester (Hrsg.), *Neutestamentliche Studien für R. Bultmann* (BZNW 21; Berlin: A. Töpelmann, 1954, [2]1957) 153 treat it as a Latinism; Torrey, *Composition* 6 as an Aramaism.

[4] The Western reading ἕως τῆς πεντηκοστῆς (D* sa mae Ephr Aug^pt Cass) simply makes more explicit that which is already in the text. I find the solution offered by W.A. Strange, *The Problem of the Text of Acts* (MSSNTS 71; Cambridge: CUP, 1992) 113-115, to regard ἕως τῆς πεντηκοστῆς as a marginal note intended for v.4 (ἀπὸ Ἱεροσολύμων μὴ χωρίζεσθαι ... ἕως τῆς πεντηκοστῆς) but wrongly inserted at the end of v.5, most attractive and preferable to the ingenious construction of Boismard, Lamouille, *Les Actes des deux apôtres 3* (EtB Ns 14; Paris: Librairie Lecoffre, J. Gabalda, 1990) 30-31, although I am hesitant to ascribe the phrase to Luke's redactional activity. See on this variant further Zahn, *Die Urausgabe der Apostelgeschichte des Lucas* (FGNK 9; Leipzig: A. Deichert, Werner Scholl, 1916) 329-330; É. Delebecque, 'Ascension et Pentecôte dans les Actes des Apôtres selon le codex Bezae', *RThom* 82 (1982) 82-84.

Spirit baptism and the call for universal mission were spoken, so it seems, on one and the same occasion.

The disciples' question concerning the restoration of the kingdom to Israel accurately reflects the mood of the post-Easter community at the time (cf. Lk 24:21). Both the resurrection and the announcement of the coming Spirit baptism would heighten the expectation of the imminent inauguration of the messianic kingdom, as prophesied in the OT and in the teaching of Jesus. As in Lk 19:11, the emphasis is on the *timing* of the event: 'is it ἐν τῷ χρόνῳ τούτῳ (= οὐ μετὰ πολλὰς ταύτας ἡμέρας) that you will restore the kingdom to Israel?'[1]. Cf. similar questions in 4 Ezra 4:33-52; 6:11-12; 2 Bar 21:18-19; 81:2 (further references in Bill. 1, 949).

The wording of v.7 is drawn from Mk 13:32 (= Mt 24:36), omitted in Lk 21:33 (without οὐδὲ ὁ υἱός) and is a typical apocalyptic *topos* (cf. 1 Thess 5:1). The term of the inauguration of the messianic reign/parousia remains undefined. Instead, the interval up to the end of the age is given purpose by the risen Lord's command for universal mission (Lk 24:47-49). Luke does not deny that God will restore the kingdom to Israel[2], but corrects the expected timing: it is not now that the kingdom will be restored[3]. Now is the time for universal mission in the power of the Holy Spirit. Vv.6-8 serve therefore to refute the idea of *Naherwartung* (see on the issue further *infra* 175-181).

*V.9* Without interruption the narrative passes into the description of the ascension, connected by ταῦτα εἰπών. The structure of the verse is that of a chiastic parallelism,

A    βλεπόντων αὐτῶν
B    ἐπήρθη
     καὶ
B'   νεφέλη ὑπέλαβεν αὐτὸν

---

[1] Lohfink, *Himmelfahrt* 154 (cf. also Dömer, *Heil Gottes* 115; Roloff, *Apg* 22-24; Zmijewski, *Apg* 56-57) over-interprets the question when he thinks to detect a three-fold Lukan concern, namely the chronological ('in dieser Zeit?'), the spatial ('für Israel'?) and the christological (wirst *du* ...) aspect. The latter two are presupposed, but are not part of the question.

[2] On the contrary, the theme is definitely a Lukan one and it is by no means clear that Luke rejects this expectation (Lk 19:11; 21:28; 24:21; Acts 3:20-21).

[3] This does not, of course, mean that Luke simply retains the old nationalistic hope on the restoration of the Davidic kingdom. Luke is too much a universalist for that. Note that in Acts 15:15-18 the nationalistic hope is redefined with the Jewish-Christian community in view. Cf. J.P. Chance, *Jerusalem, the Temple, and the New Age in Luke-Acts* (Macon, GA: Mercer, Peeters, 1988) 37-39.

A'    ἀπὸ τῶν ὀφθαλμῶν αὐτῶν,

but depending upon the question of what *kind* of chiastic parallelism it is, it gives a description of a one- or two-stage act. If καί simply annexes the two clauses to a (chrono)logical sequence, Jesus was first lifted up a certain distance into the sky before a cloud took him away from sight: 'he was taken up before their very eyes, and (καί) a cloud hid him from their sight' (NIV)[1]. That the ascension would unfold in two stages may reveal a crux: Jesus would not of himself need a vehicle for his ascent; the cloud would only prevent the spectators from looking into heaven. If, on the other hand, the two clauses are connected by a καί-*epexegeticum*, the second clause only reformulates what the first clause stated in general terms: 'he was taken up before their very eyes, that is (καί), a cloud hid him (and took him away) from their sight'[2].

If we ignore the larger context for the moment, the presence of the *cloud* causes little difficulty to the interpreter: the cloud is obviously the typical rapture cloud which in the Hellenistic [Dosiades (FGH 458 fgm 5); Apollodorus, *Bibliotheca* II 7,7; DionHal, *AntRom* I 77,2; PGrM 5,277; Lucian, *JuppTrag* 16][3] and Jewish assumption stories [1 En 39:3; GkApEzra 5:7; TAb B 8:3; 10:2; 12:1,9; Rev 11:12; Josephus, *Ant* IV viii,48 (326); cf. 2 En 3:1; SibOr 1,381 = Christian interpolation] serves as a vehicle of ascent and/or as a means to conceal the actual taking up. Which particular function should be attributed to the cloud depends at least in part upon the meaning of ὑπέλαβεν. ῾Υπολαμβάνω does not normally mean 'envelop', but 'take up by getting under' [Herodotus, *Hist* 1,24; Plato, *Rep* 5,453 D; Josephus, *Ant* XI vi,9 (238); cf. LSJM 1886]. But since composites with the prefix ὑπο- often carry the connotation 'underhand, secretly'[4], the prefix ὑπο- is not necessarily purely local. LSJM 1886 in addition gives the meaning 'take up, seize, come suddenly upon'. The phrase νεφέλη ὑπέλαβεν αὐτόν may accordingly be translated as 'a cloud suddenly came upon him' or 'a cloud enveloped him'. The cloud, then,

---

[1] So e.g. Delling, ἀναλαμβάνω, ἀνάλημψις, *ThWNT* 4 (1942) 8; C. Stam, *De hemelvaart des Heren in de Godsopenbaring van het Nieuwe Testament* (Academisch proefschrift Vrije Universiteit Amsterdam; Kampen: J.H. Kok, 1950) 42-43; Metzger, 'The Ascension of Jesus Christ', in: idem, *Historical and Literary Studies. Pagan, Jewish and Christian* (NTTS 8; Leiden: E.J. Brill; Grand Rapids: Eerdmans, 1968) 85-86.

[2] Cf. Schneider, *Apg* 1, 204; Schille, *Apg* 73. Cf. also Conzelmann, *Die Apostelgeschichte* (HNT 7; Tübingen: J.C.B. Mohr/Paul Siebeck, 1963, ²1972) 27. Note that earlier (*supra* 93) we hinted at the possibility of an epexegetical reading of Lk 24:51 as well.

[3] See further A.S. Pease, 'Some Aspects of Invisibility', *HSCP* 53 (1942) 8-10; Lohfink, *Himmelfahrt* 44; Friedrich, 'Entrückungschristologie' 65.

[4] LSJM 1875 F III, with reference to ὑποθέω, ὑποθωπεύω, ὑποκορίζομαι, ὑπόρνυμι, but many other examples could be adduced.

covers the event from the eyes of the disciples. In the light of Luke's treatment of prepositions in combination with *verba composita* elsewhere—he has a preference for unbalanced constructions[1]—ὑπέλαβεν ... ἀπὸ τῶν ὀφθαλμῶν αὐτῶν should be taken as a single construction, in which ἀπὸ τῶν ὀφθαλμῶν αὐτῶν ('away from their eyes') explicates what is already in ὑπολαμβάνω: take up (movement) secretly (concealment): a cloud enveloped him and took him away from their eyes. Just as the cloud at the transfiguration prevented the by-standers from seeing what happened and at the same time provided Moses and Elijah with access to the heavenly realm, so the ascension cloud has a double function[2].

Other interpretations of the cloud motif have been suggested. The rationalists took it as a natural cloud (fog cloud, rain cloud, dew, etc.)[3]. Others see in the cloud the Shekinah motif, the cloud of divine presence[4]. Others again think the ascension cloud is based on the parousia clouds[5] or comes directly from Dan 7:13[6]. A *direct* influence of Dan 7:13 is not likely (nothing in Dan 7:13 suggests a vertical movement of the cloud[7]). There is a connection with the parousia cloud as much as there seems to be a connection with the Transfiguration cloud. This is suggested *inter alia* by Luke's redaction of Mk 13:26. Contra Mk 13:26 (ἐν νεφέλαις) Luke speaks of a cloud in the singular (ἐν νεφέλῃ), thereby suggesting that the parousia cloud (Lk 21:27), the Transfiguration cloud (Lk 9:34-35), and the ascension cloud (Acts 1:9) are the same. The presence of the cloud is taken by some others as an indication that this is an exaltation scene[8]. It is possible that the cloud brings in the notion of theophany, but what does this imply? Clearly not that the ascending Jesus was deified! Rather that God manifested his special presence at the ascension of Jesus[9].

---

[1] Luke prefers e.g. ἐξέρχεσθαι ἀπό to ἐξέρχεσθαι ἐξ (see MGM 334). Cf. also Lk 24:50.

[2] The question whether the cloud conceals [so e.g. A. Oepke, νεφέλη, νέφος, *ThWNT* 4 (1942) 911] or is the vehicle of ascent [so already Ps-Athanasius, *In assumptionem* 5 (PG 28, 1100)] is therefore a false alternative. It has a 'Doppelfunktion': Wendt, *Apg* 67; Lohfink, *Himmelfahrt* 190-193; Luzarraga, *Tradiciones* 220-225; Dömer, *Heil Gottes* 119; Marshall, *Acts* 61. Cf. also Zmijewski, *Apg* 65-66.

[3] But also J.F. Walvoord, 'The Ascension of Christ', *BS* 121 (1964) 9!

[4] A.M. Ramsey, 'What was the Ascension?' (1951); repr. in: D.E. Nineham, *et alii* (eds.), *Historicity and Chronology in the New Testament* (TCSPCK 6; London: SPCK, 1965) 143; Bruce, *Acts* 104.

[5] E. Grässer, 'Die Parusieerwartung in der Apostelgeschichte', in: Kremer (éd.), *Actes* 113; Parsons, *Departure* 144 (cf. Lohfink, *Himmelfahrt* 187-193).

[6] N. Perrin, *Rediscovering the Teaching of Jesus* (New York, Evanston: Harper & Row, 1967) 179.

[7] Cf. R.B.Y. Scott, 'Behold, He Cometh with Clouds', *NTS* 5 (1958/59) 127-132.

[8] E.g. E. Franklin, *Christ the Lord. A Study in the Purpose and Theology of Luke-Acts* (London: SPCK, 1975) 31-32.

[9] Cf. G.E. Ladd, *A Theology of the New Testament* (Cambridge: Lutterworth, 1970) 334.

Note that as in 2 Kings 2, the emphasis of the entire section (vv.9-11) is on the notion of 'seeing': βλεπόντων αὐτῶν, ἀπὸ τῶν ὀφθαλμῶν αὐτῶν (v.9), ἀτενίζοντες, (καὶ ἰδοὺ) (v.10), [ἐμ]βλέποντες, ἐθεάσασθε (v.11)[1].

*V.10* The sudden appearance of two men in white clothing brings to mind the appearance of the two men to the women at the tomb (Lk 24:4), a parallel which is strengthened by the accompanying rebuke (Lk 24:5 τί ζητεῖτε τὸν ζῶντα μετὰ τῶν νεκρῶν; Acts 1:11 τί ἑστήκατε ἐμβλέποντες εἰς τὸν οὐρανόν;) and the revelatory word (respectively on the resurrection and the parousia). Luke thus draws a conscious parallel between the first and the last post-Easter appearance. The 'white clothes' mark the two men as heavenly messengers [2 Macc 11:8; Mk 9:3parr.; Mk 16:5parr.; Jn 20:12; Acts 10:30; *LAB* 21:2; Herm(v) IV 2,1; 3,5; Herm(s) VIII 2,3][2]. They are *angeli interpretes* (cf. Acts 10:30; 1 En 19:1; 22:3; 23:4; Rev 10:9; 19:9-10; 22:8; cf. 1 Thess 4:17), rather than Moses and Elijah[3] (if they were in view, Luke would probably have given their names, as he did in Lk 9:30).

Εἰς τὸν οὐρανὸν may be taken with ἀτενίζοντες (cf. v.11 [ἐμ]βλέποντες εἰς τὸν οὐρανόν; 7:55)[4], with πορευομένου (cf. v.11 πορευόμενον εἰς τὸν οὐρανόν; cf. Lk 24:51)[5] or with both[6]. I would prefer the first ('they were looking into the sky'), since it is the role of the angels to interpret the ascension. Πορεύομαι is to be understood as a rapture term[7], rather than a reference to the Lukan journey motif[8].

*V.11* The word of the angels (τί ἑστήκατε [ἐμ]βλέποντες εἰς τὸν οὐρανόν;) recalls the reproach of the angels in Lk 24:5. The καί is an unstressed 'also' or should be left untranslated. The obvious implication of the angelic words is 'you should *not* be standing here looking into the sky'. But

---

[1] Cf. Plutarch, *Numa* 2,4; Suetonius, *Augustus* 100,4; Seneca, *Apocolocyntosis* 1; DioCass, *RomHist* LVI 46,2; LIX 11,4. But the closer analogy is 2 Kings 2.

[2] See Van der Horst, 'Parallels' 22 for Hellenistic parallels.

[3] So J. Wellhausen, *Kritische Analyse der Apostelgeschichte* (AGWG.PH NF 15/2; Berlin: Weidmann, 1914) 2; Goulder, *Type and History in Acts* (London: SPCK, 1964) 147.

[4] RSV NEB BJ EÜ; WV (rev. ed.); Pesch, 'Anfang' 51; Bauernfeind, *Apg* 345 Anm.74.

[5] Vg; Haenchen, *Apg* 156 Anm.8; Lohfink, *Himmelfahrt* 195; WV (first edition) 'Terwijl zij Hem bij zijn hemelvaart gespannen nastaarden ...'.

[6] Stählin, *Apg* 19; Pesch, *Apg* 1, 73 Anm.4.

[7] Verbs of going are particularly favoured as rapture termini (Friedrich, 'Entrückungs-christologie' 54 Anm.58), though there is no instance of πορεύομαι, which is a favourite word of Luke and may be Luke's choice as an alternative.

[8] So Talbert, *Patterns* 114-115, following Davies, 'Purpose' 164-166.

this does not seem to correspond too well with the explanatory words that follow. For if Jesus will return in the same way from heaven as he now ascends, it is only appropriate to look into the sky (cf. Lk 21:27-28). If, on the other hand, it is the inactivity of the disciples that is the object of the angels' reproach ('why are you standing here, while you should ...'), the appeal to the parousia makes little sense. Perhaps the least unsatisfactory solution is to regard the question of the angels as criticism of the disciples' incomprehensibility: they did not realise that Jesus' departure was final: 'why are you looking into the sky as if Jesus would return any moment?'. But even so, one misses the point of the emphatic 'in the same way', that is, 'on a cloud'[1] (cf. Lk 21:27 the Son of Man coming ἐν νεφέλῃ, diff. Mk 13:26 ἐν νεφέλαις)[2]. The angelic words are then an affirmation that Jesus *will* come back, but not now[3]. At any rate, it is clear that Luke wanted to say more than was possible. In sum, the ascension is a final departure, which commences a period in which Jesus will be physically absent.

*Vv.12-14*   The disciples' return to Jerusalem (cf. Lk 24:52) is the natural reaction to the command of v.4. It is not until now—after the event—that Luke records the location of the ascension. Both that the ascension took place on a mountain and that this mountain was Mount Olivet are new pieces of information. But in this respect there is no discrepancy between Lk 24:50 and Acts 1:12[4]. Lk 24:50 situates the event somewhere between Jerusalem and Bethany (*supra* 88-89), Acts 1:12 more precisely on (the top of?) the Mount of Olives[5]. Luke adds here a precise distance: ὅ ἐστιν ἐγγὺς Ἰερουσαλὴμ σαββάτου ἔχον ὁδόν, that is, 2000 cubits = 880 m (Bill. 2, 590-594)[6]. The

---

[1] Cf. Chrysostom, *ActHom* 2,3 (PG 9, 29) (corporeally and on a cloud).

[2] It cannot be proved that for Luke οὕτως ... ὃν τρόπον (v.11) also implies that the parousia will occur on the Mount of Olives (v.12), but a christological reading of Zech 14:4 καὶ στήσονται οἱ πόδες αὐτοῦ (*sc.* the feet of Jesus!) ἐν τῇ ἡμέρᾳ ἐκείνῃ (at the parousia) ἐπὶ τὸ ὄρος τῶν ἐλαιῶν would certainly encourage this conclusion.

[3] Cf. Pesch, *Apg* 1, 73-74, who stresses that the point is that it is not *now* appropriate to stand there looking into heaven.

[4] Contra Conzelmann, *Mitte* 86 [who, incidentally, regards Bethany (and Lk 24:50-53 *in toto*) as an interpolation]. With: Menoud, 'Quarante jours' 148; Lohfink, *Himmelfahrt* 164-167; Fitzmyer, *Luke* 2, 1589-1590; Parsons, *Departure* 103-104.196.

[5] Cf. G. Dalman, *Orte und Wege Jesu* (BFChTh 2/1; Gütersloh: C. Bertelsmann, ³1924) 229: 'Wenn Apg. 1,12 die Entfernung des Oelbergs von Jerusalem auf einen Sabbatweg, also etwa 1 km, angegeben wird, muß der Gipfel gemeint sein'.

[6] According to Josephus, the distance between Jerusalem and the Mount of Olives was 5 stadia (925 m): *Ant* XX viii,6 (169); cf. also *BJ* V ii,3 (70), where 6 stadia (1110 m) is the

addition 'having a sabbath's day' shows that 'which is near Jerusalem' is not merely a geographical figure and it is certainly more than a detail to give the narrative a Jewish colouring (and so an air of antiquity). Why mention a sabbath if the ascension did not take place on a sabbath?[1] As Lohfink points out, Luke so ties the ascension within the region of Jerusalem: 'Denn ein Sabbatweg ist nach jüdischer Rechtsfiktion ja gerade die Negation jeder echten Ortsveränderung'[2]. Luke thus integrates the ascension once more into his Jerusalem perspective (*supra* 89 n.2).

That the mountain motif is a typical Hellenistic rapture *topos*[3], may be no more than a fortunate coincidence. It is also attested in Jewish rapture traditions[4] and reminds us of the Transfiguration story (Lk 9:28parr.). A more important motif lies in the specific area in which the ascension (apparently!) took place, the Mount of Olives (an inference drawn from the disciples' return from that area). On the basis of Zech 14:4, Jewish sources associate the Mount of Olives with eschatological expectations. According to Zech 14:4, the Mountain of Olives was the place where God would intervene in the eschatological battle with the nations: καὶ στήσονται οἱ πόδες αὐτοῦ ἐν τῇ ἡμέρᾳ ἐκείνῃ ἐπὶ τὸ ὄρος τῶν ἐλαιῶν[5]. The action of the Egyptian impostor referred to by Josephus, *BJ* II xiii,5 (261-263); *Ant* XX viii,6 (169-172) (cf. Acts 21:38), who assembled an army on the Mount of Olives to attack Jerusalem, is to be understood in eschatological terms, as an attempt to bring in the end by force. Later rabbinic sources refer to the Mount of Olives as the place where the righteous dead of Israel will be raised (Bill. 1, 840-842). Jesus' Triumphal Entry began, according to Luke (19:37), in this region. Since Luke

---

distance from Jerusalem of a military camp situated κατὰ τὸ Ἐλαιῶν καλούμενον ὄρος. Jn 11:18 gives 15 stadia (2730 m, Bill. 2, 544: 2957,40 m) as the distance between Jerusalem and Bethany.

[1] That the ascension actually took place on a sabbath was the opinion of Chrysostom, *ActHom* 3,1 (PG 60, 33). Among modern interpreters: H. Laible, 'An welchem Wochentag geschah die Himmelfahrt Christi? Ein Versuch', *AELKZ* 55 (1922) 313; Zahn, 'Die Himmelfahrt Jesu an einem Sabbath', *NKZ* 33 (1922) 535-541 (rejecting his earlier opinion in idem, *Apg* 1, 40-43; E. Preuschen, *Die Apostelgeschichte* (HNT 4/1; Tübingen: J.C.B. Mohr/Paul Siebeck, 1912) 26; Reicke, *Glaube und Leben der Urgemeinde. Bemerkungen zu Apg. 1-7* (AThANT 32; Zürich: Zwingli, 1957) 20; Schmithals, *Apg* 24 (cautiously).

[2] Lohfink, *Himmelfahrt* 207. This interpretation is accepted by Schneider, *Apg* 1, 205 and Hengel, 'Geographie' 160-161.

[3] Lohfink, *Himmelfahrt* 43; Van der Horst, 'Parallels' 23.

[4] E.g. in the biblical Moses tradition (Mount Sinai!) and Josephus' reinterpretation of it in *Ant* IV viii,48 (325-326) (Mount Abaris). Further: 2 Bar 76:3; *LAB* 48:1; cf. TLev 2:5ff.

[5] Ps-Athanasius, *QuaestAntDuc* (PG 28, 685.697) links Zech 14:4 to the ascension!

is familiar with the eschatological significance of the Mount of Olives, it is likely that this resounds in Acts 1:12 as well. The mention of the Mount of Olives thus heightens the eschatological perspective of the ascension.

As in Lk 24:52-53, the episode closes with the disciples' return to Jerusalem and their subsequent activities. Whereas Lk 24:53 closes rather generally with a statement on what the disciples did in that period, Acts 1:13 shifts the focus to a specific occasion, thus closing the episode with a company of disciples waiting for the events to come.

*Vv.21-22* These verses specify the qualifications of a successor to Judas. Vv.21-22 are structured after vv.1-2. We can ignore, for the moment, the many exegetical questions regarding this verse (is ἀπό inclusive or exclusive? is τὸ βάπτισμα 'Ιωάννου a generic description of the public ministry of John or does it refer to the baptism of Jesus performed by John). The important point is that Luke sets a beginning and an end to the public ministry of Jesus, the *terminus ad quem* being 'the day in which he was taken up' (here ἕως is definitely inclusive). The use of ἀνελήμφθη corresponds exactly to Lk 9:51 and Acts 1:2,11[1]. The words 'went in and out' (v.21; cf. 9:28; Jn 10:9) are far too conventional (a LXX-ism) to be taken as *ad litteram* references to the post-Easter appearances[2].

Anticipating our discussion below (chapter six), one could ask whether the ascension is here a *conditio sine qua non* for receiving power, i.e. for reconstituting the Twelve apostles. It is an event which Judas Iscariot has definitely not witnessed. However, it should be noted that it is the entire period from Jesus' baptism to the day of the ascension (including the period of post-Easter instructions!) which qualifies the successor to Judas, not only its finale.

e. *Acts 3:19-21*

If anywhere, Luke's indebtedness to Jewish rapture-preservation traditions comes to the fore in Acts 3:19-21. Luke's emphasis on salvation history and the eschatological question already prepared for by Acts 1:6[3], now receive a more

---

[1] Contra Lohfink, *Himmelfahrt* 220; Parsons, *Departure* 129-134.

[2] Cf. Haenchen, *Apg* 265 Anm.7.

[3] There is a striking correspondence between Acts 1:6 and 3:20. The strongest case for Lukan composition lies with 1:6 (the question + answer technique is a typical Lukan feature), so that 1:6 seems to be composed under the influence of 3:20 rather than *vice versa*. If Luke relies on tradition, this is to be found in Acts 3:20 rather than in 1:6. Lohfink, *Himmelfahrt* 154-157; Dömer, *Heil Gottes* 115-117; Parsons, *Departure* 142 regard vv.6-8 *in toto* as redactional.

elaborate treatment. As in Acts 1:9-11, ascension and parousia are coupled, and, significantly, that which first-century Judaism expected with regard to Elijah is here applied to Jesus.

Acts 3:1-10 is a typical 'miracle story', followed by the second apostolic missionary speech ascribed to Peter (3:12b-26). Peter's temple discourse is firmly connected with the healing incident by an editorial link (vv.11-12a). The discourse itself neatly divides into three parts: an explanation of the healing miracle to avoid a possible misunderstanding on the part of the people (vv.12b-16, containing primitive kerygmatic material in vv.13-15), an exhortation to repentance with the promise of eschatological redemption (vv.17-21), and a 'proof from Scripture' section, in which Jesus is identified as the long-awaited 'prophet like Moses' and the Jewish audience as heirs of the Abrahamic covenant (vv.22-26)[1]. The call to repentance (v.19) is prepared for by the motif of ignorance (v.17) and the motif of divine fulfilment (v.18). The act of repentance will pave the way for the coming of 'times of relief' (καιροὶ ἀναψύξεως) and the sending of the Messiah (v.20), Jesus, who now resides in heaven 'until the time of universal restoration (ἀποκατάστασις πάντων) that God has announced long ago through his holy prophets' (NRSV)[2].

The ascension is referred to in v.21, in what appears as a concessive clause: (Jesus) ὃν δεῖ οὐρανὸν (= acc. subj.) μὲν δέξασθαι κτλ. Strictly speaking, the aorist infinitive δέξασθαι (v.21) represents a punctiliar action in the past, *in concreto* Jesus' heavenly reception on the occasion of Acts 1:9-11[3]. Although δέχομαι (to receive) is not standard rapture terminology[4], the idea of

---

[1] For more detailed analyses of the structure of the speech, see R.F. Zehnle, *Peter's Pentecost Discourse. Tradition and Lukan Reinterpretation in Peter's Speeches of Acts 2 and 3* (SBL.MS 15; Nashville, New York: Abingdon, 1971) 19-43; U. Wilckens, *Die Missionsreden der Apostelgeschichte. Form- und traditionsgeschichtliche Untersuchungen* (WMANT 5; Neukirchen-Vluyn: Neukirchener, 1961, ³1974) 37-44.60-61; A. Barbi, *Il Cristo celeste presente nella Chiesa. Tradizione e Redazione in Atti 3,19-21* (AnBib 64; Roma: IBP, 1979) 98-120.

[2] As Mk 9:12 // Mt 17:11 suggests, πάντων belongs to ἀποκαταστάσεως. Accordingly, the antecedent of the relative pronoun ὧν is χρόνων (ἀποκαταστάσεως πάντων) 'the times of restoration of all things, about which God has spoken ...', not πάντων 'the times of restoration of everything that God has spoken of'. On the theme of eschatological restoration in the OT expectation, see E.L. Dietrich, שבות שוב. *Die endzeitliche Wiederherstellung bei den Propheten* (BZAW 40; Giessen: A. Töpelmann, 1925).

[3] Lygre, *Exaltation* 124-126 denies that this verse contains a specific reference to the ascension for no clear reason.

[4] In LXX δέχομαι frequently renders לקח (see Hatch-Redpath, *s.v.* δέχεσθαι), which is the standard rapture term in Hebrew. But LXX never uses δέχομαι in a rapture context. From classical Greek only some remote parallels can be adduced: Plato, *Theaetetus* 177a;

'welcoming' someone in heaven is not uncommon[1] and simply represents the rapture act from a different perspective. It cannot go unnoticed, however, that the backward reference to the ascension is framed into a larger construction, which is somewhat difficult to disentangle. The entire construction seems to have a wider reference than to the ascension alone: the present tense δεῖ (it is now necessary) together with the temporal clause ἄχρι χρόνων ἀποκαταστάσεως κτλ. expresses a temporary *condition* that will last until '(the) times of restoration'. The best solution seems to be to assume that δέξασθαι carries with it the connotation 'receive *and retain*'[2]. This would explain the curious combination of the present tense δεῖ, the aorist δέξασθαι (a backward reference to the ascension), and the *terminus ad quem* in the future. What is a matter of divine necessity (δεῖ) is not the ascension in and of itself, but the condition which followed the ascension, viz. Jesus' present dwelling in heaven. That Jesus is being kept in heaven until the parousia is now being proclaimed as a divinely-planned state of affairs. Here the problem of the 'delay' of the parousia comes clearly to the surface. The embarrassing interval separating the resurrection from the parousia appears to stand under divine control. It is God's will that Jesus is now in heaven, that is, it is God's will that the parousia has not yet taken place![3]

Though there is no principal objection to understanding Luke's words also in individualistic-spiritualised terms (καιροὶ ἀναψύξεως are experienced every time a person comes to faith)[4], the predominant perspective of Peter's temple discourse is *heilsgeschichtlich*: it is the historical Israel which is called to conversion (v.12 ἄνδρες Ἰσραηλῖται v.25 ὑμεῖς ... οἱ υἱοὶ τῶν προφητῶν καὶ τῆς διαθήκης v.26 ὑμῖν πρῶτον)[5], the blotting out of sins involves first

---

Sophocles, *Trach* 1085.

[1] Stephen prays for the reception of his soul into heaven (Acts 7:59). Cf. also 1 En 70-71.

[2] Cf. Barrett, *Acts* 1, 205 (referring to LSJM 382). He refers to Plato, *Leg* 747e, which, however, has the present participle δεχόμενοι.

[3] Wendt, *Apg* 110 comments: 'Zu dem οὐρ. μὲν steht in nicht ausgesprochenem Gegensatze der Gedanke, dass die Erde den Messias wieder aufnehmen muss, wenn der bezeichnete Zielpunkt für sein Wohnen im Himmel erreicht sein wird'.

[4] For an interpretation along these lines, see W.S. Kurz, 'Acts 3,19-26 as a Test of the Role of Eschatology in Lukan Christology', *SBL.SP* (1977) 310-311. Barrett, 'Faith and Eschatology in Acts 3', in: E. Grässer, O. Merk (Hrsg.), *Glaube und Eschatologie* (FS W.G. Kümmel; Tübingen: J.C.B. Mohr/Paul Siebeck, 1985) 12-13 calls v.20a 'an example of Luke's personalizing, or individualizing eschatology' (but without denial of the corporate or futuristic aspects). Also Ellis, 'La fonction de l'eschatologie dans l'évangile de Luc', in: Neirynck (éd.), *Luc* 303.

[5] Perhaps Luke wrestles with the question of Israel's rejection of the Gospel despite the

and foremost forgiveness of the corporate sin of having rejected and murdered the God-ordained Messiah (vv.13-15, note the emphatic ὑμεῖς)[1], and the Messiah is first and foremost the Messiah appointed for the Jewish people (v.20 τὸν προκεχειρισμένον ὑμῖν χριστὸν)[2].

That vv.19-21 is an exceptional text is already indicated by the fact that the eschatological perspective (vv.20-21) cannot be said to be a constitutive element of the 'apostolic preaching' which underlies the missionary speeches of the Book of Acts[3]. But a number of additional considerations suggest that the verses crucial to our investigation (vv.20-21) poorly fit into the present context[4]:

First of all, in the neatly composed structure of Acts 3:12b-26, vv.20-21 quite unexpectedly resume the christological kerygma, in a manner unparalleled in the other missionary speeches. The train of thought would lose little and gain in clarity if v.19 were immediately followed by v.22, esp. since vv.22-26 motivate the call to repentance (vv.17-19), not the content of vv.20-21. This may indicate that at least in vv.20-21 some foreign material has been inserted[5].

Secondly, in primitive Christology sending-terminology (ἀποστέλλω) usually refers to Jesus' historical mission (v.26!; Q Mt 10:40 // Lk 10:16; Mk 9:37 // Lk 9:48; Jn 3:17,34; 5:36; 10:36; 17:18; 1 Jn 4:9,10,14)[6]. The idea of

---

repeated chances it was given in the early period of the church. It is not clear whether Luke (like Paul) expected a future conversion of the historical Israel or whether he simply reports the historical facts.

[1] Barrett, *Acts* 1, 203.

[2] It has been argued that τὸν προκεχειρισμένον ὑμῖν χριστὸν means 'the Messiah foreordained for you', and that this pictures Jesus as *messias designatus*, not as *messias constitutus* [Robinson, Hahn, and R.H. Fuller, *The Foundations of New Testament Christology* (London: Lutterworth, 1965) 166]. But this already fails on linguistic grounds. Προχειρίζω derives from the adj. πρόχειρος 'to have or to find readily, at hand' [Michaelis, προχειρίζω, *ThWNT* 6 (1959) 863]. The meaning is 'the Messiah appointed for you', and in line with the salvation-historical character of the speech the emphasis is on ὑμῖν, the Jewish people (cf. v.22).

[3] Dupont, 'Les discours de Pierre dans les Actes et le chapitre XXIV de l'évangile de Luc', in: Neirynck (éd.), *Luc* 239-284, esp. 255-258 (in response to C.H. Dodd and B. Gärtner).

[4] For what follows see Bauernfeind, *Apg* 65-66, resumed by Lohfink, 'Christologie und Geschichtsbild in Apg 3,19-21', *BZ* 13 (1969) 224; Wilckens, *Missionsreden* 153-154.

[5] The 'un-Lukan' parts being situated between the call to repentance and conversion, and the forgiveness of sins (which are typically Lukan emphases), and the Lukan formulation v.21b (cf. Lk 1:70).

[6] Barbi, *Cristo* 39; cf. J.D.G. Dunn, *Christology in the Making. An Inquiry into the Origins of the Doctrine of the Incarnation* (London: SCM, 1980, ²1989) 38-46.

Jesus being 'sent' at the parousia is unparalleled in Luke-Acts and in the rest of the NT.

Thirdly, whereas the causal connection (ὅπως ἄν) between repentance and a future sending of the Messiah makes good sense in a pre-Christian (Baptist) or Jewish setting[1], after the historical coming of Jesus this is an exceptional claim to be made by a Christian.

Fourthly, the eschatological termini employed (καιροὶ ἀναψύξεως, χρόνοι ἀποκαταστάσεως) are unique in the NT, and difficult to connect one to another. The absence of the articles seems to suggest that they are more or less standardised terms.

Finally, a reference to the exalted Christ, constitutive for the primitive Christian preaching (Acts 2:32-36; 5:31), is lacking; the perspective is future-oriented.

This raises the question of sources/provenance. We must reckon with a complex process of adaptation, assimilation, and reinterpretation of a diversity of source-material. This complexity is evident from the widely divergent assessments of the matter. Given the popularity of Elijah in Baptist circles, O. Bauernfeind has tried to determine the *Sitz im Leben* of this tradition in Baptist circles[2]. According to J.A.T. Robinson, Acts 3:20-21 reflects a primitive rapture christology, according to which Jesus dwelt in heaven as 'Christ-elect' (*messias designatus*) from the resurrection onwards, only to be installed as the Messiah (*messias constitutus*) at the end of time[3]. F. Hahn argued in a similar vein that Acts 3:20-21a stands counter to the view that Jesus was exalted at the resurrection in that it presents Jesus as becoming Messiah only at the parousia[4]. Others claim that Luke draws from Jewish Elijah expectations and ascribe the

---

[1] References are found in Bill. 1, 162-165; W. Bousset, *Die Religion des Judentums im späthellenistischen Zeitalter* (hrsg. v. H. Gressmann; HNT 21; Tübingen: J.C.B. Mohr/Paul Siebeck, ⁴1966) 248-249.390. Cf. Zehnle, *Pentecost Discourse* 71-74; Barbi, *Cristo* 75-77.

[2] Bauernfeind, *Apg* 67-68.473-483. In addition to the authors cited in Barbi, *Cristo* 11-18, Bauernfeind has been followed by E. Plümacher, *Lukas als hellenistischer Schriftsteller. Studien zur Apostelgeschichte* (StUNT 9; Göttingen: Vandenhoeck & Ruprecht, 1972) 72; Wilson, *Luke and the Pastoral Epistles* (London: SPCK, 1979) 79; Barrett, *Acts* 1, 202.

[3] J.A.T. Robinson, *Jesus and His Coming. The Emergence of a Doctrine* (London: SCM, 1957) 140-159; idem, 'The Most Primitive Christology of All?' (1956); repr. in: idem, *Twelve New Testament Studies* (SBT 34; London: SCM, 1962) 139-153.

[4] F. Hahn, *Christologische Hoheitstitel. Ihre Geschichte im frühen Christentum* (FRLANT 83; Göttingen: Vandenhoeck & Ruprecht, 1963, ²1964) 186. Like Robinson, Hahn claimed that the post-Easter status of Christ was of an intermediate, temporary nature, on the analogy of the OT raptures of Enoch and Elijah, that is, 'als ein vorläufiger und rasch vorübergehender Zustand' (186). See the authors cited in Barbi, *Cristo* 18-25.

present passage to Lukan redaction[1].

For the present we need not go into the tradition vs. redaction debate[2]. Suffice it to say at this point that I tend to regard Lukan redaction as a feasible option. After all, the language is highly Lukan, and Luke would have had direct access to the Elijah traditions preserved in the LXX, the Gospel tradition and current Jewish apocalyptic traditions. But the issue here is how he integrates his material into the whole setting. Our concern is to find the ultimate source of inspiration, so to speak, which provides the proper context of understanding, not its intermediaries.

A. Barbi has studied the correlation between Acts 3:10-21 and Jewish apocalyptic texts[3]. Partly reproducing and partly expanding his thesis, we may note the following points of agreement in the verses under consideration, in addition, of course, to the common rapture-preservation-return pattern:

Firstly, as in the Jewish apocalypses, the duration of the Messiah's preservation in heaven is predetermined, viz. ἄχρι χρόνων ἀποκαταστάσεως πάντων κτλ. With this, compare 2 Bar 13:3; 25:1; 4 Ezra 12:32 ; cf. 2 Bar 76:2; 4 Ezra 14:9; 7:75.

Secondly, that 'times of relief' come ἀπὸ προσώπου τοῦ κυρίου ('from the face of the Lord')[4] is good apocalyptic imagery, according to which the eschatological blessings are preserved in heaven to be given at the end of times (cf. Dan 2:28; Rev 21:2; 4 Ezra 8:52; 12:32; 13:26)[5].

Thirdly, the ἀποκατάστασις[6] πάντων (restoration of all things/of all people?) is the task traditionally ascribed to the returning Elijah (Mal 3:22; Sir 48:10; Mk 9:12; Mt 17:11) and which in the course of time was ascribed to the Messiah[7].

---

[1] See the authors cited in Barbi, *Cristo* 25-33.

[2] In an article particularly addressed to the tradition-history of Acts 3:19-21, Hahn, 'Das Problem alter christologischer Überlieferungen in der Apostelgeschichte unter besonderer Berücksichtigung von Act 3,19-21', in: Kremer (éd.), *Actes* 129-154 (esp. 131-135) submitted some valid criteria for the detection of source material. Here he is much more reserved in his judgements than previously.

[3] For what follows, see Barbi, *Cristo* 45-97, whose observations are complemented by my own.

[4] Ἀπὸ προσώπου (מלפני) τοῦ κυρίου is a Semitism, not a LXX-ism: BDR 217.1a; Bauernfeind, *Apg* 68; Hahn, *Hoheitstitel* 185 and Anm.3; Lohfink, 'Christologie' 232.

[5] Cf. Barbi, *Cristo* 68-72.

[6] As in Lk 9:51 (ἀνάλημψις *pro* ἀναλαμβάνω), Luke will be responsible for replacing the verb form by a noun form.

[7] BerR 12; Bill. 1, 19. Luke omits the discussion about Elijah after the Transfiguration because the subject matter is more appropriate in the present context. The 'restoration of all

Fourthly, according to Mal 3:22 LXX, God would send (ἀποστέλλω) Elijah πρὶν ἐλθεῖν ἡμέραν κυρίου. The exceptional application of sending-terminology to Christ at the parousia is explained by reference to this passage.

Fifthly, the closest parallel to Acts 3:19-21 is found in 4 Ezra 11 (the Eagle Vision), where after the messianic woes the eagle (= Rome) is said to disappear, *ut refrigeret* (v.l. *refrigeretur*) *omnis terra et revertetur liberata de tua vi* (4 Ezra 11:46; ed. Klijn 76; tr. Metzger 549). In Greek this would read: ... ἵνα ἀναψύξαι πᾶσα ἡ γῆ καὶ ἀναζωπυρῆσαι ῥυσθεῖσα ἐκ τῆς βίας σου[1]. This period is followed by another brief, tumultuous period of terror (4 Ezra 12:2-3), so that the 'times of relief' are an *Atempause* preceding the final Messianic deliverance[2]. If there is any significance in the word order ('times of relief ... sending of the Messiah'), the καιροὶ ἀναψύξεως *precede* the sending of the Messiah. In the Malachi passage Elijah's activity is preparatory to the final messianic act (πρὶν ἐλθεῖν ἡμέραν κυρίου). If not, they are probably more or less identical to the χρόνοι ἀποκαταστάσεως, whether this is the age of salvation[3] or the messianic interim (4 Ezra 12:34)[4].

### f. Conclusions

Whatever one may say about traditions and sources of the ascension narratives, the way Luke has positioned the ascension texts at the key points of his two-volume work (at the centre and the close of the first, in the opening chapter of the second book) suggests that the ascension of Jesus is of central significance to Luke. Given the Lukan tendency to pattern his narrative around the principle of symmetry, there can be little doubt that Luke's hand has been heavily at work in Lk 24 and Acts 1. In structuring the narrative symmetrically, Luke has effected a unified composition. Luke uses ἀναλαμβάνομαι (Acts 1:2,11,22) and ἀνάλημψις (Lk 9:51) invariably as a reference to the ascension, which is not surprising when it is recognised that all these instances are redactional (= Lukan compositions).

In the preceding analysis we have found ample confirmation of the

---

things' is a still future event. See W.C. Robinson, *Der Weg des Herrn. Studien zur Geschichte und Eschatologie im Lukas-Evangelium. Ein Gespräch mit Hans Conzelmann* (ThF 36; Hamburg-Bergstedt: Herbert Reich, 1964) 18-19.

[1] Reconstruction of A. Hilgenfeld, quoted from Barbi, *Cristo* 55.

[2] Contra A. Dihle, E. Schweizer, ἀναψύχω, ἀνάψυξις, *ThWNT* 9 (1973) 665-666. A different conception is found in 2 Thess 1:7, where the idea of 'relief' (cf. 2 Bar 73:1 'rest') is expressed with the term ἄνεσις (Vg *requiem*). Here the (eschatological) relief takes place at the parousia. Cf. Acts 14:22. Cf. R. Bultmann, ἀνίημι, ἄνεσις, *ThWNT* 1 (1933) 367-368.

[3] According to mAv 4:17 'times of relief' belong to the age to come (tr. Danby 455).

[4] See the extensive discussion in Barbi, *Cristo* 143-155.

suggestion made in the previous chapter, that the biblical-Jewish rapture-preservation paradigm provides a much more systematic resemblance to the ascension of Jesus than the Graeco-Roman rapture stories. The very first mention of the ascension in Lk 9:51 points in this direction and throughout Luke's project a number of indications has confirmed this notably: the forty days, the rapture terminology, the connection with Pentecost and parousia, etc. It is noteworthy that those features in the finale of the Gospel (Lk 24:50-53) which do not 'fit' the Jewish rapture scheme betray the influence not of the Hellenistic rapture stories but of Sir 50:20-23. This means that the Lukan ascension story remains wholly within the confines of a Jewish-biblical milieu.

A particularly strong influence on the Lukan ascension narratives comes from the Elijah traditions, esp. the link of the ascension with the subsequent outpouring of the Spirit, the emphasis on the visibility of the ascension, and the double function of their (Elijah's and Jesus') ascension: it concludes the presence of the Master and at the same time (by virtue of the subsequent transferral of the Spirit) continues his ministry in the ministry of the successor. If we trace the comparison with Elijah a little further, it appears that in both cases their heavenly assumption is not the end, but inaugurates a period of temporal preservation in heaven with a view to a future eschatological return. It would be an over-simplification to claim that the Elijah story has an exclusive claim upon Luke-Acts. In the time Luke was writing, as we have seen, rapture speculations had evolved into a complex set of ideas.

In Luke-Acts the ascension theme is subordinate to the theme of apostolic witness. Of course, the influence of the Graeco-Roman rapture stories upon Lk 24 and Acts 1 should not be unduly minimalised. Formal, material and linguistic resemblances must have been unavoidable to an author who moves as easily as Luke does within the Hellenistic world, and his Gentile readers could hardly be expected not to associate Jesus' rapture with the rapture narratives of their own traditions. But in comparison with the influence of the Jewish-biblical rapture traditions their role is secondary.

The forty days have a strong associative force. They are not to prepare Jesus for his heavenly ministry, but to convince his disciples of his resurrection and to have them prepared for their future mission. The forty days have their closest parallel in the 40 days of final instructions preceding the assumption of Ezra and Baruch and reflect the rabbinic emphasis on reliable instruction.

Of course it would be premature at this stage of the investigation to draw firm conclusions about the role of the ascension in Lukan christology except for some general comments. The ascension marks the end of the ministry of Jesus and closes the period of the post-Easter appearances; it inaugurates a period in which Jesus is in heaven awaiting his parousia. But Luke not only frames the ascension in the context of the rapture-preservation-parousia (and Pentecost, for that matter); he also does so (as is most clear in Lk 24) in the framework of the resurrection-exaltation. Before we can determine the christological significance of the ascension more accurately, then, we must examine how Luke integrates his 'rapturology' into the totality of the Christ event. In the following chapters we will study the role of the ascension in the light of the resurrection-exaltation and the appearances (chapters four and five); then we will study the ascension in the light of the outpouring of the Spirit and the parousia (chapter six).

Table 1. *The Macro-Structure of Lk 24:36-53 and Acts 1:1-14*

I The Appearance of the Risen Lord (Lk 24:36-43; Acts 1:3-4)

| | |
|---|---|
| A. Appearance of the Risen Lord | (Lk 24:36) |
| B. Proofs of the Resurrection | (Lk 24:36-39,40-43) |
| C. Mealtime Setting | (Lk 24:40-43) |
| A'. Appearance of the Risen Lord | (Acts 1:3) |
| B'. Proofs of the Resurrection | (Acts 1:3) |
| C'. Mealtime Setting | (Acts 1:4) |

II The Final Instructions of the Risen Lord (Lk 24:44-49; Acts 1:3-9)

| | |
|---|---|
| A. Fulfilment Theme | (Lk 24:44-46) |
| B. Reference to Passion and Resurrection | (Lk 24:46) |
| C. Universal Mission Starting from Jerusalem | (Lk 24:47) |
| D. Motif of Witness | (Lk 24:48) |
| E. Promise of the Spirit | (Lk 24:49a) |
| F. Command to Stay in Jerusalem | (Lk 24:49b) |
| G. Empowerment with the Spirit | (Lk 24:49c) |
| B'. Reference to Passion and Resurrection | (Acts 1:3) |
| E'. Promise of the Spirit | (Acts 1:4) |
| F'. Command to Stay in Jerusalem | (Acts 1:4) |
| A'. Fulfilment Theme | (Acts 1:5) |
| C'. Universal Mission Starting from Jerusalem | (Acts 1:8) |
| D'. Motif of Witness | (Acts 1:8) |
| G'. Empowerment with the Spirit | (Acts 1:8) |

III The Departure of the Risen Lord (Lk 24:50-53; Acts 1:9-14)

| | |
|---|---|
| A. Localisation of the Event | (Lk 24:50) |
| B. Action of Jesus | (Lk 24:50) |
| C. Departure of Jesus | (Lk 24:51) |
| D. Description of the Ascension | (Lk 24:51) |
| E. The Disciples' Return to Jerusalem | (Lk 24:52) |
| F. Localisation | (Lk 24:53) |
| G. Communal Life of Worship and Prayer | (Lk 24:53) |
| B'. Action of Jesus | (Acts 1:9) |
| C'. Departure of Jesus | (Acts 1:9) |
| D'. Description of the Ascension | (Acts 1:10-11) |
| A'. Localisation of the Event | (Acts 1:12) |
| E'. The Disciples' Return to Jerusalem | (Acts 1:12) |
| F'. Localisation | (Acts 1:13) |
| G'. Communal Life of Worship and Prayer | (Acts 1:14) |

# CHAPTER FOUR

# RESURRECTION, EXALTATION AND ASCENSION
# IN EARLY CHRISTIANITY

a. *Introduction*

For Luke, the resurrection, the ascension, the outpouring of the Spirit, and the parousia are events which, though clearly separated from one another in time, together constitute a series of decisive landmarks in the unfolding of salvation history (*Heilsgeschichte*)[1].

In order to assess the function of the ascension in the theology of Luke more precisely, it is necessary to examine how the ascension ties in with these other events. The forty-day interval separating the ascension from the resurrection creates not only a chronological problem vis-à-vis the chronology of the Gospel (*supra* 89-92), but also a theological or christological problem in view of the question when—in Luke's perception—Jesus was exalted at the right hand of God. If 'exaltation' is taken in its literal sense (*exaltare* 'to lift up, to raise on high'), it is hardly justifiable *not* to speak of the ascension of Jesus as an event of exaltation.

In the two passages, however, where at least a passing reference to the exaltation would seem to be appropriate (Lk 24:50-53; Acts 1:1-11), Luke does not refer with a single word to the biblical exaltation text *par excellence*, Ps 110:1 (109:1 LXX), as he does in Acts 2:33ff. and as the author of Mk 16:19 and patristic writers do (*infra* 131-133). Nor does he allude to Dan 7:13-14, the other popular Jewish exaltation text that would contain all the necessary ingredients for a dramatic picturing of an ascension-exaltation event [so e.g. Lactantius, *Inst* IV 21,1 (PL 6, 516); *Epit* 47 (PL 6, 1055)]. Ps 68:19 (67:19 LXX) describes in an anthropomorphic manner a triumphal ascent of YHWH (to Mount Zion?), but despite the apparent suitability of the psalm in an ascension context it is notably absent in Luke's ascension story, in contrast with Eph 4:8-10 and patristic writers again [so e.g. Justin, *Dial* 39 (PG 6, 560);

---

[1] A *Forschungsbericht* on Luke's concept of salvation history is found in F. Bovon, *Luc le théologien. Vingt-cinq ans de recherches (1950-1975)* (MoBi; Neuchatel, Paris: Delachaux & Niestlé, 1978) 11-84. See also J.A. Fitzmyer, *The Gospel According to Luke I-IX. Introduction, Translation, and Notes* (AncB 28; Garden City, NY: Doubleday, 1981) 18-22.179-192.

*Dial* 87 (PG 6, 684); Irenaeus, *AdvHaer* II 20,3 (PG 7, 778; SC 294, 204); Tertullian, *AdvMarc* 5,8 (PL 2, 489)]. Luke also fails to make any reference, however brief, to the glory (δόξα) of God[1] or to report Christ's accession to a heavenly throne[2]. The intercepting cloud, moreover, an otherwise apt means to impress upon people a sense of divine presence, in fact prevents the disciples from seeing what some of them had seen on an earlier occasion (the spectacular disclosure of Christ's future heavenly glory at the Mount of Transfiguration, Lk 9:28-36) or from what Stephen was to experience later: an immediate view into the glorious abode of God, where Jesus (the Son of Man) was standing at God's right hand (Acts 7:55-56)[3].

If Luke has incorporated the ascension story to dramatise the heavenly enthronement of Jesus as Lord (Κύριος), a visualisation of the Messiah's exaltation to his throne in heaven, why this silence? Why is Luke's picture so restrained in comparison with other traditions? Why, to pose a further critical question, should Luke postpone the exaltation for forty days, whereas the early apostolic preaching is quite unanimous in regarding resurrection and exaltation as one event, a single continuous movement from grave to glory, an event, so it seems, occurring on the day of the resurrection and not disrupted by a quasi-earthbound state in which Jesus was risen but not yet exalted? And if we are right in asserting that Luke consciously patterns the ascension story on Jewish

---

[1] A conception recurring with some prominence in the *Sondergut* of Luke(-Acts) (MGM 224-225; of the 13 instances only two, Lk 9:26; 21:27, have synoptic parallels). Note that 1 Tim 3:16 has ἀνελήμφθη ἐν δόξῃ!

[2] From the time of Justin, Ps 24 (23 LXX) was used to interpret the ascension of Jesus: Justin, *Apol* 1,51 (PG 6, 404); *Dial* 36 (PG 6, 553-556); *Dial* 85 (PG 6, 676); Irenaeus, *AdvHaer* IV 33,13 (PG 7, 1081-1082; SC 100, 838); *Dem* 84 (PO 12, 719-720); Hippolytus, *In Psalmum XXIII* (according to Theodoret) (PG 10, 609); Tertullian, *AdvMarc* 5,17 (PL 2, 513); *Scorp* 10 (PL 2, 142). In ApcPe 17 (Eth), the transfiguration is portrayed in terms of the ascension, and Ps 24 is adduced (NTApo 2, 483). Further patristic references to Ps 24 are found in J.G. Davies, *He Ascended into Heaven. A Study in the History of Doctrine* (BaL 1958; London: Lutterworth, 1958) index 210 *ad loc.*; see further E. Kähler, *Studien zum Te Deum und zur Geschichte des 24. Psalms in der Alten Kirche* (VEGL 10; Göttingen: Vandenhoeck & Ruprecht, 1958). A brief discussion of the patristic exegesis of Ps 47:6 (46:6 LXX) as a prophecy to the ascension of Christ is found in C.A. Evans, 'Ascending and Descending With a Shout. Psalm 47.6 and 1 Thessalonians 4.16', in: C.A. Evans, J.A. Sanders (eds.), *Paul and the Scriptures of Israel* (JSNT.S 83; Studies in Scripture in Early Judaism and Christianity 1; Sheffield: Academic, 1993) 242-246.

[3] Note the difference between the ascension, Stephen's vision, and the Transfiguration:
Acts 1:10 ὡς ἀτενίζοντες ἦσαν εἰς τὸν οὐρανὸν [                                    ]
Acts 7:32      ἀτενίσας      εἰς τὸν οὐρανὸν εἶδεν      δόξαν θεοῦ κτλ.
Lk 9:32                                          εἶδεν τὴν δόξαν αὐτοῦ.

rapture-preservation traditions and in so doing gives it a thoroughly eschatological twist, should we perhaps not move a step further and define the meaning and function of the ascension in relation to the parousia (*in concreto*, in the context of the problem of the delay of the parousia) and *not* in relation to the resurrection kerygma? After all, from the perspective of *Religionsgeschichte* resurrection and rapture are mutually exclusive conceptualisations (*supra* 34-35), whereas in early Jewish thinking there is an intrinsic connection of rapture (*Entrückung*) to 'parousia' (= eschatological return) (*supra* chapter two).

Questions such as these justify a critical reappraisal of the theory that Luke 'historicises' the primitive exaltation kerygma and/or (to put it in more traditional words) regards the ascension 'on the fortieth day' as the occasion on which Jesus was exalted to the right hand of God. In this and the subsequent chapter we will analyse the NT resurrection-exaltation-ascension complex, with the question in mind where the exaltation of Jesus is 'located' so to speak (that is, when the heavenly reign of Christ at the right hand of God began). To assess whether or not Luke misunderstands or distorts the early apostolic resurrection-exaltation kerygma, it is necessary to explore the boundaries of early Christian resurrection and exaltation language to see whether such language connotes the notion of an ascension to heaven, and if so, what form-critical categories are put into service (§ b). An important issue to be resolved in the course of our analysis is the nature of the post-Easter appearances, those in Luke-Acts in particular. Are they appearances 'from heaven' (implying a previous ascent of Jesus thither) or do they depict Jesus in some preliminary or 'intermediate' mode of existence?[1] Because of their particular relevance to the ascension and exaltation theme a separate treatment will be given to Mk 16:9-20 (§ c) and the Fourth Gospel (§ d). To gain a general appreciation of the variety of ascension language in the NT as applied to Jesus we will turn to the other texts in the NT where ascension language is employed (§ e). By then we will have a sufficiently broad understanding of the first-century context of thought to turn to Luke-Acts and place Luke's exaltation and ascension texts in their historical and theological context (chapters five and six).

## b. *The Resurrection-Exaltation Paradigm*
There seems to be a wide measure of agreement in contemporary NT scholarship that the proclamation of Jesus' resurrection from the dead is one of

---

[1] This is e.g. the opinion of G. Lohfink, *Die Himmelfahrt Jesu. Untersuchungen zu den Himmelfahrts- und Erhöhungstexten bei Lukas* (StANT 26; München: Kösel, 1971) 274.

the earliest christological affirmations made by the post-Easter community[1]. 'Am Anfang der Verkündigung der Urgemeinde', says H. Conzelmann, voicing the current *opinio communis*, 'stand die Aussage, daß Gott den gekreuzigten Jesus nicht im Tode gelassen, sondern von den Toten auferweckt hat'[2].

From the dawn of Christianity, however, the significance of the Easter event has been understood in a variety of ways. 1 Cor 15:3ff., e.g., which is the earliest literary witness to the resurrection and post-Easter appearances, is illustrative of what we may call a biblical-*heilsgeschichtliche* or soteriological understanding of Easter. Paul reminds his Corinthian converts here of the resurrection gospel he had preached to them on his first visit to the city and which he himself in turn (at his conversion in the early or mid-30s?) had received from tradition (παρέδωκα ... ὃ καὶ παρέλαβον), namely 'that Christ died for our sins in accordance with the scriptures, and that he was buried, and that he was raised on the third day in accordance with the scriptures, and that he appeared to Cephas ...' (NRSV). The core of this pre-Pauline piece of παράδοσις reaches back at least as far as the earliest Greek-speaking community, possibly that in Palestine[3]. Unfortunately, there is no consensus of opinion on whether the interpretative statements ὑπὲρ τῶν ἁμαρτιῶν ἡμῶν and κατὰ τὰς γραφάς belong to the pre-Pauline stratum of tradition, but a good case can be made in favour of it[4]. It, at any rate, very well illustrates how the early church (Paul and possibly his predecessors) was dissatisfied with the transmission of the *nuda facta* but felt compelled to *interpret* the Easter events: death and resurrection are fulfilments of Scripture, Jesus died ὑπὲρ τῶν ἁμαρτιῶν ἡμῶν and κατὰ τὰς γραφάς (v.3) and he was raised on the third

[1] Useful bibliographies on the resurrection of Jesus are found in B.M. Metzger, *Index to Periodical Literature on Christ and the Gospels* (NTTS 6; Leiden: E.J. Brill, 1966) 36-40.480-486; E. Dhanis (éd.), *Resurrexit. Actes du Symposium International sur la Résurrection de Jésus. Roma 1970* (Roma: Libreria editrice vaticana, 1974) 651-745 (bibliography by É. Ghiberti); P. Hoffmann, 'Auferstehung Jesu Christi', *TRE* 4 (1979) 509-513; R. Bultmann, *Theologie des Neuen Testaments* (hrsg. v. O. Merk; UTB.W 630; Tübingen: J.C.B. Mohr/Paul Siebeck, 1948, ⁹1984) 653-655; J. Nolland, *Luke 18:35-24:53* (WBC 35C; Dallas, TX: Word, 1993) 1168-1176.

[2] H. Conzelmann, *Grundriß der Theologie des Neuen Testaments* (bearbeitet v. A. Lindemann; UTB.W 1446; Tübingen: J.C.B. Mohr/Paul Siebeck, 1967, ⁵1993) 46. Cf. R.H. Fuller, *The Formation of the Resurrection Narratives* (Philadelphia: Fortress, 1971, ²1980) 48: 'The resurrection of Jesus from the dead was the central claim of the church's proclamation. There was no period when this was not so'.

[3] Cf. Fuller, *Formation* 10-11; L. Goppelt, *Theologie des Neuen Testaments* (hrsg. v. J. Roloff; UTB 850; Göttingen: Vandenhoeck & Ruprecht, 1976, ³1978) 280-282.

[4] J. Jeremias, *Die Abendmahlsworte Jesu* (Göttingen: Vandenhoeck & Ruprecht, 1935, ⁴1967) 95-99; Goppelt, *Theologie* 281-282.

day κατὰ τὰς γραφάς (v.4; cf. Acts 17:3)[1]. Similarly, in Rom 4:25 Paul states that Jesus was raised (ἠγέρθη) διὰ τὴν δικαίωσιν ἡμῶν (cf. also 2 Cor 5:15).

Alongside this particular understanding of Easter we find in first-century Christian literature evidence of an 'eschatological' interpretation, which, in conformity with the hopes and expectations of Second Temple Judaism[2], regards Jesus' resurrection as a prelude or an anticipation ('the firstfruits') of the general resurrection in the end-time (Acts 4:2; 26:23; 1 Cor 15:20,23; Col 1:18; Rev 1:5; 1 Clem 24:1; cf. Mt 27:52-53)[3].

Even in what are generally held to be the oldest recoverable articulations of resurrection faith[4], namely kerygmatic formulae in the style of (θεὸς) ὁ ἐγείρας αὐτὸν / Ἰησοῦν ἐκ νεκρῶν (Rom 4:24; 8:11 (2x); 2 Cor 4:14; Gal 1:1; Col 2:12; Polyc 2:1; 12:2; cf. also Acts 13:33; 17:31; Heb 13:20; IgnSm 7:1; IgnTrall 9:2) and (ὅτι) ὁ θεὸς αὐτὸν ἤγειρεν ἐκ νεκρῶν (Rom 10:9; 1 Cor 6:14; 15:15; cf. 1 Thess 1:10; Acts 3:15; 4:10; 13:37; Polyc 1:2; cf. also Acts 2:32; 13:34), the interpretative element is not absent. The seemingly neutral affirmation that 'this Jesus God raised up (from the dead)' (Acts 2:32) proclaims the Easter event as a divine intervention in support of Jesus, an act of vindication by Heaven itself, whereby the historical mission of Jesus receives the highest possible authorisation.

The interpretative category most pertinent to the present investigation is the understanding of Easter in terms of an exaltation or instalment into an office[5].

---

[1] On 1 Cor 15:1-8 see further G.D. Fee, *The First Epistle to the Corinthians* (NICNT; Grand Rapids: Eerdmans, 1987) 717-734 (literature!), G. Lüdemann, *Die Auferstehung Jesu. Historie, Erfahrung, Theologie* (Göttingen: Vandenhoeck & Ruprecht, 1994) 50-141.

[2] On the Jewish first-century context of meaning of resurrection belief see *inter alios* G.W.E. Nickelsburg, *Resurrection, Immortality, and Eternal Life in Intertestamental Judaism* (HThS 26; Cambridge: Harvard University Press; London: OUP, 1972); *HJP* 2, 539-544 (literature n.90); H.C.C. Cavallin, *Life After Death. Paul's Argument for the Resurrection of the Dead in 1 Cor 15. Part 1: An Enquiry into the Jewish Background* (CNT 7; Lund: C.W.K. Gleerup, 1974) (literature 217-243); F. Festorazzi, 'Speranza e risurrezione nell'Antico Testamento', in: Dhanis (éd.), *Resurrexit* 5-30; G. Stemberger, 'Auferstehung der Toten I/2. Judentum', *TRE* 4 (1979) 443-450 (literature 449-450).

[3] On the tradition-history of this 'eschatological' interpretation of Jesus' resurrection, see J. Holleman, *Resurrection and Parousia. A Traditio-Historical Study of Paul's Eschatology in 1 Corinthians 15* (NT.S 84; Leiden, New York, Köln: E.J. Brill, 1996), who traces this idea back to Paul.

[4] Bultmann, *Theologie* 83-84; G. Kegel, *Auferstehung Jesu—Auferstehung der Toten. Eine traditionsgeschichtliche Untersuchung zum Neuen Testament* (Gütersloh: G. Mohn, 1970) 12-25; Hoffmann, 'Auferstehung' 479; Conzelmann, *Grundriß* 46-55.

[5] Cf. J.H. Hayes, 'The Resurrection as Enthronement and the Earliest Church Christology', *Interp.* 22 (1968) 333-345. The definition of the term 'exaltation (kerygma)' is discussed by

According to Acts 17:31 the resurrection of Jesus is proof of his divine appointment as end-time judge (cf. also 10:42). In the pre-Pauline[1] formula adopted in Rom 1:3-4 Jesus is said to be appointed 'Son of God in power' ἐξ ἀναστάσεως νεκρῶν, that is, 'as from (his) resurrection from (the) dead'[2]. Similarly, in Paul's missionary speech at Pisidian Antioch the resurrection of Jesus is considered as resurrection-to-Sonship, an affirmation which is supported by a messianic reading of Ps 2:7 LXX (Acts 13:33; cf. Heb 1:5; 5:5) (see further *infra* 158-159). In the pre-Pauline piece of tradition preserved in Phil 2:9-11 Jesus' post-death condition is described in terms of a divine act of 'super-exaltation', on which occasion Jesus was given 'the name above all names' (i.e. Κύριος / יהוה)[3], cf. Heb 1:4. In the tradition preserved in Acts 2:36, a text to which we will return later, the resurrection seems to mark the

---

F. Hahn, *Christologische Hoheitstitel. Ihre Geschichte im frühen Christentum* (FRLANT 83; Göttingen: Vandenhoeck & Ruprecht, 1963, ²1964) 126 ('die auf Grund eines Inthronisationsaktes verliehene besondere Würde und die Einsetzung in eine Machtstellung'); Ph. Vielhauer, 'Ein Weg zur neutestamentlichen Christologie? Prüfung der Thesen Ferdinand Hahns', in: idem, *Aufsätze zum Neuen Testament* (TB 31; München: Chr. Kaiser, 1965) 167-175. Lohfink, *Himmelfahrt* seems to press the point when he defines the exaltation kerygma in terms of '... 'Unsichtbarkeit' und innere Einheit mit der Auferstehung ... den Gegensatz zur lukanischen Konzeption' (98 Anm.53; cf. 81).

[1] See Fitzmyer, *Romans. A New Translation with Introduction and Commentary* (AncB 33; New York, NY: Doubleday, 1993) 229-230 (literature 239-242).

[2] The confession-like character of the phrase satisfactorily accounts for the terse formulation (the absence of articles, pronouns, and of the preposition ἐκ, for which we may have here a simple *genitivus separationis*). By the time Paul came to write Romans the reference to the resurrection of Jesus would be sufficiently clear. Note furthermore the high rate of the anarthrous usage in the immediate context (vv.1-7). See further Holleman, *Resurrection* 133-134. Perhaps on the pre-Pauline level the reference was to the general resurrection [J.D.G. Dunn, *Romans 1-8* (WBC 38A; Dallas, TX: Word, 1988) 15-16], but we cannot be sure.

[3] O. Cullmann, *Die Christologie des Neuen Testaments* (Tübingen: J.C.B. Mohr/Paul Siebeck, 1957, ⁴1966) 184-186; R.P. Martin, *Carmen Christi. Philippians ii. 5-11 in Recent Interpretation and in the Setting of Early Christian Worship* (MSSNTS 4; Cambridge: CUP, 1967) 235-247; L.W. Hurtado, *One God, One Lord. Early Christian Devotion and Ancient Jewish Monotheism* (London: SCM, 1988) 96-97 (*Yahweh*); M. Hengel, 'Setze dich zu meiner Rechten! Die Inthronisation Christi zur Rechten Gottes und Psalm 110,1', in: M. Philonenko (éd.), *Le Trône de Dieu* (WUNT 69; Tübingen: J.C.B. Mohr/Paul Siebeck, 1993) 137-138. Although there is no explicit reference to the resurrection, it is commonly agreed that this is what Paul (if not the original hymn) has in mind or what is implied, contra D. Georgi, 'Der vorpaulinische Hymnus Phil 2,6-11', in: E. Dinkler (Hrsg.), *Zeit und Geschichte. Dankesgabe an R. Bultmann zum 80. Geburtstag* (Tübingen: J.C.B. Mohr/Paul Siebeck, 1964) 274.292-293, who interprets the exaltation in terms of an *Entrückung*.

occasion on which Jesus was made (ἐποίησεν) both Christ and Lord (*infra* 156-157). In all these texts Jesus is introduced into a new stage of existence, in which he receives a higher status than he had enjoyed before, by virtue of his resurrection from the dead.

In first-century Palestinian Judaism, exaltation and throne imagery had become a popular device to glorify prominent figures of Israel's history. Many speculations were built on the plurality of thrones in Dan 7:9 (cf. Ps 122:5). See e.g. TAb A 11:4-18 (Adam); 1 En 45:3; 51:3; 55:4; 61:8; 69:27-29 (the Elect One); 11QMelch (Melchizedek); TJob 33:2-3 (Job); TBenj 10:6 (Enoch, Seth, Abraham, Isaac, Jacob); cf. bSan 38b. Such speculations were usually attributed to historical figures of the *distant* past or future. It is difficult to establish to what degree the language was taken literally. In the majority of cases it did not convey the notion of a bodily ascent (rapture), only the souls were transported to heaven (most of these exalted figures had died a natural death in the biblical tradition). Here we touch upon an important methodological issue. To what extent should exaltation and throne imagery be taken into consideration to elucidate the 'rapture' of Jesus? As we determined in chapter two, rapture does not automatically entail the idea of exaltation or enthronement. The problem is, I believe, on the exaltation side. Whereas 'rapture' (*Entrückung*) represents a relatively well-defined conceptualisation (to the exclusion of others), exaltation imagery has a wider range of connotation and is much more elusive[1]. Its semantic field reaches from a literal 'lifting up' of something (e.g. the serpent in the desert, Jn 3:14a) to a more figurative use as in the liturgical phrase 'to exalt God' (i.e. to praise Him) or 'to exalt someone to a position of honour' (as e.g. Ahasuerus' exaltation of Haman, Est 3:1 LXX). The important point is that exaltation language does not always have to be taken with strict literalness, i.e. a person exalted *by* God (to a higher rank) need not necessarily be exalted *to* God (in heaven).

As we know from the Book of Acts and other sources, the Book of Psalms (2:7; 16:8-11; 68:19; 110:1; 118:16,22 etc.) provided a rich arsenal of prooftexts for the resurrection and exaltation of Jesus[2]. It appears that the early Christian community most frequently resorted to Ps 110:1 (109:1 LXX), which speaks of an act of enthronement or exaltation of a person addressed as κύριος[3]. What originally applied to the enthronement act of an Eastern monarch[4], now became

---

[1] LSJM 1910; Bauer 1695-1696; G. Bertram, 'Der religionsgeschichtliche Hintergrund des Begriffs der 'Erhöhung' in der Septuaginta', *ZAW* 68 (1956) 57-71; idem, 'Erhöhung', *RAC* 6 (1966) 22-43; idem, ὕψος, ὑψόω, κτλ., *ThWNT* 8 (1969) 600-619.

[2] For a general assessment see J. Dupont, 'L'interprétation des Psaumes dans les Actes des Apôtres' (1962); repr. in: idem, *Études sur les actes des Apôtres* (LeDiv 45; Paris: Cerf, 1967) 283-307.

[3] As has often been noted, the frequent appeal to the Psalm in the NT (see the list of *loci citati vel allegati* in NA[27], 787) stands in marked contrast to its messianic use in contemporary Judaism. Bill. 4/1, 452-465 suspects a deliberate suppression from the part of the Jews.

[4] For the original *Sitz im Leben* of Ps 110, see H.J. Kraus, *Psalmen* 2 (BK 15; Neukirchen-

the stock-language to articulate what had happened to Jesus: the crucified Jesus had been exalted by God. From now on he was in a position of authority next to God[1].

Although the exaltation imagery of Ps 110 easily lends itself to a symbolic-figurative explanation in terms of divine appointment to a position of honour and dignity without the notion of an ascent to heaven—after all, Ps 110 was addressed to an earthly king at his accession to an earthly throne!—it seems that from the very beginning of christological reflection the belief that Jesus was 'exalted at the right hand of God' has had an overtly spatial overtone, implying a geographical transfer from earth to heaven (that is, exaltation *at* the right hand of God carried with it the thought of exaltation *to* the right hand of God)[2]. Accordingly, in several NT texts the session symbolism of Ps 110:1 is used as an expression of belief in the present exalted status (*Erhöhtsein*) of Jesus in heaven. Thus Rom 8:34 says: 'It is Christ Jesus, who died, yes, who was raised, who is at the right hand of God [ὃς καί ἐστιν ἐν δεξιᾷ τοῦ θεοῦ], who indeed intercedes for us' (NRSV)[3]. The relative remoteness from the original wording of the psalm suggests that Paul uses an expression that had already become stereotyped among Christians of this era. In Col 3:1 the believers are summoned to seek the things above (τὰ ἄνω), where the risen Christ is ἐν δεξιᾷ τοῦ θεοῦ καθήμενος. In Acts 7:55-56 Stephen sees Jesus

---

Vluyn: Neukirchener, 1961, [5]1978) 925-938; D.M. Hay, *Glory at the Right Hand. Psalm 110 in Early Christianity* (SBL.MS 18; Nashville, New York: Abingdon, 1973) 19-33 (including rabbinics); Hengel, 'Setze dich' 153-158.

[1] On the use of Ps 110 in the NT, see in addition to the classic studies of Hay, *Glory*, and M. Gourgues, *A la droite de Dieu. Résurrection de Jésus et actualisation du psaume 110:1 dans le Nouveau Testament* (EtB; Paris: Librairie Lecoffre, J. Gabalda, 1978) (literature 11-30), also: G. Dautzenberg, 'Psalm 110 im Neuen Testament', in: H. Becker, R. Kaczynski (Hrsg.), *Liturgie und Dichtung. Ein interdisziplinäres Kompendium 1. Historische Präsentation* (PiLi 1; St. Ottilien: EOS, 1983) 141-171; Hengel, 'Psalm 110 und die Erhöhung des Auferstandenen zur Rechten Gottes', in: C. Breytenbach, H. Paulsen (unter Mitwirkung von C. Gerber) (Hrsg.), *Anfänge der Christologie. FS F. Hahn zum 65. Geburtstag* (Göttingen: Vandenhoeck & Ruprecht, 1991) 43-73; idem, 'Setze dich' 108-194.

[2] Cf. O. Linton, 'The Trial of Jesus and the Interpretation of Ps cx', *NTS* 7 (1960/61) 260-261; Hahn, *Hoheitstitel* 126; B. Lindars, *Jesus Son of Man. A Fresh Examination of the Son of Man Sayings in the Gospels in the Light of Recent Research* (London: SPCK, 1983) 110; Hengel, 'Setze dich' 112-119. Contra J.A.T. Robinson, *Jesus and His Coming. The Emergence of a Doctrine* (London: SCM, 1957) 44-45.

[3] On the interrelation of the four clauses, see the varying assessments by Lohfink, *Himmelfahrt* 84-85, and C.E.B. Cranfield, *The Epistle to the Romans 1. Introduction and Commentary on Romans I-VIII* (ICC; Edinburgh: T.&T. Clark, 1975) 438-439. Lohfink's interpretation is based on a weak text-critical basis (omitting the first καί with NA[25]).

(the Son of Man) ἑστῶτα¹ ἐκ δεξιῶν τοῦ θεοῦ². The point of these confession-like formulae is that the risen Christ is now in an exalted position in heaven, ἐκ δεξιῶν (*sc.* μερῶν) or ἐν δεξιᾷ (*sc.* χειρί)³ τοῦ θεοῦ, that is, in the position of a heavenly being in the closest possible proximity to God, next in honour to Him, and hence perfectly able to intercede on behalf of his own⁴. Although these texts do not mention an ascension as a distinct event, but immediately proceed from the resurrection event to Christ's heavenly position at God's right hand, it is clear that some sort of upward journey is presupposed that accounts for the transition from earth to heaven.

In Eph 1:20-21 the session part of the psalm is exploited more emphatically with reference to an act of heavenly enthronement (*Erhöhtwerden*) subsequent to the resurrection: '... (the power) ἣν (God) ἐνήργησεν ἐν τῷ Χριστῷ ἐγείρας αὐτὸν ἐκ νεκρῶν καὶ καθίσας ἐν δεξιᾷ αὐτοῦ ἐν τοῖς ἐπουρανίοις ...' (cf. 2:6). Again, an explicit reference to an ascension is absent (the action seems to occur *in* heaven, the focus is on Christ's *position* ὑπεράνω πάσης ἀρχῆς καὶ ἐξουσίας κτλ.), but is nevertheless understood (4:9).

The important point is that, in the primitive preaching, resurrection and exaltation belong together as two sides of one coin (hence the designation 'resurrection-exaltation') and that it implies a geographical transfer from earth to heaven (hence it is possible to say that in the primitive kerygma resurrection is 'resurrection to heaven')⁵. This explains e.g. the apparent jump in the train of

---

¹ Why Jesus is here portrayed in a standing position (ἑστῶτα) is immaterial to our purpose (see the commentaries *ad loc.*). The point is that he is *in heaven*.

² See also Jesus' confession before the Sanhedrin where he anticipated a time when his opponents would see τὸν υἱὸν τοῦ ἀνθρώπου ἐκ δεξιῶν καθήμενον τῆς δυνάμεως κτλ. (Mk 14:62). Cf. Rev 14:14.

³ O. Michel, *Der Brief an die Hebräer* (KEK¹²; Göttingen: Vandenhoeck & Ruprecht, 1936, ⁶1966) 104-105, and Hengel, 'Setze dich' 125-126, suggest that ἐν δεξιᾷ is a translation variant of the more common ἐκ δεξιῶν from the Hebrew text of Ps 110:1, independent from LXX.

⁴ See Hengel, 'Setze dich', *passim*.

⁵ Cf. the judgement of Lohfink, *Himmelfahrt* 97: 'Auferweckung und Erhöhung meinen im Urchristentum dasselbe Ereignis. Die Auferweckung formuliert dieses Ereignis jedoch im Hinblick auf seinen terminus a quo, die Erhöhung im Hinblick auf seinen terminus ad quem'. Likewise Bultmann, *Theologie* 47-48.84; Goppelt, *Theologie* 285-287. Cf. also K. Berger, *Die Auferstehung des Propheten und die Erhöhung des Menschensohnes* (StUNT 13; Göttingen: Vandenhoeck & Ruprecht, 1976) 207, who speaks of 'Auferstehung in den Himmel hinein'. Further qualification of the relationship resurrection-exaltation would lead us into a tradition-historical debate which is of little relevance to the present investigation. Is 'exaltation' an interpretation of the resurrection event or is 'resurrection' simply a narrative expression of belief in Jesus' exaltation? Or were they at some early stage in the tradition

thought in 1 Thess 1:10, where the expected coming of Christ from heaven is connected with his resurrection from the dead, without an explicit statement on how he came to be in heaven[1].

Considering the close affinity between resurrection and exaltation at the right hand, it should occasion no surprise to find texts where the resurrection-exaltation complex is interpreted *expressis verbis* in terms of a literal going up to heaven, that is, in terms of an ascension in the full sense of the word. This is clearly articulated in 1 Pet 3:21-22, where baptism is said to be efficacious 'through the resurrection of Jesus Christ, ὅς ἐστιν ἐν δεξιᾷ [τοῦ] θεοῦ' (an echo of Rom 8:34!), a statement that is immediately followed by πορευθεὶς εἰς οὐρανὸν κτλ., so that we have here the logical sequence: resurrection-ascension-exaltation (*sessio ad dexteram*). After his resurrection from the dead Christ went to heaven and took his place at the right hand of God. It should be noted that the ascension part receives a relatively elaborate treatment of its own, as a victorious journey to heaven during which Christ (as subject!) overpowers the angelic forces (ὑποταγέντων αὐτῷ ἀγγέλων καὶ ἐξουσιῶν καὶ δυνάμεων). This complex of ideas is usually labelled as a 'cosmic christology', which emphasises the universality of Christ's victory over the natural and spiritual order (cf. Eph 1:21; Col 1:15-20; 2:10,15; Phil 2:9-10). Form-critically, this passage belongs to the heavenly journey type of ascension[2].

Ascension and exaltation (session) language take a prominent place in the Epistle to the Hebrews[3]. Throughout the epistle the session at the right hand

---

perhaps more or less competing interpretations of the Easter event? See J. Lambrecht, 'De oudste Christologie. Verrijzenis of verhoging?', *Bijdr.* 36 (1975) 118-144; Dupont, 'Assis à la droite de Dieu. L'interprétation du Ps 110,1 dans le Nouveau Testament' (1974); repr. in: idem, *Nouvelles Études sur les Actes des Apôtres* (LeDiv 118; Paris: Cerf, 1984) 211-216.

[1] More examples are found in Fitzmyer, 'The Ascension of Christ and Pentecost', *TS* 45 (1984) 413 n.11.

[2] Lohfink, *Himmelfahrt* 90; E. Schillebeeckx, *Jezus. het verhaal van een levende* (Baarn: H. Nelissen, 1974, ⁸1982) 589 n.40. This form-critical assessment makes it difficult to accept that πορευθεὶς εἰς οὐρανὸν is an allusion to the visible ascension from the Mount of Olives (Acts 1:9-11), as suggests e.g. V. Larrañaga, *L'Ascension de Notre-Seigneur dans le Nouveau Testament* (SPIB 50; Roma: IBP, 1938) 352-353; cf. Gourgues, *Droite* 79 n.8. This is not a typical description of an *Entrückung*. The focus is on the victorious journey itself, not on its *terminus a quo* or its destiny. Christ is the active participant, a notion not so prominent, if not absent, in Luke's rapture christology (cf. *infra* 197). In Luke-Acts the ascension of Jesus is never depicted as a victorious ascent to heaven.

[3] On the ascension-exaltation theme in Hebrews, see R.D. Kaylor, *The Ascension Motif in Luke-Acts, the Epistle to the Hebrews and the Fourth Gospel* (Diss. Duke University, 1964) 83-125; Gourgues, *Droite* 89-125.

marks the climax of Jesus' redeeming ministry. In the opening verses it is said that the Son (= Christ), after he had made purification for sins, sat down at the right hand of the Majesty on high (Heb 1:3 ἐκάθισεν ἐν δεξιᾷ, cf. 1:13). See further 8:1; 10:12; 12:2 (the perfect tense expressing a durative situation 'has sat down'). The ascension theme is also quite prominent in Hebrews. Christ is spoken of as 'having passed through the heavens' (4:14); he has entered into the inner shrine (6:20); he is exalted above the heavens (7:26); he has entered once and for all into the Holy Place (9:12-13); he has entered into heaven itself (9:24). It has been noted that, with the exception of 13:20 (which is probably traditional!), the author of Hebrews does not seem to make reference to the resurrection[1]. This is not because the *auctor ad Hebraeos* devalues the role of the resurrection in favour of the ascension but because, in his view, Christ's resurrection *is* (or is closely bound up with, or is immediately followed by) his heavenly exaltation[2]. We are to think of a description of the Easter events along the lines of a heavenly journey, refashioned after the pattern of the high priest's entrance into the Holy of Holiest, not in terms of a rapture.

Before we proceed with our inventory we need to consider the question of the nature of the post-Easter appearances in the earliest preaching. If in the earliest stage of tradition resurrection and exaltation were regarded as one event, an uninterrupted movement from grave to glory, we may infer that the appearances were *ipso facto* manifestations of the already exalted Lord, hence: appearances 'from heaven' (granted that the act of exaltation/enthronement took place *in heaven*). Paul seems to have shared this view. He regarded his experience on the road to Damascus as a revelation (ἀποκάλυψις) of God's Son in/to him (Gal 1:16), that is, as an encounter with the exalted Lord[3]. He defended his apostleship with the assertion that he had seen Ἰησοῦν τὸν κύριον (!) ἡμῶν (1 Cor 9:1)[4] and did not hesitate to put his experience on equal footing with the apostolic Christophanies (1 Cor 15:8 ὤφθη κἀμοί!). Although we will elaborate on Luke's evaluation of Paul's Damascus road experience later—Luke does *not* seem to think of it as an appearance of the

---

[1] Lohfink, *Himmelfahrt* 91-93.

[2] Cf. E. Ruckstuhl, 'Auferstehung, Erhöhung und Himmelfahrt Jesu' (1968); repr. in: idem, *Jesus im Horizont der Evangelien* (SBAB 3; Stuttgart: KBW, 1988) 195-197; Hengel, 'Setze dich' 135.

[3] H. Schlier, *Der Brief an die Galater* (KEK III¹⁴; Göttingen: Vandenhoeck & Ruprecht, 1949, ⁵1971) 55; cf. Dunn, *Christology in the Making. An Inquiry into the Origins of the Doctrine of the Incarnation* (London: SCM, 1980, ²1989) 37.

[4] Fee, *First Corinthians* 395 n.14, notes that the designation Ἰησοῦν τὸν κύριον ἡμῶν is unusual in Paul and suggests that this is semitechnical language for speaking of Christ in his resurrection, through which he became 'our Lord'.

same kind as the other appearances (*infra* 171-175)—it may be suggested that Luke would agree that Paul had had an encounter with the *exalted* Lord from heaven (Acts 9:3-7; 22:6-10; 26:12-15)[1]. It is also commonly agreed upon in biblical scholarship that the Gospel of Matthew closes with a manifestation of the already exalted Lord (Mt 28:16-20). The risen Jesus says in v.18: ἐδόθη μοι πᾶσα ἐξουσία ἐν οὐρανῷ καὶ ἐπὶ [τῆς] γῆς[2]. Gnilka comments: 'Jesus spricht von der ihm übertragenen Vollmacht. Diese Übertragung liegt schon zurück, ist als in Verbindung mit der Auferweckung stehend zu denken ...'[3]. Nothing forbids, moreover, to interpret the 'on the road' appearance to Mary Magdalene (Mt 28:9-10) in similar terms. The scene is not essentially different from the appearance to the disciples. On the contrary, both scenes describe an act of *proskynesis* as the appropriate response to the Appearing One (vv.9.17).

The structure of early Christian resurrection belief may be diagrammed as follows:

resurrection—exaltation (*sessio ad dexteram*)—appearances from heaven,

or (in case the resurrection-exaltation complex assumes cosmic dimensions),

resurrection—victorious ascent—exaltation (*sessio ad dexteram*)—appearances from heaven.

To summarise, the general conviction in the earliest Christian preaching is that as of the day of his resurrection Jesus was in heaven, seated at the right hand of God. Resurrection and exaltation were regarded as two sides of one coin; resurrection meant 'resurrection to heaven' or 'resurrection from grave to glory'. Upon further reflection on the impact of the resurrection-exaltation event upon the spiritual world, Christ's passage from grave to glory assumed cosmic dimensions: during his journey upwards Christ had defeated the angelic powers and had thereby demonstrated his universal power and authority. This explains the (undoubtedly early) amalgamation of resurrection and ascension language. From the form-critical standpoint it should be noticed that this ascent

---

[1] On the nature of the Lukan post-resurrection see further *infra* 159-163.

[2] Cf. also the Wisdom saying Mt 11:27 // Lk 10:22 πάντα μοι παρεδόθη ὑπὸ τοῦ πατρός μου, which has, however, a different statement intention and can not be held against Mt 28:18, see the commentaries *ad loc.*

[3] G. Bornkamm, 'Der Auferstandene und der Irdische. Mt. 28,16-20', in: G. Bornkamm, G. Barth, H.J. Held (Hrsg.), *Überlieferung und Auslegung im Matthäusevangelium* (WMANT 1; Neukirchen-Vluyn: Neukirchener, 1960, ⁶1970) 289-310; A. Sand, *Das Evangelium nach Matthäus übersetzt und erklärt* (RNT 1; Regensburg: F. Pustet, 1986) 596; J. Gnilka, *Das Matthäusevangelium 2. Kommentar zu Kap.14,1-28,20 und Einleitungsfragen* (HThK 2; Freiburg, Basel, Wien: Herder, 1988) 507.

assumes the form of a heavenly journey. In the earliest stage of tradition the post-resurrection appearances are appearances 'from heaven'. Although, apart from the disputed passages in Luke-Acts, the Appearing One is never said to have gone back into heaven (either after the individual appearances or at the last appearance), this seems to be the underlying assumption throughout the passages. That, e.g. Matthew does not round off his narrative with an ascension reflects the Matthean concern to stress the abiding presence of the exalted Lord in the mission of his church. Having assured his readership of the abiding presence of Jesus (v.20 καὶ ἰδοὺ ἐγὼ μεθ᾽ ὑμῶν εἰμι πάσας τὰς ἡμέρας ἕως τῆς συντελείας τοῦ αἰῶνος; cf. 18:20!), every suggestion that Jesus departed from his disciples immediately thereafter would considerably weaken the force of the statement. The readers of the First Gospel are already informed about Jesus' present whereabouts (27:64). Paul seems to have regarded Christ's appearance to him to be the last one (if we may take ἔσχατον δὲ πάντων 1 Cor 15:8 this way, see *infra* 172 n.1).

c. *The Ascension-Exaltation Paradigm (Mk 16:19)*

A quite different assessment of the relationship of resurrection, exaltation, and ascension from the one outlined above is (apart from the Lukan passages under dispute) found in just the passage, which of all the ascension texts in the NT, has the strongest affinities with Luke-Acts, the so-called 'longer ending of Mark' (Mk 16:9-20), a passage which—in general opinion—is a later addition to the original Gospel, dating from the early second century AD[1]. We have here a clear and unmistakable expression of Jesus' ascension (*Entrückung*)

---

[1] K. Aland, 'Der Schluß des Markusevangeliums', in: M. Sabbe (éd.), *L'Évangile selon Marc. Tradition et rédaction* (BEThL 34; Leuven: Leuven University Press, Peeters, 1974, [2]1988) 435-470.573-575; repr. in: Aland, *Neutestamentliche Entwürfe* (TB 63; München: Chr. Kaiser, 1979) 246-283; Metzger, *A Textual Commentary on the Greek New Testament* (Stuttgart: Deutsche Bibelgesellschaft, UBS, 1971, [2]1994) 102-107; J. Hug, *La Finale de l'Évangile de Marc (Mc 16,9-20)* (EtB; Paris: J. Gabalda, 1978); R. Pesch, *Das Markusevangelium 1. Einleitung und Kommentar zu Kap. 1,1-8,27* (HThK 2; Freiburg, Basel, Wien: Herder, 1976, [4]1984) 40-48 (literature!); W.G. Kümmel, *Einleitung in das Neue Testament* (Heidelberg: Quelle & Meyer, 1963, [21]1983) 70-73. The consensus has been challenged by W.R. Farmer, *The Last Twelve Verses of Mark* (MSSNTS 25; Cambridge: CUP, 1974); S. Zwemer, 'The Last Twelve Verses of the Gospel of Mark', in: D.O. Fuller (ed.), *Counterfeit or Genuine—Mark 16? John 8?* (Grand Rapids: Grand Rapids International Publications, 1975) 159-174 [in the same volume the classic article of J.W. Burgon, 'The Last Twelve Verses of the Gospel According to St. Mark' (1871), (condensed by D.O. Fuller) 27-130]; and J. van Bruggen, *Marcus. Het Evangelie volgens Petrus* (CNT derde serie; Kampen: J.H. Kok, 1988) 395-402.413-418.

understood in terms of his exaltation or *sessio ad dexteram Dei*.

'Ο μὲν οὖν κύριος 'Ιησοῦς μετὰ τὸ λαλῆσαι αὐτοῖς ἀνελήμφθη εἰς τὸν οὐρανὸν καὶ ἐκάθισεν ἐκ δεξιῶν τοῦ θεοῦ (Mk 16:19).

We may leave aside for the moment the question whether vv.9-20 are dependent upon Luke-Acts or not (*infra* 189-190), and concentrate upon the narrative as it now stands. Different from most of the previously studied ascension texts this is clearly an ascension of the rapture (*Entrückung*) type: the event rounds off Jesus' earthly career by his physical removal from earth to heaven by divine intervention, in the presence of eyewitnesses. The terminology employed recalls Elijah's assumption into heaven. It should be noted, however, that the author (or his source, for that matter) does what the author of Luke-Acts does *not* do, he adds an explicit reference of Ps 110:1 to the ascension of Jesus, thereby suggesting that the ascension was the occasion at (or after) which the prophetic oracle of Ps 110:1 was fulfilled.

Unfortunately, the timetable of vv.9-20 is not very clear; the resurrection, the appearances, the ascension and the exaltation all seem to occur on the same day. But given the composite character of the text we should probably not be dogmatic on this point. In the present context we are possibly to think of appearances in and around Jerusalem, but again, the author is not explicit on this and probably not interested in it. The crucial point of divergence from the primitive exaltation kerygma, however, is not the date or the locality of the ascension but the radical reassessment of the function of the resurrection, exaltation, and ascension of Jesus. The traditional sequence:

resurrection—*sessio ad dexteram*—appearances (from heaven)

has been altered into:

resurrection—appearances—ascension (rapture)—*sessio ad dexteram*.

Compared to the primitive exaltation kerygma discussed in the previous section, we should note the following divergencies. In the first place, the resurrection is no longer understood as an eschatological event that ushers in the new age or exalts Jesus to heavenly Lordship but simply as a miracle of resuscitation by which Jesus is brought back alive on the stage of history. Only at the end of the day (or later)—at any rate after a series of appearances to his followers—Jesus departs from the earth and takes his seat at the right hand of God in heaven. The time between resurrection and exaltation (session) is an intermediate period in which Jesus is risen but not yet exalted[1]. The notion that

---

[1] Cf. Gnilka, *Das Evangelium nach Markus* 2 (EKK 2; Zürich, Einsiedeln, Köln: Benziger;

Jesus appeared ἐν ἑτέρᾳ μορφῇ (v.12) does not contrast the appearance of Jesus with his pre-Easter appearing[1] or his heavenly appearance[2]. It simply contrasts the appearance to 'the two of them' with the appearance to Mary Magdalene (vv.9-11) and is readily explained as an attempt to bring two different sources (the appearance to Mary Magdalene and the Emmaus story) into accord: Jesus appeared to the two disciples not, as in the case of Mary Magdalene, in the appearance of a gardener (Jn 20:15) but as a traveller (Lk 24:15,28)[3]. The break separating the resurrection and ascension-exaltation seems to imply, in the second place, that the appearances between the resurrection and the ascension (vv.9-11,12-13,14-20) are no longer understood as 'appearances from heaven', as was the case in the earliest traditions. There is no indication in the text that Jesus has already been in heaven before his ascension recounted in v.19. The underlying thought seems to be that the appearances are temporary manifestations of the risen Jesus to his followers, after which he withdrew himself again to some hidden place on earth. In the third place, it should be noted that, in comparison with the OT-Jewish rapture traditions, the function of the rapture event is different. It is not a temporary measure to spare someone from death for an eschatological task in the future but an act of enthronement to a heavenly throne, not unlike the exaltation of Enoch as Son of Man in (the final redaction of) 1 En 70-71 (*supra* 51ff.).

### d. *The Descent-Ascent Paradigm (Fourth Gospel)*

The Fourth Gospel offers a line of development different again from the ones outlined above. In this Gospel, which offers a theological restatement of the Jesus tradition from a post-resurrection point of view, we find neither an explicit citation of nor an allusion to Ps 110. The historical mission of Jesus is portrayed in the Gospel as one single continuous movement, from his coming into the world from eternity (pre-existence) to his return thither, patterned on the scheme of the *katabasis-anabasis* of the heavenly Wisdom figure as found in Jewish wisdom literature[4]. There seems to be no room in the Fourth Gospel

---

Neukirchen: Neukirchener, 1979) 354.

[1] J. Behm, μορφή, μορφόω, κτλ., *ThWNT* 4 (1942) 757.

[2] Contra E. Schweizer, *Das Evangelium nach Markus* (NTD 1; Göttingen, Zürich: Vandenhoeck & Ruprecht, 1967, ²1968) 217-218; Van Bruggen, *Marcus* 399, who interprets ἐν ἑτέρᾳ μορφῇ as 'in een stralende, luisterrijke vorm' (with reference to Mk 9:2-4!).

[3] H.B. Swete, *The Gospel According to St Mark. The Greek Text with Introduction, Notes and Indices* (London: Macmillan, 1898, ³1909) 402; E. Lohmeyer, *Das Evangelium des Markus* (KEK II¹⁷; Göttingen: Vandenhoeck & Ruprecht, 1957, ⁸1967) 361-362; Pesch, *Markusevangelium* 2, 551-552.

[4] See C.H. Talbert, 'The Myth of a Descending-Ascending Redeemer in Mediterranean

for a separate act of exaltation; Jesus' entire life is a manifestation of the glory he possessed from eternity. His resurrection does not cause a change in status but only makes manifest what has been true from the beginning.

An immediate comparison with the synoptic tradition is difficult because the Fourth Evangelist has his own set of terminology. Jesus' departure from the world is described as ὑπάγειν (8:14,21,22; 13:33,36; 14:4,5,28; 16:5), ὑπάγειν πρὸς τὸν θεὸν (13:3), πρὸς τὸν πατέρα (16:10,17) or πρὸς τὸν πέμψαντά με (7:33; 16:5); πορεύεσθαι (14:2,3; 16:7) or πορεύεσθαι πρὸς τὸν πατέρα (14:12,28; 16:28); ἀναβαίνειν (6:62) and ἀναβαίνειν πρὸς τὸν πατέρα (20:17); μεταβαίνειν ἐκ τοῦ κόσμου (13:1) and ἀπέρχεσθαι (16:7) (cf. also 16:16-18). At various times Jesus' departure from the world is counterbalanced by a reference to the incarnation: Jesus' mission is an (ἐξ)έρχεσθαι καὶ ὑπάγειν (3:8; 8:14; 13:3; cf. 14:2 ὑπάγειν καὶ ἔρχεσθαι); ἐξέρχεσθαι καὶ πορεύειν (16:28); καταβαίνειν καὶ ἀναβαίνειν (3:13; cf. 6:62; 20:17). The saving event is characterised as Jesus' ὑψωθῆναι (3:14; 8:28; 12:32,34) and δοξασθῆναι (7:39; 11:4; 12:16,23; 13:31-32; 16:14; 17:1ff.; cf. 8:54; 12:28). Depending on the interpretation of the 'lifting up sayings', the Fourth Evangelist regards Jesus' death by crucifixion itself as the exaltation or at least regards it as part of the exaltation complex[1].

Regarding the ascension, the following texts require a further examination: Jn 3:13, 6:62 and 20:17.

*Jn 3:13* The argument is that no one can speak with authority of τὰ ἐπουράνια (v.12) unless he has been in heaven and has come down to reveal his knowledge, a condition which is fulfilled in ὁ υἱὸς τοῦ ἀνθρώπου only (cf. 1:18). What should be supplied to bring out the statement's intention is: οὗτος (the Son of Man) ἀναβέβηκεν εἰς τὸν οὐρανόν[2]. The emphasis on

---

Antiquity', *NTS* 22 (1975/76) 418-440.

[1] See W. Thüsing, *Die Erhöhung und Verherrlichung Jesu im Johannesevangelium* (NTA 21-1/2; Münster: Aschendorff, 1960, ³1979) 3-37; Ruckstuhl, 'Auferstehung' 197-199; G.C. Nicholson, *Death as Departure. The Johannine Descent-Ascent Schema* (SBL.DS 63; Chico, CA: Scholars, 1983); Th. Knöppler, *Die theologia crucis des Johannesevangeliums. Das Verständnis des Todes Jesu im Rahmen der johanneischen Inkarnations- und Erhöhungschristologie* (WMANT 69; Neukirchen-Vluyn: Neukirchener, 1994) 154-173.228-241.

[2] So rightly P. Borgen, 'Some Jewish Exegetical Traditions as Background for Son of Man Sayings in John's Gospel (Jn 3,13-14 and context)', in: M. de Jonge (éd.), *L'Évangile de Jean. Sources, rédaction, théologie* (BEThL 44; Gembloux: Duculot; Leuven: Leuven University Press, 1977) 249; J. Ashton, *Understanding the Fourth Gospel* (Oxford: Clarendon, 1991) 349-350.

exclusiveness (οὐδεὶς ... εἰ μὴ) suggests a conscious polemic against the heavenly journey traditions of Jewish apocalyptic circles, the ascents of Moses in particular[1], and goes beyond what is an otherwise accepted Jewish affirmation (cf. Prov 30:4; Deut 30:12; Bar 3:29; cf. 4 Ezra 4:8; Rom 10:6-8).

Commentators are particularly puzzled by the use of the perfect tense ἀναβέβηκεν, which seems to imply that the ascent under consideration has already taken place at the moment of speaking. Some have argued that we are to regard this as a mystical ascent during Jesus' lifetime[2], but this is not attested to elsewhere in the gospel tradition. P. Borgen thinks of an ascent prior to the incarnation, 'a pre-existent installing in office'[3]. The difficulty with these suggestions is that they do not explain the perfect tense to a satisfactory degree. In line with the normal use of the perfect tense, ἀναβέβηκεν cannot mean but 'he has ascended to heaven *and is still there*', as is correctly brought out in the interpretative gloss ὁ ὢν ἐν τῷ οὐρανῷ[4]. Augustine was aware of this and interpreted the phrase, in defence of the two natures doctrine, to mean that Jesus during his earthly ministry was simultaneously in heaven and on earth (*CommJoh* 12,8; CChr.SL 36, 125; also Cyril of Alexandria, *CommJoh* 2; PG 73, 249). But this is simply reading back later dogma into the text. The only other time that the perfect tense of ἀναβαίνω is used in the NT writings is in Jn 20:17 ('I have not yet ascended'!), so that it is reasonable to assume a connection. Since the *katabasis-anabasis* pattern is typical of the Fourth Gospel (in our verse the descent seems to precede the ascent as well), we are to explain the verse from the perspective of the Evangelist, in other words, we have here a description from a post-Easter viewpoint, when Jesus' ἀνάβασις (= his return to the Father through passion-resurrection-ascension) had already become a *fait accompli*[5].

---

[1] Bill. 2, 425; H. Odeberg, *The Fourth Gospel. Interpreted in Its Relation to Contemporaneous Religious Currents in Palestine and the Hellenistic-Oriental World* (Uppsala, Stockholm: Almquist & Wiksells, 1929; repr. Amsterdam: B.R. Grüner, 1968) 72-98; W.A. Meeks, *The Prophet-King. Moses Traditions and the Johannine Christology* (NT.S 14; Leiden: E.J. Brill, 1967) 297-301; Nicholson, *Departure* 91-93; Dunn, *The Parting of the Ways between Christianity and Judaism and their Significance for the Character of Christianity* (London: SCM; Philadelphia: TPI, 1991) 225.

[2] Cf. Odeberg, *Fourth Gospel* 72-98, esp. 94-98.

[3] Borgen, 'Exegetical Traditions' 243-258.

[4] On this *v.l.* see R. Schnackenburg, *Das Johannesevangelium 1. Einleitung und Kommentar zu Kap.1-4* (HThKNT 4; Freiburg, Basel, Wien: Herder, 1965) 406-407; Metzger, *Commentary* 174-175.

[5] So e.g. C.K. Barrett, *The Gospel According to St. John. An Introduction with Commentary and Notes on the Greek Text* (London: SCM, 1955, ²1978) 213; Schnackenburg,

*Jn 6:62* It is not immediately clear what the exact nature of the σκάνδαλον is and what is the implied apodosis of the uncompleted conditional sentence ἐὰν οὖν θεωρῆτε κτλ.: if they see the Son of Man going where he was before (ὅπου ἦν τὸ πρότερον = εἰς τὸν οὐρανόν), will then the offence caused by Jesus' self-identification as the Bread from Heaven (v.61) be removed, as his return to heaven proves that he has rightly made this claim[1]? Or does the claim that he will ascend only increase the offence, in that he claims what is allowed or even possible for no human being (Prov 30:4; Deut 30:12; Bar 3:29; cf. 4 Ezra 4:8; Rom 10:6-8)[2]? There is much to say for the view that the wording is intentionally ambiguous, the answer being dependent upon the critical judgement (the faith commitment) of the reader/hearer. For one who only sees the outward appearance of the Jesus event (the cross!) the offence remains; for one who penetrates into the inward meaning of the cross as the Messiah's path to glory and the means of salvation, the offence is alleviated[3].

To understand John's ascension theme properly, the rule 'to let John be John' (J.D.G. Dunn) is most pertinent. For the Fourth Evangelist Jesus' ἀνάβασις is not a moment in time, but a comprehensive event, a journey 'from cross to glory'. If we add to this the observation that 'seeing (θεωρέω) the Son of Man' in the Fourth Gospel usually denotes spiritual perception (6:40; 12:45)[4], it is clear that the Fourth Evangelist is not saying that Jesus' conversation partners will actually observe an ascension in the manner of Acts 1:9[5]. An immediate comparison is not in place.

---

*Johannesevangelium* 1, 405-407; R.E. Brown, *The Gospel According to John I-XII* (AncB 29; Garden City, NY: Doubleday, 1966) 132; E. Haenchen, *Das Johannesevangelium. Ein Kommentar* (hrsg. v. U. Busse; Tübingen: J.C.B. Mohr/Paul Siebeck, 1980) 224.228; Nicholson, *Departure* 95-96; Knöppler, *Theologia crucis* 233-234.

[1] Cf. Th. Zahn, *Das Evangelium des Johannes* (KNT 4; Leipzig: A. Deichert, Werner Scholl, 1908, [3.4.]1920) 359; Thüsing, *Erhöhung* 261-262; H. Ridderbos, *Het Evangelie naar Johannes. Proeve van een theologische exegese* 1 (Kampen: J.H. Kok, 1987) 161.

[2] Cf. M.-J. Lagrange, *Évangile selon St. Jean* (EtB; Paris: J. Gabalda, ²1925) 187-188; Bultmann, *Das Evangelium des Johannes* (KEK II[19]; Göttingen: Vandenhoeck & Ruprecht, 1941, [10]1968) 341.

[3] Cf. Barrett, *John* 303; Schnackenburg, *Johannesevangelium* 2, 104-105; Lindars, *The Gospel of John* (NCeB; Greenwood, SC: Attic; London: Oliphants, 1972) 272-273; D.A. Carson, *The Gospel According to John* (Leicester: IVP; Grand Rapids: Eerdmans, 1991) 300-301.

[4] W. Michaelis, ὁράω κτλ., *ThWNT* 5 (1954) 362-365.

[5] As is suggested by Zahn, *Johannes* 359-360; Lagrange, *Jean* 511-512; J.H. Bernard, *The Gospel According to St. John* 1 (ed. A.H. McNeile; ICC; Edinburgh: T.&T. Clark, 1928) 216-217; Larrañaga, *Ascension* 488; C. Stam, *De hemelvaart des Heren in de Godsopenbaring van het Nieuwe Testament* (Academisch proefschrift Vrije Universiteit Amsterdam; Kampen:

*Jn 20:17* The command μή μου ἅπτου ('don't cling to me') seems to imply that Mary had seized Jesus' feet (cf. Mt 28:9 αἱ δὲ προσελθοῦσαι ἐκράτησαν αὐτοῦ τοὺς πόδας and the interpretative gloss καὶ προσέδραμεν ἅψασθαι αὐτοῦ in the present verse) or was about to do so[1]. The point is not that Jesus did not allow Mary to touch him (for whatever reason) or that he regarded an act of *proskynesis* inappropriate for someone who failed to grasp the meaning of the new relationship that he had entered into through the resurrection. Nor is a contrast in view with Jesus' invitation to Thomas to examine the wounds caused by the nails and the spear-thrust (v.27)[2]. The issue is that Mary should not 'cling' to Jesus, not 'hold on' to him[3]. The phrase μή μου ἅπτου can best be connected with πορεύου δὲ πρὸς τοὺς ἀδελφούς μου κλτ., 'don't cling to me ... but (δέ) go to my disciples'. Mary seems to misunderstand the present occasion as the fulfilment of Jesus' promise of his abiding presence and does not realise that Jesus would be present through the Spirit (Jn 14:15-31; 16:5-33). This could only be realised after his ἀνάβασις (= Jesus' return to the Father through passion-resurrection-ascension = his glorification/exaltation) had come to completion (7:39; 16:7)[4]. If we take the larger Johannine context into consideration (the connection ascension-giving of the Spirit) and follow the Johannine understanding of Jesus' ἀνάβασις as a description of Jesus' entire passage to the Father through passion, death, resurrection and ascension, Jn 20:17 seems to make good sense. Jesus motivates his appeal not to hold on to him by stating that he has not yet ascended: οὔπω γὰρ ἀναβέβηκα (as in 3:13 perfect tense!) πρὸς τὸν πατέρα, that is, his ἀνάβασις has not yet reached completion, for the Spirit has not yet been given. But this will not take long: ἀναβαίνω (present tense, expressing imminence) πρὸς τὸν πατέρα κτλ.

In line with the Johannine use of the word, Jesus' ἀνάβασις cannot be equated with the ascension event in Acts 1[5] and it would be futile to look for a

---

J.H. Kok, 1950) 27-28.

[1] BDR 336.2c; U. Holzmeister, 'Der Tag der Himmelfahrt des Herrn', *ZKTh* 55 (1931) 59; Larrañaga, *Ascension* 480-481; Bultmann, *Johannes* 532 Anm.6; Barrett, *John* 565; Schnackenburg, *Johannesevangelium* 3, 375-376.

[2] With Brown, *John* 2, 1011. Contra Haenchen, *Johannesevangelium* 571.

[3] Brown, *John* 2, 1011-1012; Ridderbos, *Johannes* 2, 306.

[4] The line of interpretation offered here makes it unnecessary to postulate an Aramaic mistranslation underlying μή μου ἅπτου, as e.g. suggested by B. Violet, 'Ein Versuch zu Joh. 20,17', *ZNW* 24 (1925) 78-80; Michaelis, *Die Erscheinungen des Auferstandenen* (Basel: H. Majer, 1944) 74-77. The language is decidedly Johannine.

[5] J.F. Walvoord, 'The Ascension of Christ', *BS* 121 (1964) 7; Metzger, 'The Ascension of Jesus Christ', in: idem, *Historical and Literary Studies. Pagan, Jewish and Christian* (NTTS 8; Leiden: E.J. Brill; Grand Rapids: Eerdmans, 1968) 79; Carson, *John* 645.

gap in Jn 20 where the Lukan ascension story would fit in[1]. It is, of course, assumed that somewhere in the process of 'going to the Father' Jesus will depart from the earth, but the theological outlook of the Fourth Evangelist makes it impossible to make a sharp differentiation between death, resurrection, exaltation and so on[2]. The entire course of events constitutes the 'hour' of the Son of Man[3]; the entire sequence of events starting from the crucifixion is Jesus' ἀνάβασις to the Father[4].

### e. *Other Ascension Texts*

In a number of other texts in the NT ascension language is employed with reference to Jesus. These should now be examined particularly with regard to their 'statement intention' (do they presuppose or positively affirm an ascension of Jesus?), their formal structure (in which 'form' is the ascension depicted?), and their relation to the ascension in Luke-Acts.

*Mk 2:19b-20parr.* The saying on the removal of the bridegroom from the wedding festivities (Mk 2:19b-20; Mt 9:15; Lk 5:35; cf. EvThom 104) is commonly regarded as a *Gemeindebildung*[5]. If the saying is an authentic Jesus

---

[1] Usually it is assumed that Jesus' ascension took place after the appearance to Mary Magdalene and before the appearance to the disciples. Michaelis, *Erscheinungen* 76-77; P. Benoit, 'L'Ascension' (1949); repr. in: idem, *Exégèse et Théologie* 1 (Paris: Cerf, 1961) 388-389. But this is based on a mistaken contrast between the two scenes, as we noted above. The suggestion of F.F. Bruce, *The Gospel of John. Introduction, Exposition and Notes* (Grand Rapids; Eerdmans, 1983) 389, that 'the ascension referred to here may be an earlier occasion than that described in Acts 1:9 ...' must be regarded as a solution born of embarrassment.

[2] Schnackenburg, *Johannesevangelium* 3, 378.

[3] Cf. Thüsing, *Erhöhung* 75-100.

[4] Thüsing, *Erhöhung* 269-275 (Jesus' ἀναβαίνειν is a *Gesamtvorgang*). From the perspective of the Fourth Evangelist, to ask whether Jesus appears as the Exalted One is simply asking the wrong question; John's concern is not christological (the significance of Easter for Jesus) but soteriological (the significance of Easter for the disciples). See also Ridderbos, *Johannes* 2, 307-308. If one still wants to find clues, it may be pointed out that Mary after her meeting with the risen Jesus reports that she had seen 'the Lord' (= the exalted Κύριος?) (v.18) (cf. Brown, *John* 2, 1014-1015); one should also take notice of the confession of Thomas: ὁ κύριός μου καὶ ὁ θεός μου (v.28). J. Schneider, *Das Evangelium nach Johannes* (ThHK Sonderband; Berlin: Evangelische, 1976) 321 speaks of a *Zwischenzustand*, but it must be doubted whether this correctly represents the Evangelist's viewpoint.

[5] E.g. Pesch, *Markusevangelium* 1, 174-176; D. Lührmann, *Das Markusevangelium* (HNT 3; Tübingen: J.C.B. Mohr/Paul Siebeck, 1987) 63-64; R.W. Funk, M.H. Smith, *The Gospel of Mark. Red Letter Edition* (Jesus Seminar; Sonoma, CA: Polebridge, 1991) 73; M.D. Hooker,

logion, it probably circulated as an independent logion before Mark (or his source) placed it in the present context (note the catchword connection by ὁ νυμφίος).

Several scholars have suggested that ἀπήρθη ἀπ᾽ αὐτῶν ὁ νυμφίος (v.20) is a remnant of an early rapture christology[1]. The significance of this suggestion can hardly be overestimated, since, if this is the case, we have an important piece of evidence for the existence of a rapture christology in the pre-Lukan Jesus tradition. Unfortunately, it does not seem possible to confirm the suggestion. For although it seems that the Western scribe of Acts 1:9 [D ἀπήρθη ἀπὸ (ὀφθαλμῶν) αὐτῶν] has reworded his text to conform to Mk 2:20, thereby suggesting the identity of scenes, assuming such an identity violates the Markan context.

Despite voices to the contrary[2], it is hardly thinkable that the event does not include the notion of violence, because it affects the mood of the wedding guests: a bridegroom is not normally 'taken away' from the wedding festivities and if he would leave voluntarily this would not be a cause for mourning and fasting (cf. 4 Ezra 10:1-4). The violent nature of the 'taking away' is strengthened if Is 53:8 (αἴρεται ἀπὸ τῆς γῆς ἡ ζωὴ αὐτοῦ) is in the background, where the Servant of YHWH seems to die a violent death[3]. Mk 2:20, then, alludes not to the ascension of Jesus, but to his violent death on the cross. It is, however, a *veiled* allusion preparing for the more detailed passion predictions (Mk 8:31; 9:31; 10:33-34)[4]. The parallel passage Lk 5:35 does not

---

*The Gospel According to St. Mark* (BNTC; London: A.&C. Black, 1991) 98-99.

[1] Hahn, *Hoheitstitel* 126-127 Anm.4; Georgi, 'Hymnus' 292 Anm.88; cf. Lohfink, *Himmelfahrt* 97. G. Haufe, 'Entrückung und eschatologische Funktion im Spätjudentum', *ZRGG* 13 (1961) 112-113, has made appeal to the present verse to support his thesis that if the historical Jesus anticipated his future coming as Son of Man on the clouds of heaven, he must have reckoned with his bodily rapture to heaven as well.

[2] Bauer, *s.v.* ἀπαίρω, 159; W.L. Lane, *The Gospel According to Mark. The English Text with Introduction, Exposition and Notes* (NICNT; Grand Rapids: Eerdmans, 1974) 111; Fitzmyer, *Luke* 1, 599; Van Bruggen, *Marcus* 75-76; J.B. Green, *The Death of Jesus. Tradition and Interpretation in the Passion Narrative* (WUNT 2/33; Tübingen: J.C.B. Mohr/Paul Siebeck, 1988) 150.

[3] On this, see A. Schmitt, *Entrückung-Aufnahme-Himmelfahrt. Untersuchungen zu einem Vorstellungsbereich im AT* (FzB 10; Stuttgart: KBW, 1973, ²1976) 85-87, and the commentaries *ad loc.*

[4] Given the strategic position of this first (veiled!) reference to the passion, the suggestion of Haenchen, *Der Weg Jesu. Eine Erklärung des Markusevangeliums und der kanonischen Parallelen* (Berlin: W. de Gruyter, 1966, ²1968) 115, that we are to think here of Jesus being taken away 'durch Tod *und Auferstehung*' (my emphasis) is probably more than Mark wants his readers to know at this point of the story.

refer to the ascension either, since for Luke the ascension is an occasion for joy, not for grief and fasting (Lk 24:53).

*Rom 10:6-8* This is a midrash pesher on Deut 30:12-14. J.A. Fitzmyer suggests that Paul's use of ἀναβήσεται in v.6b 'makes the Christian reader think of someone 'ascending' into heaven, *as Christ Jesus did*. The allusion here to the ascension may be remote, but it is unmistakable'[1]. But if the point of v.6 is that it is unnecessary to bring Christ down because he has already come down in the incarnation, a view which many commentators embrace[2], we are not to think of Christ's ascent, but of his *descent* from heaven. The answer implied by τίς ἀναβήσεται εἰς τὸν οὐρανόν; is not 'Christ will ascend' but 'no one will ascend' (or: 'no one needs to ascend')[3]. An implied reference to an ascension of Christ may be assumed, if, as J.D.G. Dunn suggests, Paul's focus is on the *present* exalted Christ in heaven, the point being that it is not necessary for someone to ascend to heaven to bring Christ down, because his physical presence on earth is not necessary for the attainment of salvation, since the word of faith is near (v.8)[4]. But then again, the allusion to the ascension is not connected with ἀναβήσεται κτλ., but with καταγαγεῖν (which presupposes Christ's present dwelling in heaven and hence his previous ascension thither). At any rate, the reference to an ascension is very remote and only incidental to the line of argument.

*Eph 4:8-10* This is a midrash on Ps 68:19 (MT). In Ps 68 YHWH is said to have come down to earth to defeat his enemies and then to ascend upwards (to Mount Zion?) in a triumphant procession, carrying with him the spoils, which He is to bestow upon his people[5]. Christ's work of salvation is described here as a triumphal ascent to heaven with reference to Ps 68:19. Following an Aramaic targumic tradition (Targum on Ps 68:19; ed. Díez Merino 127; tr. 251; Peshitta Ps 68:19; ed. VTS 2/3, 74), Eph 4:8 has ἔδωκεν instead of ἔλαβες in

---

[1] Fitzmyer, 'Ascension' 415 (italics mine).

[2] W. Sanday, A.C. Headlam, *The Epistle to the Romans* (ICC; Edinburgh: T.&T. Clark, 1895, ⁵1902) 287; Cranfield, *Romans* 2, 525; Fitzmyer, *Romans* 590 (!).

[3] Cf. the references cited *supra* 135. For an interesting discussion of the religion-historical background of Rom 10:6-7, see J. Heller, 'Himmel- und Höllenfahrt nach Römer 10,6-7', *EvTh* 32 (1972) 478-486.

[4] Dunn, *Christology* 184-187; cf. also idem, *Romans* 2, 605, where he offers a slightly different explanation.

[5] Kraus, *Psalmen* 2, 624-638; Schmitt, *Entrückung* 332-336; M. Barth, *Ephesians. A New Translation with Introduction and Commentary* 2 (AncB 34A; Garden City, NY: Doubleday, 1974) 472-477.

the interest of a christological understanding of Pentecost. The point is that Christ's redemptive work has resulted in the giving of spiritual gifts. As in Jn 3:13, the author is thinking in terms of *katabasis* (= Christ's incarnation[1] or his *descensus ad inferos*[2]) and *anabasis* (= Christ's resurrection-exaltation to heaven). The ascension (heavenly exaltation) of Christ makes possible the outpouring of the Spirit and his gifts (Jn 7:39; Acts 2:33). Form-critically, this is a heavenly journey type of ascension[3].

*1 Tim 3:16*  The early Christian hymn adopted in 1 Tim 3:16 in all probability stems from a (Greek-speaking) Jewish-Christian milieu. The most accepted view nowadays is that the hymn consists of three two-line stanzas, each determined by a contrast of heaven and earth[4]. In addition, it is generally admitted that the Christ event begins with a reference to the incarnation (ἐφανερώθη ἐν σαρκί) and climaxes with his assumption 'in glory' (ἀνελήμφθη ἐν δόξῃ). The two most difficult parts of the hymn, which are in fact the two most pertinent to our topic, are line three (ὤφθη ἀγγέλοις) and line six (ἀνελήμφθη ἐν δόξῃ), which both refer to events in the heavenly realm, according to the conventional structuration. ὤφθη ἀγγέλοις may accordingly be interpreted as an act of presentation in the heavenly court (Jeremias) or as a reference to Christ's victorious journey through the heavens, during which He manifests his power to the angelic world (cf. AscenIs 11:23)[5]. Either way it is not very likely that we are to take the angels to be human messengers, apostles or (if one maintains the reference to angelic beings) that the angels referred to are the angels that were present at the resurrection and ascension[6]. The word ὤφθη should be correctly translated 'made himself

---

[1] Stam, *Hemelvaart* 55; F.W. Grosheide, *De Brief van Paulus aan de Efeziërs* [CNT(K); Kampen: J.H. Kok, 1960] 65; Lohfink, *Himmelfahrt* 87; Barth, *Ephesians* 2, 433-434; Gnilka, *Der Epheserbrief* (HThK 10/2; Freiburg, Basel, Wien: Herder, 1971) 208.

[2] F. Büchsel, κάτω, κατωτέρω, κατώτερος, *ThWNT* 3 (1938) 641-643; Dunn, *Christology* 186-187.

[3] Lohfink, *Himmelfahrt* 87.

[4] See W. Stenger, *Der Christushymnus 1 Tim 3,16. Eine strukturanalytische Untersuchung* (RSTh 6; Frankfurt: P. Lang; Bern: H. Lang, 1977) 35-81.235-244; R.H. Gundry, 'The Form, Meaning and Background of the Hymn Quoted in I Timothy 3.16', in: W.W. Gasque, R.P. Martin (eds.), *Apostolic History and the Gospel* (FS F.F. Bruce; Grand Rapids: Eerdmans; Exeter: Paternoster, 1970) 203-222.

[5] So e.g. L. Oberlinner, *Die Pastoralbriefe I. Kommentar zum ersten Timotheusbrief* (HThK 11/2; Freiburg, Basel, Wien: Herder, 1994) 166-167.

[6] As suggests G.W. Knight, *The Pastoral Epistles. A Commentary on the Greek Text* (NIGTC; Grand Rapids: Eerdmans, 1992) 185. Cf. W. Lock, *Pastoral Epistles. I & II*

manifest, showed himself'. Although ascension (rapture) language is tangible in line six (ἀνελήμφθη!), we are probably not to read the final line of the hymn as a reference to the event described in Acts 1:9[1], but rather as a solemn expression of Christ's heavenly exaltation at Easter[2]. It is difficult, if not impossible, to decide whether ἐν δόξῃ is circumstantial ('with glory') or local ('in glory'), or whether perhaps ἐν has replaced an original εἰς ('into glory') to conform to the hymn[3]. Probably we should not insist on a great degree of precision here, since the hymnal character of the confession would allow for a polyvalent interpretation, which is concerned with associative force, rather than with exact meaning.

*Rev 12:5* The removal of the child (= the Messiah) in the vision of the Woman and the Dragon (Rev 12:1-6) is presented in typical rapture terms: καὶ ἡρπάσθη τὸ τέκνον αὐτῆς πρὸς τὸν θεὸν καὶ πρὸς τὸν θρόνον αὐτοῦ (v.5). Here a pre-Christian (and possibly non-Jewish) myth has been taken up[4]. The idea of a snatching up of the Messiah as a child is also reflected in some Jewish sources [Ber 2:4 (5a); Bill. 1, 83; 2, 339-340] and is parallelled in the (late) Melchizedek myth in 2 En 72. On the level of John, the reference is to Jesus, but the picture is not to be taken with strict literalness, as is clear from the removal of Christ as a child, the absence of references to his death and resurrection, and so on. What we have here is a dramatic expression of God's protection of the Messiah in mythical language, applied rather artificially to the Christ event. Rev 12:5 cannot be taken to refer to the ascension of Luke-Acts[5],

---

*Timothy and Titus* (ICC; Edinburgh: T.&T. Clark, 1924) 46, who sees here angels who watched the earthly life of Christ (with reference to Lk 2:13; Mk 1:13; Jn 1:51; Lk 24:23) and who still watch His working from heaven (with reference to Eph 3:10; 1 Pet 1:12).

[1] E.g. P. Dornier, *Les Épîtres Pastorales* (SBi; Paris: J. Gabalda, 1969) 71; Knight, *Pastoral Epistles* 186. Most authors would point to the similarity of language. Here it should be noted again with all emphasis, that the verb ἀναλαμβάνομαι is sufficiently broad and well-used to be applied in a variety of contexts, see *supra* 81.

[2] So L. Brun, *Die Auferstehung Christi in der urchristlichen Überlieferung* (Oslo: H. Aschehoug & Co (W. Nygaard); Giessen: A. Töpelmann, 1925) 94; Lohfink, *Himmelfahrt* 87-89; Fitzmyer, 'Ascension' 411-412; J. Roloff, *Der erste Brief an Timotheus* (EKK 15; Neukirchen-Vluyn: Neukirchener; Zürich, Einsiedeln, Köln: Benziger, 1988) 210.

[3] See the commentaries *ad loc.* and Stenger, *Christushymnus* 215-216, for the various positions.

[4] W. Bousset, *Die Offenbarung Johannis* (KEK II[6]; Göttingen: Vandenhoeck & Ruprecht, 1896, ²1906) 346-358; R.H. Charles, *The Revelation of St. John. With Introduction, Notes and Indices. Also the Greek Text and English Translation* 1 (ICC; Edinburgh: T.&T. Clark, 1920) 298-314.

[5] Contra Charles, *Revelation* 1, 320-321; Swete, *The Apocalypse of St. John. The Greek*

but it does show that rapture motifs could be applied to Jesus in a variety of ways.

*Barn 15:9* A reminiscence of the resurrection-exaltation paradigm is found in Barn 15:9, where the resurrection and the ascension apparently are dated on one and the same day, the eighth day (that is, on Easter Sunday): διὸ καὶ ἄγομεν τὴν ἡμέραν τὴν ὀγδόην εἰς εὐφροσύνην, ἐν ᾗ καὶ ὁ Ἰησοῦς ἀνέστη ἐκ νεκρῶν καὶ φανερωθεὶς ἀνέβη εἰς οὐρανούς (ed. Funk-Bihlmeyer 29). According to L.W. Barnard, the writer simply mentioned the resurrection appearances and the ascension as a corollary to the resurrection, viewing the events as a whole without consideration of the chronological interval[1]. But in the light of our form-critical analysis above, a better explanation emerges. The 'ascension' in the sequence 'resurrection-manifestation-ascension' is not an *Entrückung* (*in concreto*, the visible ascension of Acts 1:9) but a heavenly journey, which portrays Christ's victory over death in a single continuous movement from resurrection via a heavenly journey (φανερωθεὶς may be taken as 'manifested to the heavenly powers', cf. 1 Tim 3:16 ὤφθη ἀγγέλοις!) to heaven. On Barn 15:9 see further *infra* 190-191.

### 6. *Summary and Conclusions*

In the earliest recoverable christological expressions of the early church we find evidence of the belief that the resurrection and the exaltation were more or less inseparable acts of the movement 'from grave to glory', not interrupted by interim appearances, and that since then, the resurrected Jesus was in heaven. Especially Ps 110, read quite literally, helped to articulate the exaltation belief. The suffering-vindicated Son of Man tradition and the Johannine exaltation-glorification texts provide evidence that exaltation imagery was not exclusively bound to Ps 110[2]. From his exalted position in heaven, Christ from time to time appeared to his followers, the last of these heavenly manifestations being the one to the apostle Paul on the Damascus road (Gal 1:16; 1 Cor 15:8; Acts 9:1-9; 22:1-22; 26:12-18) (*infra* 172 n.1). In this stage of tradition, resurrection and exaltation could be used almost interchangeably. In the latest sources we see that the exaltation either (1) coincides with the ascension, at the end of the resurrection day (Mk 16:19)[3], on the fortieth day (undoubtedly under the

---

*Text with Introduction, Notes, and Indices* (London: Macmillan, [2]1907; [3]1909) 151. With G.E. Ladd, *A Commentary on the Revelation of John* (Grand Rapids: Eerdmans, 1972) 170.

[1] L.W. Barnard, 'The Day of the Resurrection and Ascension of Christ in the Epistle of Barnabas', *RBen* 78 (1968) 106-107. For a discussion of older literature on Barn 15:9, see Larrañaga, *Ascension* 498-509.

[2] The suggestion of Hahn, *Hoheitstitel* 127 (now positively accepted by Hengel, 'Setze dich' 120), that it is relatively easy to trace the NT exaltation conception because it is always (*durchweg*) linked with Ps 110, gives an unrealistic and distorted picture.

[3] E.g. ActPil 14:1 (EvAp 260; tr. NTApo 1, 343); Irenaeus, *AdvHaer* III 10,6 (PG 7, 879; SC 211, 137-138).

influence of the timetable of Luke-Acts[1]), or on still another occasion[2], or (2) the exaltation was stretched out over the entire event of salvation, as in the Fourth Gospel, a journey 'from cross to glory'.

We must now turn to Luke-Acts to find Luke's position with regard to this matter.

---

[1] E.g. Lactantius, *Epit* 47 (PL 6, 1055); ConstAp V 20,2 (DCApo 1, 293-295); Ps-IgnTrall 9 (ApF II/3, 158).

[2] E.g. the Valentinians and Ophites according to Irenaeus, *AdvHaer* I 30,4 (PG 7, 703; SC 264, 382-384); ApocJas 14:30 (tr. NHL 35).

# CHAPTER FIVE

# RESURRECTION, EXALTATION AND ASCENSION IN LUKE-ACTS

a. *Introduction*

In the previous chapter we have sought to outline the various ways in which exaltation and ascension language was employed in early Christianity to interpret Jesus' post-death status. At one end of the spectrum, at the earliest recoverable stage of nascent Christianity, it became evident that Christ's exaltation to heaven or his session at the right hand of God coincided with the event of resurrection; at the other end, from the late first and early second century AD onwards, the exaltation had been detached from the resurrection and transferred to a final act of ascension at the end of a series of appearances (Mk 16:9-20) or it was interpreted as an event which stretched out over a longer period of time to cover the Easter events *in toto* (Fourth Gospel).

We must now return to Luke-Acts to find out where Luke stands on this matter. Not a few scholars would place the exaltation at the end of the line, on the same level as the longer ending of Mark and suggest that the καὶ ἐκάθισεν ἐκ δεξιῶν τοῦ θεοῦ of Mk 16:19 only brings out what is already implicit in the Lukan ascension story[1]. But even if Mk 16 turned out to be an echo of Luke-Acts it would be precarious to read Luke-Acts through the spectacles of Mk 16:19, since it would risk predetermining the terms of the argument. As we noted in the introductory section to the previous chapter, there are serious reasons to question whether Luke was very much concerned with presenting the ascension as an act of exaltation at all. Others think that Luke shares the perspective of the Fourth Evangelist and that he regards the entire sequence of death-resurrection-appearances-ascension as Christ's exaltation[2]. But we should

---

[1] E.g. B. Reicke, *Glaube und Leben der Urgemeinde. Bemerkungen zu Apg. 1-7* (AThANT 32; Zürich: Zwingli, 1957) 19. Whether or not Lk 24:50-53 and Mk 16:19 were fused already in Tatian's Diatessaron is difficult to say. It is attested e.g. in the Arabic Diatessaron (ed. Marmardji 530-531; tr. ANFa 9, 129) and the Old Italian harmony (in both the Venetian and Tuscan dialect) (ed. Todesco 171.368), but not in the (reconstructed) Syriac Diatessaron (ed. Ortiz de Urbina 299), Ephraem's Commentary (ed. LeLoir) and the Liège Diatessaron (ed. Plooij 796-797).

[2] Cf. E.E. Ellis, *The Gospel of Luke* (NCeB; Grand Rapids: Eerdmans; London: Marshall, Morgan & Scott, 1966, ²1974) 12. *Mutatis mutandis* also J.G. Lygre, *Exaltation. Considered*

not push Luke into a Johannine mould. Whatever the relationship between Luke-Acts and the Fourth Gospel, each evangelist is and remains entitled to his own views. In what follows, then, we will attempt to hear Luke's voice as much as possible from within his own context of understanding, in order to avoid trespassing the boundaries set by Luke himself.

Before we enter into a more detailed analysis of individual Lukan passages, the following overall observations may be helpful to put the critical issue in perspective.

First of all, in the narrative sections of the Book of Acts, that is, in those parts of the book where Luke is least bound to his sources and where his own theological viewpoints are most likely to surface, Luke points out, with a certain emphasis, that the *resurrection* of Jesus was the central theme of the apostolic preaching in its encounter with the non-Christian *Umwelt*, Judaism in particular (Acts 4:2,33; 17:3,18,32; 23:6-8; 25:19; 26:23). According to Acts 1:22 the twelve apostles were commissioned to be witnesses of the resurrection (although the qualifications of apostleship included their association with the risen Lord ἕως τῆς ἡμέρας ἧς ἀνελήμφθη ἀφ᾽ ἡμῶν). The theme of apostolic witness to the resurrection recurs frequently in the Book of Acts (1:22; 2:32; 3:15; 5:32; 10:40-41; 13:31)[1]. As for the Gospel, in two of the three passion predictions Luke makes reference to the resurrection 'on the third day' as the climax of Jesus' ministry (Lk 9:22; 18:33); afterwards the angels at the tomb (24:6-8) and Jesus himself (24:46) refer to these very predictions[2]. H.J. Cadbury therefore seems to be right in insisting that for Luke the resurrection is 'the distinguishing article of faith for the Christian over against the Jew'[3]. With all of Luke's emphasis on this point, he can hardly be blamed

---

*with Reference to the Resurrection and Ascension in Luke-Acts* (Diss. Princeton Theological Seminary, 1975).

[1] Cf. C.H. Talbert, *Luke and the Gnostics. An Examination of the Lukan Purpose* (Nashville, New York: Abingdon, 1966) 17-32.

[2] If the absence of the resurrection in the second of Luke's passion predictions (Lk 9:44) is intentional, its motif is to stress the seriousness of the coming passion [M. Dömer, *Das Heil Gottes. Studien zur Theologie des lukanischen Doppelwerkes* (BBB 51; Köln, Bonn: P. Hanstein, 1978) 83]. It is also possible that it reflects the use of Luke's non-Markan source, as suggest C. Colpe, ὁ υἱὸς τοῦ ἀνθρώπου, *ThWNT* 8 (1969) 447.461; I.H. Marshall, *Commentary on Luke* (NIGTC; Grand Rapids: Eerdmans, 1978) 394; T. Schramm, *Der Markus-Stoff bei Lukas. Eine literarkritische und redaktionsgeschichtliche Untersuchung* (MSSNTS 14; Cambridge: CUP, 1971) 130-136. Or has Luke perhaps transferred the phrase to 24:7?

[3] H.J. Cadbury, *The Making of Luke-Acts* (New York: Macmillan, 1927; repr. London: SPCK, 1958) 278. See also E. Haenchen, 'Judentum und Christentum in der

for deviating from the apostolic preaching[1].

Secondly, however, whereas in none of the resurrection passages just mentioned does Luke make explicit reference to the exaltation, exaltation texts generally occur in the missionary speeches, that is, on the lips of others. Does this mean that Luke subtly distances himself from the early exaltation kerygma and conveys it as an ancient relic of the primitive church only to give his narrative an air of antiquity? Does he separate the exaltation from the resurrection and postpone the heavenly enthronement of Jesus to the day of the ascension forty days later, as Acts 2:32ff. seems to imply?

In an attempt to disclose Luke's view on the matter we will now examine the principal exaltation texts in Luke-Acts that play a role in the current scholarly debate. As in chapter 3 we will follow Luke's narrative sequence (Lk 22:69; 23:42-43; 24:26; Acts 2:32-36; 5:31; 13:30-37).

### b. *The Gospel of Luke (Lk 22:69; 23:42-43; 24:26)*
Of the three sayings preserved in the Gospel of Luke which are pertinent to our topic only the first (22:69) is attested to in all three synoptic gospels; the other two (23:42-43; 24:26) are Lukan *Sondergut.*

*Lk 22:69* A comparison of the Markan and Lukan version of Jesus' reply to the high priest before the Sanhedrin (Mk 14:62 // Lk 22:69) makes it unlikely that the shorter Lukan version represents the more original form of the saying[2]. The differences between the two can be satisfactorily explained in terms of Luke's editorial work on his Markan source. In addition, no underlying source other than Mark is detectable as far as this verse is concerned[3].

---

Apostelgeschichte', *ZNW* 54 (1963) 155-187.

[1] So (rightly) Marshall, 'The Resurrection in the Acts of the Apostles', in: W.W. Gasque, R.P. Martin (eds.), *Apostolic History and the Gospel. Biblical and Historical Essays Presented to F.F. Bruce on his 60th Birthday* (Grand Rapids: Eerdmans; Exeter: Paternoster, 1970) 92-107.

[2] Contra Colpe, *ThWNT* 8, 438-439; M.-É. Boismard, *Synopse des quatre Évangiles en français* 2 (Paris: Cerf, 1972) 405-406 (short text = document B); V. Hampel, *Menschensohn und historischer Jesus. Ein Rätselwort als Schlüssel zum messianischen Selbstverständnis Jesu* (Neukirchen-Vluyn: Neukirchener, 1990) 174-185, who argue for Lukan priority of the saying.

[3] That is, if v.69 is taken by itself. For a broader source-critical analysis of Luke's passion narrative, see J.B. Green, *The Death of Jesus. Tradition and Interpretation in the Passion Narrative* (WUNT 2/33; Tübingen: J.C.B. Mohr/Paul Siebeck, 1988) 24-104, esp. 73-75, where he cautiously opts for 'a pre-Lukan, non-Markan tradition' in v.69. It seems to me that if a source underlies the larger context, its wording is more or less identical to Mk 14:62, with

(1) Ἀπὸ τοῦ νῦν is distinctly Lukan idiom[1]. As in Mt 26:29 // Lk 22:18, Matthew has ἀπ᾽ ἄρτι where Luke has ἀπὸ τοῦ νῦν. Each phrase reflects the author's diction[2]. Rather than tracing this minor agreement back to a hypothetical (Aramaic or Greek?) source[3] (or to the use of one by the other), the text of Mark itself sufficiently explains the addition: both Matthew and Luke may have felt the need to polish the awkward Markan ἐγώ εἰμι καὶ ὄψεσθε (the use of καί is strange; note the brusque change of tenses!), Luke by transposing and rephrasing ἐγώ εἰμι; Matthew by inserting πλὴν λέγω ὑμῖν (v.64), Luke and Matthew both by adding a *terminus a quo* to explain the abrupt change of tenses[4], thereby introducing a notion of imminence into Jesus' words;

(2) The most likely hypothesis to explain the absence of ὄψεσθε is that Luke, unwilling to grant the hostile Sanhedrinists a vision of the exalted Son of Man before his coming at the parousia (21:27), transposed the *verbum videndi* to the vision of Stephen (Acts 7:56) and replaced ὁράω by θεωρέω to assimilate the wording more strongly to Dan 7:13 LXX[5];

(3) Luke adds τοῦ θεοῦ to the Markan circumlocution for God, ἡ δύναμις (הגבורה Aram. גבורתא; Bill. 1, 1006-1007; cf. EvPe 5:19) for the convenience of his Hellenistic readers (cf. Lk 12:8 diff. Mt/Q 10:32; SLk 15:10)[6];

(4) The absence of καὶ ἐρχόμενον μετὰ τῶν νεφελῶν τοῦ οὐρανοῦ is also to be

---

J.A. Fitzmyer, *The Gospel According to Luke X-XXIV. Introduction, Translation, and Notes* (AncB 28A; Garden City, NY: Doubleday, 1985) 1458; J. Plevnik, 'Son of Man Seated at the Right Hand of God. Luke 22,69 in Lucan Christology', *Bib.* 72 (1991) 336-338.

[1] Lk 1:48; 5:10 (contra Mk 1:17 // Mt 4:19); 12:52; 22:18 (contra Mk 14:25 diff Mt 26:29 ἀπ᾽ ἄρτι; not in par. [?] Jn 6:53); 22:69 (contra Mk 14:62; diff Mt 26:64 ἀπ᾽ ἄρτι); Acts 18:6; outside Luke-Acts only in Jn 8:11 (*pericope de adultera*) and 2 Cor 5:16.

[2] Ἀπ᾽ ἄρτι Mt 23:39 (contra Lk 13:35 Q); 26:29 (contra Mk 14:25 diff Lk 22:18 ἀπὸ τοῦ νῦν); 26:64 (contra Mk 14:62 diff Lk 22:69 ἀπὸ τοῦ νῦν); further in Jn 13:19; 14:7; Rev 14:13). The suggestion of A. Debrunner (cf. BDR 12₃), followed by P.M. Casey, *Son of Man. The Interpretation and Influence of Daniel 7* (London: SPCK, 1979) 183-184, that in Mt 26:29 one should read ἄπαρτι ('verily') for ἀπ᾽ ἄρτι ('from henceforth'), is unlikely in the light of Matthean redaction.

[3] J. Jeremias, *Neutestamentliche Theologie 1. Die Verkündigung Jesu* (Gütersloh: G. Mohn, 1971, ³1979) 260-261; Marshall, *Commentary* 850; J. Nolland, *Luke 18:35-24:53* (WBC 35C; Dallas, TX: Word, 1993) 1110.

[4] Contra J.A.T. Robinson, *Jesus and His Coming. The Emergence of a Doctrine* (London: SCM, 1957) 49-50, who argued that Mark crossed out ἀπ᾽ ἄρτι.

[5] J. Dupont, 'Assis à la droite de Dieu. L'interprétation du Ps 110,1 dans le Nouveau Testament' (1974); repr. in: idem, *Nouvelles Études sur les Actes des Apôtres* (LeDiv 118; Paris: Cerf, 1984) 226 n.51.

[6] W. Grundmann, *Das Evangelium nach Lukas* (ThHK 3; Berlin: Evangelische, 1961, ¹⁰1984) 420; G. Schneider, *Das Evangelium nach Lukas 2* (ÖTBK 3; GTB.S 501; Gütersloh: G. Mohn; Würzburg: Echter, 1977) 470. But see also the remarks of M. Sabbe, 'The Son of Man Saying in Acts 7,56', in: J. Kremer (éd.), *Les Actes des Apôtres. Traditions, rédaction, théologie* (BEThL 48; Gembloux: Duculot, 1979) 261-262, who argues that the addition is inspired by Luke's concern to underscore the divine nature of Jesus' Messiahship.

attributed to Luke's editorial activity and reflects his tendency to deal with the delay of the parousia (cf. *infra* 178). The emphasis now falls completely on the exalted *status* of the Son of Man;

(5) The use of δέ is for stylistic reasons, the change of τὸν υἱὸν τοῦ ἀνθρώπου ... καθήμενον into ἔσται ὁ υἱὸς τοῦ ἀνθρώπου καθήμενος is required by grammar.

The crucial question in this verse is what timing Luke has in view with ἀπὸ τοῦ νῦν. In the light of Luke's use of ἀπὸ τοῦ νῦν elsewhere, it is clear that the time indication cannot be taken with strict literalness[1]. The term is used proleptically. Does it refer to the resurrection[2], the ascension[3], or to the saving event as a whole[4]? What is envisaged is a period in the near future in which the Son of Man will be seated at God's right hand, without further reflection on the moment of its inception (the emphasis is on the exalted *status* of the Son of Man). With how much precision would Luke expect his readers to take the *terminus a quo*? It may not be totally irrelevant to point out that Luke preserves the saying in a pre-Easter context, that is, before its actual fulfilment. Perhaps, then, we should not insist on too much precision and take the time indication in general terms. We may catch the statement's intention best if we paraphrase the saying 'it will not be long, before you see ...' or, 'you will very soon see ...'. But then again, Luke is writing with hindsight; did he never ask about the fulfilment of Jesus' prophetic word?

An investigation of v.69 alone does not solve the problem. Obviously Luke's larger perspective must be taken into account. But it should be noted that, in comparison with Mark, Luke's description is hardly a convincing reinterpretation of the saying in favour of the ascension, as e.g. G. Lohfink and E. Franklin would have it[5]. The effect of the excision of καὶ ἐρχόμενον μετὰ τῶν νεφελῶν τοῦ οὐρανοῦ is that the vindication of the Son of Man is brought back to the immediate future, but in this respect the difference between

---

[1] Contra Lygre, *Exaltation* 32-33.43-44.

[2] Ph. Vielhauer, 'Ein Weg zur neutestamentlichen Christologie? Prüfung der Thesen Ferdinand Hahns', in: idem, *Aufsätze zum Neuen Testament* (TB 31; München: Chr. Kaiser, 1965) 173; D.M. Hay, *Glory at the Right Hand. Psalm 110 in Early Christianity* (SBL.MS 18; Nashville, New York: Abingdon, 1973) 66; Dupont, 'Assis' 224-230.

[3] G. Lohfink, *Die Himmelfahrt Jesu. Untersuchungen zu den Himmelfahrts- und Erhöhungstexten bei Lukas* (StANT 26; München: Kösel, 1971) 237; E. Grässer, 'Die Parusieerwartung in der Apostelgeschichte', in: Kremer (éd.), *Actes* 114; R. Maddox, *The Purpose of Luke-Acts* (Studies of the New Testament and Its World; Edinburgh: T.&T. Clark, 1982) 108; Plevnik, 'Seated' 331-347.

[4] Cf. Fitzmyer, *Luke* 2, 1463.

[5] Lohfink, *Himmelfahrt* 237; E. Franklin, *Christ the Lord. A Study in the Purpose and Theology of Luke-Acts* (London: SPCK, 1975) 28-29.

Mark // Matthew and Luke is one in emphasis only. If Luke had wished to make an allusion to the ascension he could have done so much less ambiguously. If the ascension were the occasion of Christ's exaltation, why then did he eliminate the clouds, instead of reinterpreting them in conformity with the ascension cloud, in the same way he treated the Markan parousia clouds to conform them to his own cloud motif (Mk 13:26 // Lk 21:27) (*supra* 105)?

*Lk 23:42-43* Regardless of whether the penitent criminal hoped that Jesus would raise him from the dead in the age to come or that Jesus would take up his soul into heaven, the petition 'to remember him (for good)' (Ps 105:4 LXX) expresses the conviction that Jesus' imminent death would not be the end and that his royal authority would go beyond the constraints of death. If εἰς τὴν βασιλείαν σου is the correct reading ('remember me when you come into your kingdom')[1], the reference in all probability is to the period immediately after Jesus' death, when Jesus would enter into his kingdom (= realm) (cf. 24:26 παθεῖν ... καὶ εἰσελθεῖν εἰς τὴν δόξαν αὐτοῦ *v.l.* εἰς τὴν βασιλείαν). But the textual evidence is suspect and a good case can be made for adopting the reading ἐν τῇ βασιλείᾳ σου[2], which opens up the way for an eschatological interpretation: 'when you come in (or with) your kingship (Aram. במלכותך)', i.e. as king, that is, at Christ's return in glory at the parousia (so explicitly in D: ἐν τῇ ἡμέρᾳ τῆς ἐλεύσεως σου)[3]. Full force can then be given to the adverb σήμερον in Jesus' reply: it is not in the distant future, but now, at the hour of death, that the criminal will experience the fulfilment of his request: that same day he will be with Jesus in Paradise, the intermediate resting place of the souls of the righteous dead waiting for the resurrection[4].

---

[1] 𝔭⁷⁵ B L sa^mss bo^pt. This reading is accepted by B.M. Metzger, *A Textual Commentary on the Greek New Testament* (Stuttgart: Deutsche Bibelgesellschaft, UBS, 1971, ²1994) 154 and by B.D. Ehrman, *The Orthodox Corruption of Scripture. The Effect of Early Christological Controversies on the Text of the New Testament* (New York, Oxford: OUP, 1993) 233-235, who treats ἐν τῇ βασιλείᾳ σου as an 'orthodox corruption'.

[2] ℵ A C*.2 W Θ Ψ (070) *f*¹.¹³ 33 𝔐 lat sy (sa^mss bo^pt). The reading is followed by e.g. Marshall, *Commentary* 872; G. Petzke, *Das Sondergut des Evangeliums nach Lukas* (ZWKB; Zürich: Theologischer, 1990) 192. The reading εἰσελθεῖν εἰς τὴν βασιλείαν looks like a harmonisation to the more conventional phraseology, in particular to Matthean diction (Mt 5:20; 7:21 (2x); 18:3; 19:23; Mk 9:47; 10:23,24,25; Lk 10:(24,)25; Jn 3:5; Acts 14:22).

[3] Note that the phraseology is reminiscent of Lk 9:26 // Mk 8:38: ὅταν (the Son of Man) ἔλθῃ ἐν τῇ δόξῃ αὐτοῦ (cf. Mt 16:28 diff. Mk 9:1 // Lk 9:27; Mt 25:31).

[4] On the contemporary Jewish conceptions of Paradise, see W. Bousset, *Die Religion des Judentums im späthellenistischen Zeitalter* (hrsg. v. H. Gressmann; HNT 21; Tübingen:

The difficulty ·of the present saying lies in its wider christological implications. That Luke does not seem to know of a *descensus ad inferos* is one thing[1]. A more serious problem is how Jesus' entrance into Paradise at the day of crucifixion (σήμερον) relates to his resurrection 'on the third day' (Lk 9:22; 18:33). J.A. Fitzmyer thinks that 'we can only speculate about how long an interval Luke may have considered between Jesus' death and burial and his entrance into glory' (it is not stated in the Gospel tradition at what time Jesus actually rose from the dead, only that he appeared 'on the third day') and suggests taking the adverb 'today' seriously (read: literally)[2]. This is possible. On the other hand, Luke lays a certain emphasis on the 'today' of salvation elsewhere in his Gospel (2:11; 3:22; 4:21; 5:26; 13:32,33; 19:5,9), which suggests that he uses the term in a technical sense. Perhaps then we must take the 'today' of 23:43 as a standard designation for the time of messianic salvation, which begins with the resurrection and exaltation of Jesus[3]. As in 22:69 ('from now on') Luke does not seem to be particularly concerned with exact chronology. Either way, the saying cannot be said to conflict with the primitive exaltation kerygma[4].

*Lk 24:26* The critical issue in this verse revolves around the question whether Luke regards the Messiah's 'entrance into glory' (cf. 2 Bar 30:1 and *supra* 77

---

J.C.B. Mohr/Paul Siebeck, [4]1966) 282-285.488-489; P. Volz, *Die Eschatologie der jüdischen Gemeinde* (Tübingen: J.C.B. Mohr/Paul Siebeck, [2]1934) 413-418; Jeremias, *ThWNT* 5, 763-766; H. Bietenhard, *Die himmlische Welt in Urchristentum und Spätjudentum* (WUNT 2; Tübingen: J.C.B. Mohr/Paul Siebeck, 1951) 161-186; cf. Bill. 2, 264-269; 4/2, 1118-1165; *HJP* 2, 540-543.546 n.11.

[1] W. Bieder, *Die Vorstellung von der Höllenfahrt Jesu Christi. Beitrag zur Entstehungsgeschichte der Vorstellung vom sog. Descensus ad inferos* (AThANT 19; Zürich: Zwingli, 1949) 57-70.

[2] Fitzmyer, 'Today You Shall Be With Me in Paradise' (Luke 23:43)', in: idem, *Luke the Theologian. Aspects of His Teaching* (New York, Mahwah: Paulist, 1989) 220-221. Cf. also Jeremias, 'Zwischen Karfreitag und Ostern. Descensus und Ascensus in der Karfreitagstheologie des Neuen Testaments' (1949); repr. in: idem, *Abba. Studien zur neutestamentlichen Theologie und Zeitgeschichte* (Göttingen: Vandenhoeck & Ruprecht, 1966) 329.

[3] Ellis, *Luke* 268; E. Schweizer, *Das Evangelium nach Lukas* (NTD 3; Göttingen: Vandenhoeck & Ruprecht, 1982, [2]1986) 240.

[4] Contra W. Schmithals, *Das Evangelium nach Lukas* (ZBK.NT 3/1; Zürich: Theologischer, 1980) 227, it cannot be maintained that the expression 'your kingdom' presupposes the ascension of Jesus. Jesus' entry into Paradise could involve the assumption of his soul only. On the level of Luke it is quite clear that Jesus' body was in the grave immediately after death.

n.2) as an event (from the perspective of the Emmaus disciples) still in the future (i.e. either at the ascension or at the parousia) or as an already accomplished fact in the past (i.e. at the resurrection). Since the emphasis seems to be on the first part of the clause (the issue at stake is the *suffering* of the Messiah, not his exaltation-vindication), there is much to say for paraphrasing the verse as follows: 'Was it not necessary that the Messiah should suffer these things before entering into his glory?' (cf. NEB), thereby leaving the question open *when* he would enter into glory (only that it would be subsequent to the passion)[1]. Yet, if the wider Lukan context is taken into consideration, it seems that we can be a little more specific about the *terminus a quo* of the Messiah's entrance into glory. Lohfink[2] has pointed out that the structure of the verse under consideration reflects a typical statement pattern (*Aussageschema*) found elsewhere in Luke-Acts (Lk 24:46; Acts 3:18; 17:3; 26:23; cf. 14:22), and he observed that in each case the second member of the clause (each time a resurrection statement) refers to a past event. Lohfink then suggested that εἰσελθεῖν εἰς τὴν δόξαν αὐτοῦ is a Lukan stylistic variation of the traditional ἀναστῆναι ἐκ νεκρῶν (τῇ τρίτῃ ἡμέρᾳ) and there seems to be no cogent reason to question this verdict.

However, Lohfink seems to press the argument beyond its limits when he contends that, as far as Luke is concerned, εἰσελθεῖν εἰς τὴν δόξαν αὐτοῦ is a resurrection statement and *not* an exaltation statement[3]. This judgement stands or falls with the assessment of Luke's wider treatment of resurrection, ascension and exaltation. The texts Lohfink adduced to corroborate his thesis (Lk 22:69; 23:43) cannot bear the weight, as we noted above, and positive evidence that Luke relocated the exaltation to the ascension is absent, at least in the texts we have discussed so far.

Therefore, it seems to be a more natural interpretation that, for Luke, Jesus' resurrection is in some way connected with his 'entrance into glory' as an already accomplished event[4]. That is, at the resurrection Jesus entered into a new mode of existence. If we are right in suggesting that, in the earliest theology, the resurrection of Jesus implied his exaltation to heaven (i.e. to glory), then there is nothing irregular in this verse. If, finally, this line of

---

[1] *Stricto sensu* only the (divine) necessity of the impending passion and vindication is described as a past event. The imperfect ἔδει does not automatically make the following verbs events of the past as well. That the passion is considered as a past event is clear from the context, but only by implication.

[2] Lohfink, *Himmelfahrt* 236-239.

[3] Lohfink, *Himmelfahrt* 238-239.

[4] Cf. also (with some differences) Lygre, *Exaltation* 7-17.

interpretation is correct, the underlying implication (but no more than that!) is that on the Emmaus road Jesus appears as having already entered into his glory, i.e. he appears 'from heaven'[1].

c. *The Book of Acts (Acts 2:32-36; 5:31; 13:30-37)*
Apart from the ascension story in the opening chapter of the Book of Acts (Acts 1), three resurrection and exaltation texts deserve particular notice, two in the speeches of Peter in Jerusalem (Acts 2:32-36; 5:31), one in the missionary speech ascribed to Paul in Pisidian Antioch (13:30-37)[2].

*Acts 2:32-36*   Peter's Pentecost discourse (Acts 2:14-40) follows the basic structure of a primitive missionary speech[3]. The *exordium* (vv.14b-15), linking the speech to the Pentecost event (vv.1-13), is followed by a text from Scripture to interpret the event from a biblical perspective (vv.16-21 = Joel 3:1-5 LXX). Then follows a kerygmatic section on Jesus and his resurrection (vv.22-24), immediately followed by another proof-from-Scripture section, which proves the resurrection with the help of a messianic reading of Ps 15:8-11 LXX (vv.25-32), and the heavenly exaltation of Jesus and the subsequent outpouring of the Spirit, with the help of Ps 109:1 LXX (vv.33-36). Conventionally, the speech closes with a call to repentance (vv.37-40).

At first sight the speech seems to contain a quite straightforward reference to the ascension understood as the occasion of Jesus' exaltation to heaven: οὐ γὰρ Δαυὶδ ἀνέβη εἰς τοὺς οὐρανούς (v.34a), the obvious implication being that

---

[1] M.-J. Lagrange, *Évangile selon St. Luc* (EtB; Paris: J. Gabalda, 1921) 606; Fitzmyer, 'The Ascension of Christ and Pentecost', *TS* 45 (1984) 422; idem, *Luke* 2, 1538-1539.1566.

[2] Some authors take the phrase ὁ θεὸς ... ἐδόξασεν τὸν παῖδα αὐτοῦ Ἰησοῦν (Acts 3:13) as a reference to the resurrection-exaltation of Jesus [U. Wilckens, *Die Missionsreden der Apostelgeschichte. Form- und traditionsgeschichtliche Untersuchungen* (WMANT 5; Neukirchen-Vluyn: Neukirchener, 1961, ³1974) 38-39; Lygre, *Exaltation* 119-120.122-123; F. Hahn, 'Das Problem alter christologischer Überlieferungen in der Apostelgeschichte unter besonderer Berücksichtigung von Act 3,19-21', in: Kremer (éd.), *Actes* 136 (+ Anm.28)]. This is of course possible, given the following antithetical ὃν ὑμεῖς μὲν παρεδώκατε κτλ. In the present narrative context, however, it is also possible that the glorification/vindication of Jesus takes place in the miracle performed [Schneider, *Die Apostelgeschichte 1. Einleitung. Kommentar zu Kap. 1,1-8,40* (HThK 5; Freiburg, Basel, Wien: Herder, 1980) 317]. Either way there is here no reference to the ascension.

[3] C.H. Dodd, *The Apostolic Preaching and Its Developments. Three Lectures* (London: Hodder & Stoughton, 1936) (synopsis inside the back cover); Wilckens, *Missionsreden* 32-37; R.F. Zehnle, *Peter's Pentecost Discourse. Tradition and Lukan Reinterpretation in Peter's Speeches of Acts 2 and 3* (SBL.MS 15; Nashville, New York: Abingdon, 1971) 19-60 (literature in Schneider, *Apg* 1, 95).

*Jesus* (the Messiah) did go up to the heavens. This statement is immediately followed by one of the rare full quotations of Ps 110:1 in the NT (vv.34b-35). Various authors have suggested that τῇ δεξιᾷ οὖν τοῦ θεοῦ ὑψωθείς (v.33a) and ἀνέβη εἰς τοὺς οὐρανούς ... κάθου ἐκ δεξιῶν μου (v.34a) are direct references (at least in the present literary context) to the event described in Acts 1:9-11[1]. If this is so, we have here quite a significant and possibly early example of the ascension understood as exaltation or session at the right hand[2].

There are, however, several indications in the text which suggest an alternative interpretation of the words.

Firstly, the concern of the present context is to explain the miraculous events of Pentecost, *in concreto* to clarify what this has to do with Jesus of Nazareth. The argument is in two stages. At the first stage it is demonstrated that God has vindicated Jesus by raising him from the dead; this is documented with Ps 16:8-11 (15:8-11 LXX), which is taken to mean that Jesus (the Messiah) was kept from corruption[3]. At the second stage, to avoid a possible misunderstanding of the resurrection as a mere restoration to life (this would not in itself link the experience of Pentecost to Jesus!), Ps 110:1 is cited to declare that Jesus was exalted *to heaven* (the place where he must be to be able to communicate the Spirit to his disciples) and from there has poured out the Spirit. Τῇ δεξιᾷ has been put forward for the sake of emphasis; as most commentators acknowledge, it is local[4] rather than instrumental[5]. Luke thereby puts forward

---

[1] J.G. Davies, *He Ascended into Heaven. A Study in the History of Doctrine* (BaL 1958; London: Lutterworth, 1958) 29; Lohfink, *Himmelfahrt* 229; E. Kränkl, *Jesus der Knecht Gottes. Die heilsgeschichtliche Stellung Jesu in den Reden der Apostelgeschichte* (BU 8; Regensburg: F. Pustet, 1972) 150; G. Friedrich, 'Lk 9,51 und die Entrückungschristologie des Lukas', in: P. Hoffmann, N. Brox, W. Pesch (Hrsg.), *Orientierung an Jesus. Zur Theologie der Synoptiker* (FS J. Schmid; Freiburg: Herder, 1973) 67; J. Schmitt, 'Kerygme pascal et lecture scripturaire dans l'instruction d'Antioche (Act. 13,23-37)', in: Kremer (éd.), *Actes* 156; A. Weiser, 'Himmelfahrt Christi I. Neues Testament', *TRE* 15 (1986) 333; J. Zmijewski, *Die Apostelgeschichte übersetzt und erklärt* (RNT 5; Regensburg: F. Pustet, 1994) 145; C.K. Barrett, *The Acts of the Apostles 1. Preliminary Introduction and Commentary on Acts I-XIV* (ICC; Edinburgh: T.&T. Clark, 1994) 149.

[2] Under the reasonable assumption, of course, that Luke is in agreement with what he presents as *verba Petri*! Contra Haenchen, *Die Apostelgeschichte* (KEK III[17]; Göttingen: Vandenhoeck & Ruprecht, 1956, [7]1977) 189, who holds that Luke simply failed to assimilate a conflicting relic of tradition.

[3] Cf. A. Schmitt, 'Ps 16, 8-11 als Zeugnis der Auferstehung in der Apg.', *BZ NS* 17 (1973) 229-248.

[4] H. Conzelmann, *Die Apostelgeschichte* (HNT 7; Tübingen: J.C.B. Mohr/Paul Siebeck, 1963, [2]1972) 33; G. Schille, *Die Apostelgeschichte des Lukas* (ThHK 5; Berlin: Evangelische, 1983, [2]1984) 113; Schneider, *Apg* 1, 275; R. Pesch, *Die Apostelgeschichte* 1 (EKK 5;

the literal-realistic interpretation of the *sessio ad dexteram* and takes this to be a crucial element in the argumentation.

Secondly, given the use of ὑψόω (v.33; cf. Phil 2:9), the resurrection context (vv.32,33; cf. Eph 1:20; 2:6), the traditional appeal to Ps 110:1 (vv.33,34,35)[1] and the close link of the exaltation and the bestowal of the Spirit (v.33), there need be no doubt that the NT exaltation kerygma lies at the background of Acts 2:32-35[2].

Thirdly, if the conjunction οὖν (v.33) is given full (illative) force, τῇ δεξιᾷ ... τοῦ θεοῦ ὑψωθείς repeats in different words what has already been said or implied, viz. that 'this Jesus God has raised (from the dead)' (v.32)[3].

Fourthly, the phrase ἀνέβη εἰς τοὺς οὐρανούς is distinctly un-Lukan. Elsewhere, Luke never uses ἀναβαίνω in connection with the ascension and he has a pronounced preference for the singular οὐρανός instead of the plural οὐρανοί[4]. Luke is likely to have taken up this phrase from his source,

---

Neukirchen-Vluyn: Neukirchener; Zürich: Benzinger, 1986) 124; Zmijewski, *Apg* 145-146.

[5] A. Wikenhauser, *Die Apostelgeschichte übersetzt und erklärt* (RNT 5; Regensburg: F. Pustet, 1938, ⁴1961) 46; G. Stählin, *Die Apostelgeschichte* (NTD 5; Göttingen: Vandenhoeck & Ruprecht, 1962, ⁷1980) 49; F.F. Bruce, *The Acts of the Apostles. Greek Text with Introduction and Commentary* (Grand Rapids: Eerdmans; Leicester: Apollos, 1951, ³1990) 126; Barrett, *Acts* 1, 149.

[1] It is disputed whether τῇ δεξιᾷ οὖν τοῦ θεοῦ ὑψωθείς (v.33a) is an allusion to Ps 110:1. Some authors think of the influence of Ps 15:11 LXX τερπνότητες ἐν τῇ δεξιᾷ σου εἰς τέλος (significantly, the quotation of Ps 16 in vv.25-28 stops exactly at this point, obviously in view of what comes next). Unfortunately, this observation does not settle the issue: the author either preserved Ps 15:11c for v.33, or left the passage out, because it was redundant in view of the much clearer reference of Ps 110:1 in v.33. Others refer to Ps 117:16 LXX δεξιὰ κυρίου ὕψωσέν (note its context!), Bill. 2, 619; B. Lindars, *New Testament Apologetic. The Doctrinal Significance of the Old Testament Quotations* (London: SCM, 1961) 171; B. Rigaux, *Dieu l'a ressuscité* (SBFA 4; Gembloux: Duculot, 1973) 68.

[2] Lohfink, *Himmelfahrt* 226-229; Gourgues, *Droite* 173-178; Weiser, 'Himmelfahrt' 330.

[3] Οὐ (πάντες ἡμεῖς ἐσμεν μάρτυρες) refers to the resurrection [1:22 μάρτυρα τῆς ἀναστάσεως αὐτου; cf. 3:15; F. Blass, *Acta apostolorum sive Lucae ad Theophilum liber alter. Editio philologica apparatu critico, commentario perpetuo, indice verborum illustrata* (Göttingen: Vandenhoeck & Ruprecht, 1895) 58; H.J. Holtzmann, *Die Apostelgeschichte* (HC I/2; Freiburg: 1889; Tübingen, Leipzig: J.C.B. Mohr/Paul Siebeck, ³1901) 37; Schneider, *Apg* 1, 275; Bruce, *Acts GT* 126], rather than to τοῦτον τὸν Ἰησοῦν (cf. Acts 1:8 ἔσεσθέ μου μάρτυρες). On the Lukan witness motif, see Wilckens, *Missionsreden* 145-149.

[4] Of the 37 instances of οὐρανός in Lk, only five are in the plural (10:20; 11:2; 12:33; 18:22; 21:26), three of which correspond to the plural of Mt ([11:2]; 18:22; 21:26). Five times Luke changes the plural into a singular (3:21,22; 6:23; 11:13; 15:7). Only in one case Lk has a plural against Mt-Mk (12:33); 10:20 is unparalleled. Of the 26 instances of οὐρανός in Acts (MGM 729), only two have the plural (2:33; 7:56). Of the latter text the tradition-critical

presumably from a Jewish-Palestinian milieu[1]. Since Luke did not assimilate the words to his own idiom we may assume that he uses the traditional wording, which the hearers/readers would easily recognise as such (a modern author would use quotation marks).

Fifthly, the fact that Luke uses traditional material is confirmed by a comparison with other texts. The ideology of Acts 2:32ff. draws very close to Eph 4:8-10, where the ἀναβαίνω εἰς ὕψος from Ps 67:19 LXX is used in connection with Christ's resurrection-exaltation and the subsequent giving of the Spirit. One is reminded also of the Johannine connection of glorification and bestowal of the Spirit (Jn 15:26; 16:17; cf. 14:16; 7:39; cf. 20:22). Considering the intrinsic connection of exaltation and outpouring of the Spirit in the present context, there is much to say for the view that Acts 2:32ff. remotely alludes to Ps 68:19[2], and one more example of the heavenly journey type of ascension (note the use of the active mode!), i.e., a temporary journey to heaven in order to return with the gift of the Spirit (*anabasis-katabasis* pattern). Its function is distinctly different from that of a rapture (*Entrückung*), which closes one's earthly life.

The above mentioned observations easily fit the form-critical pattern of the Easter faith which we discovered in the previous chapter. If our assessment of the evidence is correct, Acts 2:33 confirms rather than contradicts our suggestion that, in the earliest preaching, the heavenly journey type of ascension is reserved for the Easter event.

A further comment on the conclusion of the argument stated in v.36 is appropriate here:

Ἀσφαλῶς οὖν γινωσκέτω πᾶς οἶκος Ἰσραὴλ ὅτι καὶ κύριον αὐτὸν καὶ χριστὸν ἐποίησεν ὁ θεός, τοῦτον τὸν Ἰησοῦν ὃν ὑμεῖς ἐσταυρώσατε.

The theology contained in this verse is probably traditional. One is reminded of early Christian confessions such as Rom 1:4 and Phil 2:9, according to which Jesus was granted a new status from the resurrection-exaltation onwards.

---

question is still unsolved, see Sabbe, 'Son of Man Saying' 241-279. According to H.E. Tödt, *Der Menschensohn in der synoptischen Überlieferung* (Gütersloh: G. Mohn, 1959) 274-276 and N. Perrin, *Rediscovering the Teaching of Jesus* (New York, Evanston: Harper & Row, 1967) 178-179, Acts 7:56 is pre-Lukan. See for the use of οὐρανός also F. Torm, 'Der Pluralis οὐρανοί', *ZNW* 33 (1934) 48-50.

[1] G. Kretschmar, 'Himmelfahrt und Pfingsten', *ZKG* 66 (1954/55) 216; Fitzmyer, 'Ascension' 434.

[2] E.g. Lindars, *Apologetic* 39.42-44.51-59; Dupont, 'Ascension du Christ et don de l'Esprit d'après Ac 2,33' (1973); repr. in: idem, *Nouvelles Études* 199-209; Gourgues, *Droite* 174-177; Barrett, *Acts* 1, 149-150.

Although the theological message of the Lukan birth narratives (Lk 1-2) is that Jesus is Son of God (Christ and Lord) from the beginning[1], it is equally clear that Luke regards the resurrection-exaltation as a special event which gives Jesus a new status which he did not possess before. So Luke could formally agree with ἐποίησεν, although he probably would have chosen a different way to express himself if he were not bound by the wording of his source. Even if Luke takes up an early piece of Christian theology to give the speech an air of antiquity (even though this would not fit his own theology), on the level of Luke the idea seems to be that, at the resurrection-exaltation, it has become manifest who Jesus was ἀπ' ἀρχῆς, namely God's Lord and Messiah[2].

The upshot of all this is that there is no justification for associating vv.33,34 with the ascension forty days after Easter[3]. In line with the primitive resurrection-exaltation paradigm ἀνέβη εἰς τοὺς οὐρανούς is only a different way of describing Jesus' entrance into his eternal glory on the day of the resurrection (Lk 24:26; cf. Eph 4:8-10; 1 Pet 3:22)[4].

*Acts 5:31*    Once it is recognised that the exaltation event referred to in Acts 2:32-36 occurred on Easter, a similar line of interpretation presents itself for Acts 5:31. In response to the crucifixion (v.30)[5] God (ὑψωθείς is now

---

[1] See R.E. Brown, *The Birth of the Messiah. A Commentary on the Infancy Narratives in the Gospels of Matthew and Luke* (AncB Reference Library; New York: Doubleday, 1977, [2]1993) 31 *et passim*; J.D.G. Dunn, *Christology in the Making. An Inquiry into the Origins of the Doctrine of the Incarnation* (London: SCM, 1980, [2]1989) 51.

[2] Marshall, *The Acts of the Apostles. An Introduction and Commentary* (TNTC 5; Leicester: IVP; Grand Rapids: Eerdmans, 1980) 80.

[3] Lohfink, *Himmelfahrt* 228-229 has argued that Luke has reinterpreted the primitive kerygma. Luke inserted οὐ πάντες ἡμεῖς ἐσμεν μάρτυρες (v.32) between the reference to the resurrection and the exaltation, thereby indicating his belief that these were two distinct events. Luke accordingly reinterpreted the ὑψωθείς (in the primitive kerygma an invisible event) as a reference to the visible ascension of Acts 1:9. But the issue is not whether or not resurrection and exaltation are distinct or not, but whether exaltation and ascension are one event.

[4] W. Michaelis, ὁράω κτλ., *ThWNT* 5 (1967) 356. Cf. Gourgues, *Droite* 167-168. Marshall, *Acts* 78, comments on v.33: 'The resurrection is to be understood as the exaltation of Jesus. It was not simply a revivification but an ascension to be with God. Peter regards this as self-evident (...)'.

[5] The question whether ἤγειρεν (v.30) refers to Jesus' historical mission [Th. Zahn, *Die Apostelgeschichte des Lucas* 1 (KNT 5; Leipzig: A. Deichert, Werner Scholl, [3]1922) 203-204 Anm.63; Bruce, *Acts GT* 172 (perhaps)] or to his resurrection [Blass, *Acta (philologica)* 87; Holtzmann, *Apg* 48; Lohfink, *Himmelfahrt* 230; R.F. O'Toole, 'Some Observations on Anistemi, 'I Raise', in Acts 3:22,26', *ScEs* 31 (1979) 85-92; Marshall, *Acts* 119; Schneider,

explicated as ὁ θεὸς ... ὕψωσεν) has exalted Jesus as Leader and Saviour 'at his right hand'[1]. As in 2:33, ὕψωσεν τῇ δεξιᾷ αὐτοῦ (v.31) does not refer to the ascension[2], but to the resurrection-exaltation.

*Acts 13:30-37*   In Paul's missionary speech in Pisidian Antioch (Acts 13:16-41), the Christ event is summarised without reference to the ascension or the exaltation[3]. It is Jesus' historical mission (vv.23-29) and his divine vindication in the resurrection from the dead (vv.30-37), which are the focal points of the proclamation. Whether ἀναστήσας Ἰησοῦν (v.33) refers to the resurrection (raised from the dead)[4] or to the historical mission of Jesus (raised as a prophet)[5] is immaterial to our purpose[6]. The point to be noted is that in the following verses the resurrection seems to build to the climax of the Christ event, the effect of which is the offer of salvation and justification (vv.38-39). Such a contention is only meaningful if the resurrection is more than a mere resuscitation and constitutes the crucial turning-point in salvation history. The resurrection initiates the Messiah's eternal reign. Again this is the traditional resurrection-exaltation concept. A series of biblical exaltation-vindication texts is used in support of the resurrection: possibly Ps 2:7 (v.33), Is 55:3 LXX

---

*Apg* 1, 395 Anm.91; Pesch, *Apg* 1, 216-217], does not seem to affect the line of our argument. A reference to the resurrection is more likely in view of the resurrection context.

[1] As in 2:33 τῇ δεξιᾷ should be taken as a local dative, see Gourgues, *Droite* 169-172 (+ 172 n.25). The *v.l.* τῇ δόξῃ αὐτοῦ (D* gig p sa; Ir^lat) is an ancient accidental error, Metzger, *Commentary* 290. The confusion of ΔΟΞΗ and ΔΕΞΙΑ is also attested in Is 62:8 (*apparatus criticus* Rahlfs 2, 649; Göttingen LXX 14, 352); Ps 16:15 (δεξιά for δόξα in Θ) (cf. Eb. Nestle in Metzger, *Commentary* 290).

[2] Lohfink, *Himmelfahrt* 230-232; Schneider, *Apg* 1, 397.

[3] On ὤφθη ἐπὶ ἡμέρας πλείους v.31, see *supra* 98 n.4, and *infra* 172 n.2.

[4] Holtzmann, *Apg* 90; Haenchen, *Apg* 395 (+ Anm.3); Lohfink, *Himmelfahrt* 232-236; Kränkl, *Jesus* 137; R.N. Longenecker, *Biblical Exegesis in the Apostolic Period* (Exeter: Paternoster, 1975; repr. Biblical and Theological Classics Library 5; 1995) 102-103; O'Toole, 'Christ's Resurrection in Acts 13:13-52', *Bib.* 60 (1979) 365-368; Marshall, *Acts* 226; K. von Zedtwitz, *Die Auferstehung Jesu in der christologischen Interpretation von Apg. 2:24-31 und 13:32-37. Eine motiv-, form- und traditionsgeschichtliche Untersuchung* (Diss. Freiburg im Breisgau, 1981) 333-335; Schneider, *Apg* 2, 137 Anm.97; Schille, *Apg* 295-296.

[5] Blass, *Acta (philologica)* 152; H.H. Wendt, *Die Apostelgeschichte* (KEK II[8]; Göttingen: Vandenhoeck & Ruprecht, 1880, [4]1899) 240; E. Preuschen, *Die Apostelgeschichte* (HNT 4/1; Tübingen: J.C.B. Mohr/Paul Siebeck, 1912) *ad loc.*; M. Rese, *Alttestamentliche Motive in der Christologie des Lukas* (StNT 1; Gütersloh: G. Mohn, 1969) 81-86; Bruce, *Acts GT* 309-10; Barrett, *Acts* 1, 645-646.

[6] If v.33 refers to the resurrection, though, we have once more an example of an exaltation text in support of the resurrection, rather than the ascension.

(v.34), and Ps 16:10 (which Luke employs as a resurrection prediction in 2:27 as well!) (v.35).

### d. *The Nature of the Lukan Post-Resurrection Appearances*

The most forceful objection to the thesis we are presently developing is that Luke does not seem to give a clear impression that he understands the post-Easter appearances as 'appearances of the already exalted Lord from heaven'[1]. Yet this seems to be the necessary corollary to the foregoing analysis.

The issue is a complex one. What are, e.g., the criteria against which the nature of the appearances can be measured? And what examples would Luke have at hand upon which to model his narrative? In the Jewish rapture tradition the motif of a post-rapture appearance is not constitutive to the rapture *Gattung*[2]. In Graeco-Roman antiquity, on the other hand, we find a large repertoire of stories about divine men appearing after their 'disappearance' and about gods who freely associate with people, not infrequently without being recognised as visitors from another world. Would they provide a plausible context of understanding for the post-resurrection appearances of Jesus?

In his stimulating analysis of the post-resurrection appearance stories in the gospel tradition, J.E. Alsup[3] has made a comparative analysis of the hellenistic θεῖος ἀνήρ appearance stories and the Gospel tradition. After having studied the appearance traditions of Apollonius of Tyana, Romulus, Aristeas of Proconnesus, Cleomedes of Astypaleia, Alcmene, Peregrinus Proteus, and Demainete[4], Alsup concludes that the hellenistic appearance stories do not offer the conceptual background for the Gospel appearances, despite the strong formal correspondence and structural similarities:

'(...) a formal analogy via the presence of similar motifs, concepts and forms of expression may well be an option, but closer consideration of the statement intention of the θεῖος ἀνήρ appearance story makes it impossible to consider these accounts as analogous in an essential sense. That is to say, both complexes share motifs like that of the figure in question being seen, recognized as a bodily reality, alive, interrupting a state of sorrow, causing a drift to rejoicing and dispelling fears, moving about or travelling, and engaging the participants in conversation, as well as the already mentioned disappearance motif, which is so key to the θεῖος ἀνήρ type; as formal categories they show a certain

---

[1] The objection of Franklin, *Christ* 31-32.

[2] Cf. E. Bickermann, 'Das leere Grab' (1924); repr. in: idem, *Studies in Jewish and Christian History* 3 (AGJU 9; Leiden: E.J. Brill, 1986) 70-81, who, however, blurs the religion-historical distinctions.

[3] J.E. Alsup, *The Post-Resurrection Appearance Stories of the Gospel Tradition. A History-of-Tradition Analysis With Text-Synopsis* (CThM 5; Stuttgart: Calwer, 1975).

[4] Alsup, *Appearance Stories* 215-238.

parallelization and correspondence. But these similarities resist their fusion into categories of identity since their statement intention as a vehicle within a particular thought-world demonstrates distinctions which are not parallel to one another'[1].

Alsup's estimation of the matter concurs with our own reservations expressed earlier about the 'transferability' of religion-historical conceptions from one religion into another (*supra* 39-40). In his search for a plausible paradigm within the OT-Jewish tradition, Alsup then turns to the anthropomorphic theophany stories of the OT and the intertestamental literature (Gen 18; Ex 3f.; Judg 6,13; 1 Sam 3; Tob 5,12; TAb B)[2]. He identifies the following structural and formal elements in the OT theophany stories: (1) verbs of seeing, encounter and action; (2) reaction of the participants (recognition or non-recognition); (3) the identity of the appearing one; (4) response and address of the appearing one; (5) content of address; (6) reaction and rejoinder; (7) culmination. On the basis of an analysis of the appearances recorded in Mt 28:16-20; Lk 24:36-49; Jn 20:19-29; Lk 24:13-33,35; Jn 21:1-14; 20:14-18, Alsup concludes: 'The OT anthropomorphic theophany stories did stand formally and essentially behind the conception of the gospel appearance stories—even though they are nowhere quoted directly—so that the formulation of the latter took place as a conscious reflex, a deliberate reaching back to this OT traditional complex, and that to the exclusion of other possibilities, to give them a definite form of expression and thereby also direction of statement'[3].

Alsup's conclusion is pertinent to our own investigation for various reasons. First of all, it should be noted that the theophanies discussed by Alsup are all in a sense 'appearances from heaven'. This is of course an essential component of the theophany *Gattung*. Secondly, the theophanies under consideration are *anthropomorphic*, which means that the character who appears is virtually unrecognisable as a heavenly being. Thirdly, Alsup identifies both the Emmaus story (Lk 24:13-33,35) and the appearance to the disciples (Lk 24:36-49) as anthropomorphic theophany stories[4]. Fourthly, Alsup arrives at his form-critical

---

[1] Alsup, *Appearance Stories* 239.

[2] Alsup, *Appearance Stories* 239-263.

[3] Alsup, *Appearance Stories* 265 (with the text italicised). Likewise L. Goppelt, *Theologie des Neuen Testaments* (hrsg. v. J. Roloff; UTB 850; Göttingen: Vandenhoeck & Ruprecht, 1976, ³1978) 290-291. See further the discussion in J.M. Guillaume, *Luc interprète des anciennes traditions sur la résurrection de Jésus* (EtB; Paris: Librairie Lecoffre, J. Gabalda, 1979) 83-92.

[4] See the Text-Synopsis inside the back cover of Alsup's book. It should be noted that Alsup puts vv.50,51 between brackets. The classification of vv.50,51 as the culmination part is rightly disputed by M.C. Parsons, *The Departure of Jesus in Luke-Acts. The Ascension Narratives in Context* (JSNT.S 21; Sheffield: JSOT, 1987) 52. Vv.36-49 are a thematic unity;

classification on the basis of the text in its present (Lukan!) form. This text bears a strong mark of Lukan redaction[1], so that we may safely assume that Luke consciously patterns the appearances after the theophany model. Tentatively it may be suggested, then, that if Alsup's categorisation of the resurrection appearances in Lk 24 as theophany stories is correct, it follows that Jesus' appearances are *ipso facto* manifestations from heaven[2].

Exegetical indications in the text itself to corroborate this hypothesis are few, if any. Admittedly, commentators have not been slow to search for evidence in support of the thesis that the Lukan appearances are manifestations of the already exalted Lord from heaven, but it must be conceded that the yield is meagre. Because the critical issue turns on the nature of the appearances during the forty-day interval, we must discard from the outset Paul's Damascus road experience. This heavenly manifestation to Paul, ranked on the same level with the other post-Easter appearances by Paul himself (1 Cor 15:8), has its own interpretative problems, which we will turn to at a later stage of the investigation. Thus we must concentrate upon the appearance stories of Lk 24 and Acts 1 themselves. So much is clear, that in Luke's description Jesus' resurrection body was of a different nature than his pre-resurrection body, proven by his capacity to make sudden entrances and disappearances (Lk 24:31,36, cf. v.51). It was a body of flesh and bones (Lk 24:39), but more than that. One cannot avoid recalling the Pauline description of the resurrection body as a σῶμα πνευματικόν (1 Cor 15:44)[3], but this does not rule out the possibility that Jesus was in some state of transition during the forty days.

Sometimes an appeal is made to the Lukan redaction of Mk 16:5. Luke adds that the disciples 'did not find the body τοῦ κυρίου 'Ιησοῦ' (Lk 24:3). This is the first time in the Gospel that Luke uses the full expression ὁ κύριος 'Ιησοῦς. If this is deliberate, it may have some significance that he does so at this particular point of the story, namely at the very dawn of the resurrection[4].

---

vv.50-53 is an independent unit requiring a formal classification of its own.

[1] We need only refer to the studies of J. Wanke, *Die Emmauserzählung. Eine redaktionsgeschichtliche Untersuchung zu Lk 24,13-35* (EThSt 31; Leipzig: St. Benno, 1973); Guillaume, *Luc interprète*; R.J. Dillon, *From Eye-Witnesses to Ministers of the Word. Tradition and Composition in Luke 24* (AnBib 82; Roma: IBP, 1978), and the commentaries *ad loc.*

[2] Cf. also K. Berger, *Die Auferstehung des Propheten und die Erhöhung des Menschensohnes* (StUNT 13; Göttingen: Vandenhoeck & Ruprecht, 1976) 497 Anm.222.

[3] That Jesus was not immediately recognised by the Emmaus disciples may not be relevant here, because this was caused by an act of divine blinding (Lk 24:16,31).

[4] So e.g. Guillaume, *Luc interprète* 19 (cautiously); cf. C.F.D. Moule, 'The Christology of Acts', in: L.E. Keck, J.L. Martyn (eds.), *Studies in Luke-Acts. Essays Presented in Honor of*

Luke may have felt it appropriate to call the risen Lord 'the Lord Jesus' from the resurrection onwards[1]. But the textual status of the reading is disputed[2] and the argument probably overly subtle[3].

Again, we should ask ourselves what kind of evidence we should in fact expect to find. A comparison with the Gospel of Matthew, which, as we noted above, closes with an appearance of the exalted Lord (*supra* 130), is most illuminating. The scenery has many parallels with Luke. Note the following points of agreement[4]:

> *v.16* the reference to the *eleven* disciples (Lk 24:33; against the twelve in Jn 20:24); the motif of the mountain (cf. Acts 1:12);
>
> *v.17* the motif of disbelief (Lk 24:41); the aorist use of ὁράω (Lk 24:39; cf. Jn 20:20); the motif of προσκύνησις (Lk 24:52);
>
> *v.18* ἐξουσία is materially parallelled in δύναμις (Lk 24:49); the authority of Jesus as the motivation to go in Matthew parallels with the empowering 'from on high' in Luke (Lk 24:49);
>
> *v.19* the name of Jesus (Lk 24:47); the universal mission (Lk 24:47); the reference to God *the Father* (Lk 24:49; cf. Jn 20:21);
>
> *v.20* καὶ [ἰδοὺ] ἐγὼ (Lk 24:49); a reference to the Spirit (Lk 24:49; cf. Jn 20:22); the promise of abiding divine presence (Lk 24:49).

Unlike Mt 28:16-20, there is no explicit reference to the exalted status of the risen Lord in Luke-Acts. But then again, in Matthew Jesus is recognised as such *through his words*. Does not the authoritative teaching of the risen Lord in Luke-Acts offer a suitable analogy? Besides, it should not be overlooked that Christ's appearance 'from heaven' at the end of Matthew's Gospel was ambiguous enough to allow room for doubt (Mt 28:17)! But are these arguments really convincing?

Perhaps we should follow a different line of argumentation. C.K. Barrett and C.H. Talbert have both suggested that Luke was writing with an anti-gnostic or

*Paul Schubert* (Nashville, New York: Abingdon, 1966) 160-161.

[1] A similar explanation is proposed by Zmijewski, *Apg* 39 vis-à-vis Acts 1:6, but there we are on still less firm ground, since we do not have there the combination κύριος ᾿Ιησοῦς.

[2] The reading is disputed by G.D. Kilpatrick, 'ΚΥΡΙΟΣ in the Gospels' (1968); repr. in: idem, *The Principles and Practice of New Testament Textual Criticism. Collected Essays Edited by J.K. Elliott* (BEThL 96; Leuven: Peeters, Leuven University Press, 1990) 210; Ehrman, *Corruption* 219.

[3] It is, however, interesting to note that in the gospel tradition the expression occurs further only in Mk 16:19.

[4] See B.J. Hubbard, *The Matthean Redaction of a Primitive Apostolic Commissioning. An Exegesis of Matthew 28,16-20* (SBL.DS 19; Missoula, MO: Scholars, 1974) 102-107.

anti-docetic bias[1]. This becomes most clear in the appearance stories, where the physical reality of the resurrection is stressed time and again: Jesus is not a ghost (Lk 24:37), he is capable of eating fish (24:43), he departs to heaven in bodily form (24:51), and so on. Tentatively, then, it may be suggested that Luke consciously toned down precisely the elements we are looking for, to avoid the false impression that Jesus' resurrection was spiritual. To counter docetism it was necessary to stress the fully human/bodily nature of the appearances. This leaves little room for supernatural flashing lights, thunderbolts, a halo, light effects, etc. as we find in the apocryphal gospel tradition [e.g. EvPe 9:35-10:42; EpAp(Eth) 51 (62); Codex Bobiensis (k) on Mk 16:3]. This would also clarify why Luke preferred to pattern the appearance stories on the analogy of the *anthropomorphic* theophany stories, and not on more spectacular disclosures of divinity (as e.g. in Ex 19:17-20). We must conclude, then, that there is no principal objection to a categorising of the post-Easter appearances recounted by Luke as 'appearances of the already exalted Lord from heaven'[2].

### e. *Summary and Conclusions*

The theory that the Lukan ascension story is the result of a radical reinterpretation or 'historicising' of the primitive exaltation kerygma (Ps 110:1), either along the lines of Mk 16 or along the lines of the Fourth Gospel, falls short of convincing proof. For Luke, the exaltation of Jesus, traditionally articulated with the help of the symbol of the session at the right hand of God, took place on the day of the resurrection, not forty days later on the day of the ascension. Luke reserves Ps 110 exclusively for the interpretation of the Easter event (resurrection-exaltation). To read the Lukan ascension story in the light of Mk 16:19 is theologically unjustified and anachronistic. Luke does not vote

---

[1] Barrett, *Luke the Historian in Recent Study* (London: Epworth, 1961) 62-64; Talbert, *Gnostics*; idem, 'An Anti-Gnostic Tendency in Lucan Christology', *NTS* 14 (1968) 259-271.

[2] So B. Weiss, *Die Evangelien des Markus und Lukas* (KEK II $^9$ Göttingen: Vandenhoeck & Ruprecht, 1876, $^4$1901) 692; Michaelis, *Die Erscheinungen des Auferstandenen* (Basel: H. Majer, 1944) 73-96; idem, *ThWNT* 5, 355-356; W. Tom, 'Waar was Jezus gedurende de veertig dagen tusschen Zijn opstanding en hemelvaart?', *GThT* 39 (1938) 404-411; idem, 'Nog eens: waar was Jezus gedurende de veertig dagen tusschen Zijn opstanding en hemelvaart?', *GThT* 40 (1939) 303-306; idem, 'Het vraagteeken gehandhaafd', *GThT* 41 (1940) 129-131; P. Benoit, 'L'Ascension' (1949); repr. in: idem, *Exégèse et Théologie* 1 (Paris: Cerf, 1961) 404-405; Bietenhard, *Himmlische Welt* 66-67; Robinson, *Coming* 134-136; Goppelt, *Theologie* 294 Anm.31; Fitzmyer, 'Ascension' 422; idem, *Luke* 2, 1538-1539; J.F. Maile, 'The Ascension in Luke-Acts', *TynB* 37 (1986) 46; Bruce, *Acts GT* 103; Hampel, *Menschensohn* 366 (+ Anm.100!).

for the Johannine option either. Unlike the Fourth Evangelist, Luke dates the exaltation on a calendar day, so to speak. He never speaks of the ascension of Jesus in terms of a *return* to heaven (*katabasis-anabasis*)[1], and he does not describe the ascension on a heavenly ascent pattern (*anabasis-katabasis* for the revelatory or redemptive purposes)[2].

The basic flaw in the theory that, for Luke, the ascension marks the moment of Christ's exaltation is that it is not sensitive to the proper distinction of 'forms' in which ascension language was employed in the ancient world and by Luke. A complicating factor that has emerged in the course of the present investigation is the imprecision with which ascension language is being used in the modern debate. The persistent speaking of *the* ascension without taking into account the semantics proper to the 'forms' employed, tends to ignore the differences between the various formal categories, and the diversity with which the particular writers fill these forms with content. The ἀνάβασις of Jesus in the Fourth Gospel, e.g., is not interchangeable with the ἀνάλημψις of Jesus in Luke-Acts. And even where 'rapture' language is used with reference to Jesus (1 Tim 3:16; Rev 12:5), we should be very cautious about over-interpretation and illicit harmonisations. The wide variety of ascension language should prevent us from assuming that all the NT writers were bound to utilise ascension or rapture language with the scenery of Acts 1:9-11 in the back of their minds.

Luke consistently presents the event of Acts 1:9-11 in terms of an *Entrückung*. For the resurrection-exaltation complex (the Easter event), he also employs ascension language (in the comprehensive sense of the word), but he does so (in the line of his sources!) with the conceptual and terminological tools of the heavenly journey type of ascension, in which Christ is the active participant and takes his rightful seat in heaven, from where he is actively involved in the affairs of his church. Such a conceptualisation is far removed from the rapture type of ascension, which puts Christ, as it were, temporarily on a sidetrack, waiting for the parousia.

---

[1] Luke does not seem to think of Jesus in terms of pre-existence, see Brown, *Birth* 141-142 *et passim* (see *index* 751 *s.v.* 'Preexistence of Jesus'); Dunn, *Christology* 50-51; K.-J. Kuschel, *Geboren vor aller Zeit? Der Streit um Christi Ursprung* (München, Zürich: R. Piper, 1990) 407-420.

[2] This would be simply reading back a Johannine conceptuality into the text. So Bengel, *Gnomon* 434: *sursum receptus est*; H.B. Swete, *The Ascended Christ. A Study in the Earliest Christian Teaching* (London: Macmillan, 1910) 6; J.H. Bernard, 'Assumption and Ascension', *ERE* 2 (1909, ²1930) 153 ('resumption'), 156-157; J.N. Geldenhuys, *Commentary on the Gospel of Luke* (NICNT; Grand Rapids: Eerdmans, 1951) 646; J.F. Walvoord, 'The Ascension of Christ', *BS* 121 (1964) 11.

The proper classification of forms proved to be particularly helpful in our understanding of Acts 2:32ff., which at face value seemed to allude to the event described in Lk 24:50-53 and Acts 1:9-11, but which on closer scrutiny appeared to be a solemn description of the Easter event as found elsewhere in the early church (Eph 4:8-10 etc.). Luke never confuses the two categories. Forty days separate the two conceptualisations! To Luke, Jesus is manifested as the Exalted One from the resurrection onwards and he does not postpone the exaltation forty days. The post-resurrection appearances described in the Gospel and Acts are all appearances of the already exalted Lord 'from glory' or 'from heaven', in which Christ temporarily condescended to human conditions. That they are devoid of supernatural accompanying phenomena such as clouds, light flashings and so on, may reflect Luke's 'anti-docetic tendency' to avoid the suggestion that the risen and exalted Lord was a πνεῦμα or φάντασμα. Although Luke ties resurrection and ascension into a fixed chronological scheme, the ascension can be spoken of as an 'exaltation' only in an attenuated sense.

Unless Mk 16:19 draws from a source, the longer ending of Mark seems to be the earliest (second-century AD) witness to the rapture-ascension of Jesus interpreted as *sessio ad dexteram Dei*. That from a very early stage of tradition the Lukan ascension narrative was read as a narrative report about Christ's session at the right hand of God must have been a virtually unavoidable consequence of the two stories being part of the canon (both conclude the life of Jesus with an ascension, thereby using the same terminology). Many early interpreters of Luke have (unconsciously or not) read the ascension story with Mk 16:19 and current dogma in the back of their minds and in doing so practised 'canonical criticism' *avant la lettre*. Ultimately this has led to the artificial distinction of the various stages of Christ's humiliation and exaltation in the dogmatic handbooks of old-Protestant orthodoxy[1]. Whatever one may say about the validity of such a harmonistic reading for the construction of a systematic theology, this is not what Luke and the primitive church were concerned about.

However, it should not go unnoticed that this is only part of the story. The primitive exaltation kerygma, in which resurrection and ascension were one event, survived in a period in which Luke-Acts had already received canonical status[2]. An author such as Jerome apparently did not notice any discrepancy between an ascension on Easter Sunday *and* one forty days later

---

[1] See H. Heppe, *Die Dogmatik der evangelisch-reformierten Kirche. Dargestellt und aus den Quellen belegt* (hrsg. v. E. Bizer; Neukirchen: Neukirchener, [1861] 1958) 387-403.

[2] See Lohfink, *Himmelfahrt* 98-109.

(*DieDomPasch*; AMar 3/2, 416.418; CChr.SL 78, 550; cf. also Tertullian, *AdvIud* 13,23; PL 2, 636-637, but probably unauthentic). This seems to indicate that Acts 1 was not universally read as a report about the *sessio ad dexteram*. If the early church regarded the resurrection as the moment of coronation or enthronement, we have also a plausible explanation for the fact that only from the fourth century AD onwards the ascension festival was celebrated as a distinct feast (*supra* 14-15 n.2).

This being said, we must turn to the remaining question: what is the role of the ascension in Lukan theology, if it is not in the first place an expression of Jesus' exaltation? How does it relate to the expectation of the parousia? What does it add to Luke's understanding of the Christ event and to christology in general?

CHAPTER SIX

# THE RAPTURE CHRISTOLOGY OF LUKE-ACTS (II)

a. *Introduction*

The question to be addressed in the present chapter is: what is the positive role of the ascension within Luke's wider concept of christology and salvation history, if it is not (or not in the first place) a narrative description of Christ's *exaltatio ad dexteram Dei*? Is it only an artistic creation from the hand of Luke to provide the Jesus story with an appropriate finale and so 'scarcely more than an editorial winding-up of the series of incidents following the resurrection', as C.H. Dodd once put it?[1] Is the ascension story only a conventional literary means to get rid of the main character of Book I to clear the scene for Book II? If Luke's ascension story served a literary-aesthetic purpose only, there would not be much sense in looking for an underlying theological (or christological) motif that inspired Luke to incorporate the story. Yet this is an assessment not many scholars have been prepared to make. There are good reasons to assume that the ascension story (also) has a polemical or tendentious function. It should be noted, for example, that a large segment of the narrative in Acts 1 reflects a concern to correct some misunderstandings (e.g. 1:3-4,6-8,11). And the repeated stress on the visibility of the ascension (Acts 1:9-11) seems to be more than a stylistic ornamentation required by the rapture *Gattung*[2]. Regardless of whether or not Luke used source material, the crucial question is: how is it that the ascension story has come to be described as it is, in this particular wording and with these particular points of emphasis?

What, then, were Luke's aims and objectives? What was (were) the critical issue(s) he wished to tackle? Which doctrinal misconception(s) did he seek to correct? And, how does the ascension story help to establish the point? In other words, what is the apologetic value of Luke's 'rapture christology'?

Unfortunately, the search for the *Sitz im Leben des Verfassers* of the ascension story is surrounded by a number of methodological intricacies. Much

---

[1] C.H. Dodd, 'The Appearances of the Risen Christ. An Essay in Form-Criticism of the Gospels' (1957); repr. in: idem, *More New Testament Studies* (Manchester: Manchester University Press, 1968) 123 n.1 with reference to Mk 16:19 and Lk 24:51.

[2] This is not to say that Lk 24 and Acts 1 have no historical core, but that is simply a different question.

depends upon hypothetical reconstructions of the eschatological views of Luke and his supposed readership, the date of composition of Luke-Acts and its assumed purpose, and the development of early Christian theologising in general. There is a long and complicated trail from the early days of the Church to the time of Luke-Acts and criteria to outline the development with reasonable confidence are either lacking or inadequate. Any attempt to come to grips with the issue of the Lukan *Sitz im Leben* is—this must be clear from the outset—inevitably speculative.

Of these, the question of the date of Luke-Acts is perhaps the least difficult. I am inclined, with a significant strand of modern scholarship, to date Luke-Acts in the 70's or 80's of the first century AD, at any rate after the Jewish war and after the fall of Jerusalem and the destruction of the temple[1]. Since these events were traditionally regarded as signs of the End[2], it should cause no surprise to see a renewed interest in apocalyptic-eschatological speculations in this very period. As we noticed in chapter two, it is in the post-70 AD period that the Jewish-apocalyptic rapture speculations gained increasing popularity. In this respect one can hardly avoid the conclusion that rapture thinking was as it were 'in the air' and that Luke has accurately caught the mood of the time.

We have already pointed out that there is a strong connection between Jesus' ascension and his parousia. As we noted in chapter two, this interconnection is inherent to the Jewish beliefs about the afterlife, the earthly-oriented eschatology and Jewish anthropology. From a first-century Jewish perspective, then, it does not cause any surprise to see that as soon as Jesus was gone the *angeli interpretes* started lecturing on the parousia[3] (Acts 1:11; cf. also 3:21).

---

[1] With e.g. F.F. Bruce, *The Acts of the Apostles. Greek Text with Introduction and Commentary* (Grand Rapids: Eerdmans; Leicester: Apollos, 1951, ³1990) 9-18 (who changed his earlier judgement). To avoid repetition of the arguments *pro et contra* see the NT introductions, the commentaries on Luke and Acts, and the literature cited in A.J. Mattill, M. Bedford Mattill, *A Classified Bibliography of Literature on the Acts of the Apostles* (NTTS 7; Leiden: E.J. Brill, 1966) 147-152. Suffice it to say at this point that I am unconvinced by the arguments put forward in support of a dating of Acts in the early 60's (62 AD) by J.A.T. Robinson, *Redating the New Testament* (London: SCM, 1976) 86-117, and C.J. Hemer, *The Book of Acts in the Setting of Hellenistic History* (ed. C.H. Gempf; WUNT 49; Tübingen: J.C.B. Mohr/Paul Siebeck, 1989) 365-410. They do not seem to acknowledge sufficiently the 'distance factor' which determines the overall pattern of Acts. The *earliest possible* date is not necessarily the *actual* date.

[2] Bill. 1, 949. It is instructive to see how Luke's contemporary, Flavius Josephus, interprets the destruction of the city and the temple with apocalyptic imagery, see Josephus, *BJ* VI v,1-3 (271-309).

[3] Not, it should be noted, on his *sessio ad dexteram*!

To put it in the most general terms: the ascension is a confirmation of the certainty of the promise of the parousia. Jesus went up to heaven not to remain there forever, but to return on the Day of Judgement.

But exegesis cannot (or at least should not) stop here. To establish more precisely *how* ascension and parousia are interconnected it is necessary to cross-examine the texts on their statement intention. As we know from common day parlance, language may take on a completely different connotation if its context changes. Inasmuch as meaning is closely connected with the context in which it stands (both the linguistic context and the life situation of the author, that is!), it is of crucial importance to know in what particular *geistesgeschichtlichen* surroundings Luke penned the ascension story. What was Luke's theological concern in telling the ascension story? Should the ascension story be perceived as a response to a misplaced form of *Naherwartung* and is it Luke's intention to say that the parousia is not an event to be expected in the near future?[1] Or is the emphatic affirmation of the certainty of the parousia to be understood as a response to critical minds who denied that there would be any parousia at all (cf. 2 Pet 3:4)?[2] Or is the angelic promise that 'this Jesus ... will come in the same way (οὕτως ... ὃν τρόπον) as you saw him go into heaven' (Acts 1:11) perhaps a response to a (Gnostic?) spiritualising tendency which asserted that the parousia had already taken place in the spiritual realm (cf. 2 Thess 2:2)?[3] With such questions in mind we must now try to describe what Ludwig Wittgenstein would call the 'language-game' (*Sprachspiel*) of the ascension[4].

b. *The Ascension and the Closure of the Time of Jesus*
In his Gospel, Luke puts special emphasis on the presence of salvation in the

---

[1] H. Conzelmann, *Die Apostelgeschichte* (HNT 7; Tübingen: J.C.B. Mohr/Paul Siebeck, 1963, [2]1972) 26-27; E. Grässer, 'Die Parusieerwartung in der Apostelgeschichte', in: J. Kremer (éd.), *Les Actes des Apôtres. Traditions, rédaction, théologie* (BEThL 48; Gembloux: Duculot, 1979) 112-117; E. Haenchen, *Die Apostelgeschichte* (KEK III[17]; Göttingen: Vandenhoeck & Ruprecht, 1956, [7]1977) 149-150.157-158.

[2] S.G. Wilson, 'The Ascension. A Critique and an Interpretation', *ZNW* 59 (1968) 277.

[3] Cf. C.H. Talbert, 'The Redaction Critical Quest for Luke the Theologian', in: *Jesus and Man's Hope* 1 (Perspective; Pittsburgh, PN: Pittsburgh Theological Seminary, 1970) 176-178.

[4] On the significance and relevance of this concept for biblical interpretation, see A.C. Thiselton, *The Two Horizons. New Testament Hermeneutics and Philosophical Description with Special Reference to Heidegger, Bultmann, Gadamer, and Wittgenstein* (Exeter: Paternoster, 1980) 357-427.

earthly ministry of Jesus, more than the other synoptic evangelists do[1].

The notion of the fulfilment of the OT messianic promise in Jesus runs as a continuous thread through the Lukan infancy narratives (Lk 1-2), especially through the *Magnificat* (Lk 1:46-55) and the *Benedictus* (Lk 1:68-79)[2]. At Jesus' presentation in the temple, Simeon declares that (in this child) his eyes have seen God's salvation (Lk 2:30). When Luke introduces John the Baptist, he extends the Isaiah quotation from Mk 3:3 to include the words καὶ ὄψεται πᾶσα σὰρξ τὸ σωτήριον τοῦ θεοῦ (Lk 3:6 = Is 40:5 LXX). There is a dramatic outburst of the activity of the Holy Spirit—promised and expected in the end-time—in the first four chapters of Luke: Luke records that John will be filled with the Holy Spirit (Lk 1:15); Elizabeth, filled with the Holy Spirit, prophesies (Lk 1:41), and so does Zechariah (Lk 1:67). Simeon is guided by the Spirit (Lk 2:25-27). The Spirit descends in visible form (σωματικῷ εἴδει) on Jesus at his baptism (Lk 3:22). In his programmatic sermon in the Nazareth synagogue Jesus claims that the prophetic words of Is 61 have been fulfilled in the audience's presence (Lk 4:21): The year of the Lord's favour is now (Lk 4:19). Later on in the ministry of Jesus, Luke reports Jesus' message to John the Baptist, about the messianic blessings present in his ministry (Lk 7:22 = Q Mt 11:4-5). After the return of the Seventy[-two] Jesus declared that he had watched 'Satan fall from heaven like a flash of lightning' (SLk 10:18 NRSV), a sure sign of his defeat. A blessing is pronounced upon the eyes that are privileged 'to see what you [the disciples] see' (Lk 10:23 NRSV). In Lk 11:20 (= Q Mt 12:28) Jesus interprets his exorcisms as proof of the present reality of the kingdom of God[3]. The presence of salvation is also expressed in Luke's special emphasis on 'today' (σήμερον), which is a keyword in his Gospel (MGM 891-892) and which refers to the time of messianic salvation present in the ministry of Jesus[4]. In Acts 10:38 it is recalled by Peter 'how God anointed Jesus of Nazareth with the Holy Spirit and with power; how he went about doing good and healing all who were oppressed by the devil, for God was with him' (NRSV).

But for Luke and his readers the period of Jesus belonged to the past, not to say the distant past; it is a *closed* epoch, at any rate (Acts 1:1-2,21-22; 10:37ff.; cf. Lk 1:1-2). Jesus is no longer physically present among his followers—those who claim to be him are impostors (Lk 21:8; cf. Acts 5:36-37; 8:9-10). By the

---

[1] I.H. Marshall, *Luke, Historian and Theologian* (Exeter: Paternoster, 1970) 116-187; F. Bovon, *Luc le théologien. Vingt-cinq ans de recherches (1950-1975)* (MoBi; Neuchatel, Paris: Delachaux & Niestlé, 1978) 255-284 (*Forschungsbericht*).

[2] See R.E. Brown, *The Birth of the Messiah. A Commentary on the Infancy Narratives in the Gospels of Matthew and Luke* (AncB Reference Library; New York, etc.: Doubleday, 1977, ²1993) 235-499.617-695; J.A. Fitzmyer, *The Gospel According to Luke I-IX. Introduction, Translation, and Notes* (AncB 28; Garden City, NY: Doubleday, 1981) 303-448.

[3] Perhaps Lk 17:21 also envisages a present understanding of the Kingdom of God, but a good case can be made for a futuristic interpretation (see the commentaries *ad loc.*).

[4] H. Flender, *Heil und Geschichte in der Theologie des Lukas* (BEvTh 41; München: Chr. Kaiser, 1965, ²1968) 135-137.

time Luke wrote Acts the Jesus event had become 'Phänomen der Geschichte', as H. Conzelmann put it[1].

Unlike the other Evangelists, Luke provides the earthly life of Jesus with a clear-cut finale, a sharp line of demarcation in time and place. The first and most obvious function of the ascension story is that it describes the final leave-taking of the risen Lord. The ascension concludes the last apostolic christophany (Lk 24:36-53; Acts 1:4-11), it concludes the period of post-resurrection appearances (Lk 24), and it concludes the public ministry of Jesus as a whole (beginning with his baptism by John), as is clear from Acts 1:1-2,21-22. The ascension, in other words, rounds off an era in salvation history. This closing function is most prominent in Lk 24. In Acts 1 the perspective broadens in that the ascension opens up a new period, the period of the Church[2].

Yet to say that the ascension functions as the dividing line between two epochs in salvation history—self-evident as such an assertion may be—catches only part of the truth. As is clear from the larger study of Luke-Acts (e.g. the Jesus-Paul and Jesus-Peter parallelisms) Luke's focus is more on that which connects the two periods than that which divides them. The function of the forty days leading up to the ascension is to ensure the continuation of Jesus' preaching. They are a 'last rehearsal' before the Church is launched into the mission of the world on the day of Pentecost, ten days later.

### c. *The Apologetic Function of the Forty Days*

With the exception of Acts 1:3, no attempt is made in the NT to affix chronological boundaries to the post-resurrection appearances. Christ's appearance at a mountain in Galilee recorded in Mt 28:16-20 cannot be dated with any precision, but probably falls shortly after the resurrection (reckoning with the time needed for the disciples' travel from Jerusalem to Galilee). In the longer ending of Mark (Mk 16:9-20)[3] the various appearances and the

---

[1] Conzelmann, *Die Mitte der Zeit. Studien zur Theologie des Lukas* (BHTh 17; Tübingen: J.C.B. Mohr/Paul Siebeck, 1954, [6]1977) 173 (see also 30.156.158.172-174); see also Haenchen, *Apg* 107-108; Grässer, *Das Problem der Parusieverzögerung in den synoptischen Evangelien und in der Apostelgeschichte* (BZNW 22; Berlin, New York: W. de Gruyter, 1957, [3]1977) 188-189.

[2] In his *Historia Ecclesiastica*, Eusebius treats the ascension (ἀνάληψις) of Jesus as a standard calendar date to date events in the early Church, see *HistEccl* II i (prologue) (2x); II i,3; II xiii,3 (quoting Justin, *Apol* 1,26); III v,2 (2x); III xxix,2 (quoting ClemAlex, *Stromata* 3,25); III xxxix,10; cf. also I xiii,4.

[3] As far as we know, the original Gospel of Mark did not record appearances at all. Mk 14:28 and 16:7 cryptically hint at a future post-resurrection manifestation of Jesus, but it is

ascension seem to have taken place on the day of resurrection, although the composite makeup of the appendix requires some caution. In the Fourth Gospel the appearances stretch out over little more than a week (cf. Jn 20:1,19,26). And if we may read the appendix to the Fourth Gospel (Jn 21) as a continuation of the preceding narrative, the period of appearances lengthens into a few weeks at the most (the only time indications are found in 21:1,14). Except for the appearance to Paul, to which we will turn later, the post-Easter appearances took place within the relatively short time-span of a few weeks or months after the resurrection. We may safely assume that in general opinion the post-Easter manifestations of the risen Lord were restricted to the early days of the Church and that the period of special appearances had come to a close. Paul, at any rate, seems to have considered Christ's appearance to him to be the last one (1 Cor 15:8)[1].

Luke-Acts sides with the tradition of the early Church in restricting the duration of the appearances. In Acts 1:3 the post-resurrection appearances occur within the time-span of forty days, that is, six weeks approximately. According to Acts 13:31, Jesus appeared to those who had come up with him from Galilee to Jerusalem ἐπὶ ἡμέρας πλείους, 'in the course of many days'[2].

During the forty days, Jesus delivered his final instructions to his disciples. This reminds us, as we noticed above (*supra* 99 + n.3), of the rabbinic emphasis on reliable instruction, and in particular the forty-day scheme of the Jewish rapture traditions of Ezra and Baruch, who instructed their disciples before they were taken up, to ensure that their teaching would survive after their departure.

That there is a note of continuity in the forty days is confirmed by the content of the instruction: during this period Jesus taught his disciples τὰ περὶ τῆς βασιλείας τοῦ θεοῦ (Acts 1:3), and in so doing reiterated what he had

---

not clear whether this is a reference to a post-Easter appearance (as Matthew obviously took it) or to the parousia.

[1] If we may take ἔσχατον in a temporal sense. So e.g. F.W. Grosheide, *De eerste brief aan de kerk te Korinthe* [CNT(K); Kampen: J.H. Kok, ²1957) 390 n.27; see also J. Roloff, *Apostolat-Verkündigung-Kirche. Ursprung, Inhalt und Funktion des kirchlichen Apostelamtes nach Paulus, Lukas und den Pastoralbriefen* (Gütersloh: G. Mohn, 1965) 49.51.55-56; J.D.G. Dunn, *Jesus and the Spirit. A Study of the Religious and Charismatic Experience of Jesus and the First Christians as Reflected in the New Testament* (London: SCM, 1975) 101. At any rate, at the time of writing, it was simply historical reality that the appearances had come to an end.

[2] G. Lohfink, *Die Himmelfahrt Jesu. Untersuchungen zu den Himmelfahrts- und Erhöhungstexten bei Lukas* (StANT 26; München: Kösel, 1971) 177 (+ Anm.40) translates correctly: 'eine größere Zahl von Tagen hindurch'.

taught them during his pre-Easter ministry (Lk 4:43; 8:1; 9:2,11,60; 10:9,11; 16:16) as a preparation for what the Church would preach afterwards (Acts 8:12; 19:8; 20:25; 28:23,31).

The function of the forty days of instruction is clearly related to the role of the apostles as eyewitnesses. It is to them that Jesus appeared and to them that he entrusted his teachings. Luke insists that Jesus had chosen them 'through the Holy Spirit' (Acts 1:2) (*supra* 96), thereby suggesting that their authoritative position in the Church was a divine ordinance. The forty days, then, are some sort of 'guarantee device' of the authentic apostolic witness[1]. In view of the threat of heresy and the danger of corruption of the gospel message which threatened the Lukan community (cf. Acts 20:29-30), the question of the authenticity of the gospel must have become acute at some point of time. Now that Jesus was no longer physically present on earth, how could his teachings be kept from corruption and heresy? The forty-day scheme of the Jewish rapture traditions provided Luke with a fit scheme to make clear that the twelve apostolic eyewitnesses were the legitimate representatives of the gospel message (Acts 1:22; 10:41-42; 13:31). The true gospel is the apostolic gospel, the gospel which was entrusted to the Twelve.

This authenticating motif, incidentally, is what Luke has in common with the (later) Gnostic claims of post-resurrection instruction. Both Luke and the Gnostics attach special significance to the post-resurrection teachings of Jesus. But whereas in Luke-Acts the teaching envisages continuity of what was publicly known of the earthly teaching of Jesus, the Gnostics exploited the post-resurrection period of teaching to convey new and secret teachings.

The authenticating function of the forty days may provide an explanation for Christ's appearance to Paul on the Damascus road, an event which Paul himself did not hesitate to add to the official list of apostolic christophanies (1 Cor 15:8; cf. 1 Cor 9:1) but which clearly falls outside the constraints of Luke's forty-day scheme. The fact that the Damascus event is significant to Luke as well is clear from the fact that he has Paul relate the story no less than three times (Acts 9:3-9; 22:6-11; 26:12-18). The way he describes the appearance, however, makes one think of a visionary experience—the Lukan Paul calls it an οὐράνιος ὀπτασία, a 'heavenly vision' (Acts 26:19)[2]—rather than a physical appearance of Jesus in line with the resurrection appearances.

---

[1] Talbert, *Luke and the Gnostics. An Examination of the Lukan Purpose* (Nashville, New York: Abingdon, 1966) 17-32.

[2] Cf. Ch. Burchard, *Der dreizehnte Zeuge. Traditions- und kompositionsgeschichtliche Untersuchungen zu Lukas' Darstellung der Frühzeit des Paulus* (FRLANT 103; Göttingen: Vandenhoeck & Ruprecht, 1970) 92-93.129-136.

To understand the issue correctly we must remember that, strictly speaking, the function of the forty days is not to date the ascension but to *delimit* the period of apostolic instruction (*supra* 98ff.). This may reveal the issue at stake. What distinguishes Paul from the Twelve is not in the first place the timing of the appearance—the Twelve apostles had seen the risen Lord before, Paul after the ascension (or before or after Pentecost for that matter[1])—but the different function of the appearances to the Jerusalem apostles from that of the appearance to Paul. Luke's periodisation has to do with the origin and authenticity of the Christian kerygma. For Luke, the Jerusalem apostles are the authentic and legitimate custodians of the faith[2]. Paul does not belong to the Twelve, he is not an apostle in this restricted sense[3]. He does not meet the (Lukan) qualifications set out in Acts 1:22[4]. From Paul's own statements in his letters as well as from the Book of Acts we know that his claim to apostolic authority and the content of his preaching were under constant attack (Gal 1-2; 1 Cor 9:1-2; 2 Cor 11:5; 12:11; 1 Thess 2:3-6; Acts 21:20-21,28; 28:17; cf. 24:5; 25:8; 23:29). Seen in this light, it is possible that Luke's presentation strikes a polemical note, presumably in defence of Paul[5]. He makes it clear that the Christian kerygma stems from the Jerusalem apostles: they were fully instructed concerning the kingdom of God during the forty days and hence are the authentic witnesses; it was not Paul who invented the Christian proclamation nor was he to be regarded as an innovator. Luke reassures his readers that the Christian kerygma as it was proclaimed by Paul goes back to and has the full support of the Jerusalem community[6].

---

[1] So Fitzmyer, *Luke* 1, 194; idem, 'The Ascension of Christ and Pentecost', *TS* 45 (1984) 422.

[2] See Talbert, *Gnostics* 17-32.49-56.

[3] It is only with reluctance that Luke calls Paul an 'apostle' (Acts 14:4,14), whereas Paul himself on various occasions made a point of it (Gal 1:1; 1 Cor 15:9; Rom 1:1f.). On Luke's view on the apostolate, see *inter alios* Roloff, *Apostolat* 169-235; J. Jervell, *Luke and the People of God. A New Look at Luke-Acts* (Minneapolis, MN: Augsburg, 1972) 75-112; G. Schneider, *Die Apostelgeschichte 1. Einleitung. Kommentar zu Kap. 1,1-8,40* (HThK 5; Freiburg, Basel, Wien: Herder, 1980) 221-232 (lit. 221-222); K. Haacker, 'Verwendung und Vermeidung des Apostelbegriffs im Lukanischen Werk', *NT* 30 (1988) 9-38.

[4] Note that his name is absent from Acts 13:31 and that Luke subtly distances Paul as preacher of the Gospel from the apostolic witnesses (v.32).

[5] In *defence* of Paul, because of Luke's otherwise positive treatment of Paul; cf. Roloff, *Apostolat* 199-211.232; Burchard, *Zeuge* 135-136. That the Lukan Paul is subordinate to the Jerusalem apostles speaks for him rather than against him.

[6] This is of course not to say that Luke wrote Acts simply as a defence for Paul. We rather must reckon with a complexity of motives and concerns.

It is difficult if not impossible to say whether the appearance to 'more than five hundred brothers and sisters at one time' (1 Cor 15:6 NRSV) falls inside or outside the forty days of Acts 1:3[1]. Assuming that Luke knew of this 'mass appearance' (which is by no means clear!), he may have suppressed it for theological reasons. So large a number of appearances would admittedly strengthen the reality of the resurrection, but it would also run counter to the theological point he wishes to make, viz. that the (pre-ascension) appearances were intended for the instruction of the apostolic witnesses. And if it was a post-ascension event, it would not fit very well to the nature of the ascension as concluding the last appearance.

### d. *The Ascension and the Expectation of the Parousia*

By the time Luke came to write Acts it was a historical reality that the promise of the imminent parousia of Jesus had not taken place. Despite the strong element of imminent expectation in the teaching of John the Baptist, Jesus and the early Christians[2], the fiery baptism announced by the Baptist had not happened, nor had Jesus made his glorious appearance on the clouds of heaven; the 'turn of the ages' had not occurred, at least not in the obvious meaning of the term. Although it is probably an oversimplification to say that the delay of the parousia had caused a deep crisis in early Christianity—a growing number of scholars express their surprise that the eschatological problem did *not* cause a deep crisis![3]—the loss of hope in the imminent parousia has put its imprint upon early Christian theologising (2 Thess 2:1-12; 2 Pet 3:1-13). To find out where Luke stands and how his rapture christology confronts the 'eschatological question' we will turn to Luke's expectation of the parousia and his understanding of the interim period.

The eschatology of Luke is a vast and most complex subject[4]. Apart from the

---

[1] For the various positions, see the commentaries *ad loc.*

[2] Dunn, *Unity and Diversity in the New Testament. An Inquiry into the Character of Earliest Christianity* (London: SCM; Valley Forge: TPI, 1977, [2]1990) 309-340.

[3] Including Conzelmann! See his *Grundriß der Theologie des Neuen Testaments* (bearbeitet v. A. Lindemann; UTB.W 1446; Tübingen: J.C.B. Mohr/Paul Siebeck, 1967, [5]1993) 348.

[4] A *Forschungsbericht* is found in Bovon, *Luc le théologien* 11-84. Older literature on Lukan eschatology is found in Mattill, Mattill, *Bibliography* 301-303; W.E. Mills, *A Bibliography of the Periodical Literature on the Acts of the Apostles 1962-1984* (NT.S 58; Leiden: E.J. Brill, 1986) index *s.v.* Eschatology. Of the literature since 1984 we mention: Bruce, 'Eschatology in Acts', in: H.W. Gloer (ed.), *Eschatology and the New Testament. Essays in Honor of G.R. Beasley-Murray* (Peabody, MA: Hendrickson, 1988) 51-63; J.T. Carroll, *Response to the End of History. Eschatology and Situation in Luke-Acts* (SBL.DS 92; Atlanta, GA: Scholars, 1988); E.E. Ellis, 'La fonction de l'eschatologie dans l'évangile de Luc', in: F. Neirynck (éd.), *L'Évangile de Luc—The Gospel of Luke. Revised and Enlarged Edition of L'Évangile de Luc. Problèmes littéraires et théologiques* (BEThL 32; Leuven:

non-controversial recognition that Luke's eschatological perspective is different from the earliest sources in that he reflects more consciously than his predecessors upon the interval which separates the time of Jesus from the final consummation at the end of history, no scholarly consensus exists on such issues as Luke's attitude towards the problem of a *delayed* parousia, his understanding of the nature of the βασιλεία τοῦ θεοῦ, his hopes and expectations about Israel, the role of the Spirit in salvation history, and so on. Luke does not offer a systematic treatment of these matters. To uncover his views we are to a large extent dependent upon scattered utterances, veiled allusions, alleged editorial operations on his sources, and so on. It is therefore not surprising to see that Lukan interpreters in the past have come to widely divergent reconstructions of Luke's eschatological conception.

According to H. Conzelmann[1] and E. Grässer[2], Luke completely abandoned belief in the imminence of the parousia and 'de-eschatologised' the original kerygma. In an attempt to provide a lasting solution for all generations to come he projected the End to the distant, unknown future and advanced the ascension as a replacement (*Ersatz*) for the imminent coming of Jesus. This means that in Luke's eyes the ascension had a strongly 'retardierende Funktion'[3]. Grässer maintains that 'der innerhalb des Neuen Testaments nur bei Lukas breit ausgebaute Topos der Himmelfahrt ein kräftiges Indiz dafür [ist], wie *uneschatologisch* Lukas im Grunde denkt'[4].

A.J. Mattill, on the other hand, labelled Luke-Acts as 'apocalyptic in nature', Luke's Gospel as 'probably the most apocalyptic of all four gospels'[5], and he went so far as to contend 'that is was *precisely because of his imminent hope* that Luke penned his two volumes'[6]. Mattill does not comment on the role of the ascension in this context, but one might expect that the significance attached to the ascension as a delaying factor would need to be qualified to a greater or lesser extent. In fact, many scholars would deny that the ascension has anything to do with a delay or an eschatological problem at all.

Before we can investigate the particular role of the ascension vis-à-vis the

---

Leuven University Press, Peeters, 1973, [2]1989) 51-65.296-303 (additional note 'Eschatology in Luke Revisited').

[1] Conzelmann, *Mitte* 87-127.

[2] Grässer, *Parusieverzögerung*; idem, 'Parusieerwartung' 99-127.

[3] Grässer, 'Parusieerwartung' 115.

[4] Grässer, 'Parusieerwartung' 116 (italics mine).

[5] Mattill, *Luke and the Last Things. A Perspective for the Understanding of Lukan Thought* (Dillsboro, NC: Western North Carolina Press, 1979) 6.

[6] Mattill, *Last Things* 233 (italics mine).

eschatological question we must have a general idea of the various components on which Luke's eschatology has been built. The following points present, in my view, a fair presentation of Luke's eschatological concerns.

Firstly, Luke retains belief in the parousia in its traditional form, i.e. as a public, visible event in the future (e.g. Lk 9:26; 12:40; 17:24,30; 18:8; 21:27; Acts 1:11; 3:20; cf. 10:42; 17:31). This stands even if there are traces here and there of a so-called 'vertical (individual) eschatology'[1].

> The evidence for such a vertical (individual) eschatology put forth in support of the theory is however far from compelling. In the Parable of the Rich Man and Lazarus (SLk 16:19-31), where immediately after death a separation takes place between righteous and unrighteous, Luke is supposed to stand under the influence of a Platonic worldview. But the argument rests on the assumption that Hades is the final state of the dead. The evidence, however, can be satisfactorily explained within the bounds of traditional OT-Jewish eschatology, where Hades designates the intermediate state of the righteous and the unrighteous dead prior to the final judgement (1 En 22; 4 Ezra 7:75-101; cf. Jude 6-7; 1 Pet 3:19-20). Lazarus, it may be assumed, is on 'the happy side of Hades' (Mattill). He is in Hades, not in Gehenna![2] This explanation would apply also to Jesus' promise to the penitent criminal (Lk 23:43) which we discussed *supra* 150-151.
>
> A stronger case can be made for Stephen (Acts 7:55-60). If the underlying implication is that Stephen immediately after his martyrdom went to heaven (the text seems to suggest this!), Stephen's fate would be exceptional (not every person is so privileged!) but not impossible in the light of first-century Jewish martyrology[3]. At any rate, Luke does not give us a hint that Stephen's case should be generalised. The same conception is found in the Book of Revelation, where we have the martyrs under the altar (i.e. in heaven) (Rev 6:9-11) and the righteous and unrighteous dead in Hades (e.g. 20:13). Luke's individual eschatology (if present) is marginal and it certainly does not obliterate a futurist eschatology[4].

Secondly, there is a firm element of imminent expectation in Luke's Gospel. Luke transmits, without any apparent sign of embarrassment, some of the

---

[1] So e.g. Barrett, 'Stephen and the Son of Man', in: W. Eltester, F.H. Kettler (Hrsg.), *Apophoreta. Festschrift für Ernst Haenchen* (BZNW 30; Berlin: A. Töpelmann, 1964) 32-38; J. Dupont, 'L'après-mort dans l'oeuvre de Luc' (1972); repr. in: idem, *Nouvelles Études sur les Actes des Apôtres* (LeDiv 118; Paris: Cerf, 1984) 358-379; Schneider, *Parusiegleichnisse im Lukas-Evangelium* (SBS 74; Stuttgart: KBW, 1975) 78-84.89-90.94-98.

[2] Cf. also J. Nolland, *Luke 9:21-18:34* (WBC 35B; Dallas, TX: Word, 1993) 829; J. van Bruggen, *Lucas. Het evangelie als voorgeschiedenis* (CNT derde serie; Kampen: J.H. Kok, 1993) 311.

[3] Cf. U. Kellermann, *Auferstanden in den Himmel. 2 Makkabäer 7 und die Auferstehung der Märtyrer* (SBS 95; Stuttgart: KBW, 1979).

[4] See further J. Ernst, *Herr der Geschichte. Perspektiven der lukanischen Eschatologie* (SBS 88; Stuttgart: KBW, 1978) 78-87; Mattill, *Last Things* 34-40; R. Maddox, *The Purpose of Luke-Acts* (Studies in the NT and Its World; Edinburgh: T.&T. Clark, 1982) 103-105.

harshest *Naherwartungslogia* preserved in the Jesus tradition (Lk 9:27 // Mk 9:1; Lk 21:32 // Mk 13:30; Lk 22:18 // Mk 14:25; cf. Jn 6:53)[1]. The apocalyptic-eschatological preaching of John the Baptist is replete with the expectation of the impending eschatological wrath (Lk 3:7,9,17). The Seventy(-two) disciples are to announce the imminent coming of the eschatological kingdom of God (Lk 10:9,11; cf. 21:31)[2]. And in the Parable of the Unjust Judge (SLk 18:1-8), which comes immediately after a set of eschatological instructions (Lk 17:20-37), God is promised to act 'quickly, speedily' (ἐν τάχει, 18:8) on behalf of his elect, viz., at the parousia of the Son of Man[3].

Thirdly, it is equally clear that the imminence of the parousia is *not* a central premise of Luke. His concern lies elsewhere. Although the absence in Lk 22:69 of the words καὶ ἐρχόμενον μετὰ τῶν νεφελῶν τοῦ οὐρανοῦ (Mk 14:62 // Mt 26:64) does not necessarily reveal Luke's embarrassment about the nonoccurrence of the parousia[4], it does make clear that the centre of interest has changed. As Luke transmits the saying, the emphasis falls completely on the exalted status of Christ in the present (i.e. the period between resurrection and parousia). Note that the notion of imminence is virtually absent in the Book of Acts[5].

Fourthly, Luke seems in fact to reckon with a longer interval between the

---

[1] Despite the many attempts to soften the uneasy directness of these sayings (including the Lukan parallel Lk 9:27!), they seem to suggest quite clearly that Jesus expected the parousia to happen within his own generation. The history of interpretation of Mk 9:1parr. has been described by M. Künzi, *Das Naherwartungslogion Markus 9,1Par. Geschichte seiner Auslegung mit einem Nachwort zur Auslegungsgeschichte von Markus 13,30Par.* (BGBE 21; Tübingen: J.C.B. Mohr/Paul Siebeck, 1977). I take 'not taste death until they see' (Mk 9:1 // Lk 9:27) as a litotes for 'certainly live to see', and 'some of those present ...' to denote an event distant enough to allow for the death of the majority of by-standers, i.e. the parousia. Van Bruggen, *Marcus. Het Evangelie volgens Petrus* (CNT derde serie; Kampen: J.H. Kok, 1988) 192-193; idem, *Lucas* 200, also understands the saying to refer to the parousia, but spiritualises 'not tasting death' along the lines of Jn 8:51-52.

[2] See W.G. Kümmel, *Verheissung und Erfüllung. Untersuchungen zur eschatologischen Verkündigung Jesu* (AThANT 6; Basel: H. Majer, 1945) 9-13 and Mattill, *Last Things* 70-79.

[3] The crux of the Parable on the level of Luke is of course the need for steadfastness and perseverance. Yet this should not undo the notion of imminence.

[4] So Conzelmann, *Mitte* 77 Anm.2.

[5] The attempt of Mattill, 'Naherwartung, Fernerwartung, and the Purpose of Luke-Acts. Weymouth Reconsidered', *CBQ* 34 (1972) 276-293, to interpret Acts 10:42; 17:31, and 24:15,25 in terms of *Naherwartung* rather than *Fernerwartung* is unconvincing. Bovon, *Luc le théologien* 58 rightly comments: 'Si Luc avait vraiment voulu souligner l'imminence il aurait pris la peine d'ajouter ταχύ ou ταχέως, comme l'a fait prudemment l'auteur de l'Apocalypse (Ap 22,20)'.

departure of Jesus and the final consummation. As a number of Lukan scholars have demonstrated, Luke's portrait of the Church, its organisation and structure, reflects a concern to define the place of the Church in the present age, and marks (to put it with due caution) a first step towards 'early Catholicism' (*Frühkatholizismus*). Luke's special interest in the organisation of the Church is not for historical reasons only. He clearly wants to provide a model of what the churches of his time and afterwards should be like[1]. This is evidence of a changed attitude. Furthermore, a number of editorial modifications reflect a concern to account for the delayed parousia[2]. In the Lukan redaction of the Markan apocalypse Luke separates events of his own time (persecution of the Church, the rise of false messiahs, the fall of Jerusalem) from the eschatological consummation[3]. The reader is instructed that οὐκ εὐθέως τὸ τέλος (Lk 21:9). Luke explicitly rejects a misguided form of *Naherwartung* (Lk 19:11)[4] and categorises it as a false doctrine (Lk 21:8). In the Parable of the Unfaithful Slave the main character says: χρονίζει ὁ κύριός μου ἔρχεσθαι (Lk 12:45, with minor alterations also in Mt 24:48), an affirmation which Luke tacitly seems to admit[5]; in the Parable of the Wicked Tenants he adds that the owner of the vineyard went abroad χρόνους ἱκανούς (Lk 20:9).

Fifthly, surveying Luke-Acts as a whole, there seems to be a certain tension between the imminent expectation and the delayed parousia. Although Luke would certainly be the first to admit that he ranked among those 'for whom it is not to know the χρονοί ἢ καιροί' of the eschatological consummation (Acts 1:7), the fact that he passed on *Naherwartungslogia* such as Lk 9:27 (Mk 9:1) and 21:32 (Mk 13:30) without significant alterations could indicate that he still expected the parousia to occur during the lives of at least some of Jesus' contemporaries [τινες τῶν αὐτοῦ (!) ἐστηκότων; ἡ γενεὰ αὕτη], that is, in Luke's own lifetime or shortly thereafter[6]. And texts that are usually put forth in support of a 'delay' theory (e.g. Lk 12:38,45; 13:6-9; 19:11,12; 20:9; 21:8) may account for the 'delay' that had *already* occurred at the time of Luke—if Luke wrote in the 70's or 80's of the first century AD the duration of the interval had already mounted to almost half a century!—and need not

---

[1] B.S. Childs, *The New Testament as Canon. An Introduction* (London: SCM, 1984) 225ff.

[2] Grässer, *Parusieverzögerung* 178-198.

[3] See the commentaries *ad loc.*

[4] Although the saying makes good sense in its historical setting, it must have evoked a strong sense of recognition on the part of Luke's readers as well.

[5] The point of the parable is not that the master does not delay his coming, but that the servant in question fails to act in accordance with this fact.

[6] Mattill, *Last Things*. Also Talbert, 'Quest' 184-185.

necessarily be extended very much beyond his own time[1]. After all, it is most unlikely that Luke would preserve these Jesus logia if he knew that they had been rendered obsolete by the subsequent course of events. The fact that he did not remove the sayings or reformulate them to soften their *prima facie* meaning suggests that he may not have given up hope of their impending fulfilment[2]. At any rate, it is not justifiable to insist that Luke *eliminates* the imminent expectation[3].

Finally, however, it should not go unnoticed that the most perplexing *Naherwartungslogia* are found in the Gospel of Luke (not in Acts!), and that these are a secure part of the Jesus tradition prior to Luke. The Book of Acts, where Luke is less bound to sources, breathes a different atmosphere. It would not be wholly out of place to say that Luke passes on the imminent expectation because this was too firm an element of the Jesus tradition to be ignored by an author whose intention was to give 'an orderly account of events that have been fulfilled among us' (Lk 1:1 NRSV). But Luke writes as an independent, self-conscious author and from a (chronological) distance, and these factors must have coloured his understanding of the effects of the eschatological preaching of Jesus. It is perhaps best to say, with W.G. Kümmel, that Luke marginalises the imminent expectation without completely abandoning it[4].

Having set out the broad parameters of Lukan eschatology we must now turn once more to Luke's rapture christology to see if and how it influences the eschatological problem. If, as we have argued above, Luke has borrowed the various components of his rapture christology from the Jewish rapture tradition, the next question is whether the rapture-preservation paradigm perhaps provides an interpretive clue to Luke's approach to the eschatological problem.

It is my contention that the Jewish rapture-preservation paradigm has provided Luke with a 'biblical' precedent for the eschatological problem, with which he could respond to various critical questions. This point may be made clear by noting the following parallels.

---

[1] Mattill, *Last Things, passim*; E. Franklin, *Christ the Lord. A Study in the Purpose and Theology of Luke-Acts* (London: SPCK, 1975) 14-15.19-20.26.

[2] Authors in defence of this position are found in Grässer, 'Parusieerwartung' 101 Anm.108.

[3] Conzelmann, *Mitte* 88.

[4] Kümmel, 'Lukas in der Anklage der heutigen Theologie' (1972); repr. in: G. Braumann (Hrsg.), *Das Lukasevangelium. Die redaktions- und kompositionsgeschichtliche Forschung* (WdF 280; Darmstadt: WBG, 1974) 426. Or, as A.N. Wilder, 'Variant Traditions of the Resurrection in Acts', *JBL* 62 (1943) 311, aptly put it long ago: 'It is true that like the Fourth Evangelist he [= the author of Luke-Acts] transmits the tradition of the Church with regard to the parousia and the Judgment but his heart is elsewhere'.

First of all, just as historical figures like Enoch and Elijah were taken up into heaven to remain there until the end-time, so Jesus had departed to heaven until his parousia. As much as Enoch and Elijah had not yet made their reentry on earth, so the promise of Jesus' return still awaited consummation.

Secondly, the fact that the Jewish-apocalyptic rapture speculations were built, without exception, around historical figures of the *distant* past (Enoch, Elijah, Moses, Ezra, Baruch, Phinehas, Melchizedek) would effectively discourage Luke's readers to maintain an overly stressed *Naherwartung*.

Thirdly, the rapture-preservation paradigm is concerned with the course of salvation history at large. The comparison suggests that the Christian community should reckon with a long interim period. The forty days of instruction by the risen Lord are preparatory to a longer period of his physical absence. After all, one does not instruct one's disciples for forty days if one expects to return shortly afterwards.

Fourthly, the Jewish apocalypses seem to have been written in the conviction that the End was near (4 Ezra 4:26,33-50; 8:61; 11:44; 2 Bar 85:10) and in a sense reflect the same tension between 'promise' and 'fulfilment' as we find in early Christian belief[1].

Fifthly, in line with the Jewish-apocalyptic conviction that the course of history stands under God's firm control, Luke not only emphasises (negatively) that the exact timing of the eschaton is God's prerogative (Acts 1:7) but also (positively) that it is God's expressed will that the parousia had not yet taken place (Acts 3:21) (*supra* 111). The rapture theme, with its emphasis on divine action, must have been particularly helpful in stressing God's initiative in what had happened to Jesus. This theocentric aspect sheds its light on the significance of the interim period, since—if it is God's will that the End has not yet come—the Church is not living in a vacuum which has escaped God's control. Rather it may live in the assurance that the interim is divinely-planned and that God has a specific purpose for his Church to fulfil, viz. the mission to the world (Lk 24:49; Acts 1:8).

---

[1] Here we must stress that the problem of the delay of the parousia is not a specifically Christian problem of a later date. Already pre-Christian Judaism has its own problem of a 'delay' of divine promises (Hab 2:3; cf. Ezek 12:21-28); see A. Strobel, *Untersuchungen zum eschatologischen Verzögerungsproblem auf Grund der spätjüdisch-urchristlichen Geschichte von Habakuk 2,2ff.* (NT.S 2; Leiden, Köln: E.J. Brill, 1961). And from the time of the apocalyptic-eschatological preaching of John the Baptist, that is, already during the earthly ministry of Jesus (!), the nonoccurrence of the day of judgement may have been an issue.

e. *The Ascension and the Outpouring of the Spirit*

The almost unavoidable corollary to Luke's rapture christology is that Luke advocates an 'absentee christology', i.e. a christology that is dominated by the (physical) absence *and present inactivity* of the exalted Lord[1]. In his study on the use of Ps 110 in early Christianity, D.M. Hay has signalled the tendency in the early Church to regard the session symbolism of Ps 110:1 as a symbol of passivity[2]. One can imagine that this would apply *a fortiori* to the rapture-preservation paradigm. The ascension opens up an interim period in which Jesus is absent. Since the ascension Christ does make his presence known but he does so in spiritual ways[3]. Christ is not actively involved in the course of history, or at least it is not Luke's main concern to develop this theme, unlike, for example, the author of Hebrews[4]. Since the ascension Jesus seems to have been put on the sidetrack as it were, waiting for his glorious comeback at the parousia (cf. 1 Thess 1:10).

However, the Book of Acts does not strike a note of despair or disillusion. Luke is far from suggesting that with Jesus' departure salvation has moved beyond the reach of man or that the Church of his time is living in a salvation-historical vacuum. On the contrary, the message of salvation realised by God in the life, death and resurrection of Jesus is now being proclaimed everywhere and salvation, forgiveness of sins, the working of the charismata, etc. are the present experience of the Christian community. Now all these have been made possible through the gift of the Spirit by the exalted Lord.

> The much-debated question whether Pentecost has eschatological significance to Luke may be answered confidently in the positive, provided that the terms of definition are clear. In the OT expectation the outpouring of the Spirit belongs to the new age (Joel 3:1-5 MT/LXX; Ezek 36:26-27). That this is so for Luke is indicated by his treatment of the Joel

---

[1] Cf. C.F.D. Moule, 'The Christology of Acts', in: L.E. Keck, J.L. Martyn (eds.), *Studies in Luke-Acts. Essays Presented in Honor of Paul Schubert* (Nashville, New York: Abingdon, 1966) 179-180; G.W. MacRae, "Whom Heaven Must Receive Until the Time'. Reflections on the Christology of Acts', *Interp.* 27 (1973) 151-165.

[2] D.M. Hay, *Glory at the Right Hand. Psalm 110 in Early Christianity* (SBL.MS 18; Nashville, New York: Abingdon, 1973) 30-31.

[3] According to the Book of Acts, Jesus now acts through his name (Acts 3:16; 4:10,30; cf. 19:13), through the Spirit (Acts 10:19; 11:12; 13:2; 15:28; 16:6-7; 19:21?; 20:22-23; 21:4,11), through visionary experiences (Acts 9:10,12; 10:3,11,17,19; 12:5; 16:8-10; 18:9-10; 22:17-18; 23:11; 26:19) and through angelic interventions (Acts 5:19; 12:7,9,23; 27:23), but these are all intermediary experiences. Cf. also O'Toole, 'Activity of the Risen Jesus in Luke-Acts', *Bib.* 62 (1981) 471-498.

[4] Cf. Dunn, *Unity* 224-225: 'In earliest Christianity, in the Synoptic tradition and in Acts hardly any [present! AZ] role is attributed to the exalted Christ'.

passage in Acts 2:17, where Luke (or his source?) replaces καὶ ἔσται μετὰ ταῦτα (Joel 3:1 LXX) by καὶ ἔσται ἐν ταῖς ἐσχάταις ἡμέραις (cf. Is 2:2 LXX), thereby making explicit the eschatological ring already present in the Joel prophecy. But to Luke the 'last days' is equivalent not to 'the Day of the Lord' at the end of history, but to the whole period of the Church: it is the entire course of events from resurrection to parousia which constitutes 'the last days'. 'Eschatological' should not be confused with the 'eschatological consummation'. Similarly, the universal mission of the Church has eschatological significance[1], but again the timetable has undergone redefinition. The command for universal mission implies a relatively long interval to enable the Church to accomplish its task. After all, the command for universal mission 'until the extremities of the earth' (Acts 1:8) is incomprehensible if the parousia was expected to occur within a few weeks or months.

It is axiomatic in biblical scholarship to regard the ascension of Jesus as *conditio sine qua non* for the outpouring of the Spirit[2]. But in the light of all that has been said before on the form-critical classification of the ascension as a rapture (*Entrückung*) and on the need to avoid reading Luke through Johannine glasses, the affirmation that the ascension is a necessary prerequisite to Pentecost is ambivalent. With the exception of Acts 2:32ff., texts that are usually brought up in support of an affirmative answer are from the Fourth Gospel (Jn 16:7; cf. 7:39; 14:18), not from Luke-Acts. This means that we may run into the methodological fallacy of letting Luke speak with a Johannine voice if we say that 'the ascension is *conditio sine qua non*' without further qualifications. What do we mean by *the* ascension? And in what sense is it a necessary condition? The underlying problem may emerge more clearly if we restate the question as follows: what is, in Luke's eyes, the connection between the rapture event (Acts 1) and the outpouring of the Spirit upon the disciples (Acts 2)?

One thing is clear from the outset. For Luke ascension and Pentecost are not simply two more or less casual dates on the church calendar. He clearly wishes to connect the ascension to the gift of the Spirit at Pentecost on a deeper level. A comparison of the first reference to the ascension (Lk 9:51) with the introductory words of the account of Pentecost (Acts 2:1), both of which are Lukan compositions (!), suggests that Luke has consciously parallelled the two events:

---

[1] So R.H. Hiers, 'The Problems of the Delay of the Parousia in Luke-Acts', *NTS* 20 (1974) 154-155; J.P. Chance, *Jerusalem, the Temple, and the New Age in Luke-Acts* (Macon, GA: Mercer, Peeters, 1988) 87-113; see also Barrett, 'The Gentile Mission as an Eschatological Phenomenon', in: Gloer (ed.), *Eschatology* 65-75.

[2] E.g. Wilder, 'Variant Traditions' 310; J.M. Robinson, 'Ascension', *IDB* 1 (1962) 246; H.H. Graham, 'Ascension', *DB(H)* (²1963) 61.

Lk 9:51    Ἐγένετο δὲ ἐν τῷ συμπληροῦσθαι τὰς ἡμέρας τῆς ἀναλήμψεως αὐτοῦ
κτλ.

Acts 2:1   Καὶ ἐν τῷ συμπληροῦσθαι τὴν ἡμέραν τῆς πεντηκοστῆς κτλ.

The close connection is clear from Lk 24 and Acts 1 as well. Both in the Gospel's finale and in the opening chapter of Acts the ascension is immediately preceded by the promise of the Spirit (Lk 24:49; Acts 1:8). In Acts 1:5 Pentecost is promised to occur οὐ μετὰ πολλὰς ταύτας ἡμέρας[1]. Luke does not doubt that it is the exalted Lord in heaven who pours out the Spirit upon the believers. The crucial question is: how does Luke understand the relationship between the two events?

First of all we must turn once more to Acts 2:33, where Jesus' heavenly exaltation at God's right hand (τῇ δεξιᾷ οὖν τοῦ θεοῦ ὑψωθείς) is followed by his receiving of the Holy Spirit (τήν τε ἐπαγγελίαν τοῦ πνεύματος τοῦ ἁγίου λαβὼν παρὰ τοῦ πατρός) and the subsequent pouring out of the Spirit upon the believers (ἐξέχεεν τοῦτο ὃ ὑμεῖς [καὶ] βλέπετε καὶ ἀκούετε). As we concluded in the previous chapter, this exaltation text does not refer to the ascension scene of Acts 1:9ff., but, in line with the early Christian kerygma, to Christ's heavenly exaltation at Easter (*supra* chapter five). Strictly speaking, then, it is the heavenly exaltation, not the ascension, which is the necessary precondition to Pentecost: the crucial point is not that Jesus had to be in heaven (or: had to leave earth) to pour out the Spirit, but that he had to receive there an exalted status, which would qualify him as the divinely appointed 'baptiser in spirit'.

If this line of interpretation is correct, the connection between Jesus' final departure and the subsequent outpouring of the Spirit must be described in different terms than Johannine theology. According to the Fourth Evangelist, Jesus had to leave the earthly scene before the Spirit could come, because the Spirit is Jesus' representative (Jn 14:18,28; 16:7). In Luke-Acts, the connection between Jesus and the Spirit is developed in a slightly different direction: Jesus must be exalted to heaven because it is only as the Exalted One that he can pour out the Spirit upon the Church.

Here we must insist that this fits nicely into the resurrection-exaltation complex. If Luke had no story on Jesus' ascension after forty days, the conclusion that he regards the exaltation (= the session at the right hand of the Father at Easter!) as *conditio sine qua non* for Pentecost would still stand. So where does the ascension fit in?

Here we may recall the influence of the Elijah story on the ascension

---

[1] On the *v.l.* ἕως τῆς πεντηκοστῆς, see *supra* 102 n.4.

narrative[1]. In 2 Kings 2 we find a straightforward connection between the ascension of Elijah and the subsequent passing of his spirit to his pupil Elisha. This parallels the ascension of Jesus and the outpouring of the Spirit at Pentecost. As the public ministry of Jesus was inaugurated by the descent of the Spirit in visible form upon him (Lk 3:21-22), so the period of the Church is initiated by the outpouring of the Spirit 'upon all flesh' (Acts 2:17) on the day of Pentecost[2]. Luke seems to make a double connection: on the one hand he connects Jesus' ascension to his parousia, on the other hand he connects the ascension to the outpouring of the Spirit upon the disciples. To put it differently, Luke exploits the rapture-preservation paradigm for *christological* reasons, the rapture-transmission of the Spirit connection of the Elijah-Elisha cycle for *salvation-historical* (soteriological/ecclesiological) reasons. The ascension and parousia are primarily concerned with what happens to Jesus; Pentecost with what happens to the Church. The ascension marks the transition point at which the Jesus event continued to be effective along two separate lines, i.e. ἐν οὐρανῷ (where the risen Lord is being kept in preservation) καὶ ἐπὶ γῆς (through the Spirit working in the Church).

## f. *The Question of Sources*

Up to this stage of the investigation we have dealt with the ascension from Luke's point of view, and we arrived at the conclusion that the ascension narrative functions as an integral part of Luke's theology of salvation history. But we cannot ignore, of course, the question of sources. Granted that Luke is the first and only NT writer who tells the story of Jesus' visible ascension after forty days, did he draw the whole or part of it from (an) earlier (written or oral) source(s)? Is the ascension story Luke's free composition or did he simply conserve what he found in his sources with little or no redactional modifications, to convey two opposite poles? Now that we have identified the OT Scripture (Gen 5:24; 2 Kings 2; Mal 3; Sir 48-50) and the Jewish-apocalyptic rapture tradition (Enoch apocalypses; 4 Ezra 14; 2 Bar 76, etc.) as

---

[1] See *inter alios* R.J. Dillon, *From Eye-Witnesses to Ministers of the Word. Tradition and Composition in Luke 24* (AnBib 82; Roma: IBP, 1978) 177-179; T.L. Brodie, *Luke the Literary Interpreter. Luke-Acts as a Systematic Rewriting and Updating of the Elijah-Elisha Narrative in 1 and 2 Kings* (Diss. Roma, 1987); idem, 'Luke-Acts as an Imitation and Emulation of the Elijah-Elisha Narrative', in: E. Richard (ed.), *New Views on Luke and Acts* (Michael Glazier; Collegeville, MN: Liturgical, 1990) 78-85.172-174.

[2] Dunn, *Baptism in the Holy Spirit. A Re-examination of the New Testament Teaching on the Gift of the Spirit in relation to Pentecostalism Today* (London: SCM, 1970) 23-54. A survey of scholarship on Luke's pneumatology is found in Bovon, *Luc le théologien* 215-254.

significant sources of inspiration for Luke's narrative presentation, it is time to pose the question whether (and if so, to what extent) Luke had points of contact in the Jesus kerygma of the early Church[1].

The quest for sources is beset by numerous complicating factors. The other gospels do not have a corresponding narrative that would provide us with a constant to measure the redactional activity of Luke[2]. Luke has the habit of rewriting his sources to such an extent that they are practically irrecoverable if such a constant is lacking. A number of studies have shown that the style and vocabulary of Lk 24 and Acts 1 are thoroughly (if not totally) Lukan, and there is no need to repeat the fine work that has been done in this area[3]. One should be careful not to attach too much significance to vocabulary and style statistics as a tool to uncover source material. Style research and word statistics may be of help to establish whether or not a given passage forms an integral part of the style and idiom of the author (in the case of Acts 1:1-5 an important argument against interpolation theories) but *not* as a means to separate tradition from redaction[4]. *If* Luke has used sources it is not very likely that we can distil them from the present text itself to any satisfactory degree.

A number of authors have tried to explain the forty days as an element of tradition[5]. However, building upon the 1962 article of Ph.H. Menoud[6], G.

---

[1] To avoid a needless confusion of terms it is necessary to distinguish between tradition, composition, and redaction. By 'tradition' I mean material present in the oral or written tradition of the early Church before Luke, by 'composition' an invention or literary creation by Luke, by 'redaction' a Lukan reformulation (editing) of traditional material.

[2] The theory of M.D. Goulder, *Luke. A New Paradigm* 2 (JSNT.S 20; Sheffield: JSOT, 1989) 794-796, that Lk 24:50-53 is Luke's re-writing of Mt 28:16-20 fails to convince. As I argued *supra* 87-88.93 (+ n.4)-94, the motifs of *proskynesis* and joy come from Sir 50:21,23, and προσεκύνησαν (Mt 28:17) is probably pre-Matthean. With regard to his overall thesis that Luke used the Gospel of Matthew, I remain equally unconvinced and still prefer the 'old paradigm'.

[3] See the statistics in V. Larrañaga, *L'Ascension de Notre-Seigneur dans le Nouveau Testament* (SPIB 50; Roma: IBP, 1938) 219-269; Lohfink, *Himmelfahrt* 163-210; J.M. Guillaume, *Luc interprète des anciennes traditions sur la résurrection de Jésus* (EtB; Paris: Librairie Lecoffre, J. Gabalda, 1979) 228-248; M.C. Parsons, *The Departure of Jesus in Luke-Acts. The Ascension Narratives in Context* (JSNT.S 21; Sheffield: JSOT, 1987) 142-143.

[4] This is one of the major weaknesses of V. Larrañaga's study. On the basis of style and word statistics he argued with a fair degree of conviction that the ascension narratives are thoroughly Lukan. Writing in the pre-redaction-critical era, he could of course not foresee that only three decades later G. Lohfink would conduct a similar line of reasoning to argue that the passage was *only* Luke's.

[5] Haenchen, 'Judentum und Christentum in der Apostelgeschichte', *ZNW* 54 (1963) 158-

Lohfink has argued with a fair degree of plausibility that the notion of the forty days is better explained in terms of Lukan redaction[1]. Unlike the resurrection 'on the third day' and Pentecost 'on the fiftieth day' Luke does not date the ascension 'on the fortieth day'. The number forty should rather be seen in the light of Luke's tendency to introduce theologically significant, round numbers into his narratives in Acts[2]. In an attempt to uncover the mechanics of Luke's choice of the number forty, Lohfink insisted that the candidate number had to be sufficiently close to the fiftieth day (Pentecost) to bring out the close chronological connection of ascension and Pentecost (Acts 1:5 οὐ μετὰ πολλὰς ταύτας ἡμέρας); further it had to be a round number with no claim of chronological exactness, since Luke did not have an exact date at his disposal; it should be a biblical number, since in texts of this sort Luke tries to write in biblical (LXX) language; and it should be a sacred number, which qualified for christological and salvation-historical purposes. The only number that met these requirements, according to Lohfink, was forty[3]. With Lohfink and others, I hold Luke responsible for fixing the interval at forty days[4]. In the light of our previous discussion, however, I am inclined to think, beyond Lohfink, that Luke has been inspired to use this biblical number more specifically under the influence of the Jewish-apocalyptic rapture tradition. That is to say, not that Luke drew the number 40 directly from 4 Ezra or 2 Baruch. Both the idea of a period of final instruction by a great teacher and the biblical number 40 were conventional enough that Luke could have made the association himself. Besides, in the pre-Christian Moses tradition, the ascent of Moses on Mount

---

160; A.R.C. Leaney, 'Why There Were Forty Days Between the Resurrection and the Ascension in Acts 1,3', in: F.L. Cross (ed.), *StEv* 4 (TU 102; Berlin: Akademie, 1968) 418; Roloff, *Apostolat* 195; W. Schmithals, *Die Apostelgeschichte des Lukas* (ZBK.NT 3/2; Zürich: Theologischer, 1982) 2.

[6] Ph.H. Menoud, 'Pendant Quarante Jours', in: W.C. van Unnik (ed.), *Neotestamentica et Patristica* (FS O. Cullmann; NT.S 6; Leiden: E.J. Brill, 1962) 148-156. Cf. *supra* 14.

[1] Lohfink, *Himmelfahrt* 176-186.

[2] Lohfink, *Himmelfahrt* 178-179, points out that Luke's account of the growth of the Church is dominated by the principle of multiplication: from the initial 12 to 120 (10 x 12) to 3000 and 5000. After the mention of 5000, when the principle has been sufficiently established, the numbers lose vividness. In Greek there is only μυρίας and μυριάδες (Acts 21:20!).

[3] Lohfink, *Himmelfahrt* 185.

[4] Menoud, 'Quarante Jours' 154-156; Lohfink, *Himmelfahrt* 176-186; M. Dömer, *Das Heil Gottes. Studien zur Theologie des lukanischen Doppelwerkes* (BBB 51; Köln, Bonn: P. Hanstein, 1978) 112-113; J.F. Maile, 'The Ascension in Luke-Acts', *TynB* 37 (1986) 48-54; J. Zmijewski, *Die Apostelgeschichte übersetzt und erklärt* (RNT 5; Regensburg: F. Pustet, 1994) 42.

Sinai and the forty days are already standard companions.

Related to this is the argument that F. Hahn has advanced. In his review of Lohfink's *Die Himmelfahrt Jesu* Hahn submitted that the alternative dates of the ascension in Gnostic circles may suggest a traditional basis for the forty days in the Lukan ascension narrative, since it was unlikely that they were all dependent upon Luke-Acts, as Lohfink held[1]. On closer scrutiny this argument cannot stand. Not only is the notion of the forty days a fixed part of a larger (Jewish-apocalyptic) scheme, but a delimitation of the post-Easter appearances must have been an unavoidable consequence of the historical fact of the cessation of the appearances and of the limited number of christophanies in the tradition of the early Church. Anyone who knew the appearances had come to an end could speculate on the date of the last appearance. The alternative ascension dates are either independent from Luke (but not earlier than Luke) or attempts to correct his chronology in the interest of tracing gnostic teachings back to the risen Lord.

Two features in the narratives themselves may point to tradition. Firstly, we have already raised the possibility (but it is obviously no more than that) that the notion of *proskynesis* was drawn from a pre-canonical appearance tradition (*supra* 93 n.4). Secondly, the precise geographical description of the location of the ascension (ἕως πρὸς Βηθανίαν, Lk 24:50) seems to reflect an accurate knowledge of local geography (cf. *supra* 88-89). Bethany does not seem to have a theological significance in the Gospel (apart from 24:50 the name only occurs in 19:29, where Luke simply retains what he found in Mk 11:1)[2]. What Luke would know from Mark is that Bethany was in the vicinity of Jerusalem and situated on the Mount of Olives (Mk 11:1; Lk 19:29; Acts 1:12). The only apologetic interest Luke would have in the mention of Bethany would be that it fits his Jerusalem-centred perspective (*supra* 89 n.2), but that still does not explain why he chose Bethany. Why not simply 'outside the city' or 'on the mount of Olives' as in Acts 1:12? We should therefore not exclude the possibility that the mention of Bethany (or better: the precise location ἕως

---

[1] F. Hahn, 'Die Himmelfahrt Jesu. Ein Gespräch mit Gerhard Lohfink', *Bib.* 55 (1974) 425.

[2] The suggestion of Conzelmann, *Mitte* 86, that Luke consistently wipes out references to Bethany is an overstatement. Of the 4 instances of Bethany which Luke found in Mark, 11:1,11,12; 14:3 (8:22 *v.l.* is secondary), he 1x retained Bethany (Lk 19:29 // Mk 11:1, contra Mt 21:1); 1x struck Bethany (Lk 7:36; contra Mk 14:3 // Mt 26:6), and 1x changed Bethany into Mount of Olives (Lk 21:37, contra Mk 11:11 (12) // Mt 21:17). The Johannine references are unparalleled (Jn 11:1,18; 12:1; 1:28 *v.l.* is a different Bethany!). Cf. also Lohfink, *Himmelfahrt* 175-167.

πρὸς Βηθανίαν) is an element which Luke inherited from tradition[1]. But it needs to be stressed that these two features (the motif of *proskynesis* and the exact location of the event) are insufficient to prove the existence of a pre-Lukan *ascension* story. At most they point more generally to a post-Easter appearance tradition.

Outside the gospel tradition there is not much comparative material at hand to come up with firm conclusions. Occasionally ascension/rapture motifs are applied to Jesus (1 Tim 3:16; Rev 12:5) but no dependency can be demonstrated. This is complicated by the fact that ascension language is often used in the context of the resurrection-exaltation paradigm, which for this reason cannot be taken as evidence.

Further we could study the non-canonical ascension stories to see whether these have left traces of an independent and pre-Lukan ascension story. Most of the material has been studied by Lohfink and his conclusions were negative[2]. In response to Lohfink, M.C. Parsons has argued, in his monograph on the departure of Jesus, that the tradition-historical quest should concentrate on the following texts: Mk 16:19; Codex Bobiensis (k) on Mk 16:3, and Barn 15:9[3]. Are these instances convincing proof to demonstrate the existence of a pre-Lukan ascension story?

*Mk 16:19*   In its present form this verse postdates Luke-Acts. However, the Markan appendix may contain source material which comes from a pre-Lukan stratum. Much has been written on the question of sources of Mk 16:9-20. I tend to regard the dependency hypothesis as the most satisfactory solution, i.e. I consider the Markan appendix as a compilation drawn from Luke-Acts and the Fourth Gospel, although I doubt whether this is a direct literary dependency. Perhaps the material reached the author through oral tradition (which accounts for the summarising character of the passage), though the ultimate source of this tradition was Lk 24 (and Acts)[4]. If, however, Mk 16:19 were independent from Luke-Acts[5], this would not automatically mean that we have proof of an

---

[1] With e.g. E. Meyer, *Ursprung und Anfänge des Christentums* 1 (Stuttgart: J.G. Cotta, 1921, [4.5]1924; repr. Darmstadt: WBG, 1962) 32; Nolland, *Luke* 3, 1227.

[2] Lohfink, *Himmelfahrt* 98-146.

[3] Parsons, *Departure* 144-148.

[4] The reverse, Luke-Acts dependent upon (proto-)Mk 16, was defended by E. Linnemann, 'Der (wiedergefundene) Markusschluß', *ZThK* 66 (1969) 255-287, but her thesis has not won much scholarly support. See the critique of K. Aland, 'Der (wiedergefundene) Markusschluß? Eine methodologische Bemerkung zur textkritischen Arbeit', *ZThK* 67 (1970) 3-13.

[5] J. Hug, *La Finale de l'Évangile de Marc (Mc 16,9-20)* (EtB; Paris: J. Gabalda, 1978) 128-153 defends independence. Likewise R. Pesch, *Das Markusevangelium 2. Kommentar zu*

independent rapture tradition, since it is not clear whether the source antedates Luke and whether it was accessible to him. At any rate, the prehistory of Mk 16:19 is much too clouded to be a reliable guide for the question of sources of Luke's ascension story.

*Codex Bobiensis (k) on Mk 16:3*     This Old Latin MS is usually dated in the fourth/fifth century AD, while the text that it preserves may go back to a second-century papyrus (in Greek?)[1]. At Mk 16:3 the text says:

> *Subito autem ad horam tertiam tenebrae diei factae sunt per totam orbem terrae, et descenderunt de caelis angeli et surgent [surgentes? surgente eo? surgit?] in claritate vivi Dei simul ascenderunt cum eo; et continuo lux facta est. Tunc illae accesserunt ad monumentum.*

What we have here is clearly a visible ascension of Jesus on the day of the resurrection. Lohfink has pointed to the striking analogy with the Gospel of Peter (EvPe 9:35-42)[2]. It cannot be denied that they are at least in a very similar *geistesgeschichtlichen* milieu. A visible ascension on the day of the resurrection is also found in EpAp(Eth) 18 (29) (tr. Schmidt 60); EpAp(Eth) 51 (62) (tr. Schmidt 154). Codex Bobiensis does not take us further back than the second century AD. It does not prove the existence of a pre-Lukan ascension story.

*Barn 15:9*     We have discussed this text already in chapter four (*supra* 143). Lohfink's suggestion, that the verse under consideration is dependent upon the scheme of Luke-Acts[3], fails to convince, as Parsons has demonstrated. However, Parsons' own suggestion, that Barn 15:9 'reflects an ascension tradition of independent stature [from Luke-Acts]'[4], is equally open to criticism. The critical question, in my view, is: does Barn 15:9 reflect an independent *rapture* tradition? As far as the text in its present shape is concerned the answer must be negative. It must be strongly doubted that φανερωθείς refers to the post-resurrection appearances of the gospel tradition.

---

Kap. *8,27-16,20* (HThK 2; Freiburg, Basel, Wien: Herder, 1977, ³1984) 545; Parsons, *Departure* 145-146.

[1] See Metzger, *The Text of the New Testament. Its Transmission, Corruption and Restoration* (New York, Oxford: Clarendon, 1964, ³1992) 73; K. Aland, B. Aland, *Der Text des Neuen Testaments. Einführung in die wissenschaftlichen Ausgaben sowie in Theorie und Praxis der modernen Textkritik* (Stuttgart: Deutsche Bibelgesellschaft, 1981, ²1989) 193.

[2] Lohfink, *Himmelfahrt* 128-129 (following the lead of A. Harnack and R. Bultmann).

[3] Lohfink, *Himmelfahrt* 121-125.

[4] Parsons, *Departure* 147.

A more likely interpretation is that it refers to Christ's manifestation in the heavenly world during his journey through the heavenly world. The scheme 'resurrection-manifestation-ascension' points to a cosmic christology along the lines of 1 Tim 3:16 (*supra* 141-142). To what extent the verse under consideration relies on sources we cannot tell. What we have here is a reminiscence of the original Easter kerygma, in which Jesus' resurrection was understood in terms of his heavenly exaltation. Barnabas, then, moves entirely within the sphere of the primitive Christian exaltation kerygma and cannot be taken as proof of a pre-Lukan rapture (visible ascension) tradition.

Both the internal (exegetical) and external evidence, then, is negative. An alternative approach would be to make an inventory of what Luke would know from tradition and to compare this to what we have in Luke-Acts.

There can be little doubt that Luke is responsible for the larger framework. A *prima facie* comparison of Luke with the other evangelists and other NT traditions shows where Luke's specific contribution lies, as becomes clear in the following diagram:

| *traditional* | *Luke* |
|---|---|
| A. resurrection-exaltation | A. resurrection-exaltation |
| B. post-Easter appearances | B. post-Easter appearances |
| C.    - | C. 40 days of final instructions |
| D.    - | D. rapture |
| E.    - | E. temporary preservation in heaven |
| F. Pentecost | F. Pentecost |
| G. parousia | G. parousia |

With the resurrection-exaltation complex (A), the post-Easter appearances (B), and the parousia (G) we are on common Christian ground. And although Luke is the first author to dramatise the 'first Christian Pentecost' (F) it is common opinion that Luke here builds on tradition as well[1]. The 'unfitting' elements (C-E) are precisely those of the Jewish rapture traditions. Since the rapture-preservation paradigm was in existence before Luke wrote (or before Christ's ascension for that matter!) Luke is likely to be responsible for having superimposed the rapture-preservation paradigm upon the traditional pattern. In doing so he was able to fill in the gap between the various isolated units to form a single movement of salvation-history, or better, he defined their mutual relationship more precisely.

Luke is the first and only NT writer to narrate Jesus' ascension on a cloud

---

[1] See the commentaries *ad loc.*, in particular Schneider, *Apg* 1, 243-247; Barrett, *The Acts of the Apostles 1. Preliminary Introduction and Commentary on Acts I-XIV* (ICC; Edinburgh: T.&T. Clark, 1994) 109-110.

forty days after the resurrection. It cannot be demonstrated positively that there was ever a rapture *narrative* before Luke. Luke's editorial hand has been too heavily at work to recover what was before him with any confidence, especially if we allow Luke the freedom to add what J.A. Fitzmyer calls 'apocalyptic stage-props' ('literary clouds, redactional angels'). This is not to say that Luke has 'invented' the ascension. Although the precise contours of the tradition are not clear we do have the building-stones: Luke knew of the post-resurrection appearances, especially those in the vicinity of Jerusalem (and from Galilee as well, but he seems to have suppressed them); he also knew that this special period had come to a close. He knew that Jesus' presence in heaven would have a fixed duration to end at the parousia on the clouds. He knew of the experience of the Spirit in the early community and that it was the exalted Christ who had poured out the Spirit. Seen in this light, we arrive at the conclusion that a good case can be made for a traditional basis of the ascension story. The character of the narrative (it describes a final departure in the context of a post-resurrection appearance) and the few un-Lukan elements in the story would point to a post-Easter appearance tradition, which Luke has remoulded with great care into the present ascension narrative. But it cannot be too strongly emphasised that we find ourselves in the sphere of hypotheses and conjectures.

g. *Conclusions*

Before passing to the final conclusions vis-à-vis the Lukan ascension story we will briefly summarise the central theses of this chapter. Different from chapter three, which was more exegetical in nature, this chapter studied the ascension in its larger context.

We approached the ascension with the assumption that to understand the function of the ascension it is necessary to take into account the larger framework in which it is embedded, *in concreto*, with reference to the resurrection-exaltation complex (which we studied in chapters four and five), the post-resurrection appearances, the forty days of final instructions, the parousia and Pentecost.

Luke is not only an outstanding historian and a good storyteller, he is also a committed theologian and evangelist. A major theological concern underlying Luke's rapture christology is found in Luke's theme of salvation history. Luke's 'rapture christology' serves in part at least as a biblical response to the problem of the 'delay' (nonoccurrence) of the parousia, in that it views the various stages of evolving salvation history as an organic unity. Luke grounds the delay of the parousia in the will of God (Acts 3:21). In Acts 1:6-8 the question of the timing remains unanswered. Instead, the disciples are instructed about their present concern, the mission of the world in the power of the Spirit.

This is typical of Luke. Without denying traditional eschatology, he manages to shift the focus back to the present situation of the Church. To Luke, the length of the interval separating resurrection from parousia does not constitute a basic problem, because the present (regardless of how long it will continue) is eschatologically qualified and the outpouring of the Spirit is an eschatological event, or at least an anticipation of the eschaton.

The forty days are a bridging period between two qualitatively different eras in salvation history, the period of Jesus and the period of the Church.

The Jewish rapture-preservation scheme provided Luke with a comprehensive design which enabled him to tie the broad lines of salvation history together, to 'streamline' as it were the various components of salvation history. The Elijah tradition enabled him to connect the ascension with the parousia *and* the outpouring of the Spirit.

Luke cannot be blamed for having *invented* the ascension story; most of the individual components were traditional. The larger paradigm, however, is Luke's.

In the present investigation we have built on the form-critical assessment of the Lukan ascension story (Lk 24:50-53; Acts 1:1-12) as a rapture story (*Entrückungserzählung*)[1]. Through an analysis of the form, structure and function of the OT and intertestamental Jewish rapture traditions we arrived at the conclusion that first-century Jews and Christians (including Luke and his readers) were not unfamiliar with the idea that some privileged people of outstanding piety had been taken up alive into the presence of God: Enoch, Elijah, Moses, Ezra, Baruch and a few other elect ones were registered (albeit with varying degrees of consent) on the list of biblical *rapti* (*supra* chapter two). When Luke puts Jesus into the rapture category he seems to do so with these illustrious Jewish examples in mind. Like the others, Jesus is marked as one who belongs to the heavenly world.

Luke's primary source of inspiration was the biblical story of Elijah's ἀνάλημψις into heaven and his expected return at the end time (2 Kings 2:1-18; Mal 3:22-23; Sir 48:9-12; 1 Macc 2:58). Luke's terminology to describe Jesus' ascension (ἀναλαμβάνομαι, Acts 1:2,11,22; ἀνάλημψις, Lk 9:51) and the nature of his eschatological activity (ἀποκαθίστημι, Acts 1:6; ἀποκατάστασις, Acts 3:21) are clear echoes of the language traditionally used in connection with Elijah. The stress on the visibility of Elijah's departure to heaven (2 Kings 2:10), the subsequent passing of the spirit from Elijah to Elisha as a means of empowerment for his future task (2 Kings 2:9-10), and the promise of his eschatological return 'to restore all things' (cf. Mal 3:23; Sir 48:12) are themes which, each in their own way, have put their imprint upon Lk 24 and the opening chapters of Acts (*supra* chapter three). The broad parameters, then, of Luke's rapture christology (ascension, pentecost, parousia) are fully comprehensible within a 'biblical' context of understanding.

At this point it is necessary to put in a methodological proviso. The focus of the present investigation has been almost exclusively on the ascension in its Jewish and Christian setting. I have attempted, as much as possible, to read Luke's ascension story 'from the inside', i.e. through the eyes of a first-century Christian who stands in the OT-Jewish tradition. This strategy was motivated

---

[1] Throughout our inquiry we have assumed the authenticity of the so-called 'longer text' of Lk 24:51,52. For a defence of this position, see A.W. Zwiep, 'The Text of the Ascension Narratives (Lk 24:50-53; Acts 1:1-2,9-11)', *NTS* 42 (1996) 219-244.

by the consideration that the 'monotheistic principle' almost inevitably must have led to a reappraisal of the meaning and function of rapture in comparison with the pagan rapture stories. That this working hypothesis proved to be correct, has been, I think, established with sufficient proof. Up to the period pertinent to our investigation, 'monotheistic raptures' do not carry the typical pagan connotations of deification and immortalisation, nor has the rapture phenomenon become a standard reward for a pious life as was the case in the Graeco-Roman world. In the OT-Jewish tradition rapture remains the privilege of only a few elect[1].

The sure affirmation that the Lukan ascension story is patterned on a Jewish (monotheistic) set of assumptions, however, does not automatically force us to deny the influence of the Graeco-Roman or Hellenistic rapture traditions upon Luke's narrative presentation. After all, the rapture repertoire of Greeks and Romans was infinitely much larger than that of Jews and Christians put together. It must have been virtually impossible for (non-Jewish) Greek readers to set aside the rapture stories of their own tradition while reading about the ascension of Jesus, and there is no reason to think that Luke eschewed the comparison with e.g. Romulus or Heracles. We must reckon with what G. Schneider observed with respect to the Lukan preface (Lk 1:1-4) and the Areopagus speech (Acts 17:22-31), that Luke works here with the principle of duality (*Zweigleisigkeit*)[2].

However, after all due allowances have been made, the validity of the central affirmation of the present thesis stands: the Jewish rapture stories provide a much more adequate context of understanding for the Lukan ascension story than the Graeco-Roman stories. Whereas the parallels with Graeco-Roman tradition are formal (common rapture terminology—unavoidable to anyone writing in Greek!—and common motifs), the Jewish rapture stories, especially the Elijah tradition and the rapture stories preserved in 4 Ezra, 2 Baruch and 2 Enoch, correspond on a more structural level. We have seen that, in the course of time, rapture speculations became part of a more comprehensive set of

---

[1] Paul's teaching on the rapture of the Church to meet the Lord in the air (ἁρπαγησόμεθα ἐν νεφέλαις, 1 Thess 4:17; cf. 1 Cor 15:51-52) and his ecstatic rapture into third heaven/paradise (2 Cor 12:2-4) lie outside the scope of the present investigation. For the questions involved, see the commentaries *ad loc.* and the literature cited there. On 2 Cor 12:2-4, see J.D. Tabor, *Things Unutterable. Paul's Ascent to Paradise in Its Greco-Roman, Judaic, and Early Christian Contexts* (Studies in Judaism; Lanham, MD: University Press of America, 1986); G. Lüdemann, *Die Auferstehung Jesu. Historie, Erfahrung, Theologie* (Göttingen: Vandenhoeck & Ruprecht, 1994) 95-106.

[2] G. Schneider, 'Der Zweck des lukanischen Doppelwerks', *BZ* 21 (1977) 48 (Anm.18).

apocalyptic-eschatological beliefs with a more or less fixed narration pattern. It is this larger model—the sequence of final instructions-rapture-preservation-eschatological return—which places the Lukan ascension story firmly in the context of the Jewish apocalyptic tradition.

A second proviso is necessary here. Although the rapture traditions preserved in 4 Ezra, 2 Baruch and the Enochic literature resemble, in many respects, the Lukan ascension story, the dates commonly assigned to these apocalypses preclude that the correspondences be explained in terms of an immediate literary dependency. Luke-Acts antedates these writings, at least in their final shape. It is possible (and perhaps likely) that Luke knew of the traditions contained therein in an earlier, pre-redactional form, but this is difficult to prove. In the final resort, however, this question is not as crucial as it may seem at first, since the raw materials of what we called the 'rapture-preservation paradigm' were provided by the OT Scripture (Gen 5:24; 2 Kings 2:1-18; Mal 3:22-23; Sir 48:9-12). Its further development in the intertestamental period involved a clarification of what was implied in the biblical tradition.

Luke has employed the rapture-preservation narration model to highlight the salvation-historical contours of the Jesus kerygma. The position of the ascension texts at the strategic points in the narrative suggests that the ascension has a structuring function. From Lk 9:51 onwards the events take place *sub specie ascensionis*; in Lk 24:50-53 and Acts 1:1-12 the ascension marks the transition from the period of Jesus to the period of the Church; in Acts 1:11 and 3:21 the ascension is connected with the parousia. Luke's primary concern was not to dramatise Easter but to clarify the inner unity which holds the great events of salvation of the past, present and future together. In utilising the rapture-preservation paradigm he managed to tie together the broad lines of salvation history, to 'streamline', as it were, its various component parts into a single scheme. To Luke, ascension and parousia belong closely together, not simply as events at two ends of the poles, but as an organic unity. The ascension is, as J.A.T. Robinson once put it in a sermon, 'the advance notice of the end'[1].

In contrast to Lohfink, we found no reason to charge Luke with having distorted or misunderstood the early apostolic preaching of Jesus' resurrection and exaltation. In line with his sources, he regards the resurrection-exaltation on Easter Sunday as the occasion of Jesus' institution to heavenly glory or at least as the moment when Christ's heavenly status became clear (depending on

---

[1] J.A.T. Robinson, 'Ascendancy', *ANQ* 5/2 (1964) 9.

the force given to ἐποίησεν in Acts 2:36). Luke sharply distinguishes the resurrection-exaltation from the ascension and never presents Jesus' ἀνάλημψις (*Entrückung*) as the occasion of his *exaltatio ad dexteram Dei* (as Mk 16:19 does!). The post-resurrection appearances recorded in Luke-Acts are all manifestations of the already exalted Lord from heaven; the ascension rounds off the last one (*supra* chapters four and five).

The *Sitz im Leben* of Luke's rapture christology is the problem of the delay (nonoccurrence) of the parousia and the subsequent questions. In a time when the Jesus event had become a distant past and the imminent expectation of the parousia had faded away, the rapture-preservation paradigm enabled Luke to maintain the certainty of the promised parousia while at the same time giving meaning to the present situation of the Church by grounding the 'delay' in the will of God (Acts 3:21). The continuity of Jesus and his teaching and the authenticity of the apostolic message—a pressing issue as time proceeded—were secured through the forty days of instructions. With the help of the Jewish rapture tradition Luke has given a biblical rationale for the interim period before the parousia: as the great historical figures of Israel's distant past were taken up into heaven and have dwelt there ever since, so Jesus would be there until the parousia. Just as Enoch, Elijah, Moses and the others did not leave their disciples and descendants behind with empty hands, but ensured that their teachings and heavenly revelations would survive, so Jesus instructed the apostles (the witnesses) during a period of forty days to ensure his teaching would continue after his departure.

An important question still to be resolved is: what type of christology comes to expression in the ascension story? Some interpreters have argued that, different from the Fourth Evangelist, Luke's christology has a 'subordinationist' undertone[1]. Whether this is a correct assessment of Luke's theological enterprise *in toto* remains to be seen. The ascension story, however, certainly does reflect a 'subordinationist' concern. The emphasis is not so much on what Jesus did, as on what happened to him (he was carried up, he was taken up, he is being preserved in heaven, etc.). Since it is God who acts upon Jesus, Jesus is marked as someone of outstanding piety, but nonetheless as someone subordinate to God. Here we are confronted with a basic weakness in

---

[1] Cf. Ph. Vielhauer, 'Zum Paulinismus der Apostelgeschichte' (1950/51); repr. in: idem, *Aufsätze zum Neuen Testament* (TB 31; München: Chr. Kaiser, 1965) 20-22; H. Braun, 'Zur Terminologie der Acta von der Auferstehung Jesu' (1952); repr. in: idem, *Gesammelte Studien zum Neuen Testament und seiner Umwelt* (Tübingen: J.C.B. Mohr/Paul Siebeck, 1962, ³1971) 173-177. Cf. also G.W. MacRae, ''Whom Heaven Must Receive Until the Time'. Reflections on the Christology of Acts', *Interp.* 27 (1973) 156f.

the rapture category from the Christian perspective: the rapture-preservation paradigm did not lend itself easily to a high christology.

The comparison with Enoch, Elijah and other saints could in the end turn against itself: Enoch, the pre-Israelite, was popular in predominantly sectarian circles; the prevailing opinion saw Elijah only as a precursor of the Messiah; the Pauline antithesis of Law and Gospel would see in Moses an anti-type rather than a type of Christ. Ezra, Baruch and the other raptured saints were relatively insignificant in the biblical tradition, and so on. Furthermore, the comparison with these historical figures would group Jesus with them, without making it clear that 'more than Enoch or Elijah is here'. And the eschatological emphasis could easily draw the focus away from the present activity of the exalted Christ.

J.A.T. Robinson and F. Hahn have argued that the earliest recoverable attempts to define the meaning of Christ were couched in terms of a rapture christology, and that only on further reflection (albeit at a very early stage) this had to make room for a high (exaltation) christology. However, we have not been able to affirm this hypothesis. On the contrary, if we are right in suggesting that Luke is responsible for having superimposed the rapture-preservation paradigm upon his sources, then historically the development has been the other way around. But does this mean that Luke has introduced a low christology at the expense of a high christology? I do not think so. The primary focus of the ascension story is salvation history, not christology. One must see the whole before one can judge the particulars. Luke's overall presentation is coloured by the early Christian christology. The inherent weakness of a rapture christology, the suggestion that Jesus is not more than Enoch or Elijah, is sufficiently counterbalanced by Luke's firm belief in Jesus' present Lordship by virtue of his resurrection-exaltation. This implies an active though distant rulership in the present and the outpouring of the Spirit at Pentecost is a dramatic illustration of the risen Lord's present activity (cf. also *supra* 182 n.3).

Finally, a question of minor significance in view of our goal to penetrate into the specifically Lukan understanding of the ascension of Jesus is that of sources. The evidence for sources is weak and fragmentary. The overall paradigm reflects the hand of Luke. It is clear that the central affirmation that Jesus had been taken up into heaven, however, was not a Lukan invention. The early Christian conviction that Jesus was now in heaven at God's right side (hence, had ascended thither) goes back to the earliest stage of Christian reflection. The constituent parts of Luke's rapture christology (the post-resurrection appearances, the biblical number 40, the fact that the period of appearances had come to a close, the conviction of Jesus' future return on the clouds of heaven) all have a firm basis in the Christian tradition prior to Luke.

It would be precarious, however, to attempt to reconstruct the exact content of the alleged sources (as e.g. R. Pesch did). Luke has a tendency to reword his sources to such an extent that they are practically irrecoverable. A few ingredients in the text seem to point to a post-resurrection appearance tradition as the source of the ascension story. This is in accordance with the character of the ascension as a final departure, but at the present state of scholarship it is difficult to say more than this.

# THE ASCENSION IN LUKE-ACTS (LK 24:50-53; ACTS 1:1-12)
## A BIBLIOGRAPHY 1900-1996

For literature on the ascension before 1900, see V. Larrañaga, *L'Ascension de Notre Seigneur dans le Nouveau Testament* (SPIB 50; traduit de l'Espagnol par G. Cazaux; Roma: IBP, 1938) vii-xi, *et passim*; B.M. Metzger, *Index to Periodical Literature on Christ and the Gospels* (NTTS 6; Leiden: E.J. Brill, 1966) 486-488; A.J. Mattill and M. Bedford Mattill, *A Classified Bibliography of Literature on the Acts of the Apostles* (NTTS 7; Leiden: E.J. Brill, 1966) 322-332; to which the following titles may be added: W. Hanna, *The Forty Days After Our Lord's Resurrection* (New York: R. Carter, 1866); D. Schenkel, 'Himmelfahrt Jesu' in: *Bibel-Lexicon. Realwörterbuch zum Handgebrauch* 3 (1871) 83-85. With a few exceptions, commentaries and literature on the resurrection have been excluded from this bibliography. For literature on the resurrection, see E. Dhanis (éd.), *Resurrexit. Actes du Symposium International sur la Résurrection de Jésus (Roma 1970)* (Roma: Libreria editrice vaticana, 1974) 651-745 (bibliography by É. Ghiberti) and the references cited *supra* 122 n.1.

1  Bernard, E.R., 'The Value of the Ascension', *ET* 12 (1900/01) 152-155.
2  Bousset, W., 'Die Himmelsreise der Seele', *ARW* 4 (1901) 136-169.229-273; repr. Libelli 71; Darmstadt: WBG, 1960, [2]1971) 83pp.
3  W., V.D., 'Jezus op de bergen', *Wat Zegt de Schrift?* 3 (1902) 78-80.
4  Belser, J.E., *Die Geschichte des Leidens und Sterbens, der Auferstehung und Himmelfahrt des Herrn nach den vier Evangelisten ausgelegt* (Freiburg im Breisgau: Herder, 1903, [2]1913) ix + 548pp. ET: *History of the Passion, Death, and Glorification of Our Saviour Jesus Christ* (Freely Adapted into English by F.A. Marks; St. Louis, MO, London: B. Herder, 1929) 668pp.
5  Schmiedel, P.W., 'Resurrection- and Ascension Narratives', *EB(C)* 4 (1903) 4039-4087.
6  Meyer, A., *Die Auferstehung Christi. Die Berichte über Auferstehung, Himmelfahrt und Pfingsten, ihre Entstehung, ihr geschichtlicher Hintergrund und ihre religiöse Bedeutung* (Tübingen: J.C.B. Mohr/Paul Siebeck, 1905) vii + 368pp.
7  J., H., 'The Ascension of Jesus Christ', *The Interpreter* 1 (1905) 411-420.
8  Soltau, W., *Himmelfahrt und Pfingsten im Lichte wahren evangelischen Christentums* (Leipzig: Dieterich, 1905).
9  Champneys, A.C., 'The Ascension', *The Interpreter* 1 (1905) 536-537.
10  Beverley, R.J., 'The Ascension', *The Interpreter* 2 (1905/06) 101-102.
11  Martin, A.S., 'Ascension', *DCG* 1 (1906) 124-128.

12 Cabrol, F., 'Ascension (Fête)', *DACL* 1/2 (1907) 2934-2943.

13 Latham, H., 'The Ascension', in: idem, *The Risen Master* (Cambridge: Deighton Bell; London: George Bell & Sons, 1907) 378-411.

14 Swete, H.B., *The Appearances of our Lord after the Passion. A Study in the Earliest Christian Tradition* (London: Macmillan, 1907) xviii + 151pp.

15 Müller, G., 'Ein Versuch zur Erklärung von Apg.1:9', *EKZ* 82 (1908) 553-554.

16 Bacon, B.W., 'The Ascension in Luke and Acts', *Exp.* (Series 7) 7 (1909) 254-261.

17 Bauer, W., *Das Leben Jesu im Zeitalter der neutestamentlichen Apokryphen* (Tübingen: J.C.B. Mohr/Paul Siebeck, 1909; repr. Darmstadt: WBG, 1965) 275-279.

18 Bernard, J.H., 'Assumption and Ascension', *ERE* 2 (1909, ²1930) 151-157.

19 Roscher, W.H., 'Die Tessarakontaden und Tessarakontadenlehren der Griechen und anderer Völker', *BVSGW* 61 (1909) 17-206.

20 Roscher, W.H., 'Die Zahl 40 in Glauben, Brauch und Schriften der Semiten', *ASGW.PH* 27 (1909) 91-138.

21 Höhn, C., 'Studien zur Geschichte der Himmelfahrt im klassischen Altertum', *Programm des Gymnasiums zu Mannheim 1909-1910* (Mannheim: Vereinsdruckerei, 1910).

22 Mangenot, E., *La Résurrection de Jésus. Suivi de deux appendices sur la crucifixion et l'ascension* (Bibliothèque Apologétique 9; Paris: Beauchesne, 1910) 377-402.

23 Swete, H.B., *The Ascended Christ. A Study in the Earliest Christian Teaching* (London: Macmillan, 1910; repr. 1916) xv + 168pp.

24 Pfister, F., 'Zu den Himmelfahrtslegenden', *Wochenschrift für klassische Philologie* 28 (1911) 81-86.

25 Tait, A.J., *The Heavenly Session of Our Lord* (London: R. Scott, 1912).

26 Norden, E., *Agnostos Theos. Untersuchungen zur Formengeschichte religiöser Rede* (Leipzig, Berlin: B.G. Teubner, 1913; repr. Darmstadt: WBG, 1956) 311-316.

27 Clarke, W.K.L., 'St. Luke and the Pseudepigrapha. Two Parallels', *JThS* 15 (1914) 597-599.

28 De Wald, E.T., 'The Iconography of the Ascension', *AJA* 19 (1915) 227-319.

29 MacLean, A.J., 'Ascension', *DAC* 1 (1915) 95-99.

30 Völter, D., 'Der Anfang der Apostelgeschichte', *PrM* 19 (1915) 93-96.

31 Martin, A.D., 'The Ascension of Christ', *Exp.* (Series 8) 16 (1918) 321-346.

32 Meyer, E., *Ursprung und Anfänge des Christentums* 1 (Stuttgart: J.G. Cotta, 1921, ⁴⋅⁵1924; repr. Darmstadt: WBG, 1962) 34-46.

33 Diels, H., 'Himmels- und Höllenfahrten von Homer bis Dante', *NJKA* 49 (1922) 239-253.

34 Laible, H., 'An welchem Wochentag geschah die Himmelfahrt Christi? Ein Versuch', *AELKZ* 55 (1922) 313.

35 Zahn, Th., 'Die Himmelfahrt Jesu an einem Sabbath', *NKZ* 33 (1922) 535-541.

36 Bickermann, E., 'Das leere Grab', *ZNW* 23 (1924) 281-292; repr. in: idem, *Studies in Jewish and Christian History* 3 (AGJU 9; Leiden: E.J. Brill, 1986) 70-81 (including a *Nachtrag* on pp.80-81).

37 Steinmetzer, F.-X., 'Aufgefahren in den Himmel, sitzet zur Rechten Gottes', *ThPQ* 77 (1924) 82-92.224-241.414-426.

38 Brun, L., *Die Auferstehung Christi in der urchristlichen Überlieferung* (Oslo: H. Aschehoug & Co (W. Nygaard); Giessen: A. Töpelmann, 1925) 3. Anhang: Die

Himmelfahrt, 90-97.

39 Holland, R., 'Zur Typik der Himmelfahrt', *ARW* 23 (1925) 207-220.

40 Michaelis, W., 'Zur Überlieferung der Himmelfahrtsgeschichte', *ThBl* 4 (1925) 101-109.

41 Martin, G., 'Ascension', *DB(V)* 1/2 (1926) 1071-1073.

42 Ropes, J.H., 'Detached Notes, Acts i,2', in: idem, *The Text of Acts* (The Beg 3; London: Macmillan, 1926) 256-261.

43 Selwyn, E.G., 'Our Lord's Ascension', *Theol.* 12 (1926) 241-244.

44 Bertram, G., 'Die Himmelfahrt Jesu vom Kreuz aus und der Glaube an seine Auferstehung', in: K.L. Schmidt (Hrsg.), *Festgabe für Adolf Deissmann zum 60. Geburtstag* (Tübingen: J.C.B. Mohr/Paul Siebeck, 1927) 187-217.

45 Bock, E., 'Von der Himmelfahrt im Alten und Neuen Testament', *Die Christengemeinschaft* 4 (1927) 45-50.

46 Fridrichsen, A., 'Die Himmelfahrt bei Lukas', *ThBl* 6 (1927) 337-341.

47 Fridrichsen, A., 'Omkring himmelfartsberetningen', *NTT* 28 (1927) 32-47.

48 Rappe, O., 'Die Bedeutung der Himmelfahrt Jesu für seine Jünger (Apg.1:1-12)', *EvBo* 64 (1927) 161-162.

49 Willink, M.D.R., 'Studies in Texts. 'A Cloud Received Him' (Acts 1,9)', *Theol.* 14 (1927) 297-299.

50 Howard, J.E., 'Acts 1:11', *ET* 39 (1927/28) 92.

51 Enslin, M.S., 'The Ascension Story', *JBL* 47 (1928) 60-73.

52 Wehring, 'Himmelfahrt II. Himmelfahrt Christi', *RGG* 2 ($^2$1928) 1898-1899.

53 Dana, H.E., 'Historical Evidence of the Ascension', *BiRev* 14 (1929) 191-209.

54 Plooij, D., 'The Ascension in the 'Western' Textual Tradition', *MNAW.L* 67 A/2 (Amsterdam: Noord-Hollandsche, 1929) 39-58 (1-17) [including an additional note by A.J. Wensinck, 56-57 (18-19)].

55 Thomas, W.H.G., 'Ascension', *ISBE* 1 (1929, $^2$1939) 263-266.

56 Schrade, H., 'Zur Ikonografie der Himmelfahrt Christi', in: F. Saxl (Hrsg.), *Vorträge der Bibliothek Warburg. Vorträge 1928-1929 über die Vorstellungen von der Himmelreise der Seele* (Leipzig, Berlin: B.G. Teubner, 1930) 66-190.

57 Holzmeister, U., 'Der Tag der Himmelfahrt des Herrn', *ZKTh* 55 (1931) 44-82.

58 Valentine, C.H., 'The Son of Man Coming in the Clouds', *Theol.* 23 (1931) 14-21.

59 Liese, H., 'In Ascensione Domini. Mc.16:14-20', *VD* 12 (1932) 129-134.

60 Wager, C.E., 'Eduard Meyer on our Lord's Ascension', *ET* 44 (1932/33) 491-495.

61 Jeremias, J., αἴρω, ἐπαίρω, *ThWNT* 1 (1933) 184-186.

62 Lake, K., 'Note 3. The Ascension', *Beg* 5 (1933) 16-22.

63 Larrañaga, V., 'La tarde de la Ascensión sobre el Olivete', *RF* 33 (1933) 77-87.

64 Lösch, St., *Deitas Jesu und antike Apotheose. Ein Beitrag zur Exegese und Religionsgeschichte* (Rottenburg a. N., Württemberg: A. Bader, 1933) xv + 137pp.

65 Ogara, F., 'De Ascensionis Christi spectatoribus (Act.Ap.1:1-22), *Gr.* 14 (1933) 37-61.

66 Schneider, J., (βαίνω) ἀναβαίνω, καταβαίνω, μεταβαίνω, *ThWNT* 1 (1933) 516-521.

67 Creed, J.M., 'The Text and Interpretation of Acts i,1-2', *JThS* 35 (1934) 176-182.

68 Larrañaga, V., 'El proemio-transición de Act.1:1-3 en los metodos literarios de la historiografia griega', *MBib* 2 (Roma: Schola typographica Pio X, 1934) 311-374.

69 Beel, A., 'Ascensio Domini juxta Act.Ap. 1:9-11', *CBrug* 35 (1935) 337-343.

70    Clarke, W.K.L., 'The Clouds of Heaven. An Eschatological Study', *Theol.* 31 (1935) 63-72.128-141; repr. in: idem, *Divine Humanity. Doctrinal Essays on New Testament Problems* (London: SPCK, 1936) 9-40

71    Grundmann, W., δεξιός, *ThWNT* 2 (1935) 37-39.

72    Gutberlet, H., *Die Himmelfahrt Christi in der bildenden Kunst von den Anfängen bis ins Hohe Mittelalter. Versuch zur geistesgeschichtlichen Erfassung einer ikonographischen Frage* (Sammlung Heitz. Akademische Abhandlungen zur Kulturgeschichte 3/3; Leipzig, etc.: 1934, ²1935).

73    Holmes-Gore, V.A., 'The Ascension and the Apocalyptic Hope. The Significance of Acts 1.6-8', *Theol.* 32 (1936) 356-358.

74    Larrañaga, V., 'Historia de la crítica en torno al misterio de la Ascensión', *EE* 15 (1936) 145-167.

75    Goossens, W., 'De valore soteriologico resurrectionis et ascensionis Christi', *CGan* 24 (1937) 9-17.

76    Larrañaga, V., 'De Ascensione Domini in Act.1:3-13', *VD* 17 (1937) 129-137.

77    Harrison, E.F., 'The Ministry of Our Lord During the Forty Days', *BS* 95 (1938) 45-55.

78    Larrañaga, V., *L'Ascension de Notre-Seigneur dans le Nouveau Testament* (SPIB 50; traduit de l'Espagnol par G. Cazaux; Roma: IBP, 1938) xiv + 662pp. = *La Ascensión del Señor en el Nuevo Testamento* (CSIC; Madrid: Instituto Francisco Suárez, 1943) 2 vols.

79    Lietzmann, H., (review of V. Larrañaga, *L'Ascension de Notre-Seigneur*), *ZNW* 37 (1938/39) 297-298.

80    Oepke, A., 'Unser Glaube an die Himmelfahrt Christi', *Luth.* (= *NKZ*) 49 (1938) 161-186.

81    Rose, H.J., 'Herakles and the Gospels', *HThR* 31 (1938) 113-142.

82    Tom, W., 'Waar was Jezus gedurende de veertig dagen tusschen Zijn opstanding en hemelvaart?', *GThT* 39 (1938) 404-411.

83    Goslinga, C.J., 'Een herhaalde Hemelvaart?', *GThT* 39 (1938) 557-560.

84    Tom, W., 'Nog eens: waar was Jezus gedurende de veertig dagen tusschen Zijn opstanding en hemelvaart?', *GThT* 40 (1939) 303-306.

85    Goslinga, C.J., 'Tot op den dag, in welken Hij opgenomen is', *GThT* 40 (1939) 519-522.

86    Hirsch, E., *Die Auferstehungsgeschichten und der christliche Glaube* (Tübingen: J.C.B. Mohr/Paul Siebeck, 1940) vii + 144pp.

87    Tom, W., 'Het vraagteeken gehandhaafd', *GThT* 41 (1940) 129-131.

88    Hirsch, E., 'Analyse des ersten Kapitels der Apostelgeschichte', in: *Frühgeschichte des Evangeliums 1.* (Tübingen: J.C.B. Mohr/Paul Siebeck, 1941, ²1951) xxx-xxxix.

89    Wensinck, A.J., 'Hemelvaart', in: *Semietische Studiën uit de nalatenschap van Prof. Dr. A.J. Wensinck* (Leiden: A.W. Sijthoff, 1941) 114-123.

90    Delling, G., ἀναλαμβάνω, ἀνάλημψις, *ThWNT* 4 (1942) 8-9.

91    Oepke, A., νεφέλη, νέφος, *ThWNT* 4 (1942) 904-912.

92    Pease, A.S., 'Some Aspects of Invisibility', *HSCP* 53 (1942) 1-36.

93    Wilder, A.N., 'Variant Traditions of the Resurrection in Acts', *JBL* 62 (1943) 307-318.

94    Michaelis, W., *Die Erscheinungen des Auferstandenen* (Basel: H. Majer, 1944) 160pp.

95    Leclercq, J., 'L'Ascension, triomphe du Christ', *VS* 72 (1945) 289-300.

96    Sahlin, H., *Der Messias und das Gottesvolk. Studien zur protolukanischen Theologie*

(ASNU 12; Uppsala: Almqvist & Wiksells, 1945) 11-18.343-347 (Exkurs 1. 'Die vierzig Tage zwischen Auferstehung und Himmelfahrt Jesu').

97 Shepherd, M.H., 'Paul and the Double Resurrection Tradition', *JBL* 64 (1945) 227-240.

98 Flicoteaux, E., 'La glorieuse ascension', *VS* 76 (1947) 664-675.

99 Zwemer, S.M., 'The Ascension', *EvQ* 19 (1947) 247-254.

100 Argyle, A.W., 'The Exaltation of Our Lord', *ET* 59 (1947/48) 190-192.

101 Senden, H. van, *Jesu Auferstehung und Himmelfahrt* (Bethel u. Bielefeld: Anstalt Bethel, 1948).

102 Benoit, P., 'L'Ascension', *RB* 56 (1949) 161-203; repr. in: idem, *Exégèse et Théologie* 1 (Paris: Cerf, 1961) 363-411.

103 Zwiep, A., 'De hemelvaart', *Uit de Levensbron. Wekelijkse predicatiën* 19 (1949) 237-252.

104 Daniélou, J., 'Les psaumes dans la liturgie de l'Ascension', *MD* 21 (1950) 40-55.

105 Ramsey, A.M., 'Ascension', in: A. Richardson (ed.), *A Theological Word Book of the Bible* (London: SCM, 1950, [20]1990) 22-23.

106 Stam, C., *De hemelvaart des Heren in de Godsopenbaring van het Nieuwe Testament* (Academisch proefschrift Vrije Universiteit Amsterdam; Kampen: J.H. Kok, 1950) 112pp.

107 Young, G.M., 'A Parallel to Act 1,9', *JThS* 1/2 (1950/51) 156.

108 Bietenhard, H., *Die himmlische Welt in Urchristentum und Spätjudentum* (WUNT 2; Tübingen: J.C.B. Mohr/Paul Siebeck, 1951) vi + 295pp.

109 Michel, A., 'Ascension de Jésus-Christ', *DThC* (1951) (Tables Générales I) 274-275.

110 Ramsey, A.M., 'What was the Ascension?', *BSNTS* 2 (1951) 43-50; repr. in: D.E. Nineham, *et alii* (eds.), *Historicity and Chronology in the New Testament* (TCSPCK 6; London: SPCK, 1965) 135-144.

111 Wikenhauser, A., 'Die Belehrung der Apostel durch den Auferstandenen nach Apg 1:3', in: N. Adler (Hrsg.), *Vom Wort des Lebens* (FS Max Meinert; NTA 1; Münster: Aschendorff, 1951) 105-113.

112 Argyle, A.W., 'The Heavenly Session of Christ', *Theol.* 55 (1952) 286-289.

113 Braun, H., 'Zur Terminologie der Acta von der Auferstehung Jesu', *ThLZ* 77 (1952) 533-536; repr. in: idem, *Gesammelte Studien zum Neuen Testament und seiner Umwelt* (Tübingen: J.C.B. Mohr/Paul Siebeck, 1962, [3]1971) 173-177.

114 Michaelis, W., 'Exegetisches zur Himmelfahrtspredigt', *RefSchw* 108 (1952) 5-8 [contra M. Werner, *SThU* 22 (1952) 83-91].

115 Ohm, T., 'Die Unterweisung und Aussendung der Apostel nach Apg 1:3-8', *ZMR* 37 (1953) 1-10.

116 Stange, C., 'Die Himmelfahrt Jesu', *ZSTh* 22 (1953) 218-222.

117 Bartsch, H.W., 'The Meaning of the Ascension', *LuthQ* 6 (1954) 44-47.

118 Conzelmann, H., *Die Mitte der Zeit. Studien zur Theologie des Lukas* (BHTh 17; Tübingen: J.C.B. Mohr/Paul Siebeck, 1954, [6]1977) 86.188-192.

119 Davies, J.G., 'The *Peregrinatio Egeriae* and the Ascension', *VigChr* 8 (1954) 93-100.

120 Fernandez y Fernandez, J., 'La Ascensión del Señor. Subió al cielo por su propia virtud', *CuBi* 11 (1954) 134-142.

121 Menoud, Ph.H., 'Remarques sur les textes de l'ascension dans Luc-Acts', in: W. Eltester (Hrsg.), *Neutestamentliche Studien für R. Bultmann* (BZNW 21; Berlin: A. Töpelmann, 1954, [2]1957) 148-156; repr. in: Menoud, *Jésus-Christ et la foi.*

*Recherches néotestamentaires* [BT (N); Neuchâtel, Paris: Delachaux & Niestlé, 1978) 76-84.

122  Michaelis, W., ὁράω κτλ., *ThWNT* 5 (1954) 315-381.

123  Schubert, P., 'The Structure and Significance of Luke 24', in: W. Eltester (Hrsg.), *Neutestamentliche Studien für R. Bultmann* (BZNW 21; Berlin: A. Töpelmann, 1954, ²1957) 165-186.

124  Traub, H., Rad, G. von, οὐρανός, οὐράνιος, ἐπουράνιος, οὐρανόθεν, *ThWNT* 5 (1954) 496-543.

125  Weterman, J.A.M., 'De Hemelvaart des Heren in het N.T.', *NKS* 50 (1954) 129-138.

126  Wulf, F., '"Und sie kehrten mit grosser Freude nach Jerusalem zurück' (Lk 24,52)', *GuL* 27 (1954) 81-83.

127  Argyle, A.W., 'The Ascension', *ET* 66 (1954/55) 240-242.

128  Stempvoort, P.A. van, 'De betekenis van λέγων τὰ περὶ τῆς βασιλείας τοῦ θεοῦ in Hand.1:3', *NThT* 9 (1954/55) 349-355.

129  Kretschmar, G., 'Himmelfahrt und Pfingsten', *ZKG* 66 (1954/55) 209-254.

130  Davies, J.G., 'The Prefigurement of the Ascension in the Third Gospel', *JThS* 6 (1955) 229-233.

131  Schweizer, E., *Erniedrigung und Erhöhung bei Jesus und seinen Nachfolgern* (AThANT 28; Zürich: Zwingli, 1955, ²1962) 195pp.

132  Iwand, H.J., 'Himmelfahrt. Apostelgeschichte 1,1-11', *GPM* 10 (1955/56) 134-143.

133  Argyle, A.W., 'Ascension and Return', *Interp.* 10 (1956) 321-322.

134  Bertram, G., 'Der religionsgeschichtliche Hintergrund des Begriffs der 'Erhöhung' in der Septuaginta', *ZAW* 68 (1956) 57-71.

135  Cadbury, H.J., 'Acts and Eschatology', in: W.D. Davies, D. Daube (eds.), *The Background of the New Testament and its Eschatology. In Honour of Charles Harold Dodd* (Cambridge: CUP, 1956) 300-321 (esp. 305-310).

136  Graß, H., *Ostergeschehen und Osterberichte* (Göttingen: Vandenhoeck & Ruprecht, 1956, ³1964) 43-51.

137  Haroutunian, J., 'The Doctrine of the Ascension. A Study of the New Testament Teaching', *Interp.* 10 (1956) 270-281 = 'La doctrina de la Ascensión. Un estudio de la enseñanza del Nuevo Testamento', *CuT* 21 (1957) 54-65.

138  Moule, C.F.D., 'The Ascension. Acts i.9', *ET* 68 (1956/57) 205-209; repr. in: idem, *Essays in New Testament Interpretation* (Cambridge, London, New York: CUP, 1982).

139  Mann, C.S., 'The New Testament and the Lord's Ascension', *CQR* 158 (1957) 452-465 [cf. G.F. Dowden, *CQR* 159 (1958) 422f].

140  Moule, C.F.D., 'The Post-Resurrection Appearances in the Light of Festival Pilgrimages', *NTS* 4 (1957/58) 58-61.

141  Reicke, B., *Glaube und Leben der Urgemeinde. Bemerkungen zu Apg. 1-7* (AThANT 32; Zürich: Zwingli, 1957) 9-26.

142  Stempvoort, P.A. van, 'Het programma van Rudolf Bultmann en de Hemelvaart in het Nieuwe Testament. Uitdaging en antwoord', *KeTh* 8 (1957) 145-166.

143  Brändle, M., 'Entmythologisierung der Himmelfahrt Christi', *GrEnt* 14 (1958/59) 207-211.

144  Davies, J.G., *He Ascended into Heaven. A Study in the History of Doctrine* (BaL 1958; London: Lutterworth, 1958) 224pp.

145 Kremers, H., 'Himmelfahrt', *EKL* 2 (1958, [2]1962) 159-161.

146 Russel, R., 'Modern Exegesis and the Fact of the Resurrection', *DR* 76 (1958) 251-264; 329-343.

147 Streeder, G.J., 'Hemelvaart', *ChrEnc* 3 ([2]1958) 425-426.

148 Stempvoort, P.A. van, 'The Interpretation of the Ascension in Luke and Acts', *NTS* 5 (1958/59) 30-42.

149 Scott, R.B.Y., 'Behold, He Cometh with Clouds', *NTS* 5 (1958/59) 127-132.

150 Bobrinskoy, B., 'Worship and the Ascension of Christ' (1959), *StLi* 2 (1963) 108-123.

151 Certeau, M. de, 'L'Ascension', *Christus* 6 (1959) 211-220.

152 Goudoever, J. van, *Biblical Calendars* (Leiden: E.J. Brill, 1959, [2]1961) 195-205.251-260.

153 Jansen, J.F., 'The Ascension, the Church and Theology', *ThTo* 16 (1959) 17-29.

154 Kümmel, W.G., 'Himmelfahrt Christi im NT', *RGG* 3 ([3]1959) 335.

155 Steck, K.G., 'Apostelgeschichte 1,1-11', in: G. Eichholz (Hrsg.), *Herr, tue meine Lippen auf. Eine Predigthilfe* 2 (Wuppertal, Barmen: E. Müller, [2]1959) 296-308.

156 Miquel, P., 'Le mystère de l'Ascension', *QLP* 40 (1959) 105-126; ET: 'Christ's Ascension and Our Glorification', *ThD* 9 (1961) 67-73.

157 Heuschen, J., *De bijbel over Hemelvaart* (4) (Roermond, Maaseik: J.J. Romen, 1960) 103pp. = *The Bible on the Ascension* (ET F. VanderHeijden; De Per, WI: St. Norbert Abbey. 1965) 105pp.

158 Heuschen, J., 'De hemelvaart des Heren in de oudste teksten van en rond het Christendom', *REcL* 47 (1960) 321-333.

159 Peifer, C., 'The Risen Christ and the Christian', *Worship* 34 (1960) 326-330.

160 Schierse, F.J., 'Himmelfahrt Christi I', *LThK* 5 (1960) 358-360.

161 Doeve, J.W., 'De hemelvaart in het Evangelie naar Lucas', *HeB* 20 (1961) 75-79.

162 Haufe, G., 'Entrückung und eschatologische Funktion im Spätjudentum', *ZRGG* 13 (1961) 105-113.

163 Schillebeeckx, E., 'Ascension and Pentecost', *Worship* 35 (1961) 336-363.

164 Schlier, H., 'Jesu Himmelfahrt nach den lukanischen Schriften', *Korrespondenzblatt des Collegium Canisianum* 95 (1961) 2-11; repr. in: *GuL* 34 (1961) 91-99; repr. in: idem, *Besinnung auf das Neue Testament. Exegetische Aufsätze und Vorträge 2* (Freiburg, Basel, Wien: Herder, 1964, [2]1967) 227-241.

165 Simon, U., *The Ascent to Heaven* (1961).

166 Squillaci, D., 'L'Ascensione in San Paolo', *PalCl* 40 (1961) 462-465.

167 Squillaci, D., 'Il salmo dell'Ascensione e della Pentecoste (Salmo 67)', *PalCl* 40 (1961) 525-530.

168 Wilckens, U., *Die Missionsreden der Apostelgeschichte. Form- und traditionsgeschichtliche Untersuchungen* (WMANT 5; Neukirchen-Vluyn: Neukirchener, 1961, [3]1974) 57 Anm.1; 150-156.233-235.

169 Dupont, J., ''ΑΝΕΛΗΜΦΘΗ (Act.i.2)', *NTS* 8 (1961/62) 154-157; repr. in: idem, *Études sur les Actes des Apôtres* (LeDiv 45; Paris: Cerf, 1967) 477-480.

170 Fürst, W., 'Himmelfahrt. Apostelgeschichte 1,1-11', *GPM* 16 (1961/62) 196-201.

171 Crehan, J.H., 'Ascension of Christ', *CDT* 1 (1962) 162-166.

172 Lohfink, G., 'Aufgefahren in den Himmel', *GuL* 35 (1962) 84-85.

173 Menoud, Ph.H., 'Pendant Quarante Jours', in: W.C. van Unnik (ed.), *Neotestamentica et Patristica* (FS. O. Cullmann; NT.S 6; Leiden: E.J. Brill, 1962) 148-156; repr. in:

Menoud, *Jésus-Christ et la foi. Recherches néotestamentaires* [BT(N); Neuchâtel, Paris: Delachaux & Niestlé, 1978] 110-118.

174  Brunner, P., 'The Ascension of Christ. Myth or Reality?', *Dialog* 1 (1962) 38-39

175  Koch, K., 'Himmelfahrt Christi', *BThW* (²1962) 650-658.

176  Robinson, J.M., 'Ascension', *IDB* 1 (1962) 245-247.

177  Strecker, G., 'Entrückung', *RAC* 5 (1962) 461-476.

178  Vellmer, E., 'Die Geschichte von Jesu Himmelfahrt und der moderne Mensch', *DtPfrBl* 62 (1962) 291-293.

179  Wenz, H., 'Ist die Geschichte von Jesu Himmelfahrt wirklich erledigt?', *DtPfrBl* 62 (1962) 222-224.

180  Wright, J.S., 'The Ascension', *NBDict* (1962, ²1982) 93.

181  Graham, H.H., 'Ascension', *DB(H)* (²1963) 60-61.

182  Haenchen, E., 'Judentum und Christentum in der Apostelgeschichte', *ZNW* 54 (1963) 155-187.

183  Hahn, F., *Christologische Hoheitstitel. Ihre Geschichte im frühen Christentum* (FRLANT 83; Göttingen: Vandenhoeck & Ruprecht, 1963, ²1964) esp. 126-132.

184  Holt, B., 'Realities of the Ascension', *Encounter* 24 (1963) 87-92.

185  Ioannides, V.Ch., Georgou, E., *al.*, ' Ἀνάλημψις, *TEE* 2 (ΚΔ) (1963) 162-166.

186  Lohfink, G., 'Der historische Ansatz der Himmelfahrt Christi', *Cath (M)* 17 (1963) 44-84.

187  Schneider, A., 'Das Evangelium der vierzig Tage', in: idem, *Gesammelte Aufsätze* (1963) 17-34.

188  Wilckens, U., 'Exaudi. Apostelgeschichte 1,6-12', *GPM* 18 (1963/64) 195-200.

189  Kaylor, R.D., *The Ascension Motif in Luke-Acts, the Epistle to the Hebrews and the Fourth Gospel* (Diss. Duke University, 1964; Ann Arbor, MI; London: UMI, 1980) xi + 217pp.

190  Robinson, J.A.T., 'Ascendancy', *ANQ* 5 (1964) 5-9.

191  Thompson, K.C., *Received up into Glory. A Study of Ascension* (SCFP 11; Westminster, New York: Faith, 1964) 108pp.

192  Wagner, J.B., *Ascendit ad coelos. The Doctrine of the Ascension in the Reformed and Lutheran Theology of the Period of Orthodoxy* (Diss. Basel; Winterthur, 1964) x + 147pp.

193  Walvoord, J.F., 'The Ascension of Christ', *BS* 121 (1964) 3-12.

194  Blenkinsopp, J., 'The Bible and the People. The Ascension as Mystery of Salvation', *CleR* 50 (1965) 369-374.

195  Flender, H., *Heil und Geschichte in der Theologie des Lukas* (BEvTh 41; München: Chr. Kaiser, 1965, ²1968) 16-18.85-98.

196  Lohfink, G., 'Wir sind Zeugen dieser Ereignisse (Apg.5.32). Die Einheit der neutestamentlichen Botschaft von Erhöhung und Himmelfahrt Jesu', *BiKi* 20 (1965) 49-52.

197  Lohfink, G., 'Was steht ihr da und schauet (Apg.1.11). Die 'Himmelfahrt Jesu' im lukanischen Geschichtswerk', *BiKi* 20 (1965) 43-48.

198  Luck, U., 'Glaube und Weltbild in der urchristlichen Überlieferung von Höllen- und Himmelfahrt Christi', in: *Collegium Philosophicum* (FS J. Rister; Stuttgart: Schwabe, 1965) 141-156.

199  Vielhauer, Ph., 'Ein Weg zur neutestamentlichen Christologie? Prüfung der Thesen

Ferdinand Hahns', in: idem, *Aufsätze zum Neuen Testament* (TB 31; München: Chr. Kaiser, 1965) 141-198.

200 Voss, G., *Die Christologie der lukanischen Schriften in Grundzügen* (SN 2; Paris: Desclée de Brouwer, 1965) 131-148.

201 Bertram, G., 'Erhöhung', *RAC* 6 (1966) 22-43.

202 Charlier, J.-P., *L'Evangile de l'enfance de l'Eglise. Commentaire de Actes 1-2* (Bruxelles, Paris, Montreal: La Pensée Catholique, 1966) 23-72.

203 Egan, J.M., 'Meaning of the Ascension', *CrCr* 18 (1966) 164-174.

204 Girock, H.J., *Himmelfahrt. Hindernis oder Hilfe für den Glauben?* (Stuttgart: Quell, 1966) 72pp.

205 Hagemeyer, O., 'Ihr seid meine Zeugen', *EuA* 42 (1966) 375-384.

206 Maly, K., 'Christi Himmelfahrt. Evangelium: Mk.16,11-20', *DAW* 3 (1966) 85-90.

207 Metzger, B.M., 'The Meaning of Christ's Ascension', *ChrTo* 10 (1966) 863-864.

208 Nibley, H., 'Evangelium Quadraginta Dierum', *VigChr* 20 (1966) 1-24.

209 Schille, G., 'Die Himmelfahrt', *ZNW* 57 (1966) 183-199.

210 Boyd, W.J., 'The Ascension according to St. John. Ch.14-17 not Pre-passion but Post-resurrection', *Theol.* 70 (1967) 207-211.

211 Duclos, V., 'Er Kristus faret op til himlen?', *Cath(K)* 24 (1967) 54-65.

212 Eisinger, W., 'Himmelfahrt. Apostelgeschichte 1,1-11', *GPM* 22 (1967/68) 238-247.

213 Quinn, J.D., 'Ascension of Jesus Christ (biblical)', *NCE* 1 (1967) 930-933.

214 Murray, J.C., 'Ascension of Jesus Christ (theological)', *NCE* 1 (1967) 933-936.

215 McNamara, M., 'The Ascension and the Exaltation of Christ in the Fourth Gospel', *Scrip.* 19 (1967) 65-73.

216 Marrevee, W.H., *The Ascension of Christ in the Works of St. Augustine* (Ottawa: University of Ottawa Press, 1967).

217 Martin, B., 'Aufgefahren in den Himmel. Gedanken eines Nicht-Theologen', *GuL* 40 (1967) 85-93.

218 Ratzinger, J., 'Christi Himmelfahrt', *GuL* 40 (1967) 80-85.

219 Seidensticker, P., *Zeitgenössische Texte zur Osterbotschaft der Evangelien* (SBS 27; Stuttgart: KBW, 1967, ²1968) 65-68.

220 Bligh, J., 'The Pattern of the Forty Days', *Tablet* 222 (1968) 413f.

221 Felix, F.M.D., 'El cristiano, sacramento de cristo (Act 1,3-11)', *CistC* 20 (1968) 97-105.

222 Kern, W., 'Das Fortgehen Jesu und das Kommen des Geistes *oder* Christi Himmelfahrt', *GuL* 41 (1968) 85-90.

223 Leaney, A.R.C., 'Why There Were Forty Days Between the Resurrection and the Ascension in Acts 1,3', *StEv* 4 (TU 102; Berlin: Akademie, 1968) 411-419.

224 Metzger, B.M., 'The Ascension of Jesus Christ', in: idem, *Historical and Literary Studies. Pagan, Jewish and Christian* (NTTS 8; Leiden: E.J. Brill; Grand Rapids: Eerdmans, 1968) 77-87.

225 Ratzinger, J., 'Himmelfahrt Christi', *SM(D)* 2 (1968) 693-696.

226 Ristow, H., 'Himmelfahrt', in: idem (Hrsg.), *Wandelt in der Liebe* (Predigtgedanken aus Vergangenheit und Gegenwart B/2; Berlin: Evangelische, 1968) 189-201.

227 Ruckstuhl, E., 'Auferstehung, Erhöhung und Himmelfahrt Jesu', in: E. Ruckstuhl, J. Pfammatter, *Die Auferstehung Jesu Christi. Heilsgeschichtliche Tatsache und Brennpunkt des Glaubens* (CiZ NF; Luzern, München: Rex, 1968) 133-183; repr. in:

Ruckstuhl, *Jesus im Horizont der Evangelien* (SBAB 3; Stuttgart: KBW, 1988) 185-218 (including a *Nachtrag*).

228  Schelkle, K.H., 'Christi Himmelfahrt', *GuL* 41 (1968) 81-85

229  Walker, W.G., *The Doctrine of the Ascension of Christ in Reformed Theology* (Ph.D. Diss. Vanderbilt University, 1968).

230  Talbert, C.H., 'An Anti-Gnostic Tendency in Lucan Christology', *NTS* 14 (1968) 259-271.

231  Wilson, S.G., 'The Ascension. A Critique and an Interpretation', *ZNW* 59 (1968) 269-281; repr. in: idem, *The Gentiles and the Gentile Mission in Luke-Acts* (MSSNTS 23; Cambridge: CUP, 1973) 88-107.

232  Balz, H., τεσσεράκοντα κτλ., *ThWNT* 8 (1969) 134-139.

233  Bertram, G., ὕψος, ὑψόω, κτλ., *ThWNT* 8 (1969) 600-619.

234  Eger, J., 'Zur Verkündigung der Himmelfahrt unseres Herrn', *LS* 20 (1969) 226-231.

235  George, A., 'Les récits d'apparitions aux Onze à partir de Luc 24,36-53', in: P. de Surgy, P. Grelot, M. Carrez, A. George, J. Delorme, X. Léon-Dufour (éds.), *La résurrection du Christ et l'exégèse moderne* (LeDiv 50; Paris: Cerf, 1969) 75-104.

236  Kaestli, J.-D., *L'eschatologie dans l'oeuvre de Luc. Ses caractéristiques et sa place dans le développement du christianisme primitif* (NSTh 22; Genève: Labor et Fides, 1969) 60-62.

237  Laconi, M., 'L'Ascensione di Christo. Divergenti e complementari testimonianze evangeliche', *RAMi* 14 (1969) 53-72.

238  Martini, C.M. *et alii*, 'Fête de l'Ascension', *Assemblées du Seigneur* 2/22 (Paris: 1969).

239  Martini, C.M., 'L'Ascension de Jésus, Act 1,1-11', *ASeign* 28 (1969) 6-11.

240  Metzger, B.M., 'The Meaning of Christ's Ascension', in: J.M. Myers, T.O. Reimherr, H.N. Bream (eds.), *Search the Scriptures* (GTS 3; FS R.T. Stamm; Leiden: E.J. Brill, 1969) 118-128.

241  Nogosek, R.J., 'The Exaltation of Christ', *BiTod* 44 (1969) 3068-3071.

242  Selman, M.R., *The Intention of the Ascension Narratives in Luke 24:50-53 and Acts 1:1-12* (Unpublished M.A. Diss. University of Bristol, 1969).

243  Thüsing, W., *Erhöhungsvorstellung und Parusieerwartung in der ältesten nachösterlichen Christologie* (SBS 42; Stuttgart: KBW, 1969) 114pp.

244  Frey, C., 'Die Himmelfahrtsbericht des Lukas nach Apg. 1:1-12; Exegetische und didaktische Problematik', *KatBl* 95 (1970) 10-21.

245  Bouwman, G., 'Die Erhöhung Jesu in der lukanischen Theologie', *BZ NS* 14 (1970) 257-263.

246  Franklin, E., 'The Ascension and the Eschatology of Luke-Acts', *SJTh* 23 (1970) 191-200.

247  Schmid, A.A., 'Himmelfahrt Christi', *LCI* 2 (1970, ²1990) 268-276.

248  Benoit, P., 'Ascension', in: X. Léon-Dufour (éd.), *VThB* (Paris: Cerf, ²1971) 87-91.

249  Fuller, R.H., *The Formation of the Resurrection Narratives* (New York: Macmillan, 1971; Philadelphia: Fortress, 1980) 120-130.

250  Lohfink, G., *Die Himmelfahrt Jesu. Untersuchungen zu den Himmelfahrts- und Erhöhungstexten bei Lukas* (StANT 26; München: Kösel, 1971) 314pp.

251  Odasso, G., 'L'Ascensione nell'Evangelo di Luca', *BeO* 13 (1971) 107-118.

252  Pesch, R., 'Der Anfang der Apostelgeschichte (Apg 1,1-11)', *EKK.V* 3 (Neukirchen: Neukirchener; Zürich: Benziger, 1971) 7-35 (in the same volume a summary of the

discussion by G. Dautzenberg, 93-94).

253  Rey Marcos, J., *La entronización de Jesús a la diestra de Dios* (Unpublished Diss., Roma, 1971).

254  Devor, R.C., 'The Ascension of Christ and the Dissension of the Church', *Encounter* 33 (1972) 340-358.

255  Francis, F.O., (review of G. Lohfink, *Die Himmelfahrt Jesu*), *JBL* 91 (1972) 424-425.

256  Rey Marcos, J., 'Sedet ad dexteram Patris. Nota sobre el 'Credo del Pueblo de Dios'', *RET* 32 (1972) 209-220.

257  Lohfink, G., *Die Himmelfahrt Jesu. Erfindung oder Erfahrung?* (KRB 18; Stuttgart: KBW, 1972) 66pp.

258  Lohfink, G., (sermon on the ascension) in: idem, *Gott ohne Masken. Predigten und Ansprachen* (Stuttgart: Calwer; Würzburg: Echter; Innsbruck: Tyrolia, 1972).

259  Ratzinger, J., 'Himmelfahrt Christi', *HTTL* 3 (1972) 290-292.

260  Schweizer, E., (review of G. Lohfink, *Die Himmelfahrt Jesu*), *ThR* 68 (1972) 18-19.

261  Villahoz, J.M., *La Ascensión a los cielos* (Diss. lic. Studii Franciscani; Jerusalem, 1972) vi + 85pp.

262  Weiser, A., (review of G. Lohfink, *Die Himmelfahrt Jesu*), in: H. Kahlefeld, O. Knoch (Hrsg.), *Die Episteln und Evangelien der Sonn- und Festtage. Auslegung und Verkündigung. Die Episteln. Lesejahre A* (Frankfurt: 1972) 279-282.

263  Boyd, W.J.P., 'The Ascension according to St. John', in: E.A. Livingstone (ed.), *StEv* 6 (TU 112; Berlin: Akademie, 1973) 20-27.

264  Czajkowski, M., *Wniebowstąpienie Jezusa* [Ascension of Jesus] (Studia z teologii św. Łukasza; Poznań: 1973) 58-71.

265  Dupont, J., 'Ascension du Christ et don de l'Esprit d'après Ac 2,33', in: B. Lindars, S.S. Smalley (eds.), *Christ and the Spirit in the New Testament. In Honour of C.F.D. Moule* (Cambridge: CUP, 1973) 219-227; repr. in: Dupont, *Nouvelles Études sur les Actes des Apôtres* (LeDiv 118; Paris: Cerf, 1984) 199-209.

266  Friedrich, G., 'Lk 9,51 und die Entrückungschristologie des Lukas', in: P. Hoffmann, N. Brox, W. Pesch (Hrsg.), *Orientierung an Jesus. Zur Theologie der Synoptiker* (FS J. Schmid; Freiburg: Herder, 1973) 48-77.

267  Harder, G., 'Himmelfahrt. Apostelgeschichte 1,1-14', *GPM* 28 (1973) 254-261.

268  Hay, D.M., *Glory at the Right Hand. Psalm 110 in Early Christianity* (SBL.MS 18; Nashville, New York: Abingdon, 1973) 176pp.

269  Luzarraga, J., *Las Tradiciones de la Nube en la Biblia y en el judaismo primitivo* (AnBib 54; Roma: IBP, 1973) 306pp. (esp. 220-225).

270  MacRae, G.W., ''Whom Heaven Must Receive Until the Time'. Reflections on the Christology of Acts', *Interp.* 27 (1973) 151-165.

271  Schmitt, A., *Entrückung-Aufnahme-Himmelfahrt. Untersuchungen zu einem Vorstellungsbereich im AT* (FzB 10; Stuttgart: KBW, 1973, ²1976) xiv + 378pp.

272  Varro, R., 'Séparé mais présent (Ascension: Luc 24,36-53)', in: G. Becquot, *Lectures d'évangiles pour les dimanches* (Année C; Paris: Seuil, 1973) 379-393.

273  Hahn, F., 'Die Himmelfahrt Jesu. Ein Gespräch mit Gerhard Lohfink', *Bib.* 55 (1974) 418-426.

274  Michiels, R., 'Eenheid van Pasen, Hemelvaart en Pinksteren', *Coll.* 20 (1974) 3-35.

275  Sabourin, L., 'The Biblical Cloud. Terminology and Traditions', *BTB* 4 (1974) 290-311.

276 Talbert, C.H., *Literary Patterns, Theological Themes, and the Genre of Luke-Acts* (SBL.MS 20; Missoula, MO: Scholars, 1974) 58-65.112-116.

277 Anon., 'Hemelvaart', in: W.H. Gispen, B.J. Oosterhoff, H.N. Ridderbos, W.C. van Unnik, P. Visser (red.), *Bijbelse Encyclopedie* 1 (Kampen: J.H. Kok, ²1975) 386-387.

278 Alsup, J.E., *The Post-Resurrection Appearance Stories of the Gospel Tradition. A History-of-Tradition Analysis With Text-Synopsis* (CThM 5; Stuttgart: Calwer, 1975) 307pp. (esp.145).

279 Lambrecht, J., 'De oudste Christologie. Verrijzenis of verhoging?', *Bijdr.* 36 (1975) 118-144.

280 Lygre, J.G., *Exaltation. Considered with Reference to the Resurrection and Ascension in Luke-Acts* (Diss. Princeton Theological Seminary, 1975; Ann Arbor, MI: UMI, 1995) 218pp.

281 Stewart, D.G., 'Ascension (of Christ)', *The Zondervan Pictorial Encyclopedia of the Bible* 1 (1975, 1976) 345-348.

282 Franklin, E., *Christ the Lord. A Study in the Purpose and Theology of Luke-Acts* (London: SPCK, 1975) 9-47.

283 Guillaume, J.M., *Luc interprète des anciennes traditions sur la résurrection de Jésus* (EtB; Paris: Librairie Lecoffre, J. Gabalda, 1979) 203-262.

284 Engelhardt, K., 'Apostelgeschichte 1,10-14', *GPM* 30 (1975/76) 240-245.

285 Talbert, C.H., 'The Myth of a Descending-Ascending Redeemer in Mediterranean Antiquity', *NTS* 22 (1975/76) 418-440.

286 Berger, K., *Die Auferstehung des Propheten und die Erhöhung des Menschensohnes. Traditionsgeschichtliche Untersuchungen zur Deutung des Geschickes Jesu in frühchristlichen Texten* (StUNT 13; Göttingen: Vandenhoeck & Ruprecht, 1976) 650pp. (esp. 170-174.471-475).

287 Lohfink, G., *Der Tod ist nicht das letzte Wort. Meditationen* (Freiburg, Basel, Wien: Herder, ⁵1976).

288 Donne, B., 'The Significance of the Ascension of Jesus Christ in the New Testament', *SJTh* 30 (1977) 555-568.

289 Geysels, L., 'Niet naar de hemel staan kijken? (Hand.1,11)', *VBS-Informatie* 8 (Boxtel: KBS, 1977) 22-27.

290 Grässer, E., 'Acta-Forschung seit 1960', *ThR* 42 (1977) 1-6.

291 Yüek Yün-feng, P., 'Yehsu shengt'ien. The Ascension of Christ', *CTUF* 9/34 (1977) 535-546.

292 Loader, W.R.G., 'Christ at the Right Hand (Ps. CX,1 in the NT)', *NTS* 24 (1977/78) 199-217.

293 Bovon, F., *Luc le théologien. Vingt-cinq ans de recherches (1950-1975)* (MoBi; Neuchatel, Paris: Delachaux & Niestlé, 1978) 181-190; ET K. McKinney; *Luke the Theologian. Thirty-Three Years of Research (1950-1983)* (PThM 12; Allison Park, PN: Pickwick, 1987) 170-177.441-446.

294 Dillon, R.J., *From Eye-Witnesses to Ministers of the Word. Tradition and Composition in Luke 24* (AnBib 82; Roma: IBP, 1978) xv + 336pp. (esp. 170-182.220-225).

295 Dömer, M., *Das Heil Gottes. Studien zur Theologie des lukanischen Doppelwerkes* (BBB 51; Köln, Bonn: P. Hanstein, 1978) 95-128.

296 Gourgues, M., *A la droite de Dieu. Résurrection de Jésus et actualisation du psaume*

*110:1 dans le Nouveau Testament* (EtB; Paris: Librairie Lecoffre, J. Gabalda, 1978) 270pp.

297 Hendrickx, H., *The Resurrection Narratives of the Synoptic Gospels* (Studies in the Synoptic Gospels; London: G. Chapman, 1978, ²1984) 97-102.

298 Hug, J., *La Finale de l'Évangile de Marc (Mc 16,9-20)* (EtB; Paris: J. Gabalda, 1978) 128-153.

299 LaVerdiere, E.A., 'The Ascension of the Risen Lord', *BT* 95 (1978) 1553-1559.

300 Barbi, A., *Il Cristo celeste presente nella Chiesa. Tradizione e Redazione in Atti 3,19-21* (AnBib 64; Roma: IBP, 1979) 199pp. (esp. 41-42.133-139).

301 Genton, N., *L'Ascension de Jésus-Christ* (Neuchâtel: Baconnière, 1979) 101pp.

302 Grässer, E., 'Die Parusieerwartung in der Apostelgeschichte', in: J. Kremer (éd.), *Les Actes des Apôtres. Traditions, rédaction, théologie* (BEThL 48; Gembloux: Duculot, 1979) 99-127, esp. 112-117.

303 Hoffmann, P., 'Auferstehung Jesu Christi', *TRE* 4 (1979) 478-513.

304 Holwerda, D.E., 'Ascension', *ISBE* 1 (1979) 310-313.

305 O'Toole, R.F., 'Luke's Understanding of Jesus' Resurrection-Ascension-Exaltation', *BTB* 9 (1979) 106-114.

306 Hofius, O., 'Himmelfahrt', *GPM* 34 (1979/80) 229-237.

307 Baird, W., 'Ascension and Resurrection. An Intersection of Luke and Paul', in: W.E. March (ed.), *Texts and Testaments. Critical Essays on the Bible and Early Church Fathers* (San Antonio: Trinity University, 1980) 3-18.

308 Delebecque, É., 'Les deux prologues des Actes des Apôtres', *RThom* 80 (1980) 628-634.

309 Gooding, D.W., 'Demythologizing Old and New, and Luke's Description of the Ascension. A Layman's Appraisal', *IBSt* 2 (1980) 95-119.

310 Kesich, V., 'Resurrection, Ascension, and the Giving of the Spirit', *GOTR* 25 (1980) 249-260.

311 Kremer, J., ἀναλαμβάνω, ἀνάλημψις, *EWNT* 1 (1980) 199-201.

312 Segal, A.F., 'Heavenly Ascent in Hellenistic Judaism, Early Christianity and Their Environment', *ANRW* II 23,2 (1980) 1333-1394.

313 Wright, J.S., 'Ascension', *IBD* 1 (1980) 129.

314 Colas, G., 'Ascension, exaltation', *Christus* 28 (1981) 78-87.

315 Dunn, J.D.G., 'Demythologizing the Ascension. A Reply to Professor Gooding', *IBSt* 3 (1981) 15-27.

316 Epp, E.J., 'The Ascension in the Textual Tradition of Luke-Acts', in: E.J. Epp, G.D. Fee (eds.), *New Testament Textual Criticism. Its Significance for Exegesis. Essays in Honour of Bruce M. Metzger* (Oxford: Clarendon, 1981) 131-145.

317 Guthrie, D., *New Testament Theology* (Leicester: IVP, 1981) 391-401.

318 Schnider, F., 'Himmelfahrt Jesu—Ende oder Anfang? Zum Verständnis des lukanischen Doppelwerkes', in: P.-G. Müller, W. Stenger (Hrsg.), *Kontinuität und Einheit* (FS F. Mußner; Freiburg: Herder, 1981) 158-172.

319 Vögtle, A., "Erhöht zur Rechten Gottes'. Braucht der Osterglaube die Krücken des antiken Weltbildes?', *Orien.* 45 (1981) 78-80.

320 Gray, J.R., 'Why the Ascension?', *ET* 93 (1982) 243-244.

321 Abba, R., 'What Does Ascension Mean?', *ET* 94 (1982) 210f.

322 Betz, O., 'Entrückung II. Biblische und frühjüdische Zeit', *TRE* 9 (1982) 683-690.

323 Delebecque, É., 'Ascension et Pentecôte dans les Actes des Apôtres selon le codex Bezae', *RThom* 82 (1982) 79-89.

324 Sabourin, L., 'The Eschatology of Luke', *BTB* 12 (1982) 73-76

325 Wißmann, H., 'Entrückung I. Religionsgeschichtlich', *TRE* 9 (1982) 680-683.

326 Donne, B.K., *Christ Ascended. A Study in the Significance of the Ascension of Jesus Christ in the New Testament* (Exeter: Paternoster, 1983) xiii + 98pp.

327 Horst, P.W. van der, 'Hellenistic Parallels to the Acts of the Apostles (1,1-26)', *ZNW* 74 (1983) 17-26.

328 Hübner, J., 'Himmel und Hölle', *TRT* 2 (⁴1983) 273-274.

329 Kasper, W., 'Christi Himmelfahrt—Geschichte und theologische Bedeutung', *IKZ* 12/3 (1983) 205-213.

330 Lambrecht, J., 'Ons Heer Hemelvaart', *IKT* 8 (1983) 164-175.

331 Toinet, P., 'Himmelfahrt als Erhöhung des Menschen' [Sermons of Leo the Great] (übers. von H.U. von Balthasar), *IKZ* 12 (1983) 238-243.

332 Toon, P., 'Historical Perspectives on the Doctrine of Christ's Ascension 1. Resurrected and Ascended: The Exalted Jesus', *BS* 140 (1983) 195-205.

333 Toon, P., 'Historical Perspectives on the Doctrine of Christ's Ascension 2. The Meaning of the Ascension for Christ', *BS* 140 (1983) 291-301.

334 Williams, R., 'Ascension of Christ', in: A. Richardson, J. Bowden (eds.), *A New Dictionary of Christian Theology* (London: SCM, 1983; repr. 1984) 44-45.

335 Dean-Otting, M., *Heavenly Journeys. A Study of the Motif in Hellenistic-Jewish Literature* (JudUmw 8; Frankfurt: P. Lang, 1984) xv + 323pp.

336 Toon, P., 'Historical Perspectives on the Doctrine of Christ's Ascension 3. The Significance of the Ascension for Believers', *BS* 141 (1984) 16-27.

337 Toon, P., 'Historical Perspectives on the Doctrine of Christ's Ascension 4. The Exalted Jesus and God's Revelation', *BS* 141 (1984) 112-119.

338 Toon, P., *The Ascension of Our Lord* (Nashville, TN: Thomas Nelson, 1984) xiv + 153pp.

339 Fitzmyer, J.A., 'The Ascension of Christ and Pentecost', *TS* 45 (1984) 409-440.

340 Fürst, T., 'Christi Himmelfahrt. Lukas 24,44-53', *GPM* 39 (1984/85) 274-280.

341 Quesada García, F., 'Las apariciones y la Ascensión en la economía salvífica', *Burg.* 26 (1985) 351-377.

342 Benéitez, M., 'Un capítulo de narrativa bíblica. Los 'encargos' de Hch 1,1-12', *MCom* 43 (1985) 329-382.

343 Kruse, M., 'Himmelfahrt. Apostelgeschichte 1,3-4(5-7)8-11', *GPM* 40 (1985/86) 290-295.

344 Tiede, D.L., 'The Exaltation of Jesus and the Restoration of Israel in Acts 1', *SBL.SP* (1985) 369-375; repr. in: *HThR* 79 (1986) 278-286.

345 LaVerdierre, E., 'The Passion-Resurrection of Jesus according to St. Luke', *ChiSt* 25 (1986) 35-50.

346 LaVerdierre, E., 'Jesus' Resurrection and Ascension', *Emmanuel* 92 (1986) 250-257.

347 Maile, J.F., 'The Ascension in Luke-Acts', *TynB* 37 (1986) 29-59.

348 Palatty, P., 'The Ascension of Christ in Luke-Acts. An Exegetical Critical Study of Luke 24.50-53 and Acts 1.2-3.9-11', *BiBh* 12 (1986) 100-117.166-181.

349 Parsons, M.C., 'A Christological Tendency in P75', *JBL* 105 (1986) 463-479.

350 Parsons, M.C., 'Narrative Closure and Openness in the Plot of the Third Gospel: The

Sense of an Ending in Luke 24:50-53', *SBL.SP* (1986) 201-223.

351   Pöhlmann, H.G., 'Himmelfahrt Christi II. Kirchengeschichtlich/Syst. Theologie', *TRE* 15 (1986) 334-341.

352   Schmidt-Lauber, H.-C., 'Himmelfahrtsfest', *TRE* 15 (1986) 341-344.

353   Weiser, A., 'Himmelfahrt Christi I. Neues Testament', *TRE* 15 (1986) 330-334.

354   Zmijewski, J., 'Apg 1 als literarischer und theologischer Anfang der Apostelgeschichte', in: idem, *Das Neue Testament. Quelle christlicher Theologie und Glaubenspraxis. Aufsätze zum Neuen Testament und seiner Auslegung* (Stuttgart: KBW, 1986) 67-84.

355   Cullianu, I.P., 'Ascension', *EncRel(E)* 1 (1987) 435-441.

356   Parsons, M.C., *The Departure of Jesus in Luke-Acts. The Ascension Narratives in Context* (JSNT.S 21; Sheffield: JSOT, 1987) 301pp.

357   Plevnik, J., 'The Eyewitnesses of the Risen Jesus in Luke 24', *CBQ* 49 (1987) 90-103.

358   Brodie, T.L., *Luke the Literary Interpreter. Luke-Acts as a Systematic Rewriting and Updating of the Elijah-Elisha Narrative in 1 and 2 Kings* (Diss. Roma, Pont. Studiorum Univ. a S. Thoma Aq. in Urbe, 1987) ix + 444pp.

359   Palmer, D.W., 'The Literary Background of Ac 1.1-14', *NTS* 33 (1987) 427-438.

360   Weinert, F.-R., *Christi Himmelfahrt. Neutestamentliches Fest im Spiegel alttestamentlicher Psalmen. Zur Entstehung des römischen Himmelfahrtsoffiziums* (Dissertationen: Theologische Reihe 25; St. Ottilien: EOS, 1987) viii + 361pp.

361   Bouwman, G., 'Der Anfang der Apostelgeschichte und der 'westliche' Text', in: T. Baarda, A. Hilhorst, G.P. Luttikhuizen, A.S. van der Woude (eds.), *Text and Testimony. Essays in Honour of A.F.J. Klijn* (Kampen: J.H. Kok, 1988) 46-55.

362   Bray, G.L., 'Ascension and Heavenly Session of Christ', in: S.B. Ferguson, D.F. Wright, J.I. Packer (eds.), *New Dictionary of Theology* (Leicester, Downers Grove, IL: IVP, 1988) 46-47.

363   Marlow, J.T.A., *A Narrative Analysis of Acts 1-2* (Diss. Golden Gate Baptist Theological Seminary, 1988) 106pp. [cf. *DAI.A* 49 (1988) 1481s.A]

364   Parsons, M.C., 'The Text of Acts 1.2 Reconsidered', *CBQ* 50 (1988) 58-71.

365   Bovon, F., 'Himmelfahrt Christi', *EKL* 2 (³1989) 522-523.

366   Mealand, D.L., 'The Phrase 'Many Proofs' in Acts 1,3 and in Hellenistic Writers', *ZNW* 80 (1989) 134-135.

367   O'Collins, G., 'Christ's Resurrection and Ascension', *America* 160 (1989) 262-263.

368   Brodie, T.L., 'Luke-Acts as an Imitation and Emulation of the Elijah-Elisha Narrative', in: E. Richard (ed.), *New Views on Luke and Acts* (Michael Glazier; Collegeville, MN: Liturgical, 1990) 78-85.172-174.

369   Hübner, E., 'Himmelfahrt. Lukas 24,(44-49)50-53', *GPM* 45 (1990/91) 233-237.

370   Mussies, G., 'Variation in the Book of Acts', *FilNT* 4 (1991) 165-182 (esp. 175-180).

371   Jones, E., 'The Origins of 'Ascension' Terminology', *ChM* 104 (1990) 156-161.

372   Spencer, F.S., (review of M.C. Parsons, *The Departure of Jesus*), *WJT* 52 (1990) 376-378.

373   Brown, R.E., *A Risen Christ in Eastertime. Essays on the Gospel Narratives of the Resurrection* (Collegeville, MN: Liturgical, 1991) 95pp.

374   Colpe, C., 'Himmelfahrt', *RAC* 15 (1991) 212-219.

375   Houlden, J.L., 'Beyond Belief. Preaching the Ascension (II)', *Theol.* 94 (1991) 173-180.

376 Plevnik, J., 'Son of Man Seated at the Right Hand of God. Luke 22,69 in Lucan Christology', *Bib.* 72 (1991) 331-347.

377 Wilcke, K., *Christi Himmelfahrt. Ihre Darstellung in der europäischen Literatur von der Spätantike bis zum ausgehenden Mittelalter* (Beiträge zur älteren Literaturgeschichte; Heidelberg: C. Winter, 1991) 505pp.

378 Nestle, D., 'Himmelfahrt. Apostelgeschichte 1,3-4(5-7)8-11', *GPM* 46 (1991/92) 247-252.

379 Giles, K., 'Ascension', *DJG* (1992) 46-50.

380 Sand, A., 'Himmelfahrt', in: M. Görg, B. Lang (Hrsg.), *NBL* 2/7 (1992) 156-160.

381 O'Carroll, M., 'Ascension', in: *Verbum Caro. An Encyclopedia on Jesus, the Christ* (Collegeville, MN: Liturgical, 1992) 12-14.

382 Gulley, N.R., 'Ascension of Christ', in: D.N. Freedman (ed.), *The Anchor Bible Dictionary* 1 (New York, London, Toronto: Doubleday, 1992) 472-474.

383 Walsh, B.J., Keesmaat, S.C., 'Reflections on the Ascension', *Theol.* 95 (1992) 193-200.

384 Ehrman, B.D., *The Orthodox Corruption of Scripture. The Effect of Early Christological Controversies on the Text of the New Testament* (New York, Oxford: OUP, 1993) 227-233.

385 Korn, M., *Die Geschichte Jesu in veränderter Zeit. Studien zur bleibenden Bedeutung Jesu im lukanischen Doppelwerk* (WUNT 2/51; Tübingen: J.C.B. Mohr/Paul Siebeck, 1993) 129-192.259-269.

386 Robinson, E., 'The Resurrection and Ascension of Our Lord', *BS* 150 (1993) 9-34 [originally published in *BS* 2 (1845) 162-189!]

387 Rius-Camps, J., 'Las variantes de la recensión occidental de los Hechos de los Apóstolos (Hch 1,1-3.4-14)', *FilNT* 6 (1993) 59-68.219-229.

388 Colpe, C. *et alii*, 'Jenseitsfahrt (I-II), Jenseitsreise', *RAC* 17 (1995) 407-543.

389 Fuller, G.C., 'The Life of Jesus, After the Ascension (Luke 24:50-53; Acts 1:9-11)', *WThJ* 56 (1994) 391-398.

390 Waltke, B.K., '"He Ascended and Sitteth ...'. Reflections on the Sixth Article of the Apostles' Creed', *Crux* 30 (1994) 2-8.

391 Neuner, J., 'He Ascended into Heaven', *VJTR* 59 (1995) 400-404.

392 Nützel, J.M., 'Entrückung III. Neues Testament', *LThK* 3 ($^3$1995) 685.

393 Milchner, H.J. (Hrsg.), *Himmelfahrt. Die Nähe Christi feiern. Predigten und liturgische Entwürfe* [DAW(S) 72; Stuttgart: 1996) 160pp.

394 Zwiep, A.W., 'The Text of the Ascension Narratives (Luke 24.50-3; Acts 1.1-2, 9-11)', *NTS* 42 (1996) 219-244.

Excurses on the ascension in commentaries. Full bibliographical descriptions are found in Bibliography C:

Harnack, *Apg* (1908) 126-130; Haenchen, *Apg* (1977) 71.142-158; Wikenhauser, *Apg* (1961) 28-32; Schneider, *Lukas* 2 (1977) 506-507; Bauernfeind, *Apg* (1980) 16-24.310-350; Roloff, *Apg* (1980) 12-13; Schneider, *Apg* 1 (1980) 208-211; Fitzmyer, *Luke* 1 (1981) 181-187.194-197; 2 (1985) 1586-1593; Schille, *Apg* (1984) 75-76; Boismard, Lamouille, *Actes* 2 (1990) 27-31.93-97.142-143.201; 3, 35-40; Zmijewski, *Apg* (1994) 68-72.

# PRIMARY SOURCES.
## 1. TEXTS, CRITICAL EDITIONS AND TRANSLATIONS

Aberbach, M., Grossfeld, B., *Targum Onkelos to Genesis. A Critical Analysis together with an English Translation of the Text. Based on A. Sperber's Edition* (Centre for Judaic Studies; Denver: Ktav; Center for Judaic Studies, University of Denver, 1982) vii + 376pp.

Aland, K., *Synopsis Quattuor Evangeliorum. Locis parallelis evangeliorum apocryphorum et patrum adhibitis* (Stuttgart: Deutsche Bibelgesellschaft, 1963, ¹³1985) xxxii + 590pp.

Aland, B., Aland, K., Karavidopoulos, J., Martini, C.M., Metzger, B.M. (eds.), *The Greek New Testament* (in cooperation with the Institute for New Testament Textual Research, Münster/Westphalia; London, Stuttgart: Deutsche Bibelgesellschaft, UBS, 1966, ³ᶜᵒʳʳ1975, ⁴1993) xiii + 61 + 918pp.

Alexander, P., '3 (Hebrew Apocalypse of) Enoch. A New Translation and Introduction', *OTP* 1 (1983) 223-315.

Andersen, F.I., '2 (Slavonic Apocalypse of) Enoch. A New Translation and Introduction. Appendix: 2 Enoch in *Merilo Pravednoe*', *OTP* 1 (1983) 91-221.

Arnaldez, R., Pouilloux, J., *et alii* (éds.), *Les oeuvres de Philon d'Alexandrie publiées sous le patronage de l'Université de Lyon* (Paris: Cerf, 1961ff.) 35 vols.

Avigad, N., Yadin, Y., *A Genesis Apocryphon. A Scroll from the Wilderness of Judaea. Description and Contents of the Scroll, Facsimiles, Transcription and Translation of Columns II, XIX-XXII* (Jerusalem: Magnes, 1956) 48 + xxii pp.

*The Babylonian Talmud* (London: Soncino, 1935-1952) 17 vols.

Barthélemy, D., Milik, J.T., *Discoveries in the Judean Desert 1. Qumran Cave 1* (Oxford: Clarendon, 1955) xi + 165pp. + xxxvii (plates).

Bartsch, H.-W., *Codex Bezae versus Codex Sinaiticus im Lukasevangelium* (Hildesheim, Zürich, New York: G. Olms, 1984) 211pp.

Benoit, P., Boismard, M.-É., *Synopse des quatre Évangiles en français* (Paris: Cerf, 1966-1972) 3 vols.

Bensly, R.L., *The Fourth Book of Ezra. The Latin Version Edited from the MSS* (TaS 3/2; Cambridge: CUP, 1895; repr. Nendeln, Liechtenstein: Kraus, 1967) xc + 107pp.

Berger, K., *Das Buch der Jubiläen* (JSHRZ 2/3; Gütersloh: G. Mohn, 1981) 275-575.

Bihlmeyer, K., *Die apostolischen Väter* 1 (Neubearbeitung der Funkschen Ausgabe; SQS 2/1; Tübingen: J.C.B. Mohr/Paul Siebeck, 1924, ³1970) lvi + 163pp.

Black, M., *The Book of Enoch or 1 Enoch. A New English Edition with Commentary and Textual Notes. In Consultation with J.C. VanderKam. With An Appendix on the 'Astronomical' Chapters (72-82) by O. Neugebauer* (SVTP 7; Leiden: E.J. Brill, 1985) xv + 467pp.

Black, M., *Apocalypsis Henochi Graece* (SVTP 3; Leiden: E.J. Brill, 1970) 1-44.

Bogaert, P., *Apocalypse de Baruch. Introduction, traduction du Syriac et commentaire* (SC 144-145; Paris: Cerf, 1969) 2 vols., 528 + 281pp.

Boismard, M.-É., Lamouille, A., *Le texte Occidental des Actes des apôtres. Reconstitution et Réhabilitation* (Paris: Éditions Recherche sur les Civilisations, Synthèse 17, 1984) 2 vols., 232 (Introduction et textes) + 356pp. (Apparat critique, Index des caractéristiques stylistiques, Index des citations patristiques).

Boismard, M.-É., Lamouille, A., *Synopsis Graece Quattuor Evangeliorum* (Paris, Louvain: Peeters, 1986) lxxviii + 418pp.

Bonnet, M., 'Acta Joannis', *AAAp* I/1 (1898; repr. Hildesheim: G. Olms, 1959) 151-216.

Box, G.H., Oesterley, W.O.E., 'The Book of Sirach', *APOT* 1 (1913) 268-517.

Box, G.H., 'IV Ezra', *APOT* 2 (1913) 542-624.

Brandenburger, E., *Himmelfahrt Moses* (JSHRZ 5/2; Gütersloh: G. Mohn, 1976) 59-84.

Braude, A.A., ...אליעזר רבי פרקי (Jerusalem: Eskol, 1972) 271pp.

Campbell Morgan, R., *The Epic of Gilgamesh. Text, Transliteration, and Notes* (Oxford: Clarendon, 1930) 92pp. + 59 plates

Charles, R.H. (ed.), *The Apocrypha and Pseudepigrapha of the Old Testament in English. With Introductions and Critical and Explanatory Notes to the Several Books* (Oxford: Clarendon, 1913; repr. 1983) 2 vols., xii + 684; xiv + 871pp.

Charles, R.H. 'Book of Enoch', *APOT* 2 (1913) 163-281.

Charles, R.H., *The Book of Enoch Translated. With an Introduction by W.O.E. Oesterley* (TED; London: SPCK, 1917, [23]1993) xxx + 154pp.

Charles, R.H., 'The Book of Jubilees', *APOT* 2 (1913) 1-82.

Charles, R.H., 'The Assumption of Moses', *APOT* 2 (1913) 407-424.

Charles, R.H., Forbes, N., '2 Enoch or the Book of the Secrets of Enoch', *APOT* 2 (1913) 425-469.

Charles, R.H., '2 Baruch or the Syriac Apocalypse of Baruch', *APOT* 2 (1913) 470-526.

Charlesworth, J.H. (ed.), *The Old Testament Pseudepigrapha* (Garden City, NY: Doubleday, 1983-1985) 2 vols., xlix + 995 (Apocalyptic Literature and Testaments); xlix + 1006pp. (Expansions of the 'Old Testament' and Legends, Wisdom and Philosophical Literature, Prayers, Psalms, and Odes, Fragments of Lost Judeo-Hellenistic Works).

Civil, M., 'The Sumerian Flood Story', in: W.G. Lambert, A.R. Millard, *Atra-ḫasīs. The Babylonian Story of the Flood* (Oxford: Clarendon, 1969) 138-145.

Clarke, E.G., with the collaboration of W.E. Aufrecht, J.C. Hurd, and F. Spitzer, *Targum Pseudo-Jonathan of the Pentateuch. Text and Concordance* (Hoboken, NJ: Ktav, 1984) xviii + 255 + 701pp.

*Codex Bezae Cantabrigiensis Quattor Evangelia et Actus Apostolorum complectens Graece et Latine sumptibus academiae phototypice repraesentatus* (Cambridge, 1899; repr. Mt. Eden, CA: Biblion) 2 vols.

Cohen, A. (ed.), *The Minor Tractates of the Talmud. Massektoth ketannoth* (London: Soncino, 1965) 2 vols., iv + 845pp.

Collins, J.J., 'Sibylline Oracles. A New Translation and Introduction', *OTP* 1 (1983) 317-472.

*The Coptic Version of the New Testament In the Southern Dialect, Otherwise Called Sahidic and Thebaic, With Critical Apparatus Literal English Translation Register of Fragments and Estimate of the Version 2. The Gospel of Luke* (Oxford: Clarendon, 1911) 479pp.

Danby, H., *The Mishna. Translated from the Hebrew with Introduction and Brief Explanatory Notes* (Oxford: OUP, 1933) xxxii + 844pp.

Dedering, S., *Apocalypse of Baruch* (Peshitta. The Old Testament in Syriac 4/3; Leiden: E.J.

Brill, 1973) iv + 50pp.

Denaux, A., Vervenne, M., *Synopsis van de eerste drie evangeliën* (Leuven: Vlaamse Bijbelstichting; Turnhout: Brepols, 1986) lxv + 332pp.

Denis, A.-M., *Fragmenta pseudepigraphorum quae supersunt graeca una cum historicorum et auctorum Judaeorum hellenistarum fragmentis* (SVTP 3; Leiden: E.J. Brill, 1970) 45-246.

Diez Macho, A., *Neophyti 1. Targum Palestinense, MS de la Bibliotheca Vaticana* (Madrid, Barcelona: CSIC, 1968-1979) 6 vols.

Díez Merino, L. (ed.), *Targum de Salmos. Edición Principe del Ms. Villa-Amil n.5 de Alfonso de Zamora* (BHBib 6; Biblia Poliglota Complutense, Tradición sefardí de la Biblia Aramea 4/1; Madrid: CSIC, Instituto 'Francisco Suárez', 1982) vii + 476pp.

Dupont-Sommer, A., *Les Écrits Esséniens Découverts près de la Mer Morte* (BH; Paris: Payot, 1959, ⁴1980) 466pp.

Dupont-Sommer, A., Philonenko, M. *et alii* (éds.), *La Bible. Écrits intertestamentaires* (Bibliothèque de la Pléiade; Paris: Gallimard, 1987) cxlix + 1903pp.

Elliger, K., Rudolph, W. (Hrsg.), תורה נבואים וכתובים *Biblia Hebraica Stuttgartensia. Editio funditus renovata* (Stuttgart: Deutsche Bibelgesellschaft, 1967, ²1984) lvii + 1574pp.

Etheridge, J.W., *The Targums of Onkelos and Jonathan Ben Uzziel on the Pentateuch with the Fragments of the Jerusalem Targum from the Chaldee* (London: Longman, Green, Longman, and Roberts, 1862-1865; repr. New York: Ktav, 1968) 2 vols., viii + 580; 668pp.

Lake, K., Oulton, J.E.L., *Eusebius. Ecclesiastical History* (LCL 153, 265; Cambridge, MA: Harvard University Press, 1926-1932; repr. London: W. Heinemann, 1980) 2 vols., lvi + 525; vii + 491pp.

Field, F., *Origenis Hexaplorum quae supersunt sive Veterum Interpretum Graecorum in totum Vetus Testamentum. Post Flaminium nobilium, Drusium, et Montefalconium adhibita etiam versione Syro-Hexaplari, concinnavit, emendavit, et multis partibus auxit* (Oxford: 1875; repr. Hildesheim: G. Olms, 1964) 2 vols., ci + 806; 1034 +77pp.

Finkelstein, L., *Sifre ad Deuteronomium. H.S. Horovitzii schedis usus cum variis lectionibus et adnotationibus* (Corpus Tannaiticum 3a/3a; 1939; repr. New York: Jewish Theological Seminary of America, 5729/1969) vi + 431pp.

Fitzmyer, J.A., *The Genesis Apocryphon of Qumran Cave 1. A Commentary* (BibOr 18; Roma: IBP,.1966) xvi + 232pp.

Forbes, N., Charles, R.H., '2 Enoch or the Book of the Secrets of Enoch', *APOT* 2 (1913) 425-469.

Freedman, H., Simon, M., *Midrash Rabbah* (London: Soncino, ³1961) 11 vols.

Friedlander, G., *Pirkê de Rabbi Eliezer. The Chapters of Rabbi Eliezer the Great according to the Text of the Manuscript Belonging to Abraham Epstein of Vienna. Translated and Annotated with Introduction* (London: Kegan Paul, Trench, Trubner: 1916; repr. New York: Hermon, 1970) lx + 490pp.

Funk, F.X. (ed.), *Didascalia et constitutiones apostolorum* (Paderborn: F. Schoeningh, 1905) 2 vols., lvi + 704; xliv + 208pp.

Funk, F.X, Diekamp, C.F. (eds.), *Patres apostolici. Textum recensuit adnotationibus criticis exegeticis historicis illustravit versionem latinam prolegomena indices addidit* (Tübingen: H. Laupp, 1901-1903) 2 vols., cli + 688; xc + 490pp.

García Martínez, F., *The Dead Sea Scrolls Translated. The Qumran Texts in English* (Leiden: E.J. Brill, 1994) lxvii + 513pp. = *Textos de Qumrán* (Colección Estructuras y Procesos, Serie Religión; Madrid: Trotta, 1992) 526pp.

Georgi, D., *Weisheit Salomos* (JSHRZ 3/4; Gütersloh: G. Mohn, 1980) 391-478.

Ginsburger, M., *Pseudo-Jonathan. Thargum Jonathan ben Usiël zum Pentateuch nach der Londoner Handschrift (Brit. Mus. add. 27031)* (Berlin: S. Calvary, 1903; repr. Hildesheim, New York: G. Olms, 1971) xxi + 366pp.

Ginzberg, L., *The Legends of the Jews* (Translated from the German Manuscript by Henrietta Szold; Phildelphia: JPS, 1909-1938; repr. 5728/1968) 7 vols.

Goeij, M. de, *Psalmen van Salomo. IV Ezra. Martyrium van Jesaja* (De Pseudepigrafen 1; Kampen: J.H. Kok, 1980) 106pp.

Goeij, M. de, *Jozef en Aseneth. Apokalyps van Baruch* (De Pseudepigrafen 2; Kampen: J.H. Kok, 1981) 143pp.

Greeven, H., Huck, A., Lietzmann, H., *Synopse der drei ersten Evangelien. Mit Beigabe der johanneischen Parallelstellen* (Tübingen: J.C.B. Mohr/Paul Siebeck, [13]1981) xli + 298pp.

Hammer, R., *Sifre. A Tannaitic Commentary on the Book of Deuteronomy. Translated from the Hebrew with Introduction and Notes* (YJS 24; New Haven, London: Yale University Press, 1986) xiv + 576pp.

Harrington, D.J., *The Hebrew Fragments of Pseudo-Philo's Liber antiquitatem Biblicarum Preserved in the Chronicles of Jerahmeel* (SBL.PS 3; Missoula, MO: SBL, 1974) vi + 74pp.

Harrington, D.J., Cazeaux, J., Perrot, C., Bogaert, P.-M., *Pseudo-Philon. Les Antiquités Bibliques* (SC 229-230; Paris: Cerf, 1976) 2 vols., 391 (introduction et texte critique); 321pp. (introduction littéraire, commentaire et index).

Harrington, D.J., Saldarini, A.J., *Targum Jonathan of the Former Prophets. Introduction, Translation and Notes* (Aramaic Bible 10; Edinburgh: T.&T. Clark, 1987) x + 320pp.

Harrington, D.J., 'Pseudo-Philo. A New Translation and Introduction', *OTP* 2 (1985) 297-377.

Hennecke, E., Schneemelcher, W. (Hrsg.), *Neutestamentliche Apokryphen in deutscher Übersetzung* (Tübingen: J.C.B. Mohr/Paul Siebeck, [4]1968, [3]1964) 2 vols., viii + 377; x + 661pp.

Higger, M., מסכתות דרך ארץ. *The Treatises Derek Erez. masseket Derek Erez Pirke Ben Azzai. Tosefta Derek Erez* (Brooklyn, NY: Moinester, 1935) 120 + 320pp.

Hodges, Z.C., Farstad, A.L., *The Greek New Testament According to the Majority Text* (Nashville, Camden, New York: Thomas Nelson, 1982, [2]1985) xlvi + 810pp.

Holladay, C.R., *Fragments from Hellenistic Jewish Authors 1. Historians* (SBL.TT 20; SBL.PS 10; Chico, CA: Scholars, 1983) xiii + 389pp.

Holmes, S., 'Wisdom of Solomon', *APOT* 1 (1913) 518-568.

Horst, P.W. van der, 'Pseudo-Phocylides. A New Translation and Introduction', *OTP* 2 (1985) 565-582.

Isaac, E., '1 (Ethiopic Apocalypse of) Enoch. A New Translation and Introduction', *OTP* 1 (1983) 5-89.

Jacobi, F. (Hrsg.), *Die Fragmente der griechischen Historiker* I-III (Berlin, Leiden: E.J. Brill, 1923-1958) 15 vols.

James, M.R., *The Biblical Antiquities of Philo. Translated from the Old Latin Version. Prolegomenon by L.H. Feldman* (LBS; 1917; repr. New York: Ktav, 1971) clxix + 280pp.

Jellinek, A., *Bet ha-Midrasch. Sammlung kleiner Midraschim und vermischter Abhandlungen aus der ältern jüdischen Literatur. Nach Handschriften und Druckwerken gesammelt und nebst Einleitungen herausgegeben* (Jerusalem: Wahrmann, 1853-1877, ³1967) 6 parts in 2 vols.

Jonge, M. de, *Testamenta XII Patriarcharum. Edited According to Cambridge University Library Ms Ff 1.24 fol. 203a-261b; with Short Notes* (PVTG 1; Leiden: E.J. Brill, 1964, ²1970) xix + 86pp.

Junod, E., Kaestli, J.-D., *Acta Johannis* (CChr.SA 1-2; Turnhout: Brepols, 1983) 2 vols., xxi + 949pp.

Kappler, W., *Maccabaeorum. Liber I* (Göttingen LXX 9; Göttingen: Vandenhoeck & Ruprecht, 1936, ³1990) 146pp.

Kautzsch, E. (Hrsg.), *Die Apokryphen und Pseudepigraphen des Alten Testaments* (Tübingen: J.C.B. Mohr, 1900; repr. 1921) 2 vols., xxxi + 507; vii + 540pp.

Klijn, A.F.J., *Die syrische Baruch-Apokalypse* (JSHRZ 5/2; Gütersloh: G. Mohn, 1976) 103-191.

Klijn, A.F.J., *Der lateinische Text der Apokalypse des Esra. Mit einem Index Grammaticus von G. Mussies* (TU 131; Berlin: Akademie, 1983) 108pp.

Klijn, A.F.J., '2 (Syriac Apocalypse of) Baruch. A New Translation and Introduction', *OTP* 1 (1983) 615-652.

Kmosko, M., *Liber apocalypseos Baruch filii Neriae. Translatus de graeco in syriacum; praefatus est, textum syriacum vocalium signis instruxit, latine vertit notis illustravit M. Kmosko)* (PS 1/2; Paris: Firmin-Didot, 1907) 1055-1306.

Knibb, M.A., *The Ethiopic Book of Enoch. A New Edition in the Light of the Aramaic Dead Sea Fragments* (Oxford, New York: Clarendon, 1978) 2 vols., xvi + 428 (Text and Apparatus); vi + 260pp. (Introduction, Translation and Commentary).

Knibb, M.A., 'Martyrdom and Ascension of Isaiah. A New Translation and Introduction', *OTP* 2 (1985) 143-176.

Kraft, R.A., Purintin, A.-E., *Paraleipomena Jeremiou* (SBL.TT 1; SBL.PS 1; Missoula, MO: SBL, 1972) 49pp.

Kramer, S.N., 'Sumerian Myths and Epic Tales', in: *ANET* 37-59.

Lambert, W.G., Millard, A.R., *Atra-Hasīs. The Babylonian Story of the Flood* (Oxford: Clarendon, 1969) xii + 198 + 11pp.

Landau, B., *Yalkut Shim'oni* ילקוט שמעוני מדרש על תורה נביאים וכתובים (Jerusalem: 1960) 2 vols., 24 + 1098 + 44pp.

Laperrousaz, E.M., *Le Testament de Moïse (généralement appelé 'Assomption de Moïse). Traduction avec introduction et notes* (Sem. 19; Paris: Adrien-Maisonneuve, 1970) xi + 140pp.

Leloir, L., *Éphrem de Nisibe. Commentaire de l'Évangile Concordant ou Diatessaron. Traduit du syriaque et de l'arménien. Introduction, traduction et notes* (SC 121; Paris: Cerf, 1966) 438pp.

Lévi, J., *The Hebrew Text of the Book of Ecclesiasticus. Edited with Brief Notes and a Selected Glossary* (SSS 3; Leiden: E.J. Brill, 1904, ³1969) xiii + 85pp.

Lightfoot, J.B., *The Apostolic Fathers. Clement, Ignatius, and Polycarp. Revised texts with Introductions, Notes, Dissertations, and Translations* (London: Macmillan, 1889, ²1890; repr. Peabody, MA: Hendrickson, 1989) 2 parts in 5 vols.

MacDonald, J., *Memar Marqah. The Teaching of Marqah* (BZAW 84; Berlin: A. Töpelmann,

1963) 2 vols., xliii + 177 (text); vi + 255pp. (translation).

Maher, M., *Targum Pseudo-Jonathan Genesis. Translated, with Apparatus and Notes* (Aramaic Bible 1B; Edinburgh: T.&T. Clark, 1992) xiv + 208pp.

Margulies, M., *Midrash haggadol on the Pentateuch. Genesis. Edited From the Various Manuscripts* (Jerusalem: Mosad Haraw Kook, 1947) 892pp.

Marmardji, A.-S., *Diatessaron de Tatien. Texte arabe établi, traduit en français, collationné avec les anciennes versions syriaques, suivi d'un évangéliaire diatessarique syriaque et accompagné de quatre planches hors texte* (Beyrouth: Imprimerie Catholique, 1935) cxl + 536pp. + 83pp.

Martin, V., Kasser, R., *Papyrus Bodmer XIV-XV. Évangiles de Luc et Jean* (Cologny, Genève: Bibliotheca Bodmeriana, 1961) 2 vols., 150 + 83pp.

McNamara, M., *Targum Neofiti 1 Genesis. Translated, with Apparatus and Notes* (Aramaic Bible 1A; Edinburgh: T.&T. Clark, 1992) xiv + 271pp.

Merk, A., *Novum Testamentum graece et latine, apparatu critico instructum* (Roma: IBP, [11]1992) 48 + 1732pp.

Metzger, B.M., 'The Fourth Book of Ezra. A New Translation and Introduction', *OTP* 1 (1983) 516-559.

Migne, J.-P., *Patrologiae cursus completus ... Series Graeca* (Paris: Petit-Montrouge, 1857-1936) 169 vols.

Migne, J.-P., *Patrologiae cursus completus ... Series Latina* (Paris: Petit-Montrouge, 1844-1855) 221 vols.

Milik, J.T., with the collaboration of M. Black, *The Books of Enoch. Aramaic Fragments of Qumran Cave 4* (Oxford: Clarendon, 1976) xvi + 439pp.

Milik, J.T., 'Dires de Moïse', *DJD* 1 (1955) 91-97; plates xviii-xix.

Mirkin, M.A., *Midrash Rabbah* (Tel-Aviv: Yabnev, 1956-1967) 11 vols.

Nestle, E., Aland, K., *Novum Testamentum Graece et Latine. Utrumque textum cum apparatu critico imprimendum curavit Eberhard Nestle* (London: UBS, [25]1969) 110 + xv + 670pp.

Nestle, E., Aland, K., *Novum Testamentum Graece. Post Eberhard Nestle et Erwin Nestle communiter ediderunt Kurt Aland, Matthew Black, Carlo M. Martini, Bruce M. Metzger, Allen Wikgren; apparatum criticum recensuerunt et editionem novis curis elaboraverunt Kurt Aland et Barbara Aland una cum Instituto studiorum textus Novi Testamenti Monasteriensi (Westphalia)* (Stuttgart: Deutsche Bibelgesellschaft, [26]1979, 8. Druck 1985) 78 + 779pp.

Nestle, E., Aland, K., *Novum Testamentum Graece. Post Eberhard et Erwin Nestle editione vicesima septima revisa communiter ediderunt Barbara et Kurt Aland, Johannes Karavidopoulos, Carlo M. Martini, Bruce M. Metzger; apparatum criticum novis curis elaboraverunt Barbara et Kurt Aland una cum Instituto Studiorum Textus Novi Testamenti Monasteriensi Westphaliae* (Stuttgart: Deutsche Bibelgesellschaft, [27]1993) 89 + 810pp.

Niese, B., *Flavii Josephi Opera. Edidit et apparatu critico instruxit* (Berlin: 1887-1895; Neudruck: Berlin, Weidmann, 1955) 7 vols.

Odeberg, H., *3 Enoch or the Hebrew Book of Enoch. Edited and Translated for the First Time with Introduction, Commentary and Critical Notes. Prolegomenon by J.C. Greenfield* (Cambridge: CUP, 1928; repr. LBS; New York: Ktav, 1973) xlvii + 192 + 179 + טע + 36pp.

Orchard, J.B., *A Synopsis of the Four Gospels in Greek. Arranged according to the Two-Gospel Hypothesis* (Edinburgh: T.&T. Clark, 1983) 342pp.

Ortiz de Urbina, I., *Vetus Evangelium Syrorum et exinde excerptum Diatessaron Tatiani* (BPM 6; Madrid: CSIC, 1967) xvi + 310pp.

Plooij, D., Philips, C.A., Bakker, A.H.A., *The Liège Diatessaron 7. Edited with a Textual Apparatus. English Translation of the Dutch Text by A.J. Barnouw* (VNAW.L 31; Amsterdam, London: Noord-Hollandsche, 1970) 673-797.

Priest, J., 'Testament of Moses. A New Translation and Introduction', *OTP* 1 (1983) 919-934.

Pritchard, J.B. (ed.), *Ancient Near Eastern Texts Relating to the Old Testament* (Princeton: Princeton University Press, 1950, ³1969) xxv + 710pp.

Rahlfs, A. (Hrsg.), *Septuaginta. Id est Vetus Testamentum graece iuxta LXX interpres)* (Stuttgart: Deutsche Bibelgesellschaft, 1935, 1979) lxix + 1184 + 941pp.

Roberts, A., Donaldson, J., Coxe, A.C., *Ante-Nicene Fathers. The Writings of the Fathers Down to A.D. 325* (1885-1887; repr. Peabody, MA: Hendrickson, 1994) 10 vols.

Robinson, J.M. (ed.), *The Nag Hammadi Library in English* (Leiden: E.J. Brill, 1977) xvi + 493pp.

Ropes, J.H., *The Text of Acts* (Beg 3; London: Macmillan, 1926) cccxx + 464pp.

Ryssel, V., 'Die Sprüche Jesus' des Sohnes Sirachs', *APAT* 1 (1900) 230-475.

Ryssel, V., 'Die Apokalypsen des Baruch', *APAT* 2 (1900) 402-446.

Sauer, G., *Jesus Sirach (Ben Sira)* (JSHRZ 3/5; Gütersloh: G. Mohn, 1976) 483-644.

Schmidt, C., *Gespräche Jesu mit seinen Jüngern nach der Auferstehung. Ein katholisch-apostolisches Sendschreiben des 2. Jahrhunderts. Nach einem koptischen Papyrus des Institut de la Mission Archéol. Française au Caire unter Mitarbeit von Herrn Pierre Lacau derzeitigem Generaldirektor der ägypt. Museen. Herausgegeben, übersetzt und untersucht, nebst drei Exkursen. Übersetzung des äthiopischen Textes von Dr. Isaak Wajnberg* (Leipzig: J.C. Hinrichs, 1919; repr. Hildesheim: G. Olms, 1967) vii + 731 + 83pp.

Schreiner, J., *Das vierte Buch Esra* (JSHRZ 5/4; Gütersloh: G. Mohn, 1981) 291-412.

Schunck, K.-D., *1. Makkabäerbuch* (JSHRZ 1/4; Gütersloh: G. Mohn, 1980) 288-373.

Scrivener, F.H., *Bezae Codex Cantabrigiensis (Being an Exact Copy, In Ordinary Type, of the Celebrated Uncial Graeco-Latin Manuscript of the Four Gospels and Acts of the Apostles, Written Early in the Sixth Century, and Presented to the University of Cambridge by Theodore Beza, A.D. 1581, Edited with a Critical Introduction, Annotations, And Facsimiles)* (Cambridge: Deighton, Bell and Co, 1864; repr. Pittsburgh, PA: Pickwick, 1978) lxiv + 453pp.

Speiser, E.A., 'Akadian Myths and Epics', *ANET* 60-119.

Sperber, A., *The Bible in Aramaic. Based on Old Manuscripts and Printed Texts* (Leiden: E.J. Brill, 1959-1973) 5 vols.

Stählin, O., Früchtel, L. (Hrsg.), *Clemens Alexandrinus. Stromata Buch I-VI* (GCS 52/2; Berlin: Akademie, 1906, ³1960) xix + 540pp.

Stone, M.E., Strugnell, J., *The Books of Elijah. Parts 1-2* (SBL.TT 18; SBL.PS 8; Missoula, MO: Scholars, 1979) ix + 110pp.

Stone, M.E., *The Testament of Abraham. The Greek Recensions* (SBL.TT 2; SBL.PS 2; Missoula, MO: SBL, 1972) viii + 89pp.

Swete, H.B., *The Old Testament in Greek According to the Septuagint* I (⁴1909) II (²1907) III (1894, ⁴1912) 3 vols.

Thackeray, H.St.J., Marcus, R., Wikgren, A., Feldman, L.H., *Josephus* (LCL; Cambridge, MA: Harvard University Press; London: W. Heinemann, 1926-1965) 10 vols.

The American and British Committees of the International Greek New Testament Project (eds.), *The Gospel According to St. Luke* (The New Testament in Greek 3; Oxford: Clarendon, 1984-1987) 2 vols., xvi + 299; 262pp.

Theodor, J., Albeck, Ch., *Midrash Bereshit Rabba. Critical Edition with Notes and Commentary. Introduction and Registers* (Jerusalem: Wahrmann, 1903-1929, ²1965) 3 vols.

Tischendorf, C., *Evangelia Apocrypha. Adhibitis plurimis codicibus graecis et latinis maximam partem nunc primum consultis atque ineditorum copia insignibus* (Leipzig: 1852, ²1876; repr. Hildesheim: G. Olms, 1966) xcv + 486pp.

Tischendorf, A.F.C., *Novum Testamentum Graece. Editio octava critica maior* (Leipzig: Giesecke & Devrient, 1869-1872) 3 vols.

Todesco, V., Vaccari, A., Vattasso, M., *Il Diatessaron in volgare italiano. Testi inediti dei secoli XIII-XIV* (StT 81; Città del Vaticano: Biblioteca Apostolica Vaticana, 1938) xii + 383pp.

Torrey, C.C., *The Lives of the Prophets. Greek Text and Translation* (JBL.MS 1; Philadelphia: SBL, 1946) 53pp.

Tromp, J., *The Assumption of Moses. A Critical Edition with Commentary* (SVTP 10; Leiden, New York, København, Köln: E.J. Brill, 1993) viii + 324pp.

Uhlig, S., *Das äthiopische Henochbuch* (JSHRZ 5/6; Gütersloh: G. Mohn, 1984) 459-780.

Vaganay, L., *L'Évangile de Pierre* (EtB; Paris: Librairie Lecoffre, J. Gabalda, 1930) xxiii + 357pp.

Vaillant, A., *Le livre des secrets d'Hénoch. Text slave et traduction française* (Paris: Institut d'Études Slaves, 1952; repr. 1976) xxvi + 125pp.

Vattioni, F., *Ecclesiastico. Testo ebraico con apparato critico e versioni greca, latina e siriaca* (Napoli: Instituto Orientale di Napoli, 1968) liv + 283pp.

Vermes, G., *The Dead Sea Scrolls in English* (London: Penguin, 1962, ³1987) xvi + 320pp.

*Vetus Testamentum Syriace. Iuxta simplicem Syrorum versionem. Ex auctoritatis societatis ad studia librorum veteris testamenti provehenda* (Institutum Peshittonianum Leidense 2/3; Leiden: E.J. Brill, 1980) xxix + 173pp.

*Nova Vulgata Bibliorum Sacrorum Editio. Sacros. oecum. concilii Vaticani II ratione habita iussu Pauli PP. VI recognita auctoritate Ioannis Pauli PP. II promulgata. Editio typica altera* (Roma: Libreria Editrice Vaticana, 1986) xxxi + 2316pp.

Wahl, O., *Apocalypsis Esdrae, Apocalypsis Sedrach, Visio Beati Esdrae* (PVTG 4; Leiden: E.J. Brill, 1977) x + 61pp.

Westcott, B.F., Hort, F.J.A., *The New Testament in the Original Greek* (Cambridge, London: Macmillan, 1881) 2 vols.; 595 + xxxi + 324 + 188pp.

Wintermute, O.S., 'Jubilees. A New Translation and Introduction', *OTP* 2 (1985) 35-142.

Yadin, Y., *The Ben Sira Scroll from Masada. With Introduction, Emendations and Commentary* (Translated and Reprinted from *Eretz-Israel* 8; Jerusalem: Israel Exploration Society, 1965) 49 + 45pp. + 9 plates.


## 2. LEXICAL AIDS, ETC.


Balz, H.R., Schneider, G. (Hrsg.), *Exegetisches Wörterbuch zum Neuen Testament* (Stuttgart, Berlin, Köln, Mainz: Kohlhammer, 1980-1983) 3 vols.

Bauer, W., *Griechisch-deutsches Wörterbuch zu den Schriften des Neuen Testaments und der frühchristlichen Literatur* (hrsg. v. K. und B. Aland; Berlin, New York: W. de Gruyter, ⁶1988) xxiv + 1796Sp.

Blass, F., Debrunner, A., *Grammatik des neutestamentlichen Griechisch* (bearbeitet v. F. Rehkopf; GTL; Göttingen: Vandenhoeck & Ruprecht, ¹⁷1990) xxi + 511pp.

Brown, C. (ed.), *The New International Dictionary of New Testament Theology* (Grand Rapids: Zondervan, rev. 1975-1978) 4 vols.

Coenen, L., Beyreuther, E., Bietenhard, H. (Hrsg.), *Theologisches Begriffslexikon zum Neuen Testament* (Wuppertal: Brockhaus, 1971, ⁴·⁷1986) 2 vols., xxxix + xv + 1536pp.

Denis, A.-M., *Concordance grecque des pseudépigraphes d'Ancient Testament. Concordance, corpus des textes, indices. Avec la collaboration d'Y. Janssens et le concours du Cetedoc* (Louvain-la-Neuve: Université Catholique de Louvain, Institut Orientaliste; Leiden: E.J. Brill, 1987) xxiii + 925pp.

Friedrich, G., Kittel, G. (Hrsg.), *Theologisches Wörterbuch zum Neuen Testament* (Stuttgart, Berlin, Köln: W. Kohlhammer, 1933-1979; repr. 1990) 11 vols.

Gesenius, W., *Hebräisches und aramäisches Handwörterbuch über das Alte Testament* (in Verbindung mit H. Zimmern, W.M. Müller und O. Weber; bearbeitet von F. Buhl; Berlin, Göttingen, Heidelberg: Springer, ¹⁷1915; repr. 1962) xix + 1013pp.

Hatch, E., Redpath, H.A. (eds.), *A Concordance to the Septuagint and the Other Greek Versions of the Old Testament. Including the Apocryphal Books* (Oxford: Clarendon, 1897; repr. Grand Rapids: Baker, ⁴1989) 2 vols., vii + 1504 + 272pp.

Jenni, E., Westermann, C. (Hrsg.), *Theologisches Handwörterbuch zum Alten Testament* (München: Chr. Kaiser; Zürich: Theologischer, 1971-1975, ⁴1984-³1984) 2 vols., lxi pp. + 942 cols.; x pp. + 602 cols.

Kraft, H., *Clavis patrum apostolicorum. Catalogum vocum in libris patrum qui dicuntur apostolici non raro occurrentium adiuvante Ursula Früchtel congessit contulit conscripsit* (Darmstadt: WBG, 1963) 501pp.

Lampe, G.W.H., *A Patristic Greek Lexicon* (Oxford: Clarendon, 1961) xlix + 1568pp.

Liddell, H.G., Scott, R., Jones, H.S., McKenzie, R., *et alii*, *A Greek-English Lexicon. With a Revised Supplement 1996* (Oxford: Clarendon, [1843], ⁹1940 / 1996) xlv + 2042 + xxxi + 320pp.

Moulton, J.H., Milligan, G., *The Vocabulary of the Greek Testament Illustrated from the Papyri and Other Non-Literary Sources* (London: Hodder & Stoughton, 1930) xxxii + 705pp.

Moulton, W.F., Geden, A.S., Moulton, H.K. (eds.), *Concordance to the Greek Testament According to the Texts of Westcott and Hort, Tischendorf and the English Revisers* (Edinburgh: T.&T. Clark, 1897, ⁵1978) xvi + 1110pp.

Rengstorf, K.H., *A Complete Concordance to Flavius Josephus* (Leiden: E.J. Brill, 1973-1983) 4 vols. + Supplement to A Complete Concordance to Flavius Josephus (Namenwörterbuch zu Flavius Josephus) (1968) (ed. by A. Schalit).

Robertson, A.T., Davis, W.H., *A New Short Grammar of the Greek Testament* (Grand Rapids: Baker, [1931], ¹⁰1958; repr. 1977) 454pp.

Soden, W. von, *Akkadisches Handwörterbuch. Unter Benutzung des lexikalischen Nachlasses von Bruno Meissner (1868-1947)* (Wiesbaden: O. Harrassowitz, 1965-1981) 3 vols.

Thayer, J.H., *A Greek-English Lexicon of the New Testament. Being Grimm's Wilke's Clavis Novi Testamenti, Translated, Revised and Enlarged* (Grand Rapids: Zondervan, [1885,

²1889] repr. n.d.) xix + 726pp.

Yoder, J.D., *Concordance to the Distinctive Greek Text of Codex Bezae* (NTTS 2; Leiden: E.J. Brill, 1961) vi + 74pp

# GENERAL BIBLIOGRAPHY

Aalders, G.Ch., *Oud-Testamentische Kanoniek* (Kampen: J.H. Kok, 1952) 415pp.

Abba, R., 'What Does Ascension Mean?', *ET* 94 (1982) 210f.

Adler, W., 'Enoch in Early Christian Literature', *SBL.SP* (1978) 271-275.

Aland, K., 'Der (wiedergefundene) Markusschluß? Eine methodologische Bemerkung zur textkritischen Arbeit', *ZThK* 67 (1970) 3-13.

Aland, K., 'Der Schluß des Markusevangeliums', in: M. Sabbe (éd.), *L'Évangile selon Marc. Tradition et rédaction* (BEThL 34; Leuven: Leuven University Press, Peeters, 1974, ²1988) 435-470.573-575; repr. in: Aland, *Neutestamentliche Entwürfe* (TB 63; München: Chr. Kaiser, 1979) 246-283.

Aland, K., Aland, B., *Der Text des Neuen Testaments. Einführung in die wissenschaftlichen Ausgaben sowie in Theorie und Praxis der modernen Textkritik* (Stuttgart: Deutsche Bibelgesellschaft, 1981, ²1989) 374pp.

Alexander, L.C.E., *The Preface to Luke's Gospel. Literary Convention and Social Context in Luke 1.1-4 and Acts 1.1* (MSSNTS 78; Cambridge, New York: CUP, 1993) xv + 250pp.

Allison, D., 'Elijah Must Come First', *JBL* 103 (1984) 256-258.

Alsup, J.E., *The Post-Resurrection Appearance Stories of the Gospel Tradition. A History-of-Tradition Analysis With Text-Synopsis* (CThM 5; Stuttgart: Calwer, 1975) 307pp.

Anon., 'Hemelvaart', in: W.H. Gispen, B.J. Oosterhoff, H.N. Ridderbos, W.C. van Unnik, P. Visser (red.), *Bijbelse Encyclopedie* 1 (Kampen: J.H. Kok, ²1975) 386-387.

Appel, H., *Die Komposition des äthiopischen Henochbuches* (BFChTh 10/3; Gütersloh: C. Bertelsmann, 1906) 101pp.

Argyle, A.W., 'The Exaltation of Our Lord', *ET* 59 (1947/48) 190-192.

Argyle, A.W., 'The Heavenly Session of Christ', *Theol.* 55 (1952) 286-289.

Argyle, A.W., 'The Ascension', *ET* 66 (1954/55) 240-242.

Argyle, A.W., 'Ascension and Return', *Interp.* 10 (1956) 321-322.

Ashton, J., *Understanding the Fourth Gospel* (Oxford: Clarendon, 1991) xvii + 599pp.

Bacon, B.W., 'The Ascension in Luke and Acts', *Exp.* (Series 7) 7 (1909) 254-261.

Baird, W., 'Ascension and Resurrection. An Intersection of Luke and Paul', in: W.E. March (ed.), *Texts and Testaments. Critical Essays on the Bible and Early Church Fathers* (San Antonio: Trinity University, 1980) 3-18.

Balz, H.R., τεσσεράκοντα κτλ., *ThWNT* 8 (1969) 134-139.

Barbi, A., *Il Cristo celeste presente nella Chiesa. Tradizione e Redazione in Atti 3,19-21* (AnBib 64; Roma: IBP, 1979) 199pp.

Barnard, L.W., 'The Day of the Resurrection and Ascension of Christ in the Epistle of Barnabas', *RBen* 78 (1968) 106-107.

Barrett, C.K., *The Gospel According to St. John. An Introduction with Commentary and Notes on the Greek Text* (London: SCM, 1955, ²1978) xvi + 638pp.

Barrett, C.K., *Luke the Historian in Recent Study* (London: Epworth, 1961) 76pp.

Barrett, C.K., 'Stephen and the Son of Man', in: W. Eltester, F.H. Kettler (Hrsg.), *Apophoreta. Festschrift für Ernst Haenchen* (BZNW 30; Berlin: A. Töpelmann, 1964) 32-38.

Barrett, C.K., 'Faith and Eschatology in Acts 3', in: E. Grässer, O. Merk (Hrsg.), *Glaube und Eschatologie* (FS W.G. Kümmel; Tübingen: J.C.B. Mohr/Paul Siebeck, 1985) 1-17.

Barrett, C.K., 'The Gentile Mission as an Eschatological Phenomenon', in: H.W. Gloer (ed.), *Eschatology and the New Testament* (1988) 65-75.

Barrett, C.K., *The Acts of the Apostles 1. Preliminary Introduction and Commentary on Acts I-XIV* (ICC; Edinburgh: T.&T. Clark, 1994) xxiii + 693pp.

Barth, M., *Ephesians. A New Translation with Introduction and Commentary* (AncB 34; Garden City, NY: Doubleday, 1974) 2 vols., xxxiv + xxxvi + 851pp.

Bartsch, H.W., 'The Meaning of the Ascension', *LuthQ* 6 (1954) 44-47.

Bauckham, R.J., 'The Martyrdom of Enoch and Elijah. Jewish or Christian?', *JBL* 95 (1976) 447-458.

Bauckham, R.J., *Jude and the Relatives of Jesus in the Early Church* (Edinburgh: T. &T. Clark, 1990) ix + 459pp.

Bauer, W., *Das Leben Jesu im Zeitalter der neutestamentlichen Apokryphen* (Tübingen: J.C.B. Mohr/Paul Siebeck, 1909; repr. Darmstadt: WBG, 1965) xv + 568pp.

Bauer, W., *Das Johannesevangelium erklärt* (HNT 6; Tübingen: J.C.B. Mohr/Paul Siebeck, 1912, ²1925) 244pp.

Bauernfeind, O., *Kommentar und Studien zur Apostelgeschichte* (hrsg. v. V. Metelmann; WUNT 22; Tübingen: J.C.B. Mohr/Paul Siebeck, 1980) xviii + 492pp.

Baum, A.D., *Lukas als Historiker der letzten Jesusreise* (TVGMS 379; Wuppertal, Zürich: Brockhaus, 1993) xi + 462pp.

Beek, M.A., 'The Meaning of the Expression 'The Chariots and Horsemen of Israel' (2 Kings 2:12)', *OTS* 17 (1972) 1-10.

Beel, A., 'Ascensio Domini juxta Act.Ap. 1:9-11', *CBrug* 35 (1935) 337-343.

Behm, J., μορφή, μορφόω, κτλ., *ThWNT* 4 (1942) 750-767.

Belser, J.E., *Die Geschichte des Leidens und Sterbens, der Auferstehung und Himmelfahrt des Herrn nach den vier Evangelisten ausgelegt* (Freiburg im Breisgau: Herder, 1903, ²1913) ix + 548pp. = *History of the Passion, Death, and Glorification of Our Saviour Jesus Christ* (Freely Adapted into English by F.A. Marks; St. Louis, MO, London: B. Herder, 1929) 668pp.

Ben-Yaacob, A. *et alii*, 'Ezra', *EJ* 6 (1971) 1104-1107.

Benéitez, M., 'Un capítulo de narrativa bíblica. Los 'encargos' de Hch 1,1-12', *MCom* 43 (1985) 329-382.

Bengel, J.A., *Gnomon Novi Testamenti in quo ex nativa verborum vi simplicitas, profunditas, concinnitas, salubritas sensuum coelestium indicatur* (Ed. III. 1773, per filium superstitem Ernestum Bengelium quondam curata, sexto recusa, emendata et e ceteris Bengelii scriptis—posthumis ex parte—suppleta et aucta opera Pauli Steudel; Stuttgart: J.F. Steinkopf, ⁸1891) xxviii + 1152pp.

Benoit, P., 'L'Ascension' (1949); repr. in: idem, *Exégèse et Théologie* 1 (Paris: Cerf, 1961) 363-411.

Benoit, P., 'Ascension', *VThB* (²1971) 87-91.

Berger, K., *Die Auferstehung des Propheten und die Erhöhung des Menschensohnes. Traditionsgeschichtliche Untersuchungen zur Deutung des Geschickes Jesu in frühchristlichen Texten* (StUNT 13; Göttingen: Vandenhoeck & Ruprecht, 1976) 650pp.

Bernard, E.R., 'The Value of the Ascension', *ET* 12 (1900/01) 152-155.

Bernard, J.H., 'Assumption and Ascension', *ERE* 2 (1909, ²1930) 151-157.

Bernard, J.H., *The Gospel According to St. John* (ed. A.H. McNeile; ICC; Edinburgh: T.&T. Clark, 1928) 2 vols., clxxxviii + 740pp.

Bertram, G., 'Die Himmelfahrt Jesu vom Kreuz aus und der Glaube an seine Auferstehung', in: K.L. Schmidt (Hrsg.), *Festgabe für Adolf Deissmann zum 60. Geburtstag* (Tübingen: J.C.B. Mohr/Paul Siebeck, 1927) 187-217.

Bertram, G., 'Der religionsgeschichtliche Hintergrund des Begriffs der 'Erhöhung' in der Septuaginta', *ZAW* 68 (1956) 57-71.

Bertram, G., 'Erhöhung', *RAC* 6 (1966) 22-43.

Bertram, G., ὕψος, ὑψόω, κτλ., *ThWNT* 8 (1969) 600-619.

Betz, O., 'Entrückung II. Biblische und frühjüdische Zeit', *TRE* 9 (1982) 683-690.

Beverley, R.J., 'The Ascension', *The Interpreter* 2 (1905/06) 101-102.

Beyer, H.W., εὐλογέω, εὐλογητός κτλ., *ThWNT* 2 (1935) 751-763.

Bickermann, E., 'Das leere Grab' (1924); repr. in: idem, *Studies in Jewish and Christian History* 3 (AGJU 9; Leiden: E.J. Brill, 1986) 70-81.

Bickermann, E., 'Die römische Kaiserapotheose', *ARW* 27 (1929) 1-27.

Bieder, W., *Die Vorstellung von der Höllenfahrt Jesu Christi. Beitrag zur Entstehungsgeschichte der Vorstellung vom sog. Descensus ad inferos* (AThANT 19; Zürich: Zwingli, 1949) 237pp.

Bietenhard, H., *Die himmlische Welt in Urchristentum und Spätjudentum* (WUNT 2; Tübingen: J.C.B. Mohr/Paul Siebeck, 1951) vi + 295pp.

Black, M., 'The Eschatology of the Similitudes of Enoch', *JThS* 3 (1952) 1-10.

Black, M., 'The 'Two Witnesses' of Rev.11.3f. in Jewish and Christian Apocalyptic Tradition', in: E. Bammel, C.K. Barrett, W.D. Davies (eds.), *Donum Gentilicum. New Testament Studies in Honour of D. Daube* (Oxford: OUP, 1978) 227-237.

Blass, F., *Acta apostolorum sive Lucae ad Theophilum liber alter. Editio philologica apparatu critico, commentario perpetuo, indice verborum illustrata* (Göttingen: Vandenhoeck & Ruprecht, 1895) x + 334pp.

Bligh, J., 'The Pattern of the Forty Days', *Tablet* 222 (1968) 413- .

Bobrinskoy, B., 'Worship and the Ascension of Christ' (1959), *StLi* 2 (1963) 108-123.

Bock, E., 'Von der Himmelfahrt im Alten und Neuen Testament', *Die Christengemeinschaft* 4 (1927) 45-50.

Boismard, M.-É., Lamouille, A., *Les Actes des deux apôtres* (EtB Ns 12-14; Paris: Librairie Lecoffre, J. Gabalda, 1990) 3 vols.

Borgen, P., 'Some Jewish Exegetical Traditions as Background for Son of Man Sayings in John's Gospel (Jn 3,13-14 and context)', in: M. de Jonge (éd.), *L'Évangile de Jean* (1977) 243-258.

Borgen, P., 'Heavenly Ascent in Philo. An Examination of Selected Passages', in: J.H. Charlesworth, C.A. Evans (eds.), *The Pseudepigrapha and Early Biblical Interpretation* (1993) 246-268.

Bornkamm, G., 'Der Auferstandene und der Irdische. Mt. 28,16-20', in: G. Bornkamm, G. Barth, H.J. Held (Hrsg.), *Überlieferung und Auslegung im Matthäusevangelium* (WMANT 1; Neukirchen-Vluyn: Neukirchener, 1960, ⁶1970) 289-310.

Böttrich, C., 'Recent Studies in the *Slavonic Book of Enoch*', *JSPE* 9 (1991) 35-42.

Bousset, W., *Der Antichrist in der Überlieferung des Judenthums des neuen Testaments und der alten Kirche. Ein Beitrag zur Auslegung der Apocalypse* (Göttingen: Vandenhoeck & Ruprecht, 1895; repr. Hildeshcim, Zürich, New York: G. Olms, 1983) vi + 186pp.

Bousset, W., 'Die Himmelsreise der Seele', *ARW* 4 (1901) 136-169.229-273; repr. Libelli 71; Darmstadt: WBG, 1960, [2]1971) 83pp.

Bousset, W., *Die Offenbarung Johannis* (KEK II[6]; Göttingen: Vandenhoeck & Ruprecht, 1896, [2]1906) iv + 468pp.

Bousset, W., *Die Religion des Judentums im späthellenistischen Zeitalter* (hrsg. v. H. Gressmann; HNT 21; Tübingen: J.C.B. Mohr/Paul Siebeck, [4]1966) xv + 576pp.

Bouwman, G., 'Die Erhöhung Jesu in der lukanischen Theologie', *BZ NS* 14 (1970) 257-263.

Bouwman, G., 'Der Anfang der Apostelgeschichte und der 'westliche' Text', in: T. Baarda, A. Hilhorst, G.P. Luttikhuizen, A.S. van der Woude (eds.), *Text and Testimony. Essays in Honour of A.F.J. Klijn* (Kampen: J.H. Kok, 1988) 46-55.

Bovon, F., *Luc le théologien. Vingt-cinq ans de recherches (1950-1975)* (MoBi; Neuchatel, Paris: Delachaux & Niestlé, 1978) 474pp.; ET K. McKinney; *Luke the Theologian. Thirty-Three Years of Research (1950-1983)* (PThM 12; Allison Park, PA: Pickwick, 1987) xvi + 510pp.

Bovon, F., 'Himmelfahrt Christi', *EKL* 2 ([3]1989) 522-523.

Boyd, W.J.P., 'The Ascension according to St. John. Ch.14-17 not Pre-passion but Post-resurrection', *Theol.* 70 (1967) 207-211.

Boyd, W.J.P., 'The Ascension according to St. John', in: E.A. Livingstone (ed.), *StEv* 6 (TU 112; Berlin: Akademie, 1973) 20-27.

Brändle, M., 'Entmythologisierung der Himmelfahrt Christi', *GrEnt* 14 (1958/59) 207-211.

Braumann, G. (Hrsg.), *Das Lukasevangelium. Die redaktions- und kompositionsgeschichtliche Forschung* (WdF 280; Darmstadt: WBG, 1974) xxiv + 436pp.

Braun, H., 'Zur Terminologie der Acta von der Auferstehung Jesu' (1952); repr. in: idem, *Gesammelte Studien zum Neuen Testament und seiner Umwelt* (Tübingen: J.C.B. Mohr/Paul Siebeck, 1962, [3]1971) 173-177.

Bray, G.L., 'Ascension and Heavenly Session of Christ', in: S.B. Ferguson, D.F. Wright, J.I. Packer (eds.), *New Dictionary of Theology* (Leicester, Downers Grove, IL: IVP, 1988) 46-47.

Brodie, T.L., *Luke the Literary Interpreter. Luke-Acts as a Systematic Rewriting and Updating of the Elijah-Elisha Narrative in 1 and 2 Kings* (Diss. Roma, Pont. Studiorum Univ. a S. Thoma Aq. in Urbe, 1987) ix + 444pp.

Brodie, T.L., 'The Departure for Jerusalem (Luke 9,51-56) as a Rhetorical Imitation of Elijah's Departure for the Jordan (2 Kgs 1,1-2,6)', *Bib.* 70 (1989) 96-109.

Brodie, T.L., 'Luke-Acts as an Imitation and Emulation of the Elijah-Elisha Narrative', in: E. Richard (ed.), *New Views on Luke and Acts* (Michael Glazier; Collegeville, MN: Liturgical, 1990) 78-85.172-174.

Brown, R.E., *The Gospel According to John. Introduction, Translation, and Notes* (AncB 29; Garden City, NY: Doubleday, 1966-1970) 2 vols., cxlvi + 1208pp.

Brown, R.E., *The Birth of the Messiah. A Commentary on the Infancy Narratives in the Gospels of Matthew and Luke* (AncB Reference Library; New York, etc.: Doubleday, 1977, [2]1993) 752pp.

Brown, R.E., *The Death of the Messiah. From Gethsemane to the Grave. A Commentary on the Passion Narratives in the Four Gospels* (AncB Reference Library; New York, London:

Doubleday, 1994) 2 vols., xxvii + 877; xix + 731pp.

Bruce, F.F., *The Acts of the Apostles. Greek Text with Introduction and Commentary* (Grand Rapids: Eerdmans; Leicester: Apollos, 1951, ³1990) xxvii + 569pp.

Bruce, F.F., *The Gospel of John. Introduction, Exposition and Notes* (Grand Rapids; Eerdmans, 1983) xii + 425pp.

Bruce, F.F., 'Eschatology in Acts', in: H.W. Gloer (ed.), *Eschatology and the New Testament* (1988) 51-63.

Bruggen, J. van, *Marcus. Het Evangelie volgens Petrus* (CNT derde serie; Kampen: J.H. Kok, 1988) 436pp.

Bruggen, J. van, *Lucas. Het evangelie als voorgeschiedenis* (CNT derde serie; Kampen: J.H. Kok, 1993) 469pp.

Brun, L., *Die Auferstehung Christi in der urchristlichen Überlieferung* (Oslo: H. Aschehoug & Co (W. Nygaard); Giessen: A. Töpelmann, 1925) 97pp.

Brunner, P., 'The Ascension of Christ. Myth or Reality?', *Dialog* 1 (1962) 38-39.

Bultmann, R., ἀνίημι, ἄνεσις, *ThWNT* 1 (1933) 367-368.

Bultmann, R., *Neues Testament und Mythologie. Das Problem der Entmythologisierung der neutestamentlichen Verkündigung* (hrsg. v. E. Jüngel; BEvTh 96; München: Chr. Kaiser, 1941; repr. ³1988) 64pp.

Bultmann, R., *Das Evangelium des Johannes* (KEK II¹⁹; Göttingen: Vandenhoeck & Ruprecht, 1941, ¹⁰1968) 8* + 563pp.

Bultmann, R., *Theologie des Neuen Testaments* (hrsg. v. O. Merk; UTB.W 630; Tübingen: J.C.B. Mohr/Paul Siebeck, 1948, ⁹1984) xix + 753pp.

Burchard, Ch., *Der dreizehnte Zeuge. Traditions- und kompositionsgeschichtliche Untersuchungen zu Lukas' Darstellung der Frühzeit des Paulus* (FRLANT 103; Göttingen: Vandenhoeck & Ruprecht, 1970) 196pp.

Burgon, J.W., 'The Last Twelve Verses of the Gospel According to St. Mark' (1871); repr. in: D.O. Fuller (ed.), *Counterfeit or Genuine—Mark 16? John 8?* (Grand Rapids: Grand Rapids International Publications, 1975) 27-130.

Burrows, E., *Tilmun, Bahrein, Paradise* (Zusatzbemerkungen von A. Deimel; BibOr 30; Roma: IBP, 1928) 34pp.

Cabrol, F., 'Ascension (Fête)', *DACL* 1/2 (1907) 2934-2943.

Cadbury, H.J., 'Commentary on the Preface of Luke', *Beg* 2 (1922) 489-510.

Cadbury, H.J., 'Lexical Notes on Luke-Acts 3. Luke's Interest in Lodging', *JBL* 45 (1926) 305-322.

Cadbury, H.J., *The Making of Luke-Acts* (New York: Macmillan, 1927; repr. London: SPCK, 1958) xii + 385pp.

Cadbury, H.J., 'Four Features of Lucan Style', in: L.E. Keck, J.L. Martyn (eds.), *Studies in Luke-Acts* (1966) 87-102.

Calvin, J., *Commentarius in Harmoniam Evangelicam* (ed. G. Baum, E. Cunitz, E. Reuss; Opera 45; RC 73; Brunswig: C.A. Schwetske / Appelhans & Pfenningstorff, 1891; repr. New York, London: Johnson; Frankfurt am Main: Minerva, 1964) 830pp.

Caquot, A., 'Remarques sur les chapitres 70 et 71 du livre éthiopien d'Hénoch', in: L. Monloubou (éd.), *Apocalypses et Theologie de l'Esperance* (Congres de Toulouse 1975; LeDiv 95; Paris: Cerf, 1977) 111-122.

Caragounis, C.C., *The Son of Man. Vision and Interpretation* (WUNT 2/38; Tübingen: J.C.B. Mohr/Paul Siebeck, 1986) ix + 310pp.

Carroll, J.T., *Response to the End of History. Eschatology and Situation in Luke-Acts* (SBL.DS 92; Atlanta, GA: Scholars, 1988) vii + 208pp.

Carson, D.A., *The Gospel According to John* (Leicester: IVP; Grand Rapids. Eerdmans, 1991) 715pp.

Casetti, P., *Gibt es ein Leben vor dem Tod? Eine Auslegung von Psalm 49* (OBO 44; Freiburg, Schweiz: Universitätsverlag; Göttingen: Vandenhoeck & Ruprecht, 1982) 315pp.

Casey, M., 'The Use of the Term 'Son of Man' in the Similitudes of Enoch', *JSJ* 7 (1976) 11-29.

Casey, M., *Son of Man. The Interpretation and Influence of Daniel 7* (London: SPCK, 1979) xv + 272pp.

Casey, P.M., *From Jewish Prophet to Gentile God. The Origins and Development of New Testament Christology* (ECL 1985-86; Cambridge: J. Clarke; Louisville, KN: Westminster, J. Knox: 1991) 197pp.

Cassuto, U., *A Commentary on the Book of Genesis* (Translated from the Hebrew by I. Abrahams; Jerusalem: Magnes, 1944-1949; ET 1961-1964) 2 vols., xviii + 323; 386pp.

Cavallin, H.C.C., *Life After Death. Paul's Argument for the Resurrection of the Dead in 1 Cor 15. Part 1: An Enquiry into the Jewish Background* (CNT 7; Lund: C.W.K. Gleerup, 1974) 301pp.

Certeau, M. de, 'L'Ascension', *Christus* 6 (1959) 211-220.

Champneys, A.C., 'The Ascension', *The Interpreter* 1 (1905) 536-537.

Charles, R.H., *The Revelation of St. John. With Introduction, Notes and Indices. Also the Greek Text and English Translation* (ICC; Edinburgh: T.&T. Clark, 1920; repr. 1985) 2 vols., cxci + 373; viii + 497pp.

Chance, J.P., *Jerusalem, the Temple, and the New Age in Luke-Acts* (Macon, GA: Mercer, Peeters, 1988) viii + 168pp.

Charlesworth, J.H., Evans, C.A. (eds.), *The Pseudepigrapha and Early Biblical Interpretation* (JSNT.S 83; Studies in Scripture in Early Judaism and Christianity 2; Sheffield: JSOT, 1993) 319pp.

Childs, B.S., *The New Testament as Canon. An Introduction* (London: SCM, 1984) xxv + 572pp.

Clarke, W.K.L., 'St. Luke and the Pseudepigrapha. Two Parallels', *JThS* 15 (1914) 597-599.

Clarke, W.K.L., 'The Clouds of Heaven. An Eschatological Study', *Theol.* 31 (1935) 63-72.128-141; repr. in: idem, *Divine Humanity. Doctrinal Essays on New Testament Problems* (London: SPCK, 1936) 9-40.

Colas, G., 'Ascension, exaltation', *Christus* 28 (1981) 78-87.

Collins, J.J., ''The Heavenly Representative'. The 'Son of Man' in the Similitudes of Enoch', in: G.W.E. Nickelsburg, J.J. Collins (eds.), *Ideal Figures in Ancient Judaism* (1980) 111-133.

Colpe, C., ὁ υἱὸς τοῦ ἀνθρώπου, *ThWNT* 8 (1969) 403-481.

Colpe, C., 'Himmelfahrt', *RAC* 15 (1991) 212-219.

Colpe, C., Dassmann, E., Engemann, E., Habermehl, P., 'Jenseitsfahrt I. Himmelfahrt', *RAC* 17 (1995) 407-466.

Colpe, C., 'Jenseitsfahrt II. Unterwelts- oder Höllenfahrt', *RAC* 17 (1995) 466-489.

Colpe, C., Habermehl, P., 'Jenseitsreise (Reise durch das Jenseits)', *RAC* 17 (1995) 490-543.

Conzelmann, H., *Die Mitte der Zeit. Studien zur Theologie des Lukas* (BHTh 17; Tübingen:

J.C.B. Mohr/Paul Siebeck, 1954, ⁶1977) viii + 242pp.

Conzelmann, H., *Die Apostelgeschichte* (HNT 7; Tübingen: J.C.B. Mohr/Paul Siebeck, 1963, ²1972) iv + 168pp.

Conzelmann, H., *Grundriß der Theologie des Neuen Testaments* (bearbeitet v. A. Lindemann; UTB.W 1446; Tübingen: J.C.B. Mohr/Paul Siebeck, 1967, ⁵1993) xx + 433pp.

Cornwall, P.B., 'On the Location of Dilmun', *BASOR* 103 (1946) 3-11.

Cranfield, C.E.B., *The Epistle to the Romans* (ICC; Edinburgh: T.&T. Clark, 1975-1979) 2 vols., xxvii + 927pp.

Creed, J.M., 'The Text and Interpretation of Acts i,1-2', *JThS* 35 (1934) 176-182.

Crehan, J.H., 'Ascension of Christ', *CDT* 1 (1962) 162-166.

Cullianu, I.P., 'Ascension', *EncRel(E)* 1 (1987) 435-441.

Cullmann, O., *Die Christologie des Neuen Testaments* (Tübingen: J.C.B. Mohr/Paul Siebeck, 1957, ⁴1966) ix + 352pp.

Czajkowski, M., *Wniebowstąpiene Jezusa* [Ascension of Jesus] (Studia z teologii św. Łukasza; Poznań: 1973) 58-71.

Dalman, G., *Orte und Wege Jesu* (BFChTh 2/1; Gütersloh: C. Bertelsmann, ³1924) viii + 427pp.

Dana, H.E., 'Historical Evidence of the Ascension', *BiRev* 14 (1929) 191-209.

Daniélou, J., 'Les psaumes dans la liturgie de l'Ascension', *MD* 21 (1950) 40-55.

Dautzenberg, G., 'Psalm 110 im Neuen Testament', in: H. Becker, R. Kaczynski (Hrsg.), *Liturgie und Dichtung. Ein interdisziplinäres Kompendium 1. Historische Präsentation* (PiLi 1; St. Ottilien: EOS, 1983) 141-171.

Davies, J.G., 'The *Peregrinatio Egeriae* and the Ascension', *VigChr* 8 (1954) 93-100.

Davies, J.G., 'The Prefigurement of the Ascension in the Third Gospel', *JThS* 6 (1955) 229-233.

Davies, J.G., *He Ascended into Heaven. A Study in the History of Doctrine* (BaL 1958; London: Lutterworth, 1958) 224pp.

Davies, J.H., 'The Purpose of the Central Section of St. Luke's Gospel', in: F.L. Cross (ed.), *StEv* 2 (TU 87; Berlin: Akademie, 1964) 164-169.

Davies, W.D., Daube, D. (eds.), *The Background of the New Testament and its Eschatology. In Honour of Charles Harold Dodd* (Cambridge: CUP, 1956) xviii + 555pp.

De Wald, E.T., 'The Iconography of the Ascension', *AJA* 19 (1915) 227-319.

Dean-Otting, M., *Heavenly Journeys. A Study of the Motif in Hellenistic-Jewish Literature* (JudUmw 8; Frankfurt: Lang, 1984) xv + 323pp.

Delebecque, É., 'Ascension et Pentecôte dans les Actes des Apôtres selon le codex Bezae', *RThom* 82 (1982) 79-89.

Delling, G., ἀναλαμβάνω, ἀνάλημψις, *ThWNT* 4 (1942) 8-9.

Devor, R.C., 'The Ascension of Christ and the Dissension of the Church', *Encounter* 33 (1972) 340-358.

Dexinger, F., 'Samaritan Eschatology', in: A.D. Crown (ed.), *The Samaritans* (Tübingen: J.C.B. Mohr/Paul Siebeck, 1989) 266-292.

Dhanis, E. (éd.), *Resurrexit. Actes du Symposium International sur la Résurrection de Jésus. Roma 1970* (Roma: Libreria editrice vaticana, 1974) xv + 766pp.

Diels, H., 'Himmels- und Höllenfahrten von Homer bis Dante', *NJKA* 49 (1922) 239-253.

Dietrich, E.L., שוב שבות. *Die endzeitliche Wiederherstellung bei den Propheten* (BZAW 40; Giessen: A. Töpelmann, 1925) vi + 66pp.

Dihle, A., Schweizer, E., ἀναψύχω, ἀνάψυξις, *ThWNT* 9 (1973) 665-666.

Dillon, R.J., *From Eye-Witnesses to Ministers of the Word. Tradition and Composition in Luke 24* (AnBib 82; Roma: IBP, 1978) xv + 336pp.

Dillon, R.J., 'Previewing Luke's Project from His Prologue (Luke 1:1-4)', *CBQ* 43 (1981) 205-227.

Dodd, C.H., *The Apostolic Preaching and Its Developments. Three Lectures* (London: Hodder & Stoughton, 1936) 240pp.

Dodd, C.H., 'The Appearances of the Risen Christ. An Essay in Form-Criticism of the Gospels' (1957); repr. in: idem, *More New Testament Studies* (Manchester: Manchester University Press, 1968) 102-133.

Dodd, C.H., *More New Testament Studies* (Manchester: Manchester University Press, 1968) vii + 157pp.

Doeve, J.W., 'De hemelvaart in het Evangelie naar Lucas', *HeB* 20 (1961) 75-79.

Dömer, M., *Das Heil Gottes. Studien zur Theologie des lukanischen Doppelwerkes* (BBB 51; Köln, Bonn: P. Hanstein, 1978) xlvii + 233pp.

Donne, B.K., 'The Significance of the Ascension of Jesus Christ in the New Testament', *SJTh* 30 (1977) 555-568.

Donne, B.K., *Christ Ascended. A Study in the Significance of the Ascension of Jesus Christ in the New Testament* (Exeter: Paternoster, 1983) xiii + 98pp.

Dornier, P., *Les Épîtres Pastorales* (SBi; Paris: J. Gabalda, 1969) 256pp.

Duclos, V., 'Er Kristus faret op til himlen?', *Cath(K)* 24 (1967) 54-65.

Dunn, J.D.G., *Baptism in the Holy Spirit. A Re-examination of the New Testament Teaching on the Gift of the Spirit in relation to Pentecostalism Today* (London: SCM, 1970) viii + 248pp.

Dunn, J.D.G., *Jesus and the Spirit. A Study of the Religious and Charismatic Experience of Jesus and the First Christians as Reflected in the New Testament* (London: SCM, 1975) xii + 515pp.

Dunn, J.D.G., *Unity and Diversity in the New Testament. An Inquiry into the Character of Earliest Christianity* (London: SCM; Valley Forge: TPI, 1977, ²1990) xli + 482pp.

Dunn, J.D.G., 'Demythologizing—The Problem of Myth in the New Testament', in: I.H. Marshall (ed.), *New Testament Interpretation* (1977, ²1979) 285-307.

Dunn, J.D.G., *Christology in the Making. An Inquiry into the Origins of the Doctrine of the Incarnation* (London: SCM, 1980, ²1989) xlvi + 443pp.

Dunn, J.D.G., 'Demythologizing the Ascension. A Reply to Professor Gooding', *IBSt* 3 (1981) 15-27.

Dunn, J.D.G., 'Was Christianity a Monotheistic Faith from the Beginning?', *SJTh* 35 (1982) 303-336.

Dunn, J.D.G., 'Let John Be John. A Gospel For Its Time', in: P. Stuhlmacher (Hrsg.), *Das Evangelium und die Evangelien* (1983) 309-339.

Dunn, J.D.G., *Romans* (WBC 38; Dallas, TX: Word, 1988) 2 vols. lxxii + 976pp.

Dunn, J.D.G., *The Parting of the Ways between Christianity and Judaism and their Significance for the Character of Christianity* (London: SCM; Philadelphia: TPI, 1991) xvi + 368pp.

Dupont, J., ''ΑΝΕΛΗΜΦΘΗ (Act.i.2)' (1961); repr. in: idem, *Études sur les actes des Apôtres* (LeDiv 45; Paris: Cerf, 1967) 477-480.

Dupont, J., 'L'interprétation des Psaumes dans les Actes des Apôtres' (1962); repr. in: idem,

*Études sur les actes des Apôtres* (LeDiv 45; Paris: Cerf, 1967) 283-307.

Dupont, J., 'L'après-mort dans l'oeuvre de Luc' (1972); repr. in: idem, *Nouvelles Études sur les Actes des Apôtres* (LeDiv 118; Paris: Cerf, 1984) 358-379.

Dupont, J., 'Ascension du Christ et don de l'Esprit d'après Ac 2,33' (1973); repr. in: idem, *Nouvelles Études sur les Actes des Apôtres* (LeDiv 118; Paris: Cerf, 1984) 199-209.

Dupont, J., 'Assis à la droite de Dieu. L'interprétation du Ps 110,1 dans le Nouveau Testament' (1974); repr. in: idem, *Nouvelles Études sur les Actes des Apôtres* (LeDiv 118; Paris: Cerf, 1984) 210-295.

Dupont, J., 'La question du plan des Actes des Apôtres à la lumière d'un texte de Lucien de Samosate' (1979); repr. in: idem, *Nouvelles Études sur les Actes des Apôtres* (LeDiv 118; Paris: Cerf, 1984) 24-36.

Egan, J.M., 'Meaning of the Ascension', *CrCr* 18 (1966) 164-174.

Eger, J., 'Zur Verkündigung der Himmelfahrt unseres Herrn', *LS* 20 (1969) 226-231.

Ehrman, B.D., *The Orthodox Corruption of Scripture. The Effect of Early Christological Controversies on the Text of the New Testament* (New York, Oxford: OUP, 1993) xiii + 314pp.

Eisinger, W., 'Himmelfahrt. Apostelgeschichte 1,1-11', *GPM* 22 (1967/68) 238-247.

Ellis, E.E., 'La fonction de l'eschatologie dans l'évangile de Luc', in: F. Neirynck (éd.), *L'Évangile de Luc* (²1989) 51-65.296-303 = Ellis, *Eschatology in Luke* (FB.B 30; Philadelphia: Fortress, 1972) xvi + 29pp.

Ellis, E.E., *The Gospel of Luke* (NCeB; Grand Rapids: Eerdmans; London: Marshall, Morgan & Scott, 1966, ²1974; repr. 1991) xxvi + 300pp.

Eltester, W. (Hrsg.), *Neutestamentliche Studien für R. Bultmann* (BZNW 21; Berlin: A. Töpelmann, 1954, ²1957) 304pp.

Engelhardt, K., 'Apostelgeschichte 1,10-14', *GPM* 30 (1975/76) 240-245.

Enslin, M.S., 'The Ascension Story', *JBL* 47 (1928) 60-73.

Epp, E.J., 'The Ascension in the Textual Tradition of Luke-Acts', in: E.J. Epp, G.D. Fee (eds.), *New Testament Textual Criticism* (1981) 131-145.

Epp, E.J., Fee, G.D. (eds.), *New Testament Textual Criticism. Its Significance for Exegesis. Essays in Honour of Bruce M. Metzger* (New York, Oxford: Clarendon, 1981) xxvii + 410pp.

Ernst, J., *Das Evangelium des Lukas übersetzt und erklärt* (RNT 3; Regensburg: F. Pustet, 1977, ²1993) 558pp.

Ernst, J., *Herr der Geschichte. Perspektiven der lukanischen Eschatologie* (SBS 88; Stuttgart: KBW, 1978) 127pp.

Evans, C.A., 'Ascending and Descending With a Shout. Psalm 47.6 and 1 Thessalonians 4.16', in: C.A. Evans, J.A. Sanders (eds.), *Paul and the Scriptures of Israel* (JSNT.S 83/Studies in Scripture in Early Judaism and Christianity 1; Sheffield: Academic, 1993) 238-253.

Evans, C.F., *Saint Luke* (TPI NT Commentaries; London: SCM; Philadelphia: TPI, 1990) xxi + 933pp.

Faierstein, M., 'Why Do the Scribes Say That Elijah Must Come First?', *JBL* 100 (1981) 75-86.

Farmer, W.R., *The Last Twelve Verses of Mark* (MSSNTS 25; Cambridge: CUP, 1974) xii + 123pp.

Fee, G.D., *The First Epistle to the Corinthians* (NICNT; Grand Rapids: Eerdmans, 1987) xxiv + 880pp.

Feldman, L.H., 'Josephus' Portrait of Moses', *JQR* 82 (1992) 285-328; 83 (1992) 7-50; 83 (1993) 301-330.

Feldman, L.H., 'Josephus' Portrait of Elijah', *SJOT* 8 (1994) 61-86.

Felix, F.M.D., 'El cristiano, sacramento de cristo (Act 1,3-11)', *CistC* 20 (1968) 97-105.

Fernandez y Fernandez, J., 'La Ascensión del Señor. Subió al cielo por su propia virtud', *CuBi* 11 (1954) 134-142.

Festorazzi, F., 'Speranza e risurrezione nell'Antico Testamento', in: E. Dhanis (éd.), *Resurrexit. Actes du Symposium International sur la Résurrection de Jésus* (1974) 5-30.

Fitzmyer, J.A., *The Gospel According to Luke* (AncB 28; Garden City, NY: Doubleday, 1981-1985) 2 vols., xxvi + xxxvi + 1642pp.

Fitzmyer, J.A., 'The Ascension of Christ and Pentecost', *TS* 45 (1984) 409-440.

Fitzmyer, J.A., 'More about Elijah Coming First', *JBL* 104 (1985) 295-296.

Fitzmyer, J.A., '"Today You Shall Be With Me in Paradise' (Luke 23:43)', in: idem, *Luke the Theologian. Aspects of His Teaching* (New York, Mahwah: Paulist, 1989) 203-233.

Fitzmyer, J.A., *Romans. A New Translation with Introduction and Commentary* (AncB 33; New York, NY: Doubleday, 1993) xxxiv + 793pp.

Flender, H., *Heil und Geschichte in der Theologie des Lukas* (BEvTh 41; München: Chr. Kaiser, 1965, ²1968) 151pp.

Flicoteaux, E., 'La glorieuse ascension', *VS* 76 (1947) 664-675.

Flusser, D., 'Lukas 9:51-56. Ein hebräisches Fragment', in: W.C. Weinrich (ed.), *The New Testament Age. Essays in Honor of Bo Reicke* 1 (Macon, MA: Mercer University Press, 1984) 165-179.

Foakes-Jackson, F.J., Lake, K. (eds.), *The Beginnings of Christianity 1. The Acts of the Apostles* (London: Macmillan, 1920-1933) 5 vols.

Fohrer, G., 'Das Geschick des Menschen nach dem Tode im Alten Testament' (1968); repr. in: idem, *Studien zu alttestamentlichen Texten und Themen (1966-1972)* (BZAW 155; Berlin, New York: W. de Gruyter, 1981) 188-202.

Fossum, J.E., *The Name of God and the Angel of the Lord. Samaritan and Jewish Concepts of Intermediation and the Origin of Gnosticism* (WUNT 36; Tübingen: J.C.B. Mohr/Paul Siebeck, 1985) xiii + 378pp.

Fraade, S.D., *Enosh and His Generation. Pre-Israelite Hero and History in Postbiblical Interpretation* (SBL.MS 30; Chico, CA: Scholars, 1984) xvi + 301pp.

Francis, F.O., (review of G. Lohfink, *Die Himmelfahrt Jesu*), *JBL* 91 (1972) 424-425.

Franklin, E., 'The Ascension and the Eschatology of Luke-Acts', *SJTh* 23 (1970) 191-200.

Franklin, E., *Christ the Lord. A Study in the Purpose and Theology of Luke-Acts* (London: SPCK, 1975) 241pp.

Franklin, F.O., 'Eschatology and History in Luke-Acts', *JAAR* 37 (1969) 49-63

Frey, C., 'Die Himmelfahrtsbericht des Lukas nach Apg. 1:1-12; Exegetische und didaktische Problematik', *KatBl* 95 (1970) 10-21.

Fridrichsen, A., 'Die Himmelfahrt bei Lukas', *ThBl* 6 (1927) 337-341.

Fridrichsen, A., 'Omkring himmelfartsberetningen', *NTT* 28 (1927) 32-47.

Friedrich, G., 'Lk 9,51 und die Entrückungschristologie des Lukas', in: P. Hoffmann, N. Brox, W. Pesch (Hrsg.), *Orientierung an Jesus. Zur Theologie der Synoptiker* (FS J. Schmid; Freiburg: Herder, 1973) 48-77.

Fuller, D.O. (ed.), *Counterfeit or Genuine—Mark 16? John 8?* (Grand Rapids: Grand Rapids

International Publications, 1975) 217pp.

Fuller, D.P., *Easter Faith and History* (Grand Rapids: Eerdmans, 1965) 279pp.

Fuller, G.C., 'The Life of Jesus, After the Ascension (Luke 24:50-53; Acts 1:9-11)', *WThJ* 56 (1994) 391-398.

Fuller, R.H., *The Foundations of New Testament Christology* (London: Lutterworth, 1965) 268pp.

Fuller, R.H., *The Formation of the Resurrection Narratives* (Philadelphia: Fortress, 1971, ²1980) xiv + 225pp.

Funk, R.W. (with M.H. Smith), *The Gospel of Mark. Red Letter Edition* (Jesus Seminar; Sonoma, CA: Polebridge, 1991) xxii + 250pp.

Fürst, T., 'Christi Himmelfahrt. Lukas 24,44-53', *GPM* 39 (1984/85) 274-280.

Fürst, W., 'Himmelfahrt. Apostelgeschichte 1,1-11', *GPM* 16 (1961/62) 196-201.

Galling, K., 'Der Ehrenname Elisas und die Entrückung Elias', *ZThK* 53 (1956) 129-148.

Gasque, W.W., Martin, R.P. (eds.), *Apostolic History and the Gospel. Biblical and Historical Essays Presented to F.F. Bruce on his 60th Birthday* (Grand Rapids: Eerdmans; Exeter: Paternoster, 1970) 378pp.

Geldenhuys, J.N., *Commentary on the Gospel of Luke* (NICNT; Grand Rapids: Eerdmans, 1951) 685pp.

Genton, N., *L'Ascension de Jésus-Christ* (Neuchâtel: Baconnière, 1979) 101pp.

George, A., 'Les récits d'apparitions aux Onze à partir de Luc 24,36-53', in: P. de Surgy, P. Grelot, M. Carrez, A. George, J. Delorme, X. Léon-Dufour (éds.), *La résurrection du Christ et l'exégèse moderne* (LeDiv 50; Paris: Cerf, 1969) 75-104.

Georgi, D., 'Der vorpaulinische Hymnus Phil 2,6-11', in: E. Dinkler (Hrsg.), *Zeit und Geschichte. Dankesgabe an R. Bultmann zum 80. Geburtstag* (Tübingen: J.C.B. Mohr/Paul Siebeck, 1964) 263-293.

Geysels, L., 'Niet naar de hemel staan kijken? (Hand.1,11)', *VBS-Informatie* 8 (Boxtel: KBS, 1977) 22-27.

Giles, K., 'Ascension', *DJG* (1992) 46-50.

Girock, H.J., *Himmelfahrt. Hindernis oder Hilfe für den Glauben?* (Stuttgart: Quell, 1966) 72pp.

Gloer, H.W. (ed.), *Eschatology and the New Testament. Essays in Honor of G.R. Beasley-Murray* (Peabody, MA: Hendrickson, 1988) xvii + 154pp.

Gnilka, J., *Der Epheserbrief* (HThK 10/2; Freiburg, Basel, Wien: Herder, 1971) xviii + 328pp.

Gnilka, J., *Das Evangelium nach Markus* (EKK 2; Zürich, Einsiedeln, Köln: Benziger; Neukirchen: Neukirchener, 1978-1979) 2 vols., 316 + 364pp.

Gnilka, J., *Das Matthäusevangelium* (HThK 1; Freiburg, Basel, Wien: Herder, 1986, ²1988-1988) 2 vols., xvi + 518; viii + 552pp.

Goldstein, J.A., *1 Maccabees. A New Translation with Introduction and Commentary* (AncB 41; Garden City, NY: Doubleday, 1976) xxiii + 593pp.

Goodenough, E.R., *By Light, Light. The Mystic Gospel of Hellenistic Judaism* (New Haven: 1935; repr. Amsterdam: Philo, 1969) xv + 436pp.

Gooding, D.W., 'Demythologizing Old and New, and Luke's Description of the Ascension. A Layman's Appraisal', *IBSt* 2 (1980) 95-119.

Goossens, W., 'De valore soteriologico resurrectionis et ascensionis Christi', *CGan* 24 (1937) 9-17.

Goppelt, L., *Theologie des Neuen Testaments* (hrsg. v. J. Roloff; UTB 850; Göttingen: Vandenhoeck & Ruprecht, 1976, ³1978) 669pp.

Goslinga, C.J., 'Een herhaalde Hemelvaart?', *GThT* 39 (1938) 557-560.

Goslinga, C.J., 'Tot op den dag, in welken Hij opgenomen is', *GThT* 40 (1939) 519-522.

Goudoever, J. van, *Biblical Calendars* (Leiden: E.J. Brill, 1959, ²1961) xii + 295pp.

Goulder, M.D., *Type and History in Acts* (London: SPCK, 1964) x + 252pp.

Goulder, M.D., *Luke. A New Paradigm* (JSNT.S 20; Sheffield: JSOT, 1989) 2 vols., xi + 824pp.

Gourgues, M., 'Exalté à la droite de Dieu (Actes 2:33; 5:31)', *ScEs* 27 (1975) 303-327.

Gourgues, M., 'Lecture christologique du Psaume 110 et fête de la Pentecôte', *RB* 83 (1976) 5-24.

Gourgues, M., *A la droite de Dieu. Résurrection de Jésus et actualisation du psaume 110:1 dans le Nouveau Testament* (EtB; Paris: Librairie Lecoffre, J. Gabalda, 1978) 270pp.

Graham, H.H., 'Ascension', *DB(H)* (²1963) 60-61.

Graß, H., *Ostergeschehen und Osterberichte* (Göttingen: Vandenhoeck & Ruprecht, 1956, ³1964) 346pp.

Grässer, E., *Das Problem der Parusieverzögerung in den synoptischen Evangelien und in der Apostelgeschichte* (BZNW 22; Berlin, New York: W. de Gruyter, 1957, ³1977) xxxiv + 257pp.

Grässer, E., 'Die Parusieerwartung in der Apostelgeschichte', in: J. Kremer (éd.), *Les Actes des Apôtres* (1979) 99-127.

Gray, J.R., 'Why the Ascension?', *ET* 93 (1982) 243-244.

Green, J.B., *The Death of Jesus. Tradition and Interpretation in the Passion Narrative* (WUNT 2/33; Tübingen: J.C.B. Mohr/Paul Siebeck, 1988) xvi + 351pp.

Green, J.B., McKnight, S., Marshall, I.H. (eds.), *Dictionary of Jesus and the Gospels* (Downers Grove, IL, Leicester: IVP, 1992) xxv + 933pp.

Grégoire, H., 'Du nouveau sur la hiérarchie de la secte Montaniste d'après une inscription grecque trouvée près de Philadelphie en Lydie', *Byzantion* 2 (1925) -

Grelot, P., 'La géographie mythique d'Hénoch et ses sources orientales', *RB* 65 (1958) 33-69.

Grelot, P., 'La Légende d'Hénoch dans les Apocryphes et dans la Bible. Son origine et signification', *RSR* 46 (1958) 5-26.181-210.

Grelot, P., 'Parwaim des Chroniques à l'Apocryphe de Genèse', *VT* 11 (1961) 30-38.

Grelot, P., 'Retour au Parwaim', *VT* 14 (1964) 155-163.

Grosheide, F.W., *De eerste brief aan de kerk te Korinthe* [CNT(K); Kampen: J.H. Kok, ²1957) 448pp.

Grosheide, F.W., *De Brief van Paulus aan de Efeziërs* [CNT(K); Kampen: J.H. Kok, 1960] 1-99.

Grundmann, W., *Das Evangelium nach Lukas* (ThHK 3; Berlin: Evangelische, 1961, ¹⁰1984) xv + 460pp.

Guillaume, J.M., *Luc interprète des anciennes traditions sur la résurrection de Jésus* (EtB; Paris: Librairie Lecoffre, J. Gabalda, 1979) 305pp.

Gulley, N.R., 'Ascension of Christ', in: D.N. Freedman (ed.), *The Anchor Bible Dictionary* 1 (New York, London, Toronto: Doubleday, 1992) 472-474.

Gundry, R.H., 'The Form, Meaning and Background of the Hymn Quoted in I Timothy 3.16', in: W.W. Gasque, R.P. Martin (eds.), *Apostolic History and the Gospel* (1970) 203-222.

Gutberlet, H., *Die Himmelfahrt Christi in der bildenden Kunst von den Anfängen bis ins*

*Hohe Mittelalter. Versuch zur geistesgeschichtlichen Erfassung einer ikonographischen Frage* (Sammlung Heitz. Akademische Abhandlungen zur Kulturgeschichte 3/3; Leipzig, etc.: 1934, ²1935).

Gutmann, J., Aberbach, M., *et alii*, 'Elijah', *EJ* 6 (1971) 632-642.

Haacker, K., Schäfer, P., 'Nachbiblische Traditionen vom Tod des Mose', in: O. Betz, K. Haacker, M. Hengel (Hrsg.), *Josephus Studien. Untersuchungen zu Josephus, dem antiken Judentum und dem Neuen Testament* (FS O. Michel; Göttingen: Vandenhoeck & Ruprecht, 1974) 147-174.

Haacker, K., 'Verwendung und Vermeidung des Apostelbegriffs im Lukanischen Werk', *NT* 30 (1988) 9-38.

Haag, E., 'Die Himmelfahrt des Elias nach 2 Kön 2,1-15', *TThZ* 78 (1969) 18-32.

Haenchen, E., *Die Apostelgeschichte* (KEK III¹⁷; Göttingen: Vandenhoeck & Ruprecht, 1956, ⁷1977) 717pp.

Haenchen, E., 'Judentum und Christentum in der Apostelgeschichte', *ZNW* 54 (1963) 155-187.

Haenchen, E., 'The Book of Acts as Source Material for the History of Early Christianity', in: L.E. Keck, J.L. Martyn (eds.), *Studies in Luke-Acts* (1966) 258-278.

Haenchen, E., *Der Weg Jesu. Eine Erklärung des Markusevangeliums und der kanonischen Parallelen* (Berlin: W. de Gruyter, 1966, ²1968) xv + 594pp.

Haenchen, E., *Das Johannesevangelium. Ein Kommentar* (hrsg. v. U. Busse; Tübingen: J.C.B. Mohr/Paul Siebeck, 1980) xxxiv + 614pp.

Hagemeyer, O., 'Ihr seid meine Zeugen', *EuA* 42 (1966) 375-384.

Hahn, F., *Christologische Hoheitstitel. Ihre Geschichte im frühen Christentum* (FRLANT 83; Göttingen: Vandenhoeck & Ruprecht, 1963, ²1964) 442pp.

Hahn, F., 'Die Himmelfahrt Jesu. Ein Gespräch mit Gerhard Lohfink', *Bib.* 55 (1974) 418-426.

Hahn, F., 'Das Problem alter christologischer Überlieferungen in der Apostelgeschichte unter besonderer Berücksichtigung von Act 3,19-21', in: J. Kremer (éd.), *Les Actes des Apôtres* (1979) 129-154.

Halperin, D.J., *The Faces of the Chariot. Early Jewish Responses to Ezekiel's Throne Vision* (TSAJ 16; Tübingen: J.C.B. Mohr/Paul Siebeck, 1988) xx + 610pp.

Hampel, V., *Menschensohn und historischer Jesus. Ein Rätselwort als Schlüssel zum messianischen Selbstverständnis Jesu* (Neukirchen-Vluyn: Neukirchener, 1990) xiv + 418pp.

Hanna, W., *The Forty Days After Our Lord's Resurrection* (New York: R. Carter, 1866)

Harder, G., 'Himmelfahrt. Apostelgeschichte 1,1-14', *GPM* 28 (1973) 254-261.

Harnack, A., *Die Apostelgeschichte* (BENT 3; Leipzig: J.C. Hinrichs, 1908) vi + 225pp.

Harnack, A., *Neue Untersuchungen zur Apostelgeschichte und zur Abfassungszeit der synoptischen Evangelien* (BENT 4; Leipzig: J.C. Hinrichs, 1911) 114pp.

Haroutunian, J., 'The Doctrine of the Ascension. A Study of the New Testament Teaching', *Interp.* 10 (1956) 270-281 = 'La doctrina de la Ascensión. Un estudio de la enseñanza del Nuevo Testamento', *CuT* 21 (1957) 54-65.

Harrison, E.F., 'The Ministry of Our Lord During the Forty Days', *BS* 95 (1938) 45-55.

Hase, K.A., *Das Leben Jesu. Lehrbuch zunächst für akademische Vorlesungen* (Leipzig: Breitkopf & Härtel, 1829, ⁵1865) xvi + 284pp.

Haufe, G., 'Entrückung und eschatologische Funktion im Spätjudentum', *ZRGG* 13 (1961)

105-113.

Hay, D.M., *Glory at the Right Hand. Psalm 110 in Early Christianity* (SBL.MS 18; Nashville, New York: Abingdon, 1973) 176pp.

Hayes, J.H., 'The Resurrection as Enthronement and the Earliest Church Christology', *Interp.* 22 (1968) 333-345.

Hayward, R., 'Phinehas—the same is Elijah. The Origin of a Rabbinic Tradition', *JJS* 29 (1978) 22-38.

Heller, J., 'Himmel- und Höllenfahrt nach Römer 10,6-7', *EvTh* 32 (1972) 478-486.

Hemer, C.J., *The Book of Acts in the Setting of Hellenistic History* (ed. C.H. Gempf; WUNT 49; Tübingen: J.C.B. Mohr/Paul Siebeck, 1989) xiv + 482pp.

Hendrickx, H., *The Resurrection Narratives of the Synoptic Gospels* (Studies in the Synoptic Gospels; London: G. Chapman, 1978, ²1984) viii + 150pp.

Hengel, M., *Die Zeloten. Untersuchungen zur jüdischen Freiheitsbewegung in der Zeit von Herodes I. bis 70 n.Chr.* (AGSU 1; Leiden, Köln: E.J. Brill, 1961) xiv + 406pp.

Hengel, M., 'Der Historiker Lukas und die Geographie Palästinas in der Apostelgeschichte', *ZDPV* 99 (1983) 147-183.

Hengel, M., 'Psalm 110 und die Erhöhung des Auferstandenen zur Rechten Gottes', in: C. Breytenbach, H. Paulsen (unter Mitwirkung von C. Gerber) (Hrsg.), *Anfänge der Christologie. FS F. Hahn zum 65. Geburtstag* (Göttingen: Vandenhoeck & Ruprecht, 1991) 43-73.

Hengel, M., 'Setze dich zu meiner Rechten! Die Inthronisation Christi zur Rechten Gottes und Psalm 110,1', in: M. Philonenko (éd.), *Le Trône de Dieu* (WUNT 69; Tübingen: J.C.B. Mohr/Paul Siebeck, 1993) 108-194.

Heppe, H., *Die Dogmatik der evangelisch-reformierten Kirche. Dargestellt und aus den Quellen belegt* (hrsg. v. E. Bizer; Neukirchen: Neukirchener, [1861] 1958) xcvi + 584pp.

Heuschen, J., *De bijbel over Hemelvaart* (4) (Roermond, Maaseik: J.J. Romen, 1960) 103pp. = *The Bible on the Ascension* (ET F. VanderHeijden; De Per, WI: St. Norbert Abbey, 1965) 105pp.

Heuschen, J., 'De hemelvaart des Heren in de oudste teksten van en rond het Christendom', *REcL* 47 (1960) 321-333.

Hiers, R.H., 'The Problems of the Delay of the Parousia in Luke-Acts', *NTS* 20 (1974) 145-155.

Himmelfarb, M., 'A Report on Enoch in Rabbinic Literature', *SBL.SP* (1978) 259-269.

Hirsch, E., *Die Auferstehungsgeschichten und der christliche Glaube* (Tübingen: J.C.B. Mohr/Paul Siebeck, 1940) vii + 144pp.

Hirsch, E., 'Analyse des ersten Kapitels der Apostelgeschichte', in: idem, *Frühgeschichte des Evangeliums 1* (Tübingen: J.C.B. Mohr/Paul Siebeck, 1941, ²1951) xxx-xxxix.

Hobbs, T.R., *2 Kings* (WBC 13; Dallas, TX: Word, 1984) xlviii + 388pp.

Hoffmann, P., 'Auferstehung Jesu Christi', *TRE* 4 (1979) 478-513.

Hofius, O., 'Himmelfahrt', *GPM* 34 (1979/80) 229-237.

Höhn, C., 'Studien zur Geschichte der Himmelfahrt im klassischen Altertum', *Programm des Gymnasiums zu Mannheim 1909-1910* (Mannheim: Vereinsdruckerei, 1910).

Holland, R., 'Zur Typik der Himmelfahrt', *ARW* 23 (1925) 207-220.

Holleman, J., *Resurrection and Parousia. A Traditio-Historical Study of Paul's Eschatology in 1 Corinthians 15* (NT.S 84; Leiden, New York, Köln: E.J. Brill, 1996) xiv + 233pp.

Holmes-Gore, V.A., 'The Ascension and the Apocalyptic Hope. The Significance of Acts

1.6-8', *Theol.* 32 (1936) 356-358.

Holt, B., 'Realities of the Ascension', *Encounter* 24 (1963) 87-92.

Holtzmann, H.J., *Die Apostelgeschichte* (HC 1/2; Freiburg: 1889; Tübingen, Leipzig: J.C.B. Mohr/Paul Siebeck, ³1901) viii + 160.

Holwerda, D.E., 'Ascension', *ISBE* 1 (1979) 310-313.

Holzmeister, U., 'Der Tag der Himmelfahrt des Herrn', *ZKTh* 55 (1931) 44-82.

Hooker, M.D., *The Gospel According to St. Mark* (BNTC; London: A.&C. Black, 1991) viii + 413pp.

Horst, P.W. van der, 'Moses' Throne Vision in Ezekiel the Dramaturg', *JJS* 34 (1983) 21-29.

Horst, P.W. van der, 'Hellenistic Parallels to the Acts of the Apostles (1,1-26)', *ZNW* 74 (1983) 17-26.

Horton, F.L., *The Melchizedek Tradition. A Critical Examination of the Sources to the Fifth Century A.D. and in the Epistle to the Hebrews* (MSSNTS 30; Cambridge, London, New York, Melbourne: CUP, 1976) xi + 192pp.

Houlden, L., 'Beyond Belief. Preaching the Ascension (II)', *Theol.* 94 (1991) 173-180.

Houtman, C., 'Elia's hemelvaart. Notities over en naar aanleiding van 2 Koningen 2:1-18', *NThT* 32 (1978) 283-304.

Howard, J.E., 'Acts 1:11', *ET* 39 (1927/28) 92.

Hubbard, B.J., *The Matthean Redaction of a Primitive Apostolic Commissioning. An Exegesis of Matthew 28,16-20* (SBL.DS 19; Missoula, MO: Scholars, 1974) xiii + 187pp.

Hübner, E., 'Himmelfahrt. Lukas 24,(44-49)50-53', *GPM* 45 (1990/91) 233-237.

Hübner, J., 'Himmel und Hölle', *TRT* 2 (⁴1983) 273-274.

Hug, J., *La Finale de l'Évangile de Marc (Mc 16,9-20)* (EtB; Paris: J. Gabalda, 1978) 268pp.

Hurtado, L.W., *One God, One Lord. Early Christian Devotion and Ancient Jewish Monotheism* (London: SCM, 1988) xiv + 178pp.

Hurtado, L.W., 'What Do We Mean by 'First-Century Jewish Monotheism'?', *SBL.SP* 32 (1993) 348-368.

Ioannides, V.Ch., Georgou, E., *et alii*, ᾽Ανάλημψις, *TEE* 2 (ΚΔ) (1963) 162-166.

Irsigler, H., *Psalm 73. Monolog eines Weisen. Text, Programm, Struktur* (MUS.ATSAT 20; St. Ottilien: EOS, 1984) xii + 404pp.

Iwand, H.J., 'Himmelfahrt. Apostelgeschichte 1,1-11', *GPM* 10 (1955/56) 134-143.

J., H., 'The Ascension of Jesus Christ', *The Interpreter* 1 (1905) 411-420.

Jacobson, H., *The Exagoge of Ezekiel* (Cambridge: CUP, 1983) 252pp.

Jansen, J.F., 'The Ascension, the Church and Theology', *ThTo* 16 (1959) 17-29.

Jeremias, J., ᾅδης, *ThWNT* 1 (1933) 146-150.

Jeremias, J., αἴρω, ἐπαίρω, *ThWNT* 1 (1933) 184-186.

Jeremias, J., Ἠλ(ε)ίας, *ThWNT* 2 (1935) 930-943.

Jeremias, J., Μωυσῆς, *ThWNT* 4 (1942) 852-878.

Jeremias, J., παράδεισος, *ThWNT* 5 (1954) 763-771.

Jeremias, J., *Neutestamentliche Theologie 1. Die Verkündigung Jesu* (Gütersloh: G. Mohn, 1971, ³1979) 314pp.

Jeremias, J., *Die Sprache des Lukasevangeliums. Redaktion und Tradition im Nicht-Markusstof des dritten Evangeliums* (KEK Sonderband; Göttingen: Vandenhoeck & Ruprecht, 1980) 323pp.

Jervell, J., *Luke and the People of God. A New Look at Luke-Acts* (Minneapolis, MN: Augsburg, 1972) 207pp.

Johnson, L.T., *The Acts of the Apostles* (SPg 5; Collegeville, MN: Liturgical, 1992) xvi + 568pp.

Jones, E., 'The Origins of 'Ascension' Terminology', *ChM* 104 (1990) 156-161.

Jonge, M. de (éd.), *L'Évangile de Jean. Sources, rédaction, théologie* (BEThL 44; Gembloux: Duculot; Leuven: Leuven University Press, 1977) 416pp.

Kähler, E., *Studien zum Te Deum und zur Geschichte des 24. Psalms in der Alten Kirche* (VEGL 10; Göttingen: Vandenhoeck & Ruprecht, 1958) 166pp.

Kasper, W., 'Christi Himmelfahrt—Geschichte und theologische Bedeutung', *IKZ* 12/3 (1983) 205-213.

Kaylor, R.D., *The Ascension Motif in Luke-Acts, the Epistle to the Hebrews and the Fourth Gospel* (Diss. Duke University, 1964; Ann Arbor, MI; London: UMI, 1980) xi + 217pp.

Keck, L.E., Martyn, J.L. (eds.), *Studies in Luke-Acts. Essays Presented in Honor of Paul Schubert* (Nashville, New York: Abingdon, 1966) 316pp.

Kegel, G., *Auferstehung Jesu—Auferstehung der Toten. Eine traditionsgeschichtliche Untersuchung zum Neuen Testament* (Gütersloh: G. Mohn, 1970) 132pp.

Keil, C.F., *Die Zwölf kleinen Propheten* (BC; Leipzig: Dörffling & Franke, ³1888) vii + 718pp.

Kellermann, U., *Auferstanden in den Himmel. 2 Makkabäer 7 und die Auferstehung der Märtyrer* (SBS 95; Stuttgart: KBW, 1979) 156pp.

Kern, W., 'Das Fortgehen Jesu und das Kommen des Geistes *oder* Christi Himmelfahrt', *GuL* 41 (1968) 85-90.

Kesich, V., 'Resurrection, Ascension, and the Giving of the Spirit', *GOTR* 25 (1980) 249-260.

Kilpatrick, G.D., *The Principles and Practice of New Testament Textual Criticism. Collected Essays Edited by J.K. Elliott* (BEThL 96; Leuven: Peeters, Leuven University Press, 1990) xxxviii + 489pp.

Klein, G., 'Lukas 1,1-4 als theologisches Programm' (1964); repr. in: G. Braumann (Hrsg.), *Das Lukasevangelium* (1974) 170-203.

Klostermann, E., *Das Lukasevangelium* (HNT 5; Tübingen: J.C.B. Mohr/Paul Siebeck, 1919, ³1975) 246pp.

Knight, G.W., *The Pastoral Epistles. A Commentary on the Greek Text* (NIGTC; Grand Rapids: Eerdmans, 1992) xxxiv + 514pp.

Knöppler, Th., *Die theologia crucis des Johannesevangeliums. Das Verständnis des Todes Jesu im Rahmen der johanneischen Inkarnations- und Erhöhungschristologie* (WMANT 69; Neukirchen-Vluyn: Neukirchener, 1994) x + 310pp.

Koch, R., 'Himmelfahrt Christi', *BThW* (²1962) 650-658.

König, E., Grossman, L., *et alii*, 'Elijah', *JE* 5 (1903, 1925) 121-129.

Korn, M., *Die Geschichte Jesu in veränderter Zeit. Studien zur bleibenden Bedeutung Jesu im lukanischen Doppelwerk* (WUNT 2/51; Tübingen: J.C.B. Mohr/Paul Siebeck, 1993) ix + 319pp.

Kraft, R.A., 'Philo (Josephus, Sirach and Wisdom of Solomon) on Enoch', *SBL.SP* (1978) 253-257.

Kramer, S.N., 'Dilmun, the Land of the Living', *BASOR* 96 (1944) 18-28.

Kränkl, E., *Jesus der Knecht Gottes. Die heilsgeschichtliche Stellung Jesu in den Reden der Apostelgeschichte* (BU 8; Regensburg: F. Pustet, 1972) xii + 239pp.

Kraus, H.J., *Psalmen* (BK 15; Neukirchen-Vluyn: Neukirchener, 1961, ⁵1978) 2 vols., vii +

1171pp.

Kreitzer, L., 'Apotheiosis of the Roman Emperor', *BA* 53 (1990) 210-217.

Kremer, J. (éd.), *Les Actes des Apôtres. Traditions, rédaction, théologie* (BEThL 48; Gembloux: Duculot, 1979) 590pp.

Kremer, J., ἀναλαμβάνω, ἀνάλημψις, *EWNT* 1 (1980) 199-201.

Kremers, H., 'Himmelfahrt', *EKL* 2 (1958, ²1962) 159-161.

Kretschmar, G., 'Himmelfahrt und Pfingsten', *ZKG* 66 (1954/55) 209-254.

Kruse, M., 'Himmelfahrt. Apostelgeschichte 1,3-4(5-7)8-11', *GPM* 40 (1985/86) 290-295.

Kümmel, W.G., *Verheissung und Erfüllung. Untersuchungen zur eschatologischen Verkündigung Jesu* (AThANT 6; Basel: H. Majer, 1945) 99pp.

Kümmel, W.G., 'Himmelfahrt Christi im NT', *RGG* 3 (³1959) 335.

Kümmel, W.G., *Einleitung in das Neue Testament* (Heidelberg: Quelle & Meyer, 1963, ²¹1983) xix + 593pp.

Kümmel, W.G., 'Lukas in der Anklage der heutigen Theologie' (1972); repr. in: G. Braumann (Hrsg.), *Das Lukasevangelium* (1974) 416-436.

Künzi, M., *Das Naherwartungslogion Markus 9,1Par. Geschichte seiner Auslegung mit einem Nachwort zur Auslegungsgeschichte von Markus 13,30Par.* (BGBE 21; Tübingen: J.C.B. Mohr/Paul Siebeck, 1977) viii + 247pp.

Kurz, W.S., 'Acts 3,19-26 as a Test of the Role of Eschatology in Lukan Christology', *SBL.SP* (1977) 309-323.

Kurz, W.S., *Reading Luke-Acts. Dynamics of Biblical Narrative* (Louisville, KN: Westminster, J. Knox, 1993) x + 261pp.

Kuschel, K.-J., *Geboren vor aller Zeit? Der Streit um Christi Ursprung* (München, Zürich: R. Piper, 1990) 834pp.

Laconi, M., 'L'Ascensione di Christo. Divergenti e complementari testimonianze evangeliche', *RAMi* 14 (1969) 53-72.

Ladd, G.E., *A Theology of the New Testament* (Cambridge: Lutterworth, 1970) 661pp.

Ladd, G.E., *A Commentary on the Revelation of John* (Grand Rapids: Eerdmans, 1972) 308pp.

Lagrange, M.-J., *Évangile selon St. Luc* (EtB; Paris: J. Gabalda, 1921) clxvii + 630pp.

Lagrange, M.-J., *Évangile selon St. Jean* (EtB; Paris: J. Gabalda, ²1925) cxcix + 551pp.

Laible, H., 'An welchem Wochentag geschah die Himmelfahrt Christi? Ein Versuch', *AELKZ* 55 (1922) 313.

Lake, K., Cadbury, H.J., *The Acts of the Apostles. English Translation and Commentary* (Beg 4; London: Macmillan, 1933) xi + 421pp.

Lake, K., 'Note 3. The Ascension', *Beg* 5 (1933) 16-22.

Lambrecht, J., 'De oudste Christologie. Verrijzenis of verhoging?', *Bijdr.* 36 (1975) 118-144.

Lambrecht, J., 'Ons Heer Hemelvaart', *IKT* 8 (1983) 164-175.

Lane, W.L., *The Gospel According to Mark. The English Text with Introduction, Exposition and Notes* (NICNT; Grand Rapids: Eerdmans, 1974) xvi + 652pp.

Larcher, C., *Le Livre de la Sagesse ou La Sagesse de Salomon* (EtB Ns 1,3,5; Paris: Librairie Lecoffre, J. Gabalda, 1983-1984) 3 vols., 1106pp.

Larrañaga, V., 'La tarde de la Ascensión sobre el Olivete', *RF* 33 (1933) 77-87.

Larrañaga, V., 'El proemio-transición de Act.1:1-3 en los metodos literarios de la historiografia griega', *MBib* 2 (Roma: Schola typographica Pio X, 1934) 311-374.

Larrañaga, V., 'Historia de la crítica en torno al misterio de la Ascensión', *EE* 15 (1936) 145-

167.
Larrañaga, V., 'De Ascensione Domini in Act.1:3-13', *VD* 17 (1937) 129-137.
Larrañaga, V., *L'Ascension de Notre-Seigneur dans le Nouveau Testament* (SPIB 50; traduit de l'Espagnol par G. Cazaux; Roma: IBP, 1938) xiv + 662pp. = *La Ascensión del Señor en el Nuevo Testamento* (CSIC; Madrid: Instituto Francisco Suárez, 1943) 2 vols.
Latham, H., 'The Ascension', in: idem, *The Risen Master* (Cambridge: Deighton Bell; London: George Bell, 1907) 378-411.
LaVerdiere, E.A., 'The Ascension of the Risen Lord', *BiTod* 95 (1978) 1553-1559.
LaVerdierre, E.A., 'Jesus' Resurrection and Ascension', *Emmanuel* 92 (1986) 250-257.
Leaney, A.R.C., *A Commentary on the Gospel According to St. Luke* (BNTC; London: A.&C. Black, 1958, ²1966) xii + 300pp.
Leaney, A.R.C., 'Why There Were Forty Days Between the Resurrection and the Ascension in Acts 1,3', in: F.L. Cross (ed.), *StEv* 4 (TU 102; Berlin: Akademie, 1968) 411-419.
Leclercq, J., 'L'Ascension, triomphe du Christ', *VS* 72 (1945) 289-300.
Liebermann, S., 'Metatron, The Meaning of His Name and His Functions', in: I. Gruenwald, *Apocalyptic and Merkabah Mysticism* (AGJU 14; Leiden: E.J. Brill, 1980) 235-241.
Liese, H., 'In Ascensione Domini. Mc.16:14-20', *VD* 12 (1932) 129-134.
Lietzmann, H., (review of V. Larrañaga, *L'Ascension de Notre-Seigneur*), *ZNW* 37 (1938/39) 297-298.
Lindars, B., *New Testament Apologetic. The Doctrinal Significance of the Old Testament Quotations* (London: SCM, 1961) 303pp.
Lindars, B., *The Gospel of John* (NCeB; Greenwood, SC: Attic; London: Oliphants, 1972) 648pp.
Lindars, B., *Jesus Son of Man. A Fresh Examination of the Son of Man Sayings in the Gospels in the Light of Recent Research* (London: SPCK, 1983) xi + 244pp.
Linnemann, E., 'Der (wiedergefundene) Markusschluß', *ZThK* 66 (1969) 255-287.
Linton, O., 'The Trial of Jesus and the Interpretation of Ps cx', *NTS* 7 (1960/61) 258-262.
Livingstone, E.A. (ed.), *Studia Evangelica 6. Papers Presented to the Fourth International Congress on Biblical Studies held at Oxford, 1969* (TU 112; Berlin: Akademie, 1973) 676pp.
Livingstone, E.A. (ed.), *Studia Evangelica 7. Papers Presented to the Fifth International Congress on Biblical Studies held at Oxford, 1973* (TU 126; Berlin: Akademie, 1982) 570pp.
Lock, W., *Pastoral Epistles. I & II Timothy and Titus* (ICC; Edinburgh: T.&T. Clark, 1924) xliv + 163pp.
Loewenstamm, S.E., 'The Death of Moses' (1958), rev. in: G.W.E. Nickelsburg (ed.), *Studies on the Testament of Abraham* (SCS 6; Missoula, MO: SBL, 1972) 185-217.
Lohfink, G., 'Aufgefahren in den Himmel', *GuL* 35 (1962) 84-85.
Lohfink, G., 'Der historische Ansatz der Himmelfahrt Christi', *Cath (M)* 17 (1963) 44-84.
Lohfink, G., 'Was steht ihr da und schauet (Apg.1.11). Die 'Himmelfahrt Jesu' im lukanischen Geschichtswerk', *BiKi* 20 (1965) 43-48.
Lohfink, G., 'Wir sind Zeugen dieser Ereignisse (Apg.5.32). Die Einheit der neutestamentlichen Botschaft von Erhöhung und Himmelfahrt Jesu', *BiKi* 20 (1965) 49-52.
Lohfink, G., 'Christologie und Geschichtsbild in Apg 3,19-21', *BZ* 13 (1969) 223-241.
Lohfink, G., *Die Himmelfahrt Jesu. Untersuchungen zu den Himmelfahrts- und*

*Erhöhungstexten bei Lukas* (StANT 26; München: Kösel, 1971) 314pp.

Lohfink, G., (sermon on the ascension) in: idem, *Gott ohne Masken. Predigten und Ansprachen* (Stuttgart: Calwer; Würzburg: Echter; Innsbruck: Tyrolia, 1972).

Lohfink, G., *Die Himmelfahrt Jesu. Erfindung oder Erfahrung?* (KRB 18; Stuttgart: KBW, 1972) 66pp.

Lohfink, G., 'Gab es im Gottesdienst der neutestamentlichen Gemeinde eine Anbetung Christi?', *BZ* 18 (1974) 161-179.

Lohfink, G., *Paulus vor Damaskus. Arbeitsweisen der neueren Bibelwissenschaft dargestellt an den Texten Apg 9,1-19; 22,3-21; 26,9-18* (SBS 4; Stuttgart: KBW, 1965) 101pp.

Lohmeyer, E., 'Galiläa und Jerusalem bei Lukas' (1936); partially repr. in: G. Braumann (Hrsg.), *Das Lukasevangelium* (1974) 7-12.

Lohmeyer, E., *Das Evangelium des Markus* (KEK II[17]; Göttingen: Vandenhoeck & Ruprecht, 1957, [8]1967, nach dem Handexemplar des Verfassers durchgesehene Ausgabe mit Ergänzungsheft bearbeitet von G. Saß, [3]1967) 8 + 368 + 44pp.

Lohse, E., πεντηκοστή, *ThWNT* 6 (1959) 44-53.

Lohse, E., *Die Auferstehung Jesu Christi im Zeugnis des Lukasevangeliums* (BSt 31; Neukirchen-Vluyn: Neukirchener, 1961) 40pp.

Loisy, A., *L'Évangile selon Luc* (Paris: E. Nourry, 1924) 600pp.

Longenecker, R.N., Tenney, M.C. (eds.), *New Dimensions in New Testament Study* (Grand Rapids: Zondervan, 1974) xiii + 386pp.

Longenecker, R.N., *Biblical Exegesis in the Apostolic Period* (Exeter: Paternoster, 1975; repr. Biblical and Theological Classics Library 5; 1995) 246pp.

Lösch, St., *Deitas Jesu und antike Apotheose. Ein Beitrag zur Exegese und Religionsgeschichte* (Rottenburg a. N. (Württemberg): A. Bader, 1933) xv + 137pp.

Luciani, F., 'Le vicende di Enoc nell'interpretazione di Filone Alessandrino', *RivBib* 31 (1983) 43-68.

Luck, U., 'Glaube und Weltbild in der urchristlichen Überlieferung von Höllen- und Himmelfahrt Christi', in: *Collegium Philosophicum* (FS J. Rister; Stuttgart: Schwabe, 1965) 141-156.

Lüdemann, G., *Das frühe Christentum nach den Traditionen der Apostelgeschichte. Ein Kommentar* (Göttingen: Vandenhoeck & Ruprecht, 1987) 285pp.

Lüdemann, G., *Die Auferstehung Jesu. Historie, Erfahrung, Theologie* (Göttingen: Vandenhoeck & Ruprecht, 1994) 227pp.

Lührmann, D., 'Henoch und die Metanoia', *ZNW* 66 (1975) 103-116.

Lührmann, D., *Das Markusevangelium* (HNT 3; Tübingen: J.C.B. Mohr/Paul Siebeck, 1987) xi + 283pp.

Luzarraga, J., *Las Tradiciones de la Nube en la Biblia y en el judaismo primitivo* (AnBib 54; Roma: IBP, 1973) 306pp.

Lygre, J.G., *Exaltation. Considered with Reference to the Resurrection and Ascension in Luke-Acts* (Diss. Princeton Theological Seminary, 1975; Ann Arbor, MI: UMI, 1995) 218pp.

MacDonald, J., *The Theology of the Samaritans* (NTLi; London: SCM, 1964) 480pp.

MacLean, A.J., 'Ascension', *DAC* 1 (1915) 95-99.

MacRae, G.W., ''Whom Heaven Must Receive Until the Time'. Reflections on the Christology of Acts', *Interp.* 27 (1973) 151-165.

Maddox, R., *The Purpose of Luke-Acts* (FRLANT 126; Göttingen, Vandenhoeck & Ruprecht;

Studies of the New Testament and Its World; Edinburgh: T.&T. Clark, 1982) 218pp.

Maile, J.F., 'The Ascension in Luke-Acts', *TynB* 37 (1986) 29-59.

Mallau, H.H., 'Baruch/Baruchschriften', *TRE* 5 (1980) 269-276.

Maly, K., 'Christi Himmelfahrt. Evangelium: Mk.16,11-20', *DAW* 3 (1966) 85-90.

Mangenot, E., *La Résurrection de Jésus. Suivi de deux appendices sur la crucifixion et l'ascension* (Bibliothèque Apologétique 9; Paris: Beauchesne, 1910) 404pp.

Mann, C.S., 'The New Testament and the Lord's Ascension', *CQR* 158 (1957) 452-465 [cf. G.F. Dowden, *CQR* 159 (1958) 422f].

Marlow, J.T.A., *A Narrative Analysis of Acts 1-2* (Diss. Golden Gate Baptist Theological Seminary, 1988) 106pp. [cf. *DAIA* 49 (1988) 1481s.A]

Marrevee, W.H., *The Ascension of Christ in the Works of St. Augustine* (Ottawa: University of Ottawa Press, 1967).

Marshall, I.H., 'The Resurrection in the Acts of the Apostles', in: W.W. Gasque, R.P. Martin (eds.), *Apostolic History and the Gospel* (1970) 92-107.

Marshall, I.H., *Luke, Historian and Theologian* (Exeter: Paternoster, 1970) 238pp.

Marshall, I.H., 'The Resurrection of Jesus in Luke', *TynB* 24 (1973) 55-98.

Marshall, I.H. (ed.), *New Testament Interpretation. Essays on Principles and Methods* (Exeter: Paternoster, 1977, ²1979) 412pp.

Marshall, I.H., *Commentary on Luke* (NIGTC; Grand Rapids: Eerdmans, 1978) 928pp.

Marshall, I.H., *The Acts of the Apostles. An Introduction and Commentary* (TNTC 5; Leicester: IVP; Grand Rapids: Eerdmans, 1980) 427pp.

Marshall, I.H., 'Acts and the 'Former Treatise'', in: B.W. Winter, A.D. Clarke (eds.), *The Book of Acts in Its Ancient Literary Setting* (1993) 163-182.

Martin, A.D., 'The Ascension of Christ', *Exp.* (Series 8) 16 (1918) 321-346.

Martin, A.S., 'Ascension', *DCG* 1 (1906) 124-128.

Martin, B., 'Aufgefahren in den Himmel. Gedanken eines Nicht-Theologen', *GuL* 40 (1967) 85-93.

Martin, G., 'Ascension', *DB(V)* 1/2 (1926) 1071-1073.

Martin, R.P., *Carmen Christi. Philippians ii. 5-11 in Recent Interpretation and in the Setting of Early Christian Worship* (MSSNTS 4; Cambridge: CUP, 1967) xii + 364pp.

Martini, C.M. *et alii*, 'Fête de l'Ascension', *Assemblées du Seigneur* 2/22 (Paris: 1969).

Martini, C.M., 'L'Ascension de Jésus, Act 1,1-11', *ASeign* 28 (1969) 6-11.

Mattill, A.J., 'Naherwartung, Fernerwartung, and the Purpose of Luke-Acts. Weymouth Reconsidered', *CBQ* 34 (1972) 276-293.

Mattill, A.J., *Luke and the Last Things. A Perspective for the Understanding of Lukan Thought* (Dillsboro, NC: Western North Carolina Press, 1979) xi + 247pp.

Mattill, A.J., Bedford Mattill, M., *A Classified Bibliography of Literature on the Acts of the Apostles* (NTTS 7; Leiden: E.J. Brill, 1966) xviii + 513pp.

Mayer, E., *Die Reiseerzählung des Lukas (Lk 9,51-19,10). Entscheidung in der Wüste* (EHS.T 554; Frankfurt etc.: P. Lang, 1996) 358pp.

McCown, C.C., 'Gospel Geography. Fiction, Fact, and Truth', *JBL* 60 (1941) 1-25; German tr. 'Geographie der Evangelien. Fiktion, Tatsache und Wahrheit', in: G. Braumann (Hrsg.), *Das Lukasevangelium* (1974) 13-42.

McNamara, M., 'The Ascension and the Exaltation of Christ in the Fourth Gospel', *Scripture* (London) 29 (1967) 65-75.

Mealand, D.L., 'The Phrase 'Many Proofs' in Acts 1,3 and in Hellenistic Writers', *ZNW* 80

(1989) 134-135.

Meeks, W.A., *The Prophet-King. Moses Traditions and the Johannine Christology* (NT.S 14; Leiden: E.J. Brill, 1967) xiv + 356pp.

Menoud, Ph.H., 'Remarques sur les textes de l'ascension dans Luc-Acts', in: W. Eltester (Hrsg.), *Neutestamentliche Studien für R. Bultmann* (BZNW 21; Berlin: A. Töpelmann, 1954, ²1957) 148-156; repr. in: Menoud, *Jésus-Christ et la foi* (1978) 76-84.

Menoud, Ph.H., 'Pendant Quarante Jours', in: W.C. van Unnik (ed.), *Neotestamentica et Patristica* (FS O. Cullmann; NT.S 6; Leiden: E.J. Brill, 1962) 148-156; repr. in: Menoud, *Jésus-Christ et la foi* (1978) 110-118.

Menoud, Ph.H., *Jésus-Christ et la foi. Recherches néotestamentaires* (BT (N); Neuchâtel, Paris: Delachaux & Niestlé, 1978) 359pp.

Metzger, B.M., *The Text of the New Testament. Its Transmission, Corruption and Restoration* (New York, Oxford: Clarendon, 1964, ³1992) ix + 310pp.

Metzger, B.M., *Index to Periodical Literature on Christ and the Gospels* (NTTS 6; Leiden: E.J. Brill, 1966) xxiii + 602pp.

Metzger, B.M., 'The Meaning of Christ's Ascension', *ChrTo* 10 (1966) 863-864.

Metzger, B.M., 'The Ascension of Jesus Christ', in: idem, *Historical and Literary Studies. Pagan, Jewish and Christian* (NTTS 8; Leiden: E.J. Brill; Grand Rapids: Eerdmans, 1968) 77-87.

Metzger, B.M., 'The Meaning of Christ's Ascension', in: J.M. Myers, T.O. Reimherr, H.N. Bream (eds.), *Search the Scriptures* (GTS 3; FS R.T. Stamm; Leiden: E.J. Brill, 1969) 118-128.

Metzger, B.M., *A Textual Commentary on the Greek New Testament* (Stuttgart: Deutsche Bibelgesellschaft, UBS, 1971, corr. ed. 1975, ²1994) xiv + 16* + 696pp.

Meyer, A., *Die Auferstehung Christi. Die Berichte über Auferstehung, Himmelfahrt und Pfingsten, ihre Entstehung, ihr geschichtlicher Hintergrund und ihre religiöse Bedeutung* (Tübingen: J.C.B. Mohr/Paul Siebeck, 1905) vii + 368pp.

Meyer, E., *Ursprung und Anfänge des Christentums* (Stuttgart: J.G. Cotta, 1921-1923, ⁴·⁵1924-1925; repr. Darmstadt: WBG, 1962) 3 vols.

Michaelis, W., 'Zur Überlieferung der Himmelfahrtsgeschichte', *ThBl* 4 (1925) 101-109.

Michaelis, W., *Die Erscheinungen des Auferstandenen* (Basel: H. Majer, 1944) 160pp.

Michaelis, W., 'Exegetisches zur Himmelfahrtspredigt', *RefSchw* 108 (1952) 5-8 (contra M. Werner, *SThU* 22 (1952) 83-91).

Michaelis, W., ὁδός, ὁδηγός κτλ., *ThWNT* 5 (1954) 42-118.

Michaelis, W., ὁράω κτλ., *ThWNT* 5 (1954) 315-381.

Michaelis, W., προχειρίζω, *ThWNT* 6 (1959) 863-865.

Michel, A., 'Ascension de Jésus-Christ', *DThC* (1951) (Tables Générales I) 274-275.

Michel, O., Μελχισεδέκ, *ThWNT* 4 (1942) 573-575.

Michel, O., *Der Brief an die Hebräer* (KEK¹²; Göttingen: Vandenhoeck & Ruprecht, 1936, ⁶1966) 564pp.

Michiels, R., 'Eenheid van Pasen, Hemelvaart en Pinksteren', *Coll.* 20 (1974) 3-35.

Milchner, H.J. (Hrsg.), *Himmelfahrt. Die Nähe Christi feiern. Predigten und liturgische Entwürfe* [DAW(S) 72; Stuttgart: 1996) 160pp.

Mills, W.E., *A Bibliography of the Periodical Literature on the Acts of the Apostles 1962-1984* (NT.S 58; Leiden: E.J. Brill, 1986) xxx + 115pp.

Miquel, P., 'Le mystère de l'Ascension', *QLP* 40 (1959) 105-126; ET 'Christ's Ascension and Our Glorification', *ThD* 9 (1961) 67-73.

Moehring, H.R., 'Rationalization of Miracles in the Writings of Flavius Josephus', in: E.A. Livingstone (ed.), *StEv* VI (TU 112; Berlin: Akademie, 1973) 376-383.

Moore, A.L., *The Parousia in the New Testament* (NT.S 13; Leiden: E.J. Brill, 1966) 248pp.

Moore, G.F., *Judaism in the First Centuries of the Christian Era. The Age of the Tannaim* (Schocken 294-295; New York: Schocken, 1927; repr. 1971) 4 parts in 2 vols., x + 552; v + 166; vii + 395 + v + 102pp.

Moule, C.F.D., 'The Ascension. Acts i.9', *ET* 68 (1956/57) 205-209 = idem, *Essays in New Testament Interpretation* (Cambridge, London, New York: CUP, 1982).

Moule, C.F.D., 'The Post-Resurrection Appearances in the Light of Festival Pilgrimages', *NTS* 4 (1957/58) 58-61.

Moule, C.F.D., 'The Christology of Acts', in: L.E. Keck, J.L. Martyn (eds.), *Studies in Luke-Acts* (1966) 159-185.

Müller, G., 'Ein Versuch zur Erklärung von Apg.1:9', *EKZ* 82 (1908) 553-554.

Murray, J.C., 'Ascension of Jesus Christ (theological)', *NCE* 1 (1967) 933-936.

Mussies, G., 'Variation in the Book of Acts', *FilNT* 4 (1991) 165-182.

Myers, J.M., *I and II Esdras. Introduction, Translation and Commentary* (AncB 42; Garden City, NY: Doubleday, 1974) xxiv + 384pp.

Neirynck, F. (éd.), *L'Évangile de Luc—The Gospel of Luke. Revised and Enlarged Edition of L'Évangile de Luc. Problèmes littéraires et théologiques* (BEThL 32; Leuven: Leuven University Press, Peeters, 1973, ²1989) x + 590pp.

Nestle, D., 'Himmelfahrt. Apostelgeschichte 1,3-4(5-7)8-11', *GPM* 46 (1991/92) 247-252.

Neuner, J., 'He Ascended into Heaven', *VJTR* 59 (1995) 400-404.

Nicholson, G.C., *Death as Departure. The Johannine Descent-Ascent Schema* (SBL.DS 63; Chico, CA: Scholars, 1983) xviii + 231pp.

Nickelsburg, G.W.E., *Resurrection, Immortality, and Eternal Life in Intertestamental Judaism* (HThS 26; Cambridge: Harvard University Press; London: OUP, 1972) 206pp.

Nickelsburg, G.W.E. (ed.), *Studies on the Testament of Moses* (SCS 4; Missoula, MO: SBL, 1973) 125pp.

Nickelsburg, G.W.E., Collins, J.J. (eds.), *Ideal Figures in Ancient Judaism. Profiles and Paradigms* (SCS 12; Missoula, MO: Scholars, 1980) xii + 258pp.

Nickelsburg, G.W.E., 'The Bible Rewritten and Expanded', in: M.E. Stone (ed.), *Jewish Writings of the Second Temple Period* (1984) 89-156.

Nielsen, J.T., *Het Evangelie naar Lucas* (PNT.N; Nijkerk: Callenbach, 1979-1983) 2 vols., 408 + 303pp.

Nogosek, R.J., 'The Exaltation of Christ', *BiTod* 44 (1969) 3068-3071.

Nolland, J., *Luke* (WBC 35; Dallas, TX: Word, 1989-1993) 3 vols.

Norden, E., *Agnostos Theos. Untersuchungen zur Formengeschichte religiöser Rede* (Leipzig, Berlin: B.G. Teubner, 1913, 1923; repr. Darmstadt: WBG, 1956) x + 410pp.

Nützel, J.M., 'Entrückung III. Neues Testament', *LThK* 3 (³1995) 685.

O'Carroll, M., 'Ascension', in: *Verbum Caro. An Encyclopedia on Jesus, the Christ* (Collegeville, MN: Liturgical, 1992) 12-14.

O'Collins, G., 'Christ's Resurrection and Ascension', *America* 160 (1989) 262- 263.

O'Toole, R.F., 'Luke's Understanding of Jesus' Resurrection-Ascension-Exaltation', *BTB* 9 (1979) 106-114.

O'Toole, R.F., 'Christ's Resurrection in Acts 13:13-52', *Bib.* 60 (1979) 361-372.

O'Toole, R.F., 'Some Observations on *Anistemi*, 'I Raise', in Acts 3:22,26', *ScEs* 31 (1979) 85-92.

O'Toole, R.F., 'Activity of the Risen Jesus in Luke-Acts', *Bib.* 62 (1981) 471-498.

O'Toole, R.F., 'Why Did Luke Write Acts (Lk-Acts)?' *BTB* 7 (1977) 66-76.

Oberlinner, L., *Die Pastoralbriefe 1. Kommentar zum ersten Timotheusbrief* (HThK 11/2; Freiburg, Basel, Wien: Herder, 1994) 1 + 312pp.

Odasso, G., 'L'Ascensione nell'Evangelo di Luca', *BeO* 13 (1971) 107-118.

Odeberg, H., *The Fourth Gospel. Interpreted in Its Relation to Contemporaneous Religious Currents in Palestine and the Hellenistic-Oriental World* (Uppsala, Stockholm: Almquist & Wiksells, 1929; repr. Amsterdam: B.R. Grüner, 1968) 336pp.

Odeberg, H., ʾΕνώχ, *ThWNT* 2 (1935) 553-557.

Oepke, A., 'Unser Glaube an die Himmelfahrt Christi', *Luth.* (= *NKZ*) 49 (1938) 161-186.

Oepke, A., νεφέλη, νέφος, *ThWNT* 4 (1942) 904-912.

Ogara, F., 'De Ascensionis Christi spectatoribus (Act.Ap.1:1-22), *Gr.* 14 (1933) 37-61.

Ohm, T., 'Die Unterweisung und Aussendung der Apostel nach Apg 1:3-8', *ZMR* 37 (1953) 1-10.

Otto, R., *Reich Gottes und Menschensohn. Ein religionsgeschichtlicher Versuch* (München: C.H. Beck, 1934, ²1940) ix + 326pp.

Overbeck, F., *Kurze Erklärung der Apostelgeschichte* (Kurzgefaßtes exegetisches Handbuch zum Neuen Testament 1/4; Leipzig: S. Hirzel, ⁴1870).

Palatty, P., 'The Ascension of Christ in Luke-Acts. An Exegetical Critical Study of Luke 24.50-53 and Acts 1.2-3.9-11', *BiBh* 12 (1986) 100-117.166-181.

Palmer, D.W., 'The Literary Background of Ac 1.1-14', *NTS* 33 (1987) 427-438.

Parsons, M.C., 'A Christological Tendency in P75', *JBL* 105 (1986) 463-479.

Parsons, M.C., 'Narrative Closure and Openness in the Plot of the Third Gospel: The Sense of an Ending in Luke 24:50-53', *SBL.SP* (1986) 201-223.

Parsons, M.C., *The Departure of Jesus in Luke-Acts. The Ascension Narratives in Context* (JSNT.S 21; Sheffield: JSOT, 1987) 301pp.

Parsons, M.C., 'The Text of Acts 1.2 Reconsidered', *CBQ* 50 (1988) 58-71.

Paulus, H.E.G., *Das Leben Jesu als Grundlage einer reinen Geschichte des Urchristentums* (Heidelberg: C.F. Winter, 1828) 2 vols., 1192pp.

Pease, A.S., 'Some Aspects of Invisibility', *HSCP* 53 (1942) 1-36.

Peifer, C., 'The Risen Christ and the Christian', *Worship* 34 (1960) 326-330.

Perkins, P., *Resurrection. New Testament Witness and Contemporary Reflection* (Garden City, NY: Doubleday, 1984; London: G. Chapman, 1985) 504pp.

Perrin, N., *Rediscovering the Teaching of Jesus* (New York, Evanston: Harper & Row, 1967) 272pp.

Pesch, R., 'Der Anfang der Apostelgeschichte (Apg 1,1-11)', *EKK.V* 3 (Neukirchen: Neukirchener; Zürich: Benziger, 1971) 7-35.

Pesch, R., *Das Markusevangelium* (HThK 2; Freiburg, Basel, Wien: Herder, 1976-1977, ⁴·³1984) 2 vols., xxiv + 480; xvi + 606pp.

Pesch, R., *Die Apostelgeschichte* (EKK 5; Neukirchen-Vluyn: Neukirchener; Zürich: Benzinger, 1986) 2 vols., 371 + 327pp.

Peters, G.N.H., 'The Ascensions of Christ', *EvR* 21 (1870) 85-111.

Petzke, G., *Das Sondergut des Evangeliums nach Lukas* (ZWKB; Zürich: Theologischer, 1990) 257pp.

Pfister, F., 'Zu den Himmelfahrtslegenden', *Wochenschrift für klassische Philologie* 28 (1911) 81-86.

Philonenko, M. (éd.), *Le Trône de Dieu* (WUNT 69; Tübingen: J.C.B. Mohr/Paul Siebeck, 1993) viii + 369pp.

Plevnik, J., 'The Eyewitnesses of the Risen Jesus in Luke 24', *CBQ* 49 (1987) 90-103.

Plevnik, J., 'Son of Man Seated at the Right Hand of God. Luke 22,69 in Lucan Christology', *Bib.* 72 (1991) 331-347.

Plooij, D., 'The Ascension in the 'Western' Textual Tradition', *MNAW.L* 67 A/2 (Amsterdam: Noord-Hollandsche, 1929) 39-58.

Plümacher, E., *Lukas als hellenistischer Schriftsteller. Studien zur Apostelgeschichte* (StUNT 9; Göttingen: Vandenhoeck & Ruprecht, 1972) 164pp.

Plummer, A., *The Gospel According to S. Luke* (ICC; Edinburgh: T.&T. Clark, 1896, ⁵1922; repr. 1981) lxxxviii + 592pp.

Pöhlmann, H.G., 'Himmelfahrt Christi II. Kirchengeschichtlich/Syst. Theologie', *TRE* 15 (1986) 334-341.

Preuschen, E., *Die Apostelgeschichte* (HNT 4/1; Tübingen: J.C.B. Mohr/Paul Siebeck, 1912) ix + 159pp.

Purvis, J.D., 'Samaritan Traditions on the Death of Moses', in: Nickelsburg, G.W.E. (ed.), *Studies on the Testament of Moses* (1973) 93-117.

Quesada García, F., 'Las apariciones y la Ascensión en la economía salvífica', *Burg.* 26 (1985) 351-377.

Quinn, J.D., 'Ascension of Jesus Christ (biblical)', *NCE* 1 (1967) 930-933.

Rainbow, P.A., 'Jewish Monotheism as the Matrix for New Testament Christology. A Review Article', *NT* 33 (1993) 78-91.

Ramsey, A.M., 'Ascension', in: A. Richardson (ed.), *A Theological Word Book of the Bible* (London: SCM, 1950, ²⁰1990) 22-23.

Ramsey, A.M., 'What was the Ascension?' (1951); repr. in: D.E. Nineham, *et alii* (eds.), *Historicity and Chronology in the New Testament* (TCSPCK 6; London: SPCK, 1965) 135-144.

Rappe, O., 'Die Bedeutung der Himmelfahrt Jesu für seine Jünger (Apg.1:1-12)', *EvBo* 64 (1927) 161-162.

Ratzinger, J., 'Himmelfahrt Christi', *SM(D)* 2 (1968) 693-696.

Ratzinger, J., 'Christi Himmelfahrt', *GuL* 40 (1967) 80-85.

Ratzinger, J., 'Himmelfahrt Christi', *HTTL* 3 (1972) 290-292.

Reicke, B., *Glaube und Leben der Urgemeinde. Bemerkungen zu Apg. 1-7* (AThANT 32; Zürich: Zwingli, 1957) 179pp.

Reicke, B., 'Instruction and Discussion in the Travel Narrative', in: K. Aland (ed.), *StEv* 1 (TU 73; Berlin: Akademie, 1959) 206-216.

Reinmuth, E., *Pseudo-Philo und Lukas. Studien zum Liber Antiquitatum Biblicarum und seiner Bedeutung für die Interpretation des lukanischen Doppelwerks* (WUNT 74; Tübingen: J.C.B. Mohr/Paul Siebeck, 1994) xi + 284pp.

Rese, M., *Alttestamentliche Motive in der Christologie des Lukas* (StNT 1; Gütersloh: G. Mohn, 1969) 227pp.

Resseguie, J.L., 'Interpretation of Luke's Central Section (Luke 9.51-19.44) since 1856', *SBTh* 5 (1975) 3-36.

Rey Marcos, J., *La entronización de Jesús a la diestra de Dios* (Unpublished Diss., Roma,

1971).

Rey Marcos, J., 'Sedet ad dexteram Patris. Nota sobre el 'Credo del Pueblo de Dios'', *RET* 32 (1972) 209-220.

Rey Marcos, J., *Jesús de Nazaret y su glorificación. Estudio de la exégesis patrística de la formula 'Sentado a la diestra de Dios' hasta el Concilio de Nicea* (CEISP 8; Salamanca, Madrid: Instituto Superior de Pastoral, 1974) 311pp.

Ridderbos, H., *Het Evangelie naar Johannes. Proeve van een theologische exegese* (Kampen: J.H. Kok, 1987-1992) 2 vols., 439 + 363pp.

Riekert, S.J., 'Stilistiese moontlikhede en die werklike of vermeende teksprobleme in die proloog van Handelinge', *NGTT* 22 (1981) 179-187.

Rigaux, B., *Dieu l'a resuscité. Exégèse et théologie biblique* (SBFA 4; Gembloux: Duculot, 1973) xii + 474pp.

Ristow, H., 'Himmelfahrt', in: idem (Hrsg.), *Wandelt in der Liebe* (Predigtgedanken aus Vergangenheit und Gegenwart B/2; Berlin: Evangelische, 1968) 189-201.

Rius-Camps, J., 'Las variantes de la recensión occidental de los Hechos de los Apóstolos (Hch 1,1-3.4-14)', *FilNT* 6 (1993) 59-68.219-229.

Robinson, E., 'The Resurrection and Ascension of Our Lord', *BS* 2 (1845) 162-189; repr. *BS* 150 (1993) 9-34.

Robinson, J.A.T., 'Ascendancy', *ANQ* 5/2 (1964) 5-9.

Robinson, J.A.T., 'The Most Primitive Christology of All?' (1956); repr. in: idem, *Twelve New Testament Studies* (1962) 139-153.

Robinson, J.A.T., *Jesus and His Coming. The Emergence of a Doctrine* (London: SCM, 1957) 192pp.

Robinson, J.A.T., 'Elijah, John and Jesus. An Essay in Detection' (1958); repr. in: idem, *Twelve New Testament Studies* (1962) 28-52.

Robinson, J.A.T., *Twelve New Testament Studies* (SBT 34; London: SCM, 1962) 180pp.

Robinson, J.A.T., *Redating the New Testament* (London: SCM, 1976) xiv + 369pp.

Robinson, J.M., 'Ascension', *IDB* 1 (1962) 245-247.

Robinson, W.C., *Der Weg des Herrn. Studien zur Geschichte und Eschatologie im Lukas-Evangelium. Ein Gespräch mit Hans Conzelmann* (ThF 36; Hamburg-Bergstedt: Herbert Reich, 1964) 70pp.

Rohde, E., *Psyche. Seelencult und Unsterblichkeitsglaube der Griechen* (mit einer Einführung von O. Weinreich; Tübingen: J.C.B. Mohr/Paul Siebeck, 1893, [9.10]1925) 2 vols., xx + 329; iii + 448pp.

Roloff, D., *Gottähnlichkeit, Vergöttlichung und Erhöhung zu seligem Leben. Untersuchungen zur Herkunft der platonischen Angleichung an Gott* (UaLG 4; Berlin: W. de Gruyter, 1970) vi + 243pp.

Roloff, J., *Apostolat-Verkündigung-Kirche. Ursprung, Inhalt und Funktion des kirchlichen Apostelamtes nach Paulus, Lukas und den Pastoralbriefen* (Gütersloh: G. Mohn, 1965) 296pp.

Roloff, J., *Die Apostelgeschichte* (NTD 5; Göttingen: Vandenhoeck & Ruprecht, 1981) 389pp.

Roloff, J., *Der erste Brief an Timotheus* (EKK 15; Neukirchen-Vluyn: Neukirchener; Zürich, Einsiedeln, Köln: Benziger, 1988) 395pp.

Ropes, J.H., 'Detached Note on [Acts] i,2', in: idem, *The Text of Acts* (Beg 3; London: Macmillan, 1926) 256-261.

Roscher, W.H., 'Die Zahl 40 in Glauben, Brauch und Schriften der Semiten', *ASGW.PH* 27 (1909) 91-138.

Roscher, W.H., 'Die Tessarakontaden und Tessarakontadenlehren der Griechen und anderer Völker', *BVSGW* 61 (1909) 17-206.

Rose, H.J., 'Herakles and the Gospels', *HThR* 31 (1938) 113-142.

Rowland, C., *The Open Heaven. A Study of Apocalyptic in Judaism and Early Christianity* (London: SPCK, 1982) xiii + 562pp.

Ruckstuhl, E., 'Auferstehung, Erhöhung und Himmelfahrt Jesu' (1968); repr. in: idem, *Jesus im Horizont der Evangelien* (SBAB 3; Stuttgart: KBW, 1988) 185-218.

Ruckstuhl, E., 'Abstieg und Erhöhung des johanneischen Menschensohnes' (1975), in: idem, *Jesus im Horizont der Evangelien* (SBAB 3; Stuttgart: KBW, 1988) 277-310.

Russel , R., 'Modern Exegesis and the Fact of the Resurrection', *DR* 76 (1958) 251-264.329-343.

Russell, D.S., *The Method and Message of Jewish Apocalyptic* (London: SCM, 1964) 464pp.

Sabbe, M., 'The Son of Man Saying in Acts 7,56', in: J. Kremer (éd.), *Les Actes des Apôtres* (1979) 241-279.

Sabourin, L., 'The Biblical Cloud. Terminology and Traditions', *BTB* 4 (1974) 290-311.

Sahlin, H., *Der Messias und das Gottesvolk. Studien zur protolukanischen Theologie* (ASNU 12; Uppsala: Almqvist & Wiksells, 1945) viii + 405pp.

Samain, E., 'La notion de APXH dans l'oeuvre lucanienne', in: F. Neirynck (ed.), *L'Évangile de Luc* (²1989) 209-238.327 (additional note by F. Neirynck).

Sand, A., *Das Evangelium nach Matthäus übersetzt und erklärt* (RNT 1; Regensburg: F. Pustet, 1986) 679pp.

Sand, A., 'Himmelfahrt', in: M. Görg, B. Lang (Hrsg.), *NBL* 2/7 (1992) 156-160.

Sanday, W., Headlam, A.C., *The Epistle to the Romans* (ICC; Edinburgh: T.&T. Clark, 1895, ⁵1902) cxii + 450pp.

Sarna, N.M., בראשית *Genesis* (JPSTC; Philadelphia, New York, Jerusalem: JPS, 5749/1989) xxxi + 414pp.

Scheftelowitz, J., 'Der Seelen- und Unsterblichkeitsglaube im Alten Testament', *ARW* 16 (1916/19) 211-232.

Schelkle, K.H., 'Christi Himmelfahrt', *GuL* 41 (1968) 81-85.

Schenkel, D., 'Himmelfahrt Jesu', *Bibel-Lexicon. Realwörterbuch zum Handgebrauch* 3 (Leipzig: 1871) 83-85.

Schierse, F.J., 'Himmelfahrt Christi 1', *LThK* 5 (1960) 358-360.

Schille, G., 'Die Himmelfahrt', *ZNW* 57 (1966) 183-199.

Schille, G., *Die Apostelgeschichte des Lukas* (ThHK 5; Berlin: Evangelische, 1983, ²1984) xxiv + 492pp.

Schillebeeckx, E., 'Ascension and Pentecost', *Worship* 35 (1961) 336-363.

Schillebeeckx, E., *Jezus. het verhaal van een levende* (Baarn: H. Nelissen, 1974, ⁸1982) 641pp.

Schlier, H., *Der Brief an die Galater* (KEK III¹⁴; Göttingen: Vandenhoeck & Ruprecht, 1949, ⁵1971) 287pp.

Schlier, H., 'Jesu Himmelfahrt nach den lukanischen Schriften' (1961); repr. in: idem, *Besinnung auf das Neue Testament. Exegetische Aufsätze und Vorträge 2* (Freiburg, Basel, Wien: Herder, 1964, ²1967) 227-241.

Schmid, A.A., 'Himmelfahrt Christi', *LCI* 2 (1970, ²1990) 268-276.

Schmid, H.H., לקח *lqh* nehmen, *THAT* 1 (1984) 878-879.

Schmid, J., *Das Evangelium nach Lukas übersetzt und erklärt* (RNT 3; Regensburg: F. Pustet, 1940, ⁴1960).

Schmidt-Lauber, H.-C., 'Himmelfahrtsfest', *TRE* 15 (1986) 341-344.

Schmiedel, P.W., 'Resurrection- and Ascension Narratives', *EB(C)* 4 (1903) 4039-4087.

Schmithals, W., *Das Evangelium nach Lukas* (ZBK.NT 3/1; Zürich: Theologischer, 1980) 240pp.

Schmithals, W., *Die Apostelgeschichte des Lukas* (ZBK.NT 3/2; Zürich: Theologischer, 1982) 248pp.

Schmitt, A., 'Die Angaben über Henoch Gen 5,21-24 in der LXX', in: J. Schreiner (Hrsg.), *Wort, Lied und Gottesanspruch. Beiträge zur Septuaginta* (FS J. Ziegler; FzB 1; Würzburg: Echter, 1972) 161-169.

Schmitt, A., *Entrückung-Aufnahme-Himmelfahrt. Untersuchungen zu einem Vorstellungsbereich im AT* (FzB 10; Stuttgart: KBW, 1973, ²1976) xiv + 378pp.

Schmitt, A., 'Ps 16, 8-11 als Zeugnis der Auferstehung in der Apg.', *BZ NS* 17 (1973) 229-248.

Schmitt, A., 'Zum Thema 'Entrückung' im Alten Testament', *BZ NF* 26 (1982) 34-49.

Schmitt, A., 'Der frühe Tod des Gerechten nach Weish 4,7-19. Ein Psalmthema in weisheitlicher Fassung', in: E. Haag, F.-L. Hossfeld (Hrsg.), *Freude an der Weisung des Herrn. Beiträge zur Theologie der Psalmen* (FS H. Groß; SBB 13; Stuttgart: KBW, 1986, ²1987) 325-347.

Schnackenburg, R., *Das Johannesevangelium* (HThK 5; Freiburg, Basel, Wien: Herder, 1965-1984) 4 vols.

Schneider, A., 'Das Evangelium der vierzig Tage', in: idem, *Gesammelte Aufsätze* (1963) 17-34.

Schneider, G., *Parusiegleichnisse im Lukas-Evangelium* (SBS 74; Stuttgart: KBW, 1975) 106pp.

Schneider, G., *Das Evangelium nach Lukas* (ÖTBK 3; GTB.S 500-501; Gütersloh: G. Mohn; Würzburg: Echter, 1977) 2 vols., 510pp.

Schneider, G., 'Der Zweck des lukanischen Doppelwerks', *BZ* 21 (1977) 45-66.

Schneider, G., *Die Apostelgeschichte* (HThK 5; Freiburg, Basel, Wien: Herder, 1980-1982) 2 vols., 520 + 440pp.

Schneider, J., (βαίνω) ἀναβαίνω, καταβαίνω, μεταβαίνω, *ThWNT* 1 (1933) 516-521.

Schneider, J., *Das Evangelium nach Johannes* (ThHK Sonderband; Berlin: Evangelische, 1976) 348pp.

Schnider, F., 'Himmelfahrt Jesu—Ende oder Anfang? Zum Verständnis des lukanischen Doppelwerkes', in: P.-G. Müller, W. Stenger (Hrsg.), *Kontinuität und Einheit* (FS F. Mußner; Freiburg: Herder, 1981) 158-172.

Schrade, H., 'Zur Ikonografie der Himmelfahrt Christi', in: F. Saxl (Hrsg.), *Vorträge der Bibliothek Warburg. Vorträge 1928-1929 über die Vorstellungen von der Himmelreise der Seele* (Leipzig, Berlin: B.G. Teubner, 1930) 66-190.

Schramm, T., *Der Markus-Stoff bei Lukas. Eine literarkritische und redaktionsgeschichtliche Untersuchung* (MSSNTS 14; Cambridge: CUP, 1971) xiii + 207pp.

Schrenk, G., ἱερός, τὸ ἱερόν κτλ., *ThWNT* 3 (1938) 221-284.

Schubert, P., 'The Structure and Significance of Luke 24', in: W. Eltester (Hrsg.), *Neutestamentliche Studien für R. Bultmann* (BZNW 21; Berlin: A. Töpelmann, 1954,

[2]1957) 165-186.

Schulz, S., *Das Evangelium nach Johannes* (NTD 4; Göttingen: Vandenhoeck & Ruprecht, 1972) 263pp.

Schürer, E., *The History of the Jewish People in the Age of Jesus Christ (175 B.C.-A.D. 135)* (A New English Version Revised and Edited by G. Vermes, F. Millar, P. Vermes and M. Black) (Edinburgh: T.& T. Clark, 1973-1987) 4 vols.

Schürmann, H., *Das Lukasevangelium* (HThK 3; Freiburg, Basel, Wien: Herder, 1969/[2]1981-1993) 2 vols., lii + 591; xxiv + 360pp.

Schweitzer, A., *Geschichte der Leben-Jesu-Forschung* (UTB.W 1302; Tübingen: J.C.B. Mohr/Paul Siebeck, 1906, [9]1984) 650pp.

Schweizer, E., *Erniedrigung und Erhöhung bei Jesus und seinen Nachfolgern* (AThANT 28; Zürich: Zwingli, 1955, [2]1962) 195pp.

Schweizer, E., *Das Evangelium nach Markus* (NTD 1; Göttingen, Zürich: Vandenhoeck & Ruprecht, 1967, [2]1968) iv + 230pp.

Schweizer, E., (review of G. Lohfink, *Die Himmelfahrt Jesu*), *ThR* 68 (1972) 18-19.

Schweizer, E., *Das Evangelium nach Lukas* (NTD 3; Göttingen: Vandenhoeck & Ruprecht, 1982, [2]1986) 263pp.

Scott, R.B.Y., 'Behold, He Cometh with Clouds', *NTS* 5 (1958/59) 127-132.

Segal, A.F., *Two Powers in Heaven. Early Rabbinic Reports about Christianity and Gnosticism* (SJLA 25; Leiden: E.J. Brill, 1977) xxiv + 313pp.

Segal, A.F., 'Heavenly Ascent in Hellenistic Judaism, Early Christianity and Their Environment', *ANRW* II 23,2 (1980) 1333-1394.

Segbroeck, F. van, *The Gospel of Luke. A Cumulative Bibliography 1973-1988* (BEThL 88; Leuven: Peeters, Leuven University Press, 1989) 241pp.

Seidensticker, P., *Die Auferstehung Jesu in der Botschaft der Evangelisten. Ein traditionsgeschichtlicher Versuch zum Problem der Sicherung der Osterbotschaft in der apostolischen Zeit* (SBS 26; Stuttgart: KBW, 1967, [2]1968) 160pp.

Selman, M.R., *The Intention of the Ascension Narratives in Luke 24:50-53 and Acts 1:1-12* (Unpublished M.A. Diss. University of Bristol, 1969).

Selwyn, E.G., 'Our Lord's Ascension', *Theol.* 12 (1926) 241-244.

Senden, H. van, *Jesu Auferstehung und Himmelfahrt* (Bethel u. Bielefeld: Anstalt Bethel, 1948).

Shekan, P.W., Di Lella, A.A., *The Wisdom of Ben Sira. A New Translation with Notes by P.W. Skekan, Introduction and Commentary by A.A. Di Lella* (AncB 39; Garden City, NY: Doubleday, 1987) xxiii + 620pp.

Shepherd, M.H., 'Paul and the Double Resurrection Tradition', *JBL* 64 (1945) 227-240.

Simon, U., *The Ascent to Heaven* (1961).

Sjöberg, E., *Der Menschensohn im äthiopischen Henochbuch* (SHVL 41; Lund: C.W.K. Gleerup, 1946, 1956) 219pp.

Skinner, J., *Genesis* (ICC; Edinburgh: T.&T. Clark, 1910, [2]1930) lxvi + 552pp.

Soltau, W., *Himmelfahrt und Pfingsten im Lichte wahren evangelischen Christentums* (Leipzig: Dieterich, 1905).

Spencer, F.S., (review of M.C. Parsons, *The Departure of Jesus*), *WJT* 52 (1990) 376-378.

Spencer, F.S., 'Acts and Modern Literary Approaches', in: B.W. Winter, A.D. Clarke (eds.), *The Book of Acts in Its Ancient Literary Setting* (1993) 381-414.

Squillaci, D., 'L'Ascensione in San Paolo', *PalCl* 40 (1961) 462-465.

Squillaci, D., 'Il salmo dell'Ascensione e della Pentecoste (Salmo 67)', *PalCl* 40 (1961) 525-530.

Stählin, G., *Die Apostelgeschichte* (NTD 5; Göttingen: Vandenhoeck & Ruprecht, 1962, [7]1980) iv + 343pp.

Stam, C., *De hemelvaart des Heren in de Godsopenbaring van het Nieuwe Testament* (Academisch proefschrift Vrije Universiteit Amsterdam; Kampen: J.H. Kok, 1950) 112pp.

Stange, C., 'Die Himmelfahrt Jesu', *ZSTh* 22 (1953) 218-222.

Steck, K.G., 'Apostelgeschichte 1,1-11', in: G. Eichholz (Hrsg.), *Herr, tue meine Lippen auf. Eine Predigthilfe* 2 (Wuppertal, Barmen: E. Müller, [2]1959) 296-308.

Steinmetzer, F.-X., 'Aufgefahren in den Himmel, sitzet zur Rechten Gottes', *ThPQ* 77 (1924) 82-92.224-241.414-426.

Stemberger, G., 'Auferstehung der Toten I/2. Judentum', *TRE* 4 (1979) 443-450.

Stempvoort, P.A. van, 'Het programma van Rudolf Bultmann en de Hemelvaart in het Nieuwe Testament. Uitdaging en antwoord', *KeTh* 8 (1957) 145-166.

Stempvoort, P.A. van, 'The Interpretation of the Ascension in Luke and Acts', *NTS* 5 (1958/59) 30-42.

Stempvoort, P.A. van , 'Het liep tegen de vijftigste dag. De betekenis van Hand.2:1', *HeB* 21 (1962) 97-103.

Stenger, W., *Der Christushymnus 1 Tim 3,16. Eine strukturanalytische Untersuchung* (RSTh 6; Frankfurt: P. Lang; Bern: H. Lang, 1977) 287pp.

Stewart, D.G., 'Ascension (of Christ)', *The Zondervan Pictorial Encyclopedia of the Bible* 1 (1975, 1976) 345-348.

Stone, M.E. (ed.), *Jewish Writings of the Second Temple Period. Apocrypha, Pseudepigrapha, Qumran Sectarian Writings, Philo, Josephus* (CRI 2/2; Assen: Van Gorcum; Philadelphia: Fortress, 1984) xxiii + 697pp.

Stone, M.E., *Fourth Ezra* (Hermeneia; Minneapolis, MN: Fortress, 1990) xxii + 496pp.

Stone, M.E., *Selected Studies in Pseudepigrapha and Apocrypha. With Special Reference to the Armenian Tradition* (SVTP 9; Leiden, New York, København, Köln: E.J. Brill, 1991) x + 473pp.

Stone, M.E., 'Coherence and Inconsistency in the Apocalypses. The Case of 'The End' in 4 Ezra' (1983); repr. in: M.E. Stone, *Selected Studies* (1991) 333-347.

Stone, M.E., 'The Question of the Messiah in 4 Ezra' (1968/1988); repr. in: M.E. Stone, *Selected Studies* (1991) 317-332.

Strack, H.L., Billerbeck, P., *Kommentar zum Neuen Testament aus Talmud und Midrasch* (München: C.H. Beck, 1922-28; repr. [8]1983) 6 vols.

Strange, W.A., *The Problem of the Text of Acts* (MSSNTS 71; Cambridge: CUP, 1992) xiii + 258pp.

Strauß, D.F., *Das Leben Jesu kritisch bearbeitet* (Tübingen: J.C.B. Mohr/Paul Siebeck, 1835; [4]1840) 2 vols.

Strauß, D.F., *Das Leben Jesu für das deutsche Volk bearbeitet* (Volksausgabe in unverkürzter Form; Stuttgart: Emil Strauß, A. Kröner, 1864, [16]o.J.) 2 vols., vii + 164; iv + 162pp.

Strecker, G., 'Entrückung', *RAC* 5 (1962) 461-476.

Streeder, G.J., 'Hemelvaart', *ChrEnc* 3 ([2]1958) 425-426.

Streeter, B.H., *The Four Gospels. A Study of Origins Treating of the Manuscript Tradition, Sources, Authorship, and Dates* (London: Macmillan, 1924, [4]1930) xxiv + 624pp.

Strobel, A., *Untersuchungen zum eschatologischen Verzögerungsproblem auf Grund der spätjüdisch-urchristlichen Geschichte von Habakuk 2,2ff.* (NT.S 2; Leiden, Köln: E.J. Brill, 1961) xxxi + 305pp.

Strobel, A., *Kerygma und Apokalyptik. Ein religionsgeschichtlicher und theologischer Beitrag zur Christusfrage* (Göttingen: Vandenhoeck & Ruprecht, 1967) 206pp.

Stuckenbruck, L.T., *Angel Veneration and Christology. A Study in Early Judaism and in the Christology of the Apocalypse of John* (WUNT 2/70; Tübingen: J.C.B. Mohr/Paul Siebeck, 1995) xviii + 348pp.

Stuhlmacher, P. (Hrsg.), *Das Evangelium und die Evangelien* (WUNT 28; Tübingen: J.C.B. Mohr/Paul Siebeck, 1983) viii + 454pp.

Swete, H.B., *The Apocalypse of St. John. The Greek Text with Introduction, Notes, and Indices* (London: Macmillan, 1906, ²1907) ccxix + 338pp.

Swete, H.B., *The Appearances of our Lord after the Passion. A Study in the Earliest Christian Tradition* (London: Macmillan, 1907) xviii + 151pp.

Swete, H.B., *The Ascended Christ. A Study in the Earliest Christian Teaching* (London: Macmillan, 1910; repr. 1916) xv + 168pp.

Tabor, J.D., *Things Unutterable. Paul's Ascent to Paradise in Its Greco-Roman, Judaic, and Early Christian Contexts* (Studies in Judaism; Lanham, MD: University Press of America, 1986) x + 155.

Tabor, J.D., "Returning to Divinity'. Josephus's Portrayal of the Disappearances of Enoch, Elijah, and Moses', *JBL* 108 (1989) 225-238.

Tait, A.J., *The Heavenly Session of Our Lord* (London: R. Scott, 1912)

Talbert, C.H., *Luke and the Gnostics. An Examination of the Lukan Purpose* (Nashville, New York: Abingdon, 1966) 127pp.

Talbert, C.H., 'An Anti-Gnostic Tendency in Lucan Christology', *NTS* 14 (1968) 259-271.

Talbert, C.H., 'The Redaction Critical Quest for Luke the Theologian', in: *Jesus and Man's Hope* 1 (Perspective; Pittsburgh, PN: Pittsburgh Theological Seminary, 1970) 171-222.

Talbert, C.H., *Literary Patterns, Theological Themes, and the Genre of Luke-Acts* (SBL.MS 20; Missoula, MO: Scholars, 1974) 159pp.

Talbert, C.H., 'The Concept of Immortals in Mediterranean Antiquity', *JBL* 94 (1975) 419-436.

Talbert, C.H., 'The Myth of a Descending-Ascending Redeemer in Mediterranean Antiquity', *NTS* 22 (1975/76) 418-440.

Tannehill, R.C., *The Narrative Unity of Luke-Acts. A Literary Interpretation* (Philadelphia, Minneapolis, MN: Fortress, 1986-1990) 2 vols., xv + 334; x + 398pp.

Teeple, H.M., *The Mosaic Eschatological Prophet* (SBL.MS 10; Philadelphia: SBL, 1957) xiii + 122pp.

Theisohn, J., *Der auserwählte Richter. Untersuchungen zum traditionsgeschichtlichen Ort der Menschensohngestalt der Bilderreden des Äthiopischen Henoch* (StUNT 12; Göttingen: Vandenhoeck & Ruprecht, 1975) xiv + 308pp.

Thiselton, A.C., *The Two Horizons. New Testament Hermeneutics and Philosophical Description with Special Reference to Heidegger, Bultmann, Gadamer, and Wittgenstein* (Exeter: Paternoster, 1980) xx + 484pp.

Thomas, W.H.G., 'Ascension', *ISBE* 1 (1929, ²1939) 263-266.

Thompson, K.C., *Received up into Glory. A Study of Ascension* (SCFP 11; Westminster, New York: Faith, 1964) 108pp.

Thüsing, W., *Die Erhöhung und Verherrlichung Jesu im Johannesevangelium* (NTA 21-1/2;

Münster: Aschendorff, 1960, [3]1979) xiv + 349pp.

Thüsing, W., *Erhöhungsvorstellung und Parusieerwartung in der ältesten nachösterlichen Christologie* (SBS 42; Stuttgart: KBW, 1969) 114pp.

Tiede, D.L., 'The Exaltation of Jesus and the Restoration of Israel in Acts 1', *SBL.SP* (1985) 369-375; repr. *HThR* 79 (1986) 278-286.

Tödt, H.E., *Der Menschensohn in der synoptischen Überlieferung* (Gütersloh: G. Mohn, 1959) 331pp.

Toinet, P., 'Himmelfahrt als Erhöhung des Menschen' [Sermons of Leo the Great] (übers. von H.U. von Balthasar), *IKZ* 12 (1983) 238-243.

Tom, W., 'Waar was Jezus gedurende de veertig dagen tusschen Zijn opstanding en hemelvaart?', *GThT* 39 (1938) 404-411.

Tom, W., 'Nog eens: waar was Jezus gedurende de veertig dagen tusschen Zijn opstanding en hemelvaart?', *GThT* 40 (1939) 303-306.

Tom, W., 'Het vraagteeken gehandhaafd', *GThT* 41 (1940) 129-131.

Toon, P., 'Historical Perspectives on the Doctrine of Christ's Ascension 1. Resurrected and Ascended: The Exalted Jesus', *BS* 140 (1983) 195-205.

Toon, P., 'Historical Perspectives on the Doctrine of Christ's Ascension 2. The Meaning of the Ascension for Christ', *BS* 140 (1983) 291-301.

Toon, P., 'Historical Perspectives on the Doctrine of Christ's Ascension 3. The Significance of the Ascension for Believers', *BS* 141 (1984) 16-27.

Toon, P., 'Historical Perspectives on the Doctrine of Christ's Ascension 4. The Exalted Jesus and God's Revelation', *BS* 141 (1984) 112-119.

Toon, P., *The Ascension of Our Lord* (Nashville, TN: Thomas Nelson, 1984) xiv + 153pp.

Torgovnick, M., *Closure in the Novel* (Princeton: Princeton University Press, 1981) x + 238pp.

Torm, F., 'Der Pluralis οὐρανοί', *ZNW* 33 (1934) 48-50.

Torrey, C.C., *The Composition and Date of Acts* (HThS 1; Cambridge, MA: Harvard University Press, 1916) 72pp.

Traub, H., Rad, G. von, οὐρανός, οὐράνιος, ἐπουράνιος, οὐρανόθεν, *ThWNT* 5 (1954) 496-543.

Unnik, W.C. van, 'Luke's Second Book and the Rules of Hellenistic Historiography', in: J. Kremer (éd.), *Les Actes des Apôtres* (1979) 37-60.

VanderKam, J.C., 'Enoch Traditions in Jubilees and Other Second-Century Sources', *SBL.SP* (1978) 229-251.

VanderKam, J.C., *Enoch and the Growth of an Apocalyptic Tradition* (CBQ.MS 16; Washington: Catholic Biblical Association of America, 1984) x + 217pp.

Varro, R., 'Séparé mais présent (Ascension: Luc 24,36-53)', in: G. Becquot, *Lectures d'évangiles pour les dimanches* (Année C) (Paris: Seuil, 1973) 379-393.

Vellmer, E., 'Die Geschichte von Jesu Himmelfahrt und der moderne Mensch', *DtPfrBl* 62 (1962) 291-293.

Verhoef, P.A., *Maleachi* (COT; Kampen: J.H. Kok, 1972) 279pp.

Vielhauer, Ph., 'Zum Paulinismus der Apostelgeschichte' (1950/51); repr. in: idem, *Aufsätze zum Neuen Testament* (1965) 9-27.

Vielhauer, Ph., 'Ein Weg zur neutestamentlichen Christologie? Prüfung der Thesen Ferdinand Hahns', in: idem, *Aufsätze zum Neuen Testament* (1965) 141-198.

Vielhauer, Ph., *Aufsätze zum Neuen Testament* (TB 31; München: Chr. Kaiser, 1965) 282pp.

Villahoz, J.M., *La Ascensión a los cielos* (Diss. lic. Studii Franciscani; Jerusalem, 1972) vi + 85pp.

Violet, B., 'Ein Versuch zu Joh. 20,17', *ZNW* 24 (1925) 78-80.

Vögtle, A., "Erhöht zur Rechten Gottes': Braucht der Osterglaube die Krücken des antiken Weltbildes?', *Orien.* 45 (1981) 78-80.

Vollert, W., 'Die Bedeutung der Himmelfahrt für Christum', *NKZ* 7 (1896) 389-427.

Vollert, W., 'Die Bedeutung der Himmelfahrt Christi für die Kirche und für den einzelnen Gläubigen', *NKZ* 7 (1896) 937-963.

Völter, D., 'Der Anfang der Apostelgeschichte', *PrM* 19 (1915) 93-96.

Volz, P., *Die Eschatologie der jüdischen Gemeinde in neutestamentlichen Zeitalter nach den Quellen der rabbinischen, apokalyptischen und apokryphen Literatur dargestellt* (Tübingen: J.C.B. Mohr/Paul Siebeck, ²1934) xvi + 458pp.

Voss, G., *Die Christologie der lukanischen Schriften in Grundzügen* (SN 2; Paris: Desclée de Brouwer, 1965) 219pp.

W., V.D., 'Jezus op de bergen', *Wat Zegt de Schrift?* 3 (1902) 78-80.

Wager, C.E., 'Eduard Meyer on our Lord's Ascension', *ET* 44 (1932/33) 491-495.

Wagner, J.B., *Ascendit ad coelos. The Doctrine of the Ascension in the Reformed and Lutheran Theology of the Period of Orthodoxy* (Winterthur, 1964; Diss. Basel) x + 147pp.

Walker, W.G., *The Doctrine of the Ascension of Christ in Reformed Theology* (Ph.D. Diss. Vanderbilt University, 1968).

Walsh, B.J., Keesmaat, S.C., 'Reflections on the Ascension', *Theol.* 95 (1992) 193-200.

Waltke, B.K., "He Ascended and Sitteth ...'. Reflections on the Sixth Article of the Apostles' Creed', *Crux* 30 (1994) 2-8.

Walvoord, J.F., 'The Ascension of Christ', *BS* 121 (1964) 3-12.

Wanke, J., *Die Emmauserzählung. Eine redaktionsgeschichtliche Untersuchung zu Lk 24,13-35* (EThSt 31; Leipzig: St. Benno, 1973) xviii + 193pp.

Wehring, 'Himmelfahrt II. Himmelfahrt Christi', *RGG* 2 (²1928) 1898-1899.

Weinert, F.D., 'The Meaning of the Temple in Luke-Acts', *BTB* 11 (1981) 85-89.

Weinert, F.-R., *Christi Himmelfahrt. Neutestamentliches Fest im Spiegel alttestamentlicher Psalmen. Zur Entstehung des römischen Himmelfahrtsoffiziums* (Diss.T 25; St. Ottilien: EOS, 1987) viii + 361pp.

Weinstock, S., *Divus Julius* (Oxford: Clarendon, 1971) xvi + 469pp.

Weiser, A., (review of G. Lohfink, *Die Himmelfahrt Jesu*), in: H. Kahlefeld, O. Knoch (Hrsg.), *Die Episteln und Evangelien der Sonn- und Festtage. Auslegung und Verkündigung. Die Episteln. Lesejahre A* (Frankfurt: 1972) 279-282.

Weiser, A., 'Himmelfahrt Christi I. Neues Testament', *TRE* 15 (1986) 330-334.

Weiss, B., *Die Evangelien des Markus und Lukas* (KEK II⁹; Göttingen: Vandenhoeck & Ruprecht, 1876, ⁴1901) iv + 694pp.

Wellhausen, J., *Kritische Analyse der Apostelgeschichte* (AGWG.PH NF 15/2; Berlin: Weidmann, 1914) 56pp.

Wendt, H.H., *Die Apostelgeschichte* (KEK II⁸; Göttingen: Vandenhoeck & Ruprecht, 1880, ⁴1899) 427pp.

Wensinck, A.J., 'Hemelvaart', in: *Semietische Studiën uit de nalatenschap van Prof. Dr. A.J. Wensinck* (Leiden: A.W. Sijthoff, 1941) 114-123.

Wenz, H., 'Ist die Geschichte von Jesu Himmelfahrt wirklich erledigt?', *DtPfrBl* 62 (1962) 222-224.

Weterman, J.A.M., 'De Hemelvaart des Heren in het N.T.', *NKS* 50 (1954) 129-138.

Wiefel, W., *Das Evangelium nach Lukas* (ThHK 3; Berlin: Evangelische, 1988) xviii + 418pp.

Wiener, A., *The Prophet Elijah in the Development of Judaism. A Depth-Psychological Study* (Littman Library of Jewish Civilization; London, Henley, Boston: Routledge & Kegan Paul, 1978) xii + 248pp.

Wieseler, K., *Chronologische Synopse der vier Evangelien. Ein Beitrag zur Apologie der Evangelien und evangelischen Geschichte vom Standpuncte der Voraussetzungslosigkeit* (Hamburg: 1843).

Wieseler, K., *Beiträge zur richtigen Würdigung der Evangelien und der evangelischen Geschichte. Eine Zugabe zu des Verfassers 'Chronologischer Synopse der vier Evangelien'* (Gotha: 1869).

Wikenhauser, A., *Die Apostelgeschichte übersetzt und erklärt* (RNT 5; Regensburg: F. Pustet, 1938, ⁴1961) 298pp.

Wikenhauser, A., 'Die Belehrung der Apostel durch den Auferstandenen nach Apg 1:3', in: N. Adler (Hrsg.), *Vom Wort des Lebens* (FS Max Meinert; NTA 1; Münster: Aschendorff, 1951) 105-113.

Wilcke, K., *Christi Himmelfahrt. Ihre Darstellung in der europäischen Literatur von der Spätantike bis zum ausgehenden Mittelalter* (Beiträge zur älteren Literaturgeschichte; Heidelberg: C.F. Winter, 1991) 505pp.

Wilckens, U., *Die Missionsreden der Apostelgeschichte. Form- und traditionsgeschichtliche Untersuchungen* (WMANT 5; Neukirchen-Vluyn: Neukirchener, 1961, ³1974) 268pp.

Wilckens, U., 'Exaudi. Apostelgeschichte 1,6-12', *GPM* 18 (1963/64) 195-200.

Wilckens, U., *Auferstehung. Das biblische Auferstehungszeugnis historisch untersucht und erklärt* (GTB.S 80; Gütersloh: G. Mohn, 1970, ³1981) 123pp.

Wilcox, M., *The Semitisms of Acts* (Oxford: Clarendon, 1965) xiii + 206pp.

Wilder, A.N., 'Variant Traditions of the Resurrection in Acts', *JBL* 62 (1943) 307-318.

Willems, G.F., 'Quelques textes rabbiniques anciens à propos du prophète Élie', in: idem (éd.), *Élie le prophète. Bible, tradition, iconographie. Colloque des 10 et 11 novembres 1985, Bruxelles* (Publication de l'Institutum Iudaicum; Leuven: Peeters, 1988) 91-114.

Williams, C.S.C., *A Commentary on the Acts of the Apostles* (BNTC; London: A.&C. Black; New York: Harper, 1957, ²1964) xvi + 301pp.

Williams, D.J., *Acts* (GNC 5; San Francisco: Harper & Row; Toronto: Fitzhenry & Whiteside, 1985; rev. ed. NIBC 5; Peabody: Hendrickson, 1990) xvi + 493pp.

Williams, R., 'Ascension of Christ', in: A. Richardson, J. Bowden (eds.), *A New Dictionary of Christian Theology* (London: SCM, 1983; repr. 1984) 44-45.

Willink, M.D.R., 'Studies in Texts. 'A Cloud Received Him' (Acts 1,9)', *Theol.* 14 (1927) 297-299.

Wilson, S.G., 'The Ascension. A Critique and an Interpretation', *ZNW* 59 (1968) 269-281.

Wilson, S.G., *The Gentiles and the Gentile Mission in Luke-Acts* (MSSNTS 23; Cambridge: CUP, 1973) xi + 295pp.

Wilson, S.G., *Luke and the Pastoral Epistles* (London: SPCK, 1979) xii + 162pp.

Winston, D., *The Wisdom of Solomon. A New Translation with Introduction and Commentary* (AncB 43; Garden City, NY: Doubleday, 1979) xxiv + 359pp.

Winter, B.W., Clark, A.D. (eds.), *The Book of Acts in its Ancient Literary Setting* (BAFCS 1; Grand Rapids: Eerdmans; Carlisle: Paternoster, 1993) 504pp.

Wißmann, H., 'Entrückung I. Religionsgeschichtlich', *TRE* 9 (1982) 680-683.

Wright, J.S., 'The Ascension', *NBDict* (1962, ²1982) 93.

Wright, J.S., 'Ascension', *IBD* 1 (1980) 129.

Young, G.M., 'A Parallel to Act 1,9', *JThS* 1/2 (1950/51) 156.

Yüek Yün-feng, P., 'Yehsu shengt'ien. The Ascension of Christ', *CTUF* 9/34 (1977) 535-546.

Zahn, Th., *Das Evangelium des Lucas* (KNT 3; Leipzig: A. Deichert, Werner Scholl, 1913, ³·⁴·1920) vi + 774pp.

Zahn, Th., *Das Evangelium des Johannes* (KNT 4; Leipzig: A. Deichert, Werner Scholl, 1908, ³·⁴·1920) vi + 729pp.

Zahn, Th., *Die Apostelgeschichte des Lucas* (KNT 5; Leipzig: A. Deichert, Werner Scholl, Bd I. ³1922; Bd. II 1921) 2 vols., 394pp. + 494pp.

Zahn, Th., *Die Urausgabe der Apostelgeschichte des Lucas* (FGNK 9; Leipzig: A. Deichert, Werner Scholl, 1916) 400pp.

Zahn, Th., 'Die Himmelfahrt Jesu an einem Sabbath', *NKZ* 33 (1922) 535-541.

Zedtwitz, K. von, *Die Auferstehung Jesu in der christologischen Interpretation von Apg. 2:24-31 und 13:32-37. Eine motiv-, form- und traditionsgeschichtliche Untersuchung* (Diss. Freiburg im Breisgau, 1981; ) x + 380 + 62pp.

Zehnle, R.F., *Peter's Pentecost Discourse. Tradition and Lukan Reinterpretation in Peter's Speeches of Acts 2 and 3* (SBL.MS 15; Nashville, New York: Abingdon, 1971) 144pp.

Zmijewski, J., 'Apg 1 als literarischer und theologischer Anfang der Apostelgeschichte', in: idem, *Das Neue Testament. Quelle christlicher Theologie und Glaubenspraxis. Aufsätze zum Neuen Testament und seiner Auslegung* (Stuttgart: KBW, 1986) 67-84.

Zmijewski, J., *Die Apostelgeschichte übersetzt und erklärt* (RNT 5; Regensburg: F. Pustet, 1994) 971pp.

Zwemer, S.M., 'The Ascension', *EvQ* 19 (1947) 247-254.

Zwemer, S., 'The Last Twelve Verses of the Gospel of Mark', in: D.O. Fuller (ed.), *Counterfeit or Genuine—Mark 16? John 8?* (Grand Rapids: Grand Rapids International Publications, 1975) 159-174.

Zwiep, A., 'De hemelvaart', *Uit de Levensbron. Wekelijkse predicatiën* 19 (1949) 237-252.

Zwiep, A.W., 'The Text of the Ascension Narratives (Luke 24.50-3; Acts 1.1-2, 9-11)', *NTS* 42 (1996) 219-244.

# INDEX OF PASSAGES

## a. OT and Apocrypha

*Genesis*

| | |
|---|---|
| 3:19 | 77 |
| 5 | 42 |
| 5:5 | 41 |
| 5:8 | 41 |
| 5:11 | 41 |
| 5:14 | 41 |
| 5:17 | 41 |
| 5:20 | 41 |
| 5:21-24 | 41, 42 |
| 5:21-31 | 47 |
| 5:22 | 42, 47 |
| 5:24 | 21, 41, 42, 44 |
| | 58, 79, 185, 196 |
| 5:24a | 42, 43 |
| 5:24b | 42 |
| 5:27 | 41 |
| 5:28-15:4 | 47 |
| 5:31 | 41 |
| 6:1-4 | 45 |
| 6:9 | 42 |
| 17:22 | 22 |
| 18 | 160 |
| 25:24 | 85 |
| 35:1 | 12 |
| 35:13 | 22 |
| 47:29 | 84 |
| 48 | 88 |

*Exodus*

| | |
|---|---|
| 2:23 | 102 |
| 3f. | 160 |
| 4:19 | 102 |
| 16:35 | 4 |
| 19:17-20 | 163 |
| 24 | 65 |
| 24:18 | 4, 71 |
| 29:38-42 | 33 |
| 30:1-9 | 33 |

| | |
|---|---|
| 34:28 | 71 |

*Leviticus*

| | |
|---|---|
| 2:13 | 101 |
| 9:22 | 32, 88 |
| 12:4 | 84 |
| 12:6 | 84 |
| 25:29 | 84 |
| 25:30 | 84 |

*Numbers*

| | |
|---|---|
| 6:13 | 84 |
| 16:9 | 50 |
| 25:11 | 75 |

*Deuteronomy*

| | |
|---|---|
| 4:46 | 68 |
| 6:13 | 93 |
| 9:9 | 71 |
| 9:18 | 71 |
| 9:25 | 71 |
| 10:8 | 50 |
| 10:10 | 71 |
| 17:12 | 50 |
| 18:5 | 50 |
| 21:17 | 58 |
| 30:12 | 135, 136 |
| 30:12-14 | 140 |
| 31:14 | 84 |
| 33 | 88 |
| 34:1-3 | 74 |
| 34:5-8 | 64 |
| 34:6 | 64, 68 |
| 34:10 | 71 |

*Joshua*

| | |
|---|---|
| 8:1 | 12 |
| 15:78 | 68 |

*Judges*
6 . . . . . . . . . . . . . . . . . . . . . . . . . . 160
6:21 . . . . . . . . . . . . . . . . . . . . . . . 22
11:36 . . . . . . . . . . . . . . . . . . . . . . 56
13 . . . . . . . . . . . . . . . . . . . . . . . . . 160
13:20 . . . . . . . . . . . . . . . . . . . . . . 93

*1 Samuel*
3 . . . . . . . . . . . . . . . . . . . . . . . . . . 160

*2 Samuel*
7:12 . . . . . . . . . . . . . . . . . . . . . . . 84
23:3 . . . . . . . . . . . . . . . . . . . . . . . 56

*1 Kings*
2:1 . . . . . . . . . . . . . . . . . . . . . . . . 84
8:11 . . . . . . . . . . . . . . . . . . . . . . . 50
8:54-61 . . . . . . . . . . . . . . . . . . . . 88
17:1 . . . . . . . . . . . . . . . . . . . . . . . 61
18:38 . . . . . . . . . . . . . . . . . . . . . . 59
19:8 . . . . . . . . . . . . . . . . . . . . 4, 12

*2 Kings*
1:1-2:6 . . . . . . . . . . . . . . . . . . . . . 80
1:10 . . . . . . . . . . . . . . . . . . . . . . . 59
1:12 . . . . . . . . . . . . . . . . . . . . . . . 59
2 . . . . . . . . 21, 33, 62, 79, 87, 106, 185
2:1-15 . . . . . . . . . . . . . . . . . . . . . . 59
2:1-18 . . . . . . . . . . . . 58, 59, 194, 196
2:1 . . . . . . . . . . . . . . . . . 58-61, 80
2:1b . . . . . . . . . . . . . . . . . . . . . . . 58
2:2 . . . . . . . . . . . . . . . . . . . . . 58, 59
2:2-15 . . . . . . . . . . . . . . . . . . . . . . 59
2:3 . . . . . . . . . . . . . . . . . . . . 41, 59
2:4 . . . . . . . . . . . . . . . . . . . . 58, 59
2:5 . . . . . . . . . . . . . . . . . . . . . . . . 41
2:6 . . . . . . . . . . . . . . . . . . . . 58, 59
2:7 . . . . . . . . . . . . . . . . . . . . . . . . 58
2:8 . . . . . . . . . . . . . . . . . . . . . . . . 58
2:9 . . . . . . . . . . . . . . . . . . 41, 58, 59
2:9-10 . . . . . . . . . . . . . . . . . . . . . 194
2:9-11 . . . . . . . . . . . . . . . . . . . . . . 15
2:10 . . . . . . . . . . . . . 41, 58, 81, 194
2:11 . . . . . . . . . . . . . . . . . 58-61, 81
2:12 . . . . . . . . . . . . . . . . . . . . . . . 58
2:12-14 . . . . . . . . . . . . . . . . . . . . . 93

2:13-14 . . . . . . . . . . . . . . . . . 58, 59
2:15 . . . . . . . . . . . . . . . . . 58, 59, 93
2:16-18 . . . . . . . . . . . . . . . . . 58, 59
2:17 . . . . . . . . . . . . . . . . . . . . . . . 41
6:17 . . . . . . . . . . . . . . . . . . . . . . . 58
7:6 . . . . . . . . . . . . . . . . . . . . . . . . 58
13:14 . . . . . . . . . . . . . . . . . . . . . . 58
19:10 . . . . . . . . . . . . . . . . . . . . . . 60
19:14 . . . . . . . . . . . . . . . . . . . . . . 60

*1 Chronicles*
1:3 . . . . . . . . . . . . . . . . . . . . . . . . 42
17:11 . . . . . . . . . . . . . . . . . . . . . . 84

*2 Chronicles*
3:6 . . . . . . . . . . . . . . . . . . . . . . . . 47
5:14 . . . . . . . . . . . . . . . . . . . . . . . 50
14:9 . . . . . . . . . . . . . . . . . . . . . . . 68
21:12 . . . . . . . . . . . . . . . . . . . . . . 63
26:9 . . . . . . . . . . . . . . . . . . . . . . . 68
29:11 . . . . . . . . . . . . . . . . . . . . . . 50

*Ezra*
7:1-5 . . . . . . . . . . . . . . . . . . . . . . 72
7:6 . . . . . . . . . . . . . . . . . . . . . . . . 72
7:11 . . . . . . . . . . . . . . . . . . . . . . . 72
7:12 . . . . . . . . . . . . . . . . . . . . . . . 72
7:21 . . . . . . . . . . . . . . . . . . . . . . . 72
10:10 . . . . . . . . . . . . . . . . . . . . . . 72
10:16 . . . . . . . . . . . . . . . . . . . . . . 72

*2 Ezra*
12:15 . . . . . . . . . . . . . . . . . . . . . . 68
13:13 . . . . . . . . . . . . . . . . . . . . . . 68
21:30 . . . . . . . . . . . . . . . . . . . . . . 68

*Nehemiah*
2:15 . . . . . . . . . . . . . . . . . . . . . . . 68
3:13 . . . . . . . . . . . . . . . . . . . . . . . 68
8:2 . . . . . . . . . . . . . . . . . . . . . . . . 72
8:5 . . . . . . . . . . . . . . . . . . . . . . . . 72
8:9 . . . . . . . . . . . . . . . . . . . . . . . . 72
8:14 . . . . . . . . . . . . . . . . . . . . . . . 72
11:30 . . . . . . . . . . . . . . . . . . . . . . 68
12:26 . . . . . . . . . . . . . . . . . . . . . . 72
12:36 . . . . . . . . . . . . . . . . . . . . . . 72

*Tobit*
5 . . . . . . . . . . . . . . . . . . . . . . . . . . . 160
6:5 . . . . . . . . . . . . . . . . . . . . . . . . . 101
8:20 . . . . . . . . . . . . . . . . . . . . . . . . 84
10:1 . . . . . . . . . . . . . . . . . . . . . . . . 84
12 . . . . . . . . . . . . . . . . . . . . . . . 12, 160
12:16-22 . . . . . . . . . . . . . . . . . . . . 87
12:20-22 . . . . . . . . . . . . . . . . . . . . 22
14:5 . . . . . . . . . . . . . . . . . . . . . . . . . 84

*Esther*
1:3 . . . . . . . . . . . . . . . . . . . . . . . . . . 84
1:5 . . . . . . . . . . . . . . . . . . . . . . . . . . 84
3:1 . . . . . . . . . . . . . . . . . . . . . . . . . 125

*1 Maccabees*
2:54 . . . . . . . . . . . . . . . . . . . . . . . . . 75
2:58 . . . . . . . . . 15, 59, 60, 75, 81, 194
4:46 . . . . . . . . . . . . . . . . . . . . . . . . . 60
9:8 . . . . . . . . . . . . . . . . . . . . . . . . . . 12
14:41 . . . . . . . . . . . . . . . . . . . . . . . . 60

*2 Maccabees*
2:4-8 . . . . . . . . . . . . . . . . . . . . . . . . 77
7 . . . . . . . . . . . . . . . . . . . . . . . . . . . 177
15:14-16 . . . . . . . . . . . . . . . . . . . . . 77
18:12 . . . . . . . . . . . . . . . . . . . . . . . . 75

*Job*
5:11 . . . . . . . . . . . . . . . . . . . . . . . . . 56
12:19 . . . . . . . . . . . . . . . . . . . . . . . . 56
38:1 . . . . . . . . . . . . . . . . . . . . . . . . . 61

*Psalms*
2:7 . . . . . . . . . . . . . . . 56, 124, 125, 158
9:9 . . . . . . . . . . . . . . . . . . . . . . . . . . 56
15:8-11 LXX . . . . . . . . . . . . . . 153, 154
15:11 LXX . . . . . . . . . . . . . . . . . . . 155
15:11c LXX . . . . . . . . . . . . . . . . . . . 155
16 . . . . . . . . . . . . . . . . . . . . . . . . . . 155
16:8-11 . . . . . . . . . . . . . . . . . 125, 154
16:10 . . . . . . . . . . . . . . . . . . . . . . . 159
16:15 LXX . . . . . . . . . . . . . . . . . . . 158
18:11 . . . . . . . . . . . . . . . . . . . . . . . . 60
21:3 LXX . . . . . . . . . . . . . . . . . . . . . 56
24 . . . . . . . . . . . . . . . . . . . . . . . . . . 120

24 (23 LXX) . . . . . . . . . . . . . . . . . 120
46:6 LXX . . . . . . . . . . . . . . . . . . . 120
47:6 . . . . . . . . . . . . . . . . . . . . . . . . 120
49 . . . . . . . . . . . . . . . . . . . . . . . . . . 45
49:16 . . . . . . . . . . . . . . . . . . . . 44, 45
50:3 . . . . . . . . . . . . . . . . . . . . . . . . . 60
59:2 // 60:2 MT . . . . . . . . . . . . . . . 68
67:19 LXX . . . . . . . . . . . . . . 119, 156
68 . . . . . . . . . . . . . . . . . . . . . . . . . 140
68:19 . . . . . . . . . . . 119, 125, 140, 156
73 . . . . . . . . . . . . . . . . . . . . . . . . . . 45
73:24 . . . . . . . . . . . . . . . . . . . . 44, 45
96:13 . . . . . . . . . . . . . . . . . . . . . . . . 56
98:9 . . . . . . . . . . . . . . . . . . . . . . . . . 56
104:3 . . . . . . . . . . . . . . . . . . . . . . . . 60
105:4 LXX . . . . . . . . . . . . . . . . . . . 150
109:1 LXX . . . . . . . . . . 119, 125, 153
110 . . . . . . . . . . . 32, 126, 133, 143
. . . . . . . . . . . . . . . . . 149, 163, 182
110:1 . . . . . . . . . . 3, 16, 32-34, 71, 119
. . . . . . . . . . . . . . 124-128, 132, 148
. . . . . . . . . . . . . . . 154, 155, 163, 182
110:4 . . . . . . . . . . . . . . . . . . . . 32, 33
111:9 . . . . . . . . . . . . . . . . . . . . . . . . 56
115:16 . . . . . . . . . . . . . . . . . . . . . . . 60
117:16 LXX . . . . . . . . . . . . . . . . . . 155
118:16 . . . . . . . . . . . . . . . . . . . . . . 125
118:22 . . . . . . . . . . . . . . . . . . . . . . 125
122:5 . . . . . . . . . . . . . . . . . . . . . . . 125

*Proverbs*
30:4 . . . . . . . . . . . . . . . . . . . 135, 136

*Ecclesiastes*
7:15 . . . . . . . . . . . . . . . . . . . . . . . . . 44
8:14 . . . . . . . . . . . . . . . . . . . . . . . . . 44

*Wisdom of Solomon*
3:2 . . . . . . . . . . . . . . . . . . . . . . . . . . 86
4:7 . . . . . . . . . . . . . . . . . . . . . . . . . . 44
4:10 . . . . . . . . . . . . . . . . . . . 42, 43, 44
4:10-14 . . . . . . . . . . . . . . . . . . . . . . 44
4:11 . . . . . . . . . . . . . . . . . . . . . . . . . 44
4:14 . . . . . . . . . . . . . . . . . . . . . . . . . 44
5:11 . . . . . . . . . . . . . . . . . . . . . . . . . 97
7:6 . . . . . . . . . . . . . . . . . . . . . . . . . . 86

10:1 .......................... 44
10:3-6 ........................ 44
10.10 ......................... 44
10:13 ......................... 44
10:16 ......................... 44
11:1 .......................... 44
12:3 .......................... 44
14:6 .......................... 44
15:14 ......................... 44
18:5 .......................... 44
18:21 ......................... 44
19:13 ......................... 97
19:14 ......................... 44
19:17 ......................... 44

*Sirach*
10:14 ......................... 56
35:22 ......................... 56
44:1-49:16 ................. 43, 88
44:16 ............... 41, 43, 44
44:16a ........................ 43
44:16b ........................ 43
44:17 ......................... 43
45:15 ......................... 32
45:23 ......................... 75
48-50 ........................ 185
48:1 ....................... 59, 61
48:2 .......................... 75
48:3 ....................... 59, 61
48:4-10 ....................... 61
48:9 ............... 15, 59-61, 81
48:9-12 .......... 44, 61, 194, 196
48:10 ........................ 114
48:11 ......................... 61
48:11c ........................ 62
48:12 ................. 60, 61, 194
49:14 .............. 41, 43, 44, 81
49:14-16 ...................... 43
49:16 ......................... 43
50 ........................ 15, 88
50:19-23 ................... 87, 93
50:20 ...................... 32, 88
50:20-22 ...................... 20
50:20-23 .................. 88, 116
50:21 ................. 88, 93, 186
50:22 ......................... 88

50:23 ..................... 88, 186

*Isaiah*
2:2 LXX ..................... 183
22:1 .......................... 68
22:5 .......................... 68
32:1 .......................... 56
40:4 .......................... 68
40:5 LXX .................... 170
42:1 .......................... 56
47:2 ......................... 101
49:6 .......................... 61
53:8 ......................... 139
53:11 ......................... 56
55:3 LXX .................... 158
57:1-2 ........................ 44
60:20 ......................... 84
61 .......................... 170
62:8 ......................... 158
63:4 .......................... 56

*Jeremiah*
7:31 .......................... 68
7:32 .......................... 68
25:34 MT (32:34 LXX) .......... 85
31:6 .......................... 12
36:26 ......................... 74
36:32 ......................... 74
39:35 // 32:35 MT ............. 68

*Lamentations*
4:18 .......................... 84

*Baruch*
3:29 .................... 135, 136

*Ezekiel*
1:4 ........................... 60
3:12-15 ....................... 81
6:3 ........................... 68
8:3 ........................... 81
11:1 .......................... 81
11:24 ......................... 81
12:21-28 ..................... 181
16:4 ......................... 101
21:31 ......................... 56

31:12 .......................... 68
35:8 .......................... 68
36:4 .......................... 68
36:26-27 .................... 182
44:15 .......................... 50
47:13-48:29 .................... 61

*Daniel*
2:28 .......................... 114
4:34 .......................... 56
7:9 .......................... 125
7:13 .................... 105, 148
7:13-14 .................... 119
7:13ff. .......................... 56

*Joel*
3:1 LXX .................... 183
3:1-5 .................... 153, 182

*Nahum*

1:3 .......................... 60

*Habakkuk*
2:2ff. .......................... 181
2:3 .......................... 181

*Zechariah*
9:9 .......................... 56
9:14 .......................... 60
14:4 .................... 33, 107, 108
14:5 .......................... 68

*Malachi*
2:6 .......................... 42
3 .......................... 79, 185
3:22 .......................... 114, 115
3:22-23 .................... 194, 196
3:22-24 .......................... 61
3:23 .......................... 194
3:23-24 .................... 60, 61

## b. Jewish Pseudepigrapha

*Apocalypse of Elijah*
4:7-19 .......................... 49
5:32 .......................... 49

*Aristeas, Letter of*
118:3 .......................... 68

*Ascension of Isaiah*
9:16 .......................... 99
11:23 .......................... 141

*Assumption of Moses*
10:12 .......................... 66

*2 Baruch*
13:3 .................... 75, 114
21:18-19 .................... 103
23:7 .......................... 56
25:1 .................... 75, 114
30:1 .................... 77, 151
32:2-4 .......................... 79
43:2 .......................... 74

44:2 .................... 36, 74
46:1 .......................... 36
46:2 .......................... 67
46:7 .......................... 74
48:30 .......................... 74
48:33 .......................... 40
48:36 .......................... 40
55:6 .......................... 75
59:5-11 .......................... 65
73:1 .......................... 115
76 .......................... 21, 185
76:1-5 .......................... 74
76:2 .................... 74, 114
76:3 .......................... 108
76:4 .................... 75, 78
78:5 .................... 36, 74
81:2 .......................... 103
84:1 .................... 36, 74
85:10 .......................... 181

*4 Baruch*
9:3 .......................... 81

*1 Enoch*

| | |
|---|---|
| 1-13 | 46 |
| 1:9 | 58 |
| 12:1-2 | 45 |
| 12:4 | 46 |
| 15:1 | 46 |
| 17-36 | 46 |
| 19:1 | 106 |
| 22 | 177 |
| 22:3 | 106 |
| 23:4 | 106 |
| 24:2 | 68 |
| 26:3 | 68 |
| 26:4 | 68 |
| 26:5 | 68 |
| 26:6 | 68 |
| 27:1 | 68 |
| 30:1 | 68 |
| 30:3 | 68 |
| 37-71 | 49, 52 |
| 39:3 | 52, 104 |
| 39:4 | 56 |
| 40:5 | 56 |
| 41:9 | 56 |
| 42 | 40 |
| 45:3 | 56, 125 |
| 45:4 | 56 |
| 46 | 55 |
| 46:2 | 53, 54 |
| 46:3 | 53, 54 |
| 46:4 | 53, 56 |
| 47:1-2 | 56 |
| 48:2 | 53 |
| 48:7 | 56 |
| 49:2 | 56 |
| 49:4 | 56 |
| 51:2 | 56 |
| 51:3 | 125 |
| 53:6 | 56 |
| 55:4 | 125 |
| 58:1-69:29 | 52 |
| 60:8 | 53 |
| 60:23 | 48 |
| 61:8 | 125 |
| 61:12 | 53 |
| 62:5 | 53 |

| | |
|---|---|
| 62:7 | 53 |
| 62:9 | 53 |
| 62:14 | 53 |
| 62:14-16 | 54 |
| 63:10 | 56 |
| 63:11 | 53 |
| 69:26 | 53 |
| 69:27 | 53 |
| 69:27-29 | 125 |
| 69:29 | 53 |
| 70-71 | 52, 53, 55-57, 111, 133 |
| 70:1 | 53 |
| 70:1-2 | 52 |
| 70:3 | 53 |
| 70:3-4 | 52 |
| 70:4 | 53 |
| 71:1 | 53 |
| 71:1-4 | 53 |
| 71:5 | 53 |
| 71:10 | 53 |
| 71:11 | 53 |
| 71:13 | 53-55 |
| 71:14 | 53-55 |
| 71:14-17 | 54, 55 |
| 71:15 | 53-55 |
| 71:16 | 54, 55 |
| 71:17 | 53-55 |
| 72-82 | 46 |
| 76:14 | 46 |
| 79:1 | 46 |
| 80-81 | 46 |
| 81:1-2 | 47 |
| 81:5 | 46 |
| 81:5ff. | 78 |
| 81:6 | 46 |
| 82:1 | 46 |
| 82:1-3 | 47 |
| 83-90 | 46 |
| 87:3 | 53 |
| 87:3-4 | 46 |
| 88:1-90:42 | 46 |
| 89:52 | 48 |
| 89:53 | 62 |
| 90:31 | 48, 53, 62 |
| 92:1 | 47 |
| 93:1 | 46 |

93:8 .......................... 62
99:3 .......................... 56
106-107 ...................... 47
106:7-8 ...................... 48
106:18 ....................... 48

*2 Enoch*
1-67 .......................... 50
3:1 ...................... 53, 104
7:4-5 ......................... 46
18:8 .......................... 50
21:1 .......................... 50
21:3 .......................... 50
22:5 .......................... 50
22:7 .......................... 50
22:8-10 ....................... 49
23:1-4 ........................ 46
24:1 .......................... 49
36:1f. ........................ 78
36:2-3 ........................ 49
39:3-5 ........................ 49
39:8 .......................... 50
40:13 ......................... 46
42:6 .......................... 50
53:2 .......................... 46
55:1-3 ........................ 49
56:1 ...................... 50, 87
57:2 ...................... 50, 87
64:4 ...................... 50, 87
64:5 ...................... 46, 50
67 ...................... 21, 49, 50
67:1 ...................... 50, 90
67:1-3 ........................ 49
67:2 ...................... 50, 53
67:3 .......................... 50
68:1-7 ........................ 49
68:1-73:9 ..................... 49
68:2 .......................... 46
71-72 ......................... 76
71 ............................ 76
71:11 ......................... 76
71:29 ......................... 76
71:33 ......................... 76
71:34 ......................... 76
71:37 ......................... 76
72 ........................... 142

72:1 .......................... 78
72:2 .......................... 76
72:6 .......................... 76

*3 Enoch*
1:9 ........................... 51
3-15 .......................... 51
3:1 ........................... 51
5:1 ........................... 51
9:2-5 ......................... 51
10:3 .......................... 51
12:5 ...................... 39, 51
15:1-2 ........................ 51
16 ............................ 51
48:1 D (90) ................... 39
48:1-12 ....................... 51
48:7 C ........................ 39

*Ezekiel the Tragedian* .............. 65

*4 Ezra*
1-2 ........................... 72
3-14 .......................... 72
4:8 ...................... 135, 136
4:26 ......................... 181
4:33-50 ...................... 181
4:33-52 ...................... 103
5:9ff. ........................ 40
6:11-12 ...................... 103
6:26 .................. 48, 62, 73
7:15 ...................... 36, 74
7:28-29 ....................... 77
7:75 ......................... 114
7:75-101 ..................... 177
8:5 ...................... 36, 74
8:20 .......................... 72
8:51 .......................... 73
8:52 ...................... 72, 114
8:53 .......................... 72
8:61 ......................... 181
10:1-4 ....................... 139
10:34 ..................... 36, 74
11 ........................... 115
11:44 ........................ 181
11:46 ........................ 115
12:2-3 ....................... 115

12:32 ..................... 73, 114
12:34 ..................... 115
12:37 38 ................... 72
13:26 ..................... 73, 114
14 ..................... 21, 75, 185
14:1-18 .................... 72
14:1-48 .................... 72
14:7-9 ..................... 72
14:9 ............. 48, 62, 73, 114
14:19-26 ................. 72, 73
14:23 ..................... 73, 78
14:24 ..................... 73
14:27-36 .................. 73
14:36 ..................... 73, 78
14:37 ..................... 73
14:42 ..................... 4, 73, 78
14:44 ..................... 73, 78
14:45 ..................... 73, 78
14:48 ..................... 72, 73
15-16 ..................... 72, 73

*Greek Apocalypse of Ezra*
1:7 ........................ 81
5:7 ..................... 22, 104
7:6 ...................... 59, 63

*Hellenistic Synagogal Prayers*
7:3 ........................ 51
8:3 ........................ 51
12:55 ...................... 51
16:8 ....................... 51

*Book of Jubilees*
prologue ................... 65
1:1-4 ...................... 65
1:26 ....................... 65
4:16-26 .................... 46
4:17 ....................... 47
4:17, 18 ................... 47
4:17-24 .................... 43
4:19 ....................... 47
4:20 ....................... 47
4:21 ..................... 42, 45, 47
4:22 ....................... 47
4:23 ..................... 46, 47, 53
4:24 ..................... 43, 47

4:25 ..................... 47, 50
4:26 ....................... 47
7:39 ..................... 36, 47
8:2 ........................ 47
10:17 .................... 43, 47
11:16 ...................... 47
21:10 ...................... 47
32:20 ...................... 22
47:9 ....................... 47

*Liber Antiquitatum Biblicarum*
1:16 ....................... 51
12:2 ....................... 69
19 ......................... 70
19:16 ...................... 69
20:2 ....................... 69
21:2 ...................... 106
32:9 ....................... 65
48:1 ..................... 36, 75, 108
48:1-2 ..................... 75

*Life of Adam and Eve*
32-37 ...................... 22

*Lives of the Prophets*
21:15 .................... 59, 63

*3 Maccabees*
3:24 ....................... 97

*4 Maccabees*
18:12 ...................... 75

*Paraleipomena Jeremiou*
3:17 ....................... 22

*Psalms of Solomon*
4:18 ....................... 81
17:28 ...................... 61
17:35 ...................... 56

*Pseudo-Eupolemus*
8-9 ........................ 57

*Pseudo-Orpheus*
32-36 ...................... 65

*Pseudo-Phocylides*
104 ........................ 39

*Sibylline Oracles*
1, 381 ..................... 104
2, 187 ..................... 59
3, 457 ..................... 68
3, 682 ..................... 68
5, 256-257 .................. 70

*Testament of Abraham (A)*
4 .......................... 81
7 .......................... 81
11:4-18 .................... 125
17 ......................... 81

*Testament of Abraham (B)*
4:4 ........................ 22
7 .......................... 81
7:18 ....................... 22
7:19-8:3 ................... 21
8 .......................... 81
8:3 ....................... 104
10:2 ...................... 104
11:3 ....................... 46
12:1 ...................... 104
12:9 ...................... 104

14:6-7 ..................... 22

*Testament of Benjamin*
10:6 ...................... 125

*Testament of Isaac*
3:16 ....................... 51

*Testament of Issachar*
1:5 ........................ 68

*Testament of Job*
33:2-3 .................... 125
52 ........................ 22

*Testament of Judah*
9:3 ........................ 22
10:2 ....................... 22

*Testament of Levi*
2:5ff. .................... 108
18:3 ....................... 81

*Testament of Moses*
1:15 ....................... 70
10:12 ...................... 81

## c. Dead Sea Scrolls, Philo, Josephus, Rabbinic Writings, etc.

*11QMelch* ..................... 125

*1QGenApocr*
2-5 ........................ 47
2:19-21b ................... 48
2:20-21 .................... 48
2:21b-23 ................... 48
5:4 ........................ 48
5:10 ....................... 48
5:24-25 .................... 48

*1QpHab*
9:12 ....................... 56

*4QEn^g ar* II, 22 ................... 46

*4QEnGiants^a* frag 8, 3 ............. 46

*4QEnGiants^b ar* II, 14 ............. 46

*4QPsJub^c (4Q227)* ................ 47

*AgBer*
67 ......................... 70

*BemR*
21:3 ....................... 75

*Ber*
2:4 (5a) ................ 77, 142

*BerR*
 12 . . . . . . . . . . . . . . . . . . . . . . . . . 114
 25·1 . . . . . . . . . . . . . . . . . . . . . 41, 44

*bSan*
 38b . . . . . . . . . . . . . . . . . . . . . . . 125

*DebR*
 3:17 . . . . . . . . . . . . . . . . . . . . . . . 70

*DEZ*
 1 . . . . . . . . . . . . . . . . . . . . . . . . . . 77
 1:18 . . . . . . . . . . . . . . . . . . . . . . . 76

Josephus
 *Ap* II 1 (1-2) . . . . . . . . . . . . . . . . . . . . 8
 *BJ* I vii, 4 (147) . . . . . . . . . . . . . . . . 68
 *BJ* II xiii, 5 (261-263) . . . . . . . . . . 108
 *BJ* V ii, 3 (70) . . . . . . . . . . . . . . . 107
 *BJ* VI ii, 8 (161) . . . . . . . . . . . . . . 68
 *BJ* VI v, 1-3 (271-309) . . . . . . . . . 168
 *Ant* I iii, 2 (79) . . . . . . . . . . . . . . . 57
 *Ant* I iii, 4 (85) . . . . . . . . . . . . 57, 67
 *Ant* I iii, 4 (85-86) . . . . . . . . . . . . 57
 *Ant* I xix, 5 (294) . . . . . . . . . . . . . 102
 *Ant* III v, 7 (95-97) . . . . . . . . . . . 68
 *Ant* III v, 7 (95-98) . . . . . . . . . . . 69
 *Ant* III v, 7 (96) . . . . . . . . . . . . . . 67
 *Ant* III v, 7 (97) . . . . . . . . . . . . . . 69
 *Ant* IV viii, 2 (189) . . . . . . . . . . . . 86
 *Ant* IV viii, 44 (302) . . . . . . . . . . . 87
 *Ant* IV viii, 48 (320) . . . . . . . . . . . 87
 *Ant* IV viii, 48 (325) . . . . . . . . . . . 67
 *Ant* IV viii, 48 (325-326) . . . . . . . . 108
 *Ant* IV viii, 48 (326) . . . . . . 57, 67, 104
 *Ant* IV viii, 49 (330) . . . . . . . . . . . 68
 *Ant* V i, 13 (39) . . . . . . . . . . . . . . 97
 *Ant* V ix, 3 (328) . . . . . . . . . . . . . 102
 *Ant* VIII i, 1 (1-2) . . . . . . . . . . . . . 8
 *Ant* IX ii, 2 (28) . . . . . . . . . 57, 62, 67
 *Ant* IX v, 2 (99) . . . . . . . . . . . . . . 63
 *Ant* XI v, 5 (158) . . . . . . . . . . . . . 71
 *Ant* XI vi, 9 (238) . . . . . . . . . . . . 104
 *Ant* XIII i, 1 (1) . . . . . . . . . . . . . . 8
 *Ant* XVII v, 6 (128) . . . . . . . . . . . . 97
 *Ant* XX viii, 6 (169) . . . . . . . . . . . 107

 *Ant* XX viii, 6 (169-172) . . . . . . . . . 108

*Joshua (Samaritan Book of)* . . . . . . . . . 70

*mAv*
 4:17 . . . . . . . . . . . . . . . . . . . . . . . 115

*Memar Marqah*
 1:9 . . . . . . . . . . . . . . . . . . . . . . . . 71
 2:8 . . . . . . . . . . . . . . . . . . . . . . 70, 71
 5:2 . . . . . . . . . . . . . . . . . . . . . . . . 71

*MHG*
 Gen 5:24 . . . . . . . . . . . . . . . . . . . . 64

*MTann*
 219 . . . . . . . . . . . . . . . . . . . . . . 68, 70
 224 . . . . . . . . . . . . . . . . . . . . . . . . 64

*Pes*
 5b . . . . . . . . . . . . . . . . . . . . . . . . . 63

*Peshitta*
 Ps 68:19 . . . . . . . . . . . . . . . . . . . . 140

Philo
 *Abr* 11 . . . . . . . . . . . . . . . . . . . . . 57
 *Abr* 17 . . . . . . . . . . . . . . . . . . . . . 44
 *Abr* 17-26 . . . . . . . . . . . . . . . . . . . 57
 *Abr* 18 . . . . . . . . . . . . . . . . . . . . . 57
 *Abr* 20-23 . . . . . . . . . . . . . . . . . . . 57
 *Imm* 136-139 . . . . . . . . . . . . . . . . . 63
 *Mut* 38 . . . . . . . . . . . . . . . . . . . . . 57
 *Plant* 2 . . . . . . . . . . . . . . . . . . . . . 8
 *Praem* 15-21 . . . . . . . . . . . . . . . . . 57
 *Praem* 17 . . . . . . . . . . . . . . . . . . . 57
 *QPL* 2 . . . . . . . . . . . . . . . . . . . . . . 8
 *QPL* 43 . . . . . . . . . . . . . . . . . . . . 39
 *Quaest in Gn* 1, 86 . . . . . . . . . . . 57, 66
 *Quaest in Ex* 2, 29 . . . . . . . . . . . 39, 65
 *Sacr* 9 . . . . . . . . . . . . . . . . . . . . . 39
 *Som* 2, 189 . . . . . . . . . . . . . . . . . . 39
 *SpecLeg* 2 . . . . . . . . . . . . . . . . . . . 8
 *Virt* 76 . . . . . . . . . . . . . . . . . . . . . 66
 *Virt* 77 . . . . . . . . . . . . . . . . . . . . . 86
 *VitMos* 1, 158 . . . . . . . . . . . . . . . . 39

*VitMos* 2, 1 . . . . . . . . . . . . . . . . . . . . . 8
*VitMos* 2, 288 . . . . . . . . . . . . . . . . . 66
*VitMos* 2, 291 . . . . . . . . . . . . . . 66, 81
*VitMos* 3, 1 . . . . . . . . . . . . . . . . . . . . 8

*PRE*
29 . . . . . . . . . . . . . . . . . . . . . . . . . . . 75
47 . . . . . . . . . . . . . . . . . . . . . . . . . . . 75

*SifDev*
355 . . . . . . . . . . . . . . . . . . . . . . . 68, 70
357 . . . . . . . . . . . . . . . . . . . . . . . . . 64

*Sot*
13b . . . . . . . . . . . . . . . . . . . . . . . . . . 64

*Suk*
5a . . . . . . . . . . . . . . . . . . . . . . . . . . . 60

*Targum*
2 Kings 1:11 . . . . . . . . . . . . . . . . . . 60
2 Kings 2:1 . . . . . . . . . . . . . . . . . . . 60
Ps 68:19 . . . . . . . . . . . . . . . . . . . . . 140

*Targum Neofiti 1*
Gen 5:24 . . . . . . . . . . . . . . . . . . . . . 43

*Targum Onkelos*
Gen 5:24 . . . . . . . . . . . . . . . . . . . 41, 43

*Targum Pseudo-Jonathan*
Gen 5:24 . . . . . . . . . . . . . . . . . . . 43, 51
Ex 6:18 . . . . . . . . . . . . . . . . . . . . . . 75
Deut 30:4 . . . . . . . . . . . . . . . . . . 63, 75
Deut 33:21 . . . . . . . . . . . . . . . . . 68, 70

*Yalkut Shim'oni*
Num 25:11 . . . . . . . . . . . . . . . . . . . . 75
Num 27:12 . . . . . . . . . . . . . . . . . 64, 65

## d. New Testament

*Matthew*
2:2 . . . . . . . . . . . . . . . . . . . . . . . . . . 93
2:8 . . . . . . . . . . . . . . . . . . . . . . . . . . 93
2:11 . . . . . . . . . . . . . . . . . . . . . . . . . 93
3:11 . . . . . . . . . . . . . . . . . . . . . . . . 101
4:9 . . . . . . . . . . . . . . . . . . . . . . . . . . 93
4:10 . . . . . . . . . . . . . . . . . . . . . . . . . 93
4:19 . . . . . . . . . . . . . . . . . . . . . . . . 148
5:13 . . . . . . . . . . . . . . . . . . . . . . . . 101
5:20 . . . . . . . . . . . . . . . . . . . . . . . . 150
7:21 . . . . . . . . . . . . . . . . . . . . . . . . 150
7:27 . . . . . . . . . . . . . . . . . . . . . . . . 101
8:2 . . . . . . . . . . . . . . . . . . . . . . . . . . 93
8:14 . . . . . . . . . . . . . . . . . . . . . . . . 101
9:15 . . . . . . . . . . . . . . . . . . . . . . . . 138
9:18 . . . . . . . . . . . . . . . . . . . . . . . . . 93
10:1 . . . . . . . . . . . . . . . . . . . . . . . . 101
10:26 . . . . . . . . . . . . . . . . . . . . . . . 101
10:32 . . . . . . . . . . . . . . . . . . . . . . . 148
10:40 . . . . . . . . . . . . . . . . . . . . . . . 112
11:2 . . . . . . . . . . . . . . . . . . . . . . . . 155
11:4-5 . . . . . . . . . . . . . . . . . . . . . . . 170

11:27 . . . . . . . . . . . . . . . . . . . . . . . 130
12:28 . . . . . . . . . . . . . . . . . . . . . . . 170
14:33 . . . . . . . . . . . . . . . . . . . . . . . . 93
15:25 . . . . . . . . . . . . . . . . . . . . . . . . 93
16:14 . . . . . . . . . . . . . . . . . . . . . 63, 77
16:28 . . . . . . . . . . . . . . . . . . . . . . . 150
17:3 . . . . . . . . . . . . . . . . . . . . . . . . . 70
17:10-13 . . . . . . . . . . . . . . . . . . . . . 63
17:11 . . . . . . . . . . . . . . . . . . . . 110, 114
18:20 . . . . . . . . . . . . . . . . . . . . . . . 131
18:22 . . . . . . . . . . . . . . . . . . . . . . . 155
18:26 . . . . . . . . . . . . . . . . . . . . . . . . 93
19:23 . . . . . . . . . . . . . . . . . . . . . . . 150
19:28 . . . . . . . . . . . . . . . . . . . . . . . . 56
20:20 . . . . . . . . . . . . . . . . . . . . . . . . 93
21:1 . . . . . . . . . . . . . . . . . . . . . . . . 188
21:17 . . . . . . . . . . . . . . . . . . . . . . . 188
21:25 . . . . . . . . . . . . . . . . . . . . . . . 101
21:26 . . . . . . . . . . . . . . . . . . . . . . . 155
23:39 . . . . . . . . . . . . . . . . . . . . . . . 148
24:36 . . . . . . . . . . . . . . . . . . . . . . . 103
24:48 . . . . . . . . . . . . . . . . . . . . . . . 179

25:31 . . . . . . . . . . . . . . . . . . . . 56, 150
26:6 . . . . . . . . . . . . . . . . . . . . . . . 188
26:15 . . . . . . . . . . . . . . . . . . . . . . 101
26:29 . . . . . . . . . . . . . . . . . . . . . . 148
26:61 . . . . . . . . . . . . . . . . . . . . . . . 98
26:64 . . . . . . . . . . . . . . . . . . 148, 178
27:52-53 . . . . . . . . . . . . . . . . . . . 123
27:55 . . . . . . . . . . . . . . . . . . . . . . 101
27:64 . . . . . . . . . . . . . . . . . . . . . . 131
28 . . . . . . . . . . . . . . . . . . . . . . . . 4, 11
28:9 . . . . . . . . . . . . . . . . 93, 130, 137
28:9-10 . . . . . . . . . . . . . . . . . . . . 130
28:16 . . . . . . . . . . . . . . . . . . . . . . 162
28:16-20 . . . . . 130, 160, 162, 171, 186
28:17 . . . . . . . . . . . . 93, 130, 162, 186
28:18 . . . . . . . . . . . . . . . . . . 130, 162
28:18-20 . . . . . . . . . . . . . . . . . . . . 23
28:19 . . . . . . . . . . . . . . . . . . . . . . 162
28:20 . . . . . . . . . . . . . . . . . . 131, 162

*Mark*
1:3 . . . . . . . . . . . . . . . . . . . . . . . . . 5
1:8 . . . . . . . . . . . . . . . . . . . . . . . . 101
1:13 . . . . . . . . . . . . . . . . . . . . . . . 142
1:17 . . . . . . . . . . . . . . . . . . . . . . . 148
1:30 . . . . . . . . . . . . . . . . . . . . . . . 101
1:45 . . . . . . . . . . . . . . . . . . . . . . . 101
2:1 . . . . . . . . . . . . . . . . . . . . . . . . . 98
2:19b-20 . . . . . . . . . . . . . . . . . . . 138
2:19b-20parr. . . . . . . . . . . . . . . . . 138
2:20 . . . . . . . . . . . . . . . . . 26, 80, 139
3:3 . . . . . . . . . . . . . . . . . . . . . . . . 170
6:7 . . . . . . . . . . . . . . . . . . . . . . . . 101
6:15 . . . . . . . . . . . . . . . . . . . . . 58, 63
8:22 . . . . . . . . . . . . . . . . . . . . . . . 188
8:28 . . . . . . . . . . . . . . . . . . . . . 58, 63
8:31 . . . . . . . . . . . . . . . . . . . . . . . 139
8:38 . . . . . . . . . . . . . . . . . . . . . . . 150
9:1 . . . . . . . . . . . . . 90, 150, 178, 179
9:1parr. . . . . . . . . . . . . . . . . . . . . . 178
9:2-10parr. . . . . . . . . . . . . . . . . . . . 63
9:2-4 . . . . . . . . . . . . . . . . . . . . . . 133
9:3parr. . . . . . . . . . . . . . . . . . . . . . 106
9:4 . . . . . . . . . . . . . . . . . . . . . . . . . 70
9:11-13 . . . . . . . . . . . . . . . . . . . . . 63
9:12 . . . . . . . . . . . . . . . . . . . 110, 114

9:31 . . . . . . . . . . . . . . . . . . . . . . . 139
9:37 . . . . . . . . . . . . . . . . . . . . . . . 112
9·47 . . . . . . . . . . . . . . . . . . . . . . . 150
9:49 . . . . . . . . . . . . . . . . . . . . . . . 101
10:23 . . . . . . . . . . . . . . . . . . . . . . 150
10:24 . . . . . . . . . . . . . . . . . . . . . . 150
10:25 . . . . . . . . . . . . . . . . . . . . . . 150
10:33-34 . . . . . . . . . . . . . . . . . . . 139
11:1 . . . . . . . . . . . . . . . . . . . . . . . 188
11:11 . . . . . . . . . . . . . . . . . . . . . . 188
11:12 . . . . . . . . . . . . . . . . . . . . . . 188
11:31 . . . . . . . . . . . . . . . . . . . . . . 101
13:2 . . . . . . . . . . . . . . . . . . . . . . . . 98
13:26 . . . . . . . . . . . . . . 105, 107, 150
13:30 . . . . . . . . . . . . . . . . . . 178, 179
13:30par. . . . . . . . . . . . . . . . . . . . . 178
13:32 . . . . . . . . . . . . . . . . . . . . . . 103
14:3 . . . . . . . . . . . . . . . . . . . . . . . 188
14:10 . . . . . . . . . . . . . . . . . . . . . . 101
14:13 . . . . . . . . . . . . . . . . . . . . . . 101
14:25 . . . . . . . . . . . . . . . . . . 148, 178
14:28 . . . . . . . . . . . . . . . . . . . . . . 171
14:58 . . . . . . . . . . . . . . . . . . . . . . . 98
14:62 . . . . . . . . 11, 127, 147, 148, 178
15:34-35 . . . . . . . . . . . . . . . . . . . . 63
16 . . . . . . . . . . . . . . . . . 145, 163, 189
16:1-8 . . . . . . . . . . . . . . . . . . . . . . . 4
16:3 . . . . . . . . . . 26, 99, 163, 189, 190
16:5 . . . . . . . . . . . . . . . . . . . . . . . 161
16:5parr. . . . . . . . . . . . . . . . . . . . . 106
16:7 . . . . . . . . . . . . . . . . . . . . 11, 171
16:9-11 . . . . . . . . . . . . . . . . . . . . 133
16:9-20 . . 121, 131, 132, 145, 171, 189
16:12 . . . . . . . . . . . . . . . . . . . . . . 133
16:12-13 . . . . . . . . . . . . . . . . . . . 133
16:14-20 . . . . . . . . . . . . . . . . . . . 133
16:19 . . . . . . . . . 3, 15, 26, 28, 81, 119
. . . . . . . . . . . 131-133, 143, 145, 162
. . . . . . . . 163, 165, 167, 189, 190, 197

*Luke*
1-2 . . . . . . . . . . . . . . . 29, 88, 157, 170
1:1 . . . . . . . . . . . . . . . . . . . . . . . . 180
1:1-2 . . . . . . . . . . . . . . . . . . . . . . 170
1:1-4 . . . . . . . . . . . . . . . . . 30, 95, 195
1:2 . . . . . . . . . . . . . . . . . . . . . . 95, 96

1:3 . . . . . . . . . . . . . . . . . . . . . . . . . . 95
1:8-20 . . . . . . . . . . . . . . . . . . . . . . 33
1:11 . . . . . . . . . . . . . . . . . . . . . . . . . 29
1:15 . . . . . . . . . . . . . . . . . . . . . . . . 170
1:20 . . . . . . . . . . . . . . . . . . . . . . . . . 96
1:23 . . . . . . . . . . . . . . . . . . . . . . 29, 84
1:26 . . . . . . . . . . . . . . . . . . . . . . . . . 29
1:38 . . . . . . . . . . . . . . . . . . . . . . . . . 23
1:41 . . . . . . . . . . . . . . . . . . . . . . . . 170
1:46-55 . . . . . . . . . . . . . . . . . . . . . 170
1:48 . . . . . . . . . . . . . . . . . . . . . . . . 148
1:52 . . . . . . . . . . . . . . . . . . . . . . . . . 56
1:57 . . . . . . . . . . . . . . . . . . . . . . . . . 85
1:67 . . . . . . . . . . . . . . . . . . . . . . . . 170
1:68-79 . . . . . . . . . . . . . . . . . . . . . 170
1:70 . . . . . . . . . . . . . . . . . . . . . . . . 112
2:6 . . . . . . . . . . . . . . . . . . . . . . . . . . 85
2:11 . . . . . . . . . . . . . . . . . . . . . . . . 151
2:13 . . . . . . . . . . . . . . . . . . . . . 29, 142
2:15 . . . . . . . . . . . . . . . . . . . . . . . . . 23
2:21 . . . . . . . . . . . . . . . . . . . . . . . . . 85
2:22 . . . . . . . . . . . . . . . . . . . . . . . . . 84
2:25-27 . . . . . . . . . . . . . . . . . . . . . 170
2:30 . . . . . . . . . . . . . . . . . . . . . . . . 170
2:37 . . . . . . . . . . . . . . . . . . . . . . . . . 94
2:45 . . . . . . . . . . . . . . . . . . . . . . . . . 29
3:5 . . . . . . . . . . . . . . . . . . . . . . . . . . 68
3:6 . . . . . . . . . . . . . . . . . . . . . . . . . 170
3:7 . . . . . . . . . . . . . . . . . . . . . . . . . 178
3:9 . . . . . . . . . . . . . . . . . . . . . . . . . 178
3:16 . . . . . . . . . . . . . . . . . . . . . . . . 101
3:17 . . . . . . . . . . . . . . . . . . . . . . . . 178
3:21 . . . . . . . . . . . . . . . . . . . . . . . . 155
3:21-22 . . . . . . . . . . . . . . . . . . . . . 185
3:22 . . . . . . . . . . . . . . . . 151, 155, 170
3:23 . . . . . . . . . . . . . . . . . . . . . . . . . 96
3:37 . . . . . . . . . . . . . . . . . . . . . . . . . 57
4:1ff. . . . . . . . . . . . . . . . . . . . . . . . . 92
4:2 . . . . . . . . . . . . . . . . . . . . . . . . . . . 4
4:8 . . . . . . . . . . . . . . . . . . . . . . . . . . 93
4:13 . . . . . . . . . . . . . . . . . . . . . . 13, 99
4:16-20 . . . . . . . . . . . . . . . . . . . . . . 13
4:19 . . . . . . . . . . . . . . . . . . . . . . . . 170
4:21 . . . . . . . . . . . . . . . . . . . . 151, 170
4:38 . . . . . . . . . . . . . . . . . . . . . . . . 101
4:43 . . . . . . . . . . . . . . . . . . . . . . . . 173

5:10 . . . . . . . . . . . . . . . . . . . . . . . . 148
5:14 . . . . . . . . . . . . . . . . . . . . . . . . 101
5:15 . . . . . . . . . . . . . . . . . . . . . . . . 101
5:26 . . . . . . . . . . . . . . . . . . . . . . . . 151
5:35 . . . . . . . . . . . . . . 33, 80, 138, 139
6:12-16 . . . . . . . . . . . . . . . . . . . . . . 96
6:13 . . . . . . . . . . . . . . . . . . . . . . . . . 96
6:23 . . . . . . . . . . . . . . . . . . . . . . . . 155
6:49 . . . . . . . . . . . . . . . . . . . . . . . . 101
7:22 . . . . . . . . . . . . . . . . . . . . . . . . 170
7:36 . . . . . . . . . . . . . . . . . . . . . . . . 188
8:1 . . . . . . . . . . . . . . . . . . . . . . . . . 173
9 . . . . . . . . . . . . . . . . . . . . . . . . . . . . 31
9:1 . . . . . . . . . . . . . . . . . . . . . . . . . 101
9:2 . . . . . . . . . . . . . . . . . . . . . . . . . 173
9:8 . . . . . . . . . . . . . . . . . . . . . . . . . . 63
9:11 . . . . . . . . . . . . . . . . . . . . . . . . 173
9:19 . . . . . . . . . . . . . . . . . . . . . . . . . 63
9:22 . . . . . . . . . . . . . . . . . . . . . 146, 151
9:26 . . . . . . . . . . . . 16, 120, 150, 177
9:27 . . . . . . . . . . . . . . . . 150, 178, 179
9:28 . . . . . . . . . . . . . . . . . . . . . . 89, 90
9:28parr. . . . . . . . . . . . . . . . . . . . . . 108
9:28-36 . . . . . . . . . . . . . . . . . . . . . . 120
9:30 . . . . . . . . . . . . . . . . . . . . . 70, 106
9:31 . . . . . . . . . . . . . . . . . . 16, 85, 86
9:32 . . . . . . . . . . . . . . . . . . . . . . . . 120
9:33 . . . . . . . . . . . . . . . . . . . . . . . . . 23
9:34-35 . . . . . . . . . . . . . . . . . . . . . . 105
9:35 . . . . . . . . . . . . . . . . . . . . . . . . . 56
9:37 . . . . . . . . . . . . . . . . . . . . . . 90, 98
9:44 . . . . . . . . . . . . . . . . . . . . . . . . 146
9:48 . . . . . . . . . . . . . . . . . . . . . . . . 112
9:51 . . . . . . . . . . . 4, 15, 22, 24, 30, 38
. . . . . . . . 80, 82-86, 96, 109, 114-116
. . . . . . . . . . . . 154, 183, 184, 194, 196
9:51ff. . . . . . . . . . . . . . . . . . . . . . . . . 7
9:51-19:10 . . . . . . . . . . . . . . . . . . . . 83
9:51-19:44 . . . . . . . . . . . . . . . . . . . . 82
9:51-56 . . . . . . . . . . . . . . . . . . . 80, 83
9:60 . . . . . . . . . . . . . . . . . . . . . . . . 173
10:9 . . . . . . . . . . . . . . . . . . . . . 173, 178
10:11 . . . . . . . . . . . . . . . . . . . . 173, 178
10:16 . . . . . . . . . . . . . . . . . . . . . . . . 112
10:18 . . . . . . . . . . . . . . . . . . . . . . . . 170
10:20 . . . . . . . . . . . . . . . . . . . . . . . . 155

10:22 . . . . . . . . . . . . . . . . . . . . . . . 130
10:23 . . . . . . . . . . . . . . . . . . . . . . . 170
10:24 . . . . . . . . . . . . . . . . . . . . . . . 150
10:25 . . . . . . . . . . . . . . . . . . . . . . . 150
11:2 . . . . . . . . . . . . . . . . . . . . . . . . 155
11:13 . . . . . . . . . . . . . . . . . . 102, 155
11:20 . . . . . . . . . . . . . . . . . . . . . . . 170
12:2 . . . . . . . . . . . . . . . . . . . . . . . . 101
12:8 . . . . . . . . . . . . . . . . . . . . . . . . 148
12:33 . . . . . . . . . . . . . . . . . . . . . . . 155
12:38 . . . . . . . . . . . . . . . . . . . . . . . 179
12:40 . . . . . . . . . . . . . . . . . . . . . . . 177
12:45 . . . . . . . . . . . . . . . . . . . . . . . 179
12:52 . . . . . . . . . . . . . . . . . . . . . . . 148
13:6-9 . . . . . . . . . . . . . . . . . . . . . . 179
13:32 . . . . . . . . . . . . . . . . . . . . . . . 151
13:33 . . . . . . . . . . . . . . . . . . . . . . . 151
13:35 . . . . . . . . . . . . . . . . . . . 16, 148
15:7 . . . . . . . . . . . . . . . . . . . . . . . . 155
15:10 . . . . . . . . . . . . . . . . . . . . . . . 148
16:9 . . . . . . . . . . . . . . . . . . . . . . . . . 56
16:16 . . . . . . . . . . . . . . . . 13, 99, 173
16:19-31 . . . . . . . . . . . . . . . . . . . . . 177
17:20-37 . . . . . . . . . . . . . . . . . . . . . 178
17:21 . . . . . . . . . . . . . . . . . . . . . . . 170
17:24 . . . . . . . . . . . . . . . . . . . . . . . 177
17:27 . . . . . . . . . . . . . . . . . . . . . . . . 96
17:30 . . . . . . . . . . . . . . . . . . . . . . . 177
18:1-8 . . . . . . . . . . . . . . . . . . . . . . 178
18:7 . . . . . . . . . . . . . . . . . . . . . . . . . 56
18:8 . . . . . . . . . . . . . . . . . . . . 177, 178
18:22 . . . . . . . . . . . . . . . . . . . . . . . 155
18:33 . . . . . . . . . . . . . . . . . . . 146, 151
19:5 . . . . . . . . . . . . . . . . . . . . . . . . 151
19:9 . . . . . . . . . . . . . . . . . . . . . . . . 151
19:11 . . . . . . . . . . . . . . . . . . . 103, 179
19:12 . . . . . . . . . . . . . . . . . . . . 80, 179
19:28-29 . . . . . . . . . . . . . . . . . . . . . . 16
19:29 . . . . . . . . . . . . . . . . . . . . 89, 188
19:37 . . . . . . . . . . . . . . . . . . . . 16, 108
19:38 . . . . . . . . . . . . . . . . . . . . . 16, 32
20:5 . . . . . . . . . . . . . . . . . . . . . . . . 101
20:9 . . . . . . . . . . . . . . . . . . . . . . . . 179
20:19 . . . . . . . . . . . . . . . . . . . . . . . . 80
21:7 . . . . . . . . . . . . . . . . . . . . . . . . . 16
21:8 . . . . . . . . . . . . . . . . . . . . 170, 179

21:9 . . . . . . . . . . . . . . . . . . . . . . . . 179
21:24 . . . . . . . . . . . . . . . . . . . . . . . . 84
21:26 . . . . . . . . . . . . . . . . . . . . . . . 155
21:27 . . . . . . . . . . . . . . . . 16, 105, 107
. . . . . . . . . . . . . . 120, 148, 150, 177
21:27-28 . . . . . . . . . . . . . . . . . . . . . 107
21:28 . . . . . . . . . . . . . . . . . . . . 56, 103
21:31 . . . . . . . . . . . . . . . . . . . . . . . 178
21:32 . . . . . . . . . . . . . . . . . . . 178, 179
21:33 . . . . . . . . . . . . . . . . . . . . . . . 103
21:37 . . . . . . . . . . . . . . . . . . . . 87, 188
22 . . . . . . . . . . . . . . . . . . . . . . . . . . . 29
22:3 . . . . . . . . . . . . . . . . . . . . . . . . . 13
22:4 . . . . . . . . . . . . . . . . . . . . . . . . 101
22:10 . . . . . . . . . . . . . . . . . . . . . . . 101
22:18 . . . . . . . . . . . . . . . . . . . 148, 178
22:39 . . . . . . . . . . . . . . . . . . . . . . . . 87
22:69 . . . . . 16, 147-149, 151, 152, 178
23:5 . . . . . . . . . . . . . . . . . . . . . . . . . 96
23:35 . . . . . . . . . . . . . . . . . . . . . . . . 56
23:42-43 . . . . . . . . . . . . . . . . . 147, 150
23:43 . . . . . . . . . . . . . . . 7, 151, 152, 177
23:49 . . . . . . . . . . . . . . . . . . . . . . . 101
24 . . . . . . . . . . . 5, 9, 12, 15, 20, 23, 25
. . . . . . . . . . 28-31, 86, 88-92, 96, 101
. . . . . . . . . . 115-117, 161, 167, 171
. . . . . . . . . . . . . . 184, 186, 189, 194
24:1 . . . . . . . . . . . . . . . . . . . . . . . . . 89
24:1-11 . . . . . . . . . . . . . . . . . . . . . . . 86
24:3 . . . . . . . . . . . . . . . . . . . . . . . . 161
24:4 . . . . . . . . . . . . . . . . . 14, 15, 106
24:5 . . . . . . . . . . . . . . . . . . . . . . . . 106
24:6-8 . . . . . . . . . . . . . . . . . . . . . . . 146
24:7 . . . . . . . . . . . . . . . . . . . . . . . . 146
24:12 . . . . . . . . . . . . . . . . . . . . . . . . 86
24:13 . . . . . . . . . . . . . . . . . . . . . . . . 89
24:13-33 . . . . . . . . . . . . . . . . . . . . . 160
24:13-35 . . . . . . . . . . . . . . . . . . 86, 161
24:15 . . . . . . . . . . . . . . . . . . . . 87, 133
24:16 . . . . . . . . . . . . . . . . . . . . . . . 161
24:21 . . . . . . . . . . . . . . . . . . . . . . . 103
24:23 . . . . . . . . . . . . . . . . . . . . . . . 142
24:26 . . . . . . . . . . . . . 7, 16, 24, 28, 77
. . . . . . . . . . . . . . 147, 150, 151, 157
24:28 . . . . . . . . . . . . . . . . . . . . 87, 133
24:28-29 . . . . . . . . . . . . . . . . . . . . . . 87

24:29 ........................ 89
24:31 ............... 23, 92, 161
24:33 .............. 29, 87, 89, 162
24:35 ........................ 160
24:35-53 ...................... 6
24:36 .......... 86, 89, 92, 118, 161
24:36-39 ..................... 118
24:36-43 ............... 23, 86, 118
24:36-49 ............... 100, 160
24:36-53 ........... 23, 86, 90, 91
.................... 94, 118, 171
24:37 ........................ 163
24:39 ................... 161, 162
24:40-43 ..................... 118
24:41 ........................ 162
24:43 ........... 91, 100, 101, 163
24:44 ...................... 9, 91
24:44-46 ..................... 118
24:44-49 ........ 23, 86, 87, 96, 118
24:44-53 ...................... 9
24:46 ............... 118, 146, 152
24:47 ............... 96, 118, 162
24:47-49 ................ 102, 103
24:48 ........................ 118
24:49 ............. 6, 15, 18, 91, 93
............ 101, 102, 162, 181, 184
24:49a ....................... 118
24:49b ....................... 118
24:49c ....................... 118
24:50 ............... 3, 6, 19, 87, 88
............ 105, 107, 118, 160, 188
24:50-51 ..................... 28
24:50-53 ........... 1, 4, 6, 8, 15, 17
............. 20, 23, 26, 29, 30, 32
............. 33, 36, 49, 50, 80, 86
.......... 88, 90, 107, 116, 118, 119
........ 145, 161, 165, 186, 194, 196
24:51 ............. 1, 7, 8, 14, 23, 29
............. 30, 32, 50, 83, 90, 92
.......... 90, 92, 96, 104, 106, 118
............ 160, 161, 163, 167, 194
24:52 ........ 1, 22, 29, 32, 50, 80, 87
.......... 88, 93, 107, 118, 162, 194
24:52-53 ..................... 109
24:53 ............. 15, 22, 23, 33, 5
.......... 80, 88, 94, 109, 118, 141

*John*
1:18 ........................ 134
1:21 ......................... 63
1:26 ........................ 101
1:28 ........................ 188
1:34 ......................... 56
1:51 ........................ 142
3:5 ......................... 150
3:8 ......................... 134
3:12 ........................ 134
3:13 ............... 134, 137, 141
3:13-14 ..................... 134
3:14 ........................ 134
3:14a ....................... 125
3:17 ........................ 112
3:34 ........................ 112
5:36 ........................ 112
6:40 ........................ 136
6:53 ................... 148, 178
6:61 ........................ 136
6:62 ............... 11, 134, 136
7:8 ......................... 84
7:33 ........................ 134
7:39 ........ 134, 137, 141, 156, 183
8:11 ........................ 148
8:14 ........................ 134
8:21 ........................ 134
8:22 ........................ 134
8:28 ........................ 134
8:51-52 ..................... 178
8:54 ........................ 134
10:9 ........................ 109
10:36 ....................... 112
11:1 ........................ 188
11:4 ........................ 134
11:18 ............... 89, 108, 188
12:1 ........................ 188
12:16 ....................... 134
12:23 ....................... 134
12:28 ....................... 134
12:32 ....................... 134
12:34 ....................... 134
12:45 ....................... 136
13:1 ........................ 134
13:3 ........................ 134
13:19 ....................... 148

13:31-32 . . . . . . . . . . . . . . . . . . . . . 134
13:33 . . . . . . . . . . . . . . . . . . . . . . . 134
13:36 . . . . . . . . . . . . . . . . . . . . . . . 134
14:2 . . . . . . . . . . . . . . . . . . . . . . . . 134
14:3 . . . . . . . . . . . . . . . . . . . . . . . . 134
14:4 . . . . . . . . . . . . . . . . . . . . . . . . 134
14:5 . . . . . . . . . . . . . . . . . . . . . . . . 134
14:7 . . . . . . . . . . . . . . . . . . . . . . . . 148
14:12 . . . . . . . . . . . . . . . . . . . . . . . 134
14:15-31 . . . . . . . . . . . . . . . . . . . . . 137
14:16 . . . . . . . . . . . . . . . . . . . . . . . 156
14:18 . . . . . . . . . . . . . . . . . . . 183, 184
14:28 . . . . . . . . . . . . . . . . . . . 134, 184
15:26 . . . . . . . . . . . . . . . . . . . . . . . 156
16:5 . . . . . . . . . . . . . . . . . . . . . . . . 134
16:5-33 . . . . . . . . . . . . . . . . . . . . . . 137
16:7 . . . . . . . . . . . . 134, 137, 183, 184
16:10 . . . . . . . . . . . . . . . . . . . . . . . 134
16:14 . . . . . . . . . . . . . . . . . . . . . . . 134
16:16-18 . . . . . . . . . . . . . . . . . . . . . 134
16:17 . . . . . . . . . . . . . . . . . . . 134, 156
16:28 . . . . . . . . . . . . . . . . . . . . . . . 134
17:1ff. . . . . . . . . . . . . . . . . . . . . . . . 134
17:18 . . . . . . . . . . . . . . . . . . . . . . . 112
20 . . . . . . . . . . . . . . . . . . . . . . . . . . 138
20:1 . . . . . . . . . . . . . . . . . . . . . . . . 172
20:12 . . . . . . . . . . . . . . . . . . . . . . . 106
20:14-18 . . . . . . . . . . . . . . . . . . . . . 160
20:15 . . . . . . . . . . . . . . . . . . . . . . . 133
20:17 . . . . . . . 11, 26, 28, 134, 136, 137
20:18 . . . . . . . . . . . . . . . . . . . . . . . 138
20:19 . . . . . . . . . . . . . . . . . . . . . . . 172
20:19-23 . . . . . . . . . . . . . . . . . . . . . . 23
20:19-29 . . . . . . . . . . . . . . . . . . . . . 160
20:20 . . . . . . . . . . . . . . . . . . . . . . . 162
20:21 . . . . . . . . . . . . . . . . . . . . . . . 162
20:22 . . . . . . . . . . . . . . . . . . . 156, 162
20:24 . . . . . . . . . . . . . . . . . . . . . . . 162
20:26 . . . . . . . . . . . . . . . . . . . . . . . 172
20:27 . . . . . . . . . . . . . . . . . . . . . . . 137
20:28 . . . . . . . . . . . . . . . . . . . . . . . 138
21 . . . . . . . . . . . . . . . . . . . . . . . . . . 172
21:1 . . . . . . . . . . . . . . . . . . . . . . . . 172
21:1-14 . . . . . . . . . . . . . . . . . . . . . . 160
21:1-23 . . . . . . . . . . . . . . . . . . . . . . . 23
21:14 . . . . . . . . . . . . . . . . . . . . . . . 172

*Acts*
1-5 . . . . . . . . . . . . . . . . . . . . . . . . . . 94
1 . . . . . . . . . . . . . 6, 9, 11, 12, 14, 15, 20
. . . . . . . . 23, 25, 26, 28, 30, 31, 86, 87
. . . . 89-91, 97, 115-116, 137, 153, 161
. . . . . . . . . 166, 167, 171, 183, 184, 186
1:1 . . . . . . . . . . . . . . . . . . . . . . . . 4, 30
1:1f. . . . . . . . . . . . . . . . . . . . . . . . . . 24
1:1-11 . . . . . . . . . . . . . . 20, 29, 88, 120
1:1-12 . . . . . . . . . . . . . . . . . 33, 194, 196
1:1-14 . . . . . . 8, 9, 80, 90, 94, 95, 118
1:1-2 . . . . . . . . . . . 1, 5, 90, 94, 95, 97
. . . . . . . . . . . . . . . 109, 170, 171, 194
1:1-3 . . . . . . . . . . . . . . . . . . . . . . . . . 8
1:1-5 . . . . . . . . . . . . . . . . . . . . . . . 6, 186
1:2 . . . . . . . . . . . . . 5, 8, 15, 22, 30, 81
. . . . . . . . . . 84, 86, 109, 115, 173, 194
1:2-14 . . . . . . . . . . . . . . . . . . . . . . . . 4
1:2-5 . . . . . . . . . . . . . . . . . . . . . . . . . 5
1:3 . . . . . . . . . . . 3-6, 8, 23, 30, 79, 94
. . . . . . 96-99, 118, 171, 172, 175, 187
1:3-12 . . . . . . . . . . . . . . . . . . . . . . . . 18
1:3-4 . . . . . . . . . . . . . . . . . . . . 118, 167
1:3-5 . . . . . . . . . . . . . . . . . . . . . . . . . 5
1:3-9 . . . . . . . . . . . . . . . . . . . . . . . 118
1:4 . . . 5, 15, 18, 98, 100, 102, 107, 118
1:4-11 . . . . . . . . . . . . . . . . . . . . 6, 171
1:4-14 . . . . . . . . . . . . . . . . . . . . 94, 100
1:4-5 . . . . . . . . . . . . . . . . . . . . . 99, 100
1:4-8 . . . . . . . . . . . . . . . . . . . . . . . . 18
1:5 . . . . . . 5, 6, 101, 102, 118, 184, 187
1:6 . . . . . . . . . . . . . . . . . 5, 6, 18, 19, 30
. . . . . . . . . . . . . . . . 98, 109, 162, 194
1:6-8 . . . . . . . . . . . . . . 18, 22, 31, 102
. . . . . . . . . . . . . . . 103, 109, 167, 192
1:6-12:25 . . . . . . . . . . . . . . . . . . . . . 32
1:6-14 . . . . . . . . . . . . . . . . . . . . . . . . 5
1:6-14a . . . . . . . . . . . . . . . . . . . . . . . 33
1:7 . . . . . . . . . . . . . . . 98, 103, 179, 181
1:8 . . . . 30, 96, 118, 155, 181, 183, 184
1:9 . . . . . . . . . . . 2, 8, 9, 18, 22, 23, 26
. . . . . . . . . . 33, 50, 83, 90, 92, 98, 103
. . . . . . . . . . . 105, 106, 118, 136, 138
. . . . . . . . . . . . . . . 139, 142, 143, 157
1:9b . . . . . . . . . . . . . . . . . . . . . . . . . 20
1:9ff. . . . . . . . . . . . . . . . . . . . . . . . . 184

1:9-11 ......... 1, 4, 9, 15, 17-20, 23
........... 28, 36, 90, 106, 110, 128
........... 154, 164, 165, 167, 194
1:9-12 ........................ 98
1:9-14 ....................... 118
1:10 ........... 31, 50, 92, 106, 120
1:10-11 .................. 50, 118
1:11 .......... 15, 20, 22, 50, 79, 81
............ 84, 106, 107, 109, 115
............ 167-169, 177, 194, 196
1:12 ............. 18, 22, 50, 89, 107
............... 109, 118, 162, 188
1:12-14 ..................... 107
1:13 ..................... 109, 118
1:14 .......................... 33
1:21 ...................... 24, 109
1:21-22 ........ 80, 94, 109, 170, 171
1:22 ................ 15, 22, 81, 84
............... 86, 87, 95, 96, 115
............ 146, 155, 173, 174, 194
2 ............................ 183
2:1 ............... 81, 86, 183, 184
2:1-13 ....................... 153
2:14-40 ...................... 153
2:14b-15 ..................... 153
2:16-21 ...................... 153
2:17 .................... 183, 185
2:22-24 ...................... 153
2:24-31 ...................... 158
2:25-28 ...................... 155
2:25-32 ...................... 153
2:27 ......................... 159
2:32 ......... 11, 123, 146, 155, 157
2:32ff. .......... 147, 156, 165, 183
2:32-35 ................... 24, 155
2:32-36 ......... 113, 147, 153, 157
2:33 ................ 11, 12, 16, 27
............... 141, 155-158, 184
2:33a .................... 154, 155
2:33ff. ....................... 120
2:33-36 ................... 16, 153
2:34 ................. 16, 155, 157
2:34a .................... 153, 154
2:34b-35 ..................... 154
2:35 ......................... 155
2:36 ............... 124, 156, 197

2:37-40 ...................... 153
2:41 ......................... 102
2:46-47 ....................... 94
3:1 ......................... 33, 94
3:1-10 ....................... 110
3:10-21 ...................... 114
3:11 .......................... 94
3:11-12a ..................... 110
3:12 ......................... 111
3:12b-16 ..................... 110
3:12b-26 ................. 110, 112
3:13 ......................... 153
3:13-15 .................. 110, 112
3:14 .......................... 56
3:15 ............... 125, 146, 155
3:16 ......................... 182
3:17 ......................... 110
3:17-19 ...................... 112
3:17-21 ...................... 110
3:18 .................... 110, 152
3:19 .................... 110, 112
3:19-21 ................. 24, 73, 80
............ 109, 112, 114, 115, 153
3:19-26 ...................... 111
3:20 ........... 109, 110, 112, 177
3:20a ........................ 111
3:20f. ........................ 26
3:20-21 .......... 79, 103, 112, 113
3:20-21a ..................... 113
3:21 ............... 79, 110, 168
............ 181, 192, 194, 196, 197
3:21b ........................ 112
3:22 .................... 112, 157
3:22-26 .................. 110, 112
3:25 ......................... 111
3:26 ............... 111, 112, 157
4:2 ................. 14, 123, 146
4:10 .................... 123, 182
4:12 .......................... 56
4:30 ......................... 182
4:33 ......................... 146
4:34 ......................... 100
5:12 .......................... 94
5:19 ......................... 182
5:30 .................... 11, 157
5:30-31 ....................... 27

5:30-32 . . . . . . . . . . . . . . . . . . . . . . 24
5:31 . . . . . . 11, 113, 147, 153, 157, 158
5:32 . . . . . . . . . . . . . . . . . . . . . . . . 146
5:36-37 . . . . . . . . . . . . . . . . . . . . . 170
5:42 . . . . . . . . . . . . . . . . . . . . . . . . 94
7:32 . . . . . . . . . . . . . . . . . . . . . . . 120
7:55 . . . . . . . . . . . . . . . . . . . . 106, 126
7:55-56 . . . . . . . . . . . . . . . . . . . . . 120
7:55-60 . . . . . . . . . . . . . . . . . . . . . 177
7:56 . . . . . . . . . 16, 126, 148, 155, 156
7:59 . . . . . . . . . . . . . . . . . . . . . . . 111
8:4 . . . . . . . . . . . . . . . . . . . . . . . . 102
8:9-10 . . . . . . . . . . . . . . . . . . . . . . 170
8:12 . . . . . . . . . . . . . . . . . . . . . 99, 173
9-11 . . . . . . . . . . . . . . . . . . . . . . . . 92
9:1-9 . . . . . . . . . . . . . . . . . . . . . . . 143
9:1-19 . . . . . . . . . . . . . . . . . . . . . . . 24
9:1-30 . . . . . . . . . . . . . . . . . . . . . . . 32
9:3-7 . . . . . . . . . . . . . . . . . . . . . . . 130
9:3-9 . . . . . . . . . . . . . . . . . . . . . . . 173
9:10 . . . . . . . . . . . . . . . . . . . . . . . 182
9:12 . . . . . . . . . . . . . . . . . . . . . . . 182
9:28 . . . . . . . . . . . . . . . . . . . . . . . 109
10:3 . . . . . . . . . . . . . . . . . . . . . . . 182
10:4 . . . . . . . . . . . . . . . . . . . . . . . . 56
10:7 . . . . . . . . . . . . . . . . . . . . . . . . 23
10:11 . . . . . . . . . . . . . . . . . . . . . . . 182
10:17 . . . . . . . . . . . . . . . . . . . . . . . 182
10:19 . . . . . . . . . . . . . . . . . . . . . . . 182
10:27 . . . . . . . . . . . . . . . . . . . . . . . . 18
10:30 . . . . . . . . . . . . . . . . . . . . . . . 106
10:34-43 . . . . . . . . . . . . . . . . . . . 5, 23
10:36 . . . . . . . . . . . . . . . . . . . . . . . . 16
10:37-38 . . . . . . . . . . . . . . . . . . . . . 96
10:37ff. . . . . . . . . . . . . . . . . . . . . . 170
10:38 . . . . . . . . . . . . . . . . . . . . . . . . 13
10:39 . . . . . . . . . . . . . . . . . . . . . . . . 95
10:40-41 . . . . . . . . . . . . . . . . . . . . 146
10:40-42 . . . . . . . . . . . . . . . . . . . . 101
10:41 . . . . . . . . . . . . . . . . . . 6, 98, 100
10:41-42 . . . . . . . . . . . . . . . . . . . . 173
10:42 . . . . . . . . . . . . . . 124, 177, 178
11:12 . . . . . . . . . . . . . . . . . . . . . . . 182
11:15 . . . . . . . . . . . . . . . . . . . . . . . . 96
11:16 . . . . . . . . . . . . . . . . . . . . . . . 101
11:19 . . . . . . . . . . . . . . . . . . . . . . . 102

12:5 . . . . . . . . . . . . . . . . . . . . . . . 182
12:7 . . . . . . . . . . . . . . . . . . . . . . . 182
12:9 . . . . . . . . . . . . . . . . . . . . . . . 182
12:10 . . . . . . . . . . . . . . . . . . . . 23, 92
12:23 . . . . . . . . . . . . . . . . . . . . . . . 182
13:1-28:31 . . . . . . . . . . . . . . . . . . . . 32
13:2 . . . . . . . . . . . . . . . . . . . . . . . 182
13:16-41 . . . . . . . . . . . . . . . . . . . . 158
13:23-29 . . . . . . . . . . . . . . . . . . . . 158
13:23-37 . . . . . . . . . . . . . . . . . . . . 154
13:30 . . . . . . . . . . . . . . . . . . . . . . . 157
13:30-37 . . . . . . . . . . . 147, 153, 158
13:31 . . . . . . . . . . . . . . . . . 5, 6, 89, 98
. . . . . . . . . . . . . . 146, 158, 172-174
13:32 . . . . . . . . . . . . . . . . . . . . . . . 174
13:32f. . . . . . . . . . . . . . . . . . . . . . . . 24
13:32-37 . . . . . . . . . . . . . . . . . . . . 158
13:33 . . . . . . . . . . . . . 123, 124, 158
13:34 . . . . . . . . . . . . . . . . . . 123, 159
13:35 . . . . . . . . . . . . . . . . . . . . . . . 159
13:37 . . . . . . . . . . . . . . . . . . . . . . . 123
13:38-39 . . . . . . . . . . . . . . . . . . . . 158
14:4 . . . . . . . . . . . . . . . . . . . . . . . 174
14:14 . . . . . . . . . . . . . . . . . . . . . . . 174
14:22 . . . . . . . . . 99, 101, 115, 150, 152
15:15-18 . . . . . . . . . . . . . . . . . . . . 103
15:28 . . . . . . . . . . . . . . . . . . . . . . . 182
16:6-7 . . . . . . . . . . . . . . . . . . . . . . 182
16:8-10 . . . . . . . . . . . . . . . . . . . . . 182
16:13 . . . . . . . . . . . . . . . . . . . . . . . . 18
16:18 . . . . . . . . . . . . . . . . . . . . . . . . 98
17:3 . . . . . . . . . . . . 101, 123, 146, 152
17:18 . . . . . . . . . . . . . . . . . . . . . . . 146
17:22-31 . . . . . . . . . . . . . . . . . . . . 195
17:31 . . . . . . . . . 56, 123, 124, 177, 178
17:32 . . . . . . . . . . . . . . . . . . . . . . . 146
18:6 . . . . . . . . . . . . . . . . . . . . . . . 148
18:9-10 . . . . . . . . . . . . . . . . . . . . . 182
18:20 . . . . . . . . . . . . . . . . . . . . . . . . 98
19:8 . . . . . . . . . . . . . . . . . . . . . 99, 173
19:13 . . . . . . . . . . . . . . . . . . . . . . . 182
19:21 . . . . . . . . . . . . . . . . . . . . . . . 182
20:9 . . . . . . . . . . . . . . . . . . . . . . . . 98
20:16 . . . . . . . . . . . . . . . . . . . . . . . . 86
20:22-23 . . . . . . . . . . . . . . . . . . . . 182
20:25 . . . . . . . . . . . . . . . . . . . . 99, 173

20:29-30 . . . . . . . . . . . . . . . . . . . . . 173
21:4 . . . . . . . . . . . . . . . . . . . . . . . . 182
21:10 . . . . . . . . . . . . . . . . . . . . . . . . 98
21:11 . . . . . . . . . . . . . . . . . . . . . . . 182
21:20 . . . . . . . . . . . . . . . . . . . . . . . 187
21:20-21 . . . . . . . . . . . . . . . . . . . . 174
21:28 . . . . . . . . . . . . . . . . . . . . . . . 174
21:38 . . . . . . . . . . . . . . . . . . . . . . . 108
22:1-22 . . . . . . . . . . . . . . . . . . . . . 143
22:6-10 . . . . . . . . . . . . . . . . . . . . . 130
22:6-11 . . . . . . . . . . . . . . . . . . . . . 173
22:17-18 . . . . . . . . . . . . . . . . . . . . 182
23:6-8 . . . . . . . . . . . . . . . . . . . . . . 146
23:11 . . . . . . . . . . . . . . . . . . . . . . . 182
23:22 . . . . . . . . . . . . . . . . . . . . . . . 101
23:29 . . . . . . . . . . . . . . . . . . . . . . . 174
24:4 . . . . . . . . . . . . . . . . . . . . . . . . . 98
24:5 . . . . . . . . . . . . . . . . . . . . . . . . 174
24:11 . . . . . . . . . . . . . . . . . . . . . . . . 98
24:15 . . . . . . . . . . . . . . . . . . . . . . . 178
24:17 . . . . . . . . . . . . . . . . . . . . . . . . 98
24:25 . . . . . . . . . . . . . . . . . . . . . . . 178
25:6 . . . . . . . . . . . . . . . . . . . . . . . . . 98
25:8 . . . . . . . . . . . . . . . . . . . . . . . . 174
25:14 . . . . . . . . . . . . . . . . . . . . . . . . 98
25:19 . . . . . . . . . . . . . . . . . . . . . . . 146
26:9-18 . . . . . . . . . . . . . . . . . . . . . . 24
26:12-15 . . . . . . . . . . . . . . . . . . . . 130
26:12-18 . . . . . . . . . . . . . . . 143, 173
26:19 . . . . . . . . . . . . . . . . . . . 173, 182
26:23 . . . . . . . . . . . . . . 123, 146, 152
27:5 . . . . . . . . . . . . . . . . . . . . . . . . . 98
27:20 . . . . . . . . . . . . . . . . . . . . . . . . 98
27:23 . . . . . . . . . . . . . . . . . . . . . . . 182
28:17 . . . . . . . . . . . . . . . . . . . . 18, 174
28:23 . . . . . . . . . . . . . . . . . 30, 99, 173
28:23-31 . . . . . . . . . . . . . . . . . . . . . 30
28:31 . . . . . . . . . . . . . . . . . 30, 99, 173

*Romans*
1:1-7 . . . . . . . . . . . . . . . . . . . . . . . 124
1:1f. . . . . . . . . . . . . . . . . . . . . . . . . 174
1:3-4 . . . . . . . . . . . . . . . . . . . . . . . 124
1:4 . . . . . . . . . . . . . . . . . . . . . . . . . 156
4:24 . . . . . . . . . . . . . . . . . . . . . . . . 123
4:25 . . . . . . . . . . . . . . . . . . . . . . . . 123

5:10 . . . . . . . . . . . . . . . . . . . . . . . . . . 7
6:4 . . . . . . . . . . . . . . . . . . . . . . . 27, 28
8:11 . . . . . . . . . . . . . . . . . . . . . . . . 123
8:34 . . . . . . . . . . . . . . . . . 11, 126, 128
10:6 . . . . . . . . . . . . . . . . . . . . . 12, 140
10:6b . . . . . . . . . . . . . . . . . . . . . . . 140
10:6-7 . . . . . . . . . . . . . . . . . . . . . . 140
10:6-8 . . . . . . . . . . . 28, 135, 136, 140
10:7 . . . . . . . . . . . . . . . . . . . . . . . . . 12
10:8 . . . . . . . . . . . . . . . . . . . . . . . . 140
10:9 . . . . . . . . . . . . . . . . . . . . . . . . 123

*1 Corinthians*
1:23 . . . . . . . . . . . . . . . . . . . . . . . . . . 7
2:2 . . . . . . . . . . . . . . . . . . . . . . . . . . . 7
6:11 . . . . . . . . . . . . . . . . . . . . . . . . . 56
6:14 . . . . . . . . . . . . . . . . . . . . . . . . 123
9:1 . . . . . . . . . . . . . . . . . . . . . 129, 173
9:1-2 . . . . . . . . . . . . . . . . . . . . . . . 174
11:18 . . . . . . . . . . . . . . . . . . . . . . . . 18
11:20 . . . . . . . . . . . . . . . . . . . . . . . . 18
14:23 . . . . . . . . . . . . . . . . . . . . . . . . 18
14:26 . . . . . . . . . . . . . . . . . . . . . . . . 18
15 . . . . . . . . . . . . . . . . . . . . . . . . . 4, 6
15:1-8 . . . . . . . . . . . . . . . . . . . . . . 123
15:3 . . . . . . . . . . . . . . . . . . . . . . . . 123
15:3ff. . . . . . . . . . . . . . . . . . . . . . . 122
15:3-5 . . . . . . . . . . . . . . . . . . . . . . . 27
15:3-8 . . . . . . . . . . . . . . . . . . . . . . . 23
15:4 . . . . . . . . . . . . . . . . . . . . . . . . 123
15:5-10 . . . . . . . . . . . . . . . . . . . . . . 26
15:5-8 . . . . . . . . . . . . . . . . . . . . . . . 97
15:6 . . . . . . . . . . . . . . . . . . . . . . . . 175
15:8 . . . . . 129, 131, 143, 161, 172, 173
15:9 . . . . . . . . . . . . . . . . . . . . . . . . 174
15:15 . . . . . . . . . . . . . . . . . . . . . . . 123
15:20 . . . . . . . . . . . . . . . . . . . . . . . 123
15:23 . . . . . . . . . . . . . . . . . . . . . . . 123
15:42-44 . . . . . . . . . . . . . . . . . . . . . 28
15:44 . . . . . . . . . . . . . . . . . . . . . . . 161
15:51-52 . . . . . . . . . . . . . . . . . . . . 195
15:52 . . . . . . . . . . . . . . . . . . . . . . . . 67

*2 Corinthians*
4:4 . . . . . . . . . . . . . . . . . . . . . . . . . . . 7
4:14 . . . . . . . . . . . . . . . . . . . . . . . . 123

5:15 . . . . . . . . . . . . . . . . . . . . . . 123
5:16 . . . . . . . . . . . . . . . . . . . . . . 148
11:5 . . . . . . . . . . . . . . . . . . . . . . 174
12:11 . . . . . . . . . . . . . . . . . . . . . . 174
12:2-4 . . . . . . . . . . . . . . . . . . . . . . 195

*Galatians*
1-2 . . . . . . . . . . . . . . . . . . . . . . 174
1:1 . . . . . . . . . . . . . . . . . . . . 123, 174
1:16 . . . . . . . . . . . . . . . . . . . 129, 144
3:1 . . . . . . . . . . . . . . . . . . . . . . . . 7

*Ephesians*
1:19-20 . . . . . . . . . . . . . . . . . . . . . 11
1:20 . . . . . . . . . . . . . . . . . . . . . . 155
1:20-21 . . . . . . . . . . . . . . . . . . . . . 127
1:21 . . . . . . . . . . . . . . . . . . . . . . 128
2:6 . . . . . . . . . . . . . . . . . . . . 127, 155
3:10 . . . . . . . . . . . . . . . . . . . . . . 142
4:7-11 . . . . . . . . . . . . . . . . . . . . . . 28
4:8 . . . . . . . . . . . . . . . . . . . . . . 140
4:8-10 . . . . 22, 120, 140, 156, 157, 165
4:9 . . . . . . . . . . . . . . . . . . . . . . 127

*Philippians*
2:5-11 . . . . . . . . . . . . . . . . . . . . . 124
2:5ff. . . . . . . . . . . . . . . . . . . . . . . 7
2:6-11 . . . . . . . . . . . . . . . . . . . . . 124
2:8 . . . . . . . . . . . . . . . . . . . . . . . 11
2:8-11 . . . . . . . . . . . . . . . . . . . 12, 27
2:9 . . . . . . . . . . . . . . . . . 11, 155, 156
2:9-10 . . . . . . . . . . . . . . . . . . . . . 128
2:9-11 . . . . . . . . . . . . . . . . . . . . . 124

*Colossians*
1:15-20 . . . . . . . . . . . . . . . . . . . . . 128
1:18 . . . . . . . . . . . . . . . . . . . . . . 123
2:10 . . . . . . . . . . . . . . . . . . . . . . 128
2:12 . . . . . . . . . . . . . . . . . . . . . . 123
2:15 . . . . . . . . . . . . . . . . . . . . . . 128
3:1 . . . . . . . . . . . . . . . . . . 11, 12, 126

*1 Thessalonians*
1:10 . . . . . . . . 12, 26, 27, 123, 128, 182
2:3-6 . . . . . . . . . . . . . . . . . . . . . 174
4:16 . . . . . . . . . . . . . . . . . . . . 27, 120

4:17 . . . . . . . . . . . . . . . . . . . 106, 195
5:1 . . . . . . . . . . . . . . . . . . . . . . 103

*2 Thessalonians*
1:7 . . . . . . . . . . . . . . . . . . . . 12, 115
2:2 . . . . . . . . . . . . . . . . . . . . . . 169
2:1-12 . . . . . . . . . . . . . . . . . . . . . 175

*1 Timothy*
3:16 . . . . . . . . . 11, 15, 22, 27, 81, 120
. . . . . . . . . . . 141, 143, 164, 189, 191

*Hebrews*
1:3 . . . . . . . . . . . . . . . . . . . . . 7, 129
1:4 . . . . . . . . . . . . . . . . . . . . . . 124
1:5 . . . . . . . . . . . . . . . . . . . . . . 124
1:13 . . . . . . . . . . . . . . . . . . . . . . 129
4:14 . . . . . . . . . . . . . . . . . . . . 27, 129
5:1 . . . . . . . . . . . . . . . . . . . . . . . 32
5:5 . . . . . . . . . . . . . . . . . . . . . . 124
6:20 . . . . . . . . . . . . . . . . . . . . . . 129
7:26 . . . . . . . . . . . . . . . . . . . . . . 129
8:1 . . . . . . . . . . . . . . . . . . . . . . 129
9:12-13 . . . . . . . . . . . . . . . . . . . . . 129
9:24 . . . . . . . . . . . . . . . . . . . . 27, 129
10:12 . . . . . . . . . . . . . . . . . . . . . . 129
11:5 . . . . . . . . . . . . . . . . . . . . . 43, 57
11:30 . . . . . . . . . . . . . . . . . . . . . . 98
12:2 . . . . . . . . . . . . . . . . . . . . . . 129
13:20 . . . . . . . . . . . . . . . . . . . 123, 129

*1 Peter*
1:12 . . . . . . . . . . . . . . . . . . . . . . 142
2:4 . . . . . . . . . . . . . . . . . . . . . . . 56
3:19 . . . . . . . . . . . . . . . . . . . . . . . 22
3:19-20 . . . . . . . . . . . . . . . . . . . . . 177
3:21 . . . . . . . . . . . . . . . . . . . . . . . 11
3:21-22 . . . . . . . . . . . . . . . . . . . . . 128
3:22 . . . . . . . . . . . . . . . . . 11, 22, 27, 157

*2 Peter*
1:15 . . . . . . . . . . . . . . . . . . . . . . . 86
3:1-13 . . . . . . . . . . . . . . . . . . . . . 175
3:4 . . . . . . . . . . . . . . . . . . . . . . 169
3:9 . . . . . . . . . . . . . . . . . . . . . . . 56

*1 John*
4:9 . . . . . . . . . . . . . . . . . . . . . . . 112
4:10 . . . . . . . . . . . . . . . . . . . . . . 112
4:14 . . . . . . . . . . . . . . . . . . . . . . 112

*Jude*
6-7 . . . . . . . . . . . . . . . . . . . . . . 177
14 . . . . . . . . . . . . . . . . . . . . . . 57, 58

*Revelation*
1:5 . . . . . . . . . . . . . . . . . . . . . . 123
1:12-18 . . . . . . . . . . . . . . . . . . . . 27
6:9-11 . . . . . . . . . . . . . . . . . . . . . 177
10:9 . . . . . . . . . . . . . . . . . . . . . . 106

11:3f. . . . . . . . . . . . . . . . . . . . . . 49
11:3-12 . . . . . . . . . . . . . . 48, 65, 70
11:3-13 . . . . . . . . . . . . . . . . . . . . 25
11:12 . . . . . . . . . . . . . . . . . . . . . 104
12:1-6 . . . . . . . . . . . . . . . . . . . . . 142
12:5 . . . . . . . . . . 26, 77, 142, 164, 189
14:13 . . . . . . . . . . . . . . . . . . . . . 148
14:14 . . . . . . . . . . . . . . . . . . . . . 127
19:9-10 . . . . . . . . . . . . . . . . . . . . 106
20:13 . . . . . . . . . . . . . . . . . . . . . 177
21:2 . . . . . . . . . . . . . . . . . . . . . . 114
22:8 . . . . . . . . . . . . . . . . . . . . . . 106
22:20 . . . . . . . . . . . . . . . . . . . . . 178

## e. Early Christian and Gnostic Writings

*Abraham of Hermonthis* . . . . . . . . . . . . 86

*Acts of John*
102 (16) . . . . . . . . . . . . . . . . . . . . 81

*Acts of Pilate*
9:25 . . . . . . . . . . . . . . . . . . . . . . . 43
14:1 . . . . . . . . . . . . . . . . . . . . . . 143
15:1 . . . . . . . . . . . . . . . . . . . . . . . 63
16:6-7 . . . . . . . . . . . . . . . . . . . . . 51

Ambrose
*De Cain et Abel* I 2, 8 . . . . . . . . . . . . 65

*Apocalypse of Paul*
20 . . . . . . . . . . . . . . . . . . . . . . . . 46

*Apocalypse of Peter*
2 . . . . . . . . . . . . . . . . . . . . . . . . . 49
17 . . . . . . . . . . . . . . . . . . . . . . . 120

*Apocryphon of James*
2:19-24 . . . . . . . . . . . . . . . . . . . . 99
14:30 . . . . . . . . . . . . . . . . . . . 99, 145

*Apostolic Constitutions (ConstAp)*
V 20, 2 . . . . . . . . . . . . . . . . . . . . 145
VIII 12, 21 . . . . . . . . . . . . . . . . . . 51

VIII 41, 4 . . . . . . . . . . . . . . . . . . . 51

Augustine . . . . . . . . . . . . . . . . . . . . 30
*CivDei* 18, 21 . . . . . . . . . . . . . . . . 39
*CommJoh* 12, 8 . . . . . . . . . . . . . . 135
*CommJoh* 74, 2 . . . . . . . . . . . . . . 65

Barnabas
15:9 . . . . . . . . . . . . 26, 143, 189, 190

Bede
*ExpLuc* 3, 9 . . . . . . . . . . . . . . . . . 82

Chrysostom
*ActHom* 1, 4 . . . . . . . . . . . . . . 98, 100
*ActHom* 2, 3 . . . . . . . . . . . . . . . . 107
*ActHom* 3, 1 . . . . . . . . . . . . . . . . 108

1 Clement
9:3 . . . . . . . . . . . . . . . . . . . . 43, 51
24:1 . . . . . . . . . . . . . . . . . . . . . . 123

Clement of Alexandria
*Stromata* 1, 23 (155, 1-7) . . . . . . . . . 65
*Stromata* 2, 15 (70, 1) . . . . . . . . . . . 44
*Stromata* 3, 25 . . . . . . . . . . . . . . . 171
*Stromata* 6, 15 (132, 2) . . . . . . . . 68, 81
*Stromata* 6, 15 (132, 2-3) . . . . . . . . . 66

Commodian
   *CarmDuoPop* 833-864 ........... 63

Cyprian
   *Mort* 23 ...................... 44

Cyril of Alexandria
   *CommJoh* 2 .................. 135

Epistula Apostolorum (Eth)
   18 (29) ................... 99, 190
   51 (62) .............. 99, 163, 190

Epiphanius
   *AdvHaer* 1, 3, *Haer* 40, 7 ........ 76

Euodius
   *EpAug* 158, 6 .................. 66

Eusebius
   *Chronicon* I 3, 2 ............... 37
   *Chronicon* I 7, 1 ............... 37
   *HistEccl* 2 (1-2) ................ 8
   *HistEccl* 8 (1) ................. 8
   *HistEccl* I xiii, 4 ............. 171
   *HistEccl* II i (prologue) .......... 171
   *HistEccl* II i, 3 ............... 171
   *HistEccl* II xiii, 3 ............. 171
   *HistEccl* III v, 2 ............. 171
   *HistEccl* III xxix, 2 ............ 171
   *HistEccl* III xxxix, 10 .......... 171
   *HistEccl* V xvi, 14 .............. 81
   *PraepEv* IX 17, 2-9 ............. 57
   *PraepEv* IX 29 ................. 65

Gospel of Peter (EvPe)
   5:19 ................... 7, 81, 148
   9:35-10:42 .................... 163
   9:35-42 .................. 26, 190
   10 ........................... 25

Gospel of Thomas
   104 ......................... 138

Gregory-Nazianzus
   *Epitaph* 92, 1 .................. 51

Hermas (s)
   VIII 2, 3 ..................... 106

Hermas (v)
   IV 2, 1 ...................... 106
   IV 2, 4 ....................... 56
   IV 3, 5 ...................... 106

Hesychius
   *Quaest* 60 .................... 89

Hippolytus
   *CommDan* 22 .................. 49
   *De Antichristo* 43 .............. 49
   *In Psalmum* XXIII ............. 120

Ignatius
   *Smyrneans* 3:3 ................ 101
   *Smyrneans* 7:1 ................ 123
   *Trallians* 9:2 ................. 123

Irenaeus
   *AdvHaer* I 10, 1 ................ 23
   *AdvHaer* I 3, 2 ................. 99
   *AdvHaer* I 30, 4 ............... 145
   *AdvHaer* I 30, 14 ............... 99
   *AdvHaer* II 20, 3 .............. 120
   *AdvHaer* II 32, 3 ............... 23
   *AdvHaer* III 10, 6 .......... 23, 143
   *AdvHaer* III 12, 1 .............. 23
   *AdvHaer* III 12, 5 .............. 23
   *AdvHaer* III 16, 8 .............. 23
   *AdvHaer* III 17, 2 .............. 23
   *AdvHaer* IV 33, 13 ............. 120
   *AdvHaer* V 5, 1 ................ 49
   *AdvHaer* V 31, 2 ............... 23
   *Dem* 41 ...................... 23
   *Dem* 83 ...................... 23
   *Dem* 84 .................. 23, 120

Jerome
   *CommAmos* III 9, 6 ............. 65
   *DieDomPasch* ................. 166

Justin
   *Apol* 1, 26 ................... 171

*Apol* 1, 50 . . . . . . . . . . . . . . . . . . . . 23
*Apol* 1, 51 . . . . . . . . . . . . . . . . . . . 120
*Dial* 19 . . . . . . . . . . . . . . . . . . . . . 43
*Dial* 36 . . . . . . . . . . . . . . . . . . . . 120
*Dial* 39 . . . . . . . . . . . . . . . . . . . . 120
*Dial* 49 . . . . . . . . . . . . . . . . . . . . . 63
*Dial* 80 . . . . . . . . . . . . . . . . . . . . . 81
*Dial* 85 . . . . . . . . . . . . . . . . . . . . 120
*Dial* 87 . . . . . . . . . . . . . . . . . . . . 120
*Dial* 105 . . . . . . . . . . . . . . . . . . . . 86

Lactantius
　*Epit* 47 . . . . . . . . . . . . . . . . 119, 145
　*Inst* IV 21, 1 . . . . . . . . . . . . . . . . . 119
　*Inst* VII 17, 1-3 . . . . . . . . . . . . . . . 63

Origen
　*Hexapla* Ps 140:4 . . . . . . . . . . . . . 100
　*HomJos* 2, 1 . . . . . . . . . . . . . . . . . . 66
　*CommMatt* 140 . . . . . . . . . . . . . . . 81
　*CommJoh* 6, 7 . . . . . . . . . . . . . . . . 75

Pistis Sophia
　1 . . . . . . . . . . . . . . . . . . . . . . . . . . . 99

Polycarp
　1:2 . . . . . . . . . . . . . . . . . . . . . . . . 123
　2:1 . . . . . . . . . . . . . . . . . . . . . . . . 123
　12:2 . . . . . . . . . . . . . . . . . . . . . . . 123

Pseudo-Athanasius
　*In assumptionem* 5 . . . . . . . . . . . . . 105
　*QuaestAntDuc* . . . . . . . . . . . . . . . . 108

Pseudo-Clement
　*Homiliae* 3, 47 . . . . . . . . . . . . . . . . 81
　*Homiliae* 11 . . . . . . . . . . . . . . . . . 100
　*Homiliae* 13, 4 . . . . . . . . . . . . . . . 100
　*Recogn* 7, 29 . . . . . . . . . . . . . . . . 100

Pseudo-Cyprian
　*MontSinSion* 5 . . . . . . . . . . . . . . . . 49

Pseudo-Ignatius
　*Trallians* 9 . . . . . . . . . . . . . . . . . . 144

Pseudo-Oecumenius
　*CommAct* 1, 4 . . . . . . . . . . . . . . . . 101

Tatian
　*Diatessaron* . . . . . . . . . . . . . . . . . . 145

Tertullian
　*AdvIud* 13, 23 . . . . . . . . . . . . . . . 166
　*AdvMarc* 5, 8 . . . . . . . . . . . . . . . . 120
　*AdvMarc* 5, 17 . . . . . . . . . . . . . . . 120
　*Anima* 50 . . . . . . . . . . . . . . . . . . . 49
　*Apol* 21 . . . . . . . . . . . . . . . . . . . . 98
　*Res* 22 . . . . . . . . . . . . . . . . . . . . . 63
　*Scorp* 10 . . . . . . . . . . . . . . . . . . . 120

Theophylact
　*ExpAct* 1, 4 . . . . . . . . . . . . . . . . . 101

Victorinus of Pettau
　*CommApc* 11, 3 . . . . . . . . . . . . . . . 77

## f. Classical and Other Ancient Writings

Antoninus Liberalis
　25, 4 . . . . . . . . . . . . . . . . . . . . . . . . 92
　33, 4 . . . . . . . . . . . . . . . . . . . . . . . 41

Apollodorus
　*Bibliotheca* II 7, 7 . . . . . . . . 38, 67, 104
　*Bibliotheca* III 2, 2 . . . . . . . . . . . . . 68

Apollonius Rhodius

*Argonautica* IV 57.58 . . . . . . . . . . . . 92

Appian
　*RomHist* 2, 1 . . . . . . . . . . . . . . . . . . 8
　*RomHist* 7, 1 . . . . . . . . . . . . . . . 8, 96

Aristotle
　*Rhetorica* I 2, 16 . . . . . . . . . . . . . . . 97

Arrian
    *Anabasis* VII 27, 3 . . . . . . . . . . . . . . 39

Artemidorus
    *Oneirocriticum* 2, 1 . . . . . . . . . . . . . . 8

Chariton
    3, 3 . . . . . . . . . . . . . . . . . . . . . . . . . 41

Cicero
    *DeoNat* II 14, 62 . . . . . . . . . . . . . . 38
    *DeoNat* III 16, 39 . . . . . . . . . . . . . 38
    *RePub* 2, 10 (17f.) . . . . . . . . . . . . . 39
    *Tusculanae* I 14, 32 . . . . . . . . . . . . 38

Dio Cassius
    *RomHist* LII 35, 5 . . . . . . . . . . . . . 39
    *RomHist* LVI 42, 3 . . . . . . . . . . . . 92
    *RomHist* LVI 46, 2 . . . . . . . . . . . 106
    *RomHist* LIX 11, 4 . . . . . . . . . . . 106
    *RomHist* LXVI 17, 3 . . . . . . . . . . . 39

Diodorus Siculus
    *Hist* I 42, 1-2 . . . . . . . . . . . . . . . . . . 8
    *Hist* II 1, 1 . . . . . . . . . . . . . . . . . . . . 8
    *Hist* II 20, 1 . . . . . . . . . . . . . . . . 60, 67
    *Hist* III 1, 1-2 . . . . . . . . . . . . . . . . . . 8
    *Hist* III 60, 3 . . . . . . . . . . . . . . 60, 67
    *Hist* IV 1, 1 . . . . . . . . . . . . . . . . . . . . 8
    *Hist* IV 1, 5 . . . . . . . . . . . . . . . . . . . . 8
    *Hist* IV 38, 5 . . . . . . . . . . . . . . 38, 41
    *Hist* IV 58, 6 . . . . . . . . . . . . . . . . . 39
    *Hist* IV 82, 6 . . . . . . . . . . . . . . . . . 68
    *Hist* V 2, 1 . . . . . . . . . . . . . . . . . . . . 8
    *Hist* V 59, 4 . . . . . . . . . . . . . . . . . 68
    *Hist* XIX 1, 10 . . . . . . . . . . . . . . . . . 8
    *Hist* XX 2, 3 . . . . . . . . . . . . . . . 8, 96

Diogenes Laertius
    *Lives* VIII 2, 68 . . . . . . . . . . . . . . 39, 41
    *Lives* VIII 2, 69 . . . . . . . . . . . . . . . 39

Dionysios Halicarnassus
    *AntRom* I 64, 4 . . . . . . . . . . . . . . . . . 41
    *AntRom* I 77, 2 . . . . . . . . . . . . . . 67, 104
    *AntRom* I 90, 2 . . . . . . . . . . . . . . . . . 8

*AntRom* II 56, 2 . . . . . . . . . . . . . . . . 60
*AntRom* II 56, 6 . . . . . . . . . . . . . . . . 39
*AntRom* VII 73-VIII 1 . . . . . . .    . . . . 8

Dosiades
    FGH 458 fgm 5 . . . . . . . . . . 38, 60, 104

Epictetus
    IV 4, 38 . . . . . . . . . . . . . . . . . . . . . . 86

Euripides
    *Andromache* 1256 . . . . . . . . . . . . . . 39
    *Helena* 1676-1677 . . . . . . . . . . . . . . 38
    *Heraclidae* 910 . . . . . . . . . . . . . . . . 38
    *Lysias* 2, 11 . . . . . . . . . . . . . . . . . . 38

Gilgamesh Epic
    11 . . . . . . . . . . . . . . . . . . . . . . . . . . . 37
    11, 196 . . . . . . . . . . . . . . . . . . . . . . . 41

Herodian
    *Hist* 3, 1 . . . . . . . . . . . . . . . . . . . . . . 8
    *Hist* 4, 1 . . . . . . . . . . . . . . . . . . . . . . 8
    *Hist* 4, 2 . . . . . . . . . . . . . . . . . . . . . 39
    *Hist* 5, 1 . . . . . . . . . . . . . . . . . . . . . . 8
    *Hist* 6, 1 . . . . . . . . . . . . . . . . . . . . . . 8
    *Hist* 7, 1 . . . . . . . . . . . . . . . . . . . . . . 8
    *Hist* 8, 1 . . . . . . . . . . . . . . . . . . . . . . 8

Herodotus
    *Hist* 1, 24 . . . . . . . . . . . . . . . . . . . 104
    *Hist* 4, 94-96 . . . . . . . . . . . . . . . . . 68

Hesiod
    *Erga* 167-173 . . . . . . . . . . . . . . . . . 38
    *Erga* 171 . . . . . . . . . . . . . . . . . . . . 36
    *fgm* 148 . . . . . . . . . . . . . . . . . . . . . 92

Homer
    *Ilias* 2, 546-550 . . . . . . . . . . . . . . . 68
    *Ilias* 20, 232 . . . . . . . . . . . . . . . . . . 39
    *Ilias* 20, 233-235 . . . . . . . . . . . . . . 38
    *Odyssey* 4, 561-565 . . . . . . . . . . . . . 38
    *Odyssey* 4, 563 . . . . . . . . . . . . . . . . 36
    *Odyssey* 20, 63-66 . . . . . . . . . . . . . . 59

Homeric Hymns
5, 208 . . . . . . . . . . . . . . . . . . . . . . . . 59

Horace
*Carm* I 2, 42-48 . . . . . . . . . . . . . . . . 60

Livy
*AUC* I 16, 1 . . . . . . . . . . . . . . . . . . . 67
*AUC* I 16, 2 . . . . . . . . . . . . . . . . . . . 60

Lucian
*ArtConscr* 55 . . . . . . . . . . . . . . . . . . . 94
*Cynicus* 13 . . . . . . . . . . . . . . . . . . . . . 38
*Hermotimus* 7 . . . . . . . . . . . . . . . . 38, 39
*JuppTrag* 16 . . . . . . . . . . . . . . . . . 104
*MortPer* 39 . . . . . . . . . . . . . . . . . . . 93

Ovid
*Metamorphoses* 8, 218-220 . . . . . . . . 39
*Metamorphoses* 10, 159-161 . . . . . . . 38
*Metamorphoses* 14, 607 . . . . . . . . . . 39

Pap Oxy
VIII 1121, 12 . . . . . . . . . . . . . . . . . 102

Pausanias
*Periegesis* VI 9, 7-8 . . . . . . . . . . . . . . 41
*Periegesis* IX 37, 7 . . . . . . . . . . . . . . 68
*Periegesis* IX 39, 2 . . . . . . . . . . . . . . 68

Petronius
*Satyricon* 17 . . . . . . . . . . . . . . . . . . 38

PGrM
5, 277 . . . . . . . . . . . . . . . . . . . . . . . . 104

Philostratus
*VitAp* 8, 29-30 . . . . . . . . . . . . . . . . . 38
*VitAp* 8, 30 . . . . . . . . . . . . . . . . . . . . 68

Pindar
*NemOd* 10, 7 . . . . . . . . . . . . . . . . . . . 39

Plato
*Leg* 747e . . . . . . . . . . . . . . . . . . . . . 111
*Rep* 5, 453 D . . . . . . . . . . . . . . . . . 104

*Theaetetus* 177a . . . . . . . . . . . . . . . . 110

Plutarch
*Camillus* 33, 7 . . . . . . . . . . . . . . . . . 67
*Numa* 2, 3 . . . . . . . . . . . . . . . . . . . . 92
*Numa* 2, 4 . . . . . . . . . . . . . . . . . . . . 106
*Romulus* 27, 5 . . . . . . . . . . . . . . 60, 67
*Romulus* 27, 7 . . . . . . . . . . . . . . . . . 60
*Romulus* 27, 8 . . . . . . . . . . . . . . 39, 93
*Romulus* 28, 6 . . . . . . . . . . . . . . . . . 41

Polybius
*Hist* II 1, 1-3 . . . . . . . . . . . . . . . . . . 96
*Hist* II 1, 1-4 . . . . . . . . . . . . . . . . . . 8
*Hist* III 1, 1-3 . . . . . . . . . . . . . . . . . 8
*Hist* IV 1, 1-2 . . . . . . . . . . . . . . . . . 96
*Hist* IV 1, 1-3 . . . . . . . . . . . . . . . . . 8

Polyhistor . . . . . . . . . . . . . . . . . . . . . 65

Seneca
*Apocolocyntosis* 1 . . . . . . . . . . . . . . 106
*Apocolocyntosis* 8-9 . . . . . . . . . . . . 39
*Apocolocyntosis* 9 . . . . . . . . . . . . . . 38
*Apocolocyntosis* 11 . . . . . . . . . . . . . 39

Sophocles
*OedCol* 1654 . . . . . . . . . . . . . . . . . 93
*OedCol* 1659f. . . . . . . . . . . . . . . . . 60
*OedCol* 1661f. . . . . . . . . . . . . . . . . 68
*OedCol* 1681 . . . . . . . . . . . . . . . . . 68
*Trach* 1085 . . . . . . . . . . . . . . . . . . 111

Suetonius
*Augustus* 100, 4 . . . . . . . . . . . . . . . 106
*Vespasian* 23, 4 . . . . . . . . . . . . . . . . 39

Xenophon
*Anabasis* II 1, 1-2 . . . . . . . . . . . . . . . 8
*Anabasis* III 1, 1 . . . . . . . . . . . . . . . 96
*Anabasis* III 1, 1-2 . . . . . . . . . . . . . . 8
*Anabasis* IV 1, 1 . . . . . . . . . . . . . . . 96
*Anabasis* IV 1, 1-2 . . . . . . . . . . . . . . 8
*Anabasis* V 1, 1-2 . . . . . . . . . . . . . . 8
*Anabasis* VII 1, 1 . . . . . . . . . . . . . . . 96
*Anabasis* VII 1, 1-2 . . . . . . . . . . . . . 8

# INDEX OF MODERN AUTHORS

Aalders, G.Ch. . . . . . . . . . . . . . . . . . . . . 61
Aberbach, M. . . . . . . . . . . . . . . . 41, 43, 63
Abrahams, I. . . . . . . . . . . . . . . . . . . . . . . 41
Adler, W. . . . . . . . . . . . . . . . . . . . . . . . . 58
Aland, B. . . . . . . . . . . . . . . . . . . . . . . . 190
Aland, K. . . . . . . . . . . . . 83, 131, 189, 190
Albeck, Ch. . . . . . . . . . . . . . . . . . . . 41, 44
Alexander, L.C.E. . . . . . . . . . . . . . . . . . 95
Alexander, P. . . . . . . . . . . . . . . . . . . . . . 51
Allison, D. . . . . . . . . . . . . . . . . . . . . . . . 63
Alsup, J.E. . . . . . . . . . . . . . . . . 159-161
Andersen, F.I. . . . . . . . . . . . . . . . . . . . . 49
Appel, H. . . . . . . . . . . . . . . . . . . . . . . . . 55
Ashton, J. . . . . . . . . . . . . . . . . . . . . . . 134
Baarda, T. . . . . . . . . . . . . . . . . . . . . . . . 96
Bacon, B.W. . . . . . . . . . . . . . . . . . . . . . . 5
Baer, H. von . . . . . . . . . . . . . . . . . . . . . 13
Bahrdt, K.F. . . . . . . . . . . . . . . . . . . . . . . 2
Balz, H.R. . . . . . . . . . . . . . . . . . . . . 73, 99
Bammel, E. . . . . . . . . . . . . . . . . . . . . . . 49
Barbi, A. . . . . . . . . . . . . . 73, 110, 112-115
Barnard, L.W. . . . . . . . . . . . . . . . . . . . 143
Barrett, C.K. . . . . . . . . . . . 49, 96, 111-113
. . . . . . . . . . . . . . . . . . 135-137, 154-156
. . . . . . . . . . . . . . . 162-163, 177, 183, 191
Barth, G. . . . . . . . . . . . . . . . . . . . . . . . 130
Barth, M. . . . . . . . . . . . . . . . . . . 140, 141
Bauckham, R.J. . . . . . . . . . . . . . . . . 49, 66
Bauer, W. . . . . . . . . . . . . . . . . . . . . . . . . 5
Bauernfeind, O. . . . . . . . . . . . . . . 101, 102
. . . . . . . . . . . . . . . . . . . . . . 106, 112-114
Baum, A.D. . . . . . . . . . . . . . . . . . . . 83-84
Beasley-Murray, G.R. . . . . . . . . . . . . . 175
Becker, H. . . . . . . . . . . . . . . . . . . . . . . 126
Beek, M.A. . . . . . . . . . . . . . . . . . . . . . . 58
Behm, J. . . . . . . . . . . . . . . . . . . . . . . . 133
Ben-Yaacob, A. . . . . . . . . . . . . . . . . . . 72
Bengel, J.A. . . . . . . . . . . . . . 91, 100, 164
Benoit, P. . . . . . . . . . . 9-11, 27, 138, 163
Berger, K. . . . . . . . . . . . . 25, 36, 41, 47
. . . . . . . . . . . . . . . . . . . 49, 77, 127, 161

Bernard, J.H. . . . . . . . . . . . . 91, 136, 164
Bertram, G. . . . . . . . . . . . . . . . . . . . 7, 125
Betz, O. . . . . . . . . . . . . . . . . . . . . 6, 64, 90
Beyer, H.W. . . . . . . . . . . . . . . . . . . . . . 87
Bickermann, E. . . . . . . . . . . 21, 40, 41, 159
Bieder, W. . . . . . . . . . . . . . . . . . . . . . . 151
Bietenhard, H. . . . . . . . . . 46, 55, 151, 163
Bihlmeyer, K., . . . . . . . . . . . . . . . . . . . 143
Bizer, E. . . . . . . . . . . . . . . . . . . . . . . . 165
Black, M. . . . . . . 45, 46, 51, 52, 55, 62, 75
Blass, F. . . . . . . . . . 10, 102, 155, 157, 158
Bogaert, P.-M. . . . . . . . . . . . . . . . . 69, 77
Boismard, M.-É. . . . . 32-34, 100, 102, 147
Bonnet, M. . . . . . . . . . . . . . . . . . . . . . . 81
Borgen, P. . . . . . . . . . . . . . . . 57, 134, 135
Bornkamm, G. . . . . . . . . . . . . . . . . . . . 130
Böttrich, C. . . . . . . . . . . . . . . . . . . . 49, 76
Bousset, W. . . . . 21, 42, 49, 113, 142, 150
Bouwman, G. . . . . . . . . . . . . . . . . . 17, 96
Bovon, F. . . . . . . . . . . . . . 1, 26, 119, 170
. . . . . . . . . . . . . . . . . . . . . . 175, 178, 185
Box, G.H. . . . . . . . . . . . . . . . . . . . . 43, 62
Brandenburger, E. . . . . . . . . . . . . . . . . . 66
Braude, A.A. . . . . . . . . . . . . . . . . . . . . . 75
Braumann, G. . . . . . . . . . . . . . 89, 95, 180
Braun, H. . . . . . . . . . . . . . . . . . . . . . . . 197
Breytenbach, C. . . . . . . . . . . . . . . . . . . 126
Brodie, T.L. . . . . . . . . . . . . . . . . . . 80, 185
Brown, R.E. . . . . . . . . . . . . 136, 137, 138
. . . . . . . . . . . . . . . . . . . . . . 157, 164, 170
Brox, N. . . . . . . . . . . . . . . . 21, 38, 81, 154
Bruce, F.F. . . . . . . . . . . . . 96, 97, 101, 105
. . . . . . . . . . . . . . 138, 141, 147, 155, 157
. . . . . . . . . . . . . . . . . . 158, 163, 168, 175
Bruggen, J. van . . . . . . . . . 83, 84, 89, 92
. . . . . . . . . . . . . . 131, 133, 139, 177, 178
Brun, L. . . . . . . . . . . . . . . . . 7, 88, 92, 142
Brunner, P. . . . . . . . . . . . . . . . . . . . . . . 10
Büchsel, F. . . . . . . . . . . . . . . . . . . . . . 141
Bultmann, R. . . . . . . . . . . 6, 11, 102, 115
. . . . . . . . . . . 122-124, 127, 136, 137, 190

Burchard, Ch. . . . . . . . . . . . . . . . 173, 174
Burgon, J.W. . . . . . . . . . . . . . . . . . . 131
Burrows, E. . . . . . . . . . . . . . . . . . . . . 37
Busse, U. . . . . . . . . . . . . . . . . . . . . . 136
Cadbury, H.J. . . . . . . . 89, 90, 95, 100, 146
Calvin, J. . . . . . . . . . . . . . . . . . . 82, 94
Campbell Morgan, R. . . . . . . . . . . . . . . 37
Caquot, A. . . . . . . . . . . . . . . . . . . . . . 52
Caragounis, C.C. . . . . . . . . . . . . 53-56, 73
Carroll, J.T. . . . . . . . . . . . . . . . . . . . 175
Carson, D.A. . . . . . . . . . . . . . . 136, 137
Casetti, P. . . . . . . . . . . . . . . . . . . . . . 45
Casey, P.M. . . . . . . . . . . . 40, 53, 54, 148
Cassuto, U. . . . . . . . . . . . . . . . . . . . . 41
Cavallin, H.C.C. . . . . . . . . . . . . . . . . 123
Ceriani, A. . . . . . . . . . . . . . . . . . . . . 66
Chance, J.P. . . . . . . . . . . . . . . . 103, 183
Charles, R.H. . . . . . . . . 46, 47, 49, 52-56
. . . . . . . . . . . . . . . . . . . . . . . . . 66, 77, 142
Charlesworth, J.H. . . . . . . . . . . . . . . . . 57
Childs, B.S. . . . . . . . . . . . . . . . . . . . 179
Civil, M. . . . . . . . . . . . . . . . . . . . . . . 37
Clarke, A.D. . . . . . . . . . . . . . . . . . 29, 91
Clarke, E.G. . . . . . . . 43, 51, 63, 68, 70, 75
Cohen, A. . . . . . . . . . . . . . . . . . . . . . 76
Collins, J.J. . . . . . . . . . . . . . . . . . . . . 52
Colpe, C. . . . . . . . . . . 36-38, 53, 146, 147
Conzelmann, H. . . . . . . 12, 13, 16, 89, 104
. . . . . . . . . . . . . . . . 107, 115, 122, 123
. . . . . . . . . . . . . . . . 154, 169, 171, 175
. . . . . . . . . . . . . . . . 176, 178, 180, 188
Cornwall, P.B. . . . . . . . . . . . . . . . . . . 37
Crane, O.T. . . . . . . . . . . . . . . . . . . . . 70
Cranfield, C.E.B. . . . . . . . . . . . . 126, 140
Creed, J.M. . . . . . . . . . . . . . . . . . . . . . 5
Cross, F.L. . . . . . . . . . . . . . . . . . 83, 187
Crown, A.D. . . . . . . . . . . . . . . . . . . . 71
Cullmann, O. . . . . . . . . . . . . 14, 124, 187
Dalman, G. . . . . . . . . . . . . . . . . . . . 107
Danby, H. . . . . . . . . . . . . . . . . . . . . 115
Daube, D. . . . . . . . . . . . . . . . . . . . . . 49
Dautzenberg, G. . . . . . . . . . . . . . . . . 126
Davies, J.G. . . . . . . . . . . . . . 7, 11, 12, 24
. . . . . . . . . . . . . . . . . . . 90, 91, 120, 154
Davies, J.H. . . . . . . . . . . . . . . . . 83, 106
Davies, W.D. . . . . . . . . . . . . . . . . . . 49

Debrunner, A. . . . . . . . . . . . . . . . . . . 148
Deimel, A. . . . . . . . . . . . . . . . . . . . . 37
Deissmann, A. . . . . . . . . . . . . . . . . . . . 7
Delebecque, É. . . . . . . . . . . . . . . . . . 102
Delling, G. . . . . . . . . . . . . . . . . . 82, 104
Dexinger, F. . . . . . . . . . . . . . . . . . . . 71
Dhanis, E. . . . . . . . . . . . . . . . . . 122, 123
Diels, H. . . . . . . . . . . . . . . . . . . . . . . 21
Dietrich, E.L. . . . . . . . . . . . . . . . . . . 110
Díez Merino, L. . . . . . . . . . . . . . . . . . 140
Diez-Macho, A. . . . . . . . . . . . . . . . . . 43
Dihle, A. . . . . . . . . . . . . . . . . . . . . . 115
Dillon, R.J. . . . . . . . . 26, 88, 95, 161, 185
Dinkler, E. . . . . . . . . . . . . . . . . . . . . 124
Dodd, C.H. . . . . . . . . . . . . 112, 153, 167
Dömer, M. . . . . . . . . . . 25, 81, 88, 91, 97
. . . . . . . . . . . . . . 103, 105, 109, 146, 187
Donne, B.K. . . . . . . . . . . . . . . . . . . . 91
Dornier, P. . . . . . . . . . . . . . . . . . . . . 142
Dunn, J.D.G. . . . . . 24-25, 39-40, 56, 112
. . . . . . . . . . . 124, 129, 135, 136, 140-141
. . . . . . . . . . . 157, 164, 172, 175, 182, 185
Dupont, J. . . . . . . . . . . 15, 30, 94, 112, 125
. . . . . . . . . . . . . 128, 148, 149, 156, 177
Ehrman, B.D. . . . . . . . . . . . . 96, 150, 162
Elliott, J.K. . . . . . . . . . . . . . . . . . . . 162
Ellis, E.E. . . . . . . . . . . . . . . . 6, 86, 111
. . . . . . . . . . . . . . . . . 145, 151, 175
Eltester, W. . . . . . . . . . . . . . 5, 15, 102, 177
Enslin, M.S. . . . . . . . . . . 5, 7, 10, 90, 100
Ernst, J. . . . . . . . . . . . . . . . . . . . . 88, 177
Etheridge, J.W. . . . . . . . . . . 63, 68, 70, 75
Evans, C.A. . . . . . . . . . . . . . . . . . 57, 120
Evans, C.F. . . . . . . . . . . . . . . . . 82, 86, 90
Faierstein, M. . . . . . . . . . . . . . . . . . . . 63
Farmer, W.R. . . . . . . . . . . . . . . . . . . 131
Fee, G.D. . . . . . . . . . . . . . . . . . . 123, 129
Feldman, L.H. . . . . . . . . . . . . . 67, 68, 69
Festorazzi, F. . . . . . . . . . . . . . . . . . . 123
Field, F. . . . . . . . . . . . . . . . . . . . . . . 100
Finkelstein, L. . . . . . . . . . . . . . 64, 68, 70
Fitzmyer, J.A. . . . . . . . . 27-28, 48, 63, 82
. . . . . . . . . . . . 89, 107, 119, 124, 128, 139
. . . . . . . . . . . 140, 142, 148, 149, 151, 153
. . . . . . . . . . . . . 156, 163, 170, 174, 192
Flender, H. . . . . . . . . . . . . . . . . . 81, 170

Flusser, D. . . . . . . . . . . . . . . . . . . . . . 83
Fohrer, G. . . . . . . . . . . . . . . . . . . . . . . 42
Fossum, J.E. . . . . . . . . . . . . . . . . . . . . 64
Fraade, S.D. . . . . . . . . . . . . . . . . . . . . 43
Franklin, E. . . . . . . . 16, 105, 149, 159, 180
Freedman, H. . . . . . . . . . . . 41, 44, 70, 75
Fridrichsen, A. . . . . . . . . . . . . . . . . . . 6-7
Friedlander, G. . . . . . . . . . . . . . . . . . . . 75
Friedrich, G. . . . . . . . . . . . . 21, 38, 43, 67
. . . . . . . . . . . . . . . . . 81-83, 104, 106, 154
Fuller, D.O. . . . . . . . . . . . . . . . . . . . . 131
Fuller, D.P. . . . . . . . . . . . . . . . . . . . . . 91
Fuller, R.H. . . . . . . . . . . . 17-18, 112, 122
Funk, F.X. . . . . . . . . . . . . . . . . . . . . . 143
Funk, R.W. . . . . . . . . . . . . . . . . . . . . . 138
Galling, K. . . . . . . . . . . . . . . . . . . . . . . 58
García Martínez, F. . . . . . . . . . . . . . . . 47
Gärtner, B. . . . . . . . . . . . . . . . . . . . . . 112
Gasque, W.W. . . . . . . . . . . . . . . 141, 147
Geldenhuys, J.N. . . . . . . . . . . . . . . . . 164
Gempf, C.H. . . . . . . . . . . . . . . . . . . . . 168
Georgi, D. . . . . . . . . . . . . . . . . . . 124, 139
Gerber, C. . . . . . . . . . . . . . . . . . . . . . . 126
Gesenius, W. . . . . . . . . . . . . . . . . . . . . 42
Ghiberti, É. . . . . . . . . . . . . . . . . . . . . . 122
Giles, K. . . . . . . . . . . . . . . . . . . . . . . . 27
Ginzberg, L. . . . . . . . . . . . . 41, 60, 63-64
. . . . . . . . . . . . . . . . . . . . . . . . . . . 71, 75
Gloer, H.W. . . . . . . . . . . . . . . . . 175, 183
Gnilka, J. . . . . . . . . . . . . . . 130, 132, 141
Goeij, M. de . . . . . . . . . . . . . . . . . . . . 77
Goldstein, J.A. . . . . . . . . . . . . . . . . . . 60
Goodenough, E.R. . . . . . . . . . . . . . . . . 57
Gooding, D.W. . . . . . . . . . . . . . . . . 24-25
Goppelt, L. . . . . . . . . . . . . . . 27, 94, 122
. . . . . . . . . . . . . . . . . . . . . 127, 160, 163
Goslinga, C.J. . . . . . . . . . . . . . . . . . . . . 9
Goulder, M.D. . . . . . . . . . . 6, 90, 106, 186
Gourgues, M. . . . . . . . . 126, 128, 155-158
Graham, H.H. . . . . . . . . . . . . . . . . . . . 183
Graß, H. . . . . . . . . . . . . . . . . . . . . . . . 91
Grässer, E. . . . . . . . . 13, 16, 105, 111, 149
. . . . . . . . . . . . . . . 169, 171, 176, 179, 180
Green, J.B. . . . . . . . . . . . . . . . . . 139, 147
Grégoire, H. . . . . . . . . . . . . . . . . . . . . 81
Grelot, P. . . . . . . . . . 37, 42, 45, 47, 48

Gressmann, H. . . . . . . . . . . . . 42, 113, 150
Groß, H. . . . . . . . . . . . . . . . . . . . . . . . 44
Grosheide, F.W. . . . . . . . . . . . . . 141, 172
Grossfeld, B. . . . . . . . . . . . . . . . . . 41, 42
Gruenwald, I. . . . . . . . . . . . . . . . . . . . 51
Grundmann, W. . . . . . . . . . . . . . . . 86, 148
Guillaume, J.M. . . . . . . . 25, 160, 161, 186
Gundry, R.H. . . . . . . . . . . . . . . . . . . . 141
Gutmann, J. . . . . . . . . . . . . . . . . . . . . . 63
Haacker, K. . . . . . . . . . . . . . . . 64, 66-68
. . . . . . . . . . . . . . . . . . . . . . . 70, 71, 174
Haag, E. . . . . . . . . . . . . . . . . . . . . 44, 59
Haenchen, E. . . . . . . . . 12-14, 56, 97, 102
. . . . . . . . . . . 106, 109, 136, 137, 139. 146
. . . . . . . . . . 154, 158, 169, 171, 177 186
Hahn, F. . . . . . . . . . . . . . . 17, 25-26, 36, 70
. . . . . . . . . . . . . . . 112-114, 124, 126, 139
. . . . . . . . . . . . . . . 143, 149, 153, 188, 198
Halperin, D.J. . . . . . . . . . . . . . . . . . . . 40
Hammer, R. . . . . . . . . . . . . . . . 64, 68, 70
Hampel, V. . . . . . . . . . . . . . . . . . 147, 163
Harnack, A. . . . . . . . . . . 4-5, 7, 9, 190
Harrington, D.J. . . . . . . . . . . . 51, 60, 65
. . . . . . . . . . . . . . . . . . . . . . . 69, 70, 75
Hase, K.A. . . . . . . . . . . . . . . . . . . 2, 10
Haufe, G. . . . . . . . . 17, 54, 69, 77, 79, 139
Hay, D.M. . . . . . . . . . . . . . 126, 149, 182
Hayes, J.H. . . . . . . . . . . . . . . . . . . . . 123
Hayward, R. . . . . . . . . . . . . . . . . . . . . 75
Headlam, A.C. . . . . . . . . . . . . . . . . . . 140
Held, H.J. . . . . . . . . . . . . . . . . . . . . . 130
Heller, J. . . . . . . . . . . . . . . . . . . . . . . 140
Hemer, C.J. . . . . . . . . . . . . . . . . . . . . 168
Hengel, M. . . . . . . . . . 64, 71, 75, 89, 108
. . . . . . . . . . . . . . . 124, 126, 127, 129, 143
Heppe, H. . . . . . . . . . . . . . . . . . . . . . 165
Heuschen, J. . . . . . . . . . . . . . . . . . . . . 10
Hiers, R.H. . . . . . . . . . . . . . . . . . . . . 183
Higger, M. . . . . . . . . . . . . . . . . . . . . . 76
Hilgenfeld, A. . . . . . . . . . . . . . . . . . . 115
Hilhorst, A. . . . . . . . . . . . . . . . . . . . . 96
Himmelfarb, M. . . . . . . . . . . . 41, 64, 76
Hobbs, T.R. . . . . . . . . . . . . . . . . . 58, 59
Hoffmann, P. . . . 21, 38, 81, 122, 123, 154
Höhn, C. . . . . . . . . . . . . . . . . . . . . . . 21
Holladay, C.R. . . . . . . . . . . . . . . . . . . 57

Holland, R. . . . . . . . . . . . . . . . . . . . . . 21
Holleman, J. . . . . . . . . . . . . . . . 123, 124
Holmes, S. . . . . . . . . . . . . . . . . . . . . 44
Holtzmann, H.J. . . . . . . . . . . . . . . 99, 102
. . . . . . . . . . . . . . . . . . . . . . 155, 157, 158
Holzmeister, U. . . . . . . . . . . 7, 15, 98, 137
Hooker, M.D. . . . . . . . . . . . . . . . . . . . 138
Horst, P.W. van der . . . . . . . 38, 39, 66, 97
. . . . . . . . . . . . . . . . . . 101, 102, 106, 108
Horton, F.L. . . . . . . . . . . . . . . . . . . . . 76
Hossfeld, F.-L. . . . . . . . . . . . . . . . . . . 44
Houtman, C. . . . . . . . . . . . . . . . . . . . . 59
Hubbard, B.J. . . . . . . . . . . . . . . . . . . 162
Hug, J. . . . . . . . . . . . . . . . . . 25, 131, 189
Hurtado, L.W. . . . . . . . . . . . . . . . 40, 124
Irsigler, H. . . . . . . . . . . . . . . . . . . . . . 45
Isaac, E. . . . . . . . . . . . . 45, 46, 48, 52-54
Jacobson, H. . . . . . . . . . . . . . . . . . . . . 66
James, M.R. . . . . . . . . . . . . . . . . . . . . 68
Jellinek, A. . . . . . . . . . . . . . . . . . . . . . 70
Jeremias, J. . . . . . . . . . . . 42, 53, 64, 68, 75
. . . . . . . . . . . . . . . 81, 122, 141, 148, 151
Jervell, J. . . . . . . . . . . . . . . . . . . . . . 174
Johnson, L.T. . . . . . . . . . . . . . 82, 96, 101
Jonge, M. de . . . . . . . . . . . . . . . . . . . 134
Jüngel, E. . . . . . . . . . . . . . . . . . . . . . . 11
Junod, E. . . . . . . . . . . . . . . . . . . . . . . 81
Kaczynski, R. . . . . . . . . . . . . . . . . . . 126
Kaestli, J.-D. . . . . . . . . . . . . . . . . . . . 81
Kähler, E. . . . . . . . . . . . . . . . . . . . . . 120
Kappler, W. . . . . . . . . . . . . . . . . . . . . 60
Kaylor, R.D. . . . . . . . . . . . . . . . . 88, 128
Keck, L.E. . . . . . . . . . . . . 13, 90, 161, 182
Kegel, G. . . . . . . . . . . . . . . . . . . . . . 123
Keil, C.F. . . . . . . . . . . . . . . . . . . . . . . 61
Kellermann, U. . . . . . . . . . . . . . . . . . 177
Kettler, F.H. . . . . . . . . . . . . . . . . . . . 177
Kilpatrick, G.D. . . . . . . . . . . . . . . . . . 162
Klein, G. . . . . . . . . . . . . . . . . . . . . . . 95
Klijn, A.F.J. . . . . . . . . . . . . . . 48, 72, 74
77, 96, 115
Klostermann, E. . . . . . . . . . . . . . . . . . 91
Kmosko, M. . . . . . . . . . . . . . . . . . . . . 74
Knibb, M.A. . . . . . . . 45, 46, 48, 52, 54, 99
Knight, G.W. . . . . . . . . . . . . . . 141, 142
Knöppler, Th. . . . . . . . . . . . . . . . 134, 136

Korn, M. . . . . . . . . . . . . . . . . . . . . . . 27
Kraft, R.A. . . . . . . . . . . . . . . . . . . . . . 57
Kramer, S.N. . . . . . . . . . . . . . . . . . . . 37
Kränkl, E. . . . . . . . . . . . . . . 25, 154, 158
Kraus, H.J. . . . . . . . . . . . . . . 45, 125, 140
Kreiswirth, M. . . . . . . . . . . . . . . . . . . 31
Kreitzer, L. . . . . . . . . . . . . . . . . . . . . . 40
Kremer, J. . . . . . . . . . . . 13, 17, 82, 94, 105
. . . . . . . . . . . . 114, 148, 149, 153, 154, 169
Kretschmar, G. . . . . . . . . . . 14-15, 19, 156
Kümmel, W.G. . . . . 90, 111, 131, 178, 180
Künzi, M. . . . . . . . . . . . . . . . . . . . . . 178
Kurz, W.S. . . . . . . . . . . . . . . . . . . . . 111
Kuschel, K.-J. . . . . . . . . . . . . . . . . . . 164
Ladd, G.E. . . . . . . . . . . . . . . . . . 105, 143
Lagrange, M.-J. . . . . . . . . . . . . . 136, 153
Laible, H. . . . . . . . . . . . . . . . . . . . . . 108
Lake, K. . . . . . . . . . . . . . . . . . . . . . . 100
Lambrecht, J. . . . . . . . . . . . . . . . . . . . 128
Lamouille, A. . . . . . . . . . . 32-34, 100, 102
Landau, B. . . . . . . . . . . . . . . . . . . 65, 75
Lane, W.L. . . . . . . . . . . . . . . . . . . . . 139
Larcher, C. . . . . . . . . . . . . . . . . . . . . . 44
Larrañaga, V. . . . . . . . . . . 1, 2, 4, 7-10, 33
. . . . . . . . . . . . . . . 37, 87, 89-91, 95, 98
. . . . . . . . . . . . . . 128, 136, 137, 143, 186
Laverdiere, E.A. . . . . . . . . . . . . . . . . . 16
Leaney, A.R.C. . . . . . . . . . . . . . . . . 6, 187
Lella, A.A. Di . . . . . . . . . . . . . 43, 61, 62
LeLoir, L. . . . . . . . . . . . . . . . . . . . . . 145
Liebermann, S. . . . . . . . . . . . . . . . . . . 51
Lindars, B. . . . . . . . . . . 126, 136, 155, 156
Lindemann, A. . . . . . . . . . . . . . . 122, 175
Linnemann, E. . . . . . . . . . . . . . . . . . . 189
Linton, O. . . . . . . . . . . . . . . . . . . . . . 126
Livingstone, E.A. . . . . . . . . . . . . . . . . 62
Lock, W. . . . . . . . . . . . . . . . . . . . . . . 141
Loewenstamm, S.E. . . . . . . . . . . . . . . . 64
Lohfink, G. . . . . . . . . . . . . . . 1, 15, 20-26
. . . . . . . . . . . . . . . 28, 33, 34, 36-39, 53
. . . . . . . . . . . . . 57, 64-68, 81, 82, 87-90
. . . . . . . . . . . 93, 97, 103-109, 112, 114
. . . . . . . . . . . 121, 124, 126-129, 139, 141
. . . . . . . . . . 142, 150, 152, 154, 155, 157
. . . . . . . . . . 158, 165, 172, 186-190, 196
Lohmeyer, E. . . . . . . . . . . . . . . . . 89, 133

Lohse, E. . . . . . . . . . . . . . . . . . . . . . . 6
Loisy, A. . . . . . . . . . . . . . . . . . . . . . . . 91
Longenecker, R.N. . . . . . . . . . . . . . . . 158
Lösch, St. . . . . . . . . . . . . . . . . . . . . . . 21
Luciani, F. . . . . . . . . . . . . . . . . . . . . . 57
Lüdemann, G. . . . . . . . . . . . . . . . 122, 195
Lührmann, D. . . . . . . . . . . . 43, 44, 58, 138
Luttikhuizen, G.P. . . . . . . . . . . . . . . . . 96
Luzarraga, J. . . . . . . . . . . . . . . 24, 92, 105
Lygre, J.G. . . . . . . . . . . . . . . . 27, 89, 110
145, 149, 152, 153
MacDonald, J. . . . . . . . . . . . . . . . . 70, 71
MacRae, G.W. . . . . . . . . . . . . . . . 182, 197
Maddox, R. . . . . . . . . . . . . . . 82, 149, 177
Maher, M. . . . . . . . . . . . . . . . . . 43, 51, 52
Maile, J.F. . . . . . . 25, 27, 28, 92, 163, 187
Mallau, H.H. . . . . . . . . . . . . . . . . . . . . 74
Marcus, R. . . . . . . . . . . . . . . . . . . . . . 62
Margulies, M. . . . . . . . . . . . . . . . . . . . 64
Marmardji, A.-S. . . . . . . . . . . . . . . . . 145
Marshall, I.H. . . . . . . . . 25, 56, 70, 88, 91
. . . . . . . . . . . . . . . 92, 101, 105, 146-148
. . . . . . . . . . . . . . . . 150, 157, 158, 170
Martin, R.P. . . . . . . . . . . . . 124, 141, 147
Martyn, J.L. . . . . . . . . . . 13, 90, 161, 182
Mattill, A.J. . . . . . . . . . . . . 168, 175-180
Mattill, M. Bedford . . . . . . . . . . . 168, 175
Mayer, E. . . . . . . . . . . . . . . . . . . . . . . 83
McCown, C.C. . . . . . . . . . . . . . . . . . . 89
McKinney, K. . . . . . . . . . . . . . . . . . . . . 1
McNamara, M. . . . . . . . . . . . . . . . . . . 43
McNeile, A.H. . . . . . . . . . . . . . . . . . . 136
Mealand, D.L. . . . . . . . . . . . . . . . . . . 97
Meeks, W.A. . . . . . . . . 64, 65, 69-71, 135
Menoud, Ph.H. . . . . . . . . . . . 5, 6, 14, 28
. . . . . . . . . . . . . . . . 102, 107, 186-187
Merk, O. . . . . . . . . . . . . . . . . . . 111, 122
Metelmann, V. . . . . . . . . . . . . . . . . . 101
Metzger, B.M. . . . . 10, 48, 72-73, 98, 100
. . . . . . . . . . . . . . 104, 115, 122, 131, 135
. . . . . . . . . . . . . . . 137, 150, 158, 190
Meyer, E. . . . . . . . . . . . . . 4-8, 89, 189
Michaelis, W. . . . . . . . . . 6-7, 9, 82, 86, 96
. . . . . . . . . . . . . . 112, 136-138, 157, 163
Michel, O. . . . . . . . . . . . . . 64, 76, 127
Milik, J.T. . . . . . . . . . . . . . . . 47, 51, 62

Mills, W.E. . . . . . . . . . . . . . . . . . . . . . 175
Mirkin, M.A. . . . . . . . . . . . . . . . . . 70, 75
Moehring, H.R. . . . . . . . . . . . . . . . . . 62
Monloubou, L. . . . . . . . . . . . . . . . . . . 52
Moore, A.L. . . . . . . . . . . . . . . . . . . . . 55
Moore, G.F. . . . . . . . . . . . . . . . . . . . . 74
Moule, C.F.D. . . . . . . . . 10, 100, 161, 182
Müller, P.-G. . . . . . . . . . . . . . . . . . . . . 83
Mußner, F. . . . . . . . . . . . . . . . . . . . . . 83
Myers, J.M. . . . . . . . . . . . . . . . . . . . . 73
Neirynck, F. . . . . . . . . . . 95, 111, 112, 175
Nestle, Eb. . . . . . . . . . . . . . . . . . . . . 158
Nicholson, G.C. . . . . . . . . . 134, 135, 136
Nickelsburg, G.W.E. . . . . . 45, 52, 64, 123
Nielsen, J.T. . . . . . . . . . . . . . . . . . . . . 92
Niese, B. . . . . . . . . . . . . . . . . . . . . . . . 69
Nineham, D.E. . . . . . . . . . . . . . . . 11, 105
Nolland, J. . . . . . . . . . . . . . . . 81, 82, 95
122, 148, 177, 189
Oberlinner, L. . . . . . . . . . . . . . . . . . . 141
Odeberg, H. . . . . . . . . . . . . . . 43, 51, 135
Oepke, A. . . . . . . . . . . . . . . . . . . . . . 105
Oesterley, W.O.E. . . . . . . . . . . . 43, 61, 62
Ortiz de Urbina, I. . . . . . . . . . . . . . . . 145
Otto, R. . . . . . . . . . . . . . . . . . . . . . . . 53
O'Toole, R.F. . . . . . . . . 27, 157, 158, 182
Palmer, D.W. . . . . . . . . . . . . . . . . . . . 95
Parsons, M.C. . . . . . . . . . . . . 23, 26-34, 82
. . . . . . . . . . . . . . . . . . . 83, 86, 87, 90
. . . . . . . . . . . . . . . 96, 105, 107, 109
. . . . . . . . . . . . . . . 160, 186, 189-190
Paulsen, H. . . . . . . . . . . . . . . . . . . . . 126
Paulus, H.E.G. . . . . . . . . . . . . . . . . . . . 2
Pease, A.S. . . . . . . . . . . . . . . 21, 39, 104
Perrin, N. . . . . . . . . . . . . 54, 56, 105, 156
Perrot, C. . . . . . . . . . . . . . . . . . . . . . . 69
Pesch, R. . . . . 18, 20, 88, 90, 102, 106-107
. . . . . . . . 131, 133, 138, 154, 158, 189, 199
Pesch, W. . . . . . . . . . . . . . . 21, 38, 81, 154
Petzke, G. . . . . . . . . . . . . . . . . . . 82, 150
Philonenko, M. . . . . . . . . . . . . . . 71, 124
Plevnik, J. . . . . . . . . . . . . . . . . . 148, 149
Plooij, D. . . . . . . . . . . . . . . . 82, 83, 145
Plümacher, E. . . . . . . . . . . . . . . . . . . 113
Plummer, A. . . . . . . . . . . . . . . . . . 10, 91
Preuschen, E. . . . . . . . . . . . . . . . 108, 158

Priest, J. .......................... 66
Purvis, J.D. .................... 64, 71
Rahlfs, A. .................... 60, 158
Rainbow, P.A. .................... 40
Ramsey, A.M. ............... 11, 105
Reicke, B. ............ 10, 83, 108, 145
Reimarus, H.S. .................. 1, 2
Reinmuth, E. .................... 34
Rengstorf, K.H. .................. 69
Rese, M. ........................ 158
Resseguie, J.L. ................... 82
Richard, E. ...................... 185
Ridderbos, H. ........... 136, 137, 138
Rigaux, B. ....................... 155
Robinson, J.A.T. ... 10, 63, 112, 113, 126
............... 148, 163, 168, 196, 198
Robinson, J.M. ................... 183
Robinson, W.C. .................. 115
Rohde, E. ..................... 21, 68
Roloff, D. ..................... 38, 39
Roloff, J. ...... 27, 94, 97, 101, 103, 122
............. 142, 160, 172, 174, 187
Ropes, J.H. ..................... 100
Rowland, C. ...................... 46
Ruckstuhl, E. ............... 129, 134
Russell, D.S. .................. 42, 46
Ryssel, V. ....................... 77
Sabbe, M. ............. 131, 148, 156
Sabourin, L. ..................... 24
Saldarini, A.J. ................... 60
Samain, E. ....................... 95
Sand, A. ........................ 130
Sanday, W. ...................... 140
Sanders, J.A. .................... 120
Sarna, N.M. ..................... 41
Sauer, G. ........................ 43
Schäfer, P. ............. 64, 66-68, 71
Scheftelowitz, J. .................. 37
Schille, G. ............. 18-19, 26, 101
....................... 104, 154, 158
Schillebeeckx, E. ................. 128
Schleiermacher, F.D.E. ............. 2
Schlier, H. ................... 88, 129
Schmid, H.H. ..................... 41
Schmid, J. ........ 21, 38, 81, 82, 91, 154
Schmidt. K.L. ..................... 7

Schmidt, C. .................. 99, 190
Schmithals, W. ................ 96, 101
....................... 108, 151, 187
Schmitt, A. ........... 21, 34, 37, 41-45
................ 58-60, 139, 140, 154
Schmitt, J. ...................... 154
Schnackenburg, R. ............ 135-138
Schneider, G. ...... 26, 95, 100, 104, 105
........ 148, 153-158, 174, 177, 191, 195
Schneider, J. .................... 138
Schnider, F. ..................... 83
Schrade, H. ...................... 21
Schramm, T. ..................... 146
Schreiner, J. ..................... 42
Schrenk, G. ...................... 94
Schubert, P. ....... 13, 15, 90, 162, 182
Schürmann, H. ................. 83, 84
Schweitzer, A. .................... 2
Schweizer, E. ......... 82, 115, 133, 151
Scott, R.B.Y. .................... 105
Segal, A.F. ................... 36, 39
Seidensticker, P. .................. 91
Shekan, P.W. ............... 43, 61, 62
Simon, M. ............. 41, 44, 70, 75
Sjöberg, E. .................. 52-55
Skinner, J. ...................... 42
Slotki, I.W. ...................... 60
Smith, M.H. ..................... 138
Speiser, E.A. .................... 37
Spencer, F.S. .................... 29
Sperber, A. ...................... 60
Stählin, G. .............. 92, 106, 155
Stam, C. .............. 104, 136, 141
Steck, O.H. ...................... 59
Stemberger, G. .................. 123
Stempvoort, P.A. van ........... 15-16
......................... 30, 88, 92
Stenger, W. ............... 83, 141, 142
Stone, M.E. ............... 45, 73, 74
Strange, W.A. ................... 102
Strauß, D.F. ............... 1-4, 10, 34
Strecker, G. .............. 21, 37, 68
Streeter, B.H. .................... 10
Strobel, A. ................... 17, 181
Stuckenbruck, L.T. ................ 40
Swete, H.B. ....... 11, 60, 133, 142, 164

Szold, H. . . . . . . . . . . . . . . . . . . . . . . 41
Tabor, J.D. . . . . . . . . . . . . . . . 67, 69, 195
Talbert, C.H. . . . . . . . . . 17, 39, 68, 86, 90
. . . . . . . . . . . . . . . . 91, 97, 106, 133, 146
. . . . . . . . . . 162-163, 169, 173, 174, 179
Tannehill, R.C. . . . . . . . . . . . . . . . . 31, 91
Teeple, H.M. . . . . . . . . . . . . . . . . . . . . 70
Theisohn, J. . . . . . . . . . . . . . . . . . . . . . 56
Theodor, J. . . . . . . . . . . . . . . . . . . 41, 44
Thiselton, A.C. . . . . . . . . . . . . . . . . . 169
Thüsing, W. . . . . . . . . . . . . 134, 136, 138
Tiede, D.L. . . . . . . . . . . . . . . . . . . . . . 82
Tischendorf, C. von . . . . . . . . . . . . . . . 8
Todesco, V. . . . . . . . . . . . . . . . . . . . . 145
Tödt, H.E. . . . . . . . . . . . . . . . . . . . . . 156
Tom, W. . . . . . . . . . . . . . . . . . . . . . 9, 163
Torgovnick, M. . . . . . . . . . . . . . . . 29-30
Torm, F. . . . . . . . . . . . . . . . . . . . . . . . 155
Torrey, C.C. . . . . . . . . . . . . . . . . 101, 102
Tromp, J. . . . . . . . . . . . . . . . . . . . . 66, 68
Uhlig, S. . . . . . . . . . . . . . . . . . . . . . . . 52
Unnik, W.C. van . . . . . . . . . . . 14, 94, 187
Vaganay, L. . . . . . . . . . . . . . . . . . . . . . 81
Vaillant, A. . . . . . . . . . . . . . . . . . . . 49, 76
VanderKam, J.C. . . . . . . . . . 41, 42, 45-47
Venturini, K.H. . . . . . . . . . . . . . . . . . . . 2
Verhoef, P.A. . . . . . . . . . . . . . . . . . . . . 61
Vielhauer, Ph. . . . . . . 17, 36, 124, 149, 197
Violet, B. . . . . . . . . . . . . . . . . . . . . . . 137
Volz, P. . . . . . . . . . . . . . . . . . . . . . . 64, 151
Walvoord, J.F. . . . . . . . . . . . 105, 137, 164
Wanke, J. . . . . . . . . . . . . . . . . . . . . . . 161
Weinert, F.D. . . . . . . . . . . . . . . . . . . . . 94
Weinrich, W.C. . . . . . . . . . . . . . . . . . . 83
Weinstock, S. . . . . . . . . . . . . . . . . . . . 40

Weiser, A. . . . . . . . . . . . . . . . 25, 154, 155
Weiss, B. . . . . . . . . . . . . . . . . . . . 88, 163
Wellhausen, J. . . . . . . . . . . . . . . . . . . 106
Wendt, H.H. . . . . . . 10, 101, 105, 111, 158
Wensinck, A.J. . . . . . . . . . . . . . . . . . . 83
WH . . . . . . . . . . . . . . . . . . . . . . . . . . . . 8
Wiefel, W. . . . . . . . . . . . . . . . . . . . 82, 86
Wiener, A. . . . . . . . . . . . . . . . . . . . . . . 60
Wieseler, K. . . . . . . . . . . . . . . . . . . . . 83
Wikenhauser, A. . . . . . . . . . . . . . . 87, 155
Wilckens, U. . . . . . . . . . 110, 112, 153, 155
Wilcox, M. . . . . . . . . . . . . . . . . . . . . . 101
Wilder, A.N. . . . . . . . . . . . . . . . . 180, 183
Willems, G.F. . . . . . . . . . . . . . . . . . . . 75
Williams, C.S.C. . . . . . . . . . . . . . . . . . 10
Williams, D.J. . . . . . . . . . . . . . . . . . . . 99
Wilson, S.G. . . . . . . . . . . . 19, 92, 113, 169
Winston, D.M. . . . . . . . . . . . . . . . . . . 44
Winter, B.W. . . . . . . . . . . . . . . . . . . 29, 91
Wintermute, O.S. . . . . . . . . . . . . . . . . 47
Wißmann, H. . . . . . . . . . . . . . . . . . . . 38
Wittgenstein, L. . . . . . . . . . . . . . . . . . 169
Woude, A.S. van der . . . . . . . . . . . . . . 96
Zahn, Th. . . . . . . . . . . . . 6, 86, 88, 89, 91
. . . . . . . . . . . . . 92, 94, 102, 108, 136, 157
Zedtwitz, K. von . . . . . . . . . . . . . . . . 158
Zehnle, R.F. . . . . . . . . . . . . 110, 113, 153
Ziegler, J. . . . . . . . . . . . . . . . . . . . . . . 42
Zmijewski, J. . . . . . . . . . . 25, 96, 101, 103
. . . . . . . . . . . . . 105, 154, 155, 162, 187
Zwemer, S. . . . . . . . . . . . . . . . . . . . . . 131
Zwiep, A.W. . . . . . . . . . . . . . 1, 30, 90, 194

# SUPPLEMENTS TO NOVUM TESTAMENTUM

ISSN 0167-9732

2. STROBEL, A. *Untersuchungen zum eschatologischen Verzögerungsproblem auf Grund der spätjüdische-urchristlichen Geschichte von Habakuk 2,2 ff.* 1961. ISBN 90 04 01582 5

6. *Neotestamentica et Patristica.* Eine Freundesgabe Herrn Professor Dr. Oscar Cullmann zu seinem 60. Geburtstag überreicht. 1962. ISBN 90 04 01586 8

8. DE MARCO, A.A. *The Tomb of Saint Peter.* A Representative and Annotated Bibliography of the Excavations. 1964. ISBN 90 04 01588 4

10. BORGEN, P. *Bread from Heaven.* An Exegetical Study of the Concept of Manna in the Gospel of John and the Writings of Philo. Photomech. Reprint of the first (1965) edition. 1981. ISBN 90 04 06419 2

13. MOORE, A.L. *The Parousia in the New Testament.* 1966. ISBN 90 04 01593 0

15. QUISPEL, G. *Makarius, das Thomasevangelium und das Lied von der Perle.* 1967. ISBN 90 04 01595 7

16. PFITZNER, V.C. *Paul and the Agon Motif.* 1967. ISBN 90 04 01596 5

17. BELLINZONI, A. *The Sayings of Jesus in the Writings of Justin Martyr.* 1967. ISBN 90 04 01597 3

18. GUNDRY, R.H. *The Use of the Old Testament in St. Matthew's Gospel.* With Special Reference to the Messianistic Hope. Reprint of the first (1967) edition. 1975. ISBN 90 04 04278 4

19. SEVENSTER, J.N. *Do You Know Greek?* How Much Greek Could the first Jewish Christians Have Known? 1968. ISBN 90 04 03090 5

20. BUCHANAN, G.W. *The Consequences of the Covenant.* 1970. ISBN 90 04 01600 7

21. KLIJN, A.F.J. *A Survey of the Researches into the Western Text of the Gospels and Acts.* Part 2: 1949-1969. 1969. ISBN 90 04 01601 5

22. GABOURY, A. *La Stucture des Évangiles synoptiques.* La structure-type à l'origine des synoptiques. 1970. ISBN 90 04 01602 3

23. GASTON, L. *No Stone on Another.* Studies in the Significance of the Fall of Jerusalem in the Synoptic Gospels. 1970. ISBN 90 04 01603 1

24. *Studies in John.* Presented to Professor Dr. J.N. Sevenster on the Occasion of His Seventieth Birthday. 1970. ISBN 90 04 03091 3

25. STORY, C.I.K. *The Nature of Truth in the 'Gospel of Truth', and in the Writings of Justin Martyr.* A Study of the Pattern of Orthodoxy in the Middle of the Second Christian Century. 1970. ISBN 90 04 01605 8

26. GIBBS, J.G. *Creation and Redemption.* A Study in Pauline Theology. 1971. ISBN 90 04 01606 6

27. MUSSIES, G. *The Morphology of Koine Greek As Used in the Apocalypse of St. John.* A Study in Bilingualism. 1971. ISBN 90 04 02656 8

28. AUNE, D.E. *The Cultic Setting of Realized Eschatology in Early Christianity.* 1972. ISBN 90 04 03341 6

29. UNNIK, W.C. VAN. *Sparsa Collecta.* The Collected Essays of W.C. van Unnik Part 1. Evangelia, Paulina, Acta. 1973. ISBN 90 04 03660 1

30. UNNIK, W.C. VAN. *Sparsa Collecta.* The Collected Essays of W.C. van Unnik Part 2. I Peter, Canon, Corpus Hellenisticum, Generalia. 1980. ISBN 90 04 06261 0

31. UNNIK, W.C. VAN. *Sparsa Collecta.* The Collected Essays of W.C. van Unnik Part 3. Patristica, Gnostica, Liturgica. 1983. ISBN 90 04 06262 9

33. AUNE D.E. (ed.) *Studies in New Testament and Early Christian Literature*. Essays in Honor of Allen P. Wikgren. 1972. ISBN 90 04 03504 4
34. HAGNER, D.A. *The Use of the Old and New Testaments in Clement of Rome*. 1973. ISBN 90 04 03636 9
35. GUNTHER, J.J. *St. Paul's Opponents and Their Background*. A Study of Apocalyptic and Jewish Sectarian Teachings. 1973. ISBN 90 04 03738 1
36. KLIJN, A.F.J. & G.J. REININK (eds.) *Patristic Evidence for Jewish-Christian Sects*. 1973. ISBN 90 04 03763 2
37. REILING, J. *Hermas and Christian Prophecy*. A Study of The Eleventh Mandate. 1973. ISBN 90 04 03771 3
38. DONFRIED, K.P. *The Setting of Second Clement in Early Christianity*. 1974. ISBN 90 04 03895 7
39. ROON, A. VAN. *The Authenticity of Ephesians*. 1974. ISBN 90 04 03971 6
40. KEMMLER, D.W. *Faith and Human Reason*. A Study of Paul's Method of Preaching as Illustrated by 1-2 Thessalonians and Acts 17, 2-4. 1975. ISBN 90 04 04209 1
42. PANCARO, S. *The Law in the Fourth Gospel*. The Torah and the Gospel, Moses and Jesus, Judaism and Christianity According to John. 1975. ISBN 90 04 04309 8
43. CLAVIER, H. *Les variétés de la pensée biblique et le problème de son unité*. Esquisse d'une théologie de la Bible sur les textes originaux et dans leur contexte historique. 1976. ISBN 90 04 04465 5
44. ELLIOTT, J.K.E. (ed.) *Studies in New Testament Language and Text*. Essays in Honour of George D. Kilpatrick on the Occasion of His Sixty-fifth Birthday. 1976. ISBN 90 04 04386 1
45. PANAGOPOULOS, J. (ed.) *Prophetic Vocation in the New Testament and Today*. 1977. ISBN 90 04 04923 1
46. KLIJN, A.F.J. *Seth in Jewish, Christian and Gnostic Literature*. 1977. ISBN 90 04 05245 3
47. BAARDA, T., A.F.J. KLIJN & W.C. VAN UNNIK (eds.) *Miscellanea Neotestamentica*. I. Studia ad Novum Testamentum Praesertim Pertinentia a Sociis Sodalicii Batavi c.n. Studiosorum Novi Testamenti Conventus Anno MCMLXXVI Quintum Lustrum Feliciter Complentis Suscepta. 1978. ISBN 90 04 05685 8
48. BAARDA, T. A.F.J. KLIJN & W.C. VAN UNNIK (eds.) *Miscellanea Neotestamentica*. II. 1978. ISBN 90 04 05686 6
49. O'BRIEN, P.T. *Introductory Thanksgivings in the Letters of Paul*. 1977. ISBN 90 04 05265 8
50. BOUSSET, D.W. *Religionsgeschichtliche Studien*. Aufsätze zur Religionsgeschichte des hellenistischen Zeitalters. Hrsg. von A.F. Verheule. 1979. ISBN 90 04 05845 1
51. COOK, M.J. *Mark's Treatment of the Jewish Leaders*. 1978. ISBN 90 04 05785 4
52. GARLAND, D.E. *The Intention of Matthew 23*. 1979. ISBN 90 04 05912 1
53. MOXNES, H. *Theology in Conflict*. Studies in Paul's Understanding of God in Romans. 1980. ISBN 90 04 06140 1
55. MENKEN, M.J.J. *Numerical Literary Techniques in John*. The Fourth Evangelist's Use of Numbers of Words and Syllables. 1985. ISBN 90 04 07427 9
56. SKARSAUNE, O. *The Proof From Prophecy*. A Study in Justin Martyr's Proof-Text Tradition: Text-type, Provenance, Theological Profile. 1987. ISBN 90 04 07468 6
59. WILKINS, M.J. *The Concept of Disciple in Matthew's Gospel, as Reflected in the Use of the Term 'Mathetes'*. 1988. ISBN 90 04 08689 7
60. MILLER, E.L. *Salvation-History in the Prologue of John*. The Significance of John 1: 3-4. 1989. ISBN 90 04 08692 7
61. THIELMAN, F. *From Plight to Solution*. A Jewish Framework for Understanding Paul's View of the Law in Galatians and Romans. 1989. ISBN 90 04 09176 9

64. STERLING, G.E. *Historiography and Self-Definition.* Josephos, Luke-Acts and Apologetic Historiography. 1992. ISBN 90 04 09501 2

65. BOTHA, J.E. *Jesus and the Samaritan Woman.* A Speech Act Reading of John 4:1-42. 1991. ISBN 90 04 09505 5

66. KUCK, D.W *Judgment and Community Conflict.* Paul's Use of Apologetic Judgment Language in 1 Corinthians 3:5-4:5. 1992. ISBN 90 04 09510 1

67. SCHNEIDER, G. *Jesusüberlieferung und Christologie.* Neutestamentliche Aufsätze 1970-1990. 1992. ISBN 90 04 09555 1

68. SEIFRID, M.A. *Justification by Faith.* The Origin and Development of a Central Pauline Theme. 1992. ISBN 90 04 09521 7

69. NEWMAN, C.C. *Paul's Glory-Christology.* Tradition and Rhetoric. 1992. ISBN 90 04 09463 6

70. IRELAND, D.J. *Stewardship and the Kingdom of God.* An Historical, Exegetical, and Contextual Study of the Parable of the Unjust Steward in Luke 16: 1-13. 1992. ISBN 90 04 09600 0

71. ELLIOTT, J.K. *The Language and Style of the Gospel of Mark.* An Edition of C.H. Turner's "Notes on Marcan Usage" together with other comparable studies. 1993. ISBN 90 04 09767 8

72. CHILTON, B. *A Feast of Meanings.* Eucharistic Theologies from Jesus through Johannine Circles. 1994. ISBN 90 04 09949 2

73. GUTHRIE, G.H. *The Structure of Hebrews.* A Text-Linguistic Analysis. 1994. ISBN 90 04 09866 6

74. BORMANN, L., K. DEL TREDICI & A. STANDHARTINGER (eds.) *Religious Propaganda and Missionary Competition in the New Testament World.* Essays Honoring Dieter Georgi. 1994. ISBN 90 04 10049 0

75. PIPER, R.A. (ed.) *The Gospel Behind the Gospels.* Current Studies on Q. 1995. ISBN 90 04 09737 6

76. PEDERSEN, S. (ed.) *New Directions in Biblical Theology.* Papers of the Aarhus Conference, 16-19 September 1992. 1994. ISBN 90 04 10120 9

77. JEFFORD, C.N. (ed.) *The* Didache *in Context.* Essays on Its Text, History and Transmission. 1995. ISBN 90 04 10045 8

78. BORMANN, L. *Philippi – Stadt und Christengemeinde zur Zeit des Paulus.* 1995. ISBN 90 04 10232 9

79. PETERLIN, D. *Paul's Letter to the Philippians in the Light of Disunity in the Church.* 1995. ISBN 90 04 10305 8

80. JONES, I.H. *The Matthean Parables.* A Literary and Historical Commentary. 1995 ISBN 90 04 10181 0

81. GLAD, C.E. *Paul and Philodemus.* Adaptability in Epicurean and Early Christian Psychagogy. 1995 ISBN 90 04 10067 9

82. FITZGERALD, J.T. (ed.) *Friendship, Flattery, and Frankness of Speech.* Studies on Friendship in the New Testament World. 1996. ISBN 90 04 10454 2

83. VAN TILBORG, S. *Reading John in Ephesus.* 1996. 90 04 10530 1

84. HOLLEMAN, J. *Resurrection and Parousia.* A Traditio-Historical Study of Paul's Eschatology in 1 Corinthians 15. 1996. ISBN 90 04 10597 2

85. MORITZ, T. *A Profound Mystery.* The Use of the Old Testament in Ephesians. 1996. ISBN 90 04 10556 5